Critica Musica

Musicology: A Book Series
Edited by Ralph Locke, Eastman School of Music, University of Rochester, New York

Volume 1	**THE EXPERIENCING OF MUSICAL SOUND** *Prelude to a Phenomenology of Music* F. Joseph Smith
Volume 2	**MUSIC AND ITS SOCIAL MEANINGS** Christopher Ballantine
Volume 3	**MUSIC, FILM, AND ART** Haig Khatchadourian
Volume 4	**LATE RENAISSANCE MUSIC AT THE HABSBURG COURT** *Polyphonic Settings of the Mass Ordinary at the Court of Rudolf II (1576–1612)* Carmelo Peter Comberiati
Volume 5	**WITNESSES AND SCHOLARS** *Studies in Musical Biography* Hans Lenneberg
Volume 6	**THE TROMBONE** *Its History and Music, 1697–1811* David M. Guion
Volume 7	**MUSIC FROM THE MIDDLE AGES THROUGH THE TWENTIETH CENTURY** *Essays in Honor of Gwynn S. McPeek* Edited by Carmelo P. Comberiati and Matthew C. Steel
Volume 8	**UNDERSTANDING THE MUSICAL EXPERIENCE** Edited by F. Joseph Smith
Volume 9	**STRAVINSKY** *The Music Box and the Nightingale* Daniel Albright
Volume 10	**MUSICAL LIFE IN POLAND** *The Postwar Years 1945–1977* Lidia Rappoport-Gelfand
Volume 11	**FROM VIVALDI TO VIOTTI** *A History of the Early Classical Violin Concerto* Chappell White
Volume 12	**THE EARLY WORKS OF FELIX MENDELSSOHN** *A Study in the Romantic Sonata Style* Greg Vitercik
Volume 13	**MUSIC IN ENGLISH CHILDREN'S DRAMA OF THE LATER RENAISSANCE** Linda Phyllis Austern
Volume 14	**THE DISSEMINATION OF MUSIC** *Studies in the History of Music Publishing* Edited by Hans Lenneberg
Volume 15	**METAPHOR** *A Musical Dimension* Edited by Jamie C. Kassler
Volume 16	**MUSIC-CULTURES IN CONTACT** *Convergences and Collisions* Edited by Margaret J. Kartomi and Stephen Blum
Volume 17	**SONGS OF THE DOVE AND THE NIGHTINGALE** *Sacred and Secular Music c. 900–c.1600* Edited by Greta Mary Hair and Robyn E. Smith
Volume 18	**CRITICA MUSICA** *Essays in Honor of Paul Brainard* Edited by John Knowles

This book is part of a series. The publisher will accept continuation orders which may be cancelled at any time and which provide for automatic billing and shipping of each title in the series upon publication. Please write for details.

Critica Musica

Essays in Honor of Paul Brainard

Edited by

John Knowles

CRC Press is an imprint of the
Taylor & Francis Group, an **informa** business

First published 1996 by Gordon and Science Publishers

Published 2018 by CRC Press
Taylor & Francis Group
6000 Broken Sound Parkway NW, Suite 300
Boca Raton, FL 33487-2742

First issued in paperback 2018

© 1996 by Taylor & Francis Group, LLC
CRC Press is an imprint of Taylor & Francis Group, an Informa business

No claim to original U. S. Government works

ISBN 13: 978-1-138-99049-4 (pbk)
ISBN 13: 978-90-5699-522-5 (hbk)

This book contains information obtained from authentic and highly regarded sources. Reasonable efforts have been made to publish reliable data and information, but the author and publisher cannot assume responsibility for the validity of all materials or the consequences of their use. The authors and publishers have attempted to trace the copyright holders of all material reproduced in this publication and apologize to copyright holders if permission to publish in this form has not been obtained. If any copyright material has not been acknowledged please write and let us know so we may rectify in any future reprint.

Except as permitted under U.S. Copyright Law, no part of this book may be reprinted, reproduced, transmitted, or utilized in any form by any electronic, mechanical, or other means, now known or hereafter invented, including photocopying, microfilming, and recording, or in any information storage or retrieval system, without written permission from the publishers.

For permission to photocopy or use material electronically from this work, please access www.copyright.com (http://www.copyright.com/) or contact the Copyright Clearance Center, Inc. (CCC), 222 Rosewood Drive, Danvers, MA 01923, 978-750-8400. CCC is a not-for-profit organization that provides licenses and registration for a variety of users. For organizations that have been granted a photocopy license by the CCC, a separate system of payment has been arranged.

Trademark Notice: Product or corporate names may be trademarks or registered trademarks, and are used only for identification and explanation without intent to infringe.

Visit the Taylor & Francis Web site at
http://www.taylorandfrancis.com

and the CRC Press Web site at
http://www.crcpress.com

British Library Cataloguing in Publication Data

A catalogue record for this book is available from the British Library.

Printed in the United Kingdom
by Henry Ling Limited

Paul Brainard

Contents

Preface ... ix

Principal Publications of Paul Brainard ... xi

Introduction to the Series ... xv

Some Considerations of the Sources of Cristóbal Galán's Music
 John H. Baron ... 1

The Speaking Body: Gaspero Angiolini's *Rhétorique Muette* and the *Ballet d'Action* in the Eighteenth Century
 Ingrid Brainard ... 15

Costanzo Festa's *Inviolata, integra et casta es Maria:* a Double Homage Motet
 Mitchell P. Brauner ... 57

Bach, Theology, and Harmony: A New Look at the Arias
 Stephen A. Crist ... 65

The Symphony and the Artist's Creed: Camille Saint-Saëns and His Third Symphony
 Ludwig Finscher ... 97

The Letter as Convention in Seventeenth-Century Venetian Opera
 Beth L. Glixon ... 125

Poetic and Musical Forms in the Laude of Innocentius Dammonis
 Jonathan Glixon ... 143

Melody and Motive in Schenker's Earliest Writings
 Allan Keiler ... 169

Twins, Cousins, and Heirs: Relationships among Editions
of Music Printed in Sixteenth-Century Venice
   Mary S. Lewis   193

Rhetoric, Rhythm, and Harmony as Keys to Schütz's *Saul, Saul,
was verfolgst du mich?*
   Eva Linfield   225

Bach's *tempo ordinario*: A Plaine and Easie Introduction
to the System
   Robert L. Marshall   249

Amorous Dialogues: Poetic Topos and Polyphonic Texture
in Some Polytextual Songs of the Late Middle Ages
   Virginia Newes   279

The Violins in Bach's St. John Passion
   Joshua Rifkin   307

French Opera in Transition: *Silvie* (1765) by Trial and Berton
   Lois Rosow   333

Kindling the Compositional Fire: Haydn's Keyboard *Phantasiren*
   Hollace A. Schafer   365

When Sources Seem to Fail: The Clarinet Parts in Mozart's
K. 581 and K. 622
   Joel Sheveloff   379

From Madrigal to Toccata: Frescobaldi and the *Seconda Prattica*
   Alexander Silbiger   403

Beethoven and Shakespeare
   Caldwell Titcomb   429

Tenors Lost and Found: The Reconstruction of Motets
in Two Medieval Chansonniers
   Mary E. Wolinski   461

Index   483

PREFACE

Critica Musica—thinking critically about music—is at the heart of Paul Brainard's long career, and of his legacy to his students, colleagues, and friends. As a scholar, performer, and teacher, Professor Brainard has embodied a thorough, meticulous, and reasoned approach to music and scholarship that has set a high standard for all who have come in contact with him.

Professor Brainard received a master's degree in Theory and Violin from the Eastman School of Music in 1951. After spending two years in the army in Germany, he stayed on to pursue a doctorate in musicology—first at Heidelberg under Thrasybulos Georgiades and then at Göttingen under Rudolf Gerber and Wolfgang Bötticher. His expertise in German allowed him to work as a translator and liner-note writer for Teldec, as a musicological translator, and as a translator of American comic books into German. The quality of his writing in German was acknowledged when he received the prize for the "best written" dissertation at Göttingen in 1960 (*Die Violinsonaten Giuseppe Tartinis*).

The essays in this book consider music from a wide variety of periods, styles, and genres, and use many different approaches and perspectives: This fairly represents Professor Brainard's own wide-ranging interests. While his areas of expertise range from chant and Notre Dame polyphony to twentieth-century analysis (his master's thesis was on Berg's *Lyric Suite*), he is probably most widely associated with music of the Baroque, especially that of Bach. His source-critical skills have informed several volumes of the *Neue Bach-Ausgabe*, for which he edited a number of specific works and served as a volume editor. (One unusual example of his remarkable source-critical intuition is the report by his secretary at Brandeis that he was able to correct her shorthand, even though he could not read it!) His abilities were recognized by Arthur Mendel, who recommended that he be assigned to edit the cantata *Ich hatte viel Bekümmernis*, BWV 21. This source situation was probably the most difficult to unravel of all the cantatas, and may have been exceeded only by that of the St. John Passion, which Mendel himself edited.

Professor Brainard's knowledge of the Baroque is not limited to one area, however, but displays great breadth, as well as depth. He is also an expert in early opera, Baroque rhythm and proportions, Handel—his article "Aria and Ritornello: New Aspects of the Comparison Handel/Bach" has been called "the best work on compositional practice in Handel's music to date"[1]—and, of course, Tartini.

---

[1] Ellen T. Harris, "Integrity and Improvisation in the Music of Handel," *Journal of Musicology* 8 (1990), p. 314.

Paul Brainard's deep understanding of the music he has studied is not merely intellectual, but has always been fed by an energetic practical involvement. In his early years, he was a professional violinist; as a doctoral student, he worked as a violin teacher. Although he decided against a career as a performer, he did not abandon performing the music he loved. He continued to perform "on the side" and eventually expanded his skills from the violin to the viol. For many years, he participated in student/faculty viol consorts, bringing his scholarly knowledge to his performances and his practical musicality to his scholarship.

As a teacher, Paul Brainard's influence has been wide ranging. In a long career at Brandeis University, as well as periods at Princeton University and the Yale Institute of Sacred Music, from which he recently retired, he set a standard for scholarly inquiry and critical evaluation that remains with his students to this day. If we often failed to meet that standard, striving to do so was one of our most formative learning experiences.

His preparation for class was legendary—he was prepared for almost any contingency, and when a student let the ball drop, he was always ready to pick it up and run with it. Although he was not the only one at Brandeis who taught the Proseminar in Musicology, he "owned it." His students benefitted from his broad education and special interests: a broad approach to the study of all musics, his "Wegweiser durch Ludwig's *Repertorium*," tempo and proportions in the early seventeenth century. It was the study of and from original materials in his classes that taught us what the "critical" meant in source criticism.

For many years, there was a general sense among his students that Professor Brainard would someday be honored by a *Festschrift*. That idea began to bear fruit shortly after his sixtieth birthday, when a group of those former students constituted themselves as an organizing committee. By the time the list of contributors had been assembled and an agreement was reached to publish this volume, his sixty-fifth birthday (and incidentally his retirement from teaching) became the occasion for presenting him with these essays.

Special thanks are due to several people. Tim Buendorf, a former student of Professor Brainard's, created the numerous musical examples. His work was made possible by support from the Yale Institute of Sacred Music and its administrator, Ruth Lackstrom; this volume is much the better for their involvement. Finally, Kathleen O'Malley provided guidance throughout the long gestation of this volume; her patience is greatly appreciated.

PRINCIPAL PUBLICATIONS OF PAUL BRAINARD

Books and Editions

Le Sonate per violino di Giuseppe Tartini. Catalogo tematico (Padua/Milan: Accademia Tartiniana di Padova/Carisch, 1975).

Giuseppe Tartini: La raccolta di sonate autografe per violino (Padua/Milan: Accademia Tartiniana di Padova/Carisch, 1976).

J. S. Bach, *Neue Ausgabe sämtlicher Werke*, ser. 2, vol. 7, *Oster-Oratorium BWV 249* (Kassel: Bärenreiter, 1977).

—ser. 2, vol. 7, *Kritischer Bericht* (1981).

—ser. 2, vol. 8, *Himmelfahrts-Oratorium BWV 11* (1978).

—ser. 2, vol. 8, *Kritischer Bericht* (1987).

—ser. 1, vol. 16, *Kantaten zum 2. und 3. Sonntag nach Trinitatis* (with George S. Bozarth and Robert Moreen, 1981).

—ser. 1, vol. 16, *Kritischer Bericht* (1984).

Italienische Violinmusik der Barockzeit, vol. 1 (Munich: Henle, 1985).

—vol. 2 (1989).

Articles and Review-Essays

"Tartini and the Sonata for Unaccompanied Violin," *Journal of the American Musicological Society* 14 (1961): 383–93 (Italian translation published in *Chigiana*, Nuova serie 6–7 [1971]:431–42).

"Documents, Pictures, and Mozart," *Fontes Artis Musicae* 9 (1962): 35–39.

"Zur Deutung der Diminution in der Mensurallehre des Michael Praetorius," *Die Musikforschung* 17 (1964): 169–74.

Article "Tartini," in *Die Musik in Geschichte und Gegenwart*, vol. 12 (Kassel: Bärenreiter, 1966), pp. 130–38.

"Bach's Parody Procedures and the St. Matthew Passion," *Journal of the American Musicological Society* 22 (1969): 241–60.

"Le Sonate a tre di Giuseppe Tartini," *Rivista Italiana di Musicologia* 6 (1969; publ. 1971): 102–26.

Review of R. L. Marshall, *The Compositional Process of J. S. Bach*. In *Journal of the American Musicological Society* 26 (1973): 483–88.

"Cantata 21 Revisited," in *Studies in Renaissance and Baroque Music in Honor of Arthur Mendel* (Kassel/Hackensack, N.J.: Bärenreiter/Joseph Boonin, 1974).

Article "Tartini," in *The New Grove Dictionary of Music and Musicians*, 6th ed. (London: Macmillan Publishers, 1980), 18:583–88.

"Über Fehler und Korrekturen der Textunterlage in den Vokalwerken J. S. Bachs," *Bach-Jahrbuch 1978*, pp. 113–39.

"The Aria and Its Ritornello: The Question of 'Dominance' in Bach," in *Bachiana et alia musicologica: Festschrift Alfred Dürr zum 65. Geburtstag*, ed. Wolfgang Rehm (Kassel: Bärenreiter, 1983), pp. 39–51.

"Aria and Ritornello: New Aspects of the Comparison Handel/Bach," in *Bach, Handel, Scarlatti: Tercentenary Essays*, ed. Peter Williams (Cambridge: Cambridge University Press, 1985), pp. 21–34.

"The Regulative and Generative Roles of Versification in the 'Thematic' Invention of J. S. Bach," in *Bach Studies*, ed. Don O. Franklin (Cambridge: Cambridge University Press, 1989), pp. 54–74.

"Proportional Notation in the Music of Schütz and His Contemporaries," *Current Musicology* 50 (1992): 21–46.

" 'Wie ernst Händel das Wort nimmt'; Adaptations, 'Outtakes', and Other Matters in *Scipione*," in *De Musica et cantu: Studien zur Geschichte der Kirchenmusik und der Oper. Helmut Hucke zum 60. Geburtstag*, ed. Peter Cahn and Ann-Katrin Heimer (Hildesheim: Georg Olms, 1993), pp. 495–511.

"The 'Non-Quoting' Ritornello in Bach's Arias," in *A Bach Tribute: Essays in Honor of William H. Scheide*, ed. Paul Brainard and Ray Robinson (Kassel/Chapel Hill, N.C.: Bärenreiter/Hinshaw, 1993), pp. 27–44.

"Bach as Theologian?," in *Reflections on the Sacred: a Musicological Perspective*, ed. Paul Brainard, Yale Studies in Sacred Music, Worship and the Arts (1994), pp. 1–7.

INTRODUCTION TO THE SERIES

The Gordon and Breach Musicology series, a companion to the *Journal of Musicological Research*, covers a creative range of musical topics, from historical and theoretical subjects to social and philosophical studies. Volumes thus far published show the extent of this broad spectrum, from *The Early Works of Felix Mendelssohn to Metaphor: A Musical Dimension*. The editors also welcome interdisciplinary studies, ethnomusicological works and performance analyses. With this series, it is our aim to expand the field and definition of musical exploration and research.

Some Considerations of the Sources of Cristóbal Galán's Music*

John H. Baron

Biography

Although the names and music of many 17th-century composers from Italy, Germany, France, and England are well known today among music students, performers, and audiences, Spanish musicians and compositions from that period remain virtually undiscovered. Despite great musicological work by Robert Stevenson and Miguel Querol to resuscitate this repertoire, it is still unknown to all but a very few enthusiasts. Yet the Spanish courts and cathedrals of the baroque were magnificent places with active musical establishments. While there assuredly are no Monteverdis or Schützes who remain to be resurrected, there are gifted men whose music is beautiful and worthy of performance today. One of the most important among these is Cristóbal Galán.

Cristóbal Galán's birth date and place are unknown, and we have only sketchy information on his early life and career.[1] Before the late 1650s and possibly as early as the 1640s, he was *maestro de capilla* in Morella and Teruel on the east coast of Spain, and in 1659 and 1660, he may have been an unordained *maestro* in the cathedral in Cagliari in Sardinia. Despite these religious positions, he published some secular songs in 1645, and it is likely that he arrived in Madrid during the early 1660s to take part in the theater of the Buen Retiro, the royal palace, where he was head of the Negro musicians in 1664 ("maestro de los ministriles negrillos del Buen Retiro").[2] From this date, we can trace Galán's footsteps fairly accurately.

---

*I am, as usual, indebted to my colleague Dan Heiple, Professor of Spanish, who has worked with me on the edition of Galán's music cited below and who has helped me analyze the sources of Galán's music.

[1] For the details of Galán's known biography with citations, see the introduction to the edition of his *Misa de Difuntos,* in *Obras Completas de Cristóbal Galán,* eds. Dan Heiple and John Baron, vol. 1 (Henryville, Penn.: Institute of Mediaeval Music, 1982), pp. vi–viii.

[2] The Ministriles performed on outdoor instruments in processions and apparently had some role in the outdoor performances of the *autos sacramentales.* Further research is necessary in this area.

He collaborated with the celebrated dramatist Calderón de la Barca in two *autos sacramentales* (sacred dramas performed outdoors with some music during Corpus Christi) that year, before leaving Madrid for a three-year appointment as *maestro de capilla* at the cathedral in Segovia, one of the most important jobs of that time. He returned to Madrid in 1667, however, as *maestro* at the Royal Descalzes Convent, partly, perhaps, to be nearer the royal theater. He set four more *autos* by Calderón and was regarded as chief composer of Calderón's *autos*. In 1680, he was named *maestro* of the royal chapel, the most prestigious position in all of Spain during the 17th century. Unfortunately, however, Galán was there only four years when he died, on September 24, 1684. His contemporaries recognized him as one of the most skillful composers of his time, and for the next half century, he was praised as the great figure in traditional, polyphonic, mid-17th-century sacred music.

The Music

Galán's music for Calderón's plays does not survive (they were lost in a fire), and only two *tonos humanos* (secular songs) have come down to us complete. But his sacred music is represented today by nearly two dozen Latin liturgical works, including two masses, and by over one hundred villancicos.[3]

The pieces range from settings for one voice and continuo to large choral works for twelve voices (three choirs) with continuo and other instruments. His preferred setting is for four or eight voices with continuo. The continuo is usually designated as organ or harp or both, with a "violon" often doubling the bass line. In a few cases, Galán doubles the bass line with a "bajón," or bassoon. When he includes treble instruments in concertato with the voices, they are either violins or "baxoncillos" ("oboes"). All the Spanish works are strophic songs with refrain (*estribillo*). The music is not easy to sing and requires experienced singers such as those who would have been available to Galán in Segovia, the Descalzes Convent, and the Royal Chapel. He favors sopranos and contraltos and apparently had many more singers with those ranges than tenors and basses.[4]

---

[3]The collected works of Galán are appearing in eleven volumes. Volumes 1–3, devoted to the Latin liturgical music, have already been issued (1982–1992). Volumes 4–11, of which volume 4 has already been published (1993), will include the villancicos and *tonos humanos* arranged according to setting (see the list according to scoring in volume 1, pp. x–xiv, and the alphabetical list in the Appendix below). Volume 5 should appear in 1995.

[4]This would be the case especially in the Descalzes Convent; Galán was also following a Spanish custom of the time favoring the higher voices (cf. Matthew D. Stroud, ed., Calderón de la Barca, *Celos Aun del Aire Matan* [San Antonio, Tex.: Trinity University Press, 1981], p. 22).

The Sources[5]

With few exceptions, Galán's music survives in manuscript part books. Each piece is a separate entity; there are only three songs that appear in collections of pieces.[6] Each part is written on an oblong folio of approximately 12 inches by 8½ inches (as in keyboard parts of the time). In some cases, the entire part is written on one side of the folio, but just as often, the *estribillo* is on one side and the strophes (*coplas*) on the other. The *coplas* are always written underneath the respective notes of the music, so that it is usually obvious what syllables are sung with a particular note or group of notes. The custom of the time was to gather all the part books of a piece together, fold the long sides in half, and cover the bundle with a sheet, on the outside of which is the composer's name, the title of the work, the number of voices required, and, where relevant, the occasion on which it was to be sung (Corpus Christi, Navidad, etc.). In some cases, folios have become separated from the bundles to which they originally belonged; either an isolated part is lying forlorn in an archive, or a bundle has fewer parts than indicated on the cover sheet.

The manuscripts are found today in numerous locations in Europe and the Americas. It is evident from the number of Galán manuscripts worldwide that his popularity was sufficient for *maestros* throughout the baroque Spanish world to collect them. In contrast to Galán and a few of his most important colleagues, most 17th- and 18th-century composers were only locally important; they are represented by large numbers of works in manuscript that cannot be found, however, outside their home churches.

Twenty-eight villancicos and seven Latin works by Galán are in the Cathedral in Segovia, but it is not at all certain if any of these were written while Galán worked there. The size of the collection does not by itself give evidence for his presence in Segovia. For instance, the largest collection of Galán manuscripts is in the Cathedral in Valladolid (forty-four villancicos and seven Latin pieces), but there is no evidence that Galán was ever there.

---

[5]As far as I know, the only study of the manuscripts of 17th-century Spanish vocal music is Paul R. Laird, *The Villancico Repertory of San Lorenzo el Real del Escorial* (Ph.D. dissertation, University of North Carolina, 1986), which is basic for any future work in the area. See also his "The Villancicos of Matías Juan de Veana," *Anuario Musical* 44 (1989): 131, which mentions the unknown copyist of the Galán manuscripts in Montserrat.

[6]In Baltazar Ferriol's manuscript collection of secular songs in Madrid, Biblioteca Nacional, Ms. N.A. 224, with Galán's three pieces on folios 50^v, 51^v, and 65^v–66. Only the tiple (treble) part survives.

As for sources in the other places where Galán worked, there are none at all in Morella, but there are four villancicos and one Latin work still in the Cathedral in Teruel. There are three manuscripts now in the Monastery of Montserrat that may have come from the Descalzes Convent; the quality of these elegant manuscripts differs markedly from that of the other Galán sources, and they were presumably written by a royal copyist in the employ of the King.[7]

The only piece of Galán that survives in the Royal Palace in Madrid is his *Ne recorderis,* which was written for the funeral of a member of the royal family and which was used subsequently for similar occasions.[8] In addition to the locations already mentioned, Galán manuscripts can be found in the Biblioteca Nacional in Madrid (three villancicos) and in the Biblioteca Central in Barcelona (eighteen villancicos); in palaces, cathedrals, or monasteries in Palencia, Burgos, Guadalupe, Valencia, Sgorbe, Ontentiente, and El Escorial; and in foreign libraries in Munich, Mexico City, Bogotá, Guatemala City, Sucre (Bolivia), and New York (Hispanic Society of America).

Several Spanish pieces survive in more than one source, which attests to their popularity.[9] The villancico *Vuele, vuele, feliz mariposa,* for three voices and continuo, is the most frequently encountered; it can be found today in archives in Valladolid (with the date 1677), Segovia, Valencia, Barcelona, and Sucre (Bolivia). *Vivir para amar solamente,* another three-voice villancico, survives in four archives: in Palencia, Barcelona, Segovia, and Valladolid. Readers can judge for themselves the special qualities of these pieces that made them so popular by consulting volume 4 of the *Obras Completas.*

Because none of the Latin works have concordances, it might be assumed that they were less well known or liked by *maestros* of the time, but there may be another explanation. The Latin works are more pretentious than the Spanish ones and would therefore have been less appealing to most choirmasters who did not benefit from the spectacular voices of the royal choirs with which Galán worked.

---

[7]The convent is closed to outsiders even today, and as far as can be ascertained, its older holdings are now in the Monastery of Montserrat. For further description, see Laird.
[8]Cf. Galán, *Obras Completas*, vol. 2 (Ottawa: The Institute of Mediaeval Music, 1992), pp. ix–xi.
[9]Detailed discussions on the differences among concordances can be found in the critical notes to Galán, *Obras Completas.*

Special Considerations

Two Latin works survive not in part books, but in score format: the *Misa a 8*[10] and a setting of *Laudate Dominum*.[11] They are both part of the same manuscript in the Valladolid Cathedral Archive and are among his works dated on the music during his lifetime: 1659 and 1660.[12] A third piece opens the manuscript, an eight-voice *Salve Regina* by Juan Batista Comes. The score probably is not in Galán's hand, since then we would be hard pressed to explain why Comes' piece is there.[13] The score is in a hurried hand with numerous abbreviations (little of the text is given), alternate versions, erasures, and even a whole page crossed out. The *Misa* is scored for two four-voice choirs with "acompañamiento" and is, apart from the abbreviations mentioned, a complete score. The *Laudate Dominum*, however, is for the same four-voice choirs but without any accompaniment, and stops in the middle (a change of meter is followed by no further notes). The Comes piece also is without accompaniment.

We need to ask why a score of Galan's music, along with so many other pieces by him, is in the Cathedral archive in Valladolid. The rubric on the cover page indicates that at the time the manuscript was being written (1659 and 1660), Galán was no longer *maestro* in Teruel and Morella and that he probably was no longer *maestro* in Cagliari.[14] If he were already in Madrid, surely this would have been indicated unless he had no position there. As has already been mentioned, there is no documentary evidence (in Valladolid cathedral or city records or in any other subsequent references to him) that Galán ever was in Valladolid. Clearly his music was well known there, so either he was there without any position or someone who

---

[10]*Obras Completas*, vol. 2.

[11]*Obras Completas*, vol. 3, appendix. Another setting of *Laudate Dominum* (vol. 3, pp. 83–113) survives in part books in Teruel.

[12]A number of Galán's villancicos survive in manuscripts that have posthumous dates. In these cases, the dates clearly point to date of performance or at least copying; they attest to Galán's continued popularity after his death.

[13]This counters our statement in *Obras Completas*, vol. 2, p. vii, where we surmise that this could be a score in Galán's hand.

[14]"Libro de Raiados de musica es de Christobal Galan maestro q fue de la Colejial iglesia de Morella y de la Catedral de Teruel y de la Sta Yglesia primicial de caller primada cerdeña y corcega 1659. En Madrid año 1659" ("Book of shining musical examples by Christobal Galán, *maestro*, who was previously at the collegial church in Morella, at the Cathedral of Teruel, and the Holy Primatial Church of the chief prelate in Cagliari in Sardinia, and Corsica, 1659. In Madrid, 1659"). The entire statement is repeated on the same page with a new date, "1660, oi miercoles 22 o cbre" ("1660, today, Wednesday, October 22"), followed by the word "finis."

knew him well was there. A pupil or former choir member who had come to Valladolid might very well have brought a large number of his former *maestro*'s compositions and, in the process of learning the craft of composition, have copied the revered *maestro*'s work into score. This would not have been a fair copy for others to use, but a private one without special care taken in its writing. Unfortunately, despite the importance of the question posed, all explanations must remain speculative at this time.

Galán's *Que os retrate Señor* is found in Teruel in both part-book format and score in what seem to be different, though contemporary, hands.[15] There are a few errors in the parts that are not found in the score, and the one error in the score is corrected in the score itself. There are two possible scenarios here. If we assume that the parts were actually used in a performance, then the *maestro da capilla* could have corrected the errors in the parts verbally without anyone writing the corrections down. He would have discovered the errors by making his own score of the piece from the part books (which Galán himself may have provided to this *maestro*) and then by correcting it.

The other scenario is that this score was the composer's own, which he wrote while he was *maestro* in Teruel, and that the parts were copied by someone other than the composer. Again, in this case, Galán would have verbally corrected the parts during rehearsals. The score is a fair copy, not a composing score, but is not as easy to read as the parts, which resemble the parts for dozens of other works by Galán. There is no resemblance between this score and that in Valladolid; the score in Valladolid is not nearly as neat as this one. Thus, unlike the Valladolid case, the score in Teruel might very well be the only example of Galán's own handwriting that we have.

The Cathedral archive in Valladolid also contains a solo song, *Serenense los mares,* for five instruments and one solo voice, with two versions of the solo voice. All the parts, including the two versions of the voice part, are gathered in one bundle with a single title cover. The voice parts have similar but not equivalent texts; there are no differences in the music. Version A[16] begins "Serense," a meaningless word that recurs three times in the *estribillo*. Version B[17] begins with what is apparently a correction of an

---

[15]There are numerous differences such as in the treble clef sign, in the capital letter *Q,* and in spelling (for example, the score has "ha-" where the part has "a-"). Furthermore, the sharp signs in the parts, leaning left, suggest a right-handed copyist, while the sharp signs in the score, leaning right, suggest a left-handed copyist.

[16]Number 13 in *Obras Completas*, vol. 4.

[17]Number 13a in *Obras Completas*, vol. 4.

erased "Serense," namely with the word "Serenense," squeezed into the space for the original meaningless word. The correct word in B, with the extra syllable, fits the music. The second and fourth occurrences of "Serenense" in B are also correct, but the third appearance reverts to the incorrect "serense." Version B also has a phrase that originally read "q'el cielo *no malogra* las dadides" (the italics are mine) but which has the italicized words replaced by "buelue en llagas." The text of Version B is that for the veiling of a new recruit for a convent, and this is reflected on the title cover with the word "Profesion" on the upper center of the page, along with the date 1673, the correct title "Serenense," and Galán's name. But at the upper right side of the title page are the words "y villa, gracias." In the fourth *copla* of Version A, there is reference to the city of Madrid. The text of A does not refer to a veiling but expresses thanks for the return of good health to the king, Carlos II, who was in Madrid. The side remark on the title page, then, refers to the villa Madrid in Version A, which the copyist is including as an afterthought, while the center remark, "Profesion," refers to Version B as the main song. Since Version A remains uncorrected (the four words "Serenense" remain "Serense") and Version B is corrected, the latter version (B) was probably the one performed and the title cover confirms this.

It seems evident that Version A precedes Version B. Not only is the text of A corrected in B, but the text of A is more important. Text A refers to the king and probably earned Galán an extra commendation if not commission, while text B refers to an anonymous girl who, whatever her social rank, would not have equaled the king. Furthermore, the poet of A is well known—Agustin Salazar y Torres—and the poem itself was published—in *Cithera de Apolo* (1694), while no poet or publication is known for B. Therefore, Version A was written first and was used as a source for Version B, B was then performed in 1673, and, as an afterthought, the copyist or editor indicated the origins of B in A on the upper right corner of the title cover.[18]

Was Galán responsible for version B as well as Version A? The two copies are seemingly in the same hand, but the corrections in B are in a different, less careful hand, which resembles the hand on the title cover. Again, two scenarios are possible. One scenario would have Galán composing both versions in Madrid and sending both versions to Valladolid to the *maestro* there, who would then have corrected a few mistakes in his

---

[18]On the upper left side of the cover is written in "y virgin de milagros" in the same hand as "y villa, gracias." At this time, we cannot explain this rubric except by the outside possibility that there was at one time a third version of the text.

own hand and written the title on the cover sheet. This scenario has the unanswered question, however, of why Galán would have sent both versions if the second (Version B) were the only one that would be performed.

A more likely scenario, however, would be one in which Galán composed both versions in Madrid and had his copyist there make both copies. In a few cases in Version B, he hurriedly made corrections and, when in performance he caught other mistakes, verbally corrected his solo singer each time an error was made whatever the version. Galán would have assembled the piece in a bundle in Madrid and written the titles on the cover at the time of Version B; then, at a later date, the bundle was brought or sent to Valladolid along with the many other Galán villancicos and Latin works.[19]

Obviously there are many questions concerning the chronology of Galán's music, and we can only speculate about most of them. A composition must have been composed by any date given on the sources; the three songs published in 1645 were already written then, as was the *Misa a 8* by 1659 and "Serenense" by 1673. But do these dates indicate the year of composition or first performance, or do they indicate dates of later copying and/or performance? The study of these questions is only at the beginning and awaits a thorough study of paper watermarks and the records of all the archives of Spain.[20] Based on handwriting alone, the only consistencies from one piece to another are in the copying of the parts, which Galán probably had done by a few professional copyists or by a royal copyist (in the Montserrat parts). A thorough investigation of the handwriting, however, and identification of the copyists also await much more study.

By publishing Galán's works, Heiple and I hope that the world will rediscover valuable Spanish music and will want to know more about it. To this end, this essay has defined some of the research and analysis that lies ahead.

---

[19]A similar situation may exist with the villancico *Hoy compiten "a nuestra Señora de la Concepcion"* (Valladolid Cathedral Mus.Ms. 63/52), a six-voice piece that has a single *estribillo* but three sets of *coplas*.

[20]Cf. Laird's dissertation. I have combed the Segovia cathedral record books for information on Galán and found some data reported in *Obras Completas*, but I have not been able to personally view the records in Teruel and Cagliari, and I have found only a few comments on him in Madrid. These remarks shed almost no light on the chronology of the works.

Appendix
Alphabetical List of Galán's Works with Spanish Text

Title	Setting	Location of Sources
A buscar la prenda	a4+bc	Segovia, Valladolid
A cantar, pajarillos	a12+bc	Valladolid
A del portal	a8+bc	Valladolid
A la flor abejuelas	a4+bc	Barcelona
A la luz más hermosa	a1+3 instr.+bc	Valladolid
Al aurora del cielo	a4+bc	Segovia, El Escorial
Al convite	a6+bc	Segovia
Al espejo que retrate	a6+3 instr.+bc	Munich
Al nacer el aurora	a1+bc	Segovia, Palencia
Al oráculo atended	a4+bc	Segovia, Barcelona
Albricias mortales	a7+bc	Valladolid
Alegres los cielos	a4+bc	Valladolid, Munich, El Escorial
Angeles a tierra, hombres al monte	a8+bc	Munich
Arder, arder, corazón	a4+bc	Segovia
Arder, arder, corazón	a4+bc	Segovia
Atención, aves	a8+instr.+bc	Teruel
Atended, oíd, la celeste	a4+bc	Burgos
Ay corderillo	a1+bc	Valladolid
Ay, arded, sentid, llorad	a4+bc	Barcelona
Ay, ay, que me anego	a4+bc	Segovia
Ay, cruel delito	a2+bc	Valladolid
Ay, mísero de ti	a4+bc	Valladolid
Bellísima hija del sol	a4+bc	Burgos

Appendix (*continued*)

Title	Setting	Location of Sources
Blanco de mi corazón	a4+bc	Teruel
Cuando María los ojos	a8+bc	Munich
Déjame, morenilla, y véte	a2+bc	Hispanic Society
Despierten las flores	a8+bc	Valladolid
Digan los dulces ecos	a8+3 instr.+bc	Valladolid
Díganme cuál es más	a1+3 instr.+bc	Valladolid
Divinos enjambres	a10+bc	Segovia
Ea, zagales, de todo elegido	a10+3 instr.+bc	Valladolid
El ave, la fiera	a8+bc	Segovia
El pronóstico nuevo	a8+bc	Guatemala City
El sol como puede encubrir	a4+bc	Valladolid
Escuchen con atención	a6+bc	Segovia
Escuchen, escuchen, con atención	a8+bc	Segovia
Fuego que se abrasa	a8+bc	Barcelona
Fuentecillas lisonjeras	a2+bc	Segovia
Gal[l]egos bailarines	a8+bc	Burgos, Segovia, Valladolid
Hoy compiten el cielo y la tierra	a6+3 instr.+bc	Valladolid
Humano ardor	a8+3 instr.+bc	Valladolid
La mariposa que busca amorosa	a4+bc	Burgos, Segorbe, Barcelona
Las angélicas voces	a8+bc	Munich
Llévame los ojos	a8+bc	Segovia, Valladolid
Los que adoran tu imagen	[incomplete]	Valladolid

Appendix (*continued*)

Title	Setting	Location of Sources
Mándasme que te coma	a4+bc	Segovia, Barcelona
Mariposa que vuelas con alas	a8+bc	Valladolid, Barcelona (2 copies)
Mariposa, no corras al fuego	a1+bc	Barcelona
No encubra el amor	a8+bc	Segovia
No es milagro	a6+3 instr.+bc	Munich
No gima nadie	a4+bc	Segovia
No, no prosigas	a2+bc	Madrid
No temas, no receles	a8+bc	Munich
Norabuena	a8+bc	Valladolid
O qué bien celébrese	a4+bc	Valladolid
O qué mal vamos, amor	a1+3 instr.+bc	Valladolid
O qué milagro de amor	a7+bc	Palencia
Oíd, troncos; oíd fieras	a8+bc	Valladolid, Barcelona
Oigan a dos sentidos	a8+bc	Barcelona
Oigan todos del ave	a11+bc	Munich
Oigan, atiendan, escuchen	a4+instr.+bc	Valladolid
Oíganos celebrar un misterio	?†	Mexico City
[Oíganos retratar un prodigio]	a2+bc	Hispanic Society
Pajarillo que cantas ausente	a1+bc	Hispanic Society
Pajarillos	a1+3 instr.+bc	Valladolid (2 copies)
[Pintar quiero una imagen]	a2+bc	Valladolid
Pues que ya tan adelante	a6+bc	Valladolid

†At this writing, we have not had access to the sources for *Oíganos celebrar un misterio*.

Appendix (*continued*)

Title	Setting	Location of Sources
Que dulcemente	a4+bc	Valladolid, Barcelona
Que ha de tener quien llegare	a2+bc	Barcelona
Que os retrate, Señor	a3+bc	Teruel
Querubes de la impirea	a8+bc	Segovia, Valladolid
Quien ha visto al placer	a7+bc	Valladolid
¿Quién ha visto el jazmín?	a7+bc	Segovia, Barcelona
Quien muere de amor	a6+bc	Segovia
Quien padece de amor	a4+3 instr.+bc	Segovia
Ramilletes canoros de pluma	a8+bc	Valladolid
Sea bien venida	a8+bc	Valladolid
Señor todo se mudó	a4+bc	Barcelona
Serénense los mares	a1+3 instr.+bc	Valladolid
Si al formarse la tierra	a4+bc	Segovia
Si del alma las alas	a7+bc	Valladolid
Si del pan el misterio	[incomplete]	Valladolid
Si me ciega el amor por ver	a5+3 instr.+bc	Segovia
Sólo sabe de amor	a1+3 instr.+bc	Valencia
Tened, tened, esferas	a4+bc	Barcelona
[Válgate Dios, Virgen pura]	a4+bc	Segovia
Vaya de jacarilla	a12+bc	Valladolid
Vengan todas las flores	a4+bc	Segovia
Vénganle todos a ver	a8+bc	Valladolid
Venid, estrellas, siguiendo	a8+bc	Barcelona
Venid, pastores siguiendo	a9+bc	Barcelona

Appendix (*continued*)

Title	Setting	Location of Sources
Vivir para amar solamente	a3+bc	Palencia, Segovia, Valladolid, Barcelona
Volved, Señor, los ojos	a1+bc	Valladolid
Vuele, vuele la flecha	a1+1 instr.+bc	Valladolid
Vuele, vuele, feliz mariposa	a3+bc	Segovia, Valladolid, Barcelona, Valencia, Sucre
Y el alborozo festivo	[incomplete]	Valladolid
[Ya los caballos]	a1+bc	Madrid

The Speaking Body: Gaspero Angiolini's *Rhétorique Muette* and the *Ballet d'Action* in the Eighteenth Century

Ingrid Brainard

Walking is natural, to dance is an art.
—Dr. Samuel Johnson

Considerable attention has been paid in recent years to the relationship of music and rhetoric. From these discussions the art of dancing and ballet has been largely excluded, presumably because an art form that uses no words would appear to be an unlikely candidate for the application of rhetorical principles.

It has even been argued that dance is not a language.[1] However, in the thinking of the representatives of the *ballet d'action* in the 18th century, it is precisely the acknowledgement that the dancing body is able to speak without words, in what became known as *la rhétorique muette*, or *l'éloquence muette*, that distinguishes the works of the new era, culminating in the great *ballets pantomimes tragiques* of Gaspero Angiolini (1731–1803),[2]

---

[1] Mark Franko, *The Dancing Body in Renaissance Choreography (c. 1416–1589)* (Birmingham, Alabama: Summa Publications, Inc., 1986), chap. 2, inter alia.

[2] Lorenzo Tozzi, *Il Balletto Pantomimo del Settecento: Gaspare Angiolini* (L'Aquila: L. U. Japadre, 1972). Gino Tani, article "G. Angiolini," in *Enciclopedia dello Spettacolo* (1954*ff*). Volume 29–30 of *Chigiana* (1975) contains a number of articles dealing with the various aspects of Angiolini's work, with his collaboration with Gluck, etc. For the acrimonious correspondence between Angiolini and Noverre, see L. Carones, "Noverre and Angiolini: Polemical Letters," *Dance Research* 5 (1987): 42*ff*. For Angiolini's place in the larger context of the Viennese Reform, see Bruce Alan Brown, *Gluck and the French Theatre in Vienna* (Oxford: Clarendon Press, 1991), and José Sasportes, "Noverre in Italia," *La Danza Italiana* 2 (Spring 1985): 39–66. See also article "Angiolini," in *Riemanns Musiklexikon*, 12th ed. (Mainz: B. Schotts Söhne, 1959); Gerhard Croll, article "Angiolini," in *The New Grove Dictionary of Music and*

those of his mentor, "the famous M. Hilverding" (1710–68), and those of his contemporary and competitor Jean-Georges Noverre (1727–1810), from the divertissements, however extravagant their staging may have been at times, that preceded them.

It may seem that the term *rhétorique* was somewhat less strictly used in the world of dance than in that of the written, declaimed or sung word, since the movement arts convey their messages or tell their tales purely through physical eloquence. However, as Patricia Ranum has shown, the "mute rhetoric" of the dance and the audible rhetoric of the singer are both founded upon the same principles of public speaking.[3] Furthermore, all writers on dance appear to be familiar with the major classical works on rhetoric such as Aristotle's *Rhetoric,*[4] Cicero's *De Oratore,*[5] and Quintilian's *Institutio Oratoria,*[6] which was the standard text used in the training of actors, orators and dancers of dramatic roles from the Renaissance through the Baroque.

Like the orator, the dancer aims to persuade, to move and to please. "The dance," says the 16th-century French canon and dancing master Thoinot Arbeau,

> is a kind of *rhétorique muette* [this, to the best of my knowledge, is the first appearance of the term in a dance context] through which the orator can, by his movements, without saying a single word, make himself understood and persuade the spectators that he is gallant [*gaillard*] and worthy of being praised, loved and cherished. Is it not in your opinion a speech [*oraison*] that he makes for himself, with his own feet, in a demonstrative genre?... And when miming [*les masquarades*] is added, it has great power to move the affections, now to anger, now to pity and commiseration, now to hate, now to love... As also Roscius made clear to Cicero when he combined his gestures and silent actions in such a fashion that in the judgment of those who were arbiters he moved the spectators as much or more than Cicero had been able to with his oratorical eloquences.[7]

Musicians, 6th ed. (London: Macmillan Publishers, 1980); and Mark Franko, *Dance as Text. Ideologies of the Baroque Body* (Cambridge: Cambridge University Press, 1993).

[3]"Audible rhetoric and mute rhetoric: the 17th-century French sarabande," *Early Music* 14/1 (Feb. 1986): 22*ff.*

[4]Trans. J. H. Freese (Harvard University Press, 1975).

[5]Trans. H. Rackham (Loeb Classical Library, 1942).

[6]Loeb Classical Library edition, 4 vols. (1959–63).

[7]*Orchésographie* (Lengres: Jehan des Preyz, 1588; later editions 1589, 1596), f. 5ᵛ: "La dance est vne espece de Rhetorique muette, par laquelle l'Orateur peult par ses mouue-

The interrelationship of dance and rhetoric occupied, explicitly or implicitly, the minds of many,[8] Angiolini included. But like Angiolini, a pragmatist whose primary concern was bodily eloquence in practical terms rather than the pursuit of an abstract theory of rhetoric, we shall in the present paper above all else attempt to recapture the physical components of the silent language of theater dance as it was practiced on the Viennese stages and elsewhere during the 18th century, without, however, losing sight of the *ars oratoria* that forms the intellectual background to the technical and expressive achievements of the Baroque ballarino.

Most of Angiolini's thoughts concerning the nature of ballet as drama, and the qualities and training required of the true dramatic dancer are contained in the two important "Dissertations" that served as introductions, and libretti, to the choreographer's masterpieces, the ballets *Don Juan ou le Festin de Pierre*[9] and *Semiramis*.[10] Both Dissertations emphasize that the works described are "Ballet Pantomimes dans le goût des Anciens": the first, *Don Juan,* for which the textual model was Molière's play, is "a Spanish tragi-comedy"; the second, *Semiramis,* after Voltaire's drama by the same name, is a "ballet pantomime tragique," purposeful, grim, without concessions to the prevailing taste of an audience that preferred, or was

---

mĕts, sans parler vn seul mot, se faire entendre, & persuader aux spectateurs, qu'il est gaillard digne d'estre loué, aymé, & chery. N'est-ce pas à vostre aduis vne oraison qu'il faict pour soy-mesme, par ses pieds propres, en gendre demonstratif?...Et quāt les masquarades y sont ioinctes, elle ha efficace grāde de mouuoir les affections, tantost à cholere, tantost à pitié & commiseration, tantost à la hayne, tantost à l'amour...Comme aussi Roscius le faisoit bien paroistre à Ciceron, quant il adjançoit ses gestes & actions muettes de telle façon, qu'au iugement de ceulx qui en estoient arbitres, il mouuoit aultant ou plus les spectateurs, que Ciceron eut peu faire par ses elocutions oratoires." The translations of this and all subsequent quotations are mine unless stated otherwise.

[8]For French 17th-century authors on this subject, see Ranum.

[9]Premier performance 17 Oct. 1761, Burgtheater, Vienna. Music by C. W. Gluck, sets and machinery by Quaglio. Angiolini danced the title role. Edition of the music and commentary in *C. W. Gluck, Sämtliche Werke,* Abteilung 2, vol. 1, *Tanzdramen* (1966), ed. R. Engländer (hereafter *SW*). An earlier reprint of the libretto, with German translation, R. Haas, "Die Wiener Ballett-Pantomime im 18. Jahrhundert und Glucks Don Juan," *Studien zur Musikwissenschaft,* Beihefte der DTÖ 10 (Vienna, 1923): 10*ff.*

[10]Premier performance 31 Jan. 1765, Burgtheater, Vienna. Music by C. W. Gluck. In the title role Mme. Trancosa, née Nency, one of Noverre's most famous pupils. Edition in *SW*. A facsimile of the complete text of the *Dissertation sur les ballets pantomimes des Anciens publiée pour servir de Programme au Ballet Pantomime Tragique Semiramis* (Milan: W. Toscanini, 1956). Synopses of both *Don Juan* and *Semiramis,* incl. history, sources etc., by Ingrid Brainard, article "Angiolini," in *Pipers Enzyklopädie des Musiktheaters,* vol. 1 (Munich: Piper, 1986), pp. 46*ff.* See also B. A. Brown, chapter 8, "Angiolini, Gluck, and Viennese Ballet-Pantomime."

used to, the lighter, entertaining type of danced spectacle. Not surprisingly, those present at the premier performance of *Semiramis* were horrified by the uncompromisingly brutal story-line ("soggetto il più terribile"). But, argues Angiolini, this time in defense of the tragic ending of *Don Juan,*

> actors please with the terrible as well as with the agreeable...Should we be forbidden to horrify in dance as [they do] in declaiming? The terror in the tragedies gives us pleasure, we cry there with a kind of sweet sensibility that enchants us. If we can arouse all the passions through a silent play, why should we be forbidden to try? If the public does not want to deprive itself of the greatest beauties of our art, it must accustom itself to be moved and to cry during our ballets.[11]

The model for Angiolini is the theater of the Greeks which, he believes, "can uniquely guide us in our plans, and that there is no tragedy in that theater that could not be treated successfully as a Ballet Pantomime."[12] By citing Lucian's *De Saltatione*[13] as a kind of poetic theory of the *danse pantomime* and by establishing the connection between his own dramatic creations and the pantomimes of the Ancients, the choreographer presents himself as the legitimate heir to a long and distinguished line of theorists whose works on aesthetics, theater, acting, and dancing reflect the reawakening of interest in the classical manifestations of these arts during the 17th and early 18th centuries: Michel de Pure,[14] Claude François Ménestrier,[15] l'Abbé Jean-Baptiste Dubos,[16] Louis de Cahusac,[17] and, in England, John

---

[11]"Les Comédiens plaisent par le terrible ainsi que par l'agréable...Nous seroit-il défendu d'épouvanter en dansant ainsi qu'en déclamant? La terreur nous fait plaisir aux Tragédies, nous y pleurons avec une espèce de sensibilité douce qui nous charme. Si nous pouvons exciter toutes les passions par un jeu muet pourquoi nous seroit-il interdit de le tenter? Si le Public ne veut pas se priver des plus grandes beautés de notre Art, il doit s'accoutumer à s'attendrir & à pleurer à nos Ballets" (*Don Juan* program, f. a5^v).

[12]"Je crois que le théâtre des Grecs doit uniquement nous guider pour nos plans, & qu'il n'y a aucune Tragédie de ce Théâtre, qui ne puisse être traitée avec succès en Ballet Pantomime" (*Semiramis* program, ff. C2*f*).

[13]Lucian de Samosata (c. 120-90); in the 16th, 17th, and 18th centuries, believed to be the author of *De Saltatione*. Trans. into French by Filbert Bretin (1582). An anonymous trans. into English, *Part of Lucian's Dialogues...done into rhyme* (1684).

[14]*Idée des Spectacles Anciens et Nouveaux* (Paris, 1668).

[15]*Traité des tournois, ioustes, carrousels et autres spectacles publics* (Paris 1669); *Des Représentations en Musique Anciennes et Modernes* (Paris, 1681); *Des Ballets Anciens et Modernes selon les Règles du Théâtre* (Paris, 1682).

[16]*Réflexions critiques sur la poésie, la peinture et la musique* (Paris, 1719).

[17]*La danse ancienne et moderne...* (Paris, 1754).

Weaver,[18] to name but a few. In the opinion of these authors, *pantomime dans le goût des Anciens,* or ballet, is at the same time the imitation and the explanation of all things natural: "Le ballet imite la nature des choses."[19] Or, as Angiolini puts it:

> The sublime of ancient dance was the pantomime, which was the art of imitating the customs, the passions, the actions of Gods, Heroes, humans, through movements and gestures executed in accordance with the music and suited to express that which one intended to represent. These movements, these gestures had to constitute, so to speak, a *running discourse;* this was *a kind of declamation, created for the eyes* [my emphases], which was made more understandable for the spectators by means of the music, which varied the sounds according to whether the Pantomimic Actor planned to express love or hate, rapture or despair.[20]

---

[18]*An Essay Towards an History of Dancing* (London, 1712); *Anatomical and Mechanical Lectures upon Dancing* (London, 1721); *The History of Mimes and Pantomimes* (London, 1728). Weaver's complete *œuvre* has been published in facsimile by Richard Ralph, *The Life and Works of John Weaver: An account of his life, writings and theatrical productions, with an annotated reprint of his complete publications* (New York: Dance Horizons, 1985). See also Selma Jeanne Cohen, "John Weaver," in *Famed for Dance: Essays on the Theory and Practice of Theatrical Dancing in England, 1660–1740* (New York: New York Public Library, 1960), pp. 35*ff,* and Richard Ralph, "Restoring Dance to Parnassus: The Scholarly Challenges of Eighteenth-Century Dance," *Dance Research* 1/1 (1983): 21*ff.*

[19]Ménestrier, *Des Ballets,* p. 291. See also Weaver, *History of Dancing,* p. 160 (Ralph, *John Weaver,* p. 652): "STAGE-DANCING was at first design'd for *Imitation;* to explain Things conceiv'd in the Mind, by the *Gestures* and *Motions* of the Body, and plainly and intelligibly representing *Actions, Manners, and Passions;* so that the Spectator might perfectly understand the *Performer* by these his *Motions,* tho' he say not a Word."

[20]"Le sublime de l'ancienne Danse étoit la Pantomime, & celleci étoit l'art d'imiter les moeurs, les passions, les actions des Dieux, des Héros, des hommes, par des mouvemens & des signes faits en cadence & propres à exprimer ce qu'on avoit dessein de représenter. Ces mouvemens, ces gestes, devoient former, pour ainsi dire, un discours suivi: c'étoit une espèce de Déclamation, faite pour les yeux, dont on rendoit l'intelligence plus aisée aux spectateurs par le moien de la Musique qui varioit les sons, suivant que l'Acteur Pantomime avoit dessein d'exprimer l'amour ou la haine, la fureur ou le désespoir" (*Don Juan* program, f. a2ᵛ). See also Weaver, *History of Mimes,* p. 7 (Ralph, *John Weaver,* p. 684): "The Mimes and Pantomimes, tho' *Dancers,* had their Names from *Acting,* that is, from *Imitation;* copying all the *Force* of the *Passions* meerly by the *Motions* of the *Body* to that degree, as to draw *Tears* from the *Audience* at their *Representations.*"

The 17th-century theorists, Ménestrier in particular, still see ballet predominantly as a pleasant entertainment,[21] a spectacle loosely constructed of several episodes, with frequent changes of scenery, and enacted by a mixture of "personnes graves & enjoüées, historiques & fabuleuses, naturelles & allégoriques";[22] the *tragédie-ballet* which was to become the lodestone of the Viennese reform of Angiolini and Gluck, was for Ménestrier "un Monstre inconnu chez les Anciens"[23] and therefore to be avoided. Gaspero Angiolini on the other hand, himself a brilliant dancer and pantomime, was a passionate advocate of the tightly structured, compact dance work for the ballet stage in which a substantial dramatic story-line drives relentlessly towards the ultimate catastrophe,[24] in which music supports the action in every detail, and the dancer is challenged at every moment to make the fullest use possible of the expressiveness of his or her entire body.

It is this expressiveness that lies at the heart of the *rhétorique muette* of all theater dance, but especially of "the most sublime kind," the *danse pantomime* "that dares to elevate itself to the representation of great tragic events."[25] "Rhetorick," declared John Weaver some forty years earlier,

> is only requir'd of a Master of *Dramatick Dances;* and then only, as far as such *Dances* have relation to the *Manners, Passions,* &c. RHETORICK is an Art of Eloquence, which arises from an elegant Choice of Words, perswasive [*sic*], and of such Force, as so to express the Passions, as to raise, or allay the Affections of Man. What *Rhetorick* is to the *Orator* in Speaking, is to the *Dancer* in Action; and an Elegance of Action consists, in adapting the Gesture to the Passions and Affections; and the *Dancer,* as well as the *Orator,* allures the Eye, and invades the Mind of the Spectator; for there is a Force, and Energy in Action, which strangely affects; and when Words will scarce move, Action will excite, and put all the Powers of the Soul in a ferment.[26]

---

[21]"Le ballet [est] pour le divertissement & le plaisir" (*Des Ballets,* p. 291).

[22]*Des Ballets,* p. 291.

[23]*Des Ballets,* p. 290.

[24]"L'Action...nous entraîne tout d'un coup à la catastrophe" (*Semiramis* program, f. B5^v).

[25]"...la danse pantomime qui ose s'élever jusqu'à représenter les grands événemens tragiques est sans contredit la plus sublime" (*Semiramis* program, f. D).

[26]*Anatomical and Mechanical Lectures,* p. 144 (Ralph, *John Weaver,* p. 1018). Similarly, *History of Dancing,* p. 123 (Ralph, *John Weaver,* p. 595).

Throughout Angiolini's two Dissertations, there are hints concerning the means by which the dancing body can transmit to the audience the manners, the thoughts, the passions of his or her role.

Prerequisite is, of course, an impeccable technique, similar to that which *la belle danse,* or *la haute danse,* of a Dupré or Vestris demands, consisting of "precision, lightness, equilibrium, flexibility, grace" ("de la justesse, de la légereté, l'équilibre, le moèleux, les graces") and enhanced by "supple and graceful" ("souples & gracieux") manipulation of the arms. "Everyone knows that it is the most beautiful, the most elegant, but also the most difficult."[27]

Here we are on relatively secure ground. The many collections of ballroom and theater dances, most of them transmitted in the notational system developed by Pierre Beauchamps and Raoul Auger Feuillet,[28] theoretical treatises,[29] the usual array of books on etiquette and education, and a wealth of pictorial representations allow us to obtain quite a clear picture of the technique of the *danse noble,* or *belle danse,* as it was practiced in France, England, Germany, Holland, Spain, Italy, Sweden, Austria, in the first half of the 18th century.[30]

---

[27]"A l'égard de la haute danse des *Dupré,* des *Vestris*...chacun sait qu'elle est la plus belle, la plus élégante, mais aussi la plus difficile" (*Semiramis* program, ff. C7^v–[C8^{vl}]); the context is Angiolini's definitions of the four genres of stage dancing: *grotesque, comique, demi-caractère* (which includes the *belle danse*), and *danse pantomime.*

[28]The notational system is explained in R. A. Feuillet, *Chorégraphie ou l'art de décrire la dance, par caractères, figures et signes démonstratifs* (Paris, 1700); trans. into English by John Weaver (1706). To his notation book, Feuillet adds a collection of sixteen salon and stage dances of his own (*Recueil de Dances*) as well as a *Recueil de Dances* by Louis Pécour. For the latter, see Anne L. Witherell, *Louis Pécour's 1700 Recueil de Dances* (Ann Arbor: UMI Research Press, 1983). Concerning Feuillet's notational system, see Francine Lancelot, "L'Ecriture de la danse: le système Feuillet," *Ethnologie Française* 1/1 (1971): 29–58. For the repertory as a whole and the technique of *la danse noble,* see Wendy Hilton, *Dance of Court & Theater. The French Noble Style 1690–1725* (Princeton: Princeton Book Co., 1981). See also Judith L. Schwartz and Christena L. Schlundt, *French Court Dance and Dance Music, A Guide to Primary Source Writings 1643–1789* (Stuyvesant, NY: Pendragon Press, 1987).

[29]E.g., Gottfried Taubert, *Rechtschaffener Tantz-Meister, oder gründliche Erklärung der Frantzösischen Tantz=Kunst* (Leipzig, 1717; the central section is a trans. of Feuillet's *Chorégraphie* into German); P[ierre] Rameau, *Le Maître à Danser* (Paris, 1725); Kellom Tomlinson, *The Art of Dancing Explained by Reading and Figures* (London, 1735); Giov. Andrea Battista Gallini, *A Treatise on the Art of Dancing* (London 1762 and later editions). More in Schwartz/Schlundt.

[30]In addition to the studies already cited, see Carol Marsh, *French Court Dance in England, 1706–1740: A Study of the Sources* (Ph.D. dissertation, City University of New York, 1985; repr. Ann Arbor: UMI Research Press, 1986). For France, see, inter alia, Rebecca Harris-Warrick, "Ballroom Dancing at the Court of Louis XIV," *Early Music*

Yet even among the elegant and seemingly conventional choreographies for the ballroom, whose moods and step sequences on the whole are predetermined by the character of the music to which they are "composed" (a Minuet differs noticeably from a Gigue, a Rigaudon from a Bourrée etc.), there are some in which the emotional and expressive content is intensified to an astonishing degree, and the floor-pattern also affected, by incorporating the principles of rhetoric. The prime example is the 17th-century Sarabande for a male solo dancer described by Father François Pomey.[31] The initial paragraphs, the Exordium, describe a variety of steps, leaps, slides and pirouettes, "the most beautiful steps ever invented for the dance" (§2). In the Narration (§§3 and 4), the emotion increases; the dancer alternates between movement and suspended poses,[32] between little skips and long steps. The Confirmation (§§5 and 6) continues such contrasts and expands the floor pattern in accordance with rhetorical figures: the dancer "moves to the right and then to the left in the gesture associated with generosity. His exaggerated pirouette seems the embodiment of hyperbole."[33] §7 makes the transition to the Peroration: "But all this was nothing compared to what was observed when this gallant began to express the emotions of his soul through the motions of his body, and reveal them in his face, his eyes, his steps and all his actions." The Peroration includes in rapid succession "languid and passionate glances", "precipitous motion"

14/1 (1986): 40–49, and Judith Chazin Bennahum, *Dance in the Shadow of the Guillotine* (Carbondale, Ill.: Southern Illinois University Press, 1988). For Sweden, see Mary Skeaping, *Ballet under the Three Crowns,* Dance Perspectives 32 (1967). For Holland, see Joan Rimmer, "Dance and dance music in the Netherlands in the 18th century," *Early Music* 14/2 (1986): 209*ff.* For Spain, see the articles by Xoán M. Carreira, "Foreign Dancers in Spain in the Second Half of the Eighteenth Century," "'Exotic' or Foreign Dancers Active in Spain, 1750–1800," and "Ballets Performed at the Teatro de los Caños del Peral, Madrid, and other Spanish Theaters, 1787–1799," in *The Origins of the Bolero School,* Studies in Dance History, 4/1 (Spring 1993), pp. 61–90.

[31]*Le dictionnaire royal augmenté* (Lyons, 1671), p. 22. The *Description* in both French and Latin is reprinted in facsimile in Ranum, p. 34; on p. 35 follows the French text with an English translation by Ranum.

[32]Domenico da Piacenza's *positura* and his concept of *fantasmata,* a sudden halt between movement sequences, come to mind immediately (cf. Paris, BN, fds. it. 972, f. 2) as does A. Cornazano's slightly more matter-of-fact remark: "Sometimes to remain still for a moment [*un tempo*] and to stop dead is not bad" ("Talhor tacere un tempo e starlo morto non e brutto") (*Libro dell'arte del danzare,* f. 7). Both treatises belong to the middle of the 15th century. Cf. Ingrid Brainard, *The Art of Courtly Äancing in the Early Renaissance* (1981), pp. 52*ff.*

[33]Ranum, p. 30.

(§8), "anger and spite...and then evoking a sweeter passion by more moderate motions, he would sigh, swoon, let his eyes wander languidly; and certain sinuous movements of the arms and body, nonchalant, disjointed and passionate" (§9). Small wonder that this dancing orator in his "enchanting dance" won as many hearts as he attracted eyes to behold him!

In the more traditional, non-pantomimic theater dances, especially those for men, the basic steps of the court dances[34] were embellished by a variety of intricate leg gestures, all manner of jumps, successions of pirouettes, and the like.[35]

As one would expect, this technique changed gradually during the years that separate the principal documents of the first decades of the century from Angiolini's creations, which, by the way, also included national dances, *balli storici*, fables and comedies.[36] The best idea of what these changes were can be gleaned from the treatise by Gennaro Magri, *Trattato Teorico-Prattico di Ballo* (Naples, 1779),[37] a rich source of information concerning the execution of the steps "and the material pertaining to them" (part 1) and ballroom dancing (part 2), with chapters on the "Duties of a Dancing Master" (2,1), "Noble Behaviour" (2,6), etc. Magri, who spent the year 1759 at the Burgtheater in Vienna, side by side with Angiolini and Pierre Michel, the great French *ballarino grotescho*,[38] represents the Italian

---

[34]For a comprehensive "Survey of the Components of the Dance," see Hilton, pp. 65*ff*.

[35]For two of innumerable examples that could be cited, see the *Entrée grave pour homme* and the *Entrée d'Apolon* in Feuillet's *Recueil* of 1700, pp. 53*ff*.

[36]See the work list in Tozzi, *Il Balletto Pantomimo*, and Robert Haas, "Der Wiener Bühnentanz von 1740 bis 1767," *Jahrbuch der Musikbibliothek Peters für 1937* (Leipzig, 1938), pp. 82*ff*. For specific examples, see the *balli* composed by Angiolini for *Antigono* and *Luzio Vero*, both 1757 at the Teatro Regio in Turin, cited in Lorenzo Tozzi, "Musica e balli al Regio di Torino (1748–1762)," *La Danza Italiana* 2 (Spring 1985): 5–21.

[37]English translation by Mary Skeaping with Irmgard Berry, *Practical and Theoretical Treatise on Dancing* (London: Dance Books, 1988). For a review of the translation, see Rebecca Harris-Warrick, *Dance Chronicle* 12/1 (1989): 140–48. Translations of passages from Magri in the present article are my own. To the brief outline of Magri's biography (p. 10 of the Introduction), which is mainly based on Hannah Winter's research (cf. *The Preromantic Ballet* [London: Pitman Publishing, 1974]), must be added four performances at the Teatro Nuovo in Padua during the years 1760–62 and 1764 (for these, see Maria Nevilla Massaro, "Il Ballo pantomimo al Teatro Nuovo di Padova (1751–1830)," *Acta Musicologica* 57 (1985): 242–43). Magri, at this time already an acclaimed and well-paid *primo ballerino grotescho*, appears to have gone back and forth between engagements in Venice (1760–63) and Vienna (1759 or slightly earlier, and 1763–64) and performances in Padua before eventually returning to Naples.

[38]Cf. Winter, p. 94. See also Magri, p. 126: "This *salto ribaltato* was invented by Monsieur Michel, the best *Ballerino grottescho* that France has produced" ("Questo salto

practice, which, after all, nurtured the talent of the young Angiolini before he became ballet master in Vienna in 1758. If one wished to stage the social dances in the banquet scene of *Don Juan*,[39] Magri would serve as well, if not better, than the earlier manuals. (See above p. 18*ff* and nn. 14 to 18.)

But, stresses Angiolini, "the steps, the jumps, the *port des bras*, the poise, the attitudes are only the alphabet of the dance,"[40] overemphasized in the training of young dancers wéth the result that "in our time the dance has degenerated to the point of being regarded only as the skill to make *entrechats* and *gambades*, to jump or run rhythmically, to carry the body or to walk with grace and without losing balance, to have flexible arms and picturesque and elegant *attitudes*. Our schools teach us nothing else."[41]

With this complaint our master is by no means alone. Noverre, in an often-quoted passage from Letter 4 of his *Lettres sur la Danse et sur les Ballets*,[42] advises the Children of Terpsichore to

> renounce cabrioles, entrechats and over-complicated steps; abandon grimaces to study sentiments, artless graces and expression; study how to make your gestures noble...; put judgment and sense into your *pas de deux*.... Renounce that slavish routine that keeps your art in its infancy; examine everything relative to the development of your talents; be original;...if you must copy, imitate nature, it is a noble model and never misleads those who follow it.[43]

---

ribaltato fu da Monsieur Michel inventato, il miglior Ballerino grottesco, che abbia dato la Francia"). High praise indeed from one colleague to the other!

[39]E.g., the *Chaconne Espagnole* (No. 19), called *Contredanse* in Regensburg; the *Contradanza/Allgemeiner Tanz* (No. 22); the Andante No. 20, which suggests a Minuet.

[40]"En effet, les pas, les sauts, le port des bras, l'à-plomb, les attitudes ne sont que l'Alphabet de la Danse" (*Semiramis* program, f. A5^v; a corresponding passage appears in the *Don Juan* booklet, f. a5^v).

[41]"La Danse a dégénéré de nos jours au point de ne plus la regarder depuis long-tems que comme l'art de faire des entrechats & des gambades, de sauter ou courir en cadence, ou tout au plus de porter le corps, ou de marcher avec grace, & sans perdre l'équilibre, d'avoir les bras moëleux, & des attitudes pittoresques & élégantes. Nos écoles ne nous apprennent pas autre chose" (*Semiramis* program, f. A4^v).

[42]1st ed., Stuttgart, 1760. English trans. by Cyril W. Beaumont (London: By the author, 1930; repr. New York: Dance Horizons, 1960). Beaumont translates the revised and enlarged edition published in St. Petersburg, 1803.

[43]"Enfants de Terpsichore, renoncez aux cabrioles, aux entrechats & aux pas trop compliqués; abadonnez les minauderie pour vous livrer aux sentiments, aux graces naïves & à l'expression; appliquez-vous à la Pantomime noble...; mettez de l'esprit & du raisonnement dans vos pas de deux.... Renoncez à cette imitation servile qui ramene insensiblement l'Art à son berceau; voyez tout ce qui est relatif à votre talent; soyez

And, shortly before Noverre, Cahusac wrote in much the same vein: "The moment will perhaps come when the spirit of reflection will enter into some kind of companionship with the mechanical production of jumps and steps."[44]

No one denies that learning to execute those jumps and steps with strength and grace, and developing nobility of bearing and elegance of posture is worth the long and exacting study, but eventually "the dancer must acquire expression, that is the skill of *parler en dansant*,"[45] which is the prime requirement for the most elevated level of theater dancing, the *danse pantomime*. If the dancer is to transmit to the audience the thoughts, the manners and the passions of his or her role, if he is to move their souls rather than merely please their eyes,[46] what is needed above all else is "the art of gesture carried to its highest degree [which] should accompany the majestic, the elegant, the delicate in *la belle danse*."[47] By its very nature the art of gesture helps to achieve the concentration that is needed in pantomimic action because it "abbreviates miraculously the discourse; with a

---

original;...copiez, mais ne copiez que la nature; c'est un beau modele, il n'égara jamais ceux qui l'ont exactement suivie" (pp. 55–56; trans. Beaumont, pp. 29–30).

[44] "Le moment viendra peut-être où l'esprit de réflexion entrera en quelque société avec la facture méchanique des sauts & des pas" (article "Geste," in Diderot/d'Alembert, *Encyclopédie*, vol. 7 [1757], p. 651–52). See also Judith Chazin Bennahum, "Cahusac, Diderot, and Noverre: Three Revolutionary Writers on the Eighteenth Century Dance," *Theatre Journal* (May 1983): 168–78.

[45] "Dans la Danse Pantomime il faut d'abord apprendre les pas ou l'Alphabet de notre langage; cet apprentissage est déja long & pénible. Il faut encore se donner la grace, la noblesse, l'élégance des attitudes...Enfin il faut acquérir l'expression, ou l'art de parler an dansant" (*Semiramis* program, f. B4). Learning the alphabet is, in fact, the first step towards oratorical competence, as Angiolini implies and as Arbeau had pointed out a century and a half earlier. From letters words are shaped, and words constitute the art of grammar in which the student "faict premierement amas de noms, verbes & aultres parties de l'oraison, puis il apprend à les lier ensemble congruement. Ainsi en l'art de dancer, il vous fault premieremēt sçauoir plusieurs particuliers mouuements, puis par le moyen des compositiõs que l'on vous donnera...sçaurez le tout" (*Orchésographie*, f. 43^v). These thoughts are echoed in Sir John Davies, *Orchestra or a poem of dancing* (1594/1596), stanzas 92–94, where the connection to rhetoric is explicitly made. On Davies, see Ingrid Brainard, "Sir John Davies' *Orchestra* as a Dance Historical Source," in *Songs of the Dove and the Nightingale: Sacred and Secular Music c. 900–c. 1600*, Australian Studies in History, Philosophy & Social Studies of Music, 3 (Sydney: Currency Press, 1994), pp. 197–99.

[46] "Dans cette danse [i.e., *la danse pantomime*] il est question de remuer l'ame, & non pas de plaire aux yeux" (*Semiramis* program, f. C4).

[47] "L'art du geste porté au suprême degré doit accompagner le majestueux, l'élégant, le délicat de la belle danse" (*Semiramis* program, f. D).

single expressive sign it often replaces a considerable number of words."[48] Besides, there is an eloquence in gesture that goes beyond the limitations of language, of age, and of educational level. "Chironomy," wrote Mattheson,

> certainly has more power than all words...Words move no one who does not understand the language; clever arguments are only for clever heads; but well-defined expressions are understood by everyone, even by children of a tender age with whom neither words nor smacks will accomplish as much as one glance. The Latins called this *Action*...without it even the best orator is worth nothing;...Words have only the tongue as their tool; but gestures have their substance [*Beistand*] in all the parts of the body.[49]

The question for us is now: What was the vocabulary of gestures that Angiolini's pantomimic dancers used, and how did they use it? The choreographer himself, to our regret, is not particularly explicit regarding the specifics of the *éloquence muette* that is so important to him. He speaks of *gestes parlans* and *signes expressifs,* mentions movements of the head, the eyes, the hands, the arms, the knees and the legs without going into details. But in his synopses of *Don Juan* and *Semiramis,* there are remarks that illuminate the affective content of certain situations, sometimes together with and at other times separate from purely physical directives.

In *Don Juan,* when the Commandeur is mortally wounded in his duel with the hero, he "withdraws to the side of the stage opposite his house, falling at every step, and leaning on his sword to remain upright." When the statue appears at the festivities in Don Juan's house and advances "gravement," the guests are "frightened" ("épouvantés"); they flee and return "trembling," expressing "by their gestures the fear that has taken hold of them." After having seen the statue to the door, Don Juan reappears "triumphant"; at the sight "terror fills all his friends." In the churchyard, Don Juan approaches the newly erected mausoleum first with "some astonishment," which gives way to "an assured mien"; his "vanity makes him tri-

---

[48]"L'art du geste...abrége [*sic*] merveilleusement le discours, qui par un seul signe expressif supplée souvant à un nombre considérable de paroles" (*Semiramis* program, f. B5).

[49]Johann Mattheson, *Der vollkommene Capellmeister* (Hamburg: 1739), chap. 6, "Von der Geberden=Kunst," p. 34, §6: "die Chironomie...hat auch wirklich mehr Nachdruck als alle Worte...Worte rühren niemand, der die Sprache nicht verstehet; scharffsinnige Sprüche schicken sich nur für scharffsinnige Köpffe; aber wolangebrachte Minen begreiffet iedermann, auch die zarten Kinder, bey welchen weder Worte noch Schläge so viel ausrichten, als ein Blick. Die Lateiner nannten solches die **Action**...ohne sie gelte der höchste Redner nichts;...Worte haben nur die Zunge zum Werckzeuge; Geberden aber haben ihren Beistand in allen Theilen des Leibes."

umph over his terror." He remains "impenitent" in spite of the admonitions of the Commandeur who "points heavenwards, taking the culprit tenderly in his arms, placing his hand several times on his heart as if to touch it by these remonstrances." Don Juan responds by shrugging his shoulders and looking at the statue "d'un air moqueur." Once the furies appear and put him in chains his passion is one of "affreux désespoir."

The first scene of *Semiramis* shows the Queen "extremely agitated," haunted by "rêves affreux." After the encounter with Ninus's ghost, she rises, "l'horreur est peinte sur son visage." "She searches everywhere for the phantom, and imagines to see it everywhere." In the second act, with the *Mages* placed to the right of the throne and the *Satrapes* to the left, Ninias "prostrates himself" before Semiramis in whose soul "remorse makes itself felt." Then, during the thunderstorm under darkening skies, "terror grips every soul" ("l'épouvante s'empare de tous les esprits"). In the third act, Semiramis "approaches the tomb trembling"; Ninus's ghost "commands her to enter into the tomb," leaving the Queen "nearly destroyed by horror and despair." After the dagger has done its job, Semiramis emerges from the tomb "pale, disheveled," "la mort peinte sur son visage," and "scarcely able to drag herself." Her women "hasten to her aid and support her." The dagger slips out of her hand. "She recognizes her son, embraces him, forgives him, falls and dies." The curtain descends as the *Mages* "disarm him [Ninias] and drag him away."

The explanation for the relative sketchiness of these directions, valuable as they are, is that in Angiolini's opinion a program needs only to present an outline of the action;[50] it is the business of the performers to fill in the details.

Beautifully and precisely executed gestures were expected of all theater persons, or orators, by an audience that was itself well-versed in these skills and therefore fully capable of evaluating the felicities and faults that they observed on stage. In the words of Dene Barnett, whose recent seminal study of 18th-century acting has brought this entire topic into new focus:

> the art of gesture...was a highly articulate art, being based on a vocabulary of gestures each with an individual meaning known to all in advance; it included many tiny and detailed expressive devices, as well as gestures and attitudes which were as large and passionate as those familiar to us in the Baroque art of Bernini; the hands and eyes were the principal instruments; a basic funcôion of the gestures was to create for the eyes of the

---

[50]This is a point of contention between Angiolini and Noverre. Cf. Angiolini's *Lettere al Sr. Noverre sugli Pantomimi, Riflessioni sopra l'uso dei Programmi ne'Balli Pantomimi* (Milan, 1773).

spectators a concrete picture of the ideas expressed by the words. Indicative and imitative gestures especially can have the vivid effect of bringing before the eyes events and things which are not on stage—events past, things distant, imaginary or abstract.[51]

Even though we are here dealing with dramatic ballet and not with acting, it is well to remember that the professions of the dancer and the actor in the period under discussion were by no means as separate as they are today. Several well-known actor-dancers, some contemporary with Angiolini, starred in the traveling companies that played an ambitious repertory of plays, operas and ballets on fairgrounds in the provinces as well as in the major cities.[52] Johann Georg Schuller and Joseph Hasslinger were actors and ballet masters for Felix Berner's company; Margaretha Liskin, who joined that troupe at age five, played "sweethearts, ingenues, soubrettes in musical pieces and plays, Ophelia in *Hamlet*, Parthenia in *Alceste*, danced in *terzettos* and filled in as *figurante*."[53] The actor-dancer-choreographer Jean-Baptiste François de Hesse (also: Deshayes; 1705–79), known especially as an interpreter of comic, grotesque and character parts, made frequent use of "Acteurs Dansans" in his works,[54] and in England the much admired Hester Santlow (c. 1690–1733) excelled as an actress as well as a dancer.[55] Justification enough to look for models, or parallels, for Angiolini's *gestes parlans* in the theater handbooks of his age.

There is, however, an author early in the 18th century whose explanations of gestures are given specifically with the dancer in mind. John Weaver (1673–1760), who described his entertainment *The Tavern Bilkers* (Drury Lane, 1702) as "THE first Entertainment that appeared on the *Eng-*

---

[51]Dene Barnett, with the assistance of Jeanette Massy-Westropp, *The Art of Gesture: The practices and principles of 18th-century acting*, Reihe Siegen, 64 (Heidelberg: C. Winter Universitätsverlag, 1987), p. 10. A review of the book, by Ingrid Brainard, *Dance Chronicle* 15/1 (1992): 94*ff.*

[52]A survey of English and German troupes in Ernst Leopold Stahl, *Shakespeare und das deutsche Theater* (Stuttgart: W. Kohlhammer, 1947).

[53]Winter, p. 147. For Berner's company, and some others, see Hermann Kaiser, *Barocktheater in Darmstadt* (Darmstadt: Eduard Roether, 1951), pp. 127*ff.*

[54]Winter, pp. 86*ff.*

[55]For a biography of Santlow, see Cohen, "Hester Santlow," in *Famed for Dance*, pp. 49*ff.* Santlow is mentioned in the titles of four choreographies in Anthony L'Abbé/ F. Le Roussau, *A NEW / COLLECTION / OF / DANCES...That have been performed both in Druy* [sic]*-Lane and Lincoln's-Inn-Fields, by the best Dancers* (c. 1725). For a facsimile of the Collection, with an introduction by C. Marsh, see Music for London Entertainment, 1660–1800, series D, vol. 2, ed. John M. Ward; (Boston: Steiner and Bell, 1991).

lish Stage, where the Representation and Story was carried on by Dancing, Action and Motion only," years later went on to produce several other "dramatick entertainments in dancing," some, like *The Tavern Bilkers,* in the grotesque style of the Italian *commedia dell'arte* ("after the manner of the Modern *Italians,* such as *Harlequin, Scaramouch,* &c"), some "in Imitation of the Ancient Pantomimes."[56] Of the latter, *The Loves of Mars and Venus* (Drury Lane, 1717) is of particular importance to us, because here, in addition to the introductory remarks to each of the six scenes, Weaver spells out precisely how a dancer would express admiration, jealousy, anger, contempt, triumphing, grief, coquetry, forgiveness, shame, etc., when these emotions were called for by the events of the story.[57]

It is tempting indeed to cite here the complete set of Weaver's gesture directives which, surprisingly, are not included in Barnett's analyses of 18th-century stage practices. But since they are readily available, I propose to go a different way. I shall juxtapose some of the dramatic and emotional peaks in Angiolini's *Don Juan* and *Semiramis* libretti with the corresponding "Passions or Affections" in Weaver as well as with relevant citations from teachers of acting and oratory in Barnett and with pertinent remarks in Magri. From these comparisons, I hope we shall be able to obtain a better idea than we have had up to now of how a dancer in the *ballet d'action* would have adapted the familiar gesture vocabulary of the tragic stage to his or her own purposes. The argument that nearly half a century separates *The Loves of Mars and Venus* from Angiolini's masterpieces and that, if the dance technique evolves noticeably during that time, why wouldn't gesture do so as well?, can be countered on the basis of Barnett's investigations, which show clearly that apart from minor differences between one author and another, the language of dramatic gesture remained comparatively stable from the beginning of the 18th to as late as the early 19th century (see p. 36 below).

In the following remarks, the pagination of the original libretto of *The Loves* appears in parenthesis after each Weaver quote. In cases where there is no key word in Angiolini's scenarios, we shall let the music be our guide or, as in the case of the duel Don Juan-Commandeur, look for documentation elsewhere.

---

[56]Cf. Weaver's own list of such shows in *Mimes and Pantomimes,* pp. 43*ff* (Ralph, *John Weaver,* pp. 720*ff*).

[57]Facsimile of the complete libretto, including the very interesting PREFACE, in Ralph, *John Weaver,* pp. 737*ff*. See also Winter, pp. 58*ff* and S. J. Cohen, ed., *Dance as a Theatre Art* (Princeton: Princeton Book Company, 1992), 2:51*ff*.

30 Ingrid Brainard

DON JUAN

The Commandeur surprises Don Juan in his house.

> Weaver: "UPBRAIDING. The Arms thrown forward; the Palm of the Hands turn'd outward; the Fingers open, and the Elbows turn'd inward to the Breast; shew *Upbraiding,* and *Despite*" (p. 21).

> Weaver: "ANGER. The left Hand struck suddenly with the right; and sometimes against the Breast; denotes *Anger*" (p. 21).

> Instructions for actors *re* "Anger": see Barnett, p. 234 (gestures) and pp. 52ff (facial expressions).

> Weaver: "INDIGNATION. When it rises to *Anguish,* and *Indignation,* it is express'd by applying the Hand passionately to the Forehead; or by steping [sic] back the right Foot, leaning the Body quite backward, the Arms extended, Palms clos'd, and Hands thrown quite back; the Head cast back, and Eyes fix'd upwards" (p. 22).

The duel Commandeur-Don Juan.

> The 18th-century director would probably rely on the fencing practices of his time;[58] he would also have taken into consideration the opposition of the parts of the body as described in the instructions by teachers of acting such as the great Dutch tragedian Johannes Jelgerhuis:

>> Apart from the mime of the face...I draw your attention to the swelling of the muscles, in the grip of the sword, in both the hands and arms; further to all these contrasts: 1st. Nothing is in one line. 2nd. The head against the neck. 3rd. The two arms, each in itself; lower and upper arms in opposition. 4th. The hands against the arms. 5th. The body flexing or curving with stylishness. 6th. Against that the contrast of the thighs and legs and the legs

---

[58] For these, see articles "Escrime," in Diderot/d'Alembert, *Encyclopédie,* vol. 5 (1755), pp. 945–47, and vol. 21 (1762), pp. 1–15. Fifteen plates of fencing positions follow the text in volume 21. In the articles, reference is made to Domenico Angelo, a well-known fencing master active in London, member of a whole dynasty of respected fencing professionals. Cf. D. Angelo, *L'Ecole des Armes, avec l'explication générale des principales attitudes et positions concernant l'Escrime* (London: 1763).

against the thighs. This figure can be called beautiful, the main standing point is over the right foot alone.[59]

How the mortally wounded Commandeur might move is explained in a passage by Magri that deals with the *Bourèè tombè* [sic]:

> This step is used in the theater in precise expressions (*atteggi precisi*), in emphatic actions: as when a personage assaulted by extreme pain, or afflicted with a mortal wound, by and by falls, with the movement of the *mezzo Tombè,* and to raise himself, driven by the ultimate natural strengths, makes use of the two simple movements, accompanying the expression with the arms.[60]

Pas de deux Don Juan-Maîtresse.

Nothing is said about the quality of this dance. But the nature of the music for this number, a "grazioso" in triple meter (*SW,* No. 21), makes Weaver's admittedly somewhat vague COQUETRY a possibility for the woman: "*Coquetry* will be seen in affected Airs, given her self throughout the whole Dance" (p. 22).

For the man, ADMIRATION might aðply: "*Admiration* is discover'd by the raising up of the right Hand, the Palm turn'd upwards, the Fingers clos'd; and in one Motion the Wrist turn'd round and Fingers spread; the Body reclining, and Eyes fix'd on the Object" (p. 21).

After having seen the Statue to the door, Don Juan returns "triumphing."

> Weaver: "TRIUMPHING. To shake the Hand open, rais'd above our Head, is an exulting Expression of *Triumph* &c." (p. 28).

The "trembling" guests.

> Possibly *terror:*
>
>> Fear violent and sudden, opens wide the eyes and mouth, shortens the nose, gives the countenance an air of wildness...draws back

---

[59]*Theoretische lessen over de gesticulatie en mimiek...* (Amsterdam, 1827), p. 66; quote after Barnett, p. 130. This passage explains a drawing, also reprinted in Barnett.
[60]Chap. 29, "Pas de Bourèè," §7, p. 67: "Questo passo si adopera in Teatro in atteggi precisi, in azione segnate; come in un Personaggio assalito da un estremo dolore, o colpito da ferita mortale, va tratto tratto cadendo, co'l movimento de mezzo Tombè, e per sollevarsi, spinto dagli ultimi sforzi naturali, si serve de'due semplici movimenti, accompagnando l'espressione con le braccia."

the elbows parallel with the sides, lifts up the open hands with the fingers spread, to the height of the breast, at some distance before it, so as to shield it from the dreadful object. One foot is drawn back behind the other, so that the body seems shrinking from the danger, and putting itself into a posture for flight.[61]

The finale of the demons, or furies, who dance around Don Juan, torches in hand.

Here it is once again Magri who provides us with details. In the chapter devoted to the *Attitudine*—"a movement of any part of our body, not just restricted to the motions of the arms, as some believe, but one that can be expressed with the head, with the eyes, with the feet, and with everything that is capable of gesturing," Magri talks about the *attitudine sforzate* which are more powerful than the *ordinarie;* these, he says, belong to the Furies. Instead of the conventional opposition of arm and leg gestures, Furies lift the same arm and leg higher than normal, "with the fingers irregular, expressing a rage whose property is the stiffening of all the limbs of the body, with eyes that scintillate, teeth that gnash, like mastiff dogs, and everything that can characterize their poisonous, spiteful, vicious essence"; their dancing must be without regularity, "with a quick dexterity in gesturing."[62] More than all other characters, Furies need physical prowess, quickness of the legs, and large and emphatic arm movements.[63]

---

[61]J[ohn] Walker, *Elements of Elocution...* (London 1781), 2:329 (quote after Barnett, p. 51). Quite similar are the directions for the ghost scene in *Hamlet* in Charles Newton, *Studies in the Science and Practice of Public Speaking, Reading and Recitation....* (c. 1817), p. 144 (quote after Barnett, p. 235): "The Eyes—Open and starting...; The Eyebrows—Rise with the Eyes...; The Mouth—Opens to receive a larger Gasp of Breath...; The Figure—Retires from the terrifying Object...; The Hands—Are thrown forward to repel Danger—or closely drawn in towards the Trunk of the Body for Self-protectéon. The whole Frame is agitated in Proportion to the Occasion."

[62]Chap. 58, "Dell'Attitudine," p. 111: "Quelle *sforzate* avranno un'atteggio più grande dell'ordinario....Esse...appartengono alle furie...Per fare una furia l'Attitudine avanti avrà alzato il braccio istesso del piede, che sta in aria, ed alto fuor di misura con le dita irregolati, esprimendo una rabbia della quale è proprio recare una rigidezza alle membra tutte del corpo, con gli occhi, che scintillano, i denti, che digrignano, come cani Mastini, e tutto ciò, che puol caratterizzare la loro essenza avvelenata, livida, e liverosa: non dovendosi mai in elleno osservare regolarità; ma soltanto una veloce destrezza nel gesteggiare."

[63]Chap. 59, "Del Gioco delle Braccia," §1, p. 114: "*Les grands bras...*che adopransi...nelle Furie, ed in simil altre azioni. Questi non ponno avere una determinata

SEMIRAMIS

The Queen's "rêves affreux" (Act 1).

> Weaver: "DISTASTE. The left Hand thrust forth with the Palm turn'd backward; the left Shoulder rais'd, and the Head bearing towards the Right, denotes an *Abhorrence*, and *Distaste*" (p. 23).

> Weaver: "DETESTATION. When both the turn'd-out Palms are so bent to the left Side, and the Head still more projected from the Object; it becomes a more passionate Form of *Detestation*, as being a redoubled Action" (p. 23).

> A picture from Gilbert Austin's *Chironomia* shows precisely this gesture, one of Aversion, which is both expressive and indicative, for "the eyes are withdrawn, the head is averted, the feet retire, and the arms are projected out extended against the object, the hands vertical."[64]

Ninus's ghost threatens the Queen.

> Weaver: "THREATS. *Threatning*, is express'd by raising the Hand, and shaking the bended Fist; knitting the Brow; biting the Nails; and catching back the Breath" (p. 22).

The words "Mon fils, va me vanger; tremble, épouse perfide" appear miraculously on the wall of Semiramis's chamber.

> Her first reaction could be one of astonishment, wonder or amazement, until it intensifies into *accablement*, i.e., being overwhelmed with sorrow.

> Weaver: "ASTONISHMENT. Both Hands are thrown up towards the Skies; the Eyes also lifted up, and the Body cast backwards" (p. 21).

---

misura, una distanza esatta, ma possono alzarsi quanto più si vuole dal sito delle altre: siccome il carattere, l'espressione, lo spirito, l'abilità dell'esecutore esigger possa."

[64]Gilbert Austin, *Chironomia: or a Treatise on Rhetorical Delivery: comprehending many precepts, both ancient and modern, for the proper regulation of the Voice, the Countenance, and Gesture. Together with an Investigation of the Elements of Gesture, and a New Method for the Notation thereof* [!]; *illustrated by many figures* (London 1806), p. 487 (picture and text reprinted in Barnett, p. 87).

> "But when...surprise reaches the superlative degree, which I take to be astonishment, the whole body is actuated; it is thrown back, with one leg set before the other, both hands elevated, the eyes larger than usual, the brows drawn up, and the mouth not quite shut"—Thomas Wilkes on acting.[65] Note the similarity of the body posture and the raised hands with Weaver's ASTONISHMENT.
>
> Weaver: "GRIEF. *Grief* is express'd by hanging down the Head, wringing the Hands; and striking the Breast" (p. 28).
>
> Gildon's description of the gesture of Grief is quite similar to Weaver's: "The Demission or hanging down of the Head is the Consequence of Grief and Sorrow."[66]

Semiramis feels remorse (Act 2).

> Weaver: "SHAME. The covering the Face with the Hand is a sign of *Shame*" (p. 28).

Ninias is disarmed and dragged away (end of Act 3).

> Possibly Weaver's "RESIGNATION. To hold out both the Hands joyn'd together, is a natural Expression of *Submission* and *Resignation*" (p. 28).

The place of the hands in the arsenal of gestures for the orator and the actor needs no additional clarification. The many sources cited by Dene Barnett, Robert Toft, Richard Ralph and others all agree on the stylized beauty of the hand at rest, on the preeminence of the right hand in declamation and the accompanying function of the left.[67]

In dance the picture is much less clear. The instruction manuals of the Baroque that are concerned with social dancing have much to say about arm movements, elbows and wrists,[68] but rarely talk about hands. When

---

[65] *A General View of the Stage* (London, 1759), p. 118; quote after Barnett, p. 47. More on the expressive gesture of Surprise, Barnett, pp. 44*ff*.

[66] [Charles Gildon], *The Life of Mr. Thomas Betterton...Wherein The Action and Utterance of the Stage, Bar, and Pulpit are distinctly consider'd...* (London: 1710), p. 43; quote after Barnett, p. 42. More on gestures of Grief in Barnett, pp. 38*ff*.

[67] For the coordination of the right and left hands, see Barnett, pp. 21-25; also pp. 95*ff* and assorted other places throughout the study.

[68] E.g., Feuillet, pp. 97*ff*. The "Seconde Partie" of Rameau is entirely devoted to the manipulation of arms, elbows and wrists; several pages of engravings illustrate the verbal directions (opposite pp. 203, 208, 212). Chapter 4 in Tomlinson is "*Of the Move-*

they do, as for instance Pierre Rameau does, they emphasize the relaxed, beautifully shaped position of the hand, "neither quite open nor quite shut,"[69] in which the thumb and the first or the middle finger may lightly touch.[70] During the execution of larger arm gestures, such as the ones used in the transition from one step to another,[71] the hand may be fully extended but must never lose the subtle coordination of the fingers.[72] In a position of rest,

> the Palms or Insides of the Hands are to our Side in a genteel easy Shape or Fashion, the whole *Arms* hanging from under the Shoulders without Force downwards, or too much Relaxation upwards, but natural and easy in a Readiness for the Elevation.[73]

There can be little doubt that the hands participated actively in the silent rhetoric of the 18th-century theater dancer as well. In addition to the hand gestures he includes in *The Loves,* Weaver also talks about the importance of the hands in the work of the ancient mimes and pantomimes who "performed all by *Gesture,* and the *Action* of Hands, Legs, and Feet, without making use of the *Tongue* in uttering their Thoughts; and in this Performance the Hands and Fingers were much made use of, and expressed

---

ment of the ARMS *in* DANCING" (pp. 152*ff*). Magri, chap. 59, is "Del Gioco delle Braccia" (pp. 113*ff*); the proper use of arms in the *Minuetto* is explained in part 2, chap. 2, especially §7 (p. 18), peripherally also in §9 and §11.

[69]Rameau, pp. 2, 199 (pp. 2, 116 in Essex's translation of Rameau, 1728). Both passages, in Essex's translation, are cited in Hilton, pp. 66, 135. See also Magri I, chap. 59, §1, p. 113: "le dita non devono stare nè serrate, nè aperte, ma moderate: il pollice, e l'indice curvati l'un verso l'altro"; the drawings from Jelgerhuis in Barnett, pp. 95–96; and the "naturall gestures of the hand and fingers" from the frontispiece of John Bulwer's *Chironomia: or, The Art of Manuall Rhetoricke* (1644), reproduced on plate 2 in Robert Toft, "Musicke a sister to Poetrie: Rhetorical artifice in the passionate airs of John Dowland," *Early Music* 12/2 (May 1984), p. 193.

[70]Rameau, p. 99, warns not to exert pressure on the fingers, because that would "cause the upper joints to stiffen, and would prevent the arms from moving with...gentleness" ("faire roidir les jointures supérieures, & empêcheroit que les bras ne se remuent avec... douceur").

[71]Cf. Hilton, especially chapter 7, "The Theory of the Arm Motions and Their Notation," (pp. 133*ff*), but also in various other contexts.

[72]A lovely engraving in Rameau, opposite p. 215, shows a gentleman ready to do a *tems de Courante;* the fingers of his right hand are extended, those of his left are curved in a "naturall gesture."

[73]Tomlinson, p. 153. Similarly Magri, part 1, chap. 59, §1, p. 114: "tenendo sempre le palme delle mani rivolte alle cosce" in preparation for a high arm gesture.

perhaps a large Share of the Performance."[74] When dealing with the different *Attitudine* in theatrical choreographies that involve precisely delineated arm gestures, Magri occasionally mentions hand positions but treats the hand in general as part of the arm,[75] as the social dance manuals do.

John Bulwer's *Chironomia: or, The Art of Manuall Rhetoricke* (1644) contains, inter alia, an "Alphabet of *Action,* or Table of Rhetoricall Indignations"[76] that shows the intricacy of the manipulation of the individual fingers in the visualization of certain affects. That this kind of precise and detailed hand- and finger-work was expected of the dancer in the *ballet d'action* as well is shown by a very similar set of pictures published nearly a century and a half after Bulwer by Abbate Vincenzo Requeno in his *Scoperta della Chironomia ossia dell'Arte di Gestire con le Mani.*[77]

Another important component in the vocabulary of the *rhétorique muette* is facial expression: "L'horreur" or "la mort est peinte sur son visage" (*Semiramis* libretto, ff. [B6ᵛ], [Cᵛ]). That meant abandoning the face mask, which for a very long time had been part of the performers' costume on stage as occasionally in the ballroom[78] and had served, together with "certain gestures and movements" and accessories as a means towards identification of personae from history, fable, etc.,[79] or neutralized a contemporary countenance in favor of the essential traits demanded by a given role.[80]

---

[74]*History of Mimes,* p. 8 (Ralph, *John Weaver,* p. 685).

[75]Chap. 58, "Dell'Attitudine" (pp. 109*ff.*). See also chap. 6, "Della Cadenza" (pp. 22*ff*) on attitudes in certain musical and dramatic situations.

[76]Bulwer, p. 95; the engraving is reproduced as plate 3 in Toft, p. 197.

[77]Parma, 1797. Requeno prescribes twenty-four hand positions for performers in pantomime and ballet, but requires fewer of orators. Three plates from the Appendix to *Scoperta* are reproduced in Winter, pp. 156–57.

[78]Angiolini bemoans that "formerly all expression was banned by covering the dancer's face with a mask" so that even solo dancers of the stature of a Dupré, or a Vestris, could "affect the spectator only mediocrily" (*Semiramis* program, f. [C8ᵛ], in the context of ôhe definition of *la danse haute*). Magri, part 2, chap. 2, §2 (pp. 15–16) points out that when a Minuetto was danced during a masked ball, the mask sometimes was kept on: "Essendo festini in maschera...ballandosi il Minuetto, quante volte la maschera si terrà sempre in viso."

[79]Ménestrier, *Des Ballets,* p. 139.

[80]De Pure, p. 257 and section 15, "Des Masques," pp. 291*ff.*

As the *ballet de cour* gradually faded into history and the *ballet d'action* asserted itself with increasing vigor,[81] the voices that were raised in protest against the mask became more and more numerous.

> It is ceòtain that the exterior movements of the face are the most expressive gestures of mankind: Why then do all the dancers in our theaters deprive themselves of the advantage that this expression, superior to all the others, would provide them?...The mask always annoys us, and is hardly ever necessary...It hinders proper breathing; it consequently diminishes the energies and is a considerable inconvenience in such exercise...No matter how well-designed and painted it is, it is always inferior to Nature's coloring, it cannot move and it can never be anything other than what it was initially; should one resist the abolition of an impediment so disadvantageous to the Dance?[82]

Noverre shares this opinion:

> Abandon those cold masks, imperfect copies of nature; they hide your features, they eclipse, so to speak, your soul, and they deprive you of the most necessary part of the expression.[83]

---

[81]The most comprehensive study of this development is Winter's book. A good survey by Wendy Thompson in the article "Dance V,1" (18th century, Theatrical), in *The New Grove Dictionary of Music and Musicians*, 6th ed. (London: Macmillan Publishers, 1980). See also Eva Campianu, "Ballet d'action in den Opern G. F. Händels," in *Händel auf dem Theater. Bericht über die Symposien 1986 und 1987. Veröffentlichungen der Internationalen Händel Akademie Karlsruhe*, ed. Hans Joachim Marx (Karlsruhe: Laaber, 1988), pp. 171–81, and Claudia Jeschke, "From Ballet de Cour to Ballet en Action: The Transformation of Dance Aesthetics and Performance at the End of the Seventeenth and Beginning of the Eighteenth Centuries," *Theatre History Studies* 11 (1991): 107–22.

[82]Cahusac, "Geste," pp. 651–52: "Il est certain que les mouvemens extérieurs du visage sont les *gestes* les plus expressifs de l'homme: pourquoi donc tous les danseurs se privent-ils sur nos théatres de l'avantage que leur procureroit cette expression supérieure à toutes les autres?...Le masque nous nuit toujours, & n'est utile presque jamais...il est impossible qu'il ne gêne pas la respiration; il diminue par conséquent les forces; & c'est un inconvénient considérable dans un pareil exercice...quelque bien dessiné & peint qu'on puisse le faire, est toûjours inférieur à la teinte de la nature, ne peut avoir aucun mouvement, & ne peut être jamais que ce qu'il a paru d'abord; peut-on se refuser à l'abolition d'un abus si nuisible à la Danse?"

[83]Letter 4, p. 55: "quittez ces masques froids, copies imparfaites de la nature; ils dérobent vos traits, ils éclipsent, pour ainsi dire, votre ame, & vous privent de la partie la plus nécessaire à l'expression."

As is so often the case, the practitioners of the art were well ahead of the theorists. Weaver had included facial expression in his gesture directives.[84] In 1728, the young Marie Sallé danced a *pas de deux* version of Camargo's famous solo *Les Caractères de la Danse* with Antoine Bandieri Laval; both dancers were unmasked.[85] In her own ballet *Pygmalion* (London, Covent Garden, 14 Feb. 1734), Sallé not only discarded the face mask but also did away with the traditional *panier* and appeared in floating muslin instead.[86] A revolution in costuming was likewise underway.

By the middle of the century, most major dramatic parts were danced without masks. Hilverding, Angiolini and Noverre are in complete agreement concerning the importance of the human countenance as a mirror of the emotions, especially in serious ballets. "The face is the tool [*organe*] of the silent scene, it is the faithful interpreter of all the movements of the Pantomime." "All our movements are purely automatic and signify nothing if the face remains mute."[87]

As an alternative to the face mask, Noverre suggests that a few strategically placed strokes of the make-up brush will emphasize the characteristic traits of a given persona without impeding the mobility of the face.[88]

---

[84]Besides the ones already cited see, for instance, "POWER. The Arm, with impetuous Agitation, directed forwards to the Person, with an awful Look, implies *Authority*" (*The Loves*, p. 22; Ralph, *John Weaver*, p. 755). Or: "CONTEMPT. *Contempt* is express'd by scornful Smiles; forbidding Looks; tossing of the Head; filliping of the Fingers; and avoiding the Object" (p. 23; Ralph, *John Weaver*, p. 756).

[85]Winter, p. 51.

[86]The hoop skirt (*panier*) is listed among several articles of costuming that Noverre would like to do away with: "Take off those enormous wigs and those gigantic head-dresses which destroy the true proportions of the head with the body; discard the use of those stiff and cumbersome hoops...which disfigure the elegance of your attitudes and mar the beauties of contour which the bust should exhibit in its different positions" ("Défaites-vous de ces perruques énormes & de ces coëffures gigantesques, qui font perdre à la tête les justes proportions qu'elle doit avoir avec le corps; secouez l'usage de ces paniers roides & guindés...qui défigurent l'élégance des attitudes, & qui effacent la beauté des contours que le buste doit avoir dans ses différentes positions") (Letter 4, pp. 55–56; trans. Beaumont, p. 29).

[87]Noverre, Letter 9, pp. 196–97: "Le visage est l'organe de la Scene muette, il est l'interprete fidelle de tous les mouvements de la Pantomime." "Tous nos mouvements sont purement automatiques & ne signifient rien, si la face demeure muette." This entire ninth letter is devoted to the subject of the masks. In the context, Noverre praises David Garrick as the most expressive of all living actors (pp. 209*ff*).

[88]Letter 9, p. 208: "Ne pourroient-ils [i.e., *les Danseurs*] pas suppléer aux dégradations du lointain, & par le secours de quelques teintes légeres & de quelques coups de pinceau distribués avec Art, donner à leurs physionomies le caractere principal qu'elle doit avoir?" A translation of this passage in Deryk Lynham, *Father of Modern Ballet: The*

But a warning comes from the actors' side of the performing community. Teachers and theorists agree that even in moments of the most violent, impassioned emotion, one must never lose sight of the ideal of pictorial beauty, neither in the face nor in the management of the entire body:

> Strong feeling makes us forget the beauty of acting...it leads us astray at times, disconcerts us and causes us to fail to observe Rightness and Deportment [*Richtigkeit und Haltung*]. We must therefore take care not to surrender entirely to emotion and passion.[89]

> The grimace has never been approved, neither in the serious, nor in the comic: but...each passion has its face.[90]

If all that has been said thus far applies to the tragic heroes of the stories, what about comic figures like the servant (*le laquais*) in *Don Juan*, who appears only as a shadowy outline in the Vienna scenario but is treated in much greater detail in the Paris version of the ballet?[91]

Whether this personage belongs in Angiolini's classification of the *grotesque* or the *comique* genre must remain an open question. Both categories involve members of the lower classes; the former includes figures of the Italian *commedia dell'arte*, peasants and herdsmen, the latter shepherds, gardeners, villagers, working people of all kinds. The former impress with their dangerous jumps, "most often disregarding the rhythm" ("le plus souvent hors de cadence"); they evoke in the spectators astonishment mixed with fear since they seem ready to kill themselves at any moment.[92] Of the latter Angiolini says that

> they are ordinarily incapable of bending [*plier*], and of maintaining balance, they dance almost always to lively and fast melodies. They would

---

Chevalier Noverre, 2nd ed. (London: Dance Books, 1972), p. 136 (see also Beaumont, p. 82).

[89] Hermann Heimark Cludius, *Grundriss der körperlichen Beredsamkeit für Liebhaber der schönen Künste, Redner und Schauspieler*, (Hamburg 1792), p. 370; quote after Barnett, p. 92.

[90] Jean-Léonor Le Gallois, sieur de Grimarest, *Traité du recitatif dans la lecture, dans l'action publique, dans la déclamation, et dans le chant...* (The Hague 1760), p. 114; quote after Barnett, p. 93.

[91] Cf. *SW*, p. xiii, esp. n. 37. For the role that comic dancing played in Molière's own theatrical productions, see Robert McBride, "Ballet: A Neglected Key to Molière's Theatre," *Dance Research* 2/1 (Spring 1984): 3–18.

[92] "Je crois que ce genre est le dernier de tous. Il ne peut exciter dans les Spectateurs qu'un étonnement mêlé de crainte, voyant leurs semblables exposés à se tuer à chaque instant" (*Semiramis* program, f. [C6ᵛ]).

40   Ingrid Brainard

not even be able to walk without falling to the slow and precise movement of the Passacaille.[93]

But when these *danseurs comiques* are at their best, one admires the combination of strength and precision in their dancing, as well as their lightness.[94]

Of the documents at our disposal that throw light on the comic and grotesque figures in the *ballets d'action* and in other productions of the musical theater such as intermedi, masquerades, operas and the like, two are of particular importance over and beyond John Weaver, who also deals with the subject of Grotesque Dancing.[95] The first is Gregorio Lambranzi's *Neue und Curieuse Theatrialische Tantz=Schul,* printed in 1716;[96] the second is Gennaro Magri's *Trattato* of 1779.

The two complement one another in most satisfactory fashion. Lambranzi, in the printed version of his book, gives us pictures of dance scenes involving from one to four personages, many of them *commedia* characters. The melody to which they dance is printed at the top of each page, and at the bottom, framed by a decorative medallion, is a brief description of the action, including the names of the main steps to be performed (cf. Plates 1, 5, 7). Magri describes the steps in detail and differentiates more often than not between their execution by a *Ballerino Serio* and by a *Grottescho,* in the process energetically breaking a lance for the latter. Both, he maintains, must be masters of all that pertains to the dance:

> If it is difficult to dance in the serious vein, it is no easier to be a true graceful comic. And as for the skill of expressing the Pantomime by means of gestures, must tèe Grottesco for his comic action have less than

---

[93]"Incapables d'ordinaire de plier, & de conserver l'à-plomb, ils dansent presque toujours sur des airs d'un mouvement vif & rapides. Ils ne pouroient même marcher sans tomber sur le mouvement lent & compassé de la Passacaille" (*Semiramis* program, f. [C7]).

[94]"Ces Danseurs comiques, s'ils sont habiles, peuvent faire admirer la force jointe à la précision & à la légéreté, & même faire rire quelquefois en tournant artistement en grimaces les gestes de contraction qui leur sont indispensables pour leurs efforts" (*Semiramis* program, f. [C7]).

[95]*History of Dancing,* pp. 164–65 (Ralph, *John Weaver,* pp. 658, 660); *Mimes and Pantomimes,* p. 56 (Ralph, *John Weaver,* p. 732).

[96]In two parts (Nürnberg, 1716); translated by F. Derra de Moroda; ed. and preface by Cyril W. Beaumont (New York: Dance Horizons, 1966); first English edition by C. W. Beaumont (London: 1928). A facsimile of Lambranzi's original drawings from the archives of the Bayerische Staatsbibliothek, Munich, with introduction and notes by Derra de Moroda (New York: Dance Horizons, 1972).

the Serio [needs] to express his Tragedy? For the *comico grazioso* as for the...Serio the action must be lively, loquacious,[97] expressive and natural...Is not the language of passion the same for both? Are not Heroes distressed by the same pangs of love as shepherds? Pastoral dance, like that of the artisan, has always been specifically for the Grottesco, and why should it not be thus in future? Those who are biased and full of prejudice mistakenly make a distinction of merit between one and the other type. Each is worthy of applause, each is skilful [*bravo*] if he expresses his action well and performs his character well.[98]

In dance-technical terms, the comic figures of the *ballet d'action* stand in a direct line of succession from the Renaissance *moresca*-dancers to the Italian *commedia dell'arte* players and the related French *forains*. Losing balance after jumps,[99] turning pirouettes with bent knees,[100] or in *ritirata, incrocciata*, or in "heel and toe" positions,[101] forced attitudes (*attitudine sforzate*), that is: exaggerated poses that are intended specifically for *Oltramontani*, for Coviello and Scaramuccia;[102] the *salto tondo* on one foot, which serves for the character of Pulcinella;[103] Truffaldino's and Scaramuccia's larger than seemly arm gestures;[104] the *Tordichamb* (*tour de*

---

[97]Winter, p. 151 translates *loquace* with "communicative." I suspect that what is meant by Magri is the *grottescho* equivalent to the *éloquence muette* of the *danseur pantomime tragique*.

[98]Magri, part 1, chap. 59, §2, pp. 116–17: "...se difficile è il ballar serio, non è più facile il vero comico grazioso. E che forse l'arte di esprimere per mezzo de'gesti la Pantomima, l'Azione comica la deve avere il Grottesco meno di quella del Serio, per esprimer questi la sua Tragica? Tanto nel comico grazioso, quanto nel...Serio l'Azione deve essere viva, loquace, espressiva, e naturale...Il linguaggio delli appassionati non è egli l'istesso? Non son soggetti gli Eroi agli affanni amorosi con le stesse angustie, come lo sono i Pastorelli. Il ballar Pastorale, come quello dell'Artiggiano è stato sempre specifico del Grottesco, e perchè non puol'esserlo, per l'avvenire? Male intendono, quei, che prevenuti, e pieni di pregiudizio, fan distinzione di merito tra l'uno, e l'altro carattere. Ognuno è degno di applauso, ognuno è bravo, se bene esprime la sua Azione, se bene eseguisce il suo Carattere."

[99]Magri, chap. 4, "Dell'Equilibrio del Corpo," pp. 20–21: "Nel Grottesco nel cader delle capriole traballa, ed alcune volte cade."

[100]Magri, chap. 45, "Della Pirola, de Pirouèttes," p. 89: "La Pirola bassa...si fa con li ginocchi piegati, e girando velocemente su la punta di un piede."

[101]Magri, chap. 45, p. 90.

[102]Magri, chap 58, "Dell'Attitudine," p. 111.

[103]Magri, chap 60, "Delle Capriole," §12, p. 130. See also in the same chapter §20: "Il *Salto dell'Impiccato* detto Saut Empedù si fa nel carattere di Pulcinella, di un'Ubbriaco, o d'altro Goffo, e talvolta si fa per bizzaria; per esser questo un salto difficile."

[104]Magri, chap. 59, "Del Gioco delle Braccia," end of §1 on p. 115 and §2, p. 116.

jambe), which is done *velocissimo* by a *mezzo carattere* dancer "*nel Grottesco si fa in Grande;*"[105] the *Tortigliè*, which is the sole property of the *Ballerini Grotteschi*[106]—all these and more are what distinguishes the movement vocabulary used by the *Grottesco* from the poised and elegant execution of many of the same steps by the *Ballerino Serio*. Add to these the *positions fausses* (the five ballet positions with the toes turned inward) that Feuillet notates[107] and that Magri assigns to the theater dances of the *ballanti Grotteschi* "in almost all their roles,"[108] and the bent torso for which notations by Jean Favier exist[109] that antedate Feuillet by about fifteen years, and the picture of an exuberant, physically demanding technique emerges with which the comic dancers amused and enchanted their audiences. One can only agree with John Weaver who explains that

> GROTESQUE *Dancing* is wholly calculated for the Stage,...and is much more difficult than the *Serious,* requiring the utmost Skill of the Performer. Yet this sort of *Dancing* seems at first View not to be so difficult...But Men of Judgment will easily perceive the Difference between a just and skilful Performance, and the ridiculous Buffoonry of...artless Ignorants. A Master or Performer of *Grotesque Dancing* ought to be a Person bred up to the Profession, and throughly [*sic*] skill'd in his Business...He must be perfectly acquainted with all Steps used in *Dancing,* and able to apply 'em properly to each *Character*...Let his Figure fill the Stage, be just to his *Characters;* pleasing, and full of Variety.... As a *Performer,* his Perfection is to become what he performs; to be capable of representing all manner of *Passions,* which *Passions* have all their peculiar *Gestures;* and that those *Gestures* be just, distinguishing and agree-

---

[105] Magri, chap. 15, "Del Tordichamb," p. 42.

[106] Magri, chap. 21, "Del Tortigliè," p. 50.

[107] *Chorégraphie,* p. 8.

[108] Magri, chap. 7, "Delle Positure de'Piedi," §2, pp. 27–28. The *positions fausees* occur several times in the "Chacoon for Harlequin...by Mr. Roussau" (n.d.), which also shows the flamboyant arm gestures and the handling of the hat typical for this personage. The first page of the choreography, in Feuillet notation, is reprinted in Hilton, p. 36.

[109] I am grateful to Dr. Rebecca Harris-Warrick for this information. In his masquerade *Le Mariage de la Grosse Cathos* (1688), Favier also uses the false positions of the feet, larger than usual steps, stumbling and staggering passages in a character dance for drunkards (No. 6: *Air des Yvrognes*). See Carol Marsh and Rebecca Harris-Warrick, "A New Source for Seventeenth-Century Ballet: *Le Mariage de la Grosse Cathos,*" *Dance Chronicle* 11/3 (1988): 398*ff*. For a complete edition of Favier's masquerade, see Rebecca Harris-Warrick and Carol Marsh, *Musical Theatre at the Court of Louis XIV. Le Mariage de la Grosse Cathos* (Cambridge: Cambridge University Press, 1994).

able in all Parts, Body, Head, Arms and Legs; in a Word, to be (if I may so say) all of a Piece.[110]

If Angiolini's dancers[111] were capable of moving the affections of their audiences by the silent rhetoric of their art, they were supported in perfect measure by the music. For Angiolini, himself a gifted composer,[112] music and dance function as one; he choreographs the music instead of superimposing a scenario on the score as Noverre was wont to do.[113] "Music is essential for the Pantomimes: it is she who speaks, we are only making the gestures"—thus a passage in the *Don Juan* program.[114] And, in the *Semiramis* Dissertation:

> Music is the poetry of the Ballets Pantomimes. We can do as little without it as an actor can do without words:...we arrange the steps, the gestures, the attitudes, the expressions of the roles that we play to the music that sounds in the orchestra.[115]

> Everything must speak in such a music...she [*la musique*] is one of our principal means to stir the passions.[116]

---

[110]*History of Dancing*, pp. 164–66 (Ralph, *John Weaver*, pp. 658–62).

[111]For the personnel of the Viennese theaters, see Robert Haas, *Gluck und Durazzo im Burgtheater* (Vienna: 1925), and idem., "Der Wiener Bühnentanz." See also F. Derra de Moroda, "The ballet masters before, at the time of, and after Noverre," *Chigiana* 29–30 (1975): 473*ff*. The part of Semiramis was danced by Mme. Trancosa, née Nency, who had been trained by Noverre in Stuttgart and "who for mime is the Ampuse of our century" but "endevoured in vain to sustain this pantomime without dances" (i.e., *Semiramis*) (Noverre, Introduction to his *Ballet des Horaces "ou petite réponse aux grandes lettres du Sieur Angiolini"* (1774; cf. Lynham, p. 77).

[112]A list of Angiolini's own ballet scores in Tozzi, *Il Balletto Pantomimo*, pp. 169–70. See also Croll, "Angiolini," and Tani, "Angiolini."

[113]See as one example the description of the creation of the *Ballet des Sauvages* for Gluck's *Iphigénie en Tauride* in the Avant-propos of Noverre's *Lettres* (St. Petersburg edition 1803). The passage is cited by Serge Lifar in his article "La Musique et le Ballet," *La Revue Musicale*, numéro spécial, (Dec.–Jan.1953): 53.

[114]F. [a8]: "La Musique est essentielle aux Pantomimes: c'est elle qui parle, nous ne faisons que les gestes."

[115]Ff. D2ᵛ–D3: "La Musique est la Poésie des Ballets Pantomimes. Nous pouvons, tout aussi peu nous en passer qu'un Acteur peut se passer de paroles...nous mettons les pas, les gestes, les attitudes, les expressions aux Rôles que nous jouons, sur la musique qui se fait entendre dans l'*Orchestre*." C. J. von Feldtenstein goes even a step further when he says, "Die Schritte sind nach dem Affekt der Musik eingerichtet" (*Die Kunst nach der Choreographie zu tanzen* [Braunschweig, 1772], p. 101).

[116]"Tout doit parler dans cette musique...elle est un de nos principaux ressorts pour émouvoir les passions" (*Semiramis* program, f. D3).

The collaboration of an imaginative and musically sensitive choreographer like Angiolini with a composer of Gluck's stature could not fail to be mutually satisfying: "M. Gluck...has perfectly grasped the terror of the action. He has made every effort to express the passions that are involved there, and the horror that reigns in the catastrophe."[117] Between them the two artists fulfilled the ideal conditions that Noverre would slightly later postulate in his *Letters,* namely that for a ballet to be a distinguished work of art the composer must have a genuine feeling for the dance[118] and the ballet master must have an understanding of music.[119]

Music had, of course, long since been credited with "Divine Rhetorical Power."[120] It

> speaks so transcendently and Communicates Its Notions so Intelligibly to the Internal, Intellectual, and Incomprehensible Faculties of the Soul; so far beyond all *Language* of *Words,* that I confess...I have been more *Sensibly, Fervently,* and *Zealously Captivated,* and drawn into *Divine Raptures,* and *Contemplations,* by Those *Unexpressible Rhetorical, Uncontroulable* [sic] *Perswasions,* and *Instructions* of *Musicks Divine Language,* than ever yet I have been, by the best *Verbal Rhetorick,* that came from any Mans Mouth, either in *Pulpit,* or elsewhere.[121]

In his passionate scores, Gluck, who in *Don Juan* and *Semiramis* reached "the highest degree of dramatic expression,"[122] affirms what earlier in the century Johann Mattheson had stated with some emphasis, namely that the job of music was not just to depict grace and pleasure ("die Anmuth und das Wolgefallen") or the milder negative emotions, but also

---

[117]"M. Gluck...a saisi parfaitement le terrible de l'Action. Il a tâché d'exprimer les passions qui y jouent, et l'épouvante qui règne dans la catastrophe" (*Don Juan* program, f. [a8]).

[118]Cf. Noverre, Letter 8, p. 163.

[119]Cf. Noverre, Letter 5, pp. 73*ff.*

[120]For the subject of music and rhetoric, see Ranum; Toft; Robin H. Wells, "The ladder of love: verbal and musical rhetoric in Elizabethan lute song," *Early Music* 12/2 (May 1984): 173*ff;* Gregory G. Butler, "The projection of affect in Baroque dance music," *Early Music* 12/2 (May 1984): 201*ff;* Dene Barnett, "La Rhétorique de l'Opéra," *XVIIe Siecle* 132/3 (1981): 336 *ff.* See also the literature listed under "Rhetoric and Music," in *The New Grove Dictionary of Music and Musicians,* 6th ed. (London: Macmillan Publishers, 1980); the article "Affektenlehre," in *Die Musik in Geschichte und Gegenwart,* vol. 1 (Kassel: Bärenreiter, 1949–51), pp. 113–21; etc.

[121]Thomas Mace, *Musick's Monument* (London, 1676), p. 118.

[122]Rudolf Gerber, *Christoph Willibald Gluck* (Potsdam: Akademische Verlagsgesellschaft Athenaion, 1950), p. 133.

"something horrible and frightful, since in these the spirit occasionally also finds a singular kind of ease."[123]

It would be fascinating and, I am sure, quite feasible to analyze the scores of our two ballets with the principles of rhetoric in mind. This, however, would be a topic large enough to deserve a study in its own right. In the present context, suffice it to say that there is little reason to doubt that Gluck quite consciously chose musical means that, while they underlined the drama that unfolded on stage, were able "to stir the affects through the musical sound."[124]

To give just a few examples: the alternating pizzicato and arco phrases and the dialogue between winds and strings in the *Don Juan pas de deux* (*SW,* No. 21) justify the coquetry and admiration suggested above (p. 31) besides underlining the contrast between the male and female gender of the proponents. The musical treatment of the *Entrée des Trembleurs* (No. 25) with its fast-moving passages and *fp* accents fits in with Mattheson's "Furcht" ("fear"), a sub-group to the affect of jealousy which is restless by nature.[125] Don Juan's bravado as he confronts the Statue, interrupted here and there by moments of doubt and hesitation (No. 24), the buffo scene of the servant with its light pizzicato (shades of Monostatos!) (No. 28), and, naturally, the encounter Don Juan-Statue in the churchyard and the grandiose finale of the Furies (Nos. 30 and 31) all offer innumerable possibilities for analysis under the headings of rhetoric and "Affektenlehre."

So does the sequence of events in *Semiramis* from the chiaroscuro coloring of the Queen's "rêves affreux" in the first scene through the noble *Danse grave et majestueuse* (No. 3)[126] to the pomp and circumstance of Ninias's entry (No. 6) in the affect of Mattheson's "Stoltz" ("pride"),[127]

---

[123]"Denn das musicalische Geschäffte, ob es gleich zu seinem Zwecke hauptsächlich die Anmuth und das Wolgefallen haben sollte; dienet doch bisweilen mit seinen Dissonantzen, oder hartlautenden Sätzen...nicht nur etwas wiedriges und unangenehmes, sondern gar etwas fürchterliches und entsetzliches vorzustellen: als woran das Gemüth auch bisweilen eine eigene Art der Behäglichkeit findet" (chap. 3, "Von der Natur= Lehre des Klanges," p. 19, §79).

[124]"Durch den Klang die Affecten [zu] erregen" (Mattheson, p. 19, §84).

[125]P. 18, §76: "Mit der lieben Eifersucht hat sowol die Klang= als Dicht=Kunst immer sehr viel zu thun: und weil diese Gemüths=Verstellung wohl aus sieben andern Leidenschaften zusammen gesetzet ist, unter welchen doch die brennende Liebe obenanstehet, Mistrauen, Begierde, Rache, Traurigkeit, Furcht und Schaam aber nebenher gehen; so kan man leicht gedencken, daß häuffige Erfindungen in der Ton=Ordnung daraus hergeleitet werden können, welche gleichwol alle, der Natur nach, auf etwas unruhiges, verdrießliches, grimmiges und klägliches ihre endliche Absichten richten müssen." See also Butler, p. 204.

[126]Cf. Mattheson's quasi-affect of "Gelassenheit", p. 19, §82.

[127]P. 18, §72.

Semiramis's admission of love (No. 7),[128] thence to the appearance of the ghost of the slain Ninus (*l'ombre vengeresse*), the Queen's attempt at flight and the deadly calm as the doors of the mausoleum close behind her (No. 10), and eventually to the drama surrounding her death (Nos. 14 and 15). Particularly poignant is the chromaticism of mm. 1–9 in No. 14, which illustrates "that sadness is a contraction of such subtle parts of our body [the reference is to the "Lebens=Geister" mentioned in the preceding paragraph], so it can easily be imagined that for this affect the small and smallest intervals are the most suitable,"[129] and the descending figures, interspersed with sighing motifs, in the final measures of No. 14 suggest not only the Queen's physical collapse, but the affect of despair: "The despair, however, [is] a total collapse of the same [i.e., "of the soul or the spirit"]."[130]

Just as the union of music with rhetorical principles became one of the most distinctive characteristics of Baroque musical production and gave shape to the progressive elements in the music theory and aesthetics of the period,[131] so did the union of dramatic dance and rhetoric produce a style of ballet and choreography that was equally progressive and powerful. The dancer's body speaks with vigor, with tenderness, with serenity or with passion, fitting the gestures to the ruling affection of the moment,[132] pleasing, persuading and instructing the spectator as an orator would,

> so that in skilful Representation of any *Character*, whether *serious* or *grotesque*, the Spectator will not only be pleas'd, and diverted with the Beauty of the *Performance*, and Symmetry of the *Movements*; but will also be instructed by the *Positions, Steps* and *Attitudes*, so as to be able to judge of the *Design* of the Performer.[133]

---

[128]Cf. Mattheson's "Liebe," p. 16, §61*ff*.

[129]Mattheson, p. 16, §57: "Weiß man hergegen, daß die Traurigkeit eine Zusammenziehung solcher subtilen Theile unseres Leibes ist, so stehet leicht zu ermessen, daß sich zu dieser Leidenschafft die engen und engesten Klang=Stuffen am füglichsten schicken."

[130]"Die Verzweiflung [ist] aber ein gäntzlicher Niedersturz derselben [i.e., "des Gemüths oder der Geister"]" (Mattheson, p. 16, §59).

[131]George J. Buelow, article "Rhetoric and Music," in *The New Grove Dictionary of Music and Musicians*, 6th ed. (London: Macmillan Publishers,1980), 15:793.

[132]"Accustom yourself to feel and soon your gestures will be the true expression of your feelings" (Cahusac, *La Danse ancienne et moderne*, p. 179).

[133]Weaver, *Anatomical and Mechanical Lectures*, pp. 144–45 (Ralph, *John Weaver*, pp. 1018–19).

> AND, as it is the Business of a *Dancer* of this kind, as well as the *Rhetorician,* to treat the Characters of the Passions, he ought to take care, that his Subjects, and the Action arising from them, have nothing in them *Immoral, Low,* or *Indecent.* I SHALL only add, That as there are many Passions, as *Love; Hatred; Grief; Joy; Despair, Hopes, Fear, Anger* &c. and others of a lesser Degree, which may be call'd Affections; as *Tranquility; Grace; Civility; Gentleness;* and the like; so there are, not only different Actions for these different Passions, and Affections; but also, Variety of Actions, for each of these Passions, or Affections; all which the Dancer ought to know, and how to vary, as his Judgment shall direct him; and to be elegant in his Choice.[134]

We do not know whether Angiolini was acquainted with the writings of his English colleague, although it is tempting to look for a connection through Gluck's visit to London in 1745–46. Be that as it may. What links the two great representatives of the danced drama is their familiarity with the principles of rhetoric and their conviction that these principles, when they are incorporated into the process of creating ballets as well as into the training of future stars of the dancing stage, will add depth and intensity to the shaping of the characters being portrayed while striking a responsive chord in the minds and hearts of an audience that was itself educated in and therefore appreciative of the skills and subtleties of Eloquence. Gaspero Angiolini's *Danseur Pantomime-tragique* thus joins the ranks of the many illustrious personalities of the Baroque theater everywhere with his *rhétorique muette* which enables him, or her,

> to express all the passions, and all the movements of the soul...and [to] make his audience feel those internal trepidations that are the language with which horror, pity, terror speak within us, and shake us to the point of growing pale, of sighing, of shuddering, and of shedding tears.[135]

---

[134] Weaver, *History of Dancing,* pp. 160–61 (Ralph, *John Weaver,* pp. 652–53).

[135] "il faut...que le Danseur Pantomime puisse exprimer tous les passions, & tous les mouvemens de l'âme...& qu'il fasse sentir aux Spectateurs ces frémissemens intérieurs, qui sont le langage avec lequel l'horreur, la pitié, la terreur parlent au-dedans de nous, & nous secouent au point de pâlir, de soupirer, de tressaillir, & de verser des larmes" (*Semiramis* program, ff. D–D^v).

Appendix of Pictures

1. Sarabande (Folie d'Espagne) in the noble style. Cf. pp. 21*ff* above. Note the finger positions; cf. p. 34 above.

2. Three gestures from Franciscus Lang, S.J., 1727:

    (1) Lang, Figure 2: Gesture of authoritative address. Cf. Weaver's POWER, cited in n. 84 above.

    Lang uses this picture to explain the proper stance as well as the gestures of both arms in relation to each other and to the torso. The relevant passages are cited in Barnett, pp. 110 and 115.

    (2) Lang, Figure 3, showing the "normal" hand posture, here used during an entrance onto the stage. Cf. Barnett, p. 96, with picuture and an extensive quotation from Lang.

    (3) Lang, Figure 7: Gesture of Grief: "One must watch that the joined hands are directed to one side or the other, right or left,...but not held in the middle of the body" (Lang, p. 49). Cf. Barnett, p. 43; see also above, p. 34.

3. Fury, or demon, from Lambranzi, 1715. Cf. p. 32 above.

4. *Pas de Deux Pantomime* from the opera *Sylvie,* by P.-M. Berton and J.-C. Trial, first performed at the Paris Opéra, 1766. Note the absence of masks! Cf. p. 37 above, and Lois Rosow's article in this volume.

Jean Dauberval (1742–1806) was *premier danseur demi-caractère* at the time this picture was painted. Marie Allard (1742–1802) had come to the Paris Opéra from Lyons in 1761. She was famous for her comic and character roles. Noverre praises the dramatic talents of both artists in Letter 11 of the 1807 edition of his *Lettres.*

The painting by Louis Carrogis *dit* Carmontelle (1717–1806) is reproduced in color in Winter, between pp. 90 and 91.

5. Comic dancer from Lambranzi 1716. Note the *position fausse* of the feet and the enormous size of the step, allowed only for grotesque and comic personages. Cf. pp. 40–43 above.

6. Pierre Dubreil dancing Scaramouche at the Paris Opera. According to Winter, p. 27, Dubreél was internationally known for this specialty.

   For Scaramuccia's larger than seemly arm gestures, cf. Magri, pp. 115–16, cited on p. 41 above. Note also the near-acrobatic quality of the leg gesture.

7. Scaramutza from Lambranzi 1716. Both the gesture of the arms and that of the legs are nearly identical with Dubreil's, except that Lambranzi's dancer does the leg gesture on the floor, while Dubreil does his *in aria*.

Plate 1. Male dancer in the Exordium of his Sarabande (Gregorio Lambranzi, *Neue und Curieuse Theatrialische Tantz=Schul* [Nürnberg, 1716], pl. 3)

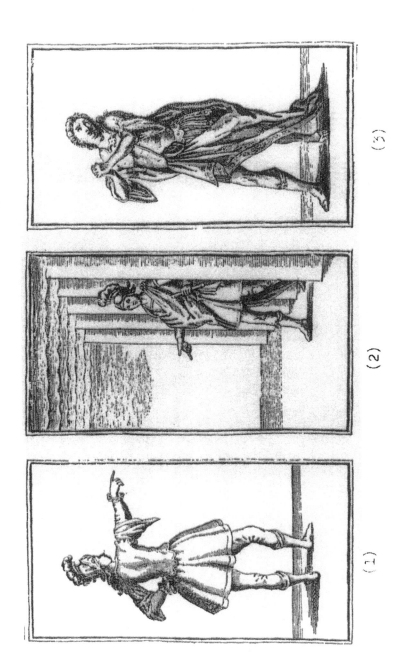

Plate 2. Gestures from Franciscus Lang, *Dissertatio de actione scenica, cum Figuris eandem explicantibus...* (Munich, 1727)

Plate 3. Fury, or demon (Lambranzi manuscript, f. 21ᵛ, 1715)

The Speaking Body 53

Plate 4. Gesture in a *ballet d'action*: Dauberval and Marie Allard in the *Pas de Deux Pantomime* from the opera *Sylvie* (1766)

Plate 5. Comic dancer (Gregorio Lambranzi, *Neue und Curieuse Theatrialische Tantz= Schul* [Nürnberg, 1716], pl. 40)

Plate 6. Pierre Dubreil in the part of Scaramouche, c. 1710 (Frontispiece to a presentation volume of his dances in Feuillet notation [Munich, n.d.])

Plate 7. Scaramutza (Scaramouche) (Gregorio Lambranzi, *Neue und Curieuse Theatrialische Tantz=Schul* [Nürnberg, 1716], pl. 25)

Costanzo Festa's *Inviolata, integra et casta es Maria:* a Double Homage Motet

Mitchell P. Brauner

The setting of the Marian sequence *Inviolata integra et casta es Maria* by Josquin Desprez is one of the monuments of Renaissance polyphony.[1] Its canonic treatment of the cantus firmus, its division of the text into three *partes,* and its decreasing of the time interval between the canonic *dux* and *comes* in each of the *partes* simply confirm that this work is a masterpiece of archetectonic construction. It stands to reason, then, that when another work appears bearing these same traits and setting the same text, the commonality demands some explanation. Costanzo Festa's setting of *Inviolata,* like Josquin's, also divides the text into three sections (unlike all other contemporary settings).[2] It is also canonic and gradually reduces the time interval between the written and realized voices.

Josquin's *Inviolata* is scored for five voices, three free and two carrying the chant melody in canon. As just noted, in each of the three sections of the motet, Josquin reduces the time interval between the *dux* and the *comes:* first three breves, then two, and finally one. The interval at which the canon is to be realized, the fifth, does not change. This canonic treatment results in a gradual integration of the texture. In the *prima pars,* the cantus firmus voices are rather distinct. The free voices begin with a slight suggestion of the chant tune but quickly explode in the series of cascades that make the piece so memorable, while the chant voices punctuate each phrase with their slower moving melody. The *secunda pars* unites free and paraphrase materials, while still keeping the free voices distinct from those

---

[1] For editions, see Albert Smijers, *et al.,* eds., *Werken van Josquin Des Prés,* 11 vols. (Amsterdam: Vereeniging voor Nederlandsche Musiekgeschiedenis, 1921–69), ser. 2, vol. 2, pp. 111–17 and Edward Lowinsky, ed., *The Medici Codex of 1518,* Monuments of Renaissance Music 3–5, 3 vols. (Chicago: University of Chicago Press, 1968), 2:231–40.

[2] See Costanzo Festa, *Opera omnia,* ed. Alexander Main and Albert Seay, Corpus mensurabilis musicae, 25, 8 vols. (N.p.: American Institute of Musicology, 1962–78), 4:96–112.

carrying the cantus firmus. Finally, the *tertia pars* unites the two elements with a chordal, antiphonal opening in which all five voices participate. The integration of the texture thus builds toward the ultimate conclusion, which may even seem to come too soon, as each *pars* is briefer than the previous one.

Like Josquin's setting, Festa's has a separate cantus firmus voice. Unlike Josquin's, however, Festa's *Inviolata* is a quadruple canon creating eight voices out of four. The original voices may be designated as Tenor I and II and Bass I and II. The level of the canon also changes in each *pars:* the octave in the *prima pars,* the fifth in the *secuna pars,* and the fourth in the *tertia pars.* At first the piece seems staid and even lugubrious, especially when compared to the Josquin with its great cascades. This results from the rather simple nature of the piece: it is almost completely chordally-based counterpoint. Even measures 33–41 of the *prima pars,* where there seems to be a greater fluidity of line, turn out really to have an essentially chordal underpinning or simply a decorated chordal texture. The only places where there seem to be truly free counterpoint come at the end of the *prima* and *secunda partes* (mm. 62–72 and 135–40). In the *prima pars,* Superius II, the *comes* of Tenor II, which carries the cantus firmus, ends two breves before the other voices (m. 66), holding an A, and the *dux* takes a line that freely interweaves with the other voices. The remaining three primary voices also take off after measure 68, and the conclusion to the *pars* becomes wonderfully exciting and complex.

The antiphony created by the canon gives Festa's *Inviolata* a polychoral character. In the *prima pars,* except for the ending, the antiphony is maintained by five-measure statements, which dovetail the entries and exits of the written and realized "choirs." In the *secunda pars,* the antiphony continues. The time between the canonic entries is shortened from four breves to three, but the lengths of the musical segments are similarly shortened. The *tertia pars* is a different matter altogether. With the canonic entries following after a one-breve rest, a polarity of echoing chordal sonorities is established that harkens directly back to the *tertia pars* of Josquin's motet. The phrases here are more extended than in the Josquin, and we do not get exact repetition on the texts *O benigna! O Regina! O Maria!* as in Josquin's setting, but rather the dialogue gradually becomes increasingly contrapuntal and complex. Most of the *tertia pars* is fully imitative and especially influenced by the dialogue between the written Tenor I and its *comes,* the realized Superius I. Until the final held note, the Superius's entries draw out the text as they mark a final musical punctuation of each phrase.

The contrast in feeling between Josquin's setting and Festa's is remarkable. The chordal nature of the latter in no way resembles the work of the older master, nor does its reliance on increasing contrapuntal intricacy. It is much heavier and thicker than Josquin's motet, as one would expect from the music of a composer who emerged in 1517. Still, the outward similarity of the two works is so close that one might guess that with the quadruple canon at three different pitch levels, Festa was trying to outdo the older master, as well as emulate and honor him.

This is not the sort of emulation and homage so widely discussed in the recent musicological literature, which cites melodic quotation almost exclusively.[3] While Festa and Josquin use the same liturgical text, that is as far as the quotation actually goes. The composers actually use different versions of the chant tune, and there is no direct melodic citation in the free voices. However, the kind of large-scale structural allusion employed by Festa directly parallels what literary scholars and art historians regard as the highest form of emulation and homage practiced in the Renaissance, and is the only form that transcends the boundaries of visual, written, and aural creativity.[4]

---

[3] Lewis Lockwood, "On Parody as Term and Concept in 16th-Century Music," in *Aspects of Medieval and Renaissance Music: A Birthday Offering to Gustave Reese*, ed. Jan La Rue (New York: W.W. Norton, 1966), pp. 560–75; Howard Mayer Brown, "Emulation, Competition, and Homage: Imitation and Theories of Imitation in the Renaissance," *Journal of the American Musicological Society* 35 (1982): 1–48; Leeman L. Perkins, "The L'Homme Armé Masses of Bunoys and Okeghem: A Comparison," *Journal of Musicology* 3 (1984): 363–94; and J. Peter Burkholder, "Johannes Martini and the Imitation Mass of the Late Fifteenth Century," *Journal of the American Musicological Society* 38 (1985): 470–523.

These approaches to the subject of emulation, homage and modelling, particularly Burkholder, have been criticized by Rob C. Wegman, "Another 'Imitation' of Busnoys's *Missa L'Homme armé*—and Some Observations on *Imitatio* in Renaissance Music," *Journal of the Royal Musical Association* 114 (1989): 196–99. Honey Meconi also criticized these approaches to the subject in "Does Imitatio exist?" *Journal of Musicology* 12 (1994): 152–78. In reviewing the use of the term "imitation" in music and in the kinds of emulation and homage these other authors have cited, she concluded that their examples do not parallel the kind of emulation and homage so prevalent in Renaissance literature.

[4] See the discussions in G. W. Pigman III, "Versions of Imitatio in the Renaissance," *Renaissance Quarterly* 33 (1980): 1–32 and Thomas M. Greene, "Petrarch and the Humanistic Hermeneutic," in *Italian Literature: Roots and Branches. Essays in Honor of Thomas Goddard Bergin*, ed. Giose Rimanelli and Kenneth John Atchity (New Haven: Yale University Press, 1976), pp. 201–24, for literary references; and E. H. Gombrich, "The Style *all'antica*: Imitation and Assimilation," in *Norm and Form*, Studies in the Art of the Renaissance, 1, 4th ed. (Chicago: University of Chicago Press, 1985), pp. 122–28, for a discussion of the use of structure and form in art. Gombrich's discussion centers on Giulio Romano's *Battle of Constantine and Maxentius at the Ponte Molle*, in which he notes Giulio's reliance on the design of a vignette from Hadrian's column for its composition. The literary studies are cited in the musicological

Despite the close affinity between Josquin's *Inviolata* and Festa's, they are not the pieces that are usually paired in the literature. Quadruple canons are so rare that this feature alone has drawn a number of writers' attention to other similar motets, particularly to two quadruple canons by Jean Mouton, *Ave Maria gemma virginum* and especially *Nesciens mater*.[5] *Ave Maria gemma virginum* is constructed such that it acts and sounds like a fully imitative eight-voice motet. *Nesciens mater* comes closer to the true antiphonal effects of a polychoral texture. However, as Anthony Carver has noted, the upper "choir" does not stand alone and is always supported by the primary voices.[6] Texturally, *Nesciens mater* resembles and sounds very similar to the *tertia pars* of Festa's *Inviolata*. In contrast to the latter, however, Mouton's work is in a single section, with the canon at the fifth.

Carver additionally notes that because of the independence of the two "choirs," Festa's *Inviolata* has the distinction of being perhaps the earliest true polychoral motet.[7] The antiphonal "choirs," though, are a result of canon, and the canon, not choral self-sufficiency, must be considered primary in the composer's mind. Although the antiphonal nature of the canonic writing is never completely obscured by the narrowing of the time interval between the *dux* and the *comes,* the antiphony does become clouded at the end of the *prima* and *secunda partes* when the texture expands into eight equal voices.

There is, however, more that binds the two *Inviolata*s and *Nesciens mater* together than separates them. It is clear that Festa took Josquin's setting of the *Inviolata* text and the increasingly narrow canonic time interval as a model on which to place his grand texture. It is also clear that *Nesciens mater,* probably the only quadruple canon that the relatively inexperienced Italian composer had available to him, acted as a model as well.[8] Both the

---

literature in the previous footnote. Pigman, Greene and Gombrich all refer to the same quotation from Petrarch (*Le familiari,* XXIII, 19, 78*ff*) for their arguments defining emulation and homage by modelling.

[5]Lowinsky, *The Medici Codex,* 1:49, says outright that *Inviolata* was modelled on *Nesciens mater,* though he gives some credence to the possibility that *Ave Maria gemma virginum* may also be an antecedent. Modern editions of *Nesciens mater* may be found in Lowinsky, *The Medici Codex,* 2:207–14 and Smijers and A. Tillman Merritt, eds., *Treize livres de motets parus chez Pierre Attaingnant,* 14 vols. (Monaco and Paris: L'Oiseau-Lyre, 1934–64), 2:43–50.

[6]Anthony F. Carver, *Cori Spezzati,* 2 vols. (Cambridge: Cambridge University Press, 1988), 1:42.

[7]Carver, 1:44.

[8]As with the Josquin, we have a structural reference to the model without quotation. I believe that *Nesciens mater,* alone, is the eight-voice antecedent by Mouton for Festa's *Inviolata. Ave Maria gemma virginum* did not circulate in Italy and appears only in a

Josquin and Mouton pieces circulated in Italy at the time that Festa emerged as a composer and singer. We can be sure that he was familiar with these works, because they were part of the repertory of the Papal Chapel when he was a member of that institution, and they were all copied at approximately the same time, ca. 1517–19, by Papal Chapel scribes. The Mouton and Josquin motets appear in the Medici Codex (Florence, Biblioteca Medicea-Laurenziana, MS aquisti e doni 666), dated 1518 and datable to before May of that year.[9] Festa's motet appears in the Vatican manuscript Cappella Sistina 46, copied by the second scribe of the Medici Codex, Claudius Gellandi, in a stage of his handwriting contemporary with that manuscript. A *terminus post quem non* of 1519 makes Festa's *Inviolata* one of his earliest surviving works. It also raises the possibility that it was composed even before he came into Papal service in 1517, and that the composition resulted from Festa's personal acquaintance with the older masters. This possibility requires a brief review of Festa's biography.[10]

Costanzo Festa served in the Papal Chapel from 1517 until his death in 1545 and provided much of its repertory. His works in all sacred genres were sung by the Sistine choir throughout the sixteenth century and some survived in the repertory even into the nineteenth.[11] Almost nothing is securely known about his biography before his entry into the Pontifical choir. He served Costanza d'Avalos, Contessa of Francavilla, in instructing her nephews Alfonso and Rodrigo d'Avalos, who were resident on the island of Ischia, off of Naples. Jeppesen, who discovered this information, believed Festa's stay on Ischia fell between 1510 and 1517, and felt the period 1515–17 to be the most probable.[12] More recently, Lewis Lockwood placed

---

later French source, a print by Attaingnant (RISM 1534[5]), and, as we shall see, Festa's motet would seem to have been composed in Rome.

[9]Jeffrey J. Dean, *The Scribes of the Sistine Chapel, 1501–1527* (Ph.D. dissertation, University of Chicago, 1984), chapters 2–5 and 7, esp. the tables on pp. 80 and 245, Figure 21 on p. 103, and pp. 94–95 and 123. See also Dean's introduction to *Vatican City, Biblioteca Apostolica Vaticana, Cappella Sistina MS 46,* Renaissance Music in Facsimile, 21 (New York: Garland, 1986), pp. v–xi. Dean describes the copy of Festa's *Inviolata* as being in the fifth phase of Gellandi's script, datable to ca. 1517–19.

[10]A summary biography may be found in Alexander Main, article "Festa, Costanzo," in *The New Grove Dictionary of Music and Musicians,* 6th ed. (London: Macmillan Publishers, 1980), 6:501.

[11]Giuseppe Baini, *Memorie Storico-Critiche della vita e della Opere di Giovanni Pierluigi da Palestrina,* 2 vols. (Rome: N.p., 1829; repr., Hildesheim: Olms, 1966), 1:215.

[12]Knud Jeppesen, article "Festa, Costanzo," in *Die Musik in Geschichte und Gegenwart,* vol. 4 (Kassel: Bärenreiter, 1955), pp. 90–102.

Festa in Ferrara on 5 March 1514. Lockwood also showed Festa to have been in contact with the Ferrarese court in July of 1516 as well.[13]

Evidence is not entirely lacking, however, about some other possible locations of employment. Festa may have been at the French court from late 1513 to early 1514. Edward Lowinsky noted that a Festa motet, *Quis dabit oculis nostris,* has exactly the same text as one by Jean Mouton written upon the death of Anne of Brittany, Queen consort to Louis XII of France, on 9 January 1514. Such compelling evidence, Lowinsky argued, must place Festa in France and as a pupil of Mouton.[14] This and a second motet, Festa's *Super flumina Babylonis,* which Lowinsky concluded was a funerary piece written for Louis XII, who died almost exactly a year later on 1 January 1515,[15] were used as evidence to support his misguided theory that the Medici Codex originated in France. Nevertheless, his connections to Ferrara seem to be more-or-less continuous, so it is less likely that he returned to France and was present at Louis XII's funeral, and, after all, *Super flumina* could have been written for anyone.

It is also possible that Festa sojourned in the Piedmont before entering Papal service.[16] He was evidently from the diocese of Turin, and the very first beneficial document concerning Festa after his entry into the Pontifical Chapel is an expectative for a benefice in Turin, Todi, or Mondovì.[17] Festa may have been born in Villafranca in Savoy, as his supposed kinsman Sebastiano Festa, the son of a musician, was born there.[18] Further, the possibility of a Piedmontese sojourn is enhanced by the fact that a substantial amount of Festa's music was copied into manuscripts for the cathedral in Casale

---

[13]Lewis Lockwood, "Jean Mouton and Jean Michel: New Evidence on French Music and Musicians in Italy, 1505–1520," *Journal of the American Musicological Society* 32 (1979): 224–30. Festa is placed in the company of the singer Bidon, Antoines Collebault, who served Savoy, Ferrara, and the papacy.

[14]Lowinsky, *The Medici Codex,* 1:48–49.

[15]Lowinsky, *The Medici Codex,* 1:42–48.

[16]The full argument is presented by David Crawford in "A Review of Costanzo Festa's Biography," *Journal of the American Musicological Society* 28 (1975): 102–11.

[17]Herman-Walther Frey, "Regesten zur päpstlichen Kapelle unter Leo X. und zu seiner Privatkapelle," *Die Musikforschung* 8 (1955): 64–65.

[18]On the presumption of Costanzo Festa's relationship to Sebastiano Festa, see Crawford, p. 103. I do not presume, as many scholars have, that Sebastiano and Costanzo Festa were brothers. They were both musicians to be sure; both came from the Piedmont; and both were clerics. Nevertheless, it is rare for two brothers born in the late 15th century to both turn to the Church for careers, unless there were an older male heir. I would think it more likely, given the evidence at hand, that Sebastiano and Costanzo were cousins—if they were related at all.

Monferrato, though much later. David Crawford concluded that the "French" motets by Festa could actually have been written in Savoy, since the courts of both countries had many ties and were on particularly good terms in 1514–15.[19] It should be noted, however, that while it was not an unusual practice for composers to write funeral motets for patrons to whom they were in proximity, it was unusual to write such motets from afar.[20]

Given the facts of and speculation about Festa's biography, there are only two logical places where he would have composed his *Inviolata*, France and Rome. Since it is far from certain that he ever was in France in his youth, the latter would seem to be the more likely choice. His familiarity with both his models is a certainty, even for the short period of time between his entry into the Papal Chapel and the copying of his motet. Both models were part of the Sistine Chapel repertory, so Festa could have composed his *Inviolata* after his arrival in Rome. Moreover, the sources do not contradict this thesis, they corroborate it. None of the pieces is to be found in the early sixteenth-century French sources; all are found in manuscripts from the Papal Chapel scriptorium. In fact, Festa's *Inviolata* does not circulate outside of the Papal Chapel. This conclusion, therefore, must be the primary explanation, if not the only one.

A French provenance for *Inviolata* rests not on sources nor archival references, but on the more shadowy area of textual interpretation, and not even on the interpretation of its own text. Festa is placed at the French court in 1513–14 because of *Quis dabit oculis nostris*. There is also no doubt, as Lowinsky notes, that Festa's music breathes an air of familiarity with the French musical scene. He writes in the common Franco-Netherlandish language, and Folengo says that his music could be mistaken for that of Josquin.[21] Although Lowinsky's conclusion of a close relationship between Mouton and Festa is encircled by his efforts to prove the Medici Codex to be of French origin, there is an apparent factual basis for that relationship. The existence of two occasional motets by different composers with the same text is so rare that it must have significance beyond the

---

[19]Crawford, *passim*.

[20]See Lowinsky's arguments *contra* Crawford in "On the Presentation and Interpretation of Evidence: Another Review of Costanzo Festa's Biography," *Journal of the American Musicological Society* 30 (1977): 112–14. Martin Staehelin has further speculated that Festa spent time in Florence studying with Isaac (rather than in France studying with Mouton), and that *Quis dabit* was originally dedicated to him and retexted for Anne. This can be dismissed as speculation. See Martin Staehelin, "Review of Edward E. Lowinsky, ed., The Medici Codex of 1518...," *Journal of the American Musicological Society* 33 (1980): 575–87, esp. 580–82.

[21]Lowinsky, *The Medici Codex*, 1:49, n. 45.

ordinary. It is unlikely that Festa would have written a funeral motet for the Queen of France on the same text as one by Mouton without physical proximity.

In actuality, however, it is not necessary for Festa to have been in contact with either Mouton or Josquin for him to have written *Inviolata* in their homage. Josquin, for instance, was resident in Condé, and no evidence places Festa in the Netherlands at any time. We have only indirect evidence for contact between Festa and Mouton, and then only for a short time. Given the source situation, it takes a leap of faith to presume Festa's familiarity with *Nesciens mater* during that brief stay. Despite speculative scenarios, Rome still seems the most likely place of origin for Festa's motet.

With his *Inviolata*, Festa intended to honor Josquin and Mouton, arguably the most highly regarded composers represented in the repertory of the Cappella Sistina in 1517–19. In looking for models, he very clearly chose those whose solidity, depth, and care in composition were well worth emulating. That is the context in which the composer who became the rising light of Roman music chose to honor the most influential composers of their generation.

Bach, Theology, and Harmony: A New Look at the Arias*

Stephen A. Crist

It has now been over fifty years since Manfred Bukofzer published "Allegory in Baroque Music."[1] In this classic essay he discusses the manifold ways Baroque composers—especially Bach—used musical devices to represent the meaning of texts in vocal works. The basis of musical allegory is a "coherent" relationship between a particular compositional procedure and some extra-musical object or idea. Bukofzer explains:

> Music does not plainly imitate what is allegorized. It produces an event in the musical sphere which is analogous to an event in the spiritual sphere.... The analogies in music may refer only to one voice or to all the voices, to the rhythm alone, to the harmony alone, to the setting and instrumentation alone, or simply to the intensity of sound. It is also possible to combine some or all of these elements.[2]

The fact that allegorical procedures, which appeal primarily to the intellect rather than the emotions, are found so frequently in the seventeenth and early eighteenth centuries led Bukofzer to characterize Baroque music as "a sort of indirect iconology of sound."[3]

---

*I owe a special debt of gratitude to Professor Paul Brainard, who first suggested to me that the Bach arias might be an especially promising topic for investigation. An abbreviated version of this essay was read at the national meeting of the American Handel Society in Washington, D. C., in November 1991, for which Professor Brainard delivered the keynote address. I wish also to thank the University Research Committee of Emory University for partial support of this project.

[1] Manfred Bukofzer, "Allegory in Baroque Music," *Journal of the Warburg and Courtauld Institutes* 3 (1939–40): 1–21.

[2] Bukofzer, p. 9.

[3] Bukofzer, p. 21. David Schulenberg has recently expressed reservations about this point of view, and about Bukofzer's use of the term "allegory," in "Expression and Authenticity in the Harpsichord Music of J. S. Bach," *The Journal of Musicology* 8 (1990): 457–58. He notes that "it has become a truism of twentieth-century literary criticism that allegory for its own sake is rather trivial, if not tedious, and this may be ultimately the case as well with musical symbolism, whether or not we apply to the latter Bukofzer's somewhat problematical term 'allegory.'...One can find...impressive complexes of symbolism

In a series of articles published in the 1980s,[4] and in his book *Tonal Allegory in the Vocal Music of J. S. Bach*,[5] Eric Chafe has explored with penetrating insight the phenomenon of "tonal allegory," which he defines as "the use of any tonal element—key, modulation, sharp sign, enharmonic change, cross relation or even the entire key structure of a lengthy work—to express a coherent relationship with something extra-musical."[6] Chafe's investigations primarily have aimed to illuminate the ways the large-scale tonal plans of complete works (particularly the cantatas and passions) allegorize various concepts of Lutheran theology. For instance, he shows that the patterns of modulation involving "downward" motion (i.e., in the flat direction on the circle of fifths) followed by "upward" motion (in the sharp direction) that are found in many cantatas represent Bach's attempt to capture

---

in some of Bach's sacred works, but...it seems to me that what we are really dealing with is essentially a variety of play, a type of sublime pun."

The choice of terminology is, indeed, problematic. Ever since Arnold Schering in the 1920s and 1930s began drawing attention to this aspect of text-music relations in Bach ("Bach und das Symbol," *Bach-Jahrbuch* 22 [1925]: 40–63; 25 [1928]: 119–37; 34 [1937]: 83–95), different authors have used a variety of terms for related phenomena, "allegory" and "symbol" being just two of the most common; and, unfortunately, Lothar Hoffmann-Erbrecht's recent attempt to systematize the terminology ("Von der Urentsprechung zum Symbol: Versuch einer Systematisierung musikalischer Sinnbilder," in *Bachiana et alia musicologica: Festschrift Alfred Dürr zum 65. Geburtstag*, ed. Wolfgang Rehm [Kassel: Bärenreiter, 1983], pp. 116–25) has not alleviated the problem. Tedious or not, though, it seems undeniable that an awareness of musical allegory is essential to understanding the vocal music of Bach and many other composers. Indeed, as John Rupert Martin has shown ("The Transcendental View of Reality and the Allegorical Tradition," in *Baroque* [New York: Harper & Row, 1977], pp. 119–53), the allegorical habit of mind extended far beyond music to embrace the art, architecture, and even the scientific writings of the period. Incidentally, Schulenberg's characterization of musical allegory as "a type of sublime pun" echoes Bukofzer's own words; with regard to the placement of sharps and flats in unexpected spots, along with the more conventional use of ascending and descending contours, to represent the words "erhöhet" and "erniedriget" in the opening chorus of Cantata 47, Bukofzer remarks that "this twofold allegory turns out to be more or less a pun" (p. 15).

[4]Eric Chafe, "Key Structure and Tonal Allegory in the Passions of J. S. Bach: An Introduction," *Current Musicology* 31 (1981): 39–54; idem, "J. S. Bach's *St. Matthew Passion:* Aspects of Planning, Structure, and Chronology," *Journal of the American Musicological Society* 35 (1982): 49–114; idem, "Allegorical Music: The 'Symbolism' of Tonal Language in the Bach Canons," *The Journal of Musicology* 3 (1984): 340–62; idem, "Luther's 'Analogy of Faith' in Bach's Church Music," *dialog* 24 (1985): 96–101; idem, "The St. John Passion: Theology and Musical Structure," in *Bach Studies,* ed. Don O. Franklin (Cambridge: Cambridge University Press, 1989), pp. 75–112.

[5]Berkeley: University of California Press, 1991.

[6]Chafe, "Key Structure," 39.

in music Luther's "analogy of faith," whereby "the whole of Scripture can be perceived in terms of a descent/ascent shape; and this in turn is the 'dynamic of faith' within the individual."[7] Similarly, he demonstrates that the harmonic groundplans and other musical details of the St. John and St. Matthew Passions illustrate the respective theological emphases of the two Gospel accounts upon which these works are based.[8]

The present study is narrower in its scope. It explores a rare but fascinating aspect of Bach's vocal music: the use of keys that exceed the normal range of modulation in the arias. Within the context of the entire corpus of arias (approximately 650 movements), such instances are relatively infrequent. Yet, taken together, they constitute a hitherto unexplored facet of Bach's allegorical approach to composition.

I

It is important to recognize at the outset that the Bach arias generally follow certain standard—almost predictable—patterns of modulation. If the first strophe of the text is set in two musical periods (A^1 and A^2) with an intervening ritornello (as is usually true of arias that end with an exact repetition of the A section, the normal *da capo* form), the first period usually modulates to the dominant (or, in minor keys, to the relative major), while the second period returns to the tonic. When the first strophe is set just once (as with arias in modified *da capo* form, or various through-composed forms),[9] the A section almost always modulates—again either to the dominant or the relative major. There is more flexibility in the modulatory schemes for the subsequent section or sections. The most common keys found here are the relatives of the tonic and dominant (iii and vi in major keys; III and III/v in minor keys). Not infrequently, however, one also encounters ii and IV in major keys, or iv and VI in minor keys. For an aria in G major, one would expect motion to D major (V) in the A section, and modulation to any or all of the following keys in the B section: A minor (ii), B minor (iii), C major (IV), and E minor (vi). The normal spectrum of tonal possibilities for a Bach aria, then, includes the tonic, dominant, subdominant, and the relative major or minor of these keys; this corresponds to what Heinichen

---

[7]Chafe, "Luther's 'Analogy of Faith'," esp. pp. 97–98; quotation on p. 97.
[8]Chafe, "J.S. Bach's *St. Matthew Passion*," esp. pp. 55–78; idem, "St. John Passion."
[9]For additional information on these forms, see my forthcoming book, *Originality and Convention: A Study of Aria Forms in the Vocal Works of J. S. Bach.*

68 Stephen Crist

called "the 'ambitus' of six keys that represent the nearest tonal relationships and the normal limit of modulation within a single movement."[10]

Although quite diverse in scoring, melodic invention, form, and other musical parameters, the vast majority of Bach's arias do not venture beyond the *ambitus* of the six closely related keys. When an aria does modulate beyond one accidental in either direction, the reason is almost always connected with some aspect of tonal allegory.

II

Let us begin with two fairly straightforward examples of the allegorical use of remote keys. The text of Cantata 164 (*Ihr, die ihr euch von Christo nennet*), by the Weimar court poet Salomon Franck, is based on the Gospel reading for the 13th Sunday after Trinity (Luke 10:23–37), which includes the Parable of the Good Samaritan. The bass recitative (movement 2) speaks disapprovingly of the unmerciful behavior of the priest and the Levite, who ignored the plight of the stranger who had been beaten by robbers on the road from Jerusalem to Jericho:

> Der Priester und Levit,
> Der hier zur Seite tritt,
> Sind ja ein Bild liebloser Christen;
> Sie tun, als wenn sie nichts von fremdem Elend wüßten,
> Sie gießen weder Öl noch Wein
> Ins Nächsten Wunden ein.
>
> The priest and the Levite
> Who step aside here
> Are an image of loveless Christians;
> They act as if they knew nothing of the misery of others,
> And they pour neither oil nor wine
> Into their neighbor's wounds.[11]

The preceding aria, for tenor, begins with a rhetorical question that applies this concern even more directly to the entire church:

---

[10] Chafe, "Key Structure," p. 39. See also Johann David Heinichen, *Neu erfundene und Gründliche Anweisung...* (Hamburg: Benjamin Schiller, 1711), pp. 262–65.

[11] Translations are mine, unless otherwise noted.

> Ihr, die ihr euch von Christo nennet,
> Wo bleibet die Barmherzigkeit,
> Daran man Christi Glieder kennet?
>
> You who call yourselves by the name of Christ,
> Where is your compassion,
> Whereby one knows Christ's members?

This is followed immediately by the response, "Alas, it is all too far from you" ("Sie ist von euch, ach, allzu weit"). The B section, in which this line is set, contains modulations to the keys of F minor (four flats, mm. 62–70) and B♭ minor (five flats, mm. 71–73), which apparently were chosen on account of their distance from the tonic G minor (two flats). The remoteness of these keys from the principal tonal center of the movement allegorizes the gulf between the merciful attitude expected of true Christians and the unmerciful behavior of the hard-hearted.

A similar example in a sharp key (F♯ minor, three sharps) is found in Tmolus's aria, "Phoebus, deine Melodei," from Cantata 201 (*Der Streit zwischen Phoebus und Pan*), where the use of the distant key of E minor (one sharp, mm. 38–39) apparently is connected with the "amazing" ("verwundernd") quality of Phoebus's music:

> Aber wer die Kunst versteht,
> Wie dein Ton verwundernd geht,
> Wird dabei aus sich verloren.
>
> But one who understands the art
> With which your notes amazingly ring,
> Thereby loses himself in it.

The use of remote tonalities in the Bach arias is rarely so readily apprehended or so localized a phenomenon as this, however. More typical are the procedures exemplified by a pair of arias from two Christmas cantatas composed in successive years. The duet for soprano and alto "Die Armut, so Gott auf sich nimmt," BWV 91/5 (first performed on Christmas Day, 1724), whose principal tonality is E minor (one sharp), contains modulations to the distant keys of F♯ minor (three sharps) and G minor (two flats). Although initially puzzling, Bach's highly unusual choice of these keys becomes intelligible when one views them in their larger context, as part of an ascending sequence of minor keys that unfolds over the course of the entire B section:

> E minor (m. 36)
>
> F♯ minor (m. 50)
>
> G minor (m. 54)
>
> A minor (m. 72)

The upward root motion is an allegory of the believer's ascent to heaven, a prominent theme of the text:[12]

> Sein menschlich Wesen machet euch
> Den Engelsherrlichkeiten gleich,
> Euch zu der Engel Chor zu setzen.
>
> His human nature makes you
> Like the angels' treasure,
> Appoints you to the angels' choir.

A year later (for the 3rd Day of Christmas, 27 December 1725), Bach composed an alto aria, "In Jesu Demut kann ich Trost," BWV 151/3:

> In Jesu Demut kann ich Trost,
> In seiner Armut Reichtum finden.
> Mir macht desselben schlechter Stand
> Nur lauter Heil und Wohl bekannt,
> Ja, seine wundervolle Hand
> Will mir nur Segenskränze winden.
>
> In Jesus's humility I can find consolation,
> In his poverty, riches.
> His poor status reveals to me
> Nothing but salvation and well-being,
> Yea, his wonderful hand
> Will make me nothing but wreaths of blessing.

This aria shares several similarities with BWV 91/5: both are in E minor; both are for an upper voice or voices; both are scored for unison strings (the earlier aria for unison violins, the latter for violins, viola, and oboe d'amore in

---

[12]Chafe identifies several other patterns of descent and ascent in Cantata 91, too. See Chafe, *Tonal Allegory*, pp. 174–76.

unison); and both use tonality to allegorize aspects of the Nativity. As Rudolf Steglich pointed out in the 1930s, the tonal focal point of this aria in Cantata 151 is the remote key of A major (three sharps), which appears at the midpoint of the B section (mm. 49–53). He saw in this passage "a radiant ray of hope" and the musical representation of "ascent into the open heavens, a view of the eternal light."[13] There is more to it than this, however. Both Schweitzer and Whittaker have noted that the melodic structure of the ritornello (and the first few measures of the vocal entrance, which is closely modeled on the ritornello) involves both successive and simultaneous patterns of descent and ascent.[14] These are linked with the idea of Christ's descent from heaven, alluded to in the aria text (which speaks of "Jesus's humility" ["Demut"], "his poverty" ["Armut"], and his "poor estate" ["schlechter Stand"]), and mentioned even more explicitly in the preceding recitative:

> Er läßt den Himmelsthron....
> Gott wird ein Mensch und will auf Erden
> Noch niedriger als wir und noch viel ärmer werden.
>
> He leaves the heavenly throne....
> God becomes a man and on earth wants
> To become even lowlier than we and far poorer still.

The theme of Christ's descent to earth is illustrated on a deeper level, however, by the aria's harmonic structure: the A-major passage occurs in the context of a stepwise descent from B minor (m. 37), to A major (m. 49), to G major (m. 68), which clearly allegorizes this aspect of the Incarnation.

It seems strange, at first, that Bach should choose A *major* here instead of A *minor,* a key within the *ambitus* of E minor that would have accomplished the same tonal descent. But in so doing he was able simultaneously to allegorize another important theological concept: the notion that the way to heaven is opened through the coming of Christ. This idea is found in the soprano aria ("For my dearest God has now chosen me for heaven")[15] and

---

[13]Rudolf Steglich, *Johann Sebastian Bach* (Potsdam: Akademische Verlagsgesellschaft Athenaion, 1935), pp. 132 ("einem strahlenden Lichtblick"), 134 ("Aufsteig in den offenen Himmel, Durchblick in das ewige Licht").

[14]Albert Schweitzer, *J. S. Bach,* trans. Ernest Newman, 2 vols. (Leipzig: Breitkopf & Härtel, 1911; repr., New York: Dover Publications, 1966), 2:350; W. Gillies Whittaker, *The Cantatas of Johann Sebastian Bach: Sacred and Secular,* 2 vols. (London: Oxford University Press, 1959), 2:162.

[15]"Denn mein liebster Gott hat mich / Nun zum Himmel auserkoren."

the tenor recitative ("You dearest Son of God, now you have opened heaven to me"),[16] but finds its most eloquent expression in the closing chorale:

> Heut schleußt er wieder auf die Tür
> Zum schönen Paradeis,
> Der Cherub steht nicht mehr dafür,
> Gott sei Lob, Ehr und Preis.

> Today he again unlocks the door
> To lovely Paradise;
> The cherub no longer stands in front,
> To God be laud, honor, and praise.

The ascent implied in these words (which inspired Steglich's remarks) is represented by another element of the alto aria's tonal plan. Beginning in the tonic E minor (one sharp), the movement modulates "upward" (i.e., in the sharpward direction on the circle of fifths), first to B minor (two sharps) at the end of the A section (m. 37), then beyond the *ambitus* to A major (three sharps) in the B section (m. 49). The display of musical ingenuity in BWV 151/3 is truly astonishing; the tonal procedures in this movement reveal a depth of theological insight virtually unparalleled in the church music of Bach's contemporaries.

III

In Baroque music theory, ascending and descending patterns are called, respectively, *anabasis* and *catabasis*.[17] Remote keys in the Bach arias almost always occur in connection with one of these types of motion. Bach employed such devices in many different ways. At its simplest, tonal *catabasis* involves direct descending root motion. For instance, in "Stumme Seufzer, stille Klagen," from the Weimar cantata for soprano solo *Mein Herze schwimmt*

---

[16]"Du teurer Gottessohn, / Nun hast du mir den Himmel aufgemacht."

[17]Walther defines *anabasis* as "a musical phrase whereby something that rises up into the air is represented. For example, on the words: He is risen, etc.; God ascends, etc.; and the like" ("ein solcher musicalischer Satz, wodurch etwas in die Höhe steigendes *exprimiret* wird. Z. E. über dir Worte: Er ist auferstanden etc. GOtt [sic] fähret auf etc. u.d.g.") and *catabasis* as "a harmonic period whereby something lowly, humble, and despicable is represented. For example, He went down; I was very humiliated; and the like" ("ein harmonischer *Periodus*, wodurch etwas niedriges, gering, und verächtliches vorgestellet wird. z. E. Er ist hinunter gefahren. Ich bin sehr gedemüthiget. u.d.g."). Johann Gottfried Walther, *Musicalisches Lexicon* (Leipzig: Wolffgang Deer, 1732; facsimile reproduction, Kassel: Bärenreiter, 1953), pp. 34, 148.

im Blut (BWV 199), the poignant descent from the tonic C minor (three flats)[18] to the distant key of B♭ minor (five flats) at the beginning of the B section (mm. 29–32) is clearly connected with the sorrowfulness of the sinner:[19]

> Und ihr nassen Tränenquellen
> Könnt ein sichres Zeugnis stellen,
> Wie mein sündlich Herz gebüßt.
>
> And you wet springs of tears
> Could provide a reliable testimony,
> How my sinful heart atoned.

Similarly, it is no accident that the brief excursion to the remote key of D minor (one flat), which lies a step below the tonic E minor (one sharp), in "Et misericordia" from the *Magnificat* (BWV 243/6) occurs on the words "timentibus eum" (mm. 17–19); clearly this modulation is connected with the idea of the fear of the Lord: "Et misericordia a progenie in progenies timentibus eum" ("And his mercy is on them that fear him throughout all generations").[20]

The tonal patterns are usually considerably more complex, however, as we saw with BWV 151/3. *Anabasis* and *catabasis* are used in two basic ways. On the one hand, the ascent or descent can involve stepwise root movement. This is the case for most of the examples discussed so far. To these can be added "Die schäumenden Wellen von Belials Bächen," BWV 81/3, a powerful tenor aria containing two examples of *anabasis* that graphically illustrate the piling up of "the foaming waves of Belial's streams."[21] The first

---

[18] In this early aria (first performed on the 11th Sunday after Trinity, 12 August 1714), Bach uses the "Dorian" notation with two flats in the signature, adding the third flat by hand throughout the movement.

[19] Wolffheim mentions the modulation to B♭ minor only in passing, and does not characterize it as unusual or comment on its possible significance. See Werner Wolffheim, "'Mein Herze schwimmt in Blut': Eine ungedruckte Solo-Kantate Joh. Seb. Bachs," *Bach-Jahrbuch* 8 (1911): 7.

[20] Spitta remarks about the colorful chromatic passage in the last measure of the voice parts (m. 31) that "the words *timentibus eum*—'On them that fear Him'—offer an opportunity for closing with an elaborate and picturesque treatment of a very interesting character," but he does not comment on the earlier passage. Philipp Spitta, *Johann Sebastian Bach,* trans. Clara Bell and J. A. Fuller-Maitland, 3 vols. (London: Novello & Co., 1889; repr. New York: Dover Publications, 1951), 2:380.

[21] Whittaker, 1:399–400 and Alfred Dürr (*Die Kantaten von Johann Sebastian Bach,* 2 vols. [Kassel: Bärenreiter and Munich: Deutscher Taschenbuch Verlag, 1971], 1:198) have described the ways in which the rising and falling of the melody represent the surging of the storm's waves.

is a pulsating series of sixteenth notes that form an ascending chromatic line—known in Baroque theory as *passus duriusculus*—from G to B in the continuo (mm. 24–31). This is followed by a sequential passage that moves upward by step from the subdominant C major (m. 75), to D minor (m. 81), a key that lies beyond the *ambitus* of the tonic G major, and on to the submediant E minor (m. 87). Unlike many of the other movements we have examined, both devices in BWV 81/3 are clearly audible—the latter not least because it is accompanied by a version of the opening measures of the ritornello transposed to successively higher pitch levels (beginning first on c^1, then on d^1, and finally on e^1).

The other main approach is through the arrangement of major and minor keys in the circle of fifths (Heinichen's "Musicalischer Circul").[22] From this point of view, movement in the sharpward direction (counterclockwise on the "Circul") constitutes "ascending" motion, while movement toward an increasing number of flats (clockwise on the "Circul") represents "descent," regardless of whether the specific pitches employed are literally higher or lower. A pair of relatively simple examples of this type of *catabasis* is found in two arias from the St. Matthew Passion, a work in which patterns of ascent and descent play a prominent role in its large-scale tonal plan as well.[23] In "Ich will bei meinem Jesu wachen," BWV 244/20, when the text takes up the themes of death, atonement, and affliction ("Meinen Tod büßet seine Seelennot..."), this is paralleled by a "descent" to B♭ minor (five flats), which lies beyond the *ambitus* of the tonic C minor (three flats):

    E♭ major (three flats, m. 31)

    F minor (four flats, m. 35)

    B♭ minor (five flats, m. 38)[24]

---

[22] For a detailed account of the conceptual development of this important device, see Chafe, *Tonal Allegory*, pp. 65–72.

[23] See Chafe, "Key Structure," pp. 45–51; idem, "J. S. Bach's *St. Matthew Passion*," pp. 55–78; idem, "Luther's 'Analogy of Faith'," pp. 100–101; idem, *Tonal Allegory*, pp. 391–423.

[24] The use of a Picardy third at the end of the B section (m. 59) surely has allegorical significance as well. The G-major chord serves dual purposes. On the one hand, it functions as the dominant that prepares for the return to the tonic C minor (in this movement, as in BWV 199/2, discussed earlier, only two flats appear in the signature). At the same time, however, it is heard as the parallel major of G minor, the key that dominates the second half of the B section (mm. 47–58). The juxtaposition of minor and major in this fashion is undoubtedly connected with the antithesis between the "bitter"

Later, in the famous soprano aria in A minor "Aus Liebe will mein Heiland sterben," BWV 244/49, flatward movement—from C major (no flats, m. 35), to F major (one flat, m. 38), to the remote key of G minor (two flats, m. 41)—begins when the text speaks of God's judgment:

Daß das ewige Verderben
Und die Strafe des Gerichts
Nicht auf meiner Seele bliebe.

That eternal ruin
And judgment's punishment
Not remain on my soul.

A more complex instance of *catabasis* is found in the alto aria "Ich sehe schon im Geist," BWV 43/9. The words "Jammer" ("wailing"), "Not" ("affliction"), and "Schmach" ("shame") call forth a striking sequential pattern involving root motion downward by thirds in the continuo: mm. 48–52 begin with the notes d, B♭, G, E♭, and C; mm. 54–57 with G, E♭, C, and A (this note is transposed up an octave from the expected AA, which would have exceeded the lower range of the cello). Simultaneously, the harmonic substance of this passage creates a more abstract kind of descent: motion towards harmonies that are increasingly distant from the tonic A minor:

> m. 48: D minor (one flat)
>
> m. 49: B♭ major (two flats)
>
> m. 50: G minor (two flats)
>
> m. 51: E♭ major (three flats)[25]
>
> m. 52: C minor (three flats)

Also, several Bach arias contain *anabasis* patterns created by sharpward motion around the circle of fifths. Schweitzer and others have noted that

---

(minor) and "sweet" (major) aspects of Christ's suffering ("Drum muß uns sein verdienstlich Leiden recht bitter und doch süße sein").
[25]Whittaker, 2:242 noted the appearance of the remote key of E♭ major, but did not comment on its connection with the subject matter of the text.

the ritornello of the bass aria in Cantata 13 (Ex. 1) embodies a duality inherent in the text:

> Ächzen und erbärmlich Weinen
> Hilft der Sorgen Krankheit nicht;
> Aber wer gen Himmel siehet
> Und sich da um Trost bemühet,
> Dem kann leicht ein Freudenlicht
> In der Trauerbrust erscheinen.

> Groaning and pitiful weeping
> Do not help worry's sickness;
> But he who looks toward heaven
> And tries to find comfort there,
> A light of joy can easily appear
> In his grieving breast.

The first half (mm. 1–4) bristles with all kinds of musical figures—including diminished and augmented intervals, chromaticism, and harsh vertical dissonances—that graphically illustrate "groaning," "pitiful weeping," and "worry's sickness." These dissolve into a diatonic passage (mm. 5–8) full of rapid scales and sequences that depicts the joy experienced by the believer who looks toward heaven.[26] The progression from sorrow to joy is allegorized at a deeper level, however, by a large-scale *anabasis* that moves from the tonic G minor (two flats) to the dominant D minor (one flat, m. 31), and ultimately to the remote key of A minor (no flats, m. 42).

Similar considerations lie behind the use of the distant key of F♯ minor in the brief Weimar aria "Jesu, der aus großer Liebe," BWV 165/3. The *anabasis,* which proceeds from the tonic E minor (one sharp) to the dominant B minor (two sharps, m. 11) before arriving in F♯ minor (three sharps, m. 17), is apparently connected with the cleansing—the progression from sin and death to grace and blessing—that comes through the waters of baptism. Although it is not mentioned directly in the text of this aria, it is a

---

[26]Schweitzer, 2:351; Whittaker, 2:148–49; Dürr, *Kantaten,* 1:185.

Example 1. BWV 13/5, mm. 1–10

prominent theme of the cantata as a whole, and of the preceding recitative in particular:

> Die sündige Geburt verdammter Adamserben
> Gebieret Gottes Zorn, den Tod und das Verderben.
> Denn was vom Fleisch geboren ist,
> Ist nichts als Fleisch, von Sünden angestecket,
> Vergiftet und beflecket.
> Wie selig ist ein Christ!
> Er wird im Geist- und Wasserbade
> Ein Kind der Seligkeit und Gnade.
> Er ziehet Christum an
> Und seiner Unschuld weiße Seide,
> Er wird mit Christi Blut, der Ehren Purpurkleide,
> Im Taufbad angetan.

> The sinful birth of Adam's condemned heirs
> Gives birth to God's wrath, death, and ruin.
> For that which is born of the flesh
> Is nothing but flesh, infected by sin,
> Polluted and defiled.
> How blessed is a Christian!
> In the Spirit- and water-bath he becomes
> A child of salvation and grace.
> He puts on Christ
> And the white silk of His innocence;
> He is dressed in Christ's blood, the crimson robe of glory,
> In the waters of baptism.

Bukofzer makes the point at some length that there is no one-to-one correspondence between particular compositional techniques and specific extra-musical obêects, that similar musical devices can allegorize different things.[27] The converse is also true: texts that share similar affective and dramatic content sometimes receive highly individual—even antithetical—musical settings. For instance, in "Mein liebster Jesus ist verloren," BWV 154/1, the despair of Jesus's parents,[28] and, by extension, of the Christian, over the loss of Jesus

---

[27]Bukofzer, pp. 6–9.

[28]The Gospel reading for the 1st Sunday after Epiphany (Luke 2:41–52), the occasion for which Cantata 154 was composed, relates the story of the twelve-year-old Jesus, who accompanied his parents to Jerusalem for the Feast of the Passover. A day into their journey home, when they realized that Jesus was not among the group of travelers, they returned to Jerusalem and found him in the temple discussing theological matters with

("O Wort, das mir Verzweiflung bringt") is represented by an extraordinarily compelling *anabasis,* which begins in the remote key of D minor (mm. 44–46), moves upward to E minor (mm. 47–48), and then to F♯ minor (mm. 49–50).[29] (The head-motive of the ritornello is also repeated at successively higher pitch levels, the first and third statements by Violin 1, the second by the tenor.) But in "Ach nun ist mein Jesus hin!" BWV 244/30, from the St. Matthew Passion, a similar sentiment—the Christian's anguish over Jesus's arrest ("Ist es möglich, kann ich schauen?" ["Is it possible, can I look?"])—is illustrated by motion through the circle of fifths in the opposite (downward) direction: from the dominant F♯ minor (three sharps, mm. 46–47), to the tonic B minor (two sharps, mm. 48–49), to the subdominant E minor (one sharp, mm. 50–51), and ultimately to the remote key of A minor (no sharps, m. 54). These examples underscore the fact that Bach's modulatory procedures are flexible in their meaning, and also testify to the remarkable scope and plasticity of Bach's creative imagination.

In the present context it is worth mentioning the alto aria "Ach, bleibe doch, mein liebstes Leben," BWV 11/4, from the Ascension Oratorio, another movement that concerns the believer's response to the departure of Jesus.

---

the teachers of the Law. Verse 48, which reports that Jesus's mother told him, "Your father and I have been anxiously searching for you," was evidently the point of departure for the text of the opening aria.

[29]*Anabasis* is also used in the soprano aria "Mein Gott, ich liebe dich von Herzen," BWV 77/3, to allegorize the spiritual ardor of the believer:

> Mein Gott, ich liebe dich von Herzen,
> Mein ganzes Leben hangt dir an.
> Laß mich doch dein Gebot erkennen
> Und in Liebe so entbrennen,
> Daß ich dich ewig lieben kann.

> My God, I love you with all my heart,
> My whole life depends on you.
> But let me understand your law
> And become so passionately in love
> That I can love you forever.

The movement's overall tonal plan involves motion "upward" through the circle of fifths: from the tonic A minor (no sharps), to the dominant E minor (one sharp, m. 21), to the distant key of B minor (two sharps, m. 42). (Immediately thereafter, in m. 44, there is a jolting, and rather puzzling, turn towards the subdominant D minor [one flat], which leads back to A minor for the close of the movement.)

The second strophe of the text reads:

> Dein Abschied und dein frühes Scheiden
> Bringt mir das allergrößte Leiden,
> Ach ja, so bleibe doch noch hier;
> Sonst werd ich ganz von Schmerz umgeben.
>
> Your parting and your early leaving
> Bring me the greatest suffering of all,
> Ah yes, then stay here yet a while;
> Otherwise I will be completely surrounded by grief.

At the beginning of the B section, where all but the last of these lines are first set, there is an *anabasis*, beginning in C major (no sharps, mm. 29–31), the relative of the tonic A minor, and moving sharpwards—first to G major and E minor (one sharp, mm. 32–35), then to the remote keys of B minor and D major (two sharps, mm. 35–41). The harmonic intensification of this passage apparently reflects the believer's distress over Christ's ascension to heaven. This aria is a parody of the third movement of a lost wedding cantata ("Auf! süß entzückende Gewalt," BWV deest), which also served as the model for the "Agnus Dei" of the B-minor Mass (BWV 232/26).[30] The version in the B-minor Mass is over a third (30 measures) shorter than BWV 11/4, and is a step lower, in G minor. Of particular interest is the fact that the "Agnus Dei" does not contain the *anabasis*. Indeed, the second vocal period (mm. 27–44) has a much simpler tonal plan (modulation from the dominant D minor back to the tonic) and is much more compact (a single section) than BWV 11/4, where the B section falls into three subsections separated by ritornellos:

$$\text{mm. 29–36} = B^1 \text{ (lines 3–5)}$$

$$\text{mm. 40–46} = B^2 \text{ (lines 3–5)}$$

$$\text{mm. 49–52} = B^3 \text{ (line 6)}$$

Although the music for the model has not been preserved, both the structure and the *Affekt* of the text[31] comport with BWV 11/4. It is possible, therefore,

---

[30]See Alfred Dürr, "'Entfernet euch, ihr kalten Herzen': Möglichkeiten und Grenzen der Rekonstruktion einer Bach-Arie," *Die Musikforschung* 39 (1986): 32–36.

[31]The second strophe of "Entfernet euch, ihr kalten Herzen" reads:

> Wer nicht der Liebe Platz will geben,
> Der flieht sein Glück, der haßt das Leben,
> Und ist der ärgsten Thorheit Freund;
> Ihr wehlt euch selber nichts als Schmerzen.

that the *anabasis* may have been present in the original aria, too, and that it was eliminated—along with a number of other major revisions—when Bach reworked the movement for the B-minor Mass.[32]

IV

Let us turn now to a remarkable movement that employs a vast array of means—including modulation to remote keys—to illustrate the meaning of its text. The tenor aria (movement 3) of Cantata 109 (*Ich glaube, lieber Herr, hilf meinem Unglauben*) speaks of vacillation between doubt and belief:[33]

> Wie zweifelhaftig ist mein Hoffen,
> Wie wanket mein geängstigt Herz!
> Des Glaubens Docht glimmt kaum hervor,
> Es bricht dies fast zustoßne Rohr,
> Die Furcht macht stetig neuen Schmerz.

> How filled with doubt is my hope,
> How my worried heart wavers!
> The wick of faith glows but dimly,
> This almost crushed reed breaks,
> Fear constantly causes new grief.

Scholars have pointed out a number of ways in which uncertainty is represented in this movement. These include: 1) the use of dotted rhythms and leaps; 2) accompaniment of the vocal line by the continuo alone or by the strings and continuo, in alternation; 3) triplet figures on the words "wanket" and "zweifelhaftig."[34] But this aria is also a virtuoso display of tonal

---

> He who does not want to make room for love,
> He flees from his happiness, he hates his life,
> And is friend to the worst foolishness;
> You yourselves choose nothing but pain.

[32]Dürr also believes that the version in the Ascension Oratorio is closer to the original than the "Agnus Dei." See Dürr, "'Entfernet euch...'," p. 33.

[33]This idea is implicit in the Biblical quotation that serves as the text for the opening chorus: "I believe, dear Lord, help my unbelief" (Mark 9:24). On the relationship of this verse to the Gospel reading for the 21st Sunday after Trinity (John 4:47-54), for which this cantata was composed, see Dürr, *Kantaten*, 2:491.

[34]See Schweitzer, 2:93, 258; Carl Otto Dreger, "Die Vokalthematik Joh. Seb. Bachs: Dargestellt an den Arien der Kirchenkantaten," *Bach-Jahrbuch* 31 (1934): 34; Whittaker, 1:684-85; Dürr, *Kantaten*, 2:493.

allegory (Ex. 2). Beginning in the tonic E minor (one sharp, mm. 25–29), there is a rapid "descent" in the flatward direction, first to C major (m. 30), then to the distant key of D minor (one flat, m. 32), which represents the negative pole of the heart's uncertainty. This is followed by a bold modulation to F♯ minor (three sharps, mm. 35–38), a key that is equidistant from E minor in the opposite (sharpside) direction, and that evidently represents the positive pole:

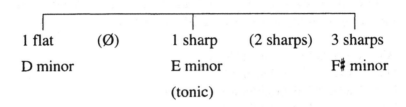

(Such a wide range of tonalities, spanning both flat and sharp keys, is not normally found in the Bach arias.[35]) In addition, the cadence in F♯ minor at m. 36 is subverted by a deceptive cadence (the dominant of F♯ minor is followed by the subdominant [iv^6] rather than the tonic). Moreover, in the last two measures of the B section (mm. 44–45), there is a sudden turn away from the dominant B minor toward the subdominant A minor. Both the deceptive cadence and the unexpected modulation underscore the instability that lies at the heart of the text.[36]

Our discussion of BWV 109/3, and the other examples cited above, raises an important question: To what extent are allegorical uses of tonality aurally perceptible? It seems undeniable that the significance of the harmonic procedures described here is lost on most listeners today. One reason for this is that we are simply not as familiar with the conventions of the genre, and are therefore not in as good a position as Bach's contemporaries to notice

---

[35]Nor, indeed, in the cantatas as a whole. Cf. Chafe's comment: "Perhaps the most striking difference between cantata and Passion…is the astonishing fact that not one of the church cantatas exhibits a range of keys that encompasses both sharp and flat areas (or systems). Close tonal relationships are overwhelmingly the norm for Bach in these works. Almost suite-like, they progress through closely related keys, often beginning and ending in the same one" ("J. S. Bach's *St. Matthew Passion*," p. 59).

[36]As Chafe points out, the tonal structure of the cantata as a whole also reflects the inner conflict between doubt and faith. See Chafe, *Tonal Allegory*, pp. 215–18.

Example 2. BWV 109/3, mm. 25–45

84 Stephen Crist

Example 2 (*continued*)

Example 2 (*continued*)

86 Stephen Crist

Example 2 (*continued*)

Bach, Theology, and Harmony 87

Example 2 (*continued*)

Example 2 (*continued*)

departures from stylistic norms.[37] More fundamentally, however, many of these procedures, particularly tonal *anabases* and *catabases*, unfold over extended spans of time. Although they were clearly an integral part of the composer's planning, they operate beneath the musical surface on a deeper level that often cannot be perceived by the ear alone. Schering's incisive remarks are relevant here:

---

[37]On the whole, the members of Bach's congregation in Leipzig—which included not only merchants but also city officials and university students and faculty—were quite well educated and musically sophisticated. As Don L. Smithers has noted: "With respect to the judging of church music, the qualifications on the part of the church attender were incomparably more favorable than today, at least in the first half of the 18th century and in a city like Leipzig. The cantata was not only listened to critically with regard to rhythm and intonation, but with regard to *Affekt,* rhetoric, and meaning as well. Not only were the performers judged critically, but also the works themselves and their points of contact with the rules of rhetoric and oratory." ("Im Blick auf die Beurteilung von Kirchenmusik waren die Voraussetzungen von seiten der Gottesdienstbesucher ungleich günstiger als heute, jedenfalls in der ersten Hälfte des 18. Jahrhunderts und in einer Stadt wie Leipzig. Nicht nur hinsichtlich Rhythmus und Intonation wurde das 'Kirchenstück' kritisch angehört, sondern ebenso in bezug auf Affekt, Rhetorik und Sinngehalt. Nicht nur die Ausführenden wurden kritisch begutachtet, sondern auch die Werke selbst und ihr Umgang mit den Vorschriften von Rhetorik und Oratorie.") Don L. Smithers, "Gottfried Reiches Ansehen und sein Einfluß auf die Musik Johann Sebastian Bachs," *Bach-Jahrbuch* 73 (1987): 113–14.

> As surely as we may assume that [Bach's] artistically experienced contemporaries—and even among the citizens of Leipzig there were many artistically experienced people—listened to his music with understanding and sound judgment, and grasped much of it (without scores!) more quickly than a later age which is farther removed from him, it may also be assumed that countless aspects of his art had no effect on the ears of his listeners. In his music there are simply some sonic occurrences which cannot be fully understood on a single and first hearing, even with the keenest ears and utmost intelligence, but which require repetition and probably even study.[38]

More recently, Chafe has reminded us, however, that when Bach employs "arcane" harmonic devices, he also takes care "to compose the movements so that countless other details that are more easily perceived and responded to match the dynamic that is 'allegorized' in the key sequences."[39]

How, then, might BWV 109/3 have been heard by the worshippers in Leipzig when it was first performed on the 21st Sunday after Trinity (17 October) in 1723? On the one hand, it seems unlikely that many listeners would be aware of the tonal distance traversed from D minor to F♯ minor, because it occurs in a fairly dissonant, highly-charged harmonic context. On the other hand, it is difficult to imagine that anyone who routinely heard at least one or two arias almost every week could fail to be jolted by the deceptive cadence at the midpoint of the B section and surprised by the abrupt turn from the dominant to the subdominant at the end. Both passages lie relatively close to the musical surface and contravene the expectation of normal cadential resolution. A moment's reflection would surely bring one to the realization that the unpredictability of the harmonic progressions is an emblem of the doubt, anxiety, and fear spoken of in the text.

Similarly, many in Bach's congregation would doubtless have recognized that the prominent ascending and descending chromatic scales in repeated sixteenth notes in the continuo that dominate the B section of the famous bass aria "Dein Wetter zog sich auf von weiten," BWV 46/3, allegorize aspects

---

[38]"So gewiß wir annehmen dürfen, daß seine kunsterfahrenen Zeitgenossen—und Kunsterfahrener gab es auch unter den Leipziger Bürgern viele—seine Musik mit Verständnis und klugem Urteil angehört und manches an ihr (ohne Partitur!) schneller aufgefaßt haben als eine spätere, von ihm ferngerückte Zeit, so gewiß darf auch angenommen werden, daß Unzähliges seiner Kunst an den Ohren seiner Hörer spurlos vorübergegangen ist. Es gibt bei ihm eben doch Klangereignisse, die sich selbst mit schärfstem Ohre und höchster Intelligenz beim einmaligen und ersten Hören nicht völlig erfassen lassen, sondern der Wiederholung, ja wohl gar des Studiums bedürfen." Schering, "Bach und das Symbol," p. 60.

[39]Chafe, "Luther's 'Analogy of Faith'," p. 101.

of the text.[40] The ascending line (mm. 45–54), which spans F to d, captures the tension inherent in the word "unerträglich" (unbearable), used here to describe the storm of God's judgment. The descending line (mm. 67–77), which returns from e to F, is connected with another facet of God's wrath. The word "Untergang" ("Da überhäufte Sünden der Rache Blitz entzünden und dir den Untergang bereiten") means both "doom" and "sinking." The latter aspect is represented by the downward direction of the chromatic scale and the descent of the vocal line to B (one of the lowest notes in the aria, m. 82), both of which are likely to have been readily understood by Bach's listeners.[41] But the simultaneous tonal "descent" to the remote key of F minor (four flats, mm. 77–87), which exceeds the *ambitus* of the tonic B♭ major, lies at a deeper level of abstraction and would probably not have been perceptible.[42]

V

If it is understandable that listeners, in Bach's time and our own, should miss the allegorical significance of remote keys in the arias, it is regrettable that scholars have, too. For, in failing to take account of this phenomenon, we have overlooked an important tool that opens new interpretive perspectives. Two final examples illustrate this point. In the soprano aria "Liebster Gott, erbarme dich," BWV 179/5 (Ex. 3), the sinner's descent into deep mire ("ich versink in tiefen Schlamm!") is vividly depicted by descending chromatic motion in the continuo (mm. 71–74) and the subsequent descent of the vocal line to b and c¹ (mm. 79–81, the lowest notes in the soprano

---

[40]Several writers, including Woldemar Voigt (*Die Kirchenkantaten Johann Sebastian Bachs: Ein Führer bei ihrem Studium und ein Berater für ihre Aufführung* [Stuttgart: J. B. Metzlersche Buchhandlung, 1918], p. 130), Arnold Schering (*Über Kantaten Johann Sebastian Bachs,* ed. Friedrich Blume [Leipzig: Koehler & Amelang, 1942], pp. 113–14), and Whittaker (1:641), have commented on these passages. Even Spitta, who normally says little about the pictorial aspect of Bach's art (see p. 94 below), was forced to admit that "the chromatic rise and fall in the middle...of the instrumental bass is highly effective" (Spitta, 2:428).

[41]If they missed it the first time, in Cantata 46 on the 10th Sunday after Trinity (1 August 1723), the Leipzig congregation had another chance just two weeks later. The bass aria "Mein Erlöser und Erhalter," BWV 69a/5 (first performed on the 12th Sunday after Trinity, 15 August), also contains striking descending and ascending chromatic lines in the continuo. Both the descent from e to B (mm. 37–42) and the ascent from d to f♯ (mm. 56–60) illustrate the words "Kreuz" ("cross") and "Leiden" ("suffering").

[42]Cf. Chafe's account of the tonal structure of Cantata 46 in *Tonal Allegory,* pp. 169–72.

Example 3. BWV 179/5, mm. 68–82

part), points that have been duly noted by Whittaker.[43] The same idea is allegorized simultaneously by an extraordinary modulation to the remote key of C minor (three flats, m. 81), which lies "deep" on the flat side of the circle of fifths with respect to the tonic A minor. But until Chafe, who mentions it briefly,[44] the only scholar who had taken note of this progression at all was Spitta, who simply stated that this aria is "quite admirable in its lavish use of harmonies and modulations."[45]

An even more striking example is found in the tenor aria "Vergibt mir Jesus meine Sünden," BWV 48/6. Here the idea of resurrection, mentioned in the second strophe of the text ("Er kann die Toten lebend machen..." ["He can raise the dead..."]), is allegorized in two ways. At the deepest level, the movement's tonal structure involves an *anabasis* that moves upward through the circle of fifths: from the tonic G minor (two flats), to the dominant D minor (one flat, m. 38), to the remote key of A minor (no flats, m. 57). Subsequently, in the ritornello between the two vocal periods of the B section (mm. 58–63), is heard one of the most arresting passages in all of Bach's vocal music (Ex. 4). As a clear and unmistakable illustration of resurrection, there is a wrenching modulation upward a half-step from A minor to B♭ major (mm. 57–63). Again, Spitta is the only one who

Example 4. BWV 48/6, mm. 41–63

---

[43]Whittaker, 1:599. Bukofzer cites a passage by Buxtehude with a similar text ("Ich versinke im tiefen Schlamm wo kein Grund ist") as "an example of the allegory of sinking" (p. 6).

[44]Chafe, *Tonal Allegory*, pp. 202–203.

[45]Spitta, 2:407.

Bach, Theology, and Harmony 93

Example 4 (*continued*)

has so much as alluded to this remarkable passage. He comments dryly that "the tenor aria is especially interesting in respect of... modulation."[46]

In Spitta's case, the overly brief treatment of arias containing conspicuous examples of tonal allegory is not attributable solely to his laconicism. Rather it reflects his position in the conflict between the proponents of absolute music and program music in the late 19th century, and his conviction that Bach adhered to the tenets of absolute music. Leo Schrade has aptly summarized the implications of this view:

> Spitta, an ardent believer in absolute, non-descriptive music, feared that Bach would become involved in the opinions held upon the music of Wagner. As a historian he knew how great a distortion such a comparison would produce. And as aesthetician he resisted even the thought that the art of sound should serve pictorial purposes. This attitude, of course, led to his embarrassment whenever he met with descriptive elements in Bach's cantatas where they are by no means rare. He made some attempt to treat them as of slight significance, or to explain them as indicative of sheer musical wit. He evaded the issue by denying the existence of any close relationship between word and tone. He "took care that no one should be misled by this or that piece of characterization into doubting for a moment that Bach was a priest of absolute music."[47]

It is more difficult to understand why subsequent generations of scholars have largely ignored this fascinating and revealing aspect of the Bach arias.

---

[46]Spitta, 3:88.

[47]Leo Schrade, "Schweitzer's Aesthetics: An Interpretation of Bach," in *The Albert Schweitzer Jubilee Book,* ed. A. A. Roback (Cambridge, Mass.: Sci-Art Publishers, n.d. [1946]), pp. 178–79. Cf. similar remarks in Schering, "Bach und das Symbol," p. 136; Friedrich Blume, *Two Centuries of Bach: An Account of Changing Taste,* trans. Stanley Godman (London: Oxford University Press, 1950), p. 66; Karl Geiringer, *Symbolism in the Music of Bach* (Washington: The Library of Congress, 1956), p. 8; and Hermann Keller, "Albert Schweitzer's Book on Bach," *Universitas* 7 (1964): 70–71. The quotation at the end of the passage from Schrade's article is from Schweitzer, 2:3. Later in life, in a 1956 letter to Breitkopf & Härtel in Leipzig, Schweitzer credited the success of his book on Bach to the fact that he "dared to contradict the dogma of Spitta and others, that Bach was absolute music, and established instead that wherever a given text contains or even only presupposes anything pictorial, he depicts this in his music." ("Den Erfolg des Buches erkläre ich mir daraus, dass ich wagte, dem Dogma von Spitta und anderen, dass Bach reine Musik sei, zu widersprechen, sondern feststellte, dass er überall, wo ein vorausgesetzter Text etwas Bildliches enthält oder auch nur voraussetzt, er dieses in seiner Musik darstellt.") Cited in Erwin R. Jacobi, "Zur Entstehung des Bach-Buches von Albert Schweitzer, auf Grund unveröffentlichter Briefe," *Bach-Jahrbuch* 61 (1975): 143–44.

Perhaps a preoccupation with philological and documentary matters since the founding of the new edition of Bach's works (*Neue Bach-Ausgabe*) and the formulation of the new chronology of the vocal music in the 1950s has diverted the attention of recent scholarship from aesthetic evaluation of this music.[48] But I hope to have shown that these incomparably rich pieces continue to repay careful analysis and provide new insight into the working of Bach's fertile compositional imagination.

---

[48]See Friedrich Blume's remarks in "The Present State of Bach Research," in *Syntagma Musicologicum II: Gesammelte Reden und Schriften 1962–1972*, ed. Anna Amalie Abert and Martin Ruhnke (Kassel: Bärenreiter, 1973), pp. 281–92.

The Symphony and the Artist's Creed: Camille Saint-Saëns and His Third Symphony

Ludwig Finscher

Camille Saint-Saëns's third, the so-called Organ Symphony, is still popular with the concert-going public despite the difficulties of its performance and despite all the changes of public taste that have been unfavorable to the "big" and especially the "Weltanschauungs" symphony of the 19th century. At the same time, it is rather unpopular with the musicological community: there is very little substantial and reliable literature on the work or, indeed, on its composer.[1]

Saint-Saëns's own generation had no difficulty with the symphony: Kretzschmar's venerable *Führer durch den Concertsaal* sheds lavish praise on it over no less than five pages.[2] Today, even where the tightness and sophistication of its motivic construction are praised or at least acknowledged, its aesthetics seem to be suspect. In his *19th Century Music*, Carl Dahlhaus regards it as an abortive attempt to write "modern" instrumental music on a classicist base, to develop the orchestral pomp and circumstance of the "big" symphony from a background of Lisztian techniques of motivic transformation (derived from Liszt's *Ce qu'on entend sur la montagne*)—abortive because these techniques would not work without their Lisztian *raison d'être*, the program.[3] But apart from the fact that this is in itself rather curiously dogmatic reasoning, the symphony comes much closer to being a symphonic poem and at the same time remaining a symphony in the wake of Beethoven's 5th than Dahlhaus (and indeed most modern authors) have thought.

---

[1] By far the best study in our context is still Daniel Martin Fallon, *The Symphonies and Symphonic Poems of Camille Saint-Saëns* (Ph.D. dissertation, Yale University, 1973). The unpublished master's thesis by Michael Houle, *Cyclic Techniques in the Symphonies of Saint-Saëns, D'Indy, Franck and Chausson* (UCLA, 1968), was not available to me, non of the UCLA libraries being able to provide me with a microfilm.

[2] Hermann Kretzschmar, *Führer durch den Concertsaal. I. Abtheilung: Sinfonie und Suite*, 3rd ed. (Leipzig: Breitkopf & Härtel, 1898), 1:688–93.

[3] Carl Dahlhaus, *Die Musik des 19. Jahrhunderts*, Neues Handbuch der Musikwissenschaft, vol. 6 (Laaber: Laaber-Verlag, 1980), pp. 242–43.

The symphony was written upon an inquiry or suggestion (not really a formal commission) from the London Philharmonic Society.[4] Saint-Saëns probably started on the work in August 1885 and finished it, after a break devoted to the *Carnaval des animaux,* in April 1886. Saint-Saëns planned to dedicate it to Franz Liszt and sought Liszt's permission, which was given in a gracious letter from Weimar in which Liszt asked to use only his name, without any title—"mettre simplement mon nom." When Liszt died on July 31, 1886, Saint-Saëns changed the dedication to "A la mémoire de Franz Liszt."[5] He conducted the first performance in London on May 19 of the same year. For this performance, he wrote a detailed analytical program note, as had been the custom for the concerts of the Philharmonic Society since 1869. Normally, these program notes were written by a member of the Society, but since the score of the symphony could not be sent to London in time, the composer himself had to do the job. This text is of fundamental importance for the understanding of the composer's intentions and of the score itself.[6]

The London premiere of the symphony went practically unnoticed in Paris, and it took a remarkably long time until the work became better known and was accepted as a masterpiece, specifically of French music, in the composer's home country. At first and to a considerable degree, the work made its career outside France and especially in Germany.[7] The reasons for this neglect of the symphony in France were complicated.[8]

On the one hand, during the 1870s Saint-Saëns's works, especially the fourth piano concerto and the symphonic poems *Le rouet d'Omphale, Phaeton,* and *La jeunesse d'Hercule,* had been denounced by a large part of the Parisian music critics as modernistic music in the wake of Liszt and Wagner—although the composer was one of the most prominent members of the Société Nationale de Musique, which had been founded after the political

---

[4]The following according to Fallon, pp. 361–64.

[5]Fallon, pp. 374–75, 479–80.

[6]The English translation of the program notes (surely approved by Saint-Saëns) is published in full in Fallon, pp. 459–71. To my knowledge, the program notes of the Philharmonic Society—the first venture of its kind—have never been studied comprehensively. They are a mine of information on analytical thought and, implicitly, on public musical taste in London in the second half of the 19th century.

[7]Instrumental in the German career of the symphony were the music journalist Otto Neitzel and the conductor Franz Wüllner; see Neitzel, *Camille Saint-Saëns* (Berlin: A. G. Liebeskind, 1899), pp. 21–25 and Kretzschmar, p. 688.

[8]For the following, cf. Michael Stegemann, *Camille Saint-Saëns* (Reinbek: Rowohlt, 1988), passim.

catastrophe of 1871 to promote French music, *ars gallica,* and especially French instrumental music as opposed to German music. On the other hand, in the very year 1886 long-standing controversies between Saint-Saëns (and his staunchest partisan, Romain Bussine) and the Wagnerites within the Société Nationale culminated in a motion by Vincent d'Indy that non-French compositions should be admitted to the concerts of the Société; when this motion passed, Saint-Saëns and Bussine left the Société. So the protagonist of *ars gallica* had been denounced by one part of the public as a Wagnerite and by one part of his colleagues as not Wagnerian enough.

To complicate matters further, Saint-Saëns's concert tour in Germany early in 1886 ended in a fiasco when rumours were spread about his French partisanship in the discussions about a *Lohengrin* performance in Paris.[9] During Saint-Saëns's first concert with the Berlin Philharmonic Orchestra on January 22, 1886, part of the public demonstrated vehemently against the composer. Following this, concerts in Kassel and other cities were cancelled, and Angelo Neumann in Prague abandoned his production of Saint-Saëns's *Henri VIII* because he feared disturbances, especially since the Czech public greeted the composer enthusiastically to demonstrate against Germanic (that is, Austrian) cultural hegemony. The aftermath of the Franco-Prussian war and of the founding of the German *Kaiserreich* in 1871 was by no means over, and Prague was a culturally divided city.[10]

---

[9]Actually, there were two scandals concerning *Lohengrin* in Paris, and Saint-Saëns was involved only in the second. In 1882, a *Lohengrin* performance in German (!) by Angelo Neumann and his troupe had been forbidden by the French government after consultations with the German ambassador, because of possible anti-German demonstrations; cf. Carl Fr. Glassenap, *Das Leben Richard Wagners* (Leipzig: Breitkopf & Härtel, 1911), 6:557–58; Ernest Newman, *The Life of Richard Wagner* (New York: Alfred A. Knopf, 1946), 4:650–51; Léon Guichard, *La musique et les lettres en France au temps du Wagnérisme* (Paris: Presses Universitaires de France, 1963), p. 57.

The second scandal started in June 1885 when rumors were spread in the press that the director of the Opéra-Comique planned to stage the opera and that the directors of the Opéra intended to circumvent Carvalho's exclusive right to perform *Lohengrin* in Paris by staging it themselves in Italian. A lively exchange of letters in the Parisian and even the provincial press followed. As an answer to an article favoring a *Lohengrin* performance in the *Revue d'Angers,* Saint-Saëns published an article in *La France,* comparing French reception of German music and German reception of French music to the disadvantage of the latter, and in no uncertain and indeed polemical and chauvinistic terms. Cf. the interesting if slightly biased account by Friedrich (Frederick) Niecks, "A Retrospective View of the Lohengrin Question in Paris," *The Monthly Musical Record* 16 (1886): 76–79; also the selective bibliography of French texts (including Baudelaire and Anatole France) in Guichard, pp. 251–52.

[10]As to the events in Berlin and Saint-Saëns's abortive German concert tour, cf. again a very balanced account by Niecks, "Art and Patriotism," *The Monthly Musical Record* 16 (1886): 99–100, 122–23.

But the composer's fame was quick to recover in Germany, due to the success of the third symphony. The work took longer to become established in France, and not until around 1900 was it hailed (more or less unanimously) as a masterpiece. Paul Dukas called it one of the most remarkable products of the French symphonic school but regretted that it was performed too rarely, due to its technical demands (that is, the necessity of an organ):

> This powerful and sweeping work is certainly one of the most remarkable products of the French symphonic school. The majority of the public, however, has had few opportunities to hear it until now, because it has only been played at the Société des Concerts du Conservatoire and the "salle d'Harcourt" due to the material means required for its execution. M. Lamoureux, having installed a large organ at the Cirque, could not inaugurate the organ better than by staging this beautiful work, whose solid style, grand design, and ingenious details attest to its authentic mastery.[11]

The symphony is described by Julien Tiersot less as a French work than as a masterpiece strongly founded in the classical (and that is, the German) tradition:

> The Third Symphony, despite tendencies that are still essentially classic, is of such grand richness of form and of such magnificent brilliance that it deserves a place in the first row of the masterpieces of the art at the end of the 19th century.... It is dedicated to the memory of Franz Liszt.... The composer has called on all the tonal resources known to the modern era....

---

[11]"Cette oeuvre, puissante et de large souffle, est certainement une des plus remarquables productions, de l'école symphonique française; et pourtant le grand public n'avait eu que peu d'occasions de l'entendre jusqu'ici, puisqu'elle n'avait encore été exécutée qu'à la Société des Concerts du Conservatoire et à la salle d'Harcourt, en raison des moyens matériels que nécessite son exécution. M. Lamoureux ayant fait installer (au Cirque) un grand orgue, ne pouvait mieux l'inaugurer qu'en montant cette belle oeuvre dont la fermeté de style, la grandeur de plan et l'ingéniosité de détails affirment une si authentique maîtrise." "Chronique musicale," *Revue hebdomadaire* 42 (1895): 310. The scarcity of big concert halls (and, implicitly, concert halls with an organ) in Paris was a kind of leitmotivic complaint of Parisian musicians and visitors alike throughout the nineteenth century and well into the 20th; cf. Jeffrey Cooper, *The Rise of Instrumental Music and Concert Series in Paris 1828–1871,* Studies in Musicology, 65 (Ann Arbor: UMI Research Press, 1983), passim. On the other hand, St. James Hall in London, the site of the first performance of the symphony, had already been built with a big organ in 1858. Saint-Saëns had played the organ in 1879 (Fallon, p. 391). Generally speaking, the concert-hall organ (on which there seems to be no comprehensive study) spread first in England, due to the Handel oratorio tradition, and much more slowly on the continent.

> From the point of view of the writing, he adopted the principle of a fundamental theme that runs through various parts of the work while constantly transforming itself in such a way that this initial theme...bursts forth in the finale with the splendor of a triumphal hymn.... The entire work, magnificently laid out, is in the best symphonic style—at the same time extensive and clear—and if, by the nature of its fundamental ideas, it reminds one of past masters, it would be nearly impossible to define which one has influenced this work directly. Is it Beethoven, or Bach, or Mozart, or Handel, or Mendelssohn, or Schumann? No, it is none of these in particular, but a little of all of them. This fusion of powerful inspiration from so many superior geniuses, occurring without effort, building on the foundation of a strong classical education, and finishing by forming a new genius, is, without a doubt, that which constitutes the best of the personality of M. Saint-Saëns.[12]

The number of German composers (among whom Bach and Handel are probably meant to evoke overtones of sacred music) thought by Tiersot to be present in Saint-Saëns's score is remarkable, but equally remarkable is the fact that the symphony's decisive unifying peculiarity, "le principe du thème fondamental," is only mentioned in passing. Five years later, however, in a context that is the more remarkable because the article generally turns a very critical eye on the composer, this principle is put into the center of the argument by Gaston Carraud:

> This is not only the most significant symphonic work that M. Saint-Saëns has produced, it is also the most significant of all his works, and the most

---

[12]"La troisième symphony, malgré des tendances toujours essentiellement classiques, est d'une si grande richesse de formes, d'un si magnifique éclat, qu'elle mérite de prendre place au premier rang des chefs-d'oeuvres de l'art à la fin du dix-neuvième siècle.... Elle est dédiée à la mémoire de Franz Liszt.... L'auteur a fait appel à toutes les ressources de la sonorité connues à l'époque moderne.... Au point de vue de l'écriture, il a adopté le principe du thème fondamental circulant à travers les diverses parties en s'y transformant incessamment, de façon que ce thème initial...arrive, dans le finale, à éclater avec la splendeur d'une hymne triomphal.... L'oeuvre entière, d'une magnifique ordonnance, est du meilleur style symphonique, à la fois large et clair; et si, par la nature des idées fondamentales, elle peut faire songer encore aux maîtres du passé, il serait bien impossible de définir duquel en particulier elle a subi l'influence directe. Est-ce de Beethoven, ou de Bach, ou de Mozart, ou de Händel, ou de Mendelssohn, ou de Schumann? Non: d'aucun spécialement, mais un peu de tous. Cette fusion de puissantes inspirations de tant de génies supérieurs, opérée de façon parfaitement normale, par le seul effet d'une forte éducation classique, et arrivant à former un génie nouveau est sans doute ce qui constitue le meilleur de la personnalité de M. Saint-Saëns." Julien Tiersot, "La Symphonie en France," *Zeitschrift der Internationalen Musikgesellschaft* 3 (1902): 391–402; quotation pp. 397–98.

perfect: the only work where his reprehensible dilettantism may have been disarmed, the only work that transcends a more than intelligent will, the only work that reaches, with moments of true intensity, some sort of interior life. I know very well that he achieves this through external means, by the artifice of writing and composition, rather than because of the substance of his ideas (which are so uneven!), but he has achieved it. Friends of M. Saint-Saëns pretend to consider this symphony stilted compared to those of Beethoven. This is a bad joke to play on Saint-Saëns. It is already a lot that the incredible magnitude of this work has not crushed it. If the work has held up, appearing simply classical, even scholastic at times, it is because of its great novelty and solidity of form. I am not talking about the connection, two by two, of its four traditional movements, which has little importance. I am talking about the systematic application of the principle of variation to the development of the symphony, which the last works of Beethoven established. I am talking about this massive unity (which is nevertheless so alive) that the composer assured through the tight relationship of all the themes, giving rise to two opposing principles of the basic theme.

One feels disappointed that neither of these two principles comes, so to speak, to its culmination. And at the height of the finale, where one expects the definitive blossoming of one of the themes, instead they fall to pieces in an apotheosis that is dazzling and robust, but of complete thematic insignificance. Even so, it is in this that one comes to recognize Saint-Saëns's soul, and one senses the real value of his ideas.[13]

---

[13]"Ce n'est pas seulement l'ouvrage symphonique le plus considérable qu'ait produit M. Saint-Saëns, c'est le plus considérable de tous ses ouvrages, et le plus parfait: le seul où son coupable dilettantisme ait désarmé, le seul qui domine une volonté un peu plus qu'intelligente, le seul qui atteigne, et avec des moments d'une véritable intensité, une sorte de vie intérieure. Je sais bien que c'est par des moyens tout extérieurs qu'il l'atteint, et par l'artifice de l'écriture et de la composition plutôt que par la substance des idées, si inégales! mais il l'atteint. Des amis de M. Saint-Saëns prétendent guinder cette symphonie en face des celles de Beethoven. C'est une maivaise blague à lui faire. C'est déjà beaucoup que sa totalité formidable ne l'ait point écrasée. Et si elle a résisté, c'est qu'avec des apparences assez simplement classiques, scolastiques même par endroits, elle a une grande nouveauté et une grande solidité de forme. Je ne parle pas de la liaison deux par deux de ses quatre "mouvements" traditionnels, que a peu d'importance. Je parle de l'application systématique au développement de la symphonie du principe de la variation, tel que l'ont établi les dernières oeuvres de Beethoven. Je parle de cette unité massive, et pourtant si vivante, que l'auteur a assurée par l'étroite parenté de tous ses thèmes, germant en deux principes opposès, du thème primordial.

On éprouve une déception qu'aucun de ces deux principes n'arrive, pour ainsi dire, à son achèvement, et qu'au point culminant du finale, où l'on attend l'épanouissement victorieux et définitif de l'un d'eux, ils s'émiettent dans une apothéose, éblouissante et robuste, mais d'une complète insignifiance thématique. C'est à quoi l'on finit tout de même par reconnaitre l'âme de M. Saint-Saëns, et l'on éprouve la valeur réelle de ses idées." "Les Concerts," *La Liberté* 42 (October 22, 1907).

The final step in the early reception of the symphony is taken by Vincent d'Indy in his *Cours de composition musicale*. On the one hand, d'Indy sees the symphony as an example of cyclic unity achieved by motivic transformation—the *sonate cyclique*, which he derives from Beethoven and which he sees as the crowning achievement in the history of the sonata and as the decisive achievement with which the French composers have surpassed (and indeed defeated) the German tradition—a teleological view of compositional history and a triumph of cultural nationalism neatly wrought in one.[14] On the other hand, the work is again analyzed at some length in the treatise's chapter on the symphony as a "conception that seems rather personal to the composer," namely the large-scale division into two movements which, however, incorporate the traditional four, similar to the design of the fourth piano concerto Op. 44 and the first violin sonata Op. 75.[15]

Saint-Saëns himself had stressed this formal peculiarity and mentioned the two other works in his program note for the London performance. He had furthermore stressed that by linking two movements each, he had changed the traditional functions of the traditional four-movement sequence: "The first, arrested in development,[16] serves as an Introduction to the *Adagio*, and the *Scherzo* is linked by the same process to the *Finale*." If this statement is strange, since the traditional functions of the four movements as well as the Beethovenian pattern culminating in the finale have been very carefully integrated into the overall plan of the symphony, the next passage is even stranger: "The composer has sought to avoid thus the endless resumptions and repetitions which more and more tend to disappear from instrumental music under the influence of increasingly developed musical culture." While the second thought of this sentence reads like a prefiguration of Schoenberg's opinion that repetition in music is an insult to the listener's intelligence,[17] the first thought is rather far from the music itself: there are a number of literal repetitions in the recapitulation of the first

---

[14]Vincent d'Indy, *Cours de composition musicale* (Paris: Durand et Cie, 1909), 2/1, pp. 375*ff*.: "La sonate cyclique." As to d'Indy's nationalism, see Charles B. Paul, "Rameau, d'Indy and French Nationalism," *The Musical Quarterly* 58 (1972): 45–56.

[15]"Conception qui paraît assez personnelle à l'auteur." D'Indy, 2/1, pp. 166*ff*.

[16]"Arrested in development" is misleading, because the first movement (in sonata form) has a complete, albeit abbreviated recapitulation. What Saint-Saëns probably means is that the recapitulation has an irregular tonal plan and an open end that develops motivically into the slow movement.

[17]"In the sphere of art-music, the author respects his audience. He is afraid to offend it by repeating over and over what can be understood at one single hearing, even if it is new, and let alone if it is stale old trash.... But an alert and well-trained mind will demand to be told the more remote matters, the more remote consequences of the simple matter that he has already comprehended. An alert and well-trained mind refuses to listen to baby-talk and requests strongly to be spoken to in a brief and straightforward language." Arnold Schoenberg, "Brahms the Progressive," *Style and Idea*, ed. Leonard Stein (London: Philosophical Library, 1975), pp. 400–401.

movement, the scherzo is repeated completely and literally after the trio, and whether the finale and especially its apotheosis is devoid of "resumptions and repetitions," listeners may decide for themselves. Either Saint-Saëns wrote his program note without much care, or he was not the best analyst of his own work. Either assumption would be borne out by the remainder of the note, which is a very simple description of the most prominent features of the score.[18]

Indeed, the symphony is much more carefully constructed than it would seem from the composer's program note: it is constructed on several levels simultaneously, and behind that construction there is a hidden meaning that can at least partially be reconstructed and understood.[19] The first level on which the symphony works is, of course, the four-movement form. The traditional sequence is obvious: the outer movements are weightier than Adagio und Scherzo, in thematic content, thematic transformation and thematic conflict; the Adagio is the lyrical and emotional core of the work, and the Scherzo (which is called a Scherzo, not in the score, but in the program note) is playful and sprightly. It is a sign of the sophistication of the symphony that this sequence is linked with the overall process of thematic transformation: the process is central in the first and crucial in the final movement, but scarcely more than episodic in the Adagio and playfully complicated and obscured in the Scherzo. On a second level, the four-movement sequence is modified after the most influential model of the 19th century, Beethoven's Fifth: like the Beethoven work, the Organ Symphony moves from C minor to C major and to a triumphant and colossal finale, and the passage from Scherzo to Finale has obvious similarities to that of Beethoven's symphony.

Only on a third level of form does Saint-Saëns's idea of four movements in two, as described in his program note, work—and perhaps not quite even there. For an unprejudiced listener who has not read the program note, it is easy to understand the Scherzo as "introduction" to the monumental Finale, but it is much more difficult to hear the first movement as "introduction" to the Adagio. The same problem arises in the fourth piano concerto Op. 44, the cyclic form of which is rather similar to that of the symphony (whereas the violin sonata Op. 75 resembles both works only superficially). The concerto is again a work that moves from C minor to a triumphant C major, it

---

[18]There is at least one observation (apart from hints at the emotional content, see below) that is helpful, because it is overlooked by most analysts (not Fallon): What Saint-Saëns calls the "final transformation" of the "initial" (main) theme (m. 610, letter EE).

[19]The best analysis by far is again Fallon, pp. 371–430. My following remarks are, needless to say, indebted to Fallon's work and can at best give some additional evidence which may be of interest.

is again designed as four movements in two, and it is again difficult to see the first movement, a magnificent quasi-Passacaglia, as "introduction" to the A♭-major Andante. It is much easier to see the Scherzo, with its reminiscences of the first movement and the Andante and its prefiguration of the Finale theme, as introduction to the latter.

Corresponding to the formal organization, the tonal plan of the symphony works on different levels at the same time: there is the traditional motion from C minor to C major, but there is also the "almost exaggerated role" ("rôle presque exagéré")[20] of the Neapolitan D♭ major. The first part opens on a D♭ sixth chord, leading over D♭$_6$–f–b$^{°7}$–G^9, which is then repeated, to C minor; in the *allegro* sonata-form movement, the process is reversed and intensified: the first subject appears in C minor, the second in D♭ major (m. 102, letter F), which is now reached not by modulation, but by an abrupt shift to A♭ (m. 90, letter E). D♭ major/minor is again prominent in the development section (along with F major), whereas the dominant of C minor is carefully avoided. In the recapitulation, D♭ is absent. The second subject appears first in F major (m. 301) and then in E major (m. 309; another half-step relation—to the F major also so prominent in the development section), only to disappear quickly and give way to a short bridge passage that finally leads from a single G to A♭ and from there to the D♭-major chord of the organ with which the slow movement begins—a shift very similar in effect to the shift to the second subject in the first movement. The middle section of the Adagio goes one step further in the expansion of the harmonic range. As the surprising E major had been introduced as a kind of substitute for F major in the recapitulation of the first movement, now E is taken up again in the shape of E minor (m. 426), and developing into a chord progression that leads back through B major (C♭ major), D major, F major, and A♭ major to the tonic D♭ major and to the beginning of the repeat of the main section (m. 439, letter V). Saint-Saëns seems to have been very proud of this progression.[21] Again one step further, the core progression (motion by minor third) is repeated three times in the coda of the movement (m. 458, letter X)—this time as D♭ major to E minor, each time an octave lower (which corresponds to the organisation of musical space at the beginning and the end of the first movement) and ending in an organ cadence over the chromatic bass line E♭–E♭♭–D♭.

---

[20]D'Indy, 2/2, p. 167. D'Indy speaks of the "rôle" of D♭ major in the first movement, seeing it as preparation of the slow movement, which is in this key, and finally as part of "une vaste cadence formée des quatre mouvements de la symphonie": C minor– D♭ major– C minor–C major.

[21]Cf. Fallon, pp. 396*ff*.

106 Ludwig Finscher

The Scherzo is the first movement in which the dominant G major plays a structurally important role, but D♭ major and F major are by no means absent. They appear first, very conspicuously, in a bridge passage leading from G major via C major, F major and A♭ major to D♭ major (mm. 25–38, the 14 measures before letter B); D♭ major comes back, juxtaposed to C minor, in the following development section (m. 55) and, again prominently, where the first Trio is for a moment inserted into the development of the second Trio (m. 150, letter H). Finally, it is hinted at and at the same time eliminated at the crucial point where the Scherzo turns into the preparation of the Finale: after the complete repeat of the Scherzo, the final bars (m. 275, letter O) turn in an abrupt shift to A♭ major instead of C major, in exact correspondence to the preparation of the D♭-major second subject in the first movement and to the shift from the end of the first to the beginning of the second movement. The ensuing Presto—the first part of the extended introduction to the Finale—starts as another repeat of the first Trio, soon interrupted and finally eliminated by the chorale melody which here appears for the first time; Saint-Saëns described this section as "a conflict...ending with the defeat of the agitated and fantastic element."[22] This section (up to m. 363, three bars after letter R) is firmly in A♭ major, from which a short bridge passage leads via E♭ major to the final C major with the entry of the organ and the first transformation of the chorale (m. 376). After this, A♭ and D♭ major reappear only fleetingly and imbedded into sequential patterns, D♭ now devoid of its former pivotal function as Neapolitan tonality. However, the idea of exploiting the contrast of the central tonality and a chromatically related one comes up again in the relation of first and second subject of the Finale proper: C major and B major.[23]

The last level on which the Organ Symphony is so very carefully constructed is the one most frequently described: thematic unity and transformation. It must be discussed here, albeit briefly, because even prominent analyses fall conspicuously short of an accurate description. As d'Indy has already demonstrated,[24] the symphony's *thème cyclique* proper is aided by the two motives that open the slow introduction: the *thème cyclique* runs through a number of transformations until it appears—"now completely transformed," as Saint-Saëns has it—in the apotheotic section before the final Allegro (m. 384, letter S), and the second motive of the introduction also reappears in different shapes. (For a list of variants of these motives,

---

[22] Fallon, p. 467.
[23] The Neapolitan relations may point back to Liszt's B-minor sonata (and further), and it is just possible (although we have no evidence) that the use of D♭ major has something to do with the most prominent D♭ major in the 19th century: that of Wagner's *Ring*.
[24] D'Indy, 2/1, pp. 382–83; 2/2, pp. 166–70.

see Appendix 1.) The process of transformation is subtle and in its very subtlety reminiscent of the techniques that Liszt had developed, above all in the piano concertos and in the symphonic poems, but it goes beyond Lisztian techniques, and its obvious aim—cyclic unity—is only one of its purposes. Its second and by no means less important purpose is to enhance the contrast between unity and transformation on the one hand and the motivically independent secondary themes (second subjects of the first and last section, second Trio of the Scherzo) and the chorale on the other. The construction could be described as dialectic: the thematic contrasts of traditional sonata-movement and scherzo forms are superimposed upon the thematic unity and transformation, and both the traditional and the Lisztian processes are crowned by the final, "complete" transformation of the *thème cyclique* and the final introduction of yet another new theme: the chorale. Attempts to understand it as another transformation of the *thème cyclique* (the most prominent example being d'Indy's analysis) are hardly convincing, due to the chorale's characteristic diastematic shape. But the melody—"calm, grave, austere" in Saint-Saëns's words—is more than just a thematic contrast. Together with the final and "complete" transformation of the *thème cyclique*, the chorale forms the climax of the symphony and unveils its meaning—the chorale as a theme stated like a theme in a classical score, not developed; the *thème cyclique* developed until it now reaches its final stage of transformation, not stated (although its appearance in the strings, surrounded by the glittering figuration of the piano *à quatre mains* and punctuated by the *piano* chords of the organ, is a stunning *coup de théatre*[25]). The chorale drives away the "agitated and fantastic element" that belongs to the thematic transformations of the *thème cyclique* and the second motive from the introduction; after a bridge passage in which the first transformation of the *thème cyclique* reappears ominously in the low strings (mm. 364–75, after letter R),[26] the chorale returns in triumph, introducing the organ with thundering C-major chords and leading to the "completely transformed" version of the *thème cyclique*. What follows is the sonata-form Finale with the *thème cyclique* as first subject, a new theme as second subject and a development in which the chorale is prominent. The final and "complete" transformation of the *thème cyclique* does not appear again—it

---

[25]The sheer sweetness of the melody and its "hit" quality—comparable again to the finale melody of the fourth piano concerto—have been exploited by Scott Fitzgerald, "If I had words" (Trax. Mod. CD 1032, *The Love Collection,* vol. 5).

[26]The use of instrumentation as a means to transform a motive and its character beyond diastematic and rhythmic transformation is one of the details in which Saint-Saëns transcends orthodox Lisztian technique. Another is the reduction of a theme to an accompaniment figure for a new theme, which appears very early in the score (first movement, Allegro, bridge theme, m. 54, five measures before letter C) and which curiously points to Brahms.

has had, so to speak, its epiphany. Again, the idea of a synthesis of Beethovenian and Lisztian thinking seems to emerge, the use of contrasting formal ideas and thematic processes even developing an allegorical meaning.

However, there is still more in the final climax of the symphony, because the chorale as well as the "complete" transformation of the *théme cyclique* are fraught with sacred associations that are at the same time Lisztian associations. They cannot have been obscure to the inner circle of Liszt's and Saint-Saëns's admirers, and they make the moment where the two melodies appear side by side the crucial moment of the symphony and the point where its meaning as hommage to Liszt is fully revealed. The beginning of the chorale is a common Gregorian intonation frequently to be found especially in Alleluja melodies (Ex. 1), but also associated with Liszt: it appears in different contexts, but always with sacred connotations, and it appears above all in the *Legende von der Heiligen Elisabeth* where the composer himself states its use and connotations in the *Schluß-Bemerkung* to the score:

> Let us finally remark that the intonation [Ex. 1] is very frequently used in Gregorian chant, e. g. in the Magnificat, the hymn "Crux fidelis" etc. The composer of this work has used it several times—among others in the Gloria fugue "Cum Sancto Spiritu" in the Gran mass, in the final chorus of the Dante symphony and in the symphonic poem *Die Hunnenschlacht*. In the present composition of the legend of the Holy Elisabeth, it forms the main motif of the chorus of the crusaders and of the march to the crusade, as it were, as musical symbol of the cross.[27]

Example 1: "Chorale" intonation

---

[27]"Schliesslich sei noch bemerkt dass die Intonation [Ex. 1] im gregorianischen Gesang sehr häufig gebraucht ist; zum Beispiel in dem [Magnificat], dem Hymnus [Crux fidelis], etc.—Der Componist dieses Werkes hat die nähmliche Tonfolge mehrmals verwendet—unter andern in der Fuge des Gloria *("cum sancto spiritu")* der Graner Messe; im Schlusschor der Dante Sinfonie, und in der symphonischen Dichtung "Die Hunnen-Schlacht."—Sie bildet, in der obliegenden Composition der Legende der heiligen Elisabeth, gleichsam als tonisches Symbol des Kreuzes, das Hauptmotif des Chors der Kreuzritter (N° III a) und des Kreuzzug-Marsches (N° III d)" (Leipzig: C.F. Kahnt Nachfolger, 1869; repr. Gregg, 1971), p. 313.

The background of the "completely transformed" version of the *thème cyclique* is more obscure and certainly more hypothetical.[28] Its opening is, to all purposes, identical with the opening of a piece originating in Paris and very popular, even notorious there in the second half of the nineteenth century, the famous "Ave Maria" by "Arcadelt," which Pierre-Louis-Philippe Dietsch—of the *Vaisseau fantôme* and the Paris première of *Tannhäuser*—published in 1842, and which really was Dietsch's four-voice arrangement of a three-voice Arcadelt chanson, *Nous voyons que les hommes font tous vertus d'aimer* (Ex. 2). And there was one composer who had

Example 2: "Arcadelt" *Ave Maria*

written a paraphrase of Dietsch's arrangement, for the organ: Liszt. That paraphrase had been published in 1865[29] and was certainly well-known to the Lisztian and organist Saint-Saëns. There is even the (faint?) possibility

---

[28]Thanks are due to my doctoral student, Gottfried Heinz, who pointed out this connection to me.
[29]Leipzig: G. W. Körner.

that the "ethereal" sound of Saint-Saëns's symphonic passage was inspired by the beginning of Liszt's work (Ex. 3).[30]

Example 3: Liszt, Paraphrase of "Arcadelt" *Ave Maria,* beginning

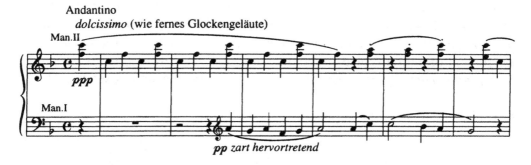

Given the fact that this very strong and twofold Lisztian connection may sound far-fetched, some additional biographical clues would be advantageous—especially so since the Dietsch-Arcadelt line, if true, implies that Saint-Saëns consciously or subconsciously composed the series of transformations of the *thème cyclique* backwards, as it were. And indeed there is a strong biographical connection between Liszt and Saint-Saëns exactly when the latter composed his symphony. On his last European tour, Liszt came to Paris not to give concerts but to have himself honoured and to renew the relations with his French friends and admirers, prominent among them his friend of long standing, Saint-Saëns.[31] Liszt lived in the town house of the Hungarian society painter Michael von Munkacsy. Parties and dinners were given there and in the house of the *Ménestrel,* and Saint-Saëns is said to have played an "active part," especially at one party at the *maison* Munkacsy. Moreover, two Liszt concerts and a performance of the Gran mass were given. From Paris Liszt travelled to London where he stayed from April 3 to April 20; in his presence, the Elisabeth oratorio was given three times (April 6, 7 and 17). When Saint-Saëns came to conduct the pre-

---

[30]There is, however, a very similar effect (a hymnlike melody in the strings, accompanied by arpeggios in the piano) in Louise Farrenc's Second Piano Quintet, E major, Op. 31 (1840), first movement. The common "father" of all this may well be the "Canto religioso" (*sic*) in the second movement of Berlioz's *Harold in Italy.*

[31]My principal sources are two reports from London, since the Liszt literature is not very explicit on this last tour: "Franz Liszt," *The Monthly Musical Record* 16 (1886): 74–75 and "Dr. Liszt in London," *The Monthly Musical Record* 16 (1886): 113–14. As to the long-standing relations between Liszt and Saint-Saëns in general, see Charles Timbrell, "Liszt and French Music," *American Liszt Society Journal* 6 (1979): 25–33.

mière of his Organ Symphony, the London music scene must have still been ringing with reverberations of these great events. Nothing could have been more apt in this situation than a symphony synthesizing the classical and the Lisztian tradition and celebrating Liszt in a musical language rich in Lisztian and sacred overtones.[32] Far from being a failed replica of Liszt's *Ce qu'on entend sur la montagne,* it is a very subtle companion piece to that prototype of the symphonic poem and declaration of (Victor Hugo's and Franz Liszt's) deism—the work of a musician who believed in Catholicism, Early Music, and Liszt.

---

[32]Although its implications were scarcely understood at the time, its impact is witnessed in the reviews that appeared in *The Musical Standard* and *The Musical World.* For the relevant passages, see Appendix 2. The fact that there is no review in *The Monthly Musical Record* is probably due to the fact that the articles on the German Saint-Saëns turbulences by Niecks (mentioned above) appeared in April, May, and June—that is, around the time of the Saint-Saëns concert. Niecks was a Wagnerian of sorts and rather on the German than on the French side, and although he tried to be fair to Saint-Saëns, he certainly had no use for a big Saint-Saëns success in London at this moment.

112   Ludwig Finscher

Appendix 1: Variants of Central Motives of the Third Symphony

a. Introduction, "motive a"

I:1

I:22

I:27

The Symphony and the Artist's Creed   113

b. Introduction, "motive b"

I:3

I:9

I:18

I:74 (letter D)

I:164 (14 after H)

I:174 (3 after I)

114   Ludwig Finscher

I:183 (2 after J)

b inv

I:216 (11 after K)

b

I:236 (3 after M)

b'

I:333 (18 after P)
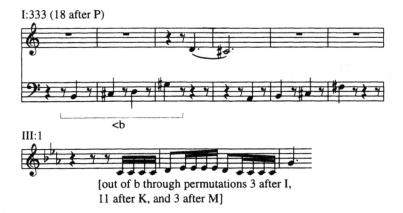
<b

III:1

[out of b through permutations 3 after I,
11 after K, and 3 after M]

III:71 (12 after C)

b retr   +   thème cyclique

c. "Thème cyclique"

I:12

I:90 (letter E)

I:92 (2 after E)

I:122 (letter G)

I:159 (9 after H)

I:196 (15 after J)

116 Ludwig Finscher

II:75 (letter U)

II:81 (6 after U)

III:17 (letter A)

III:109 (4 after F)

III:364 (4 after R)

IV:9 (letter S)

IV:25 (letter T)

The Symphony and the Artist's Creed 117

IV:131 (10 after AA)

IV:235 (letter EE)

IV:238 (3 after EE)
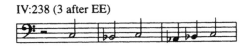

IV:241 (6 after EE)

IV:249 (14 after EE)

IV:256 (letter FF)

IV:279 (3 after GG)

d. "Chorale"

II:3

II:31 (letter R)

III:280 (5 after O)

III:320 (6 after Q)

IV:2

Appendix 2: Reviews of the Premier Performance of the Third Symphony

a. *The Musical Standard,* May 29, 1886, pp. 334–35:

Musical Intelligence

The Philharmonic Society

M. Saint-Saëns New Symphony

The fifth concert given at St. James's Hall, on the 19th inst., drew together a large audience. The chief point of interest was the production of a new symphony by the eminent French organist and writer, M. Saint-Saëns, composed expressly for the Society. M. Saint-Saëns is one of the few French musicians whose fame, both as composer and executant, extends beyond the confines of his native land. He is what few of his countrymen are, an all-round man, a fine organ player, a brilliant pianist, and a composer of much excellent music. A frequent visitor to these shores, in England his genius rightly meets with a welcome appreciation, which seems to be denied him in Germany, where—it may be remembered—owing to some hostile criticism on Wagner's works, he has literally been hunted out of the country. Freedom is not yet as complete in Germany as it is in this country. Francophobism is still an active element in certain circles; Wagnerism has been erected into a cult, and its high priests apparently seek to enforce material penalties on all who do not bend the knee to the Bayreuth idol. It is possible that the thought of the inhospitable musical treatment awarded to M. Saint-Saëns in imperfectly civilized Berlin, may have been in the mind of some of the Philharmonic audience, for his reception on this occasion was of a most friendly nature. Both after his playing of Beethoven's concerto [the fourth], as well as when he laid down the *bâton* on the conclusion of his new symphony, he was greeted with much applause....

In his new Symphony, M. Saint-Saëns has made a fresh departure. It is hardly fair, perhaps, to pronounce definitely on a work of such magnitude after a single hearing. The symphony presents certain novelties in form and instrumentation that demand a more careful examination and matured judgment than a solitary performance permits. It might therefore happen that opinions as to its merits, and the success achieved may be modified on a subsequent audition. Music is the youngest of the arts, and there is no finality in art. Like architecture, the building up of tone colour changes and varies from age to age. If we examine the scores current in the time of Bach—not to go back later—it will be found that several members of the string, wood-wind, and brass families were employed which are now obsolete; other instruments have taken their place. Moreover, our ears get modified to a certain extent by fashion. Who could listen with pleasure to such a combination as, say, ten oboes playing the violin parts, which is to be met with in certain of Bach's scores? It would sound as distressing to us as the *remplissage* of the Wagnerian *melos* would have done to our forefathers. In the onset, then, one must not be too eager to condemn M. Saint-Saëns because of his attempt to somewhat enlarge the bounds of modern orchestral resources. In some remarks on his symphony, he writes:—"The composer, believing that symphonic works should now be allowed to benefit by the progress of modern instrumentation, has made up his orchestra in the following manner: three flutes, two oboes, one English horn, two clarinets, one bass clarinet, two bassoons, one double bassoon, two horns, two valve horns, one trumpet, two valve trumpets, three trombones, one tuba, three drums, organ, pianoforte (sometimes played by two hands, sometimes by four), one triangle, one pair of cymbals, one bass drum, and the usual strings."—This copious list constitutes indeed a formidable battery of sounds! But the question to be settled is, if the effect is commensurate with the elaboration of the means employed, and not merely whether our ears are tickled with novel combinations, and sensuous tone colouring. Probably the balance of opinion will incline to credit the clever French composer with a *succès d'estime*. His experiment serves to show that certain advantages may be obtained from the united employment of all these instruments; he has pointed out the way, and it may be for others to obtain a more exalted result than has fallen to his share in the symphony under notice. A few remarks will suffice as to the form of the work. Although it contains in principle the traditional four movements, in reality it is divided into two only. The first, arrested in development, serves as an introduction to the Adagio; while in a similar way, the Scherzo is linked to the Finale. This mode of treatment is not absolutely new, examples of its partial use are to be found in the orchestral works of some of the great masters. In effect, it seems to be dictated by a desire to discard the resumption and repetitions of the old style, in favour of a leaning to the continuous melodic theory which appears to have a certain attraction for our modern writers, and is regarded by conservative classicists as tending to obliterate form as perfected in the sonata mode of construction. As to the advantage to be gained by going out of the beaten track for this inter-connection between the various movements, or the disadvantage in abandoning the usefulness of frequent repetition, metempsychosis of subjects, and completeness of finish which must characterize a movement written in the sonata mode, it would be out of place here to discourse. Some will prefer that the separate movements should each enjoy a separate individuality, while others will desire that each should be but component parts of one great whole, closely linked together by an uniformity of idea and treatment. The thematic unity which a true symphony should exhibit need not necessarily be broken by the division into strictly independent movements; but, on the other hand, it may be advanced that a continuous work ought not to bear the title of symphony, but that it must be classed as an orchestral Fantasia. And M. Saint-Saëns would have done well so to term his production. An Adagio of a few plaintive bars leads to the initial theme in C minor; this is of a sombre and agitated character, and is notable for its reiteration on synonyms of identical notes. This feature, by the way, is a peculiarity that Saint-Saëns often indulges in. We have then a second subject marked by a greater tranquility, and afterwards a clever presentation of the two themes simultaneously. The orchestration of the movement is sonorous, and occasionally marked by much power; towards the end a weird effect is produced by an extended chromatic passage on a pedal point, sustained on the contra fagotto. The Adagio is gradually led into it; it is in D flat, and the theme, of a broad contemplative character, is allotted to the strings of the orchestra, the organ sustaining chords on the flue stops. The effect is decidedly good, and the blending of tone satisfactory. Towards the close quite a novelty is introduced in the scoring. The first violins play the melody, the second have *pizzicato* chords, the organ holding soft chords, while in the lower register of the wind, short sharp bursts are emitted. The mixture and scheme of laying out is decidedly effective. The movement ends with a coda, mystical in sentiment, and unpleasantly crude as to its harmonies. The Allegro Moderato opens with an energetic figure, repetition of notes again being employed. A transformation of the intital theme of the first movement, quaintly laid out, leads to a Presto. Here, from time to time, the pianoforte is employed in arpeggios, rapid scale passages, and harmonically divided chords. Sometimes a sharp contrast of tone and effectiveness is produced, but too often the piano is swallowed up in the mass of instrumentation, and its tone is well-nigh lost. The author says that this concluding movement represents a conflict between two elements, one of an agitated and fantastic, the other of a calm and austere character. If this be so, the strife is too prolonged. Despite the ability and mastery displayed over resources of every kind, contrapuntal as well as orchestral, the movement is much too long. Climax succeeds climax, and so great is the "storm and stress," that the ear is wearied, and the mind fatigued long before the close is reached. There are many points that a musician would like to dwell upon; fugal development of much ingenuity, a clever treatment of the well known Dies Iræ, and some remarkable descending, closely knit chromatic passages, which, however, are used so frequently as to constitute a mannerism. But, on the whole, there is too much prolonged "full power" to keep the movement bright and interesting to its close. The organ is used almost throughout, and it is noteworthy, that when only the flue pipes are employed, the orchestral effect is enhanced, but so soon as the reeds and mixtures are drawn, then the blend is lost. The orchestra and organ fail to constitute one composite whole; and, doubtless owing to the acoustic variant defects of the different temperaments, there is no uniting of tone. The close of the movement is very imposing, all the instruments are employed, the orchestral wind weaving a busy figure, against short detached *fortissimo* chords on the strings, the organ majestically holding rich chords. The orchestral writer can learn many lessons from this new essay. He will mark that the pianoforte when used legitimately, accompanied by a quiet orchestra is capable of charming contrasts, but that when it is not so employed, it degenerates into a mere tinkle. As he will observe, there are times and ways in which the organ, the king of instruments, can be used with great success. But when the king is practically contending against his united courtiers, then does his voice sound harsh, and his mighty power fail to be serviceable. And the thoughtful musician will further learn how necessary it is to use self-control, and not be tempted to use all the power at command. He will observe that in the finale of this remarkable work, the music seems to run wild. It would seem that the impetuous steeds have, as it were, escaped from the control of the charioteer and literally run riot. Classical scholars will hardly need to be reminded of the fate which befell the ambitious driver of the horses of the sun. It only remains to add that the execution of the symphony considering its enormous difficulties, was exceedingly good. The players seemed to have caught some of the spirit of the composer, who conducted his work, and was greeted with hearty applause at its close.

T.L. Southgate

b. *The Musical World,* May 29, 1886, p. 349:

Philharmonic Society

The fifth Philharmonic Concert was superior to its predecessors by the fact that it introduced a novelty of almost sensational interest, if not perhaps of the highest artistic value. Philharmonic audiences do not as a rule shine by susceptibility to new impressions. They are in their tastes what they would themselves probably call classical, and what a cold world is apt to describe as narrow-minded. To rouse this kind of public to something very much like enthusiasm was a triumph for M. Saint-Saëns; the more so as his Symphony in C minor and major takes liberties with the canons of so-called classical art, which some people think as immutable as the laws of Medes and Persians. The term "new" applies to the work in more than one sense. Not only has it been written at a very recent date, but also displays some features never to our knowledge attempted by other masters. First, as regards scoring, we have not only the full modern orchestra with a more than usually large complement of brass and percussion, but to all these are superadded two instruments, the organ and the pianoforte, which when used by other composers in connexion with the orchestra are always individualities separate from it, never simple components thereof. Beethoven's Concerto in E flat has been called a symphony with an obbligato part for pianoforte; but in this work no such independent character is given to the keyed instrument. It is turned to various uses, now emphasizing a theme, now surrounding it with arpeggios. It is, in fact, part and parcel of the orchestra. That the composer was wrong in doing this merely because no one else has chosen to do it before him, only a staunch believer in the finality of established forms would venture to assert. The organ indeed adds greatly to the sonorous effect of the composer's orchestra, especially in the beautiful slow movement, to which it gives a solemn—not to say religious—character. At the same time we should be loath to see the pianoforte permanently supersede the harp, which, curiously enough, is absent from the long list of M. Saint-Saëns's instruments. Another innovation applies to the structural design of the work. It is the tendency of modern music to establish some connexion between the various movements of a symphony or concerto which in the strictly classical form are altogether separate. What Beethoven, Mendelssohn, and Schumann have done in that direction is known to every student. M. Saint-Saëns proceeds in the following manner:—He links the adagio to the opening allegro, and the finale to the scherzo, thus dividing his symphony into two instead of four sections. Apart from that he uses the first theme as a kind of leitmotive. Its presence is felt throughout the work. It appears again and again in various transformations, and finally serves as the subject of the Coda, which brings the symphony to a triumphant close. We have endeavored to indicate the general design of this interesting piece. To dwell upon the delicate and carefully considered details of the workmanship would exceed the limits of the space at our disposal, and would, moreover, necessitate an amount of technical language for which this is not the place. It will be more to the point to state that the work made a favourable impression, which we have no doubt the deliberate opinion of musicians will confirm. M. Saint-Saëns is a master of his craft, and what is more he makes the mastery subservient to the expression of a poetic idea. What that idea has been in this case, what image or what line of a poem he connects for example with the representative theme already referred to the composer has not stated; but the imaginative listener will recognize such a latent meaning, quite as distinctly as if it were couched in words, as in the case of the *Rouet d'Omphale* or the *Danse Macabre*. We cannot help thinking that the effect of M. Saint-Saëns's music would be improved if he had been less reticent. There are some composers who affix titles to their pieces which have no apparent relation to the music at all, others, who write music so simple and so consistently developed, that one enjoys it as one enjoys the murmuring of a brook or the sighing of the wind without asking for an ulterior meaning. The first division of the present symphony is of that description, but later on, as the composer's fancy grows bolder, and he assumes a little the airs of a Mephistopheles, the hearer would welcome some sort of aid to his imagination so as to comprehend the composer's flight. However that may be, the symphony was, as we said before, well received, having indeed been admirably played under the composer's own direction.

The Letter as Convention in Seventeenth-Century Venetian Opera*

Beth L. Glixon

As the genre of opera developed in Venice during the seventeenth century, librettists constantly faced the problem of either devising new plot elements, or, more commonly, rearranging preexisting ones into new configurations. The earliest operas presented in Venice treated subjects ranging from mythological, pastoral, romanzesque, and purely fictional, to historical. Operas increasingly explored the amorous problems of noble or royal figures and, especially as the century wore on, were set against a background of political intrigue in the Roman empire.[1] To a certain degree, standardization occurred in all levels of opera, from scenery and character types down to the vocabulary and phraseology found in the libretto. Operas routinely included scenes centering on passionate love duets, jealousy, confrontation between former lovers, and reconciliations perhaps brought about by a threat of suicide or murder, as well as comic staples such as an old nurse's lecherous advice and the same nurse's flirtation with a young servant.

One nearly ubiquitous ingredient, the sleep scene, provided the opportunity for a verisimilar aria, that is a lullaby, after which the librettist could lead the dramatic situation in any one of several directions: the sleeping character could talk during a dream, revealing some compromising information that would naturally be overheard; a ghost, foretelling some future success or disaster could appear in a dream; or the sleeper could become the target of an attempted murder or sexual assault. Conversely, a

---

*Earlier versions of this article were presented at the Pacific Northwest Chapter Meeting of the American Musicological Society, Seattle, 1983, and the Annual Meeting of the American Musicological Society, Philadelphia, 1984. I would like to thank Ellen Rosand and John Knowles for their helpful comments to earlier drafts of the article.

[1]The seventeenth-century opera libretto is exhaustively explored in Paolo Fabbri, *Il secolo cantante: Per una storia del libretto d'opera nel seicento* (Bologna: Mulino, 1990).

character could pretend to be asleep in order to gain information about other characters. The sleep scene became established as a convention soon after the beginnings of opera in Venice, appearing in works from the early 1640s such as Giulio Strozzi's and Francesco Sacrati's *La finta pazza* (1641),[2] Giovanni Francesco Busenello's and Claudio Monteverdi's *L'incoronazione di Poppea* (1643), Giovanni Faustini's and Francesco Cavalli's *Egisto* (1643), and Benedetto Ferrari's *Il prencipe giardiniero* (1644), and it remained a staple throughout the century.[3]

Another common practice involved the reading aloud of epitaphs, messages scrawled impulsively on any available material such as a tree, stone, or the ground, or, most frequently, letters.[4] Unlike the sleep scene, however, the letter did not gain widespread use as a convention until the 1650s.

The operatic letter had many literary precedents both in dramatic and non-dramatic genres. Letters occasionally advanced the plots of Roman comedy, for example in Plautus' *The Two Bacchides, Curculio,* and *Pseudolus*;[5] the tradition continued in its descendant, the Italian learned comedy of the sixteenth and seventeenth centuries, in authors such as Giambattista Della Porta.[6] The practice became even more widely disseminated through the *commedia dell'arte*, which often featured written arrangements for marriage as well as love letters.[7] The latter category, often the only pos-

---

[2] The dates provided here are those that appear on the librettos; they have not been adjusted to reflect the Venetian calendar, which ended on 28 February.

[3] For a discussion of the convention of the sleep scene, see Ellen Rosand, *Opera in Seventeenth-Century Venice: The Creation of a Genre* (Berkeley and Los Angeles: University of California Press, 1991), pp. 339–42. See also Fabbri, pp. 174–78.

[4] Epitaphs are read in Nicolò Minato's and Cavalli's *Artemisia* (1656, I/3 and I/10), while a previously-hidden text is revealed in a wall in Pietro Dolfin's and Antonio Sartorio's *Ermengarda* (1670, III/14); a message is scrawled on the ground in Aurelio Aureli's and Domenico Freschi's *Olimpia vendicata* (III/14), while one is incised in a tree trunk in Giulio Panciri's and Giuseppe Boniventi's *Almira* (1691, I/7).

[5] George E. Duckworth, *The Complete Roman Drama*, vol. 1 (New York: Random House, 1942).

[6] Letters appear or are referred to in several of Della Porta's plays, including *L'Olimpia* (I/3, II/6), *La trappolaria* (I/1, I/3, IV/7), and *La Carbonaria* (I/1). See Giambattista Della Porta, *Teatro*, vol. 2, *Le commedie (primo gruppo),* ed. Raffaele Sirri (Naples: Istituto universitario orientale, 1980).

[7] The plots of the commedia dell'arte frequently relied on the letter, as can be seen in the scenarios published in Flaminio Scala, *Teatro delle favole rappresentive* (Venice: Pulciani, 1611), ed. Ferruccio Marotti (Milan: Edizioni Il Polifilo, 1976). Servants often figure in the delivery. In "Il finto negromante" ("The Fake Magician"; giornata 21), the

sible means of communication between two *innamorati,* also figured prominently in the Italian *novella;* the *romanzo,* on the other hand, often featured letters communicating information between distant and exotic locations.[8] Letters also figured in plays published in Venice during the early seventeenth century written by Orfeo Buselli, Gabriello Gabrieli, Paulo Veraldo, and Giovanni Francesco Loredan the elder.[9]

Perhaps the letter found its most frequent use as a dramatic convention in Spanish drama of the seventeenth century, where it appeared in well over fifty percent of the plays by Lope de Vega, Tirso de Molina, and Calderon de la Barca.[10] The function of the letter in Spanish drama often mirrored its use in the Italian *novella.* Strict Spanish social codes forbade personal interaction between unmarried men and women, resulting, at least on the stage, in a proliferation of correspondence. Again, the mode of delivery proved a challenge: letters were tossed into windows, inserted into gloves,

---

Captain wants to send Flaminia a letter and says he will pay Arlecchino fifty scudi to drop it through her window.

[8]Letters are mentioned in a number of the *novelle* of Matteo Bandello, including the tale of Giulietta and Romeo (second part, number 9); see *Tutte le opere di Matteo Bandello* (Verona: Mondadori, 1966), 1:727–66. Giovanni Getto writes of the importance of the letter in Baroque *novelle* and *romanzi* in *Barocco in prosa e in poesia* (Milan: Rizzoli, 1969), pp. 359–60; correspondence appears frequently in the *novelle* of the members of the Venetian academy, the Incogniti (see *Novelle amorose de' signori academici incogniti* (Venice: Sarzina, 1641–51). Letters figure in four of the eight synopses of seventeenth-century *romanzi* in Albert N. Mancini, *Romanzi e romanzieri del seicento* (Naples: SEN, 1981), pp. 230–70, as well as in his discussions of the *romanzi* of Girolamo Brusoni, one of the members of the Incogniti.

[9]Orfeo Buselli, *Il disperato amante* (Venice: Angelo Salvadori, 1629); Gabriello Gabrieli, *L'innocente fanciulla* (Venice: Ciotti, 1605 [other editions of this play were published as late as 1623]); Paulo Veraldo, *L'anima dell'intrico* (Venice: Angelo Salvadori, 1629) and *L'intrigo, et torti intricati* (Venice: Alessandro Vecchi, 1610); Giovanni Francesco Loredano the elder, *Berenice* (Venice, 1601). I would like to thank my husband, Jonathan Glixon, for consulting these and other plays while on a research trip in Venice.

[10]See Henri Recoules, "Cartas y papeles en el teatro del siglo de oro," *Boletin de la Real Academia Espanola* 54 (1974): 479–496; T. Earle Hamilton, "Spoken Letters in the *comedias* of Alarcón," *Publications of the Modern Language Association* 62 (1947): 62–67; idem, "The Function of the Spoken Letter in the Plays of Tirso de Molina," in *Homage to Charles Blaise Qualia* (Lubbock: Texas Technological Press, 1962), pp. 105–12. The role of letters and writing in four Spanish plays forms the basis of Charles Marc Oriel, *Writing and Inscription in Golden Age Drama* (Ph.D. dissertation, George Washington University, 1989).

and infiltrated into the home of the recipient by ingenious servants.[11] Letters also communicated official announcements and arrangements for marriages or duels, and they revealed previously concealed information about various characters. In addition, misdelivered letters increased the complexity of plots.[12]

The development of the letter as a conventional device in opera was, of course, dependent on a class of character for whom reading was both appropriate and possible. Gods, presumably, had no need for written communication; therefore letters are absent from mythological and most pastoral librettos, both characteristic of the earliest period of Venetian opera. On the other hand, letters figured naturally in the daily affairs of rulers, the military establishment, and members of the upper class, and thus were introduced as the characters portrayed in Venetian opera became increasingly more human and urbanized.

In its simplest form, the operatic letter was identical in function to its everyday model: it served as a direct means of communication.[13] The letter frequently replaced the messenger, a more traditional bearer of operatic news, either military or civilian, and also provided a link between geographically distant characters. For example, Faustini's and Cavalli's *Ormindo* (1644) includes two letters sent from Ormindo's supposed mother in Tunis to individuals at the Moroccan court. The first (II/8), addressed to Ormindo, urges him to return home in order to help ward off an invading force. When Ormindo unsuccessfully attempts to flee the country with his lover, the king's wife, he faces death by poison. The second letter (III/13), addressed to the king, Hariadeno, reveals that Ormindo is actually Hariadeno's son. The lengthy report explains the reasons behind

---

[11]Such deliveries occur frequently in the plays of Calderon de la Barca. A letter is thrown into a window in *Dicha y desdicha del nombre* (*The Advantages and Disadvantages of a Name*) (1660?, Act III); placed into a glove in *El secreto a voces* (*The secret spoken aloud*) (1642); and infiltrated into a house by a servant in *Dicha y desdicha del nombre* (Act 1). These plays appear in English translation in Pedro Calderon de la Barca, *Four Comedies* (Lexington, Ky: University Press of Kentucky, 1980).

[12]Many of these types are discussed in Hamilton, "The Function of the Spoken Letter in the Plays of Tirso de Molina," pp. 106–107.

[13]Nearly all operatic letters are far removed from such lengthy epistolary settings as Claudio Monteverdi's "Lettere amorose" (published in 1623 in an edition of Monteverdi's *Lamento d'Arianna*), as well as verse letters modeled on Ovid's *Heroides*; see Robert Rau Holzer, *Music and Poetry in Seventeenth Century Rome: Settings of the Canzonetta and Cantata Texts of Francesco Balducci, Domenico Benigni, Francesco Melosio, and Antonio Abati* (Ph.D. dissertation, University of Pennsylvania, 1990), 1:267–74.

Ormindo's false identity, given to him at birth. Faustini intensified the poignancy of the disclosure to Hariadeno by introducing the letter just after the king has expressed regret at having ordered Ormindo's execution.

Most operatic letters were not sent from foreign lands, however, but furthered communication between residents of the same locale or community. Giacinto Andrea Cicognini's *Orontea* (1649) included three such letters: the first, an admission of love with an offer of marriage (II/18); the second, a request for a reconciliation (III/8); and the last, a challenge to a duel (III/11).[14] Perhaps owing to the success of *Orontea*, or to an increasing awareness of Spanish elements, largely a result of Cicognini's adaptations of Spanish plays,[15] or merely to the precedent of letters on the Venetian stage, the practice became much more widespread after 1650.

Nicolò Minato, who wrote librettos for Venice between 1650 and 1669, was particularly fond of using letters as a dramatic device: they play an important role in *Orimonte* (1650), his first libretto, as well as in later works.[16] One of the four letters in his *Scipione affricano* (1664) (music by Cavalli) advances the plot with extreme efficiency. The captive Siface addresses a letter to the conqueror Scipione that not only describes Siface's escape plan from a tower, but reveals that Scipione's captain, Massanissa, has been secretly hiding Siface's wife, Sofonisba. Siface has the signed letter placed on a mutilated corpse (I/16), leading Scipione to believe the attempted escape has ended in death. Siface is now free to search for his wife and seek revenge against Massanissa, who had made amorous advances towards Sofonisba; Scipione keeps the contents of the letter secret, and resolves to learn the motives behind his captain's deception (I/18).

In *Artemisia* (1656; music by Cavalli), Minato actually selected the name Artemia for one of the characters for the express purpose of using it in a letter. Artemisia, the queen, takes a love letter away from Artemia, her

---

[14] The Venetian premiere of Cicognini's *Orontea* (1649), traditionally attributed to Antonio Cesti (who composed the versions performed at Innsbruck in 1656 and Venice in 1666), was probably set by Francesco Lucio. The matter is treated in depth in Thomas Walker, "'Ubi Lucius': Thoughts on Reading *Medoro*," *Il Medoro*, Drammaturgia musicale veneta (Milan: Ricordi, 1984), 4:cxxxiv–cxl.

[15] On Cicognini's career as a dramatist, see Magda Vigilante, "Giacinto Andrea Cicognini," *Dizionario biografico degli italiani*, vol. 25 (Rome: Istituto della enciclopedia italiana, 1981): 428–31.

[16] On the librettos of Minato, see Edward Raymond Rutschman, *The Minato-Cavalli Operas: The Search for Structure in Libretto and Solo Scene* (Ph.D. dissertation, University of Washington, 1979). See also Rosand, *Opera in Seventeenth-Century Venice*, passim.

rival for the love of Meraspe, just as Artemia is signing her name, having written only the férst two syllables (III/2). Artemisia then gives the letter to Meraspe, who, seeing the abbreviated name, naturally believes the letter to be from the deliverer, Artemisia, whom he secretly loves, not from Artemia. His subsequent reply to the letter demonstrates his love for Artemisia (III/6). When the queen is accused of pursuing an improper relationship with Meraspe, she reluctantly but conveniently demonstrates that Meraspe was merely answering a letter from Artemia (III/7).

The Venetian libretto featured complex plots in the tradition of sixteenth century Italian comedy. Louise George Clubb, in a discussion of the *commedia grave*, a type of play with more serious elements than earlier comedies, writes,

> It is common to see several sets of lovers, parents, servants, and comic hangers-on, with as many encounters at cross purposes as the size of the group makes possible and as may be straightened out with a few well-planned adjustments and revelations.[17]

This description, minus the parents, could serve equally well for many operas. To traditional aids to complications such as disguise, mistaken identity, and misunderstanding, the Venetian librettists, like the Spanish playwrights, added the letter, which in their hands tended to create confusion rather than diminish it. Letters written without a proper salutation or signature invited misdelivery or misinterpretation; those that referred to characters by their stations instead of by their names were naturally ambiguous because each opera featured multiple sets of kings, princes, servants, etc.; compromising letters left unattended or in the possession of sleeping characters caused problems; and letters ripped up in anger might be reconstructed incorrectly and then misunderstood.[18]

---

[17] Louise George Clubb, "Italy and *The Comedy of Errors*," *Comparative Literature* 19 (1967): 247.

[18] This last category was given painstaking attention by Minato in his first libretto, *Orimonte* (Venice: Valvasense, 1650). Certain words of a dictated letter are assigned numbers in the libretto (II/5); the letter is subsequently ripped up, and these words then appear rearranged in a later scene (III/18–19). The original letter refers to matters of love, while the reconstruction seems to imply an act of treason; moreover, the correspondent's name, Torindo, now appears erroneously as that of another character, Orindo. The confusion, however, is resolved almost immediately, as it comes to light in the penultimate scene of the opera.

Even a well-intentioned attempt at communication with both writer and recipient present face-to-face could backfire. In Matteo Noris's and Giovanni Antonio Boretti's *Marcello in Siracusa* (1670, III/5) Mario, a Roman, and Virginia, daughter of the tyrant king of Syracuse, are secretly married. Virginia has become insanely jealous of a captured Roman woman, believing her to be Mario's former wife. After oral communication has failed, Mario finally writes Virginia a letter swearing his innocence and fidelity, and explaining the source of her confusion. When he notices that she has been eavesdropping on his soliloquy, he begins to read the letter aloud. Had Virginia merely listened, the misunderstanding would have been immediately resolved; instead, consumed by jealousy, she rips the bulk of the letter from Mario's hand and destroys it. Her subsequent denunciation of Mario leads to his arrest, and the remainder of the letter, found among the young man's possessions, is read aloud by the King, who now learns of his daughter's secret marriage to an enemy. Virginia's initial failure to listen to the letter, then, results in both Mario's and her own imprisonment.

Letters remained a prominent feature of the Venetian libretto throughout the seventeenth century. Certain librettists tended to favor the convention—Noris frequently employed as many as four or five in his librettos—while others such as Aurelio Aureli used letters more sparingly. Dictation scenes were common (with the familiar prop, the desk), and in at least two operas, Antonio Medolago's and Domenico Freschi's *Tullia superba* (1678) and Noris's and Antonio Sartorio's *I duo tiranni* (1679) letters served a diversionary function: the letter carrier attempted to murder the recipient while he read.

The convention offered seemingly endless possibilities: an intercepted letter could trigger either selfish or unselfish behavior. Adelanta in Minato's and Cavalli's *Xerse* (1654, II/4) uses a letter intended for her sister in order to further her own chances with her sister's lover, while in Pietro Dolfin's and Sartorio's *Ermengarda* (1670, III/12) Ardelinda intercepts a challenge to a duel intended for Genutio, whom she loves unrequited. She generously disguises herself as Genutio in order to save his life.

A letter could greatly complicate a plot through ambiguity (as mentioned above), or it could cut through deception and misunderstanding, as when Diocletiano, in Noris's and Carlo Pallavicino's opera of the same name (1685, III/20), discovers one of his subordinates, who had already falsely accused others of crimes he had committed, in the act of writing a treasonous letter. On a lighter, more humorous note, Breno and Nigrane, in Aureli's and Pietro Andrea Ziani's *Le fortune di Rodope e Damira* (1657, I/15), learn that they are courting the same woman when they read aloud the identical addressees of their just-written love letters: "A Rodope bella."

While some letters were merely alluded to or studied silently, the majority were read (that is, sung) aloud. At times the recipient first skimmed the contents, then began a more careful perusal. Most frequently the letter was read straight through without a break; sometimes, however, the addressee or an onlooker commented on the contents during the reading, occasionally line by line. Various sections of the letter could be repeated, either at the suggestion of the librettist or purely on the composer's initiative, as the character forced himself to assimilate some unexpected news.

In a play, an actor's rendition of a letter would demand a distinction in tone and delivery between reading and speaking. In opera, the composer bore a good deal of the responsibility for heightening the distinctions between a text read aloud and the illusion of one spontaneously spoken.[19]

Operatic letters usually involved a recitative setting within a larger context of recitative. The composer achieved separation from the surrounding material either by setting off the letter through harmonic juxtaposition or by preparing the letter with a half-cadence. Comments delivered between sections of the letter were similarly demarcated to reinforce the impression of breaking off from and then continuing the written text. Letters frequently began and ended in the same key. The nature of the vocal line cannot be so easily characterized. One might expect letters of this period to resemble the one Carlo reads at the fountain in Verdi's *Don Carlo*, that is, a text declaimed on a single note over an unchanging bass. The closest approximation to that style occurs in brief messages, but the composer always balances the music in some way; one phrase of repeated notes over a single bass note implies, even demands a change to come. Example 1, from Minato's *Seleuco* (1666), contains, for the composer, Antonio Sartorio, an uncharacteristically large number of repeated notes. Although the bass remains static for the first four measures, the vocal line finally descends by step, creating against the bass an accented dissonance that serves as the cadential approach to G. Following an interjection, the letter concludes with a melodically parallel phrase that actually continues the previous one, forming an overall stepwise descent from B to E, the new local tonic. The accented dissonance first occurs, appropriately, on the word *sposa*, as the letter from the king seems to inform the recipient that she may now marry her former lover, rather than her present fiancé, the king's son. The example shows how a potentially static declamatory formula can, instead, move forward in a dynamic manner.

---

[19]In addition, the libretto itself usually drew the listener's attention to the presence of a letter through stage directions and a change in typeface.

Example 1. Minato/Sartorio, *Seleuco* (1666), III/15 (I-Vnm, It. IV 454 [=9978])

To the prince who shows you this note you will, as his
bride, give both your hand and your faith. (Arbante, wait!)
My peace and well-being require it.

The style of recitative used in letters tends to feature restraint in ambitus as well as in intervallic and rhythmic content that contributes to a clear presentation of the text. Musical settings of letters were often strictly organized. The text of Meraspe's love letter in Minato's *Artemisia* (1656, III/6) (Ex. 2) comprises six end-stopped verses of eleven syllables with the rhyme scheme a b a b c c (it should be noted that recitative poetry was usually cast in freely alternating verses of seven and eleven syllables, largely unrhymed [*versi sciolti*]). Cavalli's musical version of the letter mirrors the poetic structure: two parallel, nearly identical antecedent and consequent phrases are followed by a third phrase divided into two parallel sections. Admittedly, the music belies the passionate nature of the poetry. Cavalli, by emphasizing the structure of the text rather than its essence, assured that the letter would be perceived as a written message; indeed, the setting of this letter strongly reflects the distinctions among operatic reading, speaking, and outright singing: had these verses occurred in another context, they undoubtedly would have received an entirely different musical treatment: either an affective, and possibly freer, recitative setting (i.e., operatic speech), or a more lyrical, fully developed aria.

Example 2. Minato/Cavalli, *Artemisia* (1656), III/6 (I-Vnm, It. IV 352 [=9876])

If you are truly my lover, I am afire. You are the sphere of my flames.
I am a martyr to your constant fire, which has already consumed me.
If I now find new life, it is because I am the phoenix arising from your fire.

Not all letters, of course, exhibited such harmonic uniformity. Megara's letter in Aureli's *Ercole in Tebe* (1671) presents a series of conditions that must be met before she will even consider Pelio's entreaties of love. In Giovanni Antonio Boretti's setting (Ex. 3), as each item is enumerated, the harmony descends by fifths, from C all the way to A♭ major. Megara's concluding remarks lead back to the original tonic.

In at least one instance, a librettist drafted a letter in more lyrical poetry, avoiding the more usual *versi sciolti* of recitative altogether. The letter in I/12 of Girolamo Castelli's *Almerico in Cipro* (1675) (Ex. 4) comprises six verses of eight syllables (the first four verses are truncated, or *tronchi*, while the last two are *versi piani*, accented on the penultimate syllable), with the rhyme scheme a b a b c c.[20] The *versi tronchi* form the

---

[20]For a discussion of versification, see Paolo Fabbri, "Istituti metrici e formali," in *Storia dell'opera italiana*, ed. Lorenzo Bianconi and Giorgio Pestelli (Turin: EDT, 1988), 6:165–233; see also Beth L. Glixon, *Recitative in Seventeenth-Century Venetian Opera:*

Example 3. Aureli/Boretti, *Ercole in Tebe* (1671), II/8 (GB-Lbl, Add. 14238)

Pelio. I am yielding to the force of my destiny. If you want me to love you, not hate you, release Ilo and let him marry Jole. I promise to marry you if Alcide does not return from the underworld. If you want me to be less severe, do not deny me your favors. Be courteous, not severe. Megara.

Its Dramatic Function and Musical Language (Ph.D. dissertation, Rutgers University, 1985), pp. 47–56.

message of the letter, while the *versi piani* identify, somewhat melodramatically, the writer. Although all six verses, by virtue of their syllabification, are typical of aria poetry, composer Antonio dal Gaudio set the first four in a rather declamatory manner (without text repetition), and the closing couplet in contrasting, affective recitative. This setting remains verisimilar in part because of its declamatory style (it never breaks out into florid "song"), but also because it is read aloud by its author, not the recipient. Indeed, although Almerico leaves the letter with the sleeping Lodicea, his beloved, she never reads it; her rival, Rosena, takes the letter and substitutes a threatening message.

Example 4. Castelli/dal Gaudio, *Almerico in Cipro* (1675), I/12 (I-Vnm, It. IV 382 [=9906])

My love, your beauty has stolen my heart. To free it I ask for nothing more than love. Thus writes a desperate one, the tormented Almerico.

As mentioned above, the familiarity of the reading (and singing) of letters in opera gave rise to the inclusion of acts of writing on stage—letter-writing and dictation scenes—each with its own musical characteristics. Dictation might transpire between master and servant, or with a sinister character forcing another to pen a false, misleading message.[21] That in Noris's and Giovanni Maria Pagliardi's *Numa Pompilio* (1674, II/11) (Ex. 5) is necessitated by a character's handicap: the would-be writer, Lucio, is blind. Letter-writing could be preceded or accompanied by aria or recitative texts either related in some way to the recipient or sender of the letter, or that addressed topics connected to writing, paper, or the like. In this instance, as a prelude to dictation, Lucio sings an aria that combines references to writing, books, and Cupid.

Example 5. Noris/Pagliardi, *Numa Pompilia* (1674), II/11 (I-Vnm, It. IV 441 [=9965])

Pluck a feather from your wings, inconstant, flying god; that fateful quill will write the miserable Iliad of a suffering heart.

---

[21]The former situation can be found in Aureli's and Freschi's *Olimpia vendicata* (1682, II/13), the latter in Adriano Morselli's and Domenico Gabrielli's *Mauritio* (1687, II/2).

Most dictation scenes were conceived by the librettist in recitative; but Adriano Morselli, in *L'incoronazione di Dario* (1684, II/2) (Ex. 6), provided the composer Domenico Freschi with the unusual opportunity of combining dictation (in recitative) with several phrases of a short aria. Argene tells Dario, whom she secretly loves, that she needs his assistance in writing down a letter, as her hand is too unsteady to accomplish the task. As Argene dictates the letter to Dario, she softly sings about him to an attending servant; with a humorous touch lacking in similar scenes, Dario must distract Argene from her singing in order to continue with the dictation.

The texts of many letters, those that go beyond a hastily scribbled warning or message, feature a three-part structure—salutation or introduction, argument, and conclusion—that, in general, is clearly projected in the musical version; indeed, recitative, with its strong and easily-directed harmonic tendencies, allowed the composer to address and reinforce effectively and efficiently the subtleties of a letter's message. While these miniature letters bear little resemblance to any actual models, they do reflect the foundation of the art of letter-writing in rhetorical theory; this relationship was first codified in the eleventh century by Alberico of Montecassino in his manual *Flores rhetorici dictaminis*.[22] Sixteenth- and seventeenth-century Italian theorists placed the letter midway between oration and conversation; letters were constructed in the same manner as an oration and, accordingly, would have enjoyed greater persuasive powers than normal conversation.[23] It seems natural, then, that operatic characters came to rely on the letter to communicate emotions they felt were too awkward or sensitive to relate in public, or to render a more convincing argument than had previously been possible during a dialogue.

---

[22]Ronald Witt, "Medieval 'Ars Dictaminis' and the Beginnings of Humanism: A New Construction of the Problem," *Renaissance Quarterly* 35 (1982): 8; see also Judith Rice Henderson, "Defining the Genre of the Letter: Juan Luis Vives's *De Conscribendis Epistolis*," *Renaissance and Reformation*, n.s. 7 (1983): 89–90.

[23]For a general discussion, see K.T. Butler, comp. *'The Gentlest Art' in Renaissance Italy. An Anthology of Italian Letters, 1459–1600* (Cambridge: University Press, 1954), p. 18. Sansovino stated that letters should have at least three sections, and at most five. See *Il secretario overo formulario di lettere missive et responsive* (Turin: gli heredi del Bevilacqua, 1580), p. 28 [many editions were also published in Venice]. Panfilo Persico stressed that the secretary needed the same skills as the orator in his *Del segretario del signor Panfilo Persico* (Venice: Combi & La Noù, 1662), pp. 12–13.; he later discusses components of the letter such as the *proemio* (introduction), *conformatione* (where the affections are moved), and the *conclusione* (p. 188).

Example 6. Morselli/Freschi, *L'incoronazione di Dario* (1684), II/2 (I-Vnm, It. IV 406 [=9930])

Argene: Write, sir: "My light."
[While Dario writes, Argene says softly to Floro, who is
    off to one side:]
Argene: Look, Floro, at that beautiful face, where sweetness
    plays, and that smile.
Dario: "My light."
Argene (to Floro): Look at those brown eyes.
Dario: I've already written "my light."
Argene: "My treasure."
Argene [to Floro]: Look at those brown eyes that shoot
    thousands of sparks into my heart.
Dario: "My treasure."
Argene: "For you I languish and die." etc.

When setting letters, many composers seem to have been concerned with presenting the text as clearly as possible, putting more emphasis on structure than on the meaning of individual words. The restricted musical attributes of the operatic letter reinforced the distinction between spontaneous speech and the inherently greater constraints of reading. The near absence of melismas and arioso, even in letters by composers who incorporated these techniques frequently in their non-epistolary recitative, tends to confirm the special consideration accorded the letter. Furthermore, by maintaining a sort of detachment in the letter itself, the composer could heighten through contrast any ensuing emotional outburst that might result from the letter's content.

Librettists undoubtedly continued to turn to the letter because of its versatility as a dramatic device. Its popularity, however, probably also reflects the importance of the letter and written communication in contemporary life. One author has hypothesized that the large number of operatic letters during this period stemmed from the perception, by the illiterate public, of letter-reading as a magical act, that is, on a level with the transformations carried out on stage by sorcerers.[24] Yet even the members of the audience with the least education, especially in Venice, which maintained a mercantile economy burdened by a huge bureaucracy, would have had contact with the written word. Although some members of the population certainly remained illiterate, contemporary archives abound in letters, reports, and receipts from men and women of a wide range of classes.[25]

---

[24]Patrick J. Smith, *The Tenth Muse: A Historical Study of the Opera Libretto* (New York: Knopf, 1970), p. 21.

[25]The papers left by lawyer and impresario Marco Faustini, housed in the Archivio di Stato di Venezia, Scuola grande di San Marco, contain hundreds of such documents, comprising letters from male and female servants, tradesmen, professionals such as doctors, and noble men and women. Much of the opera audience, at any rate (especially those who purchased opera librettos!), would have been literate. On literacy see Peter Burke, *The Historical Anthropology of Early Modern Italy* (Cambridge: Cambridge University Press, 1987), pp. 110–31; Anne Jacobson Schutte, "Teaching Adults to Read in Sixteenth-Century Venice: Giovanni Antonio Tagliente's *Libro maistrevole*," *Sixteenth Century Journal* 17 (1986): 3–16; and Paul F. Grendler, *Schooling in Renaissance Italy: Literacy and Learning, 1300–1600* (Baltimore and London: Johns Hopkins University Press, 1989). The subjects of reading and writing were taught separately. Thus, one might be literate without having perfected the skill of writing. Grendler estimates the literacy of the general male population in 1587 at 33–34 percent (p. 46).

Letter-writing in particular was both a necessity and an art. Numerous Italians published their letters, and during the sixteenth and seventeenth centuries many letter-writing manuals were published as guides for less-skilled correspondents.[26] Venice's own Francesco Sansovino published two best-sellers. The first was a general book on letter-writing, in which he instructed the reader on how to compose letters "suitably and with art on whatever subject." The second focused on love letters, providing varied examples written by illustrious men.[27] Girolamo Muzio, in his influential treatise on the duel, strongly emphasized the importance of the written challenge, and provided guidelines for its composition.[28] As we have seen, this class of letter also found its way onto the Venetian stage.

The letter, then, as presented in Venetian opera during the seventeenth century, served a double purpose: while it functioned primarily as a plot element, it was also one of the means by which various aspects of seventeenth-century life were portrayed in works set in the remote past. Recognizing its versatility, librettists writing for Venice during the early eighteenth century continued to rely on the letter (Benedetto Marcello satirized the letter scene in his *Teatro alla moda*)[29], and it remained a part of Italian opera, albeit in a more controlled manner, through the nineteenth century and into the twentieth.

---

[26]For an overview on letter writing in sixteenth- and seventeenth-century Italy, see Butler. In "Notes Toward the Study of the Renaissance Letter," in *Renaissance Genres: Essays on Theory, History, and Interpretation*, ed. Barbara Kiefer Lewalski (Cambridge, Mass.: Harvard University Press, 1986), pp. 70–101, Claudio Guillén discusses the cross-fertilization among epistles, published collections of letters, letter-writing manuals, and the use of the letter in fiction in sixteenth- and seventeenth-century Spain and Italy.

[27]Francesco Sansovino, *Il secretario overo formulario di lettere missive et responsive*; idem, *Delle lettere amorose di diversi huomini illustri* (Venice: Appresso gli Heredi di Alessandro Griffio, 1587).

[28]Girolamo Muzio, *Il duello* (Venice: Gabriel Giolito de Ferrari, 1553), pp. 26–27.

[29]Benedetto Marcello, *Il teatro alla moda* (Venice, c. 1720). Translation in Oliver Strunk, *Source Readings in Music History from Classical Antiquity Through the Romantic Era* (New York: Norton, 1950), p. 523.

Poetic and Musical Forms in the Laude of Innocentius Dammonis

Jonathan Glixon

Scholars have most often showed interest in the polyphonic lauda for its role in popular religious observances or for its stylistic relationships with the changing style of the motet in Italy at the end of the fifteenth century. The lauda repertory, however, is a surprisingly diverse and interesting one, and deserves study on its own terms. The two collections of laude published by Ottaviano Petrucci in the first decade of the sixteenth century are particularly noteworthy.[1] As I demonstrated in an earléer study,[2] Book 1, devoted to compositions by Innocentius Dammonis, contains an extraordinarily wide range of texts from several different repertories usually transmitted through distinct local source traditions. The variety of musical styles is also broad, showing that the composer was well aware of current trends in the composition of both secular and sacred music and, of course, of the traditions of the lauda itself. The second book, an anthology with connections to the Mantuan court,[3] shows the ways in which, through contrafacts and borrowings, the lauda repertory overlapped those of the motet and the frottola.

A close examination of the texts themselves, in particular those selected by Dammonis, and of their musical settings can reveal even more about the interrelationships between the repertories of lauda and frottola and the "crossover" nature of Petrucci's books.

---

[1] *Laude Libro Primo / In. dammonis /Curarum dulce lenimen* (Venice, 1508) and *Laude Libro Secondo* (Venice, 1507 [1508]). Book 2 was published in modern transcription its entirety, along with portions of Book 1 in Knud Jeppesen, *Die mehrstimmige italienische Lauda um 1500* (Leipzig: Breitkopf & Härtel, 1935). The remainder of the laude of Book 1 are transcribed in volume 2 of Francesco Luisi, *Laudario Giustinianeo* (Venice: Edizioni Fondazione Levi, 1983).

[2] Jonathan Glixon, "The Polyphonic Laude of Innocentius Dammonis," *The Journal of Musicology* 8 (1990): 19–53.

[3] William F. Prizer, "Court Piety, Popular Piety: The *Lauda* in Renaissance Mantua," paper read at the Annual Meeting of the American Musicological Society, Chicago, 1991.

Poetic Forms

The *poesia per musica* of fifteenth- and early sixteenth-century Italy can be classified into a number of distinct types.[4] Most of the forms employed in the poetry of both lauda and frottola are strophic, and these can be further classified into those with refrains and those without.

Only one purely non-strophic form is used at all frequently: the sonnet. The Italian sonnet, composed entirely of eleven-syllable lines, consists of two quatrains followed by two tercets. The two quatrains utilize identical patterns employing just two rhymes, usually $a^{11}b^{11}b^{11}a^{11} / a^{11}b^{11}b^{11}a^{11}$ or $a^{11}b^{11}a^{11}b^{11} / a^{11}b^{11}a^{11}b^{11}$. Two or three new rhymes are used in the tercets, which may or may not be identical. Typical patterns are $c^{11}d^{11}c^{11} / c^{11}d^{11}c^{11}$, $c^{11}d^{11}c^{11} / d^{11}c^{11}d^{11}$, or $c^{11}d^{11}e^{11} / c^{11}d^{11}e^{11}$. The one sonnet set by Dammonis, the anonymous dialogue *Virtù, che fai*, is a *sonetto caudato*, with the kind of two-to-four-line extension that is used fairly frequently in the lauda repertory (the responses by Virtù are indicated in italics):

Virtù, che fai in questo miser mondo?	a^{11}
Vado dispersa in ciascun paiese.	b^{11}
Ove tu alberghi et chi ti fa le spese?	b^{11}
Povera gente mersa quasi al fondo.	a^{11}
Che te inimica al tuo stato iocondo?	a^{11}
Luxuria, gulla, e giochi et altre offese.	b^{11}
Che fai tutto l'anno e ciascun mese?	b^{11}
Vigilo stento, et son redutto al fondo.	a^{11}
Perchè non regni più come solevi	c^{11}
Al tempo anticho de to degna sorte?	d^{11}
Ove son gl'homeni degni che tu havevi?	c^{11}

---

[4] Much of the following discussion is based on Don Harran, "Verse Types in the Early Madrigal," *Journal of the American Musicological Society* 22 (1969): 25–53, and William F. Prizer, *Courtly Pastimes: The Frottole of Marchetto Cara* (Ann Arbor: UMI Research Press, 1980), pp. 63–92. In my outlines of the forms, I have employed a different notation, one that I think is particularly useful for types with refrains: rhymes in the body of each strophe are indicated with the letters a, b, c, etc., while those in the refrains are indicated with x, y, and z. The number of syllables in each line is shown in superscript.

Superbia et avaritia, le porte	d^{11}
Me han serate. In questi tempi brevi	c^{11}
Le mie ragion son manchate et scorte,	d^{11}
Et le vie son si storte	d^7
De le mie schole in ciaschaduno loco,	e^{11}
Che sol abacho a venere si fa gioco.	e^{11}

The *ottava rima* in its normal strophic form was a favorite of the Renaissance epic poets Ariosto and Tasso. Its most common form in musical settings, however, was as the single-strophe *strambotto*. Like the sonnet, the *strambotto* consists entirely of eleven-syllable lines, and is usually formed of three pairs of lines with alternating rhymes followed by two lines with a third rhyme: $a^{11}b^{11}a^{11}b^{11}a^{11}b^{11}c^{11}c^{11}$.[5]

The third of the non-refrain forms, best known through its use by Dante in the *Divine Comedy*, is the strophic *capitolo* (also known as *terza rima*). Again using eleven-syllable lines, it consists of three-line strophes with linked rhymes: $a^{11}b^{11}a^{11}$ $b^{11}c^{11}b^{11}$ $c^{11}d^{11}c^{11}$ etc., sometimes ending with a quatrain. The first two strophes (of nine) of Feo Belcari's *Salve, Regina di misericordia,* set by Dammonis (No. 33), can serve as a good example of this form:

Salve, regina di misericordia,	a^{11}
Vita di dolceza di ciascun fidele,	b^{11}
Nostra speranza et fonte de concordia.	a^{11}
Nui siam concorsi sotto le toi vele,	b^{11}
Chiamando a te, che siam figliol d'Eva,	c^{11}
Per Lei sbanditi in pene si crudele.	b^{11}

The *oda*, the last of the non-refrain forms, is the least literary and the most variable. In its simplest version, it consists of three seven-syllable lines (usually rhymed abb) followed by a line of four or five syllables with a new rhyme, as in Dammonis's own *Poichè da me partisti:*

Poichè da me partisti,	a^7
O dolce eterno Dio,	b^7
Mai ben hebe il cor mio	b^7
Nè più pace.	c^4

---

[5]For an important new study of *strambotti* and their musical settings in the most important manuscript source for that genre, see Giuseppina La Face Bianconi, *Gli strambotti del codice Estense α.F.9.9* (Firenze: Leo S. Olschki Editore, 1990).

Often, the strophes are linked as in the *capitolo*: $a^7b^7b^7c^4$ $c^7d^7d^7e^4$ etc. Several simpler strophic forms may also, according to some writers,[6] be classified as *ode*. Four poems in Dammonis's collection (Nos. 15, 26, 29, and 44), with the ryhme schemes abba and equal-length lines (of 7, 8, 11, and 7 syllables respectively) fall into this broader classification, as does a fifth (No. 49) with the form $a^8b^8a^8b^8$.

The vast majority of the poems with refrains in both the frottola and the lauda repertories are variants of the Trecento *ballata*. Each strophe consists of two principal sections: the refrain, referred to as the *ripresa*, and the stanza. The stanza, in turn, is divided into two *mutazioni* or *piedi*, usually identical in structure, connected by a linking rhyme (or *concatenazione*) with the *volta*, which is often equivalent in structure to the *ripresa* and returns in the last line to one of the *ripresa* rhymes. A common form is the following:

xyyx   ab ab   bccx
ripresa   *mutazioni*   *volta*

There are, however, numerous variations of line lengths, line numbers, and rhyme schemes within this basic format.

The poetic theorists divided the trecento *ballata* into three principal classifications, depending upon the number of lines in the *ripresa*. The *ballata minore* has a two-line *ripresa* (usually rhyming xx or xy), the *ballata mezzana* a three-line *ripresa* (rhyming xyx, xyy, xxy, or even xyz), and the *ballata grande* a four-line *ripresa* (usually with the rhyme scheme xyyx, but possibly also xyxy or xyyz). *Ballate* with *riprese* of one line or more than four are also possible, but not often encountered. The *mutazioni* also vary in size, with couplets common in the *ballata minore* and *ballata mezzana* and tercets in the *ballata mezzana* and *ballata grande*. Most of the poems in the lauda repertory have four-line refrains, and would thus seem to be *ballate grandi*, but the *mutazioni* are typically couplets; *mutazioni* of three lines are extremely rare (Dammonis sets only one, Feo Belcari's *Anima che del mondo vo fuggire*).

The trecento *ballata* usually consisted of varying patterns of seven- and eleven-syllable lines. This general description also fits most of the *lauda* poetry of the quattrocento, such as this typical poem by Leonardo

---

[6]See Prizer, *Courtly Pastimes*, pp. 68–74.

Giustiniani (Petrucci 1, No. 16), a *ballata grande* with two-line *mutazioni* (in this and the following examples, the *ripresa* is indicated by italics):

Cum iubili d'amore	x^7	*ripresa*
Tutti cantando andiam a quel zardino	y^{11}	
Del dolce figliolino	y^7	
De Maria, virgo pien d'ogni odore.	x^{11}	
Andiam tutti cantando ad alta voce	a^{11}	*mutazione*
A veder Iesù bello,	b^7	
Che qui desceso de quella alta luce	a^{11}	*mutazione*
Tra'l bo e l'asinello,	b^7	
L'è nato poverello.	b^7	*volta*
Andiamo tutti e vedemo collui	c^{11}	
Ch'è venuto per noi,	c^7	
Voler salvar, il nostro redemptore.	x^{11}	

The most common *ballata*-derived form in the frottola repertory, however, contained lines all of the same length, almost always eight syllables. Written with a four-line *ripresa*, this variant of the *ballata grande* was known as the *barzelletta* or sometimes the *frottola*. The following poem by Dammonis (No. 41) is typical in its structure, though the extensive (and rather crude) use of solmization syllables in the text makes it an interesting rarity:

Sol mi sol, disse Holoferno,	x^8	*ripresa*
Mi so mire assai benigno.	y^8	
Mi fo mere sol son degno,	y^8	
Sol mi sol starò in eterno.	x^{11}	
Sol mi sol a Dio dispiacque,	a^8	*mutazione*
Mi fa mire ad lui conviene,	b^8	
Sol mi sol de qui ve nacque	a^8	*mutazione*
Gran ruina et poi gran pene.	b^8	
Privo io del summo bene,	b^8	*volta*
Et scazato nel inferno.	x^8	

Note that in the *barzelletta* the *volta* is often only two lines long, rather than being parallel to the four-line *ripresa*.

Many laude have equal-length lines, but normally of eleven syllables, or sometimes seven. Whether these should be classed as *barzellette* or *ballate* is not clear, and it may be that such a distinction is meaningless in this repertory. Of the four *ballate minori* set by Dammonis, for example, two are entirely endecasyllabic (Nos. 37 and 48), a third has all eleven-syllable lines but for one in the refrain and one in the *volta* (No. 52), and the last has all seven-syllable lines except for one eleven-syllable line in the refrain (No. 60). The entirely endecasyllabic poems seem much closer to those with varied lines than they do to the four (Nos. 35, 51, 61, and 63) that are entirely octasyllabic.

At least one of the laude set by Dammonis, *Lasso io moro,* the last in the book, can be described as a *ballata*-derived form only in a rather vague sense. It has lines of five syllables with a three-line refrain. The *mutazioni* are only one line each, and the *volta* two:

Lasso io moro	x^5	*ripresa*
Omè, ch'i moro,	x^5	
O Dio, merzè.	y^5	
La carne il mondo,	a^5	*mutazione*
O Dio iocundo,	a^5	*mutazione*
In questo fondo	a^5	*volta*
Mi tira a se.	y^5	

Distribution of the Poetic Forms

The various poetic forms outlined above appear with quite different distributions in various repertories of the late fifteenth and early sixteenth centuries, as can be seen in Table 1. In this and the following table, the Dammonis print (Petrucci, Book 1) and Petrucci's second book of laude are compared with some of the most important poetic repertories of the period.[7] The lauda is represented by two different groups, which I have labeled the Venetian and the Florentine. The Venetian group of laude are those found in a Venetian manuscript of the mid-fifteenth century[8] from the circle of the poet Leonardo Giustiniani, the most important Venetian

---

[7] That these collections are important does not, of course, mean that they are necessarily representative of the entire body of Italian poetry of the period. A determination of the distribution of poetic types throughout the complete repertories of frottole and laude (the only way to be sure that the statistics are accurate) is clearly beyond the scope of this study.

[8] Milan, private collection (formerly Venice, Biblioteca Giustinian-Recanati). This manuscript is described and edited in Luisi, vol. 1.

Table 1

Distribution of Italian Poetic Forms in Different Repertories

	Venetian laude	Florentine laude	Dammonis laude	Petrucci laude II	Petrucci frottole
strambotti	3 (2%)	6 (7%)	0 (0%)	5 (24%)	95 (15%)
sonnets	8 (5%)	0 (0%)	1 (2%)	1 (5%)	35 (5%)
capitoli	19 (13%)	4 (4%)	3 (6%)	2 (9%)	11 (2%)
ode	25 (17%)	11 (12%)	9 (17%)	2 (9%)	75 (11%)
ballate and barzellette	62 (41%)	55 (60%)	33 (64%)	6 (29%)	385 (59%)
other	33 (22%)	15 (17%)	6 (11%)	5 (24%)	52 (8%)
Total	150	91	52	21	653
(Latin texts)	3	0	13	16	–

contributor to this genre, and the first published edition (issued in Venice in 1474)[9] of works by the same man.[10] The Florentine group is made up of

---

[9]*Incomenciano le devotissime et sanctissime laude le quale compose el nobele et magnifico messere Lonardo Iustiniano* (Venice: Bartolomeo da Cremona, 1474). For a description, list of contents, and transcription of the texts, see Luisi, 1:81–90, 358–379.

[10]I have eliminated from the tabulation of this repertory those poems in the Giustinian manuscript clearly taken from other repertories, such as those widely attributed in the fifteenth century to Jacopone da Todi. I have also not included the poems printed in the other fifteenth-century publication of laude by Giustiniani, that issued in Vicenza in 1475: *Laude del excellentissimo misier Lunardo Iustiniano Patricio Venetian e de altri sapientissimi homini* (Vicenza: Leonardo Basilea, 1475) (see Luisi, 1:91–97). While

laude by Feo Belcari, as published in Florence in 1480.[11] For the secular counterpart to the lauda, the frottola, I have selected the poetry published (with musical settings) by Petrucci between 1504 and 1514.[12] It can be shown, I believe, that the greatest differences in distribution are between the two lauda text groups on the one hand and the frottole on the other, while the two lauda collections published by Petrucci fall in between, though in quite different manners.

It will be readily apparent that the most common poetic type in all of the repertories (overwhelmingly so in all except Petrucci's *Laude libro secondo*) is the *ballata* and its cousin the *barzelletta* (for the moment grouped together), amounting to between 29% and 64% of the total. *Ode* of various types make up between 9% and 17% of all repertories. The sonnet is rare throughout the sample, never amounting to more than 5% of the total. The *capitolo* is also generally rare, reaching a high point in the Venetian group, in which it represents 13% of the total, and a low point in the Petrucci frottola publications, which include a mere eleven examples out of a total of 653. Perhaps the most dramatic differences are in the distribution of the *strambotto*. While quite uncommon in the Venetian lauda repertory and in the Dammonis publication (2% and 0% respectively), and only a little more so in the Florentine lauda group, they make up nearly one quarter of the texts in Petrucci's *Laude libro secondo* and 15% of the frottola repertory (though 47, almost half of those, can be found in Book 4; in the remainder the numbers range from 0 to 9). Miscellaneous, usually unique forms make up as much as 24% of some repertories.

Other dramatic differences of distribution appear when the *ballate* and *barzellette* are analyzed in more detail, as is shown in Table 2. What can be seen first of all is the great variety of structures employed within the general form. Even beyond the divisions by *stanza* and *ripresa* length and

---

much of the contents of this publication is identical to that of the 1474 edition, the additional poems appear somewhat less tightly linked to the main repertory.

[11]*Laude di Feo Belcari* (Florence: Bartolomeo de'Libri, 1480?). A modern edition of these poems can be found in G. Galletti, *Laude spirituali di Feo Belcari, di Lorenzo di Medici, di Francesco d'Albizzo, di Castellano Castellani, e di altri...* (Florence: Molini e Cecchi, 1863). Subsequent publications (also edited in Galletti), though certainly adding to the Florentine repertory through the inclusion of laude by other local poets, also show consistent infiltration of the Venetian repertory. Therefore, I have not included them in this compilation.

[12]I have used the statistics compiled by Jeppesen, *La Frottola* (Copenhagen: Hansen, 1968), 1:34–35.

Table 2
Distribution of *Ballata/Barzelletta* Types

	Venetian laude	Florentine laude	Dammonis laude	Petrucci laude II	Petrucci frottole
7- and 11-syllable lines					
10-line strophes	–	–	–	–	1
4-line refrain	2	0	0	0	–
9-line strophes	–	–	–	–	0
3-line refrain	0	3	1	0	–
8-line strophes	–	–	–	–	0
5-line refrain	1	0	0	0	–
4-line refrain	24	12	8	0	–
3-line refrain	3	1	0	0	–
2-line refrain	0	1	0	0	–
7-line strophes	–	–	–	–	0
5-line refrain	0	0	1	0	–
3-line refrain	4	11	1	0	–
6-line strophes	–	–	–	–	0
4-line refrain	0	0	2	0	–
3-line refrain	0	0	1	0	–
2-line refrain	1	1	2	0	–
5-line strophes	–	–	–	–	0
4-line refrain	0	1	0	0	–
3-line refrain	0	1	0	0	–
4-line strophes	–	–	–	–	0
3-line refrain	0	1	0	0	–
Total	35 (56%)	32 (58%)	16 (48%)	0 (0%)	1 (0%)

Table 2 (*continued*)

	Venetian laude	Florentine laude	Dammonis laude	Petrucci laude II	Petrucci frottole
11-syllable lines					
8-line strophes	–	–	–	–	1
4-line refrain	0	8	2	0	–
2-line refrain	1	0	0	0	–
7-line strophes	–	–	–	–	0
2-line refrain	1	1	0	0	–
6-line strophes	–	–	–	–	3
4-line refrain	0	1	0	0	–
3-line refrain	0	1	0	0	–
2-line refrain	5	10	2	0	–
4-line strophes	–	–	–	–	0
2-line refrain	4	0	0	0	–
Total	11	21	4	0	4
	(18%)	(38%)	(12%)	(0%)	(1%)
7-syllable lines					
10-line strophes	–	–	–	–	0
4-line refrain	3	0	0	0	–
8-line strophes	–	–	–	–	0
4-line refrain	5	0	3	0	–
7-line strophes	0	0	0	0	1
6-line strophes	–	–	–	–	6
4-line refrain	1	0	0	0	–
4-line strophes	–	–	–	–	21
3-line refrain	1	0	0	0	–
Total	10	0	3	0	28
	(16%)	(0%)	(9%)	(0%)	(7%)

Table 2 (*continued*)

	Venetian laude	Florentine laude	Dammonis laude	Petrucci laude II	Petrucci frottole
8-syllable lines					
8-line strophes	–	–	–	–	64
4-line refrain	1	1	1	1	–
7-line strophes	0	0	0	0	1
6-line strophes	–	–	–	–	270
6-line refrain	0	0	0	2	–
4-line refrain	0	0	4	3	–
2-line refrain	0	0	4	0	–
4-line strophes	–	–	–	–	12
3-line refrain	1	0	0	0	–
2-line refrain	1	0	0	0	–
Total	3	1	9	6	347
	(5%)	(2%)	(27%)	(100%)	(90%)
Other					
9-line strophes	0	0	0	0	2
8-line strophes	3	1	0	0	0
4-line strophes	0	0	0	0	3
3-line strophes	0	0	1	0	0
Total	3	1	1	0	5
	(5%)	(2%)	(3%)	(0%)	(1%)
Total	62	55	33	6	385

syllable count there is remarkable variety, not shown in the table. The poets use both numerous variations of rhyme schemes in the refrains and many different patterns of line-length alternations. For example, in the eight *ballate* in the Dammonis collection with seven- and eleven-syllable lines, eight-line stanzas, and a four-line refrain, there are five different patterns:

$$x^7y^7y^7x^7 \quad a^7b^7a^7b^7 \quad b^7c^7c^7x^{11} \quad \text{(No. 3)}$$
$$x^7y^7y^7x^7 \quad a^7b^{11}a^7b^{11} \quad b^7c^7c^7x^7 \quad \text{(No. 54)}$$
$$x^{11}y^7y^7x^{11} \quad a^{11}b^7a^{11}b^7 \quad b^{11}c^7c^7x^{11} \quad \text{(Nos. 27, 62)}$$
$$x^{11}y^7y^{11}x^7 \quad a^{11}b^7a^{11}b^7 \quad b^7c^{11}c^7x^{11} \quad \text{(Nos. 16, 30, 32)}$$
$$x^7y^7y^7z^{11} \quad a^7b^{11}a^7b^{11} \quad b^7c^7c^7z^{11} \quad \text{(No. 40)}$$

Similar degrees of variation occur throughout the collection.

The standard *ballata*, with alternating seven- and eleven-syllable lines, comprises about half of the poems in this general classification in the two lauda text repertories and in the Dammonis book. On the other hand, there are none in Petrucci's *Laude libro secondo*, and only one in the ten books of Petrucci frottole. *Ballata*-type poems composed entirely of eleven-syllable lines are well represented in the same three repertories (especially so in the Florentine lauda), but are nearly absent in the other two. Those with seven syllables in each line are fairly common (16%) in the Venetian lauda, but entirely absent in the Florentine lauda and *Laude libro secondo*. The numbers in the other two groups are in between.

The distribution of poems with eight-syllable lines, that is *barzellette*, is almost exactly the opposite. While *barzellette* are only 5% of this overall group in the Venetian laude, and only 2% in the Florentine, they make up 90% of those in the frottola collections and 100% in *Laude libro secondo*. Dammonis's collection shows an intermediary position, with a figure of 27%.

The distribution figures shown in Tables 1 and 2 indicate that in some respects, both Dammonis and, even more so, the anonymous compiler of *Laude libro secondo*, were moving away from the established poetic types of the quattrocento lauda towards those of the newly popular frottola. Dammonis's move was primarily in the addition of *barzellette* to the standard *ballate*. He did this not only by selecting the single *barzelletta* in Belcari's 1480 publication, along with four that appeared in later Florentine books, but by writing three himself. The compiler of *Laude libro secondo* selected no standard *ballate*, the mainstay of the traditional lauda repertory, but only *barzellette*, and also added a significant number of *strambotti*, quite rare in other collections of laude. That there are similarities between the poetic types represented in *Laude libro secondo* and in the Petrucci frottole should not be surprising, as the two repertories share, at least in part, a common origin at the Mantuan court.[13]

Latin poetry is also included in some of the lauda collections, in the form of hymns. There are seven such hymns (with strophes of three to five lines each) in the Dammonis collection (two of which are also found in the Venetian lauda tradition), and one in Petrucci's *Laude libro secondo*.[14]

Musical Forms

The musical forms utilized by Dammonis in composing his laude are as varied as the poetry he sets (see the "Musical Forms" column of the Appendix). While many are, of course, quite simple and straightforward, suiting both the poetry and the performance situation,[15] others are considerably more complicated, and demonstrate once again Dammonis's creative abilities and apparent love of variety.[16]

Dammonis set nearly all of the simple strophic texts, whether *ode*, *capitoli*, Latin hymns, or others, in a straightforward strophic manner, writing a single setting to be repeated as many times as needed. In nineteen of the twenty-seven settings of simple strophic poems, this single strophe is through composed, as in the *oda Aimè, dolce mio Dio* (No. 8; see Ex. 1).

In two other settings (Nos. 24 and 28), Dammonis has made a through-composed setting of a pair of strophes, in order to reduce the number of repetitions of musical material. In one of these, however, the *capitolo O*

---

[13]On the Mantuan origin of Petrucci, Book 2, see Prizer, "Court Piety." The principal composers represented in the frottola collections published by Petrucci are Marchetto Cara and Bartolomeo Tromboncino, both employed by Isabella d'Este, marchioness of Mantua.

[14]Additionally, both of Petrucci's lauda publications include sizable numbers of Latin prose texts or single strophes of hymns or sequences, which are rare or non-existent in the other repertories. Six of the thirteen Latin texts in Dammonis's collection are of this type, as are fifteen of the sixteen in the second book. Musical settings of such texts are perhaps better thought of as simple motets than as real laude.

[15]See Glixon, pp. 41–43.

[16]Elsewhere I have demonstrated the variety of textures and compositional techniques employed by Dammonis. See Glixon, pp. 30ff.

156   Jonathan Glixon

Example 1. Dammonis, *Aimè, dolce mio Dio*

madre del Signore (No. 28), the melodic lines for the second, third, and sixth lines clearly echo that of the opening line (Ex. 2).

In six of the simple strophic settings (indicated in the Appendix by the abbreviation S-IR), Dammonis introduced a certain amount of internal repetition into the setting of the single strophe. This may be an exact repetition, indicated by repeat signs (Nos. 26 and 45), or may involve some amount of variation, either for adjacent lines (Nos. 15 and 49), or to give a sense of rounding or return (Nos. 10 and 47). Only once, in the first of his two versions of *Verbum caro factum est* (No. 11), did Dammonis abandon the normal technique of setting strophic poems strophically. In this case, Dammonis composed six different elaborate cantus-firmus settings, each to be used for two strophes (repeat signs are indicated). This, of course, resulted in a much longer composition; whereas most of the settings of strophic poems have between twenty and forty measures, *Verbum caro* has 118.

In the frottola repertory, sonnets are usually composed as partially strophic works, with one setting repeated for the two quatrains and another for the two tercets, or even a single setting repeated for all four sections (abbreviated for the tercets).[17] Dammonis, however, sets the single sonnet in his collection, *Virtù, che fai* (No. 36) in a nearly through-composed manner, as diagrammed below:

         Text: a b b a   a b b a   c d c   d c d   d e e
         Music: A B A B   C D C D   E F G   H I J   K L M

---

[17] See Prizer, *Courtly Pastimes*, pp. 112–14.

Example 2. Dammonis, *O madre del Signore*[18]

Double bars after the A, B, C, D, and G sections separate the responses by Virtue from the questions (see above, p. 144). The final response, covering the last two tercets, is designated as *"secunda pars"* in the original publication, and contains no internal divisions.

As with the poetry, the most varied and interesting musical settings are the *ballate* and *barzellette*. These can be divided, first of all, into two broad categories: those in which the *ripresa* and the *stanza* share the same musical material (indicated as B1 in the Appendix; in the Petrucci publication the settings of this type invariably have only the *ripresa* text underlaid), and those in which they receive different settings. The latter can be subdivided

---

[18]The superius does not sing the fifth line of poetry, so I have substituted the tenor, which carries the melody at that point.

into those in which the *ripresa* is a variant or abbreviation of the *stanza* (indicated B2) and those in which the music for the two sections is completely different (B3).

The basic form of the single-setting type can be illustrated by the setting of *Jesù fami morire* (No. 65; see Ex. 3), which can be diagrammed as follows:

    Text: x y y x   a b a b b x

    Music: A B B C   A B A B B C[19]

Similar settings of poems with four-line *volte* have the following appearance:

    Text: x y y x—   a b a b b c c x

    Music: A B B C D   A B A B B C C D

Four of Dammonis laude (Nos. 5, 27, 41, and 65) employ this simplest of structures. Two others (Nos. 6 and 20) differ only in that each has one line that is varied slightly instead of being repeated exactly.

This form is nearly identical to the simplest of the frottola settings of *barzellette*. However, while in the lauda the *ripresa* is repeated in its entirety after each *stanza*, in many frottole the *ripresa* is sung complete only once, at the beginning, with an abbreviated version, the refrain, used afterwards. In the settings in the Petrucci frottola books, this refrain usually has a separate varied setting with an extended cadential passage.[20] It is notable, in light of the distribution of text types discussed above (p. 148), that nearly all of the *barzelletta* settings in Petrucci's *Laude libro secondo* include this frottola-type refrain.

---

[19]Note that in the following diagrams and descriptions, I have always treated the music of the *stanza* as the starting point, with that of the *ripresa*, where not completely identical, being indicated as the repeat or variant. While this may seem counter-intuitive, the greater completeness and better musical logic of the *stanze* in this repertory has led me to take this approach.

[20]On the musical settings of the *barzelletta* in the frottola repertory see Prizer, *Courtly Pastimes,* pp. 116–24.

Laude of Innocentius Dammonis 159

Example 3. Dammonis, *Jesù fami morire*

Dammonis introduces a simple variation in four laude: in Nos. 38, 46, 58, and 62, the second half of the *concatenazione* is given new material:

```
Text:      x y y x     a b a b b x
Music:     A B C D     A B A B C D
```

This results in a *ripresa* that is through composed.

The setting of *Al bel fonte* (No. 25) has an added sophistication that is much more common in the settings with varied or different *ripresa* settings. In these, the final line of the *stanza* is similar or identical to an earlier phrase. Whereas in those with varied or different *riprese* this rounding is to the final line of the *ripresa*, here it is to the *mutazioni*:

```
Text:      x y y x     a b a b b x
Music:     A B C B     A B A B C B
```

160   Jonathan Glixon

In two of the single-setting *ballate* with four-line *volte* (Nos. 31 and 54), Dammonis ignores the parallelism of the *volta* with the *ripresa*, treating the *volta* as a pair of couplets that can share the same setting:

>   Text: x y y x   a b a b b c c x
>   Music, No. 31:   A B B A'   A B A B B A' B A'
>   Music, No. 54:   A B C D   A B A B C D C D

Several times, Dammonis used only a portion of the musical material of the *stanza* in the *ripresa*, omitting one or more phrases, in some cases because the *ripresa* has fewer lines than usual, and in others because he had provided individual settings for more of the lines in the *stanza* than normal. An example of the former situation is *O peccatori, ti moverai tu mai* (No. 48), which has a *ripresa* of only two lines:

>   Text: x x   a b a b b x
>   Music: A B   A B A B C D

A similar situation occurs in *Fuzite christiani* (No. 39), in which the "C" music is omitted (and the "A" material is presented in a slightly varied form):

>   Text: x y z   a b a b b c d
>   Music: A' B D   A B A B B C D

and in *Anima che del mondo vo fugire* (No. 57). In the latter, unusually, the music for the *ripresa* is taken not from the beginning of the *stanza* but from the end (note that the poem itself is quite varied from the normal *ballata* form):

>   Text: x x y   a b a b a b c c y
>   Music: E E' F   A B A B C D E E' F

In Nos. 30 and 32, Dammonis has provided more music for the *stanza* than he could use in the *ripresa*, even though of normal length. The stanza of *Maria, madre de Dio* (No. 32), in fact, is practically through-composed:

    Text: x y y x   a b a b b c c x

    Music: B' C E G   A B C D E F F G

The *stanze* of two additional laude, Nos. 40 and 64, are set normally, but in each case Dammonis has chosen to omit the "C" music from the refrain (No. 64 is diagrammed):

    Text: x y y x   a b a b b c c x

    Music: A B B D'   A B A B B C C' D

The final group of eleven *ballate* or *barzellette* have different settings for the *ripresa* and *stanza*. These may be entirely different or may, in some cases, include references one to another. In one instance, *Spirito sancto, amore* (No. 3) Dammonis even employs different meters for the two sections (Ex. 4).

In order to produce a sense of rounding off where the settings of *ripresa* and *stanza* are entirely different, the final line of the *stanza* usually repeats or reflects the second line of the *mutazione*.

In three cases (Nos. 50, 60, 61), Dammonis has, to at least some extent, distorted the poetic form of the *ballata* in his setting by composing new music for the second *mutazione*. This is clearly seen in the structure of *Nostra interna et vera pace* (No. 50):

    Text: x y y x   a b a b b x

    Music: X Y D' E'   A B C D D E

Example 4. Dammonis, *Spirito sancto, amore*

In the simpler *Io son quel misero ingrato* (No. 61) the distortion is minimized by rhythmic parallels and melodic reminiscences (Ex. 5).

Finally, in two cases Dammonis chose not to set the poems in a manner to reflect the *ballata* form, but rather as simple strophic compositions. In *Anima benedetta* (No. 56), each eight-line *stanza* is treated as a repeated four-line, through-composed strophe:

Text:	x y y x	a b a b	b c c x
Music:	A B C D	A B C D	A B C D

L'amor a me venendo (No. 59) is set in two-line strophes, subdividing what should be four eight-line strophes with a four-line refrain into eight-

Example 5. Dammonis, *Io son quel misero ingrato*

een two-line strophes (most probably the *ripresa* was sung only at the beginning in both this example and the previous one):

    Text: x y—   y x—   a b—   a b—   b c—   c x—

    Music: A B B'   A B B'   A B B'   A B B'   A B B'   A B B'

* * *

As is so often the case, neglected repertories can, when studied carefully, reveal unrecognized riches and complexities. The laude of Innocentius Dammonis are no exception. Containing a collection of poetry of a diversity practically unequalled for the period, musical textures and styles drawn from several different repertories (the traditional lauda, the frottola, and the motet), and a variety of often sophisticated and sensitive responses to the numerous poetic forms, this book displays the workings of a curious and creative mind. While Dammonis was certainly not a composer of the first rank (nor probably even of the second), his lack of talent was compensated for by a full measure of that often praised (but too often neglected) Renaissance imperative, *varietas*.

Appendix

Poetic and Musical Forms of the Dammonis Laude

KEY

On the attributions and sources of the texts, see Jonathan Glixon, "The Polyphonic Laude of Innocentius Dammonis," *The Journal of Musicology* 8 (1990): 19–53.

Language: **I**—Italian; **L**—Latin.

Poetic Form: B—*ballata/barzelletta* (the first number or pair of numbers indicates the number of syllables in each strophe, and the number of lines in the refrain; following are the number of lines in each strophe, and the number of syllables in each line; e.g, B-7/11-6+4 indicates that the poem has lines of 7 and 11 syllables, a 6-line strophe, and a 4-line refrain); **O**—*oda* (standard form); **Ov**—*oda* (variant form; see text); **C**—*capitolo*; **So**—sonnet; **H**—hymn; **St**—other strophic form; **Pr**—prose; **R**—refrain.

Musical Form: TC—through-composed; **S-TC**—strophic, each strophe through-composed; **S2-TC**—strophic, each pair of strophes through-composed; **S-IR**—strophic, some internal repetition in each strophe (see text).

Ballata/barzelletta forms: **B1**—single setting for refrain and strophe; **B2**—refrain is a variation on or portion of strophe; **B3**—refrain set to different music than strophe; **r**—rounded (end of strophe recalls end of refrain); **c**—the two lines of the *concatenazione* are given different settings; **x**—phrase structure does not correspond to poetic structure (see text).

No.	ff.	Title	Author or Origin	Poetry Language	Form	Strophes	Musical form
1	2v–3	*Te invocamus*	liturgical	L	Pr	–	TC
2	3v–4	*Adoramus te Christe*	liturgical fragment?	L	Pr	–	TC
3	4v–5	*Spirito sancto, amore*	Leonardo Giustiniani	I	B-7/11-8+4	10+R	B3r
4	5v–6	*Ubi caritas et amor*	hymn parody	L	Pr	–	TC
5	6v–7	*Da che tu m'hai Idio*	Feo Belcari	I	B-11-8+4	6+R	B1
6	7v–8	*Da che to m'hai, Iesù*	C. Castellani	I	B-11-8+4	6+R	B1
7	8v	*Poichè da me partisti*	Dammonis	I	O	13	S-TC

Appendix (*continued*)

No.	ff.	Title	Author or Origin	Language	Form	Strophes	Musical form
8	9	*Aimè, dolce mio Dio*	?	I	O	14	S-TC
9	9v–10	*Iesu dulcis memoria*	Bernard of Clairvaux	L	H	47	S-TC
10	10v–11	*Salve, mundi salutare*	Bernard of Clairvaux	L	H	17	S-IR
11	11v–14	*Verbum caro factum est*	attrib. Jacopone	L	H	11	TC
12	14v–15	*Verbum caro factum est*	attrib. Jacopone	L	H	11	S-TC
13	15v	*Laudiam l'amor divino*	attrib. Jacopone	I	St+R	11+R	S-TC
14	16	*Tutti debiam cantare*	?	I	O	13	S-TC
15	16v	*Amor, Iesù divino*	?	I	Ov	11	S-IR
16	17–18	*Cum iubili d'amore*	Leonardo Giustiniani	I	B-7/11-8+4	3+R	B3rx
17	18v–19	*Ave Maria gratia plena*	liturgical	L	Pr	–	TC
18	19v	*O gloriosa vergine Maria*	Leonardo Giustiniani	I	C	9	S-TC
19	20	*Stabat mater dolorosa*	attrib. Jacopone	L	H	17	S-TC
20	20v–21	*Vergine benedecta*	Bianco da Siena?	I	B-7/11-7+5	8+R	B1
21	21v	*Ave, virgo gloriosa*	liturgy-derived?	L	H	6	S-TC
22	22	*Gaude virgo mater Christi*	prosa for B.V.M	L	H	6	S-TC
23	22v–23	*Gaude virgo mater Christi*	prosa for B.V.M	L	H	6	S-TC
24	23v–24	*Gaude flore virginali*	rhymed prayer	L	H	6	S2-TC
25	24v	*Al bel fonte sacro*	C. Castellani	I	B-8-6+4	4+R	B1rc
26	25	*O Maria, divina stella*	Simon Pallaio	I	Ov	7	S-IR
27	25v–26	*O madre sancta*	C. Castellani	I	B-7/11-8+4	6+R	B1
28	26v–28	*O madre del Signore*	?	I	C	35	S2-TC
29	28v	*Madre, che festi*	Leonardo Giustiniani	I	Ov	9	S-TC
30	29–30	*Maria, del ciel regina*	Leonardo Giustiniani	I	B-7/11-8+4	7+R	B2x
31	30v	*Maria, misericordia*	Leonardo Giustiniani	I	B-7-8+4	11+R	B1x

Appendix (*continued*)

No.	ff.	Title	Author or Origin	Language	Form	Strophes	Musical form
32	31–32	*Maria, madre de Dio*	Leonardo Giustiniani	I	B-7/11-8+4	8+R	B2x
33	32v–33	*Salve, regina di misericordia*	Feo Belcari	I	C	9	S-TC
34	33v–34	*Salve regina, o germinante ramo*	Leonardo Giustiniani	I	St+R	3+R	S-TC
35	34v–35	*Maria drent alla tua corte*	?	I	B-8-6+2	6+R	B3rc
36	35v–37	*Virtù, che fai*	?	I	So	–	see text
37	37v–38	*Como dinanzi a Christo*	Bianco da Siena?	I	B-11-6+2	9+R	B3rc
38	38v–39	*Sempre te sia in diletto*	Bianco da Siena	I	B-7/11-6+3	9+R	B1c
39	39v–40	*Fuzite christiani*	Leonardo Giustiniani	I	B-7/11-7+3	8+R	B2r
40	40v–41	*O vero amor celeste*	Leonardo Giustiniani	I	B-7/11-8+4	11+R	B2r
41	41v–42	*Sol mi sol*	Dammonis	I	B-8-6+4	2+R	B1
42	42v–43	*Dammi il tuo amore*	Feo Belcari	I	St	3	S-TC
43	43v	*Peccatori, perchè seti*	Leonardo Giustiniani	I	St	11	S-TC
44	44	*Humilmente t'envocho*	Leonardo Giustiniani	I	Ov	21	S-TC
45	44v–45	*Pianzeti, christiani*	Leonardo Giustiniani	I	St	11	S-IR
46	45v–46	*De piangeti amaramente*	Dammonis	I	B-8-6+4	3+R	B1c
47	46v–47	*Popul mio, popul ingrato*	Leonardo Giustiniani	I	St	10	S-IR
48	47v–48	*O peccatore, ti moverai*	L. Giustiniani?	I	B-11-6+2	5+R	B2c
49	48v–49	*O croce alma mirabile*	Leonardo Giustiniani	I	Ov	11	S-IR
50	49v–50	*Nostra interna et vera pace*	Dammonis	I	B-8-6+4	3+R	B3rx
51	50v–51	*Chi vol pace*	Feo Belcari	I	B-8-6+2	5+R	B3rc
52	51v–52	*Dapoi che te lasciai*	attrib. Bianco da Siena	L	B-7/11-6+2	3+R	B3rc
53	52v	*Salve regina glorie*	?	L	H	8	S-TC
54	53	*O stella matutina*	Leonardo Giustiniani	I	B-7/11-8+4	5+R	B1x
55	53v–54	*Adoramus te, O Iesu*	liturgy-derived?	L	Pr	–	TC

Appendix (*continued*)

No.	ff.	Title	Author or Origin	Language	Form	Strophes	Musical form
56	54ᵛ	Anima beneditta	?	I	St (B-7-8+4	15 7+R)†	S-TC
57	55–56	Anima che del mondo	Feo Belcari	I	B-7/11-9+3	7+R	B2x
58	56ᵛ	Se voi gustar l'amore	Francesco d'Albizo	I	B-7/11-6+4	3+R	B1c
59	57	L'amor a me venendo	Bianco da Siena	I	St (B-7-8+4	18 4+R)†	S-IR
60	57ᵛ–58	Nel to furore	?	I	B-7/11-6+2	8+R	B3rx
61	58ᵛ–59	Io son quel misero	Lorenzo de' Medici	I	B-8-6+2	9+R	B3rx
62	59ᵛ–60	O Iesù dolce	Leonardo Giustiniani	I	B-7/11-8+4	8+R	B1c
63	60ᵛ–61	Peccatori, ad una voce	Lorenzo Tornabuoni	I	B-8-6+2	5+R	B3
64	61ᵛ–62	Questa è quella croce	?	I	B-8-8+4	6+R	B2r
65	62ᵛ–63	Iesù, fami morire	Feo Belcari	I	B-7/11-6+4	3+R	B1
66	63ᵛ	Lasso, io moro	?	I	B-5-4+3	6+R	B3x

† Although the poem is strophic, Dammonis set it as a *ballata/barzelletta*.

Melody and Motive in Schenker's Earliest Writings

Allan Keiler

1.

There has been a growing interest in recent years in the earlier and less mature writings of Heinrich Schenker, and in the many musical and intellectual influences on his work. We have as yet, however, only the barest outline of any developmental or intellectual narrative, and much of that outline has been manipulated so as to suggest a narrative that is often at odds with the evidence of the various stages of Schenker's work. As I have suggested elsewhere,[1] much of these earlier stages has been seen as anticipating in important ways his more mature ideas. A usual theme has been to characterize Schenker as systematically moving from middle-ground structures to more background structures. This gradual search for the most prototypical and universal properties of tonal music and the laws of harmonic prolongation can thus be portrayed as a relentless and uninterrupted progression in which every stage plays its role in the search for ultimate truths. One can hardly fail to see the similarity between this process of intellectual search and achievement and the actual levels of prolongation that make up the typical Schenkerian analysis.

Of course, if the earliest stages of the narrative process should at some point stand revealed, the result is often surprising and casts a shadow forward over later stages that can rarely be reconciled easily with that light projected backward from the most mature periods. Many themes emerge from a clearer understanding of the full complexity inherent in Schenker's early work that could be explored with profit in relation to later stages. One might, for example, follow Schenker's changing views on musical form, or trace the gradual change in his thinking about the succession of historical changes in the development of Western music, or the change in his views on important composers, for example, Wagner.

One of the most fruitful themes that might be pursued for most of the course of Schenker's long career is what I would call the path away from

---

[1]"The Origins of Schenker's Thought: How Man Is Musical," *Journal of Music Theory* 33/2 (Fall, 1989): 273–99.

melody. It is important because, in spite of the importance that melody plays in his earliest writings, it remains a promise that is never kept in any systematic or exhaustive way in his later work. One of the most important themes of this subject is the gradual interconnection of melody with voice-leading and motivic processes, topics that would become more and more important during later stages. And when the subject shifts definitively toward motivic structure, the long perspective that comes about makes for a narrative with some internal logic, and yet one with surprises and hesitations as well. It is the first stages of this long narrative that I wish to take up here.

2.

One recent writer on music theory has observed that there occurred "a general revival of interest in melody from both musical and philosophical circles around 1900."[2] In these terms, we could see the primary importance that Schenker attributes to melody, so concretely felt if not always sufficiently argued in his essay "Der Geist der musikalischen Technik,"[3] as an important precursor to the theoretical and psychological interest given to the study of melody in the first years of the present century. This comparison would prove, however, misleading not only from the perspective of the decades to come, but from those previous to the early writings of Schenker as well.

Before Schenker, the study of melody among music theorists did give rise, in the German theoretical tradition, to occasional programmatic eloquence. Perhaps the most important is the polemical volume of A. B. Marx, *Die alte Musiklehre im Streit mit unserer Zeit,* in which he summed up what he saw as the state of affairs with respect to the study of melody at the beginning of the 1840s:

> Now one should at least hope to find some theory of melody, since melody is the simpler substance, preceding and taking precedence over harmony, which by itself alone cannot form an art work, in the way, as is well known, that melody can (for example, in natural song [*Naturgesang,* that is, melody as it comes about spontaneously in nature]). But *a theory of melody is lacking altogether.* One has been content to criticize or forbid certain melodic turns, steps etc., and, to be sure, from very inadequate and one-sided

---

[2] Lee A. Rothfarb, *Ernst Kurth as Theorist and Analyst* (Philadelphia: University of Pennsylvania Press, 1988), p. 13.
[3] *Musikalisches Wochenblatt* 26/19–26 (2, 9, 16, 23, 30 May, 13, 20 June 1895): 245–46, 257–59, 273–74, 285–86, 297–98, 309–10, 325–26. I have discussed this essay in some detail in Keiler, "Origins of Schenker's Thought."

views. Then there are a series of individual, equally inadequate observations on the relationship of two or more voices to each other. That is all. How a melody may be formed in and of itself—nowhere are we told that. Indeed, it is considered to be impossible to go further in this regard.[4]

One has only to remember the profoundly comprehensive and even spiritual significance that Marx gave to the world of experience, feeling, and learning that made up his conception of the *Kompositionslehre*, the only place in which he could realize his programmatic call for the study of melody, to see that by the end of the century very little of what he had hoped for had come to pass. At the dawn of the new century, it was rather the impetus from ethnomusicological studies, experimental work in the acoustics and physiology of hearing, and the overwhelming stylistic revolutions of the second part of the nineteenth century that all worked together to produce new interest and scholarship in the study of melody.[5]

But what shall we make of the importance that Schenker attributes to melody in his early essay "Der Geist der musikalischen Technik," within the musical traditions of his youth? Schenker does not stand apart in this regard, but we have to look beyond the isolated instances of official recognition given to the study of melody, to the areas of philosophy and especially aesthetics and, of course, to those writings that were overwhelmingly affected by evolutionary thought during the latter part of the nineteenth century. Above all it is the Romanticist view of the artist, who expresses the profoundest essence of his imagination without conscious thought when the individuality and uniqueness of musical utterance and the deepest strains of personality are welded together, that seizes on melody as the truest expression of musical instinct and creativity. Is there a more urgent expression of the Romanticist view than E. T. A. Hoffmann's?

> The primary and most superior element in music, that which seizes the human spirit with wonderful magic power, is melody.... This should be song,

---

[4]"Nun sollte man wenigstens hoffen, die Lehre von der Melodie zu finden, da Melodie die einfachere Substanz ist und der Harmonie vor- und vorangeht, dir für sich allein kein Kunstwerk bilden kann, wie es die Melodie (z. B. im Naturgesange) bekanntlich vermag. Aber—d i e L e h r e v o n d e r M e l o d i e f e h l t ü b e r a l l. Man hat sich begnügt, gewisse Wendungen, Schritte u. s. w. zu tadeln oder zu verbieten,—und zwar aus sehr unzulänglichen und einseitigen Gesichtspunkten; sodann hat man über das Verhalten zweier oder mehrerer Stimmen gegen einander eine Reihe einzelner, ebenfalls unzulänglicher Betrachtungen angestellt. Das ist alles. Wie eine Melodie an und für sich zu bilden sei,—das erfahren wir nirgends. Ja, man hat es sogar für unmöglich gehalten, hier weiter zu kommen." Adolph Bernhard Marx, *Die alte Musiklehre im Streit mit unserer Zeit* (Leipzig: Breitkopf und Härtel, 1841), p. 16. Unless otherwise noted, all translations in this essay are mine.

[5]See Rothfarb, pp. 13*ff*.

streaming free and unforced directly from the breast of man, who himself is the instrument that resounds in the most wonderful, the most secret sounds of nature. Melody, which in this way is not singable, can only remain a series of individual tones, which strive in vain to become music.[6]

In the German philosophical tradition, of course, this Romanticist perspective was transformed and developed so as to give melody a position of the highest ranking significance. Hegel's view will sound the most familiar:

Melody, as contrasted with time-measure, rhythm, and harmony, is the free-sounding soul itself in music. It is rooted in the rhythmically measured movements and harmonic relations of sounds we have been discussing, and can indeed in no way give itself existence apart from them. But its submission to their laws rather enhances than restricts its essential freedom.[7]

And the more abstract idea of Schelling, in which melody, although absorbing into itself the other musical elements, thus becomes the primary unity within multiplicity, only echoes in a different way than Hegel how melody achieves its preeminent status as the highest content of music as it makes use of and gives expression to harmony and rhythm toward its own ends.

If we make our way toward the first decade of Schenker's work, these same ideas resound in many contexts. Perhaps no more concrete expression of the primacy of melody can be found during this period than the writings of Wagner, in which it is nearly a commonplace that melodic expression is seen as part of the deepest level of the creative imagination. Here the common metaphor is the birth process rather than the germination and growth of plants of Goethe, for example, and it is no mere coincidence that it is on Beethoven, who came soon enough to be seen universally as the unparalleled prototype of the Romanticist's unconscious and demonic creative force,

---

[6]"Das Erste und Vorzüglichste in der Musik, welches mit wunderbarer Zauberkraft das menschliche Gemüt ergreift, ist die Melodie.... Diese soll Gesang sein, frei und ungezwungen unmittelbar aus der Brust des Menschen strömen, der selbst das Instrument ist, welches in den wunderbarsten, geheimnisvollsten Lauten der Natur ertönt. Die Melodie, die auf diese Weise nicht singbar ist, kann nur eine Reihe einzelner Töne bleiben, die vergebens danach streben, Musik zu werden." "Über einen Ausspruch Sacchinis und über den sogenannten Effekt in der Musik," *Kreisleriana,* zweite Reihe, No. 6; in *E. T. A. Hoffman. Musikalische Novellen und Aufsätze,* ed. Edgar Istel (Regensburg: Gustav Bosse, n.d.), p. 150; translated in *E. T. A Hoffmann's Musical Writings,* ed. David Charlton (Cambridge: Cambridge University Press, 1989), p. 156.

[7]*Hegel: On the Arts,* abridged and translated with an Introduction by Henry Paolucci (New York: Ungar, 1979), pp. 135–36.

that Wagner lavished his most sympathetic descriptions of the wedding of melody and the act of musical creation:

> With Beethoven...we recognize the natural life-urge that gives birth to melody from the inner organism of music. In his most important works, he in no way presents melody as something already completed at the beginning, but rather he lets it *come to birth* before our eyes to a certain extent organically; he consecrates us in this act of birth, by leading it before us in its organic necessity.[8]

We should not be tempted to make too much of what is too easily seen as a paradox in the attitudes about the study of melody during the nineteenth century. The very mystery surrounding the concrete strategies and principles of melody became in the writings of philosophers and aestheticians, and in those creative artists who gave voice to the problems of creation, the surest sign of the ultimate unfathomability of the creative act and of melody, its most characteristic and natural expression. Ambros, for example, in a moment of unusually dispassionate observation, makes this very connection:

> Music possesses, however, besides rhythm, the two elements of harmony and melody. To seek to explain the effect of a piece of music from the rhythm alone means, therefore, to overlook its two other equally essential elements; it means to set down the effect of a tragedy by Sophocles or Shakespeare to the credit of the *metre*. Even if harmony admits in any case of an additional explanation through agreeable or disagreeable convulsions of the auditory nerves by means of consonances or dissonances, yet in the case of the third element of music, which is almost the most essential one, namely, *melody*, a physiological theory for explaining its charm would hardly be so easy to establish.[9]

---

[8]"Bei Beethoven...erkennen wir den natürlichen Lebensdrang, die Melodie aus dem inneren Organismus der Musik heraus zu gebären. In seinen wichtigsten Werken stellt er die Melodie keinesweges als etwas von vornherein Fertiges hin, sondern er läßt sie aus ihren Organen heraus gewissermaßen vor unseren Augen g e b ä r e n; er weiht uns in diesen Gebärungsakt ein, indem er ihn uns nach seiner organischen Nothwendigkeit vorführt." Richard Wagner, "Oper und Drama: Die Oper und das Wesen der Musik," in *Gesammelte Schriften und Dichtungen,* Bd. 3 (Leipzig: E. W. Fritzsch, 1872), pp. 384–85.

[9]"Die Musik besitzt aber, nebst dem Rhythmus auch noch die beiden Elemente der Harmonie und Melodie. Die Wirkung einer Musik aus dem Rhythmus allein erklären wollen, heißt also die beiden andern gleich wesentlichen Elemente derselben außer Acht zu lassen, es heißt so viel, als die Wirkung eines Trauerspieles von Sophokles oder Shakespeare auf Rechnung des V e r s m a ß e s setzen. Läßt die Harmonie allenfalls auch noch eine physiologische Erklärung durch angenehme oder widrige Erschütterung der

Examples such as these, which locate melody at the very center of the creative process as the most immediate and unmistakable index of a composer's personality and musical style, could be multiplied with ease. Such views were part of the general intellectual tradition of Schenker's youth and period of studies. And, of course, the impact of such ideas must have been greatest from those works that played a more direct role in Schenker's early musical training and experience. These would include not only Hanslick's influencial monograph *Vom Musikalisch-Schönen*,[10] but other works on aesthetics and the development of the musical instinct, such as Hausegger's *Die Musik als Ausdruck*.[11] These two works alone reveal how the belief in the primacy of melody could find a natural place in works of widely divergent purposes and of different attitudes, both aesthetic as well as analytic and even historical.

By the last decade or so of the last century, when Schenker's earliest essays and reviews on music were written, there was already a tradition reaching well back into the century that saw melody as the central and most characteristic attribute of musical style and the musical personality. In spite of the significance and influence of this belief, little real theory of melody emerged during these decades.

Perhaps it would be worthwhile to emphasize here not the commonality of sentiment and belief in the primacy of melody that links Schenker with his contemporaries, for example, with Hanslick and Hausegger, but to point out, however briefly, some of those differences. For Hanslick, melody was the defining attribute of his doctrine of the beautiful; this is announced, in fact, at the very start of the third chapter of his famous monograph:

> The primordial stuff of music is *regular and pleasing sound.* Its animating principle is *rhythm:* rhythm in the larger scale as the co-proportionality of a symetrical structure; rhythm in the smaller scale as regular alternating motion of individual units within the metric period. The material out of which

---

Gehörnerven durch Consonanzen oder Dissonanzen zu, so dürfte bei dem dritten Elemente der Musik, das beinahe das wesentlichste ist, der M e l o d i e eine physiologische Theorie zur Erklärung ihres Zaubers schwerlich so leicht aufzustellen sein." Wilhelm August Ambros, *Die Grenzen der Musik und Poesie. Eine Studie zur Aesthetik der Tonkunst* (Leipzig: Heinrich Matthes, 1855), pp. 40–41. Translated by J. H. Cornell, *The Boundaries of Music and Poetry* (New York: G. Schirmer, 1893), pp. 39–40.

[10]It was the seventh edition of Hanslick's monograph, (Leipzig, 1885), that caused a new round of polemical discussion, just at the outset of Schenker's career as a writer on music. Schenker knew personally some of the participants of this debate, and its influence on him is discussed in Keiler, "Origins of Schenker's Thought."

[11]Friedrich von Hausegger, *Die Musik als Ausdruck,* 2nd ed. (Vienna: Carl Konegen, 1887).

the composer creates, of which the abundance can never be exaggerated, is the entire system of *tones,* with their latent possibilites for melodic, harmonic, and rhythmic variety. Unconsumed and inexhaustible, *melody* holds sway over all, as the basic form of musical beauty.[12]

For over fifty years, Hanslick's attitude toward melody changed very little. "Independent, symmetrically articulated melody" ("selbständige, symmetrisch gegliederte Melodie") was how he described it in a review of Verdi's *Otello,* melodies that do not make unreasonable demands on the memory: "How much more directly the musical invention flows, how these painfully sweet melodies can pursue us, even when we are not thinking at all of their relationship to the opera."[13]

In the fifth section of his *Die Musik als Ausdruck,* Hausegger takes up in earnest the problem of melody, and how much do his initial ideas remind us of Schenker's thought and language, emphasizing as they do universal competence and primordial appearance:

> Melody! That is what we demand above all from music. Where this is lacking, there the soul of music is missing. The development of our Western music distinguishes itself as the striving to allow melody as the victorious principle to result from the tone masses that group themselves according to different specifications and to allow art, so wonderfully enriched in means, to become once again, in accordance with its essence, what it was in its original simplicity. And we find that, despite all historical influences, the conditions that underlie the effectiveness of melody are no different from what they were formerly and have always been.[14]

---

[12]"Das Urelement der Musik ist W o h l l a u t, ihr Wesen R h y t h m u s. Rhythmus im großen, als die Übereinstimmung eines symmetrischen Baues, und Rhythmus im kleinen, als die wechselndgesetzmäßige Bewegung einzelner Glieder im Zeitmaß. Das Material, aus dem der Tondichter schafft, und dessen Reichtum nicht verschwenderisch genug gedacht werden kann, sind die gesammten T ö n e, mit der in ihnen ruhenden Möglichkeit zu verschiedener Melodie, Harmonie und Rhythmisierung. Unausgeschöpft und unerschöpflich waltet vor allem die M e l o d i e, als Grundgestalt musikalischer Schönheit." Eduard Hanslick, *Vom Musikalisch-Schönen,* 10th ed. (Leipzig: Johann Ambrosius Barth, 1902), p. 73. Translated by Jeffrey Payzant, *The Musically Beautiful* (Indianapolis, Ind.: Hackett Publishing Co., 1986), p. 28.

[13]"Wie viel unmittelbarer strömt da die musikalische Erfindung, wie können diese schmerzlich süßen Melodien uns verfolgen, auch wenn wir gar nicht an ihren Zusammenhang mit der Oper denken!" Eduard Hanslick, *Musikalisches und Litterarisches.* Vol. 5 of *Moderne Oper,* 2nd ed. (Berlin: Allgemeiner Verein für Deutsche Litteratur, 1889), pp. 72, 73.

[14]"Melodie! Das ist es, was wir vor Allem vom Tonstücke fordern. Wo es an solcher fehlt, da mangelt die Seele der Musik. Die Entwickelung unserer abendländischen Musik kennzeichnet sich als das Streben, aus den sich nach verschiedenen Bestimmungen gruppirenden Tonmassen die Melodie als siegreiches Princip hervorgehen und so die wunderbar an Mitteln bereicherte Kunst wieder ihrer Wesenheit nach das werden zu

And yet, the very first programmatic assertion of Hausegger about the nature of melody takes us far indeed from Schenker's perspective:

> I therefore believe, despite the absence of detailed results of research, to be able to assert that unshakable laws or prohibitions of melodic succession can be explained by laws or limitations of sound expression with reference to the human organism.[15]

Could there be anything more alien both to the spirit and substance of Schenker's work, even at the early stage that we are considering, than the illustrative analysis provided by Hausegger of Donna Anna's aria "Or sai che l'onore" from *Don Giovanni*, in which the purely physiological substratum of his thinking is illustrated by constant reference to quickness of pulse, heartbeat and various bodily motions in an attempt to explain the expressive power of Donna Anna's aria?[16] As I hope to make clear in the next sections of this essay, Schenker's way came to lie elsewhere.

3.

When one considers the importance that melody plays in Schenker's earliest writings, it is surprising that so little of the essay "Der Geist der musikalischen Technik" is concerned with melody. In the fifth section, he says only that the particular mood [*Stimmung*] of the musical content of a piece is inextricably bound up with melodic ideas. In the next section is the first occurrence of a conviction with which the entire essay ends, that the essential nature of music consists of bringing forth melodies.[17] Only in the last paragraph of the entire essay does Schenker take up the question of melody with any insistence, and the discussion here is not the usual comparative one in which melody is set beside and integrated with the other primary elements of music. One original feature of Schenker's discussion is that he emphasizes melody not as a musical parameter so much as the creative melodic impulse. Indeed, the emphasis is not unlike that given to

---

lassen, was sie in ihrer ursprünglichen Einfachheit war. Und wir finden, daß trotz allen historischen Einflüssen, die Bedingungen der Wirksamkeit dieser Melodie keine anderen geworden sind, als sie ehevor und stets waren." Hausegger, pp. 158–59.

[15]"So viel glaube ich, trotz dem Abhandensein detaillirter Erforschungsresultate, behaupten zu dürfen, daß unumstößliche Gesetze der Melodieführung oder absolute Unzulässigkeiten in derselben sich auf Gesetze des Lautausdruckes oder Grenzen desselben im menschlichen Organismus zurückführen lassen." Hausegger, p. 161.

[16]Hausegger, pp. 165–69.

[17]Schenker, "Der Geist" (May 30), p. 297.

the properties of universal musical competence that forms the subject matter of the first half of the essay. It is not only that Schenker characteristically describes melody as an inherent property of the musical instinct toward creativity; the primeval character of melodic creation is described in such a way as to give the feeling of great antiquity:

> *The real nature of music is to create melodies* which, like folksongs, live with each other free and independently, like families, conciliatory, and which, like the first people in paradise, can romp about in the paradise of music, naked and unclothed.[18]

Melody, like articulated speech, is part of man's earliest means of expression.

The other characteristic aspect of Schenker's discussion of melody is that it is embedded in a discussion of the relationship of form and content. I have discussed elsewhere some of Schenker's ideas about form and content primarily in relation to Hanslick's doctrines.[19] Here I will try to summarize them more independently of their original polemical context, and this discussion should enable us to make some comparisons between this earliest period of Schenker's work and his more mature thinking. In Schenker's view during this period, form is too often emphasized at the expense of content, which is primary. Although he admits that formal categories and their aesthetic and dramatic implications often stimulate the creative process during each period of musical development, form is still, in the end, "an abstraction, a representation that does not reside in the ear."[20] In spite of the propensity shown in the writing of music history to utilize formal categories and form types as the basis for stylistic comparison and the judgements underlying stylistic change, any study of music history that does this is to be admonished for giving undue attention to form: "The content carries and is responsible for everything."[21] In fact, the variety of titles based on formal categories and even on the mood and character of a piece—sonata, intermezzo, capriccio, etc.—that are used by composers with such frequency

---

[18]"Die eigentliche Natur der Musik ist Melodien zu schaffen, die, wie die Volkslieder, frei und unabhängig mit einander leben, familienähnlich und versöhnlich, und die, wie die ersten Menschen im Paradies, nackt und unbekleidet im Paradies der Musik sich herumtummeln können." Schenker, "Der Geist" (June 20), p. 326.

[19]Keiler, "Origins of Schenker's Thought."

[20]"Eine Abstraction, eine Vorstellung, die nicht im Ohr ihren Sitz hat." Schenker, "Der Geist" (June 20), p. 326.

[21]"Alles trägt und verantwortet nur der Inhalt." Schenker, "Der Geist" (June 20), p. 326.

turn attention away from the individuality of musical content: "It may even have been a conscious thought that the title actually says nothing and its relationship with the content extends no further than the mere announcement that something is about to sound."[22] And at the center of the individual musical content is melody.

As for the rest of Schenker's writings during this period, there is not to be found any technical or comprehensive theory of melody, although many programmatic discussions about melody can be found. The predominant role of melody in Schenker's musical thinking is for the most part in keeping with the natural and largely intuitive and uncritical priority assigned to melody throughout the second half of the nineteenth century. Perhaps it is wisest here to let Schenker's own writings speak for themselves, as they reflect his many-sided commitment to the significance of melody.

Many of Schenker's articles are concerned with the evaluation, not only of individual works heard for the first time, but of individual composers and of contemporary stylistic developments in specific musical genres. In this context, the importance of melody as a basis for stylistic definition and comparison can be seen in nearly every article in which such stylistic questions are taken up. Perhaps it is Schenker's article "Johannes Brahms,"[23] that should be taken as the most representative in this regard. The primary role that the study of melody is meant to assume in the understanding and evaluation of any composer's work is announced in this article almost in the form of a credo: "It is only the power of melody that legitimizes a composer as a great one."[24]

There is another programmatic statement in this article on Brahms, which we must give in its entirety, not only because of the light that it sheds on Schenker's approach to the study of melody, but perhaps even more important, because it is so much in opposition to the discussion in the essay "Der Geist der musikalischen Technik" about the relation of language and melody, in which he attempted to reject organicism as a fundamental property of musical structure.[25] The context of that argument was the creative process and the argument rested on the relationship of musical content to the coherent and conscious will of the composer. In that argument, a piece is coherent

---

[22]"Er mag selbst im Bewusstsein gehabt haben, dass der Titel eigentlich Nichts sagt und seine Verwandtschaft mit dem Inhalt über die blosse billige Ankündigung, es werde bald Etwas 'erklingen,' nicht weiter hinausreicht." Schenker, "Der Geist" (June 20), p. 326.

[23]Heinrich Schenker, "Johannes Brahms," *Die Zukunft* 19 (May 8, 1897): 261–65.

[24]"Nur die Melodiekraft ist es aber, die einen Tondichter als einen großen legitimirt." Schenker, "Johannes Brahms," p. 262.

[25]I have discussed this argument at some length in Keiler, "Origins of Schenker's Thought."

only when the materials themselves (and from the discussion as a whole, one cannot avoid the impression that by musical content Schenker has in mind a single dominant musical idea, perhaps a motive or group of motives, all of whose variations are related in a narrow way to the principal idea) take over completely the unconscious creative impulses of the composer, so that any attempts to control and manipulate from the outside are prevented. In these cases, there is actually music that could be considered organic as far as the organization of its content is concerned. Otherwise, any attempt to claim that any music is organic has to be considered a merely subjective impression by the listener who in a natural and instinctive way uses the language of organicism to portray and evaluate properties that are not in any way intrinsic to the music. This language tends to come from one's experience with language, and from the long association that music has with language, where the language of organicism is appropriate.

In the Brahms essay, this is what Schenker has to say about the general nature of melody and melodic logic:

> Just as in the art of speech or of writing one may distinguish between thoughts that rustle in the wind of icy conceptuality, because they speak more of abstract concepts than of that which has been seen or heard, and other thoughts, which indeed *only* speak of things seen or heard, and therefore reflect the colorful sensuality of life—in the same way in music, abstract musical thoughts can be distinguished from musical thoughts that are melodies. Logic is inherent in both categories of thoughts, otherwise they would not be thoughts at all. While in conceptual musical thoughts, so to speak, everything is cold logic, one sees in the others, that is, melodies, a juice running like blood. As if they came out of the mouth of a rosy young girl or boy and drew the breath of ardent life in itself, so sound the melodies of all great masters. Also in absolute music (therefore not merely, for example, in song) they are similar to song or speech, and there steals over us the desire to think up vigorous words to accompany the pulsating sounds.[26]

---

[26]"Wie in der Kunst der Sprache oder Schrift man unterscheiden dürfte zwischen Gedanken, die von eisiger Begriffskälte durchweht sind, weil sie mehr von abstrakten Begriffen als von Gesehenem oder Gehörtem, und den anderen Gedanken, die eben nur von gesehenen oder gehörten Dingen sprechen und so die farbige Sinnlichkeit des Lebens wiedergeben,—genau so lassen sich in der Musik abstrakte Tongedanken von Tongedanken unterscheiden, die Melodien sind. Beiden Gattungen von Gedanken ist Logik immanent, sonst wären sie überhaupt keine Gedanken. Während aber in den sozusagen begrifflichen Tongedanken die kalte Logik Alles ist, sieht man in den anderen, den Melodien, einen Saft wie Blut rinnen. Als kämen sie aus dem Munde eines blühenden Mädchens oder Jünglings und führten den Athem heißen Lebens in sich, so klingen die Melodien aller großen Meister. Sie sind auch in der absoluten Musik (also

In this passage it is clear first of all that Schenker does not warn against the comparison between language (and the language of thought) and music in any way, but takes it as one that is mutually insightful. And, of course, the context has shifted here from the polemical and abstract one of the essay of two years before, "Der Geist der musikalischen Technik," to the biographical and stylistically descriptive one about Brahms. Here Schenker claims that even for melodic content that is cold and calculated, not alive and spontaneous, there is a ruthless logic of organization such that continuations make sense, stucture is coherent, and beginning, middle and end appear completely in place. And even though this logic is not discussed in terms of organicism (indeed, the term is not mentioned), there is no mistaking that Schenker's understanding of the logic of melodic content in this essay is entirely in keeping with those instances described in the earlier one, about which the term organic would be perfectly appropriate for him.

The theoretical implications of this passage from Schenker's essay on Brahms have more value for us than its immediate application to Brahms's style, for Schenker goes on to defend rather than to explain or illustrate:

> A great, individual power of melody was given to the master Brahms, and only the inadequacies of his contemporaries brought it about that one saw an unplowed field with dialectically proliferating weeds instead of sumptuous arches of melodies.[27]

And about those works that seem in any way deficient to Schenker, he is less likely to give precise reasons than to ascribe the lack to the character and psychology of the composer, in a way that is wholeheartedly in keeping with the nineteenth century's attempt to wed life and work in a mutually causal and explanatory fashion:

> While several of his major works, above all the *German Requiem* and the *Four Serious Songs,* arose from an exceptionally strong stimulus in his life, such a stimulus seems to have been almost entirely lacking in the case of his symphonies.[28]

---

nicht blos z. B. im Liede) dem Gesange oder der Rede ähnlich und es beschleicht uns ordentlich Lust, zu den blutwarmen Tönen lebensvolle Worte zu denken." Schenker, "Johannes Brahms," p. 262.

[27]"Dem Meister Brahms war eine große, eigenthümliche Melodiekraft gegeben und nur eine Unzulänglichkeit seiner Zeitgenossen bewirkte, daß man statt des üppigen Melodiebodens ein brachliegendes Feld mit dialektisch wucherndem Unkraut sah." Schenker, "Johannes Brahms," p. 262.

[28]"Während mehre seiner Hauptwerke, wohl in erster Linie das 'Deutsche Requiem' und die 'Vier ernsten Gesänge,' aus einer überaus kräftigen Anregung im Leben entstanden sind, scheint seinen Sinfonien eine solche Anregung fast ganz gefehlt zu haben." Schenker, "Johannes Brahms," pp. 262–63.

In this case, for once, Schenker does not let the matter drop, and his discussion of Brahms's melodic technique in the four symphonies provides unexpected insight into his ideas concerning melodic content and construction during this period:

> Rather here he seems to have drawn his inspiration almost solely from the laws of art: he penetrated so deeply into the knowledge of Beethoven's symphonic technique that it was possible for him almost to equal it, in relation to the concentration and nimbleness of the thoughts, to the vital forward striving of the symphonic development and, most of all, in relation to what musicians call an organic, thematic method of working.[29]

How unceremoniously the term organic crops up in this description; the term in this context has the feel of general usage, to be sure, but nothing in the context suggests at all that Schenker is uncomfortable with its meaning. It seems that in this essay Schenker means by organic, at least in the context of melodic style and content, the motivically derived and concentrated processes of Beethoven's style, which are a customary vantage point from which to trace a compositional lineage for Brahms's motivic language. Melodic content that is organized organically, in other words, seems to be for Schenker content that depends on an economy of motivic material, where a musical surface with differing themes and contrasting motives can be shown to derive from one or a small repertory of motivic shapes. The argumentative position about organicism that Schenker made so much of in his earlier essay is here replaced by a position in which "organic" is simply an alternative term for Brahms's technique of motivic economy and transformation.

The Brahms essay is no more helpful than this. But it does draw our attention for the first time, in a context outside of the more philosophical and abstract essay "Der Geist der musikalishen Technik," to a connection of importance for Schenker: that between melody and motivic content. And while we should not be struck by Schenker's emphasis on the importance of the motive and on motivic repetition or transformation even in these earliest writings, the complicated development that these ideas will undergo throughout the history of Schenker's writings will give us more than one occasion to pause in surprise and reflection. Perhaps the first such occasion

---

[29]"Vielmehr schien er hier seine Inspiration fast nur von den Gesetzen der Kunst bezogen zu haben; er drang so tief in die Erkenntniß der Sinfonietechnik Beethovens ein, daß es ihm möglich wurde, sie fast ganz zu erreichen, in Bezug auf die Konzentrirtheit und Schlagfertigkeit der Gedanken, auf lebensvolles Vorwärtsstreben der sinfonischen Handlung und am Meisten in Bezug auf Das, was die Musiker eine organische, thematische Arbeitmethode nennen." Schenker, "Johannes Brahms," p. 263.

will come from considering another essay of this period, "Notizen zu Verdis Falstaff."[30] It is not only the fact that Schenker uses Wagnerian principles of music drama as the basis for the most sustained and detailed of his comments about Verdi's late style, in this case the composer's last opera. While it is surprising to see Schenker on such easy terms with Wagner's music in view of his later and well-known position about Wagner's compositional style, it was common enough in the reception history of Verdi's later works in Germany, from *Don Carlos* on, to make stylistic comparisons, with various ends in mind, with Wagner's music. Indeed, no discussion of late nineteenth century opera, of whatever national origin or stylistic character, could escape some contact with Wagnerism in German critical writings of this period. But we can still learn much, in spite of this almost automatic connection to principles of Wagnerian music drama, by taking careful notice of the different ways, psychologically as well as musically or aesthetically, in which different writers respond to Wagner. Any artistic figure of such compelling dimensions as Wagner, quite apart from the merely musical questions of influence, rejection or assimilation that have to be faced in most stylistic discussions of opera in the late nineeeenth century, must make his significance felt in the more personal and psychological spheres of ego development and myth formation. What is negotiated in one way on the musical level may not be so negotiated on the more private level of wish and need. And, of course, it is essential to understand the artistic and personal influence of Wagner on a young man during a crucially formative period in his intellectual development. In this regard, a simple yet useful comparison might be made between Schenker's essay on Verdi's *Falstaff* and Eduard Hanslick's review of Verdi's *Otello*, written only three years earlier.[31]

Hanslick's review was written on the occasion of the first Viennese performance of Verdi's penultimate opera, near the end of his career, when he was less than a decade away from retirement. On its own terms, his review of *Otello* is perceptive and surprisingly comprehensive in the general knowledge and understanding shown to the wide span of Verdi's works. But our interest here lies in the ways in which Wagner appears during the course of the discussion. In fact, comparison, even allusion to Wagner occurs at only a single juncture of the essay, and that at a place where Hanslick has described the characteristics of Verdi's late style as they are manifested in *Otello*. But the affect of the passage is wholly one of detachment, distance and sober reflection, without a single suggestion of the personal and passionate involvement of a lifetime's confrontation with Wagner's works. The whole

---

[30]Heinrich Schenker, "Notizen zu Verdis Falstaff," *Die Zukunft* 3 (June 3, 1893): 474–76.

[31]Hanslick, *Musikalishes und Litterarisches,* pp. 69–79.

reference to Wagner, in fact, has the character of a wise father's counsel to a son's attitude constantly led astray by uncritical passion and unreflective hero-worship:

> Whoever wishes to designate all that with the general and current designation 'Wagnerian' may do so. In *Otello* Verdi['s practice] coincides in many ways with Wagnerian principles. That he arrived at this style only through Wagner['s example], perhaps even adopted it from Wagner—that can be believed only by one who does not know *Don Carlos*, which appeared twenty years before *Otello*, at a time when Verdi had heard nothing by Wagner but the *Tannhäuser* Overture. Verdi still knows nothing today of Wagner's last works, the foundation of 'the real Wagner style.' An opera like *Otello*, in which neither leitmotive nor endless orchestral melody, but rather the singing voices hold sway, to which as the highest will the orchestra is subordinated even in its most significant moments, has nothing in common with the style of *Tristan* and *Siegfried*. *Otello* is different from *Aida* and *La Traviata*, but it is still unmistably Verdian; there is not one scene in it whose music could be said to imitate Wagner.[32]

At least in this review, there is not a trace of undue influence of Wagnerism to interfere with Hanslick's judgement. In Schenker's essay on Verdi's *Falstaff*, on the other hand, it is just the opposite. One has the impression there, in fact, that somewhere behind the scenes Schenker is engaged with some imaginary antagonist who identifies with the Wagnerian side of Schenker's thinking and personality and who goads him continually into retreating a step or two whenever Schenker is inclined to be unconditionally positive about Verdi. At the very end of the essay, for example, in discussing the characteristic short melodic fragments that recur in *Falstaff*, associated generally with a single personage, Schenker says:

> An idea of charming originality in *Falstaff* is that of typically bestowing on a few words of a few characters a fixed melodic formula. But I beg for

---

[32]"Wer das Alles mit dem allgemeinen landläufigen Ausdrucke 'Wagnerisch' bezeichnen will, der mag es thun. Verdi trifft im Othello vielfach mit Wagnerschen Grundsätzen zusammen. Daß er diesen Stil erst durch Wagner erfaßt, etwa gar von Wagner angenommen habe, das kann nur glauben, wer seinen 'Don Carlos' nicht kennt, der zwanzig Jahre vor Othello erschienen ist, zu einer Zeit, da Verdi von Wagner nichts als die Tannhäuser=Ouvertüre gehört hatte. Von Wagners letzten, 'den eigentlichen Wagnerstil' begründenden Werken kennt Verdi heute noch nichts. Eine Oper, in welcher, wie im 'Othello,' weder Leitmotive noch die unendliche Orchester=Melodie regieren, sondern die Singstimmen, denen, als oberstem Willen, das Orchester auch in seinen bedeutsamsten Momenten untergeordnet ist, hat mit dem Tristan= und Siegfriedstil nichts gemein. 'Othello' ist anders als Aïda und die Traviata, aber er ist doch unverkennbar Verdisch; nicht Eine Scene steht darin, deren Musik Wagner nachgebildet wäre." Hanslick, *Musikalisches und Litterarisches*, pp. 73–74.

heaven's sake that such thin, airy spider's threads not be confused with the essence of the leitmotive, which concerns itself not with the painting of some incidental features, but with the greatest character painting.[33]

Schenker's praise of Verdi may be sincere, but it is rarely more than reward, and from a Wagnerian perspective that is very nearly defensive hero-worship, when it is not banner waving. The same tone and purpose recurs often in Schenker's writings during this period, yet what I find surprising and certainly suggestive is that there is hardly a sustained reference to Wagner's music to give the suggestion that it is, after all, from the music itself that Schenker's sentiments are derived. It is not Wagner's music, apparently, but rather Wagner's theories about his music, and surely about other musical and aesthetic doctrines, that had this profound hold on Schenker, at least for a few years during this period.

Perhaps it is still another passage from Schenker's essay on Verdi's *Falstaff* that will suggest at least one reason for the strong hold that Wagner's doctrines held for Schenker, the passage, in fact, where Schenker deals with the melodic style of Verdi. As usual the appraisal is based on a comparison with Wagner:

> Do not think here of Wagner's *Meistersinger von Nürnberg*, in which the broader, more easy-going humor and the frequently misunderstood leitmotive system have made easy similar and, as many feel, model adaptations. Wagnerian themes are more plastic, more typical, and in livelier, more varied relationships to the events on stage than are Verdi's melodies. The motivic work of Wagner, as well as other means he employs to form larger sections, entails the inestimable advantage that it constantly elucidates, solidifies and leaves its mark, so to speak, on the essential elements of his music. Through the introduction of leitmotives, part of whose function is that they are immediately understood, an appearance of causality, of logic, I would like to say, is brought to the orchestra, and all of the music must then, of course, give the impression of an animated, changeable newness, which still appears to be in some way known.[34]

---

[33]"Von liebenswürdiger Originalität ist in 'Falstaff' der Einfall, einige Worte einiger Personen mit einem feststehenden Tonfall typisch zu bedenken. Aber ich bitte um Himmelswillen nur, solche dünne, durch die Luft ziehenden Spinnenfäden nicht mit dem Wesen des Leitmotivs zu verwechseln, das keine Ausmalung kleiner zufälliger Züge, sondern größte Charaktermalerei treibt." Schenker, "Notizen zu Verdis Falstaff," p. 476.

[34]"Man denke hier nicht an die 'Meistersinger von Nürnberg' Wagners, in denen der breitere, behäbigere Humor, und das so vielfach verkannte Leitmotivsystem die ähnliche und, wie Viele meinen, auch vorbildliche Adaptirung erleichtert haben. Wagnerische

In any context that was not already marked by some point of special interest, this careful and fully approving statement of Wagner's leitmotive method would call for very little comment. But not so here. We have here an even clearer statement than was the case in the Brahms essay of Schenker's ability to see the problem of organic unity independently of the more abstract compositional and aesthetic questions of the long essay of two years later. For Wagner's leitmotive technique is a carefully premeditated system (Schenker chooses that very word: *Leitmotifsystem*), and one that Schenker could hardly have thought was carried out and applied in Wagner's music without so much as an inkling of conscious thought or willful care. And yet in the very comprehensiveness of that application lies its effect of causality and logic. The descriptive language and attitude in this example seem to me different from those expressed in Schenker's assessment of Brahms's melodic or motivic style only to the degree that it is itself more extreme and thoroughgoing.

Why then should Wagner's leitmotive technique have produced from Schenker here and elsewhere so complete and uncritical a response? A reasonable explanation is simply that it represented for Schenker during this period, more in the language and conviction with which it was presented and defended by Wagner and others than in the results it gave rise to musically or aesthetically, the readiest and most defendable example of an organic and comprehensive theory of musical content. Later, when Schenker came to examine it in the light of his emerging ideas of harmonic prolongation, his attitude about Wagner's music changed decisively. And if it was not so much Wagner's music but his theories that made so deep an impression on Schenker during this period, then it would not have been all that difficult to change his mind about Wagner's music in a way that would seem to many as unusual. For the time being at any rate, Schenker had little original idea of his own about the nature of musical content beyond the concepts of repetition and motivic economy and organic unity to go on, and so

---

Themen sind plastischer, typischer, und in lebhaftern, vielfacheren Beziehungen zum Bühnenereigniß als die Verdischen Melodien. Die motivische Arbeit Wagners und noch jede andere Art, die er anwendet, um größere Theile zu bilden, bringt den unschätzbaren Vortheil mit sich, daß sie die wesentlichen Elemente seiner Musik gleichsam immer neu erläutert, befestigt und einprägt. Durch die Einführung der Leitmotive, deren Beruf es mit sich bringt, daß sie eben so bald verstanden werden, wird außerdem in das Orchester ein Schein von Kausalität, von Logik möchte ich sagen, hineingebracht, und die Gesammtmusik muß dann freilich den Eindruck eines bewegt und wechselvoll Neuen machen, das doch immer wieder irgend bekannt zu sein scheint." Schenker, "Notizen zu Verdis Falstaff," p. 475.

Wagner's system of leitmotives became for him something to fill a void rather than the foundation for a more personal theory of musical content.

4.

Schenker's article on Brahms's *Five Songs for Mixed Choir a Capella, Op. 104*,[35] falls within the same period as his other early writings that we have been discussing. Of all of Schenker's writings on musical repertory during this period, it is the one that best illustrates his more technical analytic thinking, although it is disappointing, of course, when compared to the suggestiveness and ingenuity of his middle period work, or to the technical mastery of his late writings. Because the article on the five songs Op. 104 was about recent music, newly published, rather than a more general appreciation of Brahms's style, Schenker was expected both to evaluate and to describe in more detail than was usual. In much of this article, his descriptions of the melodic style of the songs are limited to general expressive character, relationships to the text, large scale melodic contour, and points of greatest tension and relaxation. His more detailed observations are mainly about motivic content and relationships, especially in the central three songs, where his attention to motivic content is most insistent and continuous.

In the second song, "Nachtwache II," it is first the descending fourth motive that seizes on Schenker's attention, as he points out how this motive of the watchman occurs especially in the two bass parts (Ex. 1).

Example 1. Brahms, "Nachtwache II," Op. 104/2

---

[35]Heinrich Schenker, "Kritik: Johannes Brahms. Fünf Gesänge für gemischten Chor a capella, Op. 104," *Musikalisches Wochenblatt* 23/33–36 (18, 25 August, 1 September 1892): 409–12, 425–26, 437–38.

Schenker not only emphasizes the expressive character of the successive transformations of this motive in the first part of the song, but he makes clear his own excitement at even this simple process of motivic content:

> Even more worthy of admiration, perhaps, is the way Brahms fulfilled the form of the question "Ruhn sie? rufet das Horn" by rhythmic means:

> And now as the horn's "aus Osten" is brought to mind, answering with "Sie ruhn!", the melodic progression turns as if instinctively in the opposite direction:

> and again one hears in Bass II and Tenor, and finally in Alto II the motive of the horn in the affirmative form of the inverted leap of a fourth:

> like a part of reality from the very texture of the mood.[36]

It is not Brahms's use of the principal motive in mm. 5–7, but Schenker's own obsessive reaction to its exploitation that is striking in his description: "The motive, which appears with the words 'und aus Osten das Horn' is to

---

[36]"Noch bewunderswerther vielleicht, wie Brahms mit Mitteln der Rhythmik die Form der Frage bei den Worten: 'ruhn sie? rufet das Horn' gelöst hat:...Und wie nun des Hornes 'aus Osten' gedacht wird, das entgegengeruft: 'sie ruhn,' wendet sich wie instinctiv die Tonfolge der Melodie in der Gegenrichtung:...und wieder hört man im Bass II und Tenor und endlich Alt II das Motiv des Hornes in der bejahenden Form des umgekehrten Quartsprunges:...wie ein Element der Wirklichkeit aus dem Gewebe der Stimmung heraus!" Schenker, "Op. 104," p. 410.

be sure no longer new, but what freedom in the alteration of the fourth leap, in the partial augmentation of the soprano!"[37]

In the final section of the song, it is the unifying character of the motive that Schenker emphasizes:

> New motives and melodies bring us first the words "hülle in Frieden dich ein," in free and strict imitation, which chase one another in voices full of life, but one hears here clearly and often the old familiar motive of the horn in the version of the answer sounding now and then (especially in Bass II), as if it wanted to set us again on the ground where we stood.[38]

The thought here is colorful rather than precise; nonetheless, it cannot escape attention how similar is Schenker's attitude here about the recurrence of the horn motive in the lowest part, to the importance he gives to the actual recurrence of the Stufe in the bass during the course of some harmonic prolongation in his later writings. Here again, as I have pointed out earlier in this essay, Schenker's conceptual inclinations have to be seen apart from the particular musical problems to which they are applied in these early writings; they often reappear more strikingly later on when they are seen in their more familiar guise.

So far the examples of motivic relationships that Schenker illustrates in the second song are closely related and rather transparent. But there is another that he establishes, which is deeper and, for once, really suggestive of his later thinking. The connection is between the soprano parts of mm. 3–4 and 10–12. The whole passage is worth quoting:

> I come now to a consideration of the melody of the chorus. It is this melody that gives first of all the impression of a romantic enchantment by virtue of its particular qualities; and in its womb rests the germ of all of the harmonic interpretations that bestow on it its distinctive physiognomy. Consider now the following patterns:

---

[37]"Das Motiv, das bei den Worten 'und aus Osten das Horn' erscheint, ist zwar nicht mehr neu, aber welche Freiheit in der Aenderung des Quartsprunges, in der theilweisen Vergrösserung im Sopran!" Schenker, "Op. 104," p. 411.

[38]"Neue Motive und Melodien bringen uns erst die Worte 'hülle in Frieden dich ein,' in freien und strengen Nachahmungen, die in den lebensvollen Stimmen einander jagen, aber man hört hier deutlich und oft das alte, bekannte Motiv des Hornes in der Fassung der Antwort zwischendurch erklingen (besonders im Bass II), als wollte es uns wieder auf den Boden stellen, auf dem wir früher gestanden." Schenker, "Op. 104," p. 411.

Melody and Motive 189

and

Peculiar to both is the original step of the second, which finds its way into the pure harmonic series of tones without thereby doing away with its own harmonic meaning.[39]

In these brief remarks the fundamental relationship between the horizontalization of the triad as a primary means of generating musical content and the prolongational effect of passing motion seems clear. One wonders how deeply these ideas were a part of Schenker's harmonic thinking during this period. Certainly they resonate in the final remark that Schenker makes in this passage:

The melodic pattern of the soprano at its conclusion is:

---

[39]"Ich komme nun zu der Betrachtung der Melodie des Chores. Sie ist es ja, die durch ihre Eigenart zunächst den Eindruck romantischen Zaubers gibt, und in ihrem eigenen Schoosse ruhen ja die Keime all der harmonischen Interpretationen, die ihr die bestimmte Physiognomie verleihen. Nun sehe man die folgenden Gebilde:...Eigenthümlich ist Beiden der originelle Secundenschritt, der sich in die reine harmonische Tonreihe hineindrängt, ohne dabei auf einen eigenen harmonischen Sinn zu verzichten." Schenker, "Op. 104," p. 411.

190 Allan Keiler

> How characteristic is its motion downward and the elementary decomposing of the triad in measures three and four.[40]

Schenker's discussion of the third song, "Letztes Glück," is the shortest of the essay, but it is the only one that is devoted entirely to the question of motivic organization. Only here does Schenker consider motivic relationship and melodic content from the point of view of the organization of the entire song. First, tonal organization and melodic content are related:

> "Complete congruence reveals itself in the pattern of the four keys that govern the piece—F minor–A♭ major, F major–F minor. The melody is also divided into four parts and thus intensifies the suppleness of the motives [that the composer] conceived."[41]

But this relationship is carried further when Schenker suggests that the partial return of the first melodic group in the fourth part of the song, and the similarities of melodic construction of the central sections are related textually and symbolically as well. It is, of course, the motivic similarites of the central sections that we wonder about because Schenker does not describe them at all; but what Schenker must have had in mind is clear enough. There is first of all the descending third motive presented first in m. 19 in the soprano and repeated a step higher in the next measure; the process is interrupted only by the cadential figure but is taken up again with the words "lebt das Herz in Frühlingsträumen," now repeated and filled in with passing motion (Ex. 2).

Example 2. Brahms, "Letztes Glück," Op. 104/3

---

[40]"Das melodische Gebilde des Soprans am Schluss lautet:...Wie charakteristisch sein Neigen zur Tiefe und die elementare Dreiklangszerlegung im Takt 3 und 4!" Schenker, "Op. 104," p. 411.

[41]"Die vollständige Congruenz zeigt sich in der Ordnung der vier Tonarten, die das Stück beherrschen—F moll–As dur, F dur–F moll. Die Melodie theilt sich ebenfalls in vier Gruppen und steigert so die Plastik der gedanklichen Motive." Schenker, "Op. 104," p. 425.

In the soprano part of the third section, "Noch verweilt ein Sonnenblick," the ascending sequence of downward thirds continues (Ex. 3).

Example 3. Brahms, "Letztes Glück," Op. 104/3

And surely the motivic reference of the words "bei den späten Hagerosen" to the beginning of the soprano part of the second section would not have been missed by Schenker. Indeed, the matching of beginning and end points in the central section motivically only serves to mirror the large scale melodic matching of first and fourth sections.

5.

The path away from melody in Schenker's writings was a long and arduous one. Schenker did not join his early interest in the many-faceted and personal language of melodic structure and melodic style with methodological or analytic explicitness or consistency. The move toward motivic structure came early, and the first stage of that predilection, in the earliest writings of Schenker, is what I have tried to describe here. Another stage of considerable importance was reached in the *Tonwille*, for example, where voice leading was often interpreted in the most varied and adventuresome ways in all of Schenker's work, as he strove to account for motivic and sometimes even melodic content in ways that would force the notion of voice leading into directions that were never taken up again. As other topics concerned with the development of Schenker's work are examined, we should have before us a more acurate view of the delicate and complicated path from which the mature ideas of Schenker gradually emerged. Ultimately, of course, there is no approach to the interpretation of the growth and development of scholarly work that is entirely free from ideological pressure. I have argued that much of the work in this area seeks to impose, consciously or unconsciously, the same kind of organicist doctrine of beliefs on the historical development of Schenker's work as underlies Schenker's own theoretical ideas. If I, on the other hand, have tried to emphasize such themes as conflict, divergence and richness of possiblity, then it is to encourage a less rigid and dogmatic approach to Schenker's work, and to try to assign him an accurate place as part of the historical record of music theory from which many stages of growth, departure, and new interpretation can proceed.

Twins, Cousins, and Heirs: Relationships among Editions of Music Printed in Sixteenth-Century Venice

Mary S. Lewis

In the middle years of the sixteenth century, the two leading Venetian music printers, Antonio Gardano and Girolamo Scotto, frequently published the same music—even the same collections of pieces—at approximately the same time, and at other times produced new editions of each other's work within a year or two after the previous edition had appeared.

Many questions have arisen regarding the relationship of these similar editions. We do not know if Gardano or Scotto ever jobbed out projects to each other, if they copied each other's publications, or if they obtained their music through different channels. Sorting out the relationships among these sources should contribute to our understanding of the dynamics of music publishing in Venice in the mid-sixteenth century, and of the way these printers chose, gathered, edited, printed, promoted, and distributed the music they dispersed all over Europe. We can then form a better picture of the nature of the repertory published in Venice, and about the printers' sources of supply.

Since we have no documentary evidence in the form of agreements, letters, contracts, or lawsuits regarding the paired or similar editions, we must turn to the sources themselves for clues about their relationship, which can best be found by comparing the readings of some of the pieces they hold in common. Such a comparison may tell us if one publisher indeed copied the work of the other verbatim, or if more complex processes were involved. Presumably, the closer the correspondence of readings between two editions, the more likely the possibility one was copied—with or without permission—from the other. Heretofore only Thomas Bridges has worked to any extent on the readings, primarily those of the editions of Arcadelt's first book of madrigals.[1] My own work in this area is far from complete,

---

[1] Thomas Bridges, *The Publishing of Arcadelt's First Book of Madrigals,* 2 vols. (Ph.D. dissertation, Princeton University, 1982), passim.

and this report is preliminary, but I believe we can learn something from it of the dynamics of the music publishing process in Venice.

Interpretations of The Related Editions

Table 1 lists in chronological order the closely-related pairs or groups of editions that the two printers produced from 1539 through 1550. Scholars have ventured a variety of opinions regarding the implications of these closely-related publications. At one extreme are those who suggest that Gardano and Scotto were involved in cooperative ventures, farming out work to each other as necessary, or at least that they coexisted in a state of *laissez-faire*. The opposite, and until recently more widely-held view, has represented them as pirates, plagiarizing each other's material in a bitter and protracted rivalry to gain the upper hand in a lucrative business.[2]

One of the first to address the problem of the paired editions was Robert Eitner, who wrote in 1907:

> Although the publishers themselves again and again acquired a printing privilege...it was so little observed that often a pirate edition appeared, even in the same year as the first print, especially if the work itself proved popular.... It is truly comical how one accused the other of theft, for scarcely had the one made a fortunate success, than the other would certainly make a reprint from it.[3]

More recently, Claudio Sartori maintained that Scotto was the principal culprit, and that he and Gardano entered into a price war that lowered the quality of their publications—a claim, incidentally, that I have been unable to substantiate.[4] Samuel Pogue, in his study of Moderne, seems to have accepted Eitner's view, as he refers to the "plagiarizing rivalry that existed between Gardano and Scotto in Venice."[5]

---

[2]These opinions are discussed in Mary S. Lewis, *Antonio Gardano, Venetian Music Printer 1538–1569: A Descriptive Bibliography and Historical Study. Vol. I. 1538–1549* (New York: Garland, 1988), pp. 30–31.

[3]Robert Eitner, *Biographisch-Bibliographisch Quellen-Lexikon der Musiker und Musikgelehrten der christlichen Zeitrechnung bis zur Mitte des neunzehnten Jahrhunderts* (Leipzig: Breitkopf & Härtel, 1898–1904; repr. New York: Musurgia, n.d.), 4:149, cited and translated in Richard Agee, *The Privilege and Venetian Music Printing in the Sixteenth Century* (Ph.D. dissertation, Princeton University, 1982), p. 51.

[4]Claudio Sartori, article "Scotto" in *Die Musik in Geschichte und Gegenwart,* vol. 12 (Kassel: Bärenreiter, 1965), p. 435.

[5]Samuel Pogue, *Jacques Moderne: Lyons Music Printer of the Sixteenth Century* (Geneva: Librairie Droz, 1969), p. 55.

Table 1

Related Pairs 1539–50: Antonio Gardano & Girolamo Scotto

(RISM numbers are given in boldface type.)

1539	Jachet *Liber I Motetti a 5* (Scotto)	**J6**
1540	Jachet *Liber I Motetti a 5* (Gard)	**J7**
1539	Gombert *Motetti a 4 libro primo* (Scotto)	**G2977**
1541[4]	Gombert *Motetti a 4 libro primo* (Scotto)	**G2978**
1541	Gombert *Motetti a 4 libro primo* (Gard)	**G2974**
1539	Willaert *Famosissimi Adriani Willaert,...musica quatuor vocum* (Scotto)	**W1106**
1545	Willaert *Adriani Willaert...musica quatuor vocum* (Gard)	**W1107**
1539	Willaert *Motetti d'Adriano Willaert, Libro II a 4 voci* (Scotto)	**W1108**
1545	Willaert *Adriani Willaert...musica quatuor vocum...liber II* (Gard)	**W1109**
1539	Arcadelt *Terzo libro madrigali* (Scotto)	**A1374**
1541[11]	Arcadelt *Terzo libro madrigali* (Gard)	**A1376**
1539	Jachet *Motetti a 4* (Scotto)	**J9**
1544	Jachet *Motetti a 4* (Scotto)	**J10**
1545	Jachet *Motetti a 4* (Gard)	**J11**
1540[3]	*Quinque missae* (Scotto)	**M3575**
1543[1]	*Quinque missarum* (Scotto)	**M3578**
1547[4]	*Quinque missarum* (Gard)	**M3589**
1540[18]	*Le dotte et eccellente* (Scotto)	
1541[17]	*Le dotte et eccellente* (Gard)	
1540[19]	Veggio *Madrigali a 4* (Scotto)	**V1087**
1545	Veggio *I[o] Lib. madrigali a 4* (Gard)	**V1088**
1540[20]	*Di Verdelot tutti li madrigali del Primo et Secondo Libro* (Scotto)	
1541[18]	*Di Verdelot tutti li madrigali del Primo et Secondo Libro* (Gard)	

Table 1 (*continued*)

1541	Gombert *Motetti libro secondo a 4* (Scotto)	**G2987**
1542	Gombert *Motetti libro secondo a 4* (Gard)	**G2988**
1541	Nola *Canzone villanesche a 4* (Scotto)	
1545	Nola *Canzone villanesche a 4* (Gard)	**N774**
1542²	*Sex missae* (Scotto)	
1547³	*Sex Misse* (Gard)	**G2975**
1542³	*Missae cum 4 v* (Scotto)	
1544³	*Liber IV Missarum quinque* (Gard)	**M3588**
1542	Rore *Primo libro a 5* (Scotto)	**R2479**
1544	Rore *Madrigals a 5* (Scotto)	**R2489**
1544	Rore *Primo libro a 5* (Gard)	**R2480**
1544¹⁷	Rore II Lib. madr a 5 (Gard)	
1542⁹	Morales *Magnificats* (Scotto)	**M3592**
1545	Morales *Magnificats* (Gard)	**M3594**
1543	Lupacchino *Madrigali a 4* [Gard]	**L3050**
1543	Lupacchino *Madrigali a 4* (Scotto)	**L3081**
1543	Reulx *Madrigali a 4* (Scotto)	**R1204**
1543	Reulx *Madrigali a 4* (Gard) ("ristampate & corretti.")	**R1205**
1543²	*Musica quinque vocum* (Scotto)	
1549⁶	*Musica quinque vocum* (Gard)	
1543⁵	*Morales hispani, et multorum exemiae artis virorum musica* (Scotto)	
1546⁹	*Morales hispani, et multorum exemiae artis virorum musica* (Gard)	
1544	Corteccia. *Libro primo madrigali a quatro* (Scotto)	**C4157**
1547	Corteccia. *Libro primo madrigali a quatro* (Gard)	**C4158**
1544¹	*Sex missae* (Gard)	
1544²	*Liber I missarum quinque* (Scotto)	

Table 1 (*continued*)

1544	Morales *Missarum quinque cum 4 voc. lib. II* (Scotto)	**M3584**
1544[5]	Morales *Missarum quinque cum 4 voc. lib. II* (Gard)	**M3585**
1544	*Canzone villanesche...di M. Adriano* (Scotto)	
1545[20]	*Canzone villanesche...di M. Adriano* (Gard)	**W1115**
1548[11]	*Canzon villanesche...di messer Adriano* (Scotto)	**W1116**
[**1548**[11a]]	*Canzon villanesche...di messer Adriano* (Gard)	**W1117**
1546[32]	Rotta. *Intabolatura de lauto* (Gard)	**R2799**
1546[33]	Rotta. *Intabolatura de lauto* (Scotto)	
1548[7]	*Madrigali de la fama a quatro* (Gard)	
1548[8]	*Madrigali de la fama a quatro* (Scotto)	
1548[9]	*Di Cipriano Rore et di altri eccellentissimi musici il terzo libro di madrigali* (Scotto)	
1548[10]	*Musica di Cipriano Rore sopra le stanze del Petrarcha* (Gard)	
1549[4]	*Excellentis. autorum...Fructus* (Scotto)	
1549[5]	*Excellentis. autorum...Fructus* (Gard)	
1549[7]	*Primo libro mot. a 5* (Scotto)	
1549[8]	Rore *Terzo libro mot. a 5* (Gard)	
1549[9a]	*Musica quatuor vocum...moteta* (Gard)	
1549[9]	*Musica quatuor vocum...moteta* (Scotto)	
1549[12]	*Electiones diversorum motetorum distincte quatuor vocibus* (Gard)	
1549[15]	*Di Verdelot elletione de motetti non piu stampate a quatro voce* (Scotto)	
1549[30]	*Lib. terzo de d. autori...a 4 a notte negre* (Scotto)	
1549[31]	*Il vero terzo libro di madr. di div. aut. a note negre* (Gard)	
1549	M. Mathias Fiamengo *La Bataglia taliana* (Gard)	**M1404**
1550	M. Mathias Fiamengo *La Bataglia taliana* (Scotto)	**M1405**

198   Mary S. Lewis

Daniel Heartz was one of the first to suggest an alternative theory.[6] He pointed out that Gardano and Scotto used the same type faces for music and texts in their earliest publications, and suggested that "their sharing of types raises the possibility that the relationship was one of collusion more than competition."[7] Heartz credited Gardano with originating that first, shared type face, thus like Sartori placing Scotto in the role of imitator, though we have no evidence to support the primacy of either printer in the venture.

A serious challenge to Eitner's view was undertaken by Thomas Bridges, who believes that the presence of a dedication by Scotto in a book of duos composed by Ihan Gero and published in 1541 by Gardano, "shows that Scotto not only commissioned Gero to compose the pieces, but also commissioned Gardano to print them," and that "the mere existence of this book, which Scotto and Gardane cooperated to produce, should dispel the notion that the two of them were locked in 'cutthroat' competition."[8] Bridges hypothesizes that "the fact that [Gardane and Scotto] regularly reprinted each other's editions...without incident, suggests at least an informal agreement to tolerate such reprinting."[9]

Richard Agee has pointed out that neither printer "ever accused the other of theft," nor did they ignore "the privileges issued by the Doge and the Venetian Senate."[10] He adds that "the reprinting by Scotto of a work privileged by Gardano or by Gardano of a work [privileged] by Scotto is rare," and concludes that "no bitter rivalry developed" between the two.[11]

Thus arguments have been put forward to support the idea of a fierce rivalry between the two printers based on the reprinting of each other's work, supposed accusations of theft, an unsubstantiated price war, and alleged violation of copyright. Other scholars, arguing for a cooperative arrangement, point to the sharing of the earliest type face, the Gero dedication of 1541, and respect by each for the other's copyrights (privileges).

In support of Agee's claim, none of the titles listed in Table 1 bears notice of a privilege. For whatever reason, Gardano and Scotto did not seek out the copyright protection inherent in a privilege for these works, and thus any

---

[6] Daniel Heartz. *Pierre Attaingnant, Royal Printer of Music: A Historical Study and Bibliographical Catalogue* (Berkeley: Univ. of California Press, 1969), p. 159.

[7] When he speaks here of "sharing of types," Heartz is referring to the use by both printers of type manufactured from the same punches and matrixes, not the sharing of the actual pieces of type.

[8] Bridges, p. 131.

[9] Bridges, p. 132.

[10] Agee, p. 52.

[11] Agee, p. 53.

republishing would have been legal. Thus, since there is no evidence to support violation of copyright, theories suggesting a price war, theft, or claims of piracy and plagiarism lack substantiation.

Evidence from Comparison of Readings

For the first stage of the readings study, I have selected pieces from a variety of pairs, attempting to identify different situations and complexes of circumstances. I have only been able to compare a few pieces from each of the pairs to be discussed, taking soundings, identifying pairs that invite more careful scrutiny. Even so, I have been able to establish a continuum of degrees of relationships between pairs of editions, one that ranges from direct, exact copying to reliance on separate exemplars from different source traditions. The following discussion will present examples of pairs that appear to fall at different points along that continuum.

On the basis of the evidence presented by the readings and to be described below, I have classified the paired editions in Table 2, dividing them into three groups: (1) Those that provide evidence of direct and virtually unaltered copying and which I have designated "twins"; (2) those that reveal evidence of copying with revisions, sometimes suggesting the use of more than one exemplar—the "heirs" of my title; and (3) those whose readings point to two separate transmissions—the "cousins."

The types of evidence that help determine the relationship between a pair of prints are summarized in Table 3. The characteristics of the evidence for the first category are a direct result of the way the printers worked. When making a new edition, a printer seems not surprisingly to have used the earlier edition as copy for the typesetter, entering as many changes as possible in that copy. Thus, we can often see from one edition to the next such telltale marks of direct copying as line endings at the same places in the piece or the reproduction of an error or idiosyncrasy from the earlier edition. Such activity only makes common sense for a printer producing a second or third edition of his own output. However, it raises questions of propriety—at least from our point of view—when two printers are involved. I have placed editions in the first category—direct copying—only if there were few if any editorial changes and copying appeared to be almost mechanical.

The second category—revised copying—presents a more complex picture that includes some of the evidence of direct copying—corresponding line endings, for instance. However, one also encounters such editorial emendations as altered text underlay and changes in accidentals. Even more

Table 2

Selected Pairs by Relationship Category Based on Contents and Chronology

Twins
Same year, same contents.

1548[11]	*Canzon villanesche...di messer Adriano* (Scotto)
[1548[11a]]	*Canzon villanesche...di messer Adriano* (Gard)
1549[9]	*Musica quatuor vocum...moteta.* (Scotto)
1549[9a]	*Musica quatuor vocum...moteta.* (Gard)

Parallel Editions
Same year, part of contents same.

1548[7]	*Madrigali de la fama a quatro* (Gard)
1548[8]	*Madrigali de la fama a quatro* (Scotto)
1548[9]	*Di Cipriano Rore et di altri eccellentissimi musici il terzo libro di madrigali* (Scotto)
1548[10]	*Musica di Cipriano Rore sopra le stanze del Petrarcha* (Gard)
1549[12]	*Electiones diversorum motetorum distincte quatuor vocibus* (Gard)
1549[15]	*Di Verdelot elletione de motetti non piu stampate a quatro voce* (Scotto)

Republished Editions
Different years, all or part of contents same.

1543[5]	*Morales hispani, et multorum exemiae artis virorum musica* (Scotto)
1546[9]	*Morales hispani, et multorum exemiae artis virorum musica* (Gard)
1544	*Canzone villanesche...di M. Adriano* (Scotto)
1545[20]	*Canzone villanesche...di M. Adriano* (Gard)
1540[20]	*Di Verdelot tutti li madrigali del Primo et Secondo Libro* (Scotto)
1541[18]	*Di Verdelot tutti li madrigali del Primo et Secondo Libro* (Gard)

Table 3

Criteria for Determining Relationships Between Pairs

I	**Evidence for direct copying**
	Same line endings
	Reproduction of mistakes or idiosyncracies
	Close readings with only slight variants
II	**Evidence for revised copying and/or more than one source**
	Same line endings
	Reproduction of mistakes or idiosyncracies
	Omission of ligatures
	Improved or altered text underlay
	Differences in accidentals
	New attributions
	Added text
III	**Evidence for separate transmission**
	Significant variants
	New attributions
	New text
	Addition of ligatures
	Compositional variants
	Little correspondence in line endings
	Significant differences in text placement

substantive changes, such as new attributions or added stanzas of text suggest fresh input from a source other than the earlier edition.

Finally, pairs in the third category show evidence—in the form of stemmatically significant variants—of separate transmissions. Such variants could include the addition of ligatures, substitution of one section of music for another, or substantial compositional revisions.

Direct Copying

Direct and unaltered copying of all or part of one edition appears to be rare between Gardano and Scotto. Most instances occur between "twin" editions—those that were published in the same year with identical contents. Occasionally a pair of editions appeared initially as twins (1549[9] and 1549[9a] in Table 2), but more often, one or more earlier editions preceded the twins. For instance, editions of Willaert's *Canzone villanesche* had already appeared in 1544 and 1545 when in 1548 Gardano and Scotto both published editions of the collection (Appendix, group I). These editions are a classic case of "twin" prints, containing the same pieces, in the same order, and with almost identical readings.

Even the wording, typography, and layout of the title pages correspond; however, on Scotto's title page, the *A* of *Canzon* is chipped, while on Gardano's it is undamaged, and of course the printer's marks and impressum differ. In the body of the work, the type faces and initials, as well as the orthography of the text in the signature line differ, but line endings correspond with one exception: in the final piece, Scotto's second staff ends before the two semiminims at the end of Gardano's staff.

Scotto and Gardano use the same page layout, but Scotto has roman numerals at the top of the page, while Gardano uses arabic. Scotto's *TAVOLA* heading is set in small Roman type rather than Gardano's large italics, but Scotto, in accordance with his usual custom, uses the same arabic numerals as Gardano, even though he uses roman numerals in the body of the work.[12] Occasionally, an insignificant spelling variant can be found, but text placement is identical.

The 1548 edition of the *Canzone Villanesche* was either some sort of cooperative edition, or one printer must have directly copied the work of the other. If the latter is true, who did the copying? Possibly the two publishers agreed to share the task of producing the edition; but the popular and lucrative nature of the publication—it went through six editions in all—argues against such cooperation. Cooperation, with shared resources and risk, would be better suited to a publication with less of a guaranteed return on investment than Willaert's songs. Furthermore, duplication of typesetting effort and expense would hardly seem to be a way to reduce financial risk. Finally, a simultaneous venture would probably not have produced the near-photographic similarity found in the two prints, for the chances of two typesetters coming up time after time with the same line lengths and text underlay seems remote. The 1548 editions agree to a considerable extent with Gardano's of 1545 in terms of line endings and text underlay. Either or both typesetters for the 1548 editions could have used that of 1545 as a guide. But major discrepancies in other areas exist between the 1548 and 1545 editions, discrepancies to be discussed below.

---

[12]I would like to thank Jane Bernstein for providing information on Scotto's conventions in the printing of tables of contents.

In 1549, both Gardano and Scotto published editions of a collection of motets whose identical titles commenced *Musica Quatuor Vocum* (Appendix, group II). Both editions contain the same contents in the same order. The majority are new works, but older music, some dating back nearly two decades, fills out the editions. There can be little doubt that in the two 1549 editions of the *Musica quatuor vocum* one printer copied from the other, for line endings correspond regularly, and in several motets there is almost no divergence between the two editions. The few variants primarily involve text underlay, with Gardano's edition placing the text more carefully than Scotto's, separating syllables, especially final ones, and occasionally supplying an additional text repeat. In this case, there was no earlier edition to use as a model, so the correspondence in line endings must indicate copying. Again, there is no evidence for determining which edition served as exemplar, though one might regard Gardano's texting as an improvement over Scotto's. Neither edition bears a privilege, and both claim priority in the title page statement that the works therein are published here for the first time.[13]

Thus we have in the Willaert *Canzone* of 1548 and the *Musica quatuor vocum* of 1549 two sets of twins—editions with the same contents and with similar wording on their title pages, and with identical or extremely close readings pointing to direct copying. One pair represents reprinting by both publishers of editions published a few years before, while many works in the other had not previously appeared in Venice.[14] In neither case was there any violation of copyright nor any attempt to disguise the source for the copying edition.

The presence of variants does not in itself rule out direct copying. For example, in 1540 Scotto assembled what he called "all the madrigals of Verdelot's first and second books for four voices, with the addition of the madrigals of the same author not printed before. Added are still other madrigals newly composed by Messer Adriano, and by other excellent musicians" (Appendix, group III). Scotto's title points to the fact that much of this music was not new; it had in fact been published in the 1530s in Venice and Rome. In the following year, Gardano printed a new edition of this enormous collection of sixty-eight madrigals, changing only one piece. (See 1541[18] in Appendix, group III.) However, Gardano reordered the music

---

[13] "...nunc primum soliciti cura in lucem producta."

[14] For concordances, see Lewis, *Antonio Gardano*, pp. 659–61.

completely, and noted on the title page that he had "emended many errors." (Ex. 1 shows one of these corrections.)

Example 1. C. Festa, *Amanti il servir*

a. Scotto's version from 1540[20], bassus, No. XXXX, fourth staff

b. Gardano's version from 1541[18], p. 8, bassus, fourth staff

In his title, Gardano was careful not to claim novelty for the madrigals by Verdelot that Scotto had added, but he did retain Scotto's phrase describing Willaert's madrigals as newly composed. His edition was apparently based on Scotto's, for line endings frequently correspond, and both omit a repeat of the last phrase of *Madonna qual certezza* that is present in the subsequent editions. Besides an occasional alteration of a pitch, Gardano used minor color more than Scotto did. In one madrigal, *Passer mai solitario*, Gardano changed Scotto's mistaken O time signature to a ¢. Wherever Scotto's edition used a ligature, Gardano substituted two semibreves, for until 1545 he had no ligatures in his fonts. In another instance he changed Scotto's white breve to a blackened one (Ex. 2).

Example 2. Willaert, *Grat'e benigna*

a. Scotto's version of 1540[20], No. XXXIII, bassus, third staff

b. Gardano's version from 1541[18], p. 39, bassus, third staff

Overall, then, Gardano's editorial changes are minor, and his claim to have corrected many errors in Scotto's work seems inflated. However, his assertion would have suggested to the public that Scotto's edition was inaccurate, a move not calculated to endear him to his colleague. And yet, Gardano's edition appeared in the same year as the Gero duos he published with Scotto's dedication, a circumstance Bridges has pointed to as an indication of friendship and cooperation between the two printers.[15]

Revised Copying

While the existence of copying, the direction of copying and the source of variants are clear in the Verdelot editions, the situation becomes increasingly murky when we turn to two pairs of editions that present evidence of copying, but also signs of changes based either on substantial editorial intervention or information gleaned from a separate source tradition.

Such a problem pair involves a collection of motets that Scotto published in 1543, and that has proven particularly vexing because of confusion surrounding the attributions—or lack of attributions—for its contents (Appendix, group IV). The title given in the Appendix describes an edition containing motets by Morales and many others, but those others are never named, as no ascriptions are given within the body of the work. Three years later, Gardano published an edition containing sixteen of these motets, plus four new ones. Gardano's title is strikingly similar to Scotto's, but shorter, and he omits Scotto's claim that the works are newly published. The resemblance of the two titles suggests that Gardano's edition was based at least in part on Scotto's. Like Scotto, Gardano gave no attributions.

Scotto could have omitted the attributions for a number of reasons. Perhaps he simply did not know the names of the composers. Or he may have wanted to use Morales's name to boost sales, but preferred to obscure the fact that few works in the edition were by the great Spanish composer. Gardano, who must have used Scotto's collection as one source in compiling his own, seems either to have chosen to follow Scotto's lead, or to have had no further information on the authorship of the music.

However, in putting together a new edition Gardano was not content simply to reproduce Scotto's version. His departures from Scotto's readings are so substantial they suggest either detailed re-editing or the incorporation of material from a different source. Gardano corrected a few pitches, in the manner of Example 3.

---

[15]Bridges, p. 131.

Example 3. [anon], *Cumque audissent* (*II^a pars* of *Ingrediente*)

a. Scotto's edition (1543[5]), bassus, f. 16, first staff

b. Gardano's edition (1546[9]), bassus, p. XXIII, first staff

Gardano also reworked Scotto's text placement extensively. His changes include realigning syllables, sometimes even changing which phrase of text is assigned to a particular musical phrase. (For instance, Ex. 4: Scotto's would appear to be the better reading, as it repeats the previous text phrase, while Gardano's version begins with the second word of the next phrase, "pueri hebreorum.")

Example 4. [anon], *Ingrediente*

a. Scotto's edition (1543[5]), tenor, f. 15, second staff

b. Gardano's edition (1546[9]), tenor, p. XXII, second staff

Gardano's version also includes more repetitions of words and phrases (see Ex. 5), although sometimes the exact reverse is true (Ex. 6).

Example 5. [anon], *Paulus apostolus*

a. Scotto's edition (1543[5]), altus, f. 21, staves 1–3

b. Gardano's edition (1546[9]), altus, p. XXX, staves 1–3

Example 6. [Morales]. *Sancta Maria succurre miseris*

a. Scotto's edition (1543[5]), tenor, f. 6ᵛ, staves 1–2

b. Gardano's edition (1546[9]), altus, p. XIIII

Gardano uses more ligatures than Scotto, as we can see in Example 7,

Example 7. [anon], *Cumque audissent*

a. Scotto's edition (1543[5]), tenor, f. 16, staves 3–4

b. Gardano's edition (1546[9]), tenor, p. XXIII, staves 3–4

but occasionally omits a ligature where one is found in Scotto's version, or breaks a ligature into two notes, to accommodate a differently aligned text (Ex. 8).

Example 8. [anon], *Ingrediente*

a. Scotto's edition (1543[5]), tenor, f. 15[v], staff 6

b. Gardano's edition (1546[9]), tenor, p. XXII, staff 6

The addition of ligatures is suggestive of a separate source, or at least of substantial re-editing. In a separate study, I have maintained that printers would seldom have added ligatures while copying from another edition that lacked them.[16] Much more editorial intervention is needed to add ligatures than for the shuffling about of text.

In another piece in this collection, *Inter natos mulierum*, three of the four voice parts in the two editions are exchanged. Thus, Scotto's cantus is marked tenor in Gardano's edition, Scotto's altus becomes Gardano's superius, and Scotto's tenor becomes Gardano's altus. In Gardano's altus, the clef is C4, not C3 as in Scotto's edition, but the notes remain in the same places on the staves, thus yielding different pitches. I have suggested elsewhere that this sort of confusion in assignment of voice part indications may point to reliance at some stage on an exemplar with each voice of each piece written on a separate sheet, and that this sort of confusion may indicate two different transmissions.[17] The fact that the Scotto edition is itself in partbooks may in fact be the cause of the mix-up. But the voice indications are clearly marked on each page of Scotto's edition. Again, Gardano may have used more than one source for these pieces. None of the works from these two editions that I compared have line endings that correspond, but it seems inconceivable that Gardano did not make some use of Scotto's earlier edition in preparing his own. This pair warrants further study, for it poses as many questions as it answers.

The 1548 editions of Willaert's *Canzone villanesche* discussed earlier were not the first to appear. Most of these pieces had been published three years before by Gardano in an edition with somewhat different contents (see Appendix, group I). Gardano's, in turn, was a new edition of a Scotto print of 1544 that survives only as a fragment, and whose exact contents are only partially known.[18] The 1548 editions omit some pieces from 1545, add two new ones, and reassign one, changing the order slightly. We cannot tell who decided on the contents and order of the 1548 editions, nor why both Gardano's and Scotto's editions contained the same revisions.

But while the two 1548 editions were almost identical, significant variants are found between the 1544 and 1545 editions. In the single altus gathering surviving from 1544 (see Appendix, group I), Scotto gave no attributions; these were supplied by Gardano in 1545. Likewise, Scotto only provided the first stanzas of strophic pieces in 1544, but Gardano printed the subsequent stanzas the following year. Either Gardano used a source other than Scotto's, one with attributions and complete texts, or he used material that had been available but that Scotto had chosen not to print. There are a

---

[16]Mary S. Lewis, "Rore's Setting of Petrarch's 'Vergine bella,'" *Journal of Musicology* 4 (1985–86): 382.

[17]Lewis, "Vergine bella," pp. 365–409.

[18]I would like to thank Jane Bernstein for calling this edition to my attention.

few pitch differences between the two editions' versions of Willaert's *Cingari simo venite a giocare* (Ex. 9).

Example 9. Willaert, *Cingari simo*

a. Scotto's version of 1544, altus, f. 2ᵛ, staves 4–5

b. Gardano's version (1545[26]), altus, p. 4, staff 3

The two editions vary in their indication of triple meter, with Scotto using $\phi\frac{3}{2}$, while Gardano uses ¢3. In one madrigal, *A quand'a quand'havea*, Gardano exchanged Scotto's altus and tenor parts, and his order was retained in subsequent editions. Gardano's 1545 edition, then, is a complete revision of the material in Scotto's 1544 version, with alternative readings drawn from at least one other source. The 1548 editions retain the revisions in Gardano's 1545 books.

Thus, in the so-called Morales motets and the early editions of Willaert's *Canzone villanesche*, we see some evidence and opportunity for copying, in these cases by Gardano, but not without considerable editorial intervention. In several instances, material from another transmission may have been involved in the re-editing.

Separate Transmissions

Finally, we will look now at three pairs in which evidence from the readings makes copying less likely. One example of such a situation is a pair of editions, both published in the same year, whose contents parallel, but do not exactly duplicate, each other. In 1548 both Scotto and Gardano published collections entitled *Madrigali de la fama* that are so similar in their contents that they might almost be twins (Appendix, group V). Scotto probably originated the project, for one of the firm's printer's marks, used on the title page of the *Fama* collection, presents Fame, personified as a winged female figure blowing a horn and holding a tablet with the initials O.S.M. (for Ottavianus Scotus Modoetiensis.) It was not unusual to base a title on a printer's mark or other emblem appearing on the title page. Gardano's *Mottetti del Frutto*, Moderne's *Motteti del fiore*, Buglhat's *Motetti de la Simia*, and Scotto's *Madrigali del Labarinto* all feature on their title pages a woodcut with a figure corresponding to the title—a bowl of fruit, a bunch of flowers, a monkey, or a labyrinth. Gardano's title to his parallel edition of Scotto's *Fama* collection retains the reference to La Fama, but otherwise differs considerably from Scotto's. Both titles, however, claim their music is newly printed and corrected with diligence. Only Scotto's title mentions that the madrigals are newly composed, but Gardano names their three composers—Francesco Manara, Francesco Viola, and Cipriano Rore. Gardano prints the same madrigals as Scotto, but regroups them by composer, and adds one more by Rore. The rearrangement cannot be to disguise piracy, for Gardano's title identifies his edition with Scotto's. Perhaps Gardano may have been attempting to cash in on the success of a popular edition. The revised ordering and new madrigal may represent Gardano's attempt to improve on Scotto's work or to market it more effectively.

The readings from this pair are contradictory. Line endings rarely correspond, and variants consist almost exclusively of small differences in text underlay. Gardano's edition is often and uncharacteristically less careful about separating the final syllable of a word and placing it under the last note of a phrase. On the other hand, he unexpectedly uses more ligatures. Had Gardano done a thorough editorial reworking of the *Fama* material, we would expect the new ligatures to have been accompanied by more precise underlay than is found in his edition. I suspect that the two printers obtained separate copies of the same repertory and each published it with his own order, text underlay, and ligatures, but that Scotto was first on the market with his edition, and Gardano made the best of the situation by invoking Scotto's title and symbol. He could have done this quite late in the printing process, since the first gathering with the title page was usually the last to be printed.

A different and more complex example involves a pair of parallel editions with a core repertory in common that both Gardano and Scotto published in 1548 as Rore's Third Book of Madrigals (Appendix, group VI). Elsewhere, I have shown that the core repertory of seventeen pieces appearing in both books, all written by Rore and his circle, was probably transmitted to Gardano and Scotto by two different routes, although both copies stemmed from the same exemplar.[19] The titles indicate Scotto's edition was probably published first, for only he claims the madrigals to be new. But his edition also has several unique readings, both in the labeling of voice parts,

---

[19]Lewis, "Vergine bella," pp. 397–406.

and in the interpretation of presumed text repeat signs from some earlier source.[20] The nature of these variants, and the evidence of the titles, rules out Gardano's edition as Scotto's source. Gardano's text underlay disagrees with Scotto's, particularly in repeated phrases, and he again includes ligatures where Scotto has none. In this case, we can see that Gardano's ligatures stem, not from editorial decisions made in his shop, but from a different source than Scotto's, for the ligatures in Gardano's edition agree exactly with those found in a Ferrarese-Venetian manuscript believed to be close to Rore, Wolfenbüttel 293.[21] I have speculated that Scotto's versions of the core repertory were transmitted to him by Paulo Vergelli, a Paduan musician who was active in Venice from at least 1542, who signed the dedication for the edition, while Gardano obtained his exemplars either from the composer Perissone Cambio, the signer of a dedication in some copies of Gardano's edition, or even from Rore himself.[22] Thus, what on first glance appears to be a case of plagiarism is, in fact, a case of parallel publication from different source transmissions.

A third pair of parallel editions with a central repertory in common is that published in 1549 by Scotto and Gardano as "a selection of motets for four voices, newly printed, by Verdelot and others" (Appendix, group VII). Its core repertory consists of twelve works, eleven by composers of an earlier generation—Verdelot and Silva—with just one piece by a contemporary Venetian, Jachet Berchem. The remainder of Gardano's edition is also heavily weighted towards an older generation—Manchicourt, M. Ihan, Claudin, Lupus, and still more Verdelot—and some of the motets found here were initially published by French printers. Only Ihan Gero is from the ranks of those contemporary composers published most often by Gardano and Scotto. The works Scotto includes along with the core repertory are by similar composers, with one work by Willaert representing the modern Venetian school. In his title, Scotto claims that the Verdelot motets were newly printed, and that the other motets were newly composed. It indeed appears that only two of the Verdelot motets that Scotto published, *Victime paschali laudes* and *Gaudeamus omnes in domino* had in faāt been printed before (by Attaingnant). The others can be found in earlier manuscripts, especially the Newberry-Oscott Partbooks of 1528. Gardano's repertory is

---

[20]For examples of these differing interpretations, see Lewis, "Vergine bella," pp. 381–82. For a discussion of differences in voice-part labeling, see p. 388.

[21]Wolfenbüttel, Herzog August Bibliothek, Codex Guelf 293 Musica Handschr. For more information on this manuscript and its relationship to Gardano's edition, see Lewis, "Vergine bella," pp. 366–67, 371–77, 381–91, 401–403.

[22]Lewis, "Vergine bella," pp. 404–405.

more varied in its background, ranging from music originally published by Attaingnant in the 1530s to works such as Gero's *Deus qui sedes super thronum* that have no earlier concordances.

Much more variance is found between the two editions of the selected motets than in most other paired prints. Three of the motets are transposed, being in high clefs in one edition, low in the other. One of these, the anonymous *Salve regina* that opens Gardano's collection, is attributed to Verdelot in Scotto's edition. The piece appears with the same ascription and clefs as Scotto's in the manuscript Bergamo 1208D, which Jeppesen dated around 1545.[23] Thus, Gardano's edition appears to belong to a separate transmission. Similarly, the two other transposed works, both by Verdelot, may have reached Scotto and Gardano by different routes. *Hesterna die dominus* is separated from its *secunda pars* in Scotto's edition, and only the *prima pars* is transposed down a fourth. Colin Slim has pointed out that the transposition in Scotto's edition makes no sense musically, and speculates that "perhaps by transposing *Hesterna die* and by substituting a new second part Scotto was seeking to disguise the similarity of his edition to that of his rival, Gardane."[24] But if that had been Scotto's aim, he would have started with the title page, which, like the *Madrigali de la Fama*, emphasizes rather than diminishes the relationship between the two prints. Since no other source, including those closest to Verdelot, gives *Hesterna die* in low clefs, we must assume that Scotto either received a corrupt version or revised the motet for reasons of his own. Scotto's version departs from Gardano's in numerous other ways. First of all, it has an ornamented cadence that also occurs in the Newberry-Oscott partbooks and thus was unlikely to have been an invention of Scotto or his editor. Furthermore, Scotto includes several accidentals not in Gardano's edition or the Newberry-Oscott partbooks, and finally, Scotto's version differs substantially in its application of text repetition. Scotto was probably working from a separate source, and thus neither he nor Gardano copied *Hesterna die* from the other.

Gaudeamus omnes, the other transposed piece, is in low clefs in Gardano's edition. Slim suggests Gardano may have considered the tessitura of the original version, also found in the Newberry-Oscott partbooks and other sources, to be too high, and transposed it for practical reasons. Scotto's edition again has ornamented cadences but this time they are not replicated

---

[23]Knud Jeppesen, "A Forgotten Master of the Early Sixteenth Century: Gaspar de Albertis." *Musical Quarterly* 44 (1958): 311–28.

[24]H. Colin Slim, *A Gift of Madrigals and Motets* (Chicago: University of Chicago Press, 1972), p. 130.

in the Newberry-Oscott partbooks or any other source. Several other pitch readings in Scotto's version are unique (Exx. 10 and 11).

Example 10. Verdelot. *Gaudeamus omnes*

a. Scotto's edition (1549[15]), cantus, No. III, staff 4

b. Gardano's edition (1549[12]), cantus, p. 7, staff 4

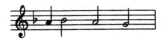

Example 11. Verdelot. *Gaudeamus omnes*

a. Scotto's edition (1549[15]), tenor, p. III, staff 5

b. Gardano's edition (1549[12]), tenor, p. 7, staff 5

Scotto's edition is also alone in omitting the few ligatures in the piece. Therefore, it is unlikely that either printer copied this piece from the other.

The readings of Verdelot's *Ad dominum cum tribularer* reveal a similar situation. Scotto's edition has one unique musical reading (Ex. 12). As in *Gaudeamus omnes* it lacks the ligatures of the other sources, and frequently omits text repeats.

None of the motets in this pair of editions correspond significantly in line endings. Thus, if one of the printers did copy from the other, the revision was much more intense than in other pairs that demonstrate more secure evidence for copying. The readings of the pieces compared so far suggest separate source traditions for much of the repertory in this print, but it is difficult to imagine how Gardano and Scotto might have acquired separate

Example 12. Verdelot. *Ad dominum cum tribularer*

a. Scotto's edition (1549[15]), altus, No. VIII, staff 2

clamavi

b. Gardano's edition (1549[12]), altus, p. 13, staff 2

cla - - - mavi

sources of this repertory—older, not primarily local, and somewhat out of fashion. We can accept dual transmission of new music by local composers such as we have seen in Rore's third madrigal book, but it is harder to explain for the selected motets of 1549, unless the printers had acquired the diverging sources earlier, when most of the music was new.

If we return now to Table 2, we can see that there is no correlation between the date of publication and point on the relationship continuum, and therefore no evidence from the readings of any consistent change in the relationship of the two printers over these years.

Even at this stage of investigation, evidence emerges that the two printers did copy each other's editions at times; however, that copying was not as frequent nor usually as mechanical as a simple comparison of tables of contents might suggest. In fact, a number of publications that first appear to have involved copying or re-editing actually represent separate transmissions of the same repertory.

How, then, does the evidence of the readings contribute to our understanding of the relationship between the two printers and the significance of the relationship for the history of music publishing?

Virtually every known paired edition belongs to a repertory whose popularity is attested by its appearance in numerous sources. In order to maintain a thriving business, the publishers had first of all to acquire the music from this repertory, a process that involved both the publishers and their agents.[25] The readings in the paired editions suggest that from time to time each publisher's agents sent him separate copies of the latest works of such composers

---

[25]See Jane Bernstein, "Girolamo Scotto and the Venetian Music Trade," in *Atti del XIV Congresso della Società Internazionale di Musicologia: Trasmissione e recezione delle forme di cultura musicale* (Torino: EDT, 1990), 1:295–305.

as Jachet, Rore, or Morales, and when these repertories were insufficient to fill an entire volume, the printers added whatever individual works they could acquire. The results of such a process were at least some of those editions we have called "cousins." If one or the other printer acquired and published without privilege a significant group of new works, and the other's supplier was slow in acquiring that music, the second printer might then prepare his own edition, using his rival's work as a starting point. The readings again show that usually one was reluctant to simply reproduce the other's version, but revised and rearranged it, at times employing his own sources as they became available. The results are the revised copies, or "heirs." Finally, when a particular volume proved unusually popular, and the market appeared ready to absorb more copies than the original first or even second editions had provided, the printers seemed more willing simply to copy each other, in order to produce twin prints like the 1548 Willaert *Canzone*. Usually, one of the twins represented a revision of an earlier edition.

As Agee has pointed out, evidence that Gardano and Scotto violated each other's copyright or complained about pirating or other illegal activities is rare. We have seen that none of the pairs examined here involved privileged material. Their references to each other were usually indirect, as claims to have corrected and emended each other's editions, a claim that graced almost every title page of the time. They seem to have identified a repertory with potential for commercial success, and to have taken advantage of opportunities to publish as much of that repertory as possible without encroaching on each other's legal rights. They may have conferred (colluded seems far too dramatic a word).

All this activity was partly in response to public demand for the music of certain composers and for certain genres. At the same time, the appearance of multiple editions of certain works made them more available, and undoubtedly reinforced the popularity and dispersion of particular repertories. While both satisfying and creating the public's demand for new music, Gardano and Scotto seem neither to have colluded, nor to have been fiercely competitive, but rather to have coexisted, and to have managed between them to create a virtual monopoly on music printing in Italy, one whose outlines will become clearer as we continue to study their publications.

Twins, Cousins, and Heirs 217

Appendix
Pairs: Complete Titles and Contents

I

1544

Canzone villanesche alla napolitana di M. Adriano Wigliaret a quatro voci, con alcuni Madrigali da lui nuovamente composti & diligentemente corretti, con la Canzona di Ruzante. Con la giunta di alcune altre Canzone Villanesche alla Napolitana a Quatro Voci, composte da M. Francesco Corteccia non piu viste ne stampate, nuovamente poste in luce. Venetiis Apud Hieronymum Scotum. M.D.XLIIII.

2	Madonna io non lo so
2ᵛ	Vecchie retrose non valete
3	Madonna mia famme
3ᵛ	Cingari simo venit'a giocare
4	A quand'a quand'havea
4ᵛ	Un giorno mi prego una vedovella

[remaining contents unknown]

1545[20]

Canzone Villanesche alla napolitana di M. Adriano Wigliaret a quatro voci con la Canzona di Ruzante. Con la gionta di alcune altre canzone villanesche alla napolitana di Francesco silvestrino ditto chechin et di francesco corteccia novamente stampate con le soe stanze. Primo libro a quatro voci. Venetijs Apud Antonium Gardane. M.D.XXXXV.

(Page numbers in the right hand column refer to the Scotto edition of 1548 [1548[11]].)

I	Adriano	Sempre mi ride	1
II	Adriano	O dolce vita mia	5
III	Adriano	Madonn'io non lo so	3
IIII	Adriano	Cingari simo	4
V	Adriano	Vecchie letrose non valete	7
VI	Adriano	Madonna mia famme	6
VII	Fran. silvestrino	Se mille volte	
VIII	Fran. silvestrino	O dio se vede chiaro	9
IX	Adriano	Un giorno mi prego	8
X	Fran. silvestrino	Si come bella sei	
XI	Adriano	A quand'a quand'havea	10
XII	Adriano	O bene mio fa	11
XIII	Fran. Corteccia	Madonn'io t'haggi'amato	
XIII	[anon]	Madonna mia io son un poverello	
XIIII	Adriano	Sospiri miei d'oime	13
XV	Fran. Corteccia	Le vecchie per invidia	14

1548[11]

Canzon villanesche alla napolitana di messer Adriano a quattro voci con la canzon di Ruzante. Libro primo. (Venice: G. Scotto. 1548)

Contents as above, omitting VII, X, XIII (both), and adding:

2	Adriano	Zoia zentil che per secreta
12	Piersson	Buccucia dolce
14	Adriano	Le vecchie per invidia [new attribution]

1548[11a]

Canzon villanesche alla napolitana di messer Adriano a quatro voci con la Canzon di Ruzante. Libro primo. In Venetia Appresso di Antonio Gardane. 1548.

Contents same as 1548[11].

Signature lines
1548[11] Primo Libro di canzone alla Napolitana di Messer Adriano a quatro
1548[11a] Primo Libro di canzone alla napolitana di M. Adriano a 4

* * * * *

II

1549[9]

Musica quatuor vocum que materna lingua moteta vocantur ab optimis & varijs authoribus elaborata, paribus vocibus decantanda nunc primum soliciti cura in lucem producta. Cum quatuor vocibus. Venetijs Apud Antonium Gardane. 1549.

Contents: Motets by Ihan Gero (6), N. Gombert, Consilium (2), Iachet, Adriano (2), D. Finot (3), Morales, Yvo, Verdelot, anon (2)

1549[9a]

Musica quatuor vocum, que materna lingua moteta vocantur ab optimis & varijs authoribus elaborata, paribus vocibus decantanda, nunc primum soliciti cura, in lucem producta. Venice, G. Scotto, 1549.

Same contents in same order as in Gardano's edition (1549[9]).

* * * * *

III

1540[20]

Di Verdelotto tutti li madrigali del Primo, et Secondo Libro a quatro voci, con la gionta de i madigali del medesmo auttore, non piu stampati. Aggiontovi anchora altri madrigali novamente composti da messer Adriano, et da altri eccellentissimi musici, come appare ne la seguente tavola. Apud Hieronymum Scotum. 1540.

1541[18]

Di Verdelot tutti li Madrigali del Primo et Secondo Libro, a quatro voci: novamente ristampati, et da molti errori emendati. Con la gionta de i madrigali del medesmo auttore. Aggiontovi anchora altri madrigali novamente composti da Messer Adriano, et da altri eccellentissimi musici. MDXXXXI Excudebat Venetiis, apud Antonium Gardane.

>Same contents as 1540[20], but in totally different order. One piece from the 1540 edition, Arcadelt's *Amor, quando più lieta*, is omitted in 1541[18], and a piece by Maistre Jan, *Deh perche si veloce passo*, is included instead.

*****

IV

1543[5]

Moralis hispani, et multorum eximiae artis virorum musica cum vocibus quatuor, vulgo motecta cognominata: cuius magna pars paribus vocibus cantanda est: reliqua vero plena voce apta est decantari, hactenus non typijs excussa, nunc autem in lucem prodit. [Venice: G. Scotto, 1543]

1546[9]

Moralis hispani et multorum eximiae artis virorum musica cum vocibus quatuor vulgo motecta cognominata quatuor vocum. Venetijs Apud Antonium Gardane. M.D.XXXXVI.

>Contents of 1543[5] (No attributions are given.)
>(Pieces in italics also appear in 1546[9]. The numbers in the right-hand column are the locations of the pieces in that edition.)

2	Candida virginitas	
	II Que meruit dominum	
2ᵛ	Regina coeli letare	
3	*Clementissime Christe confessor*	IIII
	II Sancte pater Egidi	V

4	*Inter natos mulierum*	XXVIII
4ᵛ	*II Fuit homo missus a deo*	XXIX
5	Regina coeli letare	
5ᵛ	*In illo tempore dixit Iesus discipulis suis*	VI
6	*II Dicebant ergo*	VII
6ᵛ	*Sancta Maria succurre miseris*	XIIII
7ᵛ	*Ave domine Iesu Christe...lumen coeli*	I
8	*II Ave domine Iesu Christe...splendo*	II
8ᵛ	*III Ave domine Iesu Christe...vita*	III
9	*Ad dominum cum tribularer*	XXVI
10	Adest dies celebris	
11	O quam veneranda es virgo Maria	
11ᵛ	Cum inducerent puerum Iesum	
12	O Beatum pontificem Martinum	
13	*Inclina domine aurem tuam*	XV
13ᵛ	*II Deduc me domine*	XVI
14	*III Domine deus miserator*	XVII
14ᵛ	*Immutemur habitu*	X
15	*II Iusta vestibulum et altare*	XI
15ᵛ	*Ingrediente domino*	XXII
16	*II Cunque audissent quod Iesus*	XXIII
16ᵛ	*Martinus abrahe*	VIII
17	In tua pacientia	
17ᵛ	*In illo tempore stabat autem*	XXXV
18	*Miserere nostri deus omnium*	XII
18ᵛ	*II Innova signa & immuta*	XIII
19	Cantate domino canticum novum	
19ᵛ	II Cantate ei & psallite	
20ᵛ	*Signum crucis*	IX
	II Hec arbor	IX
21	*Paulus apostolus spirans*	XXX
21ᵛ	*II Quis es domine. Ego sum Iesus*	XXXI
22	*Ecce amica mea, colomba mea*	XXXIII
22ᵛ	*II Flores apparuerunt in terra*	XXXIIII
23	*In illo tempore...nolite timere*	XXXII

1546[9] includes the following motets that are not in 1543[5]:

XVIII	Victime paschali laudes
XIX	II Surrexit Christus spes nostra
XX	Pastore dicite quid nam vidistis
XXI	II Infantem vidimus
XXIIII	Hec est vera fraternitas
XXV	II Ecce quam bonum
XXXVI	Sancta et immaculata virginitas
XXXVII	II Benedicta tu in mulieribus

There are no attributions in 1546[9].

* * * * *

V

1548[8]

Madrigali de la fama a quatro voce composti novamente da diversi eccellentissimi musici con iudicio raccolti et con diligentia stampati. Fora del solito modo corretti, come a ciascuno facendone prova sara palese. Venetijs MDXLVIII Apresso Hieronimo Scotto.

(The numbers to the right indicate the location of the piece in Gardano's edition.)

I	Francesco Viola	Cibo dolce & soave	IX
		II Et com'interso chiaro	IX
II	Francesco Manari	Lasso mi trova Amore	XXV
III	Francesco Viola	Come poss'io scoprir	X
IIII	Cipriano Rore	La bella nett'ignuda	I
V	Cipriano Rore	La giustitia immortale	II
VI	Francesco Manari	Pien d'un vago pensier	XXIIII
VI		II Ben s'io non erro	XXV
VII	Francesco Viola	Altro che lagrimar	XI
VIII	Cipriano Rore	Com'havran fin le doloroso	V
IX	Francesco Manari	Tal'hor m'assal'in mezz'a	XXVII
X	Francesco Viola	Lasso s'io tremo	VII
XI	Cipriano Rore	Anchor che co'l partire	III
XII	Francesco Viola	A quante vol t'avien	VIII
XIII	Francesco Viola	In picciol tempo	XX
XIIII	Francesco Viola	Felice chi di spensa	XXI
XV	Francesco Manari	Un si nuovo de sio	XXXIIII
XVI	Francesco Viola	Occhi sopr'al mortal	XXII
XVII	Francesco Viola	Chi non conosce Amore	XVI
XVIII	Francesco Manari	Amor dentr'al mio cor	XXVIIII
XIX	Francesco Viola	Pensai ch'ad ambi'havesse	XI
XX	Francesco Manari	Il fiero passo ove	XXVIII
XXI	Francesco Viola	Altri con lieti suoni	XVII
XXII	Francesco Viola	Si vaga pastorel	XVIII
XXIII	Francesco Viola	Vivo sol di speranza	XIIII
XXIIII	Cipriano Rore	Chi con eterna legge	VI
XXV	Francesco Viola	Poi che nostro server	XII
XXVI	Francesco Viola	Deh perche non credete	XIII
		II Se da vostr'occhi	XIII
XXVII	Francesco Viola	Siepi che'l bel giardin	XV
		II Voi provedete Amore	XV
XXVIII	Francesco Manari	Satiati Amor	XXIII
XXIX	Francesco Viola	La verginella e simil'a	XVIIII
XXX	Cipriano Rore	Linconstantia che sec'han	IIII
XXXI	Francesco Manari	Dolc'amoros'ardore	XXXII
XXXII	Francesco Manari	Amor scorta mi	XXX
XXXIII	Francesco Viola	Mirando vostr'angeli	XXIII
XXXIIII	Francesco Manari	Tal guida fummi'l giovi	XXXIII
XXXV		II Ma perch'ogn'hor	XXXIII
XXXVI	Francesco Manari	O che liev'e ingannar	XXVII

1548[7]

Madrigali de la fama a quatro voci composti da l'infrascritti Autori, Nouamente con diligentia stampati & corretti Cypriano De Rore, Francesco Da la Viola, Francesco Manara. In Venetia Appresso di Antonio Gardane. D.M.XLVIII [sic].

>Gardano rearranged the contents to group them by author, and added one more madrigal by Rore, *Quel foco che tanti anni,* on p. V.

*****

VI

1548[9]

Di Cipriano Rore et di altri eccellentissimi musici il terzo libro di madrigali a cinque voce novamente da lui composti et non piu messi in luce. Con diligentia stampati. Musica nova & rara come a quelli che la canteranno & udiranno sara palese. Venetiis, Apresso Hieronimo Scotto. MDXLVIII.

1548[10]

Musica di Cipriano Rore sopra le stanze del Petrarcha in laude della Madonna, Et altri Madrigali a cinque voci, Con cinque Madrigali di due parte l'uno del medesmo autore bellissimi non piu veduti. Insieme quatro Madrigali nuovi a Cinque di Messer Adriano. Libro Terzo. In Venetia Apresso di Antonio Gardane. M.D.XLVIII.

>(In the list of contents, numbers to the left represent locations in Scotto's edition, those to the right, in Gardano's. Those pieces appearing in both editions are given in italics.)

3-8	*Rore*	*Vergine bella 1-6*	*1-6*
9	*Rore*	*Lasso che mal*	*7*
10	*Rore*	*S'honest'amor*	*8*
11	Perissone	Amor m'ha posto	
12	*Rore*	*Quando fra l'altre*	*12*
13	Donato	S'una fed'amorosa	
14	*Willaert*	*Amor da che*	*20*
15	Willaert	Dove sei tu	
16	*Rore*	*Quel vag'impallidir*	*10*
17	*Rore*	*Qual donn'attend'a*	*12*
18	Martinengo	Quelle fiamme	
19	*Willaert*	*Mentr'al bel*	*26*
20	Zarlino	Lauro gentile	
21	*Willaert*	*Se la gratia divina*	*23*
22	Martinengo	Poi ch'io vi veggio	
23	*Rore*	*Se voi potesti*	*16*
24	*Willaert*	*Ne l'amare & fredd'onde*	*24*
25	*Rore*	*Si travagliat'el folle*	*14*

Gardano added the following madrigals to his edition:

22	Rore	Pommi ove'l sol
29	Rore	Quand'io veggio
30	Rore	L'augel sacro
32	Rore	Ite rime
34	Rore	S'amor la viva
36	Rore	Scarco di doglia

* * * * *

VII

1549[12]

Electiones diversorum motetorum distincte quatuor vocibus, nunc primum in lucem misse Auctore excellenti musico Verdeloto Et quorundam musicantium aliorum meditationes musices dulcissime, summa cum diligentia excusse, ad satisfactionem canentium. Cum quatuor vocibus. Venetijs Apud Antonium Gardane. 1549

1549[15]

Di Verdelot elletione me motetti non piu stampati a quatro voce di Verdelotto et di altri diuersi eccelentissimi autori nouamente fatta et con somma diligentia corretissimi posti in luce Libro primo. Venetiis Apud Hieronymum Scottum. DM XLIX [sic].

The core repertory shared by these two editions follows. The first page number and attribution are Gardano's, the second Scotto's. Motets transposed between one edition and the other are indicated by an *.

	Gardano	Scotto
Salve regina*	1, [anon]	1, Verdelot
II Eia ergo advocata	2	II
Hesterna die dominus*	3, Verdelot	XV, Verdelot
II Heri enim rex noster	4	XVI
Gaudeamus omnes in domino*	7, [anon]	III, Verdelot
Ad dominum cum tribularer	13, Verdelot	VIII, Verdelot
II Heu mihi domine	14	IX
Contristamur domine	24, Adrea de Silva	XIX, Andrea de Silva
Sit vox et iubilatio nostra	25, Andreas de Silva	XX, Andrea de Silva
Victime paschali laudes	27, Verdelot	IIII, Verdelot
II Sepulchrum christi	28	V
O quam gloriosum	29, Andreas de Silva	XXX, Andrea de Silva
II Sancti et iusti	30	XXXI
Gaude Maria virgo	31, Verdelot	VI, Verdelot
II Gabrielem Archangelum	32	VII
Verba mea aurebus	33, Andreas de Silva	XVII, Andrea de Silva
II Odisti omnes	34	XVIII
Gaudete omnes	35, Verdelot	XI, Verdelot
Unica lux venetum	38, Iachet Berchem	XXI, Iachet Berchem

Gardano's edition also includes the following works:

5	[anon]	Recordare domine testamenti
6		II Quiescat domine ira tua
8	Verdelot	Domine deus qui conteris
9	Ihan Gero	Deus qui sedes super thronum
10		II Tibi derelictus est pauper
11	Mancicourt	Adorna thalamum tuum sion
12		II Suscipiens Simeon Iesus
15	Lupus	Usquequo domine
16	Verdelot	Illumina oculos meos [other sources give this as II^a pars of previous piece]
17	Claudin	Euntes ibant et flebant
18		II Tunc repletum est gaudio
19	M. Ihan	Levita Laurentius
20		II Beatus Laurentius orabat
21	[anon]	Congratulamini mihi omnes
22		II Tulerunt dominum
23	M. Ihan	Cum audissent apostoli
26	M. Ihan	In viam pacis salutis
37	Archadelt	Hodie beata virgo

Scotto's edition includes the following pieces in addition to the core repertory:

9	Verdelot	Sancta Maria succurre
13	Verdelot	Levita laurentius
		II Beatus laurentius
23	A. de Silva	Regina celi letare
24	Consilium	Quo abiit dilectus
		II Quoniam beata
26	Lasson	Antoni pater inclyte
		II O Antoni pater
28	Adriano	Victime paschali laude
		II Surrexit Christus

Rhetoric, Rhythm, and Harmony as Keys to Schütz's *Saul, Saul, was verfolgst du mich?*

Eva Linfield

The concerto *Saul, Saul, was verfolgst du mich?*, SWV 415, from *Symphoniae sacrae* III has been recognized as an outstanding piece of music ever since Carl von Winterfeld initiated the Schütz revival 150 years ago. Winterfeld singled it out in his study *Johannes Gabrieli und sein Zeitalter* in a chapter devoted to "Johannes Gabrieli's Schüler, Heinrich Schütz."[1] He transcribed the piece (a transcription to which I will refer later) and offered a sensitive analysis of some of the composition's technical aspects as well as its broader meaning.

Brahms, being very much interested in early music, performed *Saul* from Winterfeld's edition in an unsuccessful concert of January 6, 1864, with the Singakademie in Vienna. Clara Schumann wrote to Brahms concerning this concert:

> I heard that you had done the sort of old sacred pieces that people in Vienna don't like—is that true? Surely you did other things as well, and then one or two such old pieces could perhaps be pleasing![2]

(Brahms had performed, contrary to Clara's sense of what might seem reasonable, works by Schütz, Gabrieli, Rovetta, and Eccard; however, also something more "up-to-date" by Beethoven and Mendelssohn.)

Nowadays the concerto appears in music history anthologies for college survey classes and is discussed in books specializing in the music of the Baroque era, for example, those of Manfred Bukofzer and Claude Palisca.[3]

---

[1] Carl von Winterfeld, *Johannes Gabrieli und sein Zeitalter,* 3 vols. (Berlin: Schlesingersche Buch und Musikhandlung, 1834; repr. Hildesheim: Georg Olms, 1965), 2:168–212. *Saul* is discussed on p. 197; its transcription is in 3:92.

[2] Quoted in Virginia Hancock, *Brahms's Choral Compositions and His Library of Early Music,* Studies in Musicology, 76 (Ann Arbor, Mich., 1983), pp. 3, 101.

[3] Manfred F. Bukofzer, *Music in the Baroque Era: From Monteverdi to Bach* (New York, 1947), p. 93; Claude V. Palisca, *Baroque Music,* 2d ed. (Englewood Cliffs, N.J., 1981), pp. 109–12.

Since *Saul* is one of the most tightly composed and powerful sacred concertos in all of the *Symphoniae sacrae* collections,[4] it is, despite its widespread exposure, worthy of a more detailed analysis or at least one that adopts a different approach from that usually undertaken. I will, in particular, concern myself with the overall affection (*affectio*) that Schütz represents in *Saul* and will show how technical devices, rhetorical figures, and rhythmic and harmonic aspects lead to different levels of meaning in the composition.

When Winterfeld talks about part III of the *Symphoniae sacrae* as the most significant collection in which the seeds of oratorio are revealed, we will, no doubt, agree. For this particular composition, it is striking what effects Schütz achieves in setting so short a text. With only two verses from the Bible, he creates a mini-oratorio that focuses on Saul as the protagonist. The work shares certain features with what the Italians characterized as *stile rappresentativo*. One becomes immediately aware that Schütz's main concern here is not the dramatic and expressive setting of individual words—although the level of single-word expression contributes to the overall achievement of the piece—but that his interest lies in the gesture of the music as it helps to conceptualize the text and present a message visually, and, in the case of *Saul,* vivify the account of a dramatic incident.

In an article on Bach's canons, Eric Chafe discusses allegory as an underlying concept of Baroque art.[5] He develops its importance to music relying in part on Walter Benjamin's discussion of the dialectic of allegory and its conflict between "cold, facile technique" or convention on the one hand and an "eruptive expression" on the other. Benjamin sees the dualism of Baroque art exemplified through allegory, which, he says, "is both, convention and expression."[6] Chafe defines convention as the bringing of a concept down to the earthly and finite, and he connects expression with the elevation of the material through its significance.[7] In Baroque art, there-

---

[4]*Symphoniae sacrae* I, (Venice, 1629); *Symphoniae sacrae* II, (Dresden, 1647); *Symphoniae sacrae* III (Dresden, 1650).

[5]Eric Chafe, "Allegorical Music: The 'Symbolysm' of Tonal Language in the Bach Canons," *Journal of Musicology* 3 (1984): 340–62. See also Chafe's *Tonal Allegory in the Vocal Music of J. S. Bach* (Berkeley, Los Angeles, Oxford, 1991), particularly chap. 1, "Theology and Tonal Allegory in the Music of J. S. Bach."

[6]Walter Benjamin, *Ursprung des deutschen Trauerspiels* (Berlin, 1928; Frankfurt a. M., 1972), pp. 193–94: "Denn die Allegorie ist beides, Konvention und Ausdruck; und beide sind von Haus aus widerstreitend.... Die Allegorie des siebzehnten Jahrhunderts ist nicht Konvention des Ausdrucks, sondern Ausdruck der Konvention.... Die gleiche Antinomik ist's, die bildnerisch begegnet im Konflikt der kalten, schnellfertigen Technik mit dem eruptiven Ausdruck der Allegorese."

[7]Chafe, "Allegorical Music," p. 346.

fore, materiality (that is, artistic devices) is initially separate from significance.

Since the final goal of that art lies in moving the affections, we can extend the concept of allegory as a product of convention and expression to the concept of affection. The dualism or conflict in allegory also exists in the description of affection, in the seemingly contradictory elements of (1) the dogmatic aspect of "affection" associated with musical figures, formulas, and "cold" techniques in general, and (2) "affection" as an expressive force.

By the time of Schütz's composition *Saul,* rhetorical figures belonged to a convention. They had been codified and catalogued continually by theorists from the sixteenth century until the time of Schütz's own pupil Christoph Bernhard. Their conventional use serves a concrete concept, a finite meaning: in more recent times, Unger, for example, in his book on music and rhetoric, lists fifteen figures for *Saul* with their specific conventional meanings.[8] But the technical devices, including rhetorical figures, are not in themselves necessarily expressive or affective. Rather they can become an expressive force through the composer's manipulation of a context. In that respect, Chafe is correct that "analysis of affect is the highest aim that criticism of Baroque art can have."[9]

A taxonomic chart may suggest the different levels of such an analysis (Fig. 1):

Figure 1: Affection and allegory

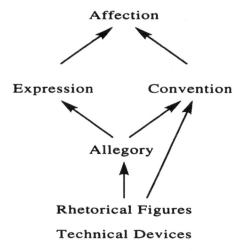

---

[8]Hans-Heinrich Unger, *Die Beziehungen zwischen Musik und Rhetorik im 16.–18. Jahrhundert* (Würzburg, 1941; repr. Hildesheim, 1969). An analysis of the rhetorical figures can be found on pp. 138–40.
[9]Chafe, "Allegorical Music," p. 346.

Example 1: Schütz, *Saul, Saul, was verfolgst du mich?*, mm. 20–23

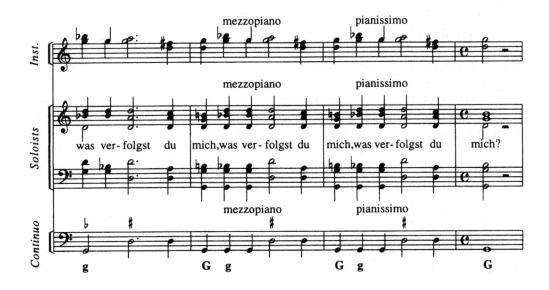

An example of musical affection rooted in an allegorical concept strikes us in measures 20–23 (Ex. 1).[10] Schütz employs what Athanasius Kircher, for example, calls a *mutatio modi,* a shift from a G-minor to a G-major chord.[11] Several short statements of "Was verfolgst du mich?" each end on a major triad, a musical-technical convention employed at phrase endings in the seventeenth century. This convention is, however, not as important as the constant juxtaposition of the B♮ with B♭, that is, of *mi contra fa.* Applying the tree in Figure 1 to this pattern, the B♮ can be accounted for as a

---

[10]As point of reference, I am using the *Stuttgarter Schützausgabe,* ed. Günter Graulich and Paul Horn (Stuttgart, 1969). In addition to an *Einzelausgabe* of this edition by Hänssler-Verlag, *Saul* is easily accessible in Claude V. Palisca's *Norton Anthology of Western Music,* 2d ed. (New York, 1988), I:469–79, and in Sarah Fuller, ed., *The European Musical Heritage, 800–1750* (New York: McGraw-Hill, Inc., 1987), pp. 336–46. Because of the reduced note values and modern clefs, this edition will be for most musicians much easier to read than Philipp Spitta's edition of Schütz's *Symphoniae sacrae, dritter Theil, erste Abtheilung,* vol. 11 of *Sämmtliche Werke* (Leipzig, 1891; repr. Wiesbaden, 1972), pp. 100*ff.* Spitta's edition, however, closely represents the original print, which the reader may want to consult, particularly with regard to my discussion of the concerto's rhythm.

[11]Athanasius Kircher, *Musurgia universalis* (Rome, 1650; facs. repr., ed. Ulf Scharlau, Hildesheim and New York, 1970), I:672–75.

rhetorical figure, namely an *interrogatio*. Bernhard talks about its use in the *stylus theatralis:*

> Questions are commonly expressed by raising the pitch a second from its preceding syllable.[12]

In this case, however, an *interrogatio* could refer to either B♭ or B♮, raising the voice a minor or a major second from A in the tenor. As such, it would count as a purely technical device, contributing to the affection through a musical convention. This passage is significant because its multilevel meaning takes the left-hand branch of the tree through allegory and expression to affection. The *mutatio modi* achieves a striking flickering, suggesting flashes of light. Although the words themselves do not evoke the association with light, it is clearly the context in which they appear that inspired Schütz. I quote from the New English Bible: "In the middle of the day, I saw a light from the sky, more brilliant than the sun, shining all around me and my travelling companions" (Acts 26:13). Johann Kuhnau stresses the causal connection between hermeneutics, that is, the *inventio*[13] stimulated by allegory, and the moving of the affections:

> Apart from the importance of understanding the art of moving the affections and skillfully expressing everything, I deem it necessary not to be a stranger in hermeneutics and to understand the correct *sensum* [sense] and *scopum* [broader meaning] of the words.[14]

---

[12]"Die Fragen werden gemeinem Brauche nach am Ende eine *Secunde* höher als die vorhergehende Sylbe gesetzt." Christoph Bernhard, *Die Kompositionslehre Heinrich Schützens in der Fassung seines Schülers Christoph Bernhard,* ed. Joseph Müller-Blattau, 2d ed. (Kassel, 1963), p. 83. All translations in the present article are my own.

[13]Music theorists borrowed the term *inventio* from the classical discipline of rhetoric. Gallus Dressler may have been the first to use it in his *Praecepta musicae practicae* (1563), which he devoted exclusively to the art of composition. *Inventio* refers to a basic concept and an initial idea of a composition. The term is commonly used in the Baroque period. Mattheson, for example, discusses it as late as the 18th century as a music-rhetorical feature in the opening section of *Der vollkommene Kapellmeister* (Hamburg: Christian Herold, 1739; facs. ed., Kassel: Bärenreiter, 1954).

[14]"Denn ausser dem, dass man sich auff das Artificium die Affectus zu moviren, und sonsten alles geschicklich zu exprimiren wohl verstehen solte, so hielt ich vor nöthig, dass man in der Hermeneutica kein Frembdling wäre, und den rechten *Sensum* und *Scopum* der Worte allemahl wohl capirte." Quoted after Bernhard Friedrich Richter, "Eine Abhandlung Joh. Kuhnaus," *Monatshefte für Musik-Geschichte* 34 (1902): 150.

Although Kuhnau's advice dates from 1709—a preface to some cantata texts—it seems obvious that Schütz worked with the same concept and embedded his concerto in the *sensus* and *scopus* of the Biblical context.

Another allegorical meaning of the same passage might be explored through the writings of Andreas Werckmeister. He attaches to his treatise *Musicae mathematicae hodegus curiosus, oder Richtiger musicalischer Wegweiser*...(Musical Road Sign) from 1686 an appendix with the title "Of allegory and ethics in music" ("Von der allegorischen und moralischen Music") in which he links tonal musical materials directly to metaphysical/theological meaning. Werckmeister speaks about the nature of the major and minor third:

> The third has two natures: one sounds magnificent, perfect, majestic, the other humble, imperfect, slavelike.... These are best compared to the godly as opposed to the human nature.[15]

Against this background, we can hear the *mutatio modi* as a juxtaposition of "du" and "mich": "you," referring to Saul, the addressee, the sinner as the blinded slave, and "me," referring to the pure, magnificent voice of Christ.

Winterfeld eliminated the fast shift from G minor to G major, letting the B♮ stand only in its habitual place at the end of a phrase segment. He interpreted the unusual technical device as a mistake in the original print and, in "cleaning up" the print, distorted the subtle significance intended by Schütz and neutralized the intense meaning or *scopum*, that is, he literally "entschärfte" ("de-activated") the text.[16]

Schütz employs another *mutatio modi* in the opening section. The first eight measures are tonally rooted in D minor. The shift to D major occurs in measure 17 (Ex. 2). The stunning light that blinded Saul is at this point musically expressed with explosive power: the "cold and facile techniques," as Benjamin called them, feed into both branches of the tree, through allegory, expression, and convention to affection. Schütz magnifies the iconic

---

[15]"Der mittelste *clavis* in dieser *Triade* zwo Naturen mit sich führet / da denn die eine prächtig / vollkommen / Majestätisch / die andere aber Demüthig / unvollkommen / knechtisch klinget und lautet.... Wie kan dieses besser vergleichen werden als mit der Göttlichen und Menschlichen Natur...?" Andreas Werckmeister, "Von der allegorischen und moralischen Music," in *Musicae mathematicae hodegus curiosus* (Frankfurt a. Main and Leipzig: Theodor Philipp Calvisius, 1686; facs. repr. Hildesheim: Georg, Olms, 1972), p. 148.

[16]The verb "entschärfen" appropriately plays with a linguistic pun. Literally it means to "remove sharpness." The verb's basic reference is, however, to "defusing" or "deactivating" a bomb (a not inappropriate metaphor).

implications of the context by overlapping a number of rhetorical figures that impact on the affections:

1. The change of mode with what Werckmeister calls the "majestic" major third (*mutatio modi*).

2. The addition of two four-voice *capellae* (*paranomasia*) suddenly expanding the texture from two to sixteen voices and filling out the registral space.

   It needs to be mentioned here that the concerto bears the title "mit 8 Stimmen" ("for eight voices"), namely six *favoriti* singers and two obbligato violins—the continuo is always left out in the count. The *complementi*, as Schütz states in the title and again in the preface to the print, can be added "nach Belieben" ("if one pleases"); they are not obligatory to the composition. Since, however, the printer invested in printing separate partbooks for two *capellae* or *complementi*, it is clear that the effect of the large scoring reflects Schütz's ideal of a sonority and is in full support of the composition's basic concept.

3. The dynamic indication of an additional *forte* marking (*auxesis*).

4. A percussive rhythmic activity caused by the interlocking of the opening syncopated *exclamatio* "Saul, Saul" at a rhythmic delay of a breve. The increase in rhythmic intensity creates a vivid sense of arrows of light striking on each breve.

The opening, leading to the extraordinary tutti explosion, is remarkable in its spatial layout (Ex. 2). In four duets, the six *favoriti* singers and the obbligato violins rise gradually, encompassing a registral span of three and a half octaves. Again, Kuhnau's notion of *scopus* seems at work. "We all fell to the ground, and then I heard a voice talking to me" (Acts 26:14) is the text immediately preceding Christ's address to Saul. Schütz describes the voice reaching down to the bottom, where Saul, the sinner, lies having fallen off his horse. The spatial, highly effective buildup of the music corresponds to textual imagery that allegorizes the rise from earth to heaven and the move toward light and toward God. This most intense realism also recalls the depiction of this scene by Caravaggio, where Paul is overwhelmed by the beam of heavenly light that both blinds the outward eye and brings

Example 2: Schütz, *Saul, Saul, was verfolgst du mich?*, mm. 1–17

Rhetoric, Rhythm, and Harmony   233

Example 2 (*continued*)

inner illumination.[17] Werckmeister describes his theory of the spatial layout of the four different octaves as an allegory of the four elements:

> A sensitive musician will know how to apply this properly, namely that the earth is the heaviest element and therefore placed on the very bottom [of the register], that the others must follow.[18]

The low register in Baroque music has its conventional association with earth, for Schütz here with the fall to the ground.[19]

Each of the voice pairs concludes its question "Was verfolgst du mich?" on a *cadentia duriuscula,* a rhetorical figure discussed by Bernhard as a "somewhat strange dissonance" ("eine etwas seltsame *Dissonantz*"), a "harshness" ("eine Härtigkeit") that he warns composers to use only with

---

[17]The writings of the German mystic Jacob Böhme (1575–1624) offer certain striking analogies to the work of Baroque painters like Caravaggio and Rembrandt, and to this composition by Schütz, regarding an allegorical interpretation of light and dark. Böhme writes in his book *Aurora* (Görlitz, 1612) about his visions of light representing a divine force fighting against darkness, which he associates with death and evil forces. See Jacob Böhme, *Sämtliche Schriften: Faksimile-Neudruck der Ausgabe von 1730,* vol. 1, *Aurora, oder Morgenröthe im Aufgang,* ed. Will-Erich Peuckert (Stuttgart, 1955). Schütz might well have been familiar with Böhme's somewhat abstruse speculations, since *Aurora* went through a couple of reprints during the seventeenth and early eighteenth centuries. Martin Gregor-Dellin advances the idea that Schütz and Böhme might actually have met in Dresden. At Pentecost, 1624, a social gathering took place in honor of Böhme to which "hohe Herren" were invited, Schütz possibly being one of them. See *Heinrich Schütz: Sein Leben, sein Werk, seine Zeit* (Munich, 1984), pp. 127–28.

[18]"Ein verständiger *Musicus* wird schon die *Application* zu machen wissen / dass nehmlich die Erde das schwereste *Element* ist / und unten seinen Sitz habe / die andern aber darnach folgen müssen" (Werckmeister, p. 145).

[19]The association of high and low pitch with ethical qualities originated with the ancients. During the age of Humanism, much Greek theory was transmitted by Boethius's sixth-century treatise *De institutione musica.* He discusses the dependency of low and high pitch qualities on the frequency and density of the pitches' pulsation and also speaks of harmony of the four elements; see A. M. S. Boethius, *Fundamentals of Music,* trans. Calvin M. Bower (New Haven and London, 1989), I:9–12. Many of the aesthetic questions in Baroque music were first addressed by members of the Florentine Camerata. In attaching moral qualities to the threefold division of pitch and mode into low, intermediate, and high register, Bardi evokes Aristotle, who advanced the concept that "in melodies the mutations [low, intermediate, high] are of moral character"; see Bardi's letter to Caccini on "Ancient Music and Good Singing," in Claude V. Palisca, *The Florentine Camerata: Documentary Studies and Translations* (New Haven and London, 1989), particularly p. 109. Although, to a large extent, Baroque aesthetics reinterpreted theoretical concepts of the ancients, the three registers continued to be associated with similar qualitative attributes.

careful "judgement" ("*Judicio*").[20] Schütz boldly used this figure, compounding the simultaneous dissonances with the harshest voice leading—parallel seconds. The importance of a connection between the musical rhetorical figure and its aspect of "affection" is described by Werckmeister:

> All dissonances are far removed from perfection, which is the reason for their sad and somewhat confused nature.[21] When these dissonances are presented through music to a person who is already sad, depressed, as well as disturbed, this person will become yet more disturbed and agitated because he identifies with those emotions.[22]

According to Werckmeister's statement, composition with harsh dissonances does not only express the affection of the text, but, at the same time, affects the listener's temperament and state of mind. The dissonance figures in *Saul* thus belong to a *stile rappresentativo,* as the Italians would have referred to such a manner of scenic representation, as well as to a music that moves the passions of the listener.[23]

---

[20]Bernhard, p. 82.

[21]Intervals of greatest perfection are those whose proportions consist of the lowest numbers, that is, the unison (1:1, or proportion of equality), the octave (2:1), the fifth (3:2), and the fourth (4:3). The basis for perfection is thus rooted in the law of mathematics.

[22]"Alle *dissonantien* sind von der Vollkommenheit weit abgelegen / derohalben sind sie trauriger und etwas verwirreter Natur. Wenn den denselbigen einen bevorab traurigen / schwermüthigen und gleichsam bestürtzten Menschen durch die Music vorgetragen werden / so wird derselbe dadurch noch bestürtzter und bewegter gemacht / weil er seines gleichen findet" (Werckmeister, p. 84).

[23]Kircher, in his *Musurgia* (part 2, chap. 5, p. 581), makes the distinction between *stylus expressus,* depending on structural or qualitative phenomena, and *stylus impressus,* which is connected with the individual's personality and temperament, and influenced by passion as well as actively affecting passions:

> Musical style is both, impressive and expressive; the impressive style incorporates the leaning of the mood towards this or that style, depending on man's natural temperament. The expressive style consists in a certain manner of how to compose.
>
> (*Stylus musicus* ist zweyfach, *impressus vel expressus;* der eingetruckte *stylus* ist die Zuneigung deß Gemüts zu disem oder jenem *stylo, dependiret* von deß Menschen seinem natürlichen Temperament; der ausgetruckte *stylus* ist ein gewisse weis / vorgeschriben / wie man componiren solle.)

Shortly after Kircher's publication of *Musurgia* in Rome, an abbreviated version had already appeared in German translation: Andreas Hirsch, *Phil. Extract und Auszug/aus des Weltberühmten Teutschen Jesuitens Athanasii Kircheri von Fulda/Musurgia Universali...* (Schwäbisch Hall, 1662; facs. repr. Kassel, 1988), p. 157.

Schütz uses rhythm as another device of compositional manipulation. There are some rhythmic and notational ambiguities in *Saul* that Schütz may have employed for the sake of *confusio* (a figure more closely referring to ambiguity than to actual confusion), and that further contribute to the intensification of the dramatic affection of the composition. The mensural indication is C$^3_1$ and changes after the interrogative text phrase to C. Already at the very beginning of the concerto, rhythmic ambiguity exists with respect to the accent distribution. The basso continuo pattern of o. (dotted breve), o (breve), ♩ (semibreve) assumes a grouping of 2 times 3 semibreves until the following coloration where, of course, the accent distribution changes to 3 times 2 semibreves (Ex. 2). This shift occurs in each of the opening four phrases. At the same time, the melodic lines of the vocal and instrumental parts stay clearly in a 3 times 2 semibreve accentual pattern, which thus creates a cross-accentuation. Not only does Schütz open with a syncopated questioning phrase, he somewhat startles the listener with this jerkiness of cross-accentuation. Just before the shift to the duple mensuration, he introduces a new rhythmic energy: a rhythmic acceleration through redistributing the accents into a smaller triple grouping of three ♩ (minims) (see Ex. 1). This rhythmic intensification coincides with a *noëma*—a homophonic declamation of the question "Was verfolgst du mich?"—now repeated in close succession and with a reduction in dynamics to *pianissimo*. The rhythmic element mimics the insistent penetration of the question "Was verfolgst du mich?" and characterizes, together with the harmonic shifts of the *mutatio modi,* an overall agitated affection of the passage.

But how does the duple mensuration relate to the triple of the beginning? A proportional triple/duple relation does not make any musical sense. If one looks ahead at the ritornello in measure 34 (Ex. 3), it becomes clear that musically this material is identical with the first ritornello notated as a triple. Common sense would, therefore, prescribe the same *tactus* for the later ritornello section, in which case we are dealing with an example of "spielmännische Reduktion," that is, no proportion.[24] The initial unit—a semibreve beat—would now equal that of a semiminim, with the notation based on a 1:4 reduction in the *note nere* notation. The 1:4 reduction does not involve a speeding up of the music itself. The acceleration here is merely rooted in the notational system and could, in this case, be labeled as "Augenmusik," a purely visual speeding up and intensification.

---

[24]This is a term Paul Brainard used in his paper "Proportion and Pseudo-Proportion in 17th-Century Rhythm: Some Hypotheses," given at the Annual Meeting of the American Musicological Society, Philadelphia, 1984. I am grateful to him for providing me with a copy of his paper.

Example 3: Schütz, *Saul, Saul, was verfolgst du mich?*, mm. 34–38

Comparing the opening with the ritornello section notated in duple meter also confirms the duple grouping of the semibreve pattern at the beginning, although coloration is not used in the melody parts.

Another possibility, for which there is, however, no notational indication in the print, is a proportion between the faster triple section in measures 21–22 and the following duple. This results in ₵ ³/₁ ♩♩♩ = ₵ ♩ (three minims in ₵ ³/₁ = one minim in ₵). This solution would make, from the performance-practice point of view, good musical sense. The faster triple would actually seem more "natural" as a point of reference, while the performer would have to go through a complicated intellectual process in order to reestablish the initial slower *tactus*. Assuming this proportion, the later ritornello music moves slightly faster: the speeding up of the beat is very much in line with the composition's general intensification.

A notational oddity is worth pointing out here: it consists of an irregularity of the *Mensurstrich* indication. In the duple section of the original print, a *Mensurstrich* is placed before the two *fusae* almost consistently throughout the parts (Ex. 4). This *Mensurstrich* appears to be a phrasing

Example 4: Schütz, *Saul, Saul, was verfolgst du mich?*

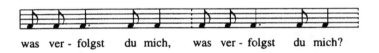

indication disrupting the regularity of the mensuration grouping. It corresponds to the mensural distribution of the beginning and provides yet another clue suggesting that the initial triple and the later duple keep the same (or possibly slightly sped up) *tactus* (Ex. 5). The *Mensurstrich* before the arsis underlines the rhythmic impact of the *fusae* with their percussive quality. It also confirms that this music is not conceived metrically, but that it is governed by a fluid declamatory rhythm within the mensural notational system.

Example 5: Schütz, *Saul, Saul, was verfolgst du mich?*, triple and duple rhythms

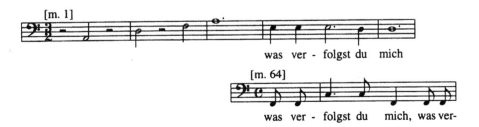

The story of Paul's conversion from the adamant anti-Christian, Saul, to a follower of the Christian belief is mentioned three times in the Book of Acts. The literature on Schütz's composition cites Acts 9, verses 4 and 5, as the source of the text. In fact, the text is taken from Acts 26, verse 14. Only there do we find the second-sentence warning "Es wird dir schwer werden, wider den Stachel zu löcken" ("lecken" in Schütz). The different context in which the story appears is of prime importance: whereas in Acts 9 the story is told as an historical account in a third-person narrative, it is Paul himself who pictures the event of his conversion in Acts 26. Direct speech naturally imprints an action more vividly on the listener than does indirect speech. In this connection, we must also look at the circumstances under which Paul delivers his report, circumstances that must have contributed to Schütz's inspiration and *inventio* for setting these words. Paul has been accused by the Jews of creating and following a new law that focuses on preaching about Christ. He has been taken to court by the Pharisees and defends himself first before the Roman procurator, Festus. Although he does not understand Paul's Christian utterances, Festus prosecutes him reluctantly, believing in Paul's innocence. Subsequently Festus has Paul deliver his report before the Caesarean king, Agrippa. The direct parallel between Paul's situation and that of Christ, defending himself before Pontius Pilate, is remarkable. Paul was standing trial because of his belief in the resurrection of the dead. Christ was the long-awaited Messiah who would rise from the dead. Schütz's setting vividly depicts the dialectic of an eschatological concept: death of Saul, the sinner, and his resurrection as Paul, the Christian, alluding on a higher level to Christ, the redeemer.

In the central section, "Es wird dir schwer werden, wider den Stachel zu löcken," Schütz expresses Saul's struggle against his destiny and, ultimately, the inevitability of fighting against the law. Biblical commentaries indicate that Luke quotes here a Greek aphorism appearing in works by Pindar, Euripides, and Aeschylus. An interesting parallel is provided by Aeschylus's *Prometheus Unbound:* there Prometheus, rebelling against the new law enforced by Zeus, here Saul, rebelling against the new Christian law.

Schütz exposes the text first in a solo whose melodic contour and rhythmic action reflect single-word expression (Ex. 6; faster declamation on "Stachel," a *saltus duriusculus* [a "rather harsh leap"]—a leap of a descending minor sixth—on "löcken"). The text finds its most complex work-

Example 6: Schütz, *Saul, Saul, was verfolgst du mich?*, mm. 24–28

240   Eva Linfield

ing-out, however, in a *fuga,* in this case referring to a technique of imitation (Ex. 7). *Fuga* is used here as a musical rhetorical figure. The strict

Example 7: Schütz, *Saul, Saul, was verfolgst du mich?*, mm. 45–57

Example 7 (*continued*)

rules of its contrapuntal technique mirror, on a musically conventional level, the concept of "law," a concept that dictates confinement and constraint. Saul's most rebellious behavior against that law is demonstratively exposed in the treatment of the *soggetto*. Its motion in parallel thirds, at times consecutive major thirds, creates "forbidden" and intentionally awkward cross relations as in measure 39 (Ex. 8), or in measure 53 (Ex. 9). In measure 53, the tritone F/B♮ sticks out harmonically and melodically, and the original leap of a fourth has been widened to an ascending sixth, still ascending in parallels and thus violating traditional rules of counterpoint as they had been codified by Zarlino.[25]

---

[25]Zarlino warns against progressions from one imperfect consonance to another of the same species, particularly in two-part writing—exactly the situation here. See Gioseffo Zarlino, *Le Istitutioni Harmoniche* (Venice, 1558), 3:178; trans. Guy A. Marco and Claude V. Palisca, *The Art of Counterpoint* (New Haven, 1968), 3:62.

Example 8: Schütz, *Saul, Saul, was verfolgst du mich?*, mm. 39–41

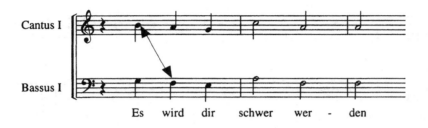

Example 9: Schütz, *Saul, Saul, was verfolgst du mich?*, mm. 53–54

With the beginning of the *fuga* in measure 45, a most extraordinary harmonic progression sets in: a fast descent through the circle of fifths from G–C–F–B♭–E♭–A♭ (see Ex. 7). Hexachordal or modal transpositions to A♭ were rare in seventeenth-century composition and not discussed by theorists until late in the century. The note A♭ itself was described as a "wolf" tone on keyboard instruments in mean-tone tuning, referring to its characteristic out-of-tuneness. During this harmonic "fall," and at the point of the *fuga*'s densest texture, Schütz increases the tension with what must have seemed to the seventeenth-century ear a dissonant cluster. The augmented interval in measure 49 is striking (Ex. 10). Although the basso continuo anticipates the lowest note of the texture—the new phrase begins in that dissonant measure on G in *bassus* I—the ear is, nevertheless, aware of the approach to the dissonance with an ascent of a "rather harsh" major sixth in the basso continuo.[26] (The leap of the major sixth in the basso continuo

---

[26]Both Zarlino and Bernhard considered such leaps to be in bad taste. Bernhard would not allow them in *contrapunctus gravis;* but in *contrapunctus luxurians*—and here only in the second, least restrained category of contrapuntal writing, in *stylus theatralis*—they can serve as expressive licenses (cf. Bernhard, p. 78).

from measure 48 to measure 49 is not analogous to the one in measure 46, which functions as part of a *basso seguente* and occurs on an unaccented beat.)

Example 10: Schütz, *Saul, Saul, was verfolgst du mich?* mm. 48–49

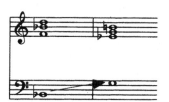

(Winterfeld undertook another editorial clean-up in measure 49. He removed the stunning dissonance by changing the B♮ to a B♭, a change that, unfortunately, also made its way into *The Norton Scores*.[27]) This most insidious dissonance marks Schütz's introduction of a quasi counterfugue with the inverted headmotive in measure 49, leading to another cluster in measure 55 before resolving to a D-major chord in measure 57. The greatest dialectical tension in *Saul,* measures 45–57 (see Ex. 7), coincides with a divergence between the harmonic downwards motion into remote key areas, a *catabasis,* and the melodic upwards motion, an *anabasis,* extending into the composition's highest register, saved again for the violins as last voices to enter with the motive in measures 52 and 54. (This spatial and registral expansion is conceptually analogous to the concerto's opening.) Here, at the center of the concerto, Schütz expresses through a carefully planned manipulation of musical complexities a manifesto of the allegorical dialectic between death and resurrection, the crux of the Christian law.

With the overlap of the *fuga* and the *exclamatio* "Saul" in measures 60–63, Schütz creates textual and musical intensification âefore leading to the last section, a return to the interrogative phrase. The tenor cuts through the full texture with a diatonic ascent in sustained note-values (Ex. 11). It pulls with it the whole viscous musical apparatus in an ascent of parallel harmonies from F–G–A. The final segment rests statically on the chord-exchange A/D with the tenor calling "Saul" on a reiterated pitch A

---

[27]*The Norton Scores: An Anthology for Listening,* 3d ed., ed. Roger Kamien (New York, 1977), 1:99. *The Norton Anthology of Western Music,* see n. 10 above, gives the correct reading.

Example 11: Schütz, *Saul, Saul, was verfolgst du mich?*, mm. 65–74

Example 11 (*continued*)

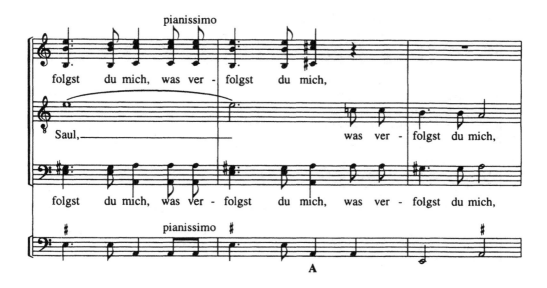

(Ex. 12). The concerto closes with a notated general pause, what Joachim Burmeister and Joachim Thuringus referred to as an *aposiopesis,* after a gradual thinning out of texture and dynamics.[28] (Winterfeld omits the general pause in his transcription, as does the editor of *The Norton Scores.*) Unger, in his book on rhetoric in music, mentions the rare employment of a final general pause and its significance as a representation of death.[29] We may think of Schütz's notated final silence as allegory for the "dying" echo between neasures 75 and 80. In that context, the rest would operate, in musically absolute terms, as the final point of a decrescendo. In a transfigurational sense, we could also view the finality of this silence as a music-liguistic transferal from persecution to death.

---

[28]See, for example, Joachim Burmeister, *Musica poetica* (Rostock, 1606), p. 62: "Aposiopesis is a figure that causes, through a certain sign, absolute silence in all voices" ("Aposiopesis est quae silentium totale omnibus vocibus signo certo posito confert"). See also Joachim Thuringus, *Opusculum bipartitum* (Berlin, 1624), p. 126. Thuringus may have been directly influenced by Burmeister.

[29]Unger, p. 140, n. 31. Unger gives seven examples of rests ending compositions by Schütz and makes a convincing case for their affective meaning.

Example 12: Schütz, *Saul, Saul, was verfolgst du mich?*, mm. 75–80

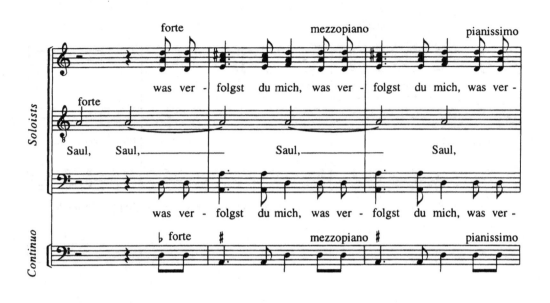

The last section, measures 64–80, resembles the opening passage, measures 17–23 (see Ex. 1). Most of the rhetorical devices are recalled. Schütz, however, reinforces the musical gesture with multiple repeats (*anaphora*) of the penetrating *noëma* figure "Was verfolgst du mich?" and with the introduction of a quasi cantus firmus in augmentation, signifying the personification of the tenor as *vox Christi*. Both affection as a visual/musical gesture and affection as a musical/allegorical expression are present and now magnified by the juxtaposition of the harmonic ascent and the final harmonic stasis. In this section once again, Schütz crystallizes the concept of an antithesis germane to an eschatological interpretation. The allegorical superstructure deals with death versus resurrection, perceived on the next level down through the Biblical context. In the verses immediately following the text set by Schütz, in Acts 26:17–18, Paul recalls Christ's words: "I send you to open their eyes [of the Jews and the Gentiles] and turn them from darkness to light, from the dominion of Satan to God." The textual oppositions "darkness to light" and "Satan to God" provide what Kuhnau calls *sensus* and *scopus*—the higher allegorical meaning is, of course, death and resurrection. On the lowest and most immediate level of perception, the abundance of Schütz's rhetorical devices comes into play and creates the intended affection through skillfully manipulated techniques belonging to the realm of convention.

In discussing certain analytical points in *Saul*, I have tried to show that musical-technical devices such as rhetoric, rhythm, and harmony all contribute to moving the affections, the final goal of music during this period; or as Kircher wrote in 1650 in his *Musurgia universalis:* "affectus totius musicae finis" ("The aim of all music is to create affection"). The correlation of technical means yields, however, an analysis that is dependent on extra-musical aspects, namely on allegory and, as Kuhnau suggested, on *scopus* and *sensus* of the context. This somewhat obscure thinking is typical of German Baroque art and is best described by the German word "Hintergründigkeit" ("cryptic or abstruse matter"). It lies deep in the cryptic exegetical meaning that constitutes the major *inventio* for Schütz's composition.

Bach's *tempo ordinario:*
A Plaine and Easie Introduction to the System

Robert L. Marshall

The initial impetus for this inquiry came from a question posed by Arthur Mendel during a coffee break in a Bach seminar some thirty years ago. Why, he asked, did Bach notate the last movement of the fifth Brandenburg Concerto in two-four time, with triplets (Ex. 1):

Example 1. Brandenburg Concerto No. 5, BWV 1050/3, original notation

rather than in six-eight time (Ex. 2)?

Example 2. Brandenburg Concerto No. 5, BWV 1050/3, hypothetical version

At the least, the composer could have avoided any ambiguity as to whether the upbeat was to be rendered as a strict sixteenth or assimilated into the prevailing triplet pattern. Mendel offered no definitive explanation for Bach's puzzling notation, but he suggested that the reason probably had to do with the desired tempo.

As to that tempo: Bach informs us in this case that it is to be *allegro.* But he obviously could have put the same designation above a 6/8 movement just as well. At all events, it is worth noting that Bach frequently provides tempo designations for movements in instrumental ensemble works; moreover, the markings are often quite nuanced: for example *adagio o vero Largo* (in the Concerto for Two Harpsichords senza ripieno, BWV

1061a),[1] *allegro moderato* (in the Sonata for Viola da Gamba and Harpsichord, BWV 1027), *andante un poco* (in the Sonata for Violin and Harpsichord, BWV 1015).

In other repertories, however, Bach's practice is altogether different. Tempo designations are notoriously rare, for example, in Bach's organ and keyboard compositions, apart from dance headings in suite movements. Of the 96 movements of the *Well-Tempered Clavier,* only seven carry tempo marks: the B-minor prelude and fugue of Book I, the preludes in G minor and B minor of Book II, and the closing sections of the C-minor and E-minor preludes of Book I and of the C♯-major prelude of Book 2.

In the vocal works, the very limited presence (and, implicitly, the equally limited need) of tempo indications is just as striking. They appear in the sources of about 120 of Bach's 250 extant vocal compositions.[2] But that number is misleading; for typically only one movement—occasionally two (hardly ever more)—of a vocal work has a tempo marking. Accordingly, if we take the average number of movements in a vocal composition to be seven, then Bach's surviving vocal works contain some 1,750 movements, of which well over ninety percent get by with no tempo markings.

In an earlier study, I presented a preliminary compilation of tempo designations in the Bach sources and attempted to draw some practical

---

[1] The tempo designation in the surviving set of parts is autograph. In the sources for the more familiar version of this concerto, with ripieno accompaniment in the outer movements, BWV 1061 (all dating no earlier than the second half of the eighteenth century), the second movement is marked simply *adagio*. See *Johann Sebastian Bach: Neue Ausgabe sämtlicher Werke* [*Neue Bach-Ausgabe;* hereafter *NBA*], ser. 7, vol. 5, ed. Karl Heller and Hans-Joachim Schulze (Kassel: Bärenreiter, 1985), *Kritischer Bericht* (1990) [hereafter *KB*].

[2] The original sources that survive for approximately 225 vocal works by Bach consist of about 170 autograph scores and 175 sets of original performing parts. For some 125 compositions, both the scores and the parts survive; about 50 works are transmitted only in scores, while another 50 survive only in the original parts. Finally, some 25 vocal compositions are preserved only in secondary sources. (Owing to the difficulties and ambiguities entailed in establishing a precise, definitive count, it seems prudent to present these and the following statistics rounded off to the nearest five.)

Occasional tempo marks appear in some 95 of the 175 sets of parts and in about 40 of the 170 autograph scores. (Almost half of the 40 autographs containing tempo indications, incidentally, are composing scores.) Since there is an overlap of about twenty works among these 135 "marked" sources (i.e., about twenty compositions survive in both a score and a set of parts containing tempo indications), a total of about 115 vocal compositions are transmitted with tempo indications in original sources. When one adds to this number the five vocal works containing tempo indications that survive only in secondary sources, one arrives at the number of 120 for vocal compositions with tempo indications.

lessons from them.[3] I suggested that tempo markings were rarely necessary in keyboard works, since the choice of tempi in a solo repertory could be left to the taste and skill of the performer. I remarked further that in vocal works "character and meaning of the text normally suffice to define the *Affekt* and thereby suggest the appropriate tempo."[4] I could also have mentioned that, since Bach himself normally conducted the performances of his vocal music, he was able to dictate the desired tempo of every number in every composition with complete precision and therefore really had no need to write down any tempo indications in this repertory at all. But then, why are there any at all?

There is yet another well-known reason why Bach's music, like that of his contemporaries, makes so little use of tempo markings. The tempo of a baroque composition was not just implicit in its *Affekt:* it was embodied in the notation. Musical practice in the early eighteenth century was still predicated on the (pre)existence of a normal, relatively constant beat—a *tempo ordinario*—whose rate was linked to such natural human activities and functions as the leisurely stride and, more commonly, to the human pulse rate. This association made its first documented appearance in the *Musica practica* of Ramos de Pareia (1482), and was still invoked almost three hundred years later in Johann Joachim Quantz's flute treatise of 1752.[5]

---

[3] Robert L. Marshall, "Tempo and Dynamic Indications in the Bach Sources: A Review of the Terminology," in *Bach, Handel, Scarlatti: Tercentenary Essays*, ed. Peter Williams (Cambridge: Cambridge University Press, 1985), pp. 269–75; reprinted in slightly revised form in Robert L. Marshall, *The Music of Johann Sebastian Bach: The Sources, the Style, the Significance* (New York: Schirmer Books, 1989), pp. 255–70. Further references are to the revised version.

[4] Marshall, p. 268.

[5] See Curt Sachs, *Rhythm and Tempo: A Study in Music History* (New York: Norton, 1953), pp. 202–203. Quantz writes in his famous chapter on accompaniment (Chapter 17): "The means that I consider the most useful as a guide for tempo is the more convenient because of the ease with which it is obtained, since everyone always has it upon himself. It is the pulse beat at the hand of a healthy person." Johann Joachim Quantz, *On Playing The Flute*, trans. Edward R. Reilly, 2nd ed. (New York: Schirmer Books, 1985), p. 283. The original reads: "Das Mittel welches ich zur Richtschnur des Zeitmaaßes am dienlichsten befinde, ist um so viel bequemer, je weniger Mühe es kostet, desselben habhaft zu werden, weil es ein jeder immer bey sich hat. Es ist **der Pulsschlag an der Hand eines gesunden Menschen**" [Boldface in the original]. Johann Joachim Quantz, *Versuch einer Anweisung die Flöte traversiere zu spielen*, 3rd ed. (Breslau: Johann Friedrich Korn, 1789); facsimile edition, ed. Hans-Peter Schmitz (Kassel: Bärenreiter, 1953), p. 261.

There is no doubt about the relevance of the *tempo ordinario* to a proper historical understanding of tempo in Bach's music. Nonetheless, the composer's own understanding of the concept does not seem to have received much systematic investigation. The possibility that Bach's time signatures prescribe proportionally related tempi, however, has been argued by Walter Gerstenberg and Ulrich Siegele.[6] Most recently, Don O. Franklin has reopened the issue in two provocative studies that postulate the existence of specific, proportional, tempo relationships obtaining between consecutive sections or movements of a work—between a prelude and the following fugue, or between successive movements of a cantata or mass—based on the conspicuous or anomalous absence, in original or reliable sources, of a fermata between the affected movements.[7]

For the rest, most observers have been content merely to acknowledge the existence of the *tempo ordinario* and its pertinence for Bach.[8] Erwin Bodky, however, in an ambitious effort, divided the keyboard works into groups sharing the same time signatures, similar rhythmic patterns, and presumably similar affective qualities; he thereupon proceeded to assign an appropriate tempo to each group and each work.[9] As Bodky concedes, however, such an endeavor, even when carried out with intelligence and sensitivity, is subjective and inevitably "arbitrary" (p. 120).

What follows does not pretend to be a comprehensive study of the vast and elusive issue of tempo in the music of Bach. On the contrary, its objec-

---

[6] Walter Gerstenberg, "Die Zeitmasse und ihre Ordnungen in Bachs Musik," *Freunde der Bachwoche Ansbach: Jahresgabe 1952*; repr. in *Johann Sebastian Bach*, ed. Walter Blankenburg. Wege der Forschung, 170 (Darmstadt: Wissenschaftliche Buchgesellschaft, 1970): 129–49; Ulrich Siegele, "Zur Verbindung von Praeludium und Fuga bei J. S. Bach," in *Kongreßbericht Kassel 1962* (Kassel: Bärenreiter, 1963), pp. 164–67; and Siegele, "Bemerkungen zu Bachs Motetten," *Bach-Jahrbuch 1962*, pp. 33–57.

[7] Don O. Franklin, "Die Fermate als Notationsmittel für das Tempoverhältnis zwischen Präludium und Fuge," in *Beiträge zur Bachforschung: 9/10. Bericht über die Wissenschaftliche Konferenz zum VI. Internationalen Bachfest der DDR, Leipzig 1989* (Leipzig, 1991), pp. 138–56; and "The Fermata as Notational Convention in the Music of J. S. Bach," in *Convention in Eighteenth- and Nineteenth-Century Music: Essays in Honor of Leonard G. Ratner*, ed. Wye J. Allanbrook, Janet M. Levy, and William P. Mahrt (New York: Pendragon Press, 1992), pp. 345–81.

[8] See, for example, Hermann Keller, *Das Wohltemperierte Klavier von Johann Sebastian Bach: Werk und Wiedergabe* (Kassel: Bärenreiter, 1965), especially pp. 32–33. The most extensive discussion of the topic appears in Thomas E. Hoekstra, *Tempo Considerations in the Choral Music of Johann Sebastian Bach* (Ph.D. dissertation, University of Iowa, 1974). See also the helpful review of some of the main issues in Paul Badura-Skoda, *Bach Interpretation: Interpreting Bach at the Keyboard* (Oxford: Clarendon Press, 1993), pp. 71–91.

[9] Erwin Bodky, *The Interpretation of Bach's Keyboard Works* (Cambridge, MA: Harvard University Press, 1960).

tive is quite limited: to formulate a small number of simple propositions, or "rules," that enunciate in concise fashion the general principles that seem to be governing Bach's notational practices with respect to rhythm and meter insofar as they may have implications for determining the tempo—or the tolerable tempo range—of a composition. In contrast to the studies of Gerstenberg, Siegele, and Franklin, the focus here is primarily on the individual continuous work or movement. But, needless to say, any conclusions that may be drawn here regarding the tempo of individual movements will inevitably carry consequences for the tempo relationship that may obtain between paired or adjacent movements or among the sections of larger compositions.

The fundamental premise underlying the present attempt is that Bach's notational practice not only assumed a *tempo ordinario*, but that it was in essence a system and, accordingly (at least in principle), that it was both rational and consistent. The assumption that Bach's notation embodies a rational system suggests, among other things, that Bach must have had a "reason" for notating the Brandenburg theme as shown in Example 1 rather than in the simpler notation of Example 2; it would have been irrational, in a rational system, to choose a more complicated notation over a simpler one, if both notations had exactly the same meaning.

As to the system's consistency: here the converse should hold, i.e., the same notation should mean the same thing from work to work. But in all things human, consistency has its limits. Bach's notation undeniably has its share of idiosyncracies, redundancies, ambiguities, and arbitrary elements—as much as any other man-made system: human language, for example. Moreover, even a perfectly consistent system, in the hands of a fallible mortal, could be used less than perfectly; and we must assume that even Johann Sebastian Bach may, on occasion, have notated a work in one way when another would have been more appropriate or effective. He could have done so through thoughtlessness—or perhaps as a matter of expediency.

I. The tempo of the *tempo ordinario*

During the baroque era, the normal tempo was referred to as either *tempo ordinario* or *tempo giusto*.[10] According to Sébastien Brossard, however, *tempo ordinario* primarily designated common time in contemporary

---

[10] See David Fallows, articles "Tempo giusto," and "Tempo ordinario," in *The New Grove Dictionary of Music and Musicians*, 6th ed. (London: Macmillan Publishers, 1980), 18:685.

Italian usage.[11] Handel seems to have had both meanings in mind when he employed the heading *a tempo ordinario* for movements in common time like the choruses "Lift up your heads" and "Their sound is gone out" from *Messiah*. Bach, for his part, evidently never made use of the expression *tempo ordinario;* but *a tempo giusto* appears at least three times in his compositions.[12] In all three instances, the purpose of the term is clearly not to suggest a particular tempo but rather to prescribe strict, i.e., measured time in a recitative-like movement. That is, Bach uses the term exactly as he does *a tempo* and *a battuta*.[13]

By far the most common meter in Bach's music is common time. Therefore, it seems safe to designate the quarter-note in C time as representing the normal, "ordinary" beat. As Curt Sachs pointed out, "the metronomical value of both...the stride and the heartbeat lies between M.M. 60 and M.M. 80."[14] Since contemporary accounts testify that Bach's normal tempo was "very lively,"[15] it seems historically justified to posit the speed of Bach's normal beat—his personal *tempo ordinario*—at the high end of the normal human pulse rate: namely, M.M. = ca. 80. If we can believe Quantz's assertion that during Bach's generation tempi were quite a bit slower than during his own, then we can be quite certain that a basic beat of M.M. 80 would have struck Bach's contemporaries as a "very lively" tempo, indeed.[16]

---

[11]Sébastien de Brossard, *Dictionaire de Musique,* 2nd ed. (Paris: Christophe Ballard, 1705; repr. Hilversum: Frits Knuf, 1965), p. 154.

[12]In the heading of the *Choral et Recit à tempo giusto,* "Auf sperren sie den Rachen weit," BWV 178/5 (composed for 30 July 1724); at the arioso passage (m. 13) of "Wenn einstens die Posaunen schallen," BWV 127/4 (composed for 11 February 1725); and in the heading of the recitative "Hochteurer Mann," BWV 210/9 (composed between 1738 and 1741).

[13]The term *a tempo giusto* should have been listed along with *a tempo* and *a battuta* in Marshall, note 25.

[14]Sachs, *Rhythm and Tempo,* p. 203. The medical profession puts the average human pulse rate at 72 per minute. See Hoekstra, p. 12.

[15]In the words of the *Necrolog:* "of the tempo, which he generally took very lively, he was uncommonly sure." ("und im Zeitmasse, welches er gemeiniglich sehr lebhaft nahm, [war er] überaus sicher.") Translated in Hans T. David and Arthur Mendel, *The Bach Reader,* 2nd ed. (New York: Norton, 1966), p. 222; original in Hans-Joachim Schulze, ed., *Bach-Dokumente, III: Dokumente zum Nachwirken Johann Sebastian Bachs* (Kassel: Bärenreiter, 1972), p. 87.

[16]"What in former times was considered to be quite fast would have been played almost twice as slow as in the present day." Quantz, *On Playing the Flute,* p. 285. ("Was in vorigen Zeiten recht geschwind gehen sollte, wurde fast noch einmal so langsam gespielt, als heutiges Tages." *Versuch einer Anweisung,* p. 263)

It cannot be emphasized sufficiently that the *tempo ordinario,* whether defined as ♩ = M.M. 80 or anything else, was by no means a fixed metronomic point but rather—like baroque chamber pitch—encompassed a fairly generous amplitude. This is already clear from its traditional association with such a variable standard as the human pulse. In Bach's case, it may have extended from M.M. 72 to 88—or even further in each direction, depending on the acoustical conditions, the technical abilities of the musicians, and any number of ineffable subjective circumstances of the moment. Nonetheless, in light of Bach's documented preference for "very lively" tempi, I shall adopt M.M. 80 for the calculations to follow, even though the figure 72, being readily divisible by 2, 3, 4, 6, and 12, would be more convenient.

Now to our postulates. We begin with the following six rules:

Time Signatures

1. The principal considerations in the choice of time signature are (a) the rate of surface motion, and (b) the grouping of surface rhythms.

2. The numerator establishes the organization of the meter (duple, triple, compound) by defining the groupings of the various rhythmic levels.

3. The denominator establishes the unit of measure—and the approximate speed—as derived from the normal binary ratios prevailing under *tempo ordinario.*

Time Signatures and Note-Values

4. The choice of denominator determines the usual number of subdivisions of the beat: the lower the denominator (2 or 4), the larger the number of subdivisions available.

5. Conversely, the higher the denominator (8 or 16), the fewer subdivisions available.

6. By the same token, the higher the denominator (8 or 16), the larger the number of multiples (macro-groupings) of the beat available.

Rules 1 and 2 are self-evident and need no explanation. Rule 3, on the contrary, is crucial to all that will follow here. It maintains that the unit of measure established by the denominator is always derived from the *binary* ratios pevailing under *tempo ordinario.* That is: if the denominator is 4, then the unit of measure is the quarter-note; if the denominator is 8, then the unit of measure—but not necessarily the beat—is an eighth-note normally twice as fast as the quarter. That is, if the quarter-note = M.M. 80, then the eighth-note = M.M. 160. (The actual beat under an 8-denominator, however, is often the dotted quarter, as in $^6_8$.)

The practical consequences of Rules 4, 5, and 6 regarding the relationship between the denominator and the number of subdivisions (or multiples) of the beat are these: In C or $^3_4$ time (i.e., low denominators), there are normally two active subdivisions of the quarter-note beat—eighths and sixteenths—which accommodate the prevailing units of rhythmic activity:

$$♩→♫→♬♬$$

In $^3_8$ or $^6_8$ time, on the other hand (i.e., high denominators), there is normally only one significant subdivision of the eighth-note beat—sixteenths: ♪→♫. And there is generally no subdivision at all of the sixteenth-note unit under 16-denominator signatures. Rule 6, finally, attests to the phenomenon of increasing numbers of beat multiples (at the expense of subdivisions) available under the higher denominators, namely: four with denominator 8: $^3_8$, $^6_8$, $^9_8$, $^{12}_8$; five (theoretically six) with denominator 16: ($^3_{16}$), $^6_{16}$, $^9_{16}$, $^{12}_{16}$, $^{18}_{16}$, $^{24}_{16}$.

In application these propositions produce the patterns of metrical organization shown in Table 1. An immediate attraction of this schema is that it draws a meaningful tempo distinction between triplet subdivisions (triplet eighths) in 4-denominator meters and the eighths in compound 8-denominator meters. It thus offers an answer to our original question about the theme from the fifth Brandenburg Concerto. Example 1 is based on a quarter-note pulse. Accordingly, if ♩ = M.M. 80, then the triplet eighths proceed at a rate of 240, and the sixteenths at a quite brisk 480. This tempo is perhaps reflected in the *allegro* heading, but presumably it would have prevailed even in the absence of a tempo designation. (The primary purpose of the tempo marking here was surely to confirm the reestablishment of the *tempo ordinario* after the *Adagio/Affettuoso* second movement.[17]) Had Bach notated the movement in $^6_8$—analogous to his choice of *Allegro* $^{12}_8$ for the final movement of the sixth Brandenburg

---

[17]The heading of the movement in the autograph score and in the solo parts reads *Affetuoso,* but the indication in the *tacet* (but likewise autograph) ripieno parts for this movement reads *Adagio tacet.* See *Brandenburgische Konzerte,* facsimile edition of the autograph score, ed. Peter Wackernagel (Leipzig: Edition Peters, [1960]); and *Brandenburgishes Konzert Nr. 5, D-Dur, BWV 1050,* facsimile edition of the original parts, ed. Hans-Joachim Schulze (Leipzig: Edition Peters, 1975).

Bach's *tempo ordinario*   257

Table 1

Patterns of Metrical Organization

I. Unit (denominator) = ♩ (=M.M. "80")
    Time Signatures: 2/4, 3/4, C, 6/4
    a. Simple binary divisions on all rhythmic levels:
       Subdivision 2:   ♬ = 320 (2 × 160)
       Subdivision 1:   ♪ = 160 (2 × 80)
       Beat: ♩ = 80
    b. Ternary division of the quarter:
       Subdivision 2:   ♬ = 480 (2 × 240)
       Subdivision 1:   ♪ = 240 (3 × 80)
       Beat: ♩ = 80
    c. Ternary division of the eighth:
       Subdivision 2:   ♬ = 480 (3 × 160)
       Subdivision 1:   ♪ = 160 (2 × 80)
       Beat: ♩ = 80

II. Unit (denominator) = ♪ (= M.M. "160")
    Time Signatures: 3/8, 6/8, 9/8, 12/8
    Subdivision 1:   ♬ = 320 (binary grouping)
    Beat: ♪ = 160
    Multiple: ♩. = >52

III. Unit (denominator) = ♬ (= M.M. "320")
    Time Signatures: 6/16, 9/16, 12/16, 18/16, 24/16
    Beat: ♬ = 320 (ternary grouping)
    Multiple 1:   ♬. = <108 [♪ = 160]
    Multiple 2:   ♩. = >52

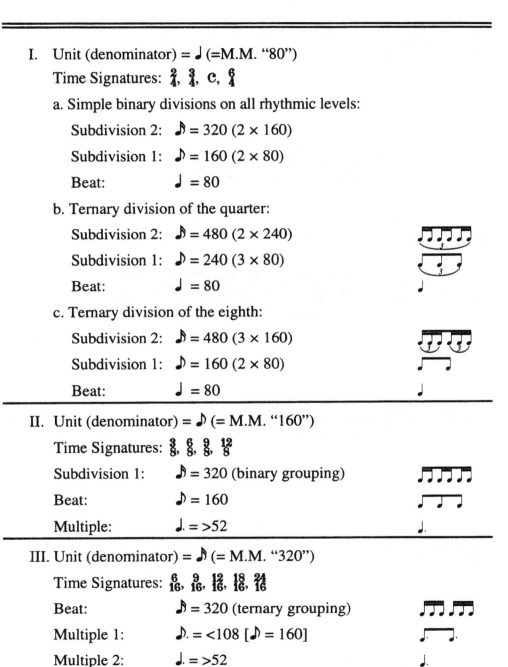

258 Robert L. Marshall

Example 3. The Final Movements of the Brandenburg Concertos: Incipits

a. BWV 1046/4

b. BWV 1047/3

c. BWV 1048/2

d. BWV 1049/3

e. BWV 1051/3

concerto—the prevailing unit of motion, acccording to our model, would have been a leisurely ♪ = M.M. 160, with the sixteenths at 320—a tempo in effect too slow by a third ([♪] 160:240 = [♪] 320:480 = 2:3).[18]

The variety of meters (and, consequently, of tempi) encountered among the final movements of the six Brandenburg Concertos is striking (Ex. 3). In addition to the curious meter of the fifth Brandenburg, we find ¾ *Menuet*, 2/4 *Allegro assai*, 12/8 *Allegro* (prevailing sixteenths), ¢ *Presto*, 12/8 *Allegro* (prevailing eighths).[19]

Our table asserts further that 6/8 and 12/16 prescribe the same rate of motion for the smallest prevailing note values, namely, ♪ = 320, but grouped differently (3 × 2 instead of 2 × 3) (Ex. 4).

Example 4

a. *Well-Tempered Clavier,* Book I: Fugue in G Major, BWV 860/2

b. *Well-Tempered Clavier,* Book II: Fugue in C♯ Minor, BWV 873/2

On the other hand, the rate of motion on the next higher rhythmic level diverges substantially: 6/8 ♪ = 160 vs. 12/16 ♪. = <108 (i.e., one-third of 320).

---

[18]As for the treatment of the dotted notes in the finale of the fifth concerto, they are to be assimilated with the triplets. According to his pupil, Johann Friedrich Agricola, Bach assimilated the rhythms "in extremely fast tempi" ("bey der äußersten Geschwindigkeit"). See Erwin R. Jacobi, "Neues zur Frage 'Punktierte Rhythmen gegen Triolen' und zur Transkriptionstechnik bei J. S. Bach," *Bach-Jahrbuch 1962,* pp. 88–96, especially p. 90.

[19]A tempo of about ♩. = ca. M.M. >52 (♪ = ca. M.M. 160) for the final movement of the sixth concerto—or for the opening 3/8 *Allegro* movement of the fourth concerto—as implied by the use of the 8-denominator, may, admittedly, seem too slow for modern listeners accustomed to high tech tempi.

260 Robert L. Marshall

If Bach wanted a rate for ternary sixteenths substantially quicker than M.M. 320, then he notated them as triplet sixteenths in ₵ time (Ex. 5).

Example 5

a. *Well-Tempered Clavier,* Book I: Prelude in D Minor, BWV 851/1

b. *Well-Tempered Clavier,* Book II: Fugue in D Minor, BWV 875/2

This distinction may explain Bach's occasional use of the double time signatures ₵+12/8, ₵+24/16, or 3/4+18/16. Their purpose, presumably, is to establish the quarter-note as the unit of measure—along with its implications for the *tempo ordinario*—but with the internal organization of the compound meter. That is, the double time signature is presumably synonymous with a simple 4-denominator signature with triplet indications for the sixteenths—but spared the composer the bother of adding innumerable triplet signs (Ex. 6).

Example 6. *Well-Tempered Clavier,* Book I: Prelude in G Major, BWV 860/1

Whenever duple and triple subdivisions of the same unit were to be combined, however, then Bach was obliged to choose a 4-denominator—regardless of the desired tempo (Ex. 7).[20]

---

[20]Bach did not have a notation that would have enabled him to prescribe duplets in a compound meter.

Example 7. *Well-Tempered Clavier,* Book II: Fugue in D Minor, 875/2, m. 6

II. Modifications of the *tempo ordinario*

We must now introduce two further rules:

7. As the normal number of subdivisions of a beat is exceeded, the pulse rate is retarded.

8. Conversely, if the normal number of subdivisions of the beat is not used, the pulse rate is accelerated.

Rule 7 explains that the introduction of, for example, thirty-second notes in C time as the prevailing unit of rhythmic activity slows the beat to below ♩ = M.M. 80; and the introduction of sixteenth-notes in ¢ time as the prevailing unit of activity slows the beat to below 𝅗𝅥 = M.M. 80. Rule 8, for its part, reveals that in a composition, for example, in 9/8 with few or no sixteenths, the beat is faster than in a 9/8 composition with prevailing sixteenth-note motion. (See Section III below.)

Rules 7 and 8 acknowledge and confirm the importance attached by eighteenth-century theorists to the smallest prevailing note values in a composition in determining the proper tempo. According to C. P. E. Bach:

> The pace of a composition, which is usually indicated by several well-known Italian expressions, is based on its general content as well as on the fastest notes and passages contained in it. Due consideration of these factors will prevent an allegro from being rushed and an adagio from being dragged.[21]

---

[21]Carl Philipp Emanuel Bach, *Essay on the True Art of Playing Keyboard Instruments,* trans. William J. Mitchell (New York: Norton, 1949), p. 151. The original reads: "Der Grad der Bewegung läßt sich so wohl nach dem Inhalte des Stückes überhaupt, den man durch gewisse bekannte italiänische Kunstwörter anzuzeigen pflegt, als besonders aus den geschwindesten Noten und Figuren darinnen beurtheilen. Bey dieser Untersuchung wird man sich in den Stand setzen, weder im Allegro übereilend, noch im Adagio zu

Bach's pupil Johann Philipp Kirnberger is more specific:

> Regarding note values, dance pieces involving sixteenth and thirty-second notes have a slower tempo than those that tolerate only eighth and at most sixteenth notes as the fastest note values in the same meter...thus the *tempo giusto* is determined by the meter and by the longer and shorter note values of a composition.[22]

Tempo Designations. We may reasonably assume that Bach resorted to verbal tempo designations in order to refine or modify the tempi that would otherwise have been implied by the usual combinations of time signatures and rhythmic values. My earlier survey revealed that there are no fewer than forty-five tempo designations in the Bach sources, of which the six principal terms, in order of increasing velocity, are: *adagio, largo, andante, allegro, vivace,* and *presto.* Moreover, *allegro* could be shown, under normal circumstances, i.e. with a quarter-note unit and prevailing sixteenth-note motion, to represent—or, more commonly, to restore—the *tempo ordinario.*[23] Example 8 provides a representative sampling of Bach's use of the most common tempo designations.

Example 8

a. Sonata in G Minor for Unaccompanied Violin, BWV 1001/1

---

schläfrig zu werden." Carl Philipp Emanuel Bach, *Versuch über die wahre Art, das Clavier zu spielen.* Facsimile reprint of the 1st edition (Berlin, 1753 and 1762), ed. Lothar Hoffmann-Erbrecht (Leipzig: VEB Breitkopf & Härtel, 1957), p. 121.

[22]Johann Philipp Kirnberger, *The Art of Strict Musical Composition,* trans. David Beach and Jurgen Thym (New Haven: Yale University Press, 1982), p. 377. The original reads: "In Ansehung der Notengattungen haben die Tanzstücke, worin Sechszehntel und Zweyunddreyßigtheile vorkommen, eine langsamere Taktbewegung, als solche, die bey der nemlichen Taktart nur Achtel, höchstens Sechzehntel, als die geschwindesten Notengattungen vertragen....Also wird das *Tempo giusto* durch die Taktart und durch die längeren und kürzeren Notengattungen eines Stückes bestimmt." Johann Philipp Kirnberger, *Die Kunst des reinen Satzes in der Musik* (Berlin, 1776–79; facs. repr. Hildesheim: Olms-Verlagsbuchhandlung, 1968), 2:107.

[23]Marshall, pp. 264f.

Example 8 (*continued*)

b. Sonata in C Major for Unaccompanied Violin, BWV 1005/1

c. Mass in B Minor: Opening of Kyrie I, BWV 232/1

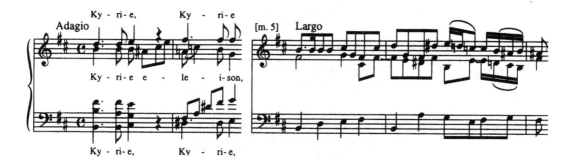

d. Sonata in C Major for Unaccompanied Violin, BWV 1005/3

e. Concerto in C Major for Two Harpsichords, BWV 1061a/2

264 Robert L. Marshall

Example 8 (*continued*)

f. Concerto in the Italian Style, BWV 971/2

g. Sonata for Violin and Cembalo obbligato, BWV 1015/3

h. Sonata for Violin and Cembalo obbligato, BWV 1019/1

i. Sonata for Flute and Cembalo obbligato, BWV 1032/1

Example 8 (*continued*)

j. Mass in B Minor: Opening of Gloria, BWV 232/4

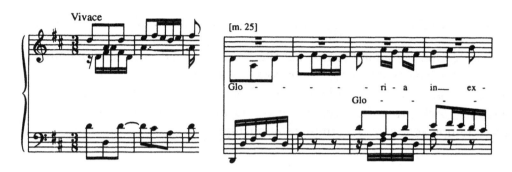

k. Clavier Toccata in F♯ Minor, BWV 910/3

l. Concerto in the Italian Style, BWV 971/3

The frequent association of the slowest of Bach's common tempo designations, *adagio* (or its synonyms *lente* and *grave*), with prevailing thirty-second note motion strongly suggsts that the term normally (but not invariably) signalled something approaching a simple augmentation or doubling of the duration (or perhaps the subdivision) of the beat. At the other extreme, too, *presto* presumably increases the speed of the beat beyond *allegro* (i.e., the *tempo ordinario*) in some simple ratio. As a matter of practicality, given the "liveliness" of Bach's *tempo ordinario,* that ratio is hardly likely to exceed 3:2. We can, then, assign the following approximate "real time" values to the mid- and endpoints of Bach's tempo designations:

adagio 𝄴 ♩ = ca. 40   *allegro* 𝄴 ♩ = ca. 80   *presto* 𝄴 ♩ (𝄵 ♩) = ca. 120

As for the remaining terms: despite the occasional, inevitable inconsistencies, the basic conceptual framework—and Bach's practice in general—places *andante* between *adagio* and *allegro, largo* between *adagio* and *andante,* and *vivace* between *allegro* and *presto.*[24] Table 2 summarizes, and attempts to concretize, these relationships.

Table 2

Bach's Principal Tempo Designations
(with Hypothetical Metronomic Values)

Designation	Tempo Unit	M.M. Value
adagio	𝄴 ♩	= ca. 40
largo	𝄴 ♩	= ca. 50?
andante	𝄴 ♩	= ca. 60
allegro	𝄴 ♩	= ca. 80 (*tempo ordinario*)
vivace	𝄴 ♩	= ca. 100
presto	𝄴 ♩ (𝄵 ♩)	= ca. 120

Once again, these metronomic values must be understood as representing the hypothetical medians of normal ranges extending perhaps as much as ten metronomic points in either direction. It is certainly clear from the extensive thirty-second note figuration in the second movement of the "Italian" Concerto (Ex. 8f), for example, that the tempo in this instance must be considerably closer to ♩ = 50 than to ♩ = 60. The primary purpose of the *andante* designation for this movement, no doubt, is to avoid the excessively slow (*adagio*) tempo otherwise suggested by the prevalence of thirty-second notes.

Moreover, Bach did not observe these terminological distinctions rigidly. Don O. Franklin has argued persuasively that in the Organ Prelude

---

[24] The evidence and argumentation are set forth in Marshall, pp. 265–67.

and Fugue in G Major, BWV 541, the tempo relationship between the prelude—in ¾ time and marked *vivace*—and the fugue—in common time and with no tempo marking (i.e., implicitly *allegro*)—is ¾ ♩. = ₵ ♩, i.e., 3:2 (Ex. 9).[25]

Example 9. Prelude and Fugue in G Major for Organ, BWV 541

Nor is it certain that *largo* should invariably be understood as prescribing a significantly different (i.e., faster) tempo than *adagio*. In the Concerto for Two Harpsichords, BWV 1061a, Bach seems to have equated the two. On the other hand, the successive autograph indications *adagio...largo* at the beginning of the Mass in B Minor strongly suggest a meaningful distinction between them. (See Figure 1 and Exx. 8c and 8e.)

Figure 1. Mass in B Minor, BWV 232, original performance parts

---

[25]Franklin, "The Fermata," pp. 353, 356.

There are, then, always exceptions. In some compositions the *tempo ordinario* undoubtedly remains unchanged, despite the presence of thirty-seconds, when the latter function in a clearly ornamental context (Ex. 10).

Example 10

a. *Well-Tempered Clavier,* Book I: Fugue in D Major, BWV 850/2

b. *Well-Tempered Clavier,* Book I: Prelude in B♭ Major, BWV 866/1

or in virtuoso passage work of the sort displayed, for example, in the cadenza of the fifth Brandenburg Concerto. For its part, an *adagio* designation need not be associated either with thirty-second notes or, apparently, with anything like a strict augmentation of the *tempo ordinario*. The aria "Mein teurer Heiland" from the St. John Passion carries a double time signature: 12/8 in the basso solo and continuo parts and C in the chorus parts (and its colla parte instruments), along with an *adagio* indication in the continuo parts.[26] The basso and the continuo parts elaborate the 12/8 theme, while the chorus presents the chorale verse in quarter-notes (Ex. 11).

The normal tempo C ♩ = 80 would be readily appropriate for this chorale (as it is for virtually all of Bach's chorales), but it seems rather hurried for the obbligato parts. Yet it is difficult to imagine that the *adagio* indication—which appears only in the continuo parts—calls in this case for a tempo anything like twice as slow as the *tempo ordinario*. Most likely it prescribes only a slightly slower tempo here (♩ = 60?). Perhaps it is to be understood as an instruction to the continuo players to regard their part as "in 12"—a possibility reinforced by the movement's rapid harmonic rhythm.

---

[26] See the *NBA*, 2/4, ed. Arthur Mendel, *KB*, p. 267.

Example 11. St. John Passion, "Mein teurer Heiland," BWV 245/32, mm. 3–6

At the other tempo extreme, compositions in *alla breve* notation usually manifest prevailing eighth-note motion and often carry the designation *vivace* or *presto* confirming the shift of the beat to the next higher rhythmic level, i.e., to the half-note, and the adoption of a fast tempo. For true *alla breve* movements, Bach seems, for the most part, to have preferred the time signatures 2 or 𝟐, rather than ¢.[27] Indeed, the not uncommon occurence of a ¢ signature in conjunction with prevailing sixteenth motion (even if combined with a quick tempo marking) surely implies—in conformity with Rule 7, above—not a literal doubling but rather only a slight acceleration of the *tempo ordinario:* that is, faster than C♩ = 80, but slower than ¢♩ = 80. The first movements of no fewer than five of the six Brandenburg Concertos are notated in this fashion. (Of these only the fifth carries a tempo indication: *allegro.*)

The B-minor prelude from Book 2 of the *Well-Tempered Clavier* presents yet a different case. The movement was originally notated in C with prevailing sixteenth-note and occasional thirty-second note motion but then rewritten in ¢ with the tempo designation *allegro.*[28] The introduction of an *alla breve* signature in this instance does not seem to have been motivated by a desire to increase the tempo. If anything, the *allegro* designation affirms the *tempo ordinario*. Bach's concern here, rather, may have been to avoid the trivialization of the quick figures throughout the prelude or perhaps to synchronize the barring and downbeat emphasis with the movement's characteristic whole-note rate of harmonic change (Ex. 12).

III. Compound Time Signatures and the *tempo ordinario*

We must consider further the case of 8-denominators, i.e., compound meters. The basic position that has been advocated here so far is that the denominator establishes the eighth-note as the temporal unit in these meters and that its normal temporal value, derived from the *tempo ordinario*, is equivalent to the ordinary, binary eighth, namely, ♪ = ca. M.M. 160. This

---

[27] I am indebted to Joshua Rifkin for this observation.

[28] The original notation is preserved in a manuscript copied by Bach's pupil and son-in-law, Johann Christoph Altnikol. See Don O. Franklin, "Reconstructing the *Urpartitur* for WTC II: a study of the 'London autograph' (BL Add. MS 35021)," in *Bach Studies*, ed. Don O. Franklin (Cambridge: Cambridge University Press, 1989), p. 265, n. 48.

Example 12

a. *Well-Tempered Clavier,* Book II: Prelude in B Minor, BWV 893/1, original notation

b. Well-Tempered Clavier, Book II: Prelude in B Minor, BWV 893/1, final version

in turn establishes the value of the dotted quarter as ♩. = ca. >M.M. 52. This tempo is not implausible for pieces with prevailing motion in sixteenths where the beat is normally on the eighth-note, as in the Fugue in G Major, BWV 860/2 (Ex. 4a, above) and the Fugue in G Major, BWV 884/2 (Ex. 13):

Example 13. *Well-Tempered Clavier,* Book II: Fugue in G Major, BWV 884/2

perhaps also the Prelude in C♯ Major, BWV 848/1 (Ex. 14):

Example 14. *Well-Tempered Clavier,* Book I: Prelude in C♯ Major, BWV 848/1

But ♩. = >M.M. 52 is certainly too slow for most compositions with prevailing eighth-note motion (Ex. 15).

Example 15

a. *Well-Tempered Clavier,* Book I: Prelude in E Major, BWV 854/1

b. *Well-Tempered Clavier,* Book II: Fugue in G♯ Minor, BWV 887/2

The beat in such compositions no doubt is not on the eighth but on the dotted quarter. According to Kirnberger, in fact, the 8-denominator meters are to be understood fundamentally as triplet subdivisions of the 4-denominators: 2/4 ♩ = 6/8 ♩. (= ca. M.M. 80). Kirnberger claims that the differences between 9/8 and 3/4 or between 6/8 and 2/4 do not involve tempo at all but only the manner of performance:

> The 9/8 meter of three triple beats that is derived from 3/4 has the same tempo as 3/4, but the eighth notes are performed more lightly than in 3/4. It is a mistake to consider this meter as a 3/4 meter whose beats consist of triplets. He who has only a moderate command of performance knows that triplets in 3/4 meter are played differently from eighths in 9/8 meter. The former are played very lightly and without the slightest pressure on the last note, but the latter heavier and with some weight on the last note. The former never or only rarely permit a harmony to be sounded with the last note, but the latter do very often. The former do not permit any arpeggiations [subdivisions?] in sixteenth notes, but the latter do very easily. If the two meters were not distinguished by special qualities, all gigues in 6/8 could also be written in 2/4; 12/8 would be a C meter, and 6/8 a 2/4 meter. How senseless this is can easily be discovered by anyone who rewrites, for example, a gigue in 12/8 or 6/8 meter in C or 2/4 meter.[29]

---

[29]Kirnberger, *The Art,* p. 396. The original reads: "Der aus dem 3/4 Takt entstehende Neunachteltakt von drey triplirten Zeiten hat die Bewegung des 3/4 Taktes, doch werden die Achtel leichter als in 3/4 vorgetragen. Man irret sich, wenn man diese Taktart für einen 3/4 Takt hält, dessen Zeiten aus Triolen bestehen: wer nur einigermaßen den Vortrag in seiner Gewalt hat, weiß, daß Triolen in dem 3/4 Takt anders vorgetragen

Kirnberger's insistence on $\quarternote = \dottedquarter$ rather than $\eighthnote = \eighthnote$ equivalence between 4-denominator and 8-denominator time signatures, as we have seen, is quite plausible—at least for compositions with prevailing eighth-note motion. On the other hand, the assumption of eighth-note equivalence that has enabled us to posit a meaningful tempo distinction between triplet eighths in common time and the corresponding units in compound meters is corroborated by Bach's own notation of the "Gloria" from the Mass in B Minor. As Arthur Mendel observed, the "Gloria," in 3/8 time and marked *Vivace,* ends with a hemiola cadence that leads directly into the "Et in terra pax" movement, notated in C.[30] The hemiola unambiguously defines the tempo relation between the two movements as 3/8 $\eighthnote$ = C $\eighthnote$. Mendel also pointed out that the 100-measure "Gloria" contains 302 eighth-notes (100 × 3 (+2)), the 76-measure "Et in terra" contains 606 eighth-notes (76 × 8), and saw this 1:2 ratio as further confirmation of the $\eighthnote = \eighthnote$ tempo relationship (Ex. 16).

Example 16. Mass in B Minor: Gloria, BWV 232/4, m. 99, to 232/5, m. 2

As to the absolute tempo: according to the reasoning advanced earlier, the *vivace* designation would seem to call for a tempo of $\eighthnote$ = ca. M.M. 200 (i.e., $\quarternote$ = ca. M.M. 100).

---

werden, als Achtel in dem 3/8 Takt. Jene werden ganz leicht und ohne den geringsten Druck auf der letzten Note, diese hingegen schwerer und mit etwas Gewicht auf der letzten Note vorgetragen. Jene vertragen gar nicht oder doch selten eine anschlagende Harmonie auf der letzten Note, diese hingegen sehr oft. Jene vertragen keine Brechungen in Sechszehntel, diese aber ganz leicht. Wären beyde Taktarten nicht durch besondere Eigenschaften von einander unterschieden, so müsten alle Giguen im 6/8 auch in den 2/4 Takt versetzt werden können, der 12/8 wäre ein C Takt, und der 6/8 ein 2/4 Takt; wie widersinnig dieses sey, kann jeder leicht selbst erfahren, der z.B. ein Gigue in 12/8 oder 6/8 Takt in dem C oder 2/4 Takt versetzt." Kirnberger, *Die Kunst,* 2:129.

[30]Arthur Mendel, "A Note on Proportional Relationships in Bach Tempi," *The Musical Times* 100 (1959): 683–85.

In the Sanctus of the B-minor Mass, we encounter the same combination of meters between the "Sanctus" and the "pleni sunt coeli" sections as we found in the "Gloria" movement—but in reverse order. It would seem to follow, however, that they must be governed by the same relation. That is, the tempo relation between the opening of the movement, in ₵, and the "pleni sunt coeli" section, in ⅜, should, once again, as Bernard Rose suggested, be based on eighth-note equivalence: ₵ (binary) ♪ = ⅜ ♪, or ₵ ♩ = ⅜ ♩.[31] This, reasonably enough, would render the (melismatic) triplet eighths in the opening ₵ section 50 percent faster than the (syllabic) eighths of the ⅜ "pleni": ₵ ♪³ = ca. M.M. 240 vs. ⅜ ♪ = ca. M.M. 160 (Ex. 17).

Example 17. Mass in B Minor, BWV 232/22

a. Opening of the Sanctus

b. Opening of the Pleni section

Furthermore, the proportions of the two sections of the movement argue in this instance, too, for the proposed tempo relation. The 47-measure "Sanctus" is the equivalent of 376 (binary) eighth-notes in length (47 mm. × 8 eighth-notes per measure); the 121-measure "pleni" 363 eighth-notes (121 × 3)—virtually a 1:1 ratio. (The binary division of the quarter-note in the "Sanctus" section is in fact represented beneath the prevailing triplets—in the timpani part with its rhythm: ♩♫♫ .)

Mendel discounted the testimony of these proportions and argued rather for ₵ ♩ = ⅜ ♩. in this movement. Drawing on "the practical experience of conducting the work," he finds that "Dr. Rose's suggested proportion of ⅜ ♩ = ₵ ♩ makes either the ₵ too fast or the ⅜ too slow."[32] This, of course, is an explicitly personal judgement. On the other hand, some might find that

---

[31] Bernard Rose, "A Further Note on Bach Tempi," *The Musical Times* 101 (1960): 107.
[32] Arthur Mendel, "Bach Tempi: A Rebuttal," *The Musical Times* 101 (1960): 251.

declaiming the "pleni" text at ♪ = ca. M.M. 240 (as implied by Mendel's suggestion, and, of course, still assuming a *tempo ordinario* of M.M. 80) is uncomfortably rushed. Moreover, since the tempo relation $\frac{3}{8}$ ♩. = 𝄵 ♩ ($\frac{3}{8}$ ♪ = 𝄵 $\overset{-3}{♪}$) would result in an equivalence between the triplet eighths in the "Sanctus" and the eighth-note units in the "pleni," there would be effectively no tempo change at all between the two sections, which would raise the question why Bach bothered to change the meter at all.

In sum, there are evidently two different tempi for compositions in 8-denominator meters. In conformity with our Rule 8 (and with Kirnberger's description), for pieces with prevailing eighth-note motion the *tempo ordinario* is represented by the dotted quarter: ♩. = ca. M.M. 80 (♪ = ca. M.M. 240). For pieces containing significant sixteenth-note motion, however, the *tempo ordinario* is represented by the eighth-note: ♪ = ca. M.M. 160 (♩. = ca. >M.M. 52).[33]

Let us consider, in conclusion, the large-scale temporal organization of a multi-movement composition. The funeral ode, *Laß Fürstin, laß noch einen Strahl*, BWV 198, composed for the cermonies held on 17 October 1727 for Queen Christiane Eberhardine, is a ten-movement work. It survives only in a composing score;[34] the autograph—as usual—contains no tempo markings. But in this case—as usual—none were necessary: a consistent *tempo ordinario* of approximately 80 seems to work quite well for the entire composition (Ex. 18).

The salient point, however, is that retaining the *tempo ordinario* through the entire composition is not at all a prescription for monotony. Quite the contrary: the contrast and juxtaposition of different meters (𝄴, $\frac{3}{4}$, 𝄵, $\frac{12}{8}$), and especially the diversity of surface motion prevailing from one movement to the next—from even eighth-notes in the recitatives to dotted sixteenths and thirty-seconds (Movement 1) to mixed duplet and triplet sixteenths (Movement 3) to ternary eighths of different values (Movement 5 vis-à-vis Movement 10)—produce a fully satisfying variety with respect

---

[33] Don Franklin reaches the same conclusion—at least with respect to relative tempi. For the Prelude and Fuge in A Major, BWV 888, from the *Well-Tempered Clavier II*, wherein the prelude, notated in $\frac{12}{8}$, proceeds in eighth-note motion, Franklin prescribes the tempo relation: (prelude) $\frac{12}{8}$ ♩. = 𝄵 ♩ (fugue). Moreover, his discussion of the Gloria and Sanctus movements from the Mass in B Minor, accepts, as does ours, eighth-note equivalence between the $\frac{3}{8}$ and 𝄴 sections. See Franklin, "The Fermata," pp. 352, 355, and pp. 372–74, 377, n. 43, respectively.

[34] See the *NBA*, I/38, ed. Werner Neumann, *KB*, pp. 98–119.

to the *perceived* tempo throughout the work.[35] At the same time, the relation of the entire composition to a single underlying, unifying *tactus* imparts to the whole a fundamental unity that is both intellectually profound and aesthetically compelling.[36] But this, after all, is only what one expects from a well-regulated composition from the pen of Johann Sebastian Bach.[37]

Example 18. *Laß, Fürstin,* BWV 198: Movement Incipits

---

[35]As usual there is some question as to the tempo of the 12/8 movements. The presence of sixteenths in No. 5, the aria "Wie starb die Heldin so vergnügt" (see especially mm. 43–45, 52), suggests that ♪ = M.M. 160 (♩. = M.M. >52) is a plausible tempo. Conversely, the unbroken eighth-note motion of the final chorus, "Doch Königin! du stirbest nicht," suggests ♩. = M.M. 80.

[36]It does not seem that the presence or absence of movement-ending fermatas has any connection with the existence of a pervasive *tactus* and hence a rational tempo relation governing the movements of this work, as propounded in Franklin, "The Fermata." Nor is it clear that the omission of concluding fermatas in four movements in the cantata autograph was deliberate or significant. There are fermatas at the ends of Movements 1, 6, and 7; 8, 9, and 10–that is, the first and last two movements of Part I, and all three movements of Part II of the cantata.

[37]I am indebted to Don O. Franklin for making a copy of his essay "The Fermata as Notational Convention" available to me before its publication and to Mark Kroll, Joshua Rifkin, and David Schulenberg for many valuable suggestions and comments.

Bach's *tempo ordinario* 277

Example 18 (*continued*)

278 Robert L. Marshall

Example 18 (*continued*)

Amorous Dialogues: Poetic Topos and PolyphonicTexture in Some Polytextual Songs of the Late Middle Ages*

Virginia Newes

In a series of important studies of the arias of Johann Sebastian Bach, Paul Brainard has demonstrated convincingly that the composer's melodic invention was generated by a keen sensitivity to the prosody, syntax, and affect of the text as well as by more abstract musical concerns.[1] Indeed, in Bach's time, mastery of the poet's craft was considered an integral part of the craft of composition,[2] reflecting a continuing predominance in the Baroque era of vocal over instrumental music. Turning to composers of earlier centuries, we find that they too looked on the text as a prime source of musical invention. Like Bach, song composers of the late Middle Ages were thoroughly grounded in prosody and versification; in fact, most of them probably composed their own poetic texts. These poet-composers were also well versed in the thematic commonplaces of the rhetorical tradition that flourished in troubadour and trouvère poetry and reached a high point in the thirteenth-century *Romance of the Rose*. Although— judging at least from the text underlay in the manuscript copies that have come down to us— they may not always have been sensitive to details of correct accentuation, they were clearly aware of the nuances of poetic theme and genre, an area of investigation that has received too little scholarly attention. This study

---

*An earlier version of this paper appeared in *Sonus* 12 (1991): 66–86. I should like to thank the editors for permission to publish this material here.

[1] Paul Brainard, "The Aria and its Ritornello: The Question of 'Dominance' in Bach," in *Bachiana et alia Musicologica: Festschrift Alfred Dürr zum 65. Geburtstag*, ed. Wolfgang Rehm (Kassel: Bärenreiter, 1983), pp. 39–51; "Aria and Ritornello: New Aspects of the Comparison Handel/Bach," in *Bach, Handel, Scarlatti: Tercentenary Essays*, ed. Peter Williams (Cambridge: Cambridge University Press, 1985), pp. 2–33; "The Regulative and Generative Roles of Verse in Bach's 'Thematic' Invention," in *Bach Studies*, ed. Don O. Franklin (Cambridge: Cambridge University Press, 1989), pp. 54–74.

[2] Brainard, "The Regulative and Generative Roles of Verse," p. 55.

will explore the thematic and structural rather than prosodic, metrical, or affective relationships between text and music in a small group of late fourteenth-century polytextual chansons. Even though surface clarity is obscured in these songs by the polyphony of multiple texts, the polyphonic texture itself can be understood as a symbolic representation of a textual theme.

Polytextual songs first begin to appear in France around the middle of the fourteenth century,[3] more than a hundred years after the emergence of the polytextual motet. Indeed, they have often been looked on as archaic holdovers from the compositional patterns of the motet. In one view, chansons with more than one text represent an intermediate stage in a chronological progression leading from the motet, with two or more independently texted parts over a borrowed tenor, to the late fourteenth-century polyphonic song with a single texted part and one or more untexted accompanying parts.[4] This evolutionary model obscures, however, the position of the polytextual chanson as an independent genre, distinct from both the motet and the single-texted chanson.

There are two principal types of polytextual songs, which we can distinguish as "combinative" or "simultaneous." Combinative chansons—in this period most often virelais—feature a pre-existing tenor whose text and melody are borrowed from a popular rondeau or virelai and combined with one or more texts in the upper parts.[5] This study will focus on polytextual chansons of the simultaneous type, that is, songs whose multiple texts and melodies were newly composed and intended from their inception to be performed together. The texts of these chansons may represent a dialogue involving two or three protagonists, or parallel statements of a single idea, or one text may serve as a *response* to the other. Such paired texts usually share a single meter and rhyme scheme and, in the case of ballades, identical refrains. The interlocking nature of the chanson texts can be linked to some unusual polyphonic textures and, in one instance, even points to the correct realization of a canon.

---

[3]Margaret Paine Hasselman, *The French Chanson in the Fourteenth Century* (Ph.D. dissertation, University of California, Berkeley, 1970), p. 111.

[4]Hasselman, pp. 111–35.

[5]On combinative chansons of the late fifteenth century, see Maria Rika Maniates, "Combinative Chansons in the Dijon Chansonnier," *Journal of the American Musicological Society* 23 (1970): 228–81. Three fourteenth-century combinative chansons are edited by Gordon Greene in *French Secular Music. Manuscript Chantilly Musée Condé 564*, Polyphonic Music of the Fourteenth Century, 18 (Monaco: L'Oiseau-Lyre, 1981), No. 4, and *French Secular Music. Virelais*, Polyphonic Music of the Fourteenth Century, 21 (Monaco: L'Oiseau-Lyre, 1987), Nos. 24 and 26.

To illustrate how one fourteenth-century poetic topos, the amorous dialogue, gave rise to musical textures that depart from established norms, I will examine settings by Machaut and his successors of seven poetic dialogues in the courtly tradition. They are listed in Table 1, numbers 3 to 9.

Departing significantly from the configuration of a single texted cantus with untexted tenor and contratenor that prevails in most French chansons from the mid-century on, these settings of two or three simultaneously-declaimed texts employ several divergent polyphonic textures: three equal voices, including a canon for three voices at the unison; two equal voices; equal-voice duet with accessory tenor; duet with harmonically essential tenor; duet with tenor-contratenor canon. Since in all seven songs two or three texts are apparently intended to be sung simultaneously rather than in sequence, none of them can be said to represent dialogue in a directly realistic way. In fact, hearing and understanding the texts is next to impossible in performance. Nevertheless, I believe that the various polyphonic textures of these settings are all genre-specific in their adaptation to an unusual performance requirement: simultaneous declamation of the parts of a sequential dialogue.

Before focusing more narrowly on musical settings of amorous dialogues, we should explore the tradition of text pairing in general and its place within the larger medieval tradition of citation and imitation. My point of departure will be the lyric insertions in Guillaume de Machaut's narrative poem, *Le Livre du Voir-Dit* (The Book of the True Tale), a late work that in many ways represents a summation of his entire artistic career. As is well known, more than half of the lyrics in the *Voir-Dit* form pairs, with related subjects, verse forms, and rhymes,[6] demonstrating the importance of matching texts in Machaut's poetic world. Furthermore, the exchange of letters and poems between the poet and his young admirer can be seen as an expansion on the theme of the amorous dialogue as a poetic topos. Finally, the paired lyrics in Machaut's narrative have links both to earlier conventions of dialogue poetry and to a chain of imitations, beginning with his own settings of lyric poetry outside the *Voir-Dit* and continuing with songs by his younger contemporaries and successors.

---

[6]Sarah Jane Williams, "The Lady, the Lyrics and the Letters," *Early Music* 5 (1977): 465.

Table 1

Fourteenth-Century Amorous Dialogs

KEY

Manuscript sigla are according to *Répertoire international des sources musicales.*

CMM: *French Secular Compositions of the Fourteenth Century,* ed. Willi Apel, Corpus mensurabilis musicae, 53 (American Institute of Musicology, 1970)

Ludwig: *Guillaume de Machaut. Musikalische Werke,* ed. Friedrich Ludwig (Leipzig: Breitkopf und Härtel, 1926–54)

PMFC: *Polyphonic Music of the Fourteenth Century* (Monaco: L'Oiseau-Lyre).

Reaney: Gilbert Reaney, "The Ballades, Rondeaux, and Virelais of Guillaume de Machaut: Melody, Rhythm, and Form," Acta Musicologica 27 (1955): 57–58.

Composer	Sources	Incipits	Genre	No. of Voices
1. T. Paien/ Machaut	Ludwig, No. 34 PMFC 3, No. 34	*Quant Theseus, Hercules* *Ne quier veoir*	ballade	4
2. F. Andrieu	F-CH564, f. 52 Ludwig, No. 41 PMFC 19, No. 84	*Armes, amours* *O flours des flours*	ballade	4
3. Machaut	Reaney, pp. 57–58 Ludwig, No. 17 PMFC 3, No. 17	*Sans cuer m'envois* *Amis dolens* *Dame par vous*	ballade	3
4. Machaut	Ludwig, No. 29 PMFC 3, No. 29	*De triste cuer* *Quant vrais amans* *Certes, je di*	ballade	3
5. Johannes Vaillant	F-CH564, f. 26^v CMM, No. 116 PMFC 18, No. 31	*Dame doucement* *Doulz amis*	rondeau	3
6. Vaillant	F-CH564, f. 17^v CMM, No. 118 PMFC 18, No. 12	*Ma dame ce que vous* *Tres doulz amis* *Cent mille fois*	rondeau	3
7. Anon.	F-Pn6771, f. 53^v CMM, No. 134 PMFC 20, No. 32	*Dame vaillans de pris* *Amis de tant que vous* *Certainement puet on*	ballade	3
8. Anon.	F-Sm222, f. 78 CMM, No. 282 PMFC 22, No. 76a	*Dame de pris* *Tres douls amis*	rondeau	4
9. Matteo da Perugia	I-MOe5.24, f. 48^v–49 CMM, No. 65 PMFC 22, No. 12	*Par vous m'estuet* *Soyes par moy*	rondeau	2

In their exchange of paired texts, Machaut and "Toute-Belle" act as mirrors for one another, displaying their virtuosity at matching each other's rhymes and meters:

> Ains me respondi proprement
> De tel metre et de tel rime
> Com li rondiaus, que j'ay fait, rime.[7]

> (And so she answered me appropriately
> In like meter and like rhyme
> As the rondeau, which I made, rhymes.)

Although we can be fairly sure that Peronne d'Armentières or someone like her served as inspiration for the *Voir-Dit*,[8] it is unlikely that Machaut intended their story to be understood literally as a "True Romance."[9] To a sophisticated courtly audience, a poet's originality lay as much in the artful reworking of familiar themes and word plays as in novelty of plot and situation. In fact, the *Voir-Dit*, even more than the earlier *Remede de Fortune*, is a highly self-conscious reflection on the creative process, embedded in a demonstration of epistolary prose, octosyllabic rhymed couplets, and fixed lyric forms that amounts to a treatise on literary practice in the vernacular.[10]

> Le Voir-Dit veuil je qu'on appelle
> Ce traitie que je fais pour elle.[11]

> (The True Tale I wish it to be called
> This treatise I am making for her.)

---

[7] Guillaume de Machaut, *Le Livre du Voir-Dit*, ed. Paulin Paris (Paris: Société des bibliophiles français, 1875), lines 2716–18.

[8] Machaut, *Voir-Dit*, introduction; Paula Higgins, "Parisian Nobles, a Scottish Princess, and the Woman's Voice in Late Medieval Song," *Early Music History* 10 (1991): 145–200.

[9] According to Daniel Poirion, the title signifies Machaut's promise that in this narrative he will his express true feelings rather than simulated emotions (*Le Poète et le prince. L'Evolution du lyrisme courtois de Guillaume de Machaut à Charles d'Orléans* [Paris: Presses universitaires de France, 1965], p. 199).

[10] Jacqueline Cerquiglini, *Un Engin si soutil: Guillaume de Machaut et l'écriture au XIVe siècle* (Paris: H. Champion, 1985), pp. 10, 16.

[11] Machaut, *Voir-Dit*, lines 430–31.

In spite of Toute-Belle's frequent entreaties and Guillaume's promises, only a few of the lyric insertions in the *Voir-Dit* were ever set to music. The only paired lyrics from the narrative that Machaut actually combined in a polytextual chanson are the ballades *Quant Theseus, Hercules et Jazon* and *Ne quier veoir la biaute d'Absalon* (Table 1, No. 1). The first ballade is attributed in the *Voir-Dit* to one Thomas Paien, who has been identified as a Breton jurist who taught at the Sorbonne in the third quarter of the fourteenth century;[12] the second is Machaut's *response*, which employs the same meter and rhyme scheme (but without duplicating any rhyming words) and concludes each stanza with Paien's refrain.

Two passages in the *Voir-Dit* that refer to the double ballade are of particular significance. First, the poet takes pains to tell Toute-Belle in a letter just how difficult the matching game is: in presenting his ballade first, Thomas Paien has skimmed the fat from the pot ("il a pris toute la graisse du pot"), preempting the best rhyming words.[13] Secondly, Machaut seems to have been just as proud of his musical setting of the two ballade texts as he was of his *response* to Paien's poem. Eagerly awaiting Toute-Belle's critical appraisal, he writes that he has composed it for four voices, implying that this is something out of the ordinary;[14] "normal" song texture calls for only one texted voice with two untexted accompanying parts.[15]

Machaut's ballade *response* was quoted in turn in a ballade by the poet and chronicler Jean Froissart,[16] and his double ballade must have served as a model for F. Andrieu's setting of Eustache Deschamps's lament on Machaut's death (Table 1, No. 2).[17] Emulation, exemplified both in the matching

---

[12]*Guillaume de Machaut. Musikalische Werke*, ed. Friedrich Ludwig (Leipzig: Breitkopf und Härtel, 1926–54), 2:69. Machaut could, of course, have written Paien's ballade himself, just as he may also have composed poetry and prose in Toute-Belle's name.

[13]Machaut, *Voir-Dit*, letter 35.

[14]Machaut, *Voir-Dit*, letter 37.

[15]On the exceptional status of four-voice harmony in fourteenth-century secular polyphony, see Gilbert Reaney, "Fourteenth-century Harmony and the Ballades, Rondeaux and Virelais of Guillaume de Machaut," *Musica Disciplina* 7 (1953): 139–41.

[16]Froissart's ballade echoes Machaut's with the opening line "Ne quier veoir Medee ne Jason," and ends with the same refrain. Jean Froissart, *Ballades et Rondeaux*, ed. Rae S. Baudouin (Geneva: Droz, 1978), pp. 11–12; cited in Cerquiglini, p. 99.

[17]The musical and textual links between these two works and three other ballades from the late fourteenth and early fifteenth centuries are explored in Virginia Newes, "The Bitextual Ballade from the Manuscript Torino J.II.9 and Its Models," in *The Cypriot-French Repertory of the Manuscript of Torino J.II.9. International Musicological Congress, Paphos, 20–25 March 1992*, ed. Ludwig Finscher and Ursula Günther (Neuhausen: Hänssler, 1995).

lyrics of the *Voir-Dit* and in the myriad textual and musical citations embedded in fourteenth and fifteenth-century chansons, was an important part of the rhetorical tradition.[18] None of the treatises on the "second rhetoric" (defined in fifteenth-century poetic theory as the art of poetry in the vernacular) has anything to say, however, either about citations or about paired lyrics, although these manuals do provide lengthy word catalogs that professional poets could draw upon in their search for matching rhymes.[19] Nor does Machaut mention ballade or rondeau pairs among the poetic genres he enumerates in the *Prologue* that precedes the *Dit dou Vergier* in the later manuscripts. Still, the structural importance he accorded matching lyrics in the *Voir-Dit* speaks for itself. As we have seen, this late work can be read as Machaut's own exposition of the second rhetoric, the summation of a rich tradition of both narrative and lyric poetry in the vernacular.

The exchange of lyric poems between Machaut and Toute-Belle is central to the narrative structure of the *Voir-Dit;* at the same time, it is a vehicle for virtuoso play with matching meter and rhyme whose roots can be found in earlier traditions. The poetic dialogue in matching ballade or rondeau stanzas harks back to the *tenso,* or debate song, of which some ninety examples dating from the late twelfth to the late thirteenth century have survived in Provençal and Old French sources.[20] In the *tenso,* two singers, addressing each other by name or by epithet, engage in a question-and-answer or attack-and-response dialogue, exchanging opinions and invectives in alternating strophes or strophe pairs that share matching metrical structures and rhyme schemes. Traces of the earlier debate song can still be seen in Machaut's amorous dialogue and in paired ballades and rondeaux by his contemporaries and successors, and it is against this background that they must be understood. By the fourteenth century, however, the poetic exchange had been enriched (and carried a step further away from reality) by the personified attributes of love and its perils in the allegorical tradition of the *Roman de la Rose*. Furthermore, matching stanzas were now shaped according to the highly prescriptive conventions of the fixed forms, challenging the poet to new heights of rhyming artifice. In musical settings, the dialogue form gave rise to a variety of polyphonic textures, each of

---

[18]Ursula Günther, "Zitate in französischen Liedsätzen des Ars Nova und Ars Subtilior," *Musica Disciplina* 26 (1972): 53–68.

[19]Ernest Langlois, *Recueil des arts de seconde rhétorique* (Paris: Imprimerie nationale, 1902); Edmond Faral, *Les Arts poétiques du XIIe et du XIIIe siècle* (Paris: H. Champion, 1923), p. 197.

[20]Sebastian Neumeister, *Das Spiel mit der höfischen Liebe. Das altprovenzalische Partimen* (Munich: Wilhelm Fink, 1969), p. 15; Alfred Jeanroy, *La Poésie lyrique des troubadours*, vol. 2, *Les Genres* (Toulouse: E. Privat; Paris: H. Didier, 1934), pp. 245–67.

which attempted to represent symbolically the poetic exchange between two or three protagonists.

In his canonic ballade *Sans cuer m'envois / Amis dolens / Dame par vous* (Table 1, No. 3), Machaut used the successive entries of the three voices to represent a dialogue in the sequence lover–lady–lover. The three ballade texts (labelled A, B, and C in Ludwig's edition) are identical not only in metrical structure but also in rhyme, and the same refrain (except for a change of speaker from lover to lady in voice B) completes each of the nine stanzas. Text A, beginning "Sans cuer m'envois, dolens et esploures" ("Downhearted you send me away, suffering and tearful"), seems to recall the first line of a rondeau from the *Voir-Dit:* "Sans cuer, dolens, de vous departir." In his narrative, Machaut disingenuously claims to have composed this poem while "on his way" ("en chemin") to meet Toute-Belle;[21] in fact, we know that the rondeau (No. 4 in Ludwig's edition) and its music had already circulated some years before the *Voir-Dit,* since they were included in manuscript C (F-Pn 1586), the earliest of the Machaut manuscripts, which was copied before 1356.[22] In the *Voir-Dit,* the lady reassures her lover with a rondeau that echoes his, beginning "Sans cuer de moy pas ne vous partirez" ("Downhearted you shall not part from me"). In the same vein, Machaut's second ballade text (voice B), "Amis dolens maz et desconfortes" ("My friend, most sad and discouraged"), is a reassuring response by the lady to her lover's complaint of hard-hearted dismissal; in the third ballade, beginning "Dame, par vous me sens reconfortes" ("Lady, I feel consoled by you"), the lover expresses his gratitude to the lady for the encouragement she has granted him.

It is the dialogue sequence of the three ballades that provides the clue to the correct mode of performance, not stated explicitly in the sources. Unaccompanied canons in the fourteenth and fifteenth centuries were normally notated as a single melodic line, with either a *signum congruentiae* or a verbal instruction providing the clue to canonic realization. In all but one of the six sources of *Sans cuer m'envois / Amis dolens / Dame par vous*, however, the same melody is written out in full for each of the three voices, each one having its own text. The exception is manuscript E (F-Pn 9221), a late source copied after Machaut's death,[23] which gives the ballade melody

---

[21]Kevin Brownlee, *Poetic Identity in Guillaume de Machaut* (Madison: University of Wisconsin Press, 1984), p. 101.

[22]On the dating of the Machaut manuscripts, see François Avril, "Les Manuscrits enluminés de Guillaume de Machaut," in *Guillaume de Machaut. Colloque-Table ronde organisée par l'Université de Reims* (Paris: Klinksieck, 1982), pp. 118–24.

[23]Avril, p. 128.

only once; here the melody is underlaid with the first stanza of voice A and followed by its remaining two strophes and the six strophes of voices B and C, all written continuously without music. Thus there is no indication whatsoever in manuscript E that the ballade is polyphonic.[24] In manuscripts B (F-Pn 1585), Vg (US-NYw), C (F-Pn 1586), and F-G (F-Pn 22545–22546), voice B is preceded by two *longa* rests, the time interval at which it must follow voice A in strict canon. None of these manuscripts, however, has rests at the beginning of voice C telling us how long it should wait before beginning to sing.

In Ludwig's edition of the canonic ballade, prepared during the 1920s,[25] as well as in Schrade's edition of 1956,[26] voice C's entry is placed at the beginning of the second *longa* measure, between that of voices A and B. This not only contradicts the sequential placement of the voices in the manuscripts, but produces several unacceptably harsh dissonances. If we read the texts in their logical order, however, the solution is apparent: voice C, representing the lover's answer to the lady, has to follow voice B at the same time interval at which B follows A. The correct solution was proposed by Laurence Feininger in 1937[27] and published in transcription by Gilbert Reaney in 1955.[28] Example 1 is based on Reaney's solution.

According to Reaney, Machaut looked on canon as a variant of monody.[29] Analysis of *Sans cuer m'envois / Amis dolens / Dame par vous*, however, shows its melody to have been conceived with the special rhythmic and harmonic requirements of canonic realization in mind, resulting in a structure that differs in important respects from that of Machaut's single monophonic ballade (No. 37 in Ludwig's edition), as well as from the melodies of his other polyphonic ballades.

---

[24] Clues to canonic realization are also lacking in MS E for the two canonic lais (Nos. 16 and 17 in Ludwig's edition) and for the retrograde canon *Ma fin est mon commencement* (Rondeau No. 14).

[25] *Machaut. Musikalische Werke*, vol. 1, *Balladen, Rondeaux, und Virelais*, pp. 16–17.

[26] Leo Schrade, ed., *The Works of Guillaume de Machaut*, Polyphonic Music of the Fourteenth Century, 3 (Monaco: L'Oiseau-Lyre, 1956), p. 88.

[27] Laurence Feininger, *Die Frühgeschichte des Kanons* (Emsdetten: H. & J. Leichte, 1937), p. 13.

[28] Gilbert Reaney, "The Ballades, Rondeaux, and Virelais of Guillaume de Machaut: Melody, Rhythm, and Form," *Acta Musicologica* 27 (1955): 57–58.

[29] Reaney, "The Ballades, Rondeaux, and Virelais," p. 51.

Example 1. Machaut, *Sans cuer m'envois / Amis dolens / Dame par vous*

Amorous Dialogues 289

Example 1 (*continued*)

Example 1 (*continued*)

First of all, Machaut's canonic ballade is unique in that it makes no provision for an *ouvert* cadence. (See measure 8 in voice A, measure 10 in voice B, and measure 12 in voice C.) The stereotypical fourteenth-century ballade consists of a couplet, an epilogue, and a refrain; the two sections of the couplet have matching rhymes and are sung to the same music, first with an open, then with a closed cadence. The lack of an *ouvert* cadence in the canonic ballade is linked to the performance of the couplet as a "circular" canon: after arriving at the first cadence, each voice in turn returns immediately to the beginning to sing the second two couplet lines. If the first section were to end on A, the most likely cadential pitch for the *ouvert* ending of a ballade with G final, it would form a dissonant fourth with voice C at measure eight, voice B would not harmonize with voice A in measure 10, and C would conflict with B in measure 12. A cadence on D results in either an awkward unison at measure 8 or dissonant fourths in measures 10 and 12.[30]

A close look at the notation in the manuscripts points to another anomaly in the melody: the continuity between couplet and epilogue. Normally, at the end of a ballade couplet, all voices come to a full stop, marked by a stroke through the entire staff. In all sources of *Sans cuer m'envois / Amis dolens / Dame par vous*, however, the usual stroke separating the couplet from the epilogue is lacking. Furthermore, there are no rests at the beginning of the second section in voice B indicating a new imitative departure. Thus, in spite of the parallel octaves that result in measures 13 and 15, voice A, once it has repeated the couplet, must continue immediately with the epilogue rather than waiting for the other voices to cadence.

Further evidence that Machaut's ballade melody must be realized as a three-voice canon can be found in its phrase structure and rhythmic patterns. Frequent rests and long notes at the ends of phrases, while awkward in monophonic performance, serve two important functions in canonic realization. On the one hand, they are used to stretch out canonic segments to a uniform length; at the same time, these pauses leave rhythmic voids that demand to be filled in by complementary activity in the canonic voices.

The pitch structure of the melody demonstrates yet another feature of canonic writing: Machaut had to "compose out" an underlying harmonic plan in regularly alternating segments. Thus, the first half of each *longa* measure always produces some form of the principal "perfect" sonority g-d-g´, while the second half outlines a subsidiary harmony. In Machaut's

---

[30]*Ouvert* endings are similarly avoided in Machaut's canonic lais, which are also circle canons. See Virginia Newes, "Turning Fortune's Wheel: Musical and Textual Design in Machaut's Canonic Lais," *Musica Disciplina* 45 (1991): 109.

non-canonic songs, progressions between perfect sonorities are usually longer and less metrically regular.

Within the rather rigid rhythmic and harmonic confines just outlined, Machaut set the text of voice A line by line, marking the customary caesura after the fourth syllable in lines 1, 2, 3, 4, 7, and 8 by a breve or a rest, and allotting at least the space of a breve to the end of each line. The beginning of the epilogue departs from this pattern in order to conform to the irregular structure of lines 5 and 6. Line 5, a *vers coupé* of seven rather than ten syllables, runs into line 6: "Si qu'einssi sans cuer durer / Ne porroie, ne telz maulz endurer." Opening with an augmented fourth G-C♯—a sharply differentiating gesture of the kind Machaut often used at the beginning of a ballade's second section—the melody follows the sense of the text by observing the enjambment between lines 5 and 6. Yet the musical elision, which conforms so well to the enjambment of lines 5 and 6 in text A, violates the sense of the corresponding lines in stanza 1 of text B. As we so often find in settings of strophic poetry, the melody was composed to fit the initial stanza of the ballade without regard to the stanzas that follow.

Machaut's only other triple ballade, *De triste cuer / Quant vrais amans / Certes, je di* (Table 1, No. 4), presents an exchange, not between a lover and his lady, but between a poet and two other speakers. The three protagonists are discussing the effects of unrequited love on poetic inspiration, defined in troubadour/trouvère terms as "joie":[31] can the lovelorn poet assume a voice that denies his true emotional state? As Machaut has already stated in the *Remede de Fortune*, he who does not compose according to his feelings is guilty of falsification:

> Car qui de sentement ne fait
> Son oeuvre et son chant contrefait.[32]

The artistic dilemma depicted here, with its paradoxical non-solution, might easily have been disputed in a court of love, or in a debate poem of the more elaborate genre known as the *partimen* or *joc-partit* (*jeu-parti* in Old French). Speaking in the first person, the poet (voice A) complains that his stricken heart can produce only sad songs; his heart is blacker than a berry, sad, suffering, and weeping tears of blood. In this condition, to feign

---

[31]On the role of *joie* in poetic creation, see Poirion, p. 74, and Leonard Johnson, *Poets as Players. Theme and Variation in Late Medieval French Poetry* (Stanford, Calif.: Stanford University Press, 1990), pp. 30–33.

[32]Guillaume de Machaut, *Le Jugement du roy de Behaigne and Remede de Fortune*, ed. James I. Wimsatt and William W. Kibler (Athens, Ga.: University of Georgia Press, 1988), p. 189, lines 407–408; quoted in Poirion, p. 198

Joy would surely be contrary to Nature. His companion (voice B) agrees: a lover rejected by his lady can only weep; even memory will torment him, and he cannot be expected to sing joyfully. The third speaker sympathizes with the lover's distress, but resolves the dilemma by finding a source of inspiration as powerful as Joy. Remaining in a state of unfulfilled Desire, the rejected lover will be a better poet than any successful lover could hope to be. He who enjoys the mercy of his lady has what he desires; therefore Desire, the source of inspiration, no longer possesses him and will retreat in disarray. At least from the standpoint of poetic inspiration, the unhappy lover is better off than the happy one.

The fictitious nature of this exchange recalls the stylized argument of the *jeu-parti*. In this debate game, the topic or dilemma, usually a problem of courtly love, is set by the first speaker. He states two possible solutions and invites his partner to choose one of these alternatives, agreeing to defend the other one himself.[33] As in the *tenso*, the discussion in the *jeu-parti* takes place in alternating stanzas of matching structure and rhyme. Since there is often no winner, the partners may call on an impartial judge to settle the dilemma: this is the role assumed by the third speaker (voice C) in Machaut's ballade.[34]

Let us turn now to considerations of polyphonic texture in *De triste cuer / Quant vrais amans / Certes, je di* (Ex. 2). The setting is for three non-canonic but polyphonically equal voices, another significant departure from the hierarchical three-voice configuration found in almost all of Machaut's later ballades. As in the canonic ballade, the three voice parts, each underlaid with its own text, follow one another in the manuscripts in sequence, and the nine stanzas are linked by an identical metrical structure, rhyme scheme, and refrain. Phrase lengths in the three voices seldom coincide, however, and in only a few instances does the declamation appear to have been arranged so as to synchronize matching rhymes. In contrast to the syllabic declamation in *Sans cuer m'envois / Amis dolens / Dame par vous,* on the other hand, occasional melismas reduce text conflict by allowing one or the other text to be heard without interference from the other voices.

---

[33] Neumeister, pp. 15–20; Jeanroy, p. 247; A. Klein, "Die altfranzösischen Minnefragen," *Marburger Beiträge zur romanischen Philologie* 1 (Marburg, 1911). For a discussion of the "demande d'amour" theme in the poetry of Boccaccio, Deschamps, and Chaucer, see Geoffrey Chaucer, *The Parlement of Foulys*, ed. D. S. Brewer (Edinburgh: Thomas Nelson and Sons, 1960), p. 10.

[34] In Machaut's *Jugement du roy de Behaigne,* an elaboration on a favorite *jeu-parti* theme, the royal patron is invited to decide whether the knight whose lady is faithless suffers more than the lady whose lover has died.

294 Virginia Newes

Example 2. Machaut, *De triste cuer / Quant vrais amans / Certes, je di*, mm. 1–21

Example 2 (*continued*)

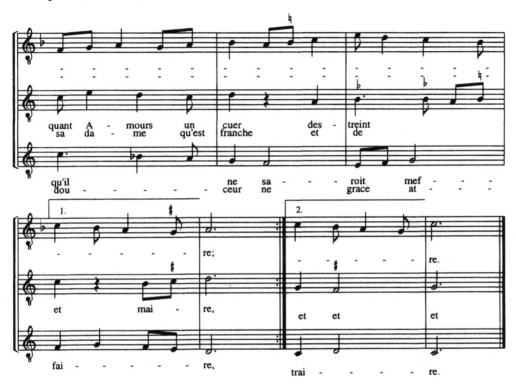

Maintaining their polyphonic independence throughout, the three parts are equivalent in rhythmic activity, and similar, although not quite identical, in melodic range. In fact, no voice is designated as "tenor" in the manuscripts. The reason might be that, with the exception of combinative chansons incorporating a preexisting song tenor, the tenor in secular songs in Machaut's time was understood to be a textless voice. Voice B is only slightly lower than the other two parts, and functions alternately as cantus and tenor. It crosses frequently with the treble voices, yet assumes the role of harmonic support at the principle cadences, taking the lower final against the upper octave and the fifth in the other two parts.

Machaut's choice of an equal-voice texture for his two triple ballades can be contrasted with the treble-duet-plus-tenor disposition found in two polytextual chansons by a younger contemporary, Johannes Vaillant. Vaillant, the composer of a double and a triple rondeau (Table 1, Nos. 5 and 6) as well as three other chansons included in the Chantilly manuscript, is believed to be identical with the Johannes Vaillant who, according to the *Regles de la seconde rhetorique,* had a music school in Paris ("lequel tenoit a Paris escolle de musique") and whose teachings are reported in a

Example 3. Vaillant, *Dame, doucement fortrait / Doulz amis de cuer parfait,* mm. 1–21

Hebrew treatise from the late fourteenth century.[35] He may also be the author of a treatise on intervals and instrumental tunings included in the Berkeley theory manuscript.[36]

Like Machaut's canonic ballade, Vaillant's double rondeau *Dame, doucement fortrait / Doulz amis de cuer parfait* (Ex. 3) depicts a dialogue between a lover and his lady, and once again the texts are matched in metrical structure and rhyme scheme while studiously avoiding duplication of the rhyming words. The two cantus parts have the same rate of rhythmic activity and share the D octave range; at cadences they are either a fifth apart or converge on a unison. The untexted accompanying tenor, lying a fifth lower than the texted parts, belongs to a type found in some of Machaut's early songs but abandoned in his later works: since the upper voices form a harmonically self-sufficient pair, the tenor fills no essential supporting role and could easily be omitted. The cadences in measures 14, 16, and 21 of Vaillant's rondeau may be compared with the 8-5-1 cadences in Machaut's ballade *De triste cuer / Quant vrais amans / Certes, je di.*

Far more than in Machaut's ballade, there seems to be an attempt in Vaillant's rondeau to avoid conflict between simultaneously-declaimed texts. Voice B begins two and one-half measures after voice A, and declamation is arranged throughout so that the two texts almost never conflict. Indeed, syllables are distributed so sparsely in this largely melismatic setting that the poetic syntax nearly becomes lost.

Vaillant's triple rondeau, *Ma dame, ce que vous / Tres doulz amis / Cent mille fois,* represents another dialogue between lover and lady (Ex. 4). Machaut's canonic ballade, *Sans cuer m'envois / Amis dolens / Dame par vous,* may have served as Vaillant's model, since his three texts, like Machaut's, represent the sequence pleading lover (voice A), reassuring lady (voice B), grateful lover (voice C).

Although they do not share matching rhymes, the texts are nonetheless interrelated: in her rondeau, the lady echoes her lover's words "prommis" and "nomme," and even makes a pun on his name in line 6: "Pour ce que t'es en tout nomme Vaillant."[37]

---

[35] Ursula Günther, article "Vaillant, Jehan," in *The New Grove Dictionary of Music and Musicians,* 6th ed. (London: Macmillan, 1980), 19:487.

[36] Christopher Page, "Fourteenth-century Instruments and Tunings: a Treatise by Jean Vaillant? (Berkeley, MS 744)," *Galpin Society Journal* 33 (1980): 17–20.

[37] Ursula Günther, "Johannes Vaillant," in *Speculum Musicae Artis: Festgabe für Heinrich Husmann zum 60. Geburtstag,* ed. Heinz Becker and Reinhard Gerlach (Munich: Fink, 1970), p. 184.

Example 4. Vaillant, *Ma dame ce que vous / Tres doulz amis / Cent mille fois,* mm. 1–9

A. Ma dame, ce que vous m'avez prommis,
   A vous amer et desirer m'a mort,
   C'est que de vous seray nomme amis,
   Ma dame, ce que vous m'avez prommis,
   Si vous supli qu'en oubli ne soye mis,
   Car pour vray trop avanceroyt ma mort.
   Ma dame, ce que vous m'avez prommis,
   A vous amer et desirer m'a mort.

B. Tres doulz amis, tout ce que prommis t'ay
    Est tout certain, ne t'en iray faillant,
    Mais sans fausser entierement tendray,
    Tres doulz amis, tout ce que prommis t'ay,
    C'est que toudis loyalment t'ameray,
    Pour ce que t'es en tout nomme Vaillant.
    Tres doulz amis, tout ce que prommis t'ay
    Est tout certain, ne t'en iray faillant.

C. Cent mille fois, ma douce dame chere,
    De vostre humble response vous mercy.
    Comme celle que j'ay plus qu'autre chiere,
    Cent mille fois, ma douce dame chere,
    Veuillies dont fayre a mon cuer bone chiere,
    Quar chascun jour se met en vo mercy,
    Cent mille fois, ma douce dame chere,
    De vostre humble response vous mercy.

A. My lady, that which you have promised me,
    Has bound me to love and desire you,
    So that I should be named your lover,
    My lady, that which you have promised me,
    So I beg you that I not be forgotten,
    For in truth it would hasten my death.
    My lady, that which you have promised me,
    Has bound me to love and desire you.

B. Most sweet friend, all that I have promised you
    Is entirely sure, I'll not depart deceiving you,
    But without falsehood I'll give entirely,
    Most sweet friend, all that I have promised you,
    So that I'll always love you faithfully,
    Since you are called Valiant without exception.
    Most sweet friend, all that I have promised you
    Is entirely sure, I'll not depart deceiving you.

C. One hundred thousand times, my dear sweet lady,
    I thank you for your modest response.
    As the one whom I hold more dear than any other,
    One hundred thousand times, my dear sweet lady,
    Would that you may grant fair welcome to my heart,
    For every day I place myself at your mercy.
    One hundred thousand times, my dear sweet lady,
    I thank you for your modest response.

The distribution of the voice parts, on the other hand, makes no attempt at realistic characterization. The part of the lover is assigned to two voices of decidedly different range: one is a treble in the same range as the lady's part; the other lies an octave below it in the tenor range and functions alternately as part of the contrapuntal dialogue and as harmonic support.

With the anonymous triple ballade *Dame vailans de pris / Amis, de tant que vous / Certainement puet on* (Table 1, No. 7), we return once more to the texture of three equal voices employed in Machaut's polytextual ballades (Ex. 5). Three protagonists join in a celebration of love: a lover

Example 5. Anonymous, *Dame vailans de pris / Amis de tant que vous / Certainement puet on*, mm. 1–11, 49–68

Amorous Dialogues 301

Example 5 (*continued*)

(voice A) makes a declaration to his lady with a pledge to keep their love secret; the lady (voice B) then bestows her favor; finally, an impartial commentator (voice C) sententiously repeats the rules of courtly love, stressing the importance of the pledge of secrecy ("estre secreis, vrays et loyalz amis") that serves as the refrain in all three voices (m. 52). The three texts, which although they share the same refrain have no other matching rhymes, are assigned as in Machaut's ballades *Sans cuer m'envois / Amis dolens / Dame par vous* and *De triste cuer / Quant vrais amans / Certes, je di* to three voices of equal range that continually cross and exchange roles. The voice exchange culminates in a lively fanfare-like passage based on hocketing thirds and fifths that marks the end of both couplet and refrain in an extended musical rhyme.

The triple ballade is preserved without attribution in its unique source, Paris, Bibliothèque nationale, nouv. acq. fr. 6771 ("Reina"). Compiled in the Veneto during the second and third decades of the fifteenth century, this manuscript preserves a mixed French, Flemish, and Italian secular repertory from the fourteenth century, with a supplement devoted to French works of the Dufay period.[38] Although there are no composer attributions in the section containing fourteenth-century French chansons, seven of them have concordances in the Chantilly manuscript, demonstrating intersections between this repertory and Vaillant's sphere of activity. I suggest that the anonymous triple ballade was composed either by Vaillant himself, or by another composer emulating him. Its rhythmic and melodic style are consistent with Vaillant's, and the cadential imitations cited above recall a less extended imitation on a triadic motive near the end of Vaillant's double rondeau. A textual allusion may provide further support for this hypothesis. Although such epithets were common currency in courtly love poetry, the "Dame vailans de pris" might possibly be a punning reference to the name of the composer of at least two other dialogue songs. The web of citations may extend even further to the texts of a lover/lady double rondeau in the Strasbourg manuscript (Table 1, No. 8). Its opening lines "Dame de pris" and "Tres douls amis" could refer back to the "Dame vailans de pris" of the anonymous ballade and the "Doulz amis" of Vaillant's double rondeau. I have traced elsewhere the transmission of model patterns for retrograde motet tenors and retrograde rondeaux.[39] A similar process of emulation may well have been at work among dialogue chansons.

---

[38]*Handschriften mit mehrstimmiger Musik des 14., 15. und 16. Jahrhunderts,* ed. Gilbert Reaney, Répertoire international des sources musicales, B IV³ (Munich: G. Henle, 1972), p. 485; Kurt von Fischer, "The Manuscript Paris, Bibl. Nat., nouv. acq. fr. 6771 (Codex *Reina* = PR)," *Musica Disciplina* 10 (1957): 37–78; John Nádas, *The Transmission of Trecento Secular Polyphony: Manuscript Production and Scribal Practices in Italy at the End of the Middle Ages* (Ph.D. dissertation, New York University, 1985), pp. 110–215.

[39]Virginia Newes, "Writing, Reading and Memorizing: The Transmission and Resolution of Retrograde Canons from the 14th and Early 15th Centuries," *Early Music* 18

Early in the fifteenth century, a new type of poetic dialogue appears on the scene, one in which the exchange takes place not between stanzas, but in short "conversational" phrases within the stanza itself;[40] in polyphonic settings, the entire text is now assigned to a single voice part rather than to two or three equal voices.[41] Polytextual settings of the older type of dialogue poetry are still found, however, in sources copied at least until the middle of the century. Since these later chansons lie outside the scope of this study, I will conclude with a polytextual rondeau from the turn of the century by an Italian composer writing in the French tradition.

Active at Francophile courts in Milan and Pavia in the late fourteenth and early fifteenth centuries, Matteo da Perugia tried his hand at almost every category of French as well as Italian polyphony current at the time. The subject of his double rondeau *Par vous m'estuet / Soyes par moy* (Table 1, No. 9) is the by now familiar theme of pleading lover/reassuring lady, and I believe that Matteo consciously chose to imitate here a specific sub-genre of the French chanson, the amorous dialogue (Ex. 6). The texture of two equal-range voices without accompaniment is unusual in this period and, in this case, probably genre-specific.[42] The two voices cross frequently, exchanging discant and tenor functions and alternating syllabic declamation with melisma in such a way that both texts can be heard most of the time. Another unusual feature, which is, so far as I know, unique in Italian sources of this period, is the rondeau's low notated tessitura with signatures of two flats in both voices. The symbolic use of low-clef flat signatures had already begun to appear in sources of French music by the late fourteenth century.[43] Quite possibly the unusual notation in Matteo's rondeau reflects the melancholy cast of the texts.

(1990): 218–34. In the Strasbourg double rondeau, the contratenor is derived by reading the tenor backwards.

[40] Omer Jodogne, "La ballade dialoguée dans la littérature française médiévale," in *Fin du moyen âge et renaissance: mélanges de philologie française offerts à Robert Guiette* (Antwerp: De nederlandsche Boekhandel, 1961), pp. 71–85.

[41] An example of the new type of dialogue chanson is Paullet's *J'aim. Qui? Vous. Moy?*, transcribed in *Early Fifteenth-Century Music,* ed. Gilbert Reaney, Corpus mensurabilis musicae, 11 (American Institute of Musicology, 1959), 2:102.

[42] One other example that comes to mind is Johannes Ciconia's *Aler m'en veus en estrange patrie*, a single-texted virelai in which the two voices are linked through voice exchange and imitation, transcribed in *The Works of Johannes Ciconia,* ed. Margaret Bent and Anne Hallmark, Polyphonic Music of the Fourteenth Century, 24 (Monaco: L'Oiseau-Lyre, 1985), No. 44.

[43] See the rondeau *Fuemeux fume* by Solage, transcribed in *French Secular Compositions of the Fourteenth Cntury,* ed. Willi Apel, Corpus mensurabilis musicae, 53 (American Institute of Musicology, 1970), vol. 1, No. 97 and *French Secular Music:*

Example 6. Matteo da Perugia, *Par vous m'estuet / Soyes par moy*, mm. 1–15

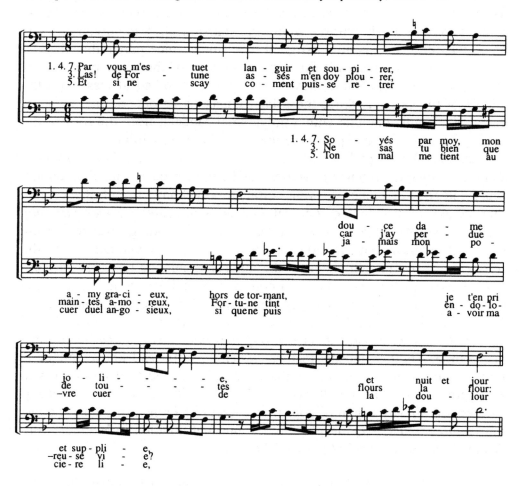

As I have demonstrated, polytextual songs in at least one clearly delineated genre, the dialogue chanson, had their own *raison d'être* based on the composer's decision to set multiple texts, texts that were conceived as equal, coordinated, and essential parts of a whole rather than as successive grafts onto a pre-existing framework. Yet many uncertainties remain about the relationship between text and music in these chansons. A preliminary conclusion might be that immediate intelligibility of the texts was not of prime conern to composers of fourteenth and early fifteenth-century polyphony. We know very little, however, about the performance of medieval

---

Manuscript Chantilly, Musée Condé 564, ed. Gordon K. Greene, Polyphonic Music of the Fourteenth Century, 19 (Monaco: L'Oiseau-Lyre, 1981), No. 98.

polyphonic songs, and even less about the preparation and expectations of their audiences. Were motet and chanson texts declaimed one after the other before being sung simultaneously, or were they perhaps circulated in advance among a sophisticated and increasingly literate courtly audience?[44]

Viewed in the light of Renaissance ideals of correct declamation, emotive content, and madrigalian word painting, late medieval attitudes toward text setting have seemed arbitrary and abstract; it is only relatively recently that we have begun to untangle in fourteenth-century polyphony the complex webs of interaction between poetry and music that are more often rhetorical and symbolic than directly pictorial.[45] In polytextual songs, the simultaneous performance of dialoguing texts serves to symbolize their structural interrelationship in much the same way that a medieval painting depicts the unity of present, past, and future events by including them in a single picture plane.

---

[44] On the increased literacy of the French nobility in the fourteenth century and the resultant shift from recitation to silent reading, see Poirion, p. 170.

[45] Some important studies are Wolfgang Dömling, "Aspekte der Sprachvertonung in den Balladen Guillaume de Machauts," *Die Musikforschung* 25 (1972): 301–307; Georg Reichert, "Das Verhältnis zwischen musikalischer und textlicher Struktur in den Motetten Machauts," *Archiv für Musikwissenschaft* 13 (1956): 197–216; Ursula Günther, "Das Wort-Ton-Problem bei Motetten des späten 14. Jahrhunderts," in *Festschrift Heinrich Besseler zum 60. Geburtstag* (Leipzig: Institut für Musikwissenschaft der Karl Marx Universität, 1961), pp. 163–78; Kevin Brownlee, "Machaut's Motet 15 and the *Roman de la rose*: The Literary Context of *Amours qui a le pouoir / Faus samblant m'a deceü / Vidi Dominum*," *Early Music History* 10 (1991): 1–14; Margaret Bent, "Deception, Exegesis and Sounding Number in Machaut's Motet 15," *Early Music History* 10 (1991): 15–27.

The Violins in Bach's St. John Passion

Joshua Rifkin

Bach's St. John Passion comes down to us in two main sources: a score begun by the composer near the end of the 1730s but mostly copied a decade later by another scribe; and a set of parts documenting at least four different performances over a span of twenty-five years.[1] While the score presents a relatively smooth appearance, the parts confront the reader with a minefield of insertions, deletions, reworkings, and reinstatements, all carried out by an equally daunting variety of means: crossing out, writing in, cutting away, sewing over. No one attempting to steer a path through this terrain will likely venture forth without the guidance provided by Arthur Mendel's critical report to his edition of the Passion in the *Neue Bach-Ausgabe*.[2] Not that Mendel makes the going easy—to put it mildly. But he does seem to have gone everywhere first and virtually never to have put a foot wrong. In one instance, however, I have found it impossible to follow Mendel's lead.

The issue turns on a pair of autograph leaves found as inserts in the violin parts and shown here as Plates 1 and 2. In Mendel's running pagination of the materials, they bear the numbers 361–62 and 363–64; in Table 1—to which readers may wish to refer for orientation throughout this article—

---

[1] The two manuscripts survive in the Staatsbibliothek zu Berlin—Preußischer Kulturbesitz under the call numbers Mus. ms. Bach P 28 and Mus. ms. Bach St 111, respectively. For descriptions, see *Johann Sebastian Bach: Neue Ausgabe sämtlicher Werke* [*Neue Bach-Ausgabe;* hereafter *NBA*], ser. 2, vol. 4, ed. Arthur Mendel, *Kritischer Bericht* (Kassel: Bärenreiter, 1974) [hereafter Mendel], pp. 12–60. On the dates of the various sources and performances, see Mendel, pp. 69–72 and 75–76, as well as Yoshitake Kobayashi, "Zur Chronologie der Spätwerke Johann Sebastian Bachs: Kompositions- und Aufführungstätigkeit von 1736 bis 1750," *Bach-Jahrbuch* 74 (1988): 20, 44, and 63; see also n. 4, below. Readers not already familiar with the intricacies of the Passion might find it useful to consult the easily digestible overview of its versions and sources in Alfred Dürr, *Die Johannes-Passion von Johann Sebastian Bach: Entstehung, Überlieferung, Werkeinführung* (München: Deutscher Taschenbuch-Verlag; Kassel: Bärenreiter, 1988), pp. 13–43.

[2] See the preceding note.

Table 1

(a) Violin parts, inserts, and cover-sheets to the St. John Passion, BWV 245

Violin parts

B 5	Violin I, 1724	[*NBA:* Violino I [I]; *BG:* Violino I [b]]
B 6	Violin I, 1725	[*NBA:* Violino I [II]; *BG:* Violino I [a]]
B 7	Violin I, 1749	[*NBA:* Violino I [IV]; *BG:* Violino I [c]]
B 8	Violin II, 1724	[*NBA:* Violino II [I]; *BG:* Violino II [b]]
B 9	Violin II, 1725	[*NBA:* Violino I [II]; *BG:* Violino I [b] (*recte* II [a])]

Inserts and cover-sheets

	Pages	NBA 2/4	Contents	Date
i 361	361–62	B 6 [III]	Nos. 19–20 [V obl. 1], (21a), 21b [WW 1]	1732
i 363	363–64	B 6 [III]	Nos. 19–20 [V obl. 2], (21a), 21b [WW 2], (21c)	1732
i 365	365–66*	B 9 [III]	Nos. (19–20), 21b [Soprano], (21c)	1732
i 377	377–78*	B 6 [III]	Nos. 25b [WW 1], (25c)	1732
i 379	379–80*	B 9 [III]	Nos. 25b [Soprano], (25c)	1732
i 507	507–508*	B 5 [III]	Nos. (21a), 21b [Soprano], (21c)	1749
i 526	527–28	—	No. 35 [Traverso]	1749
i 513	513–14*	B 5 [IV]	Nos. (25a), 25b [WW 2], (25c)	1749

* = cover-sheet
V obl = Violin obbligato
WW = Woodwind (Flute & Oboe)
( ) = tacet marking or rests

Table 1 (*continued*)

(b) Movements of the St. John Passion cited above and elsewhere in this article

No. 18	Evangelista: "Da sprach Pilatus zu ihm"
No. 19	Arioso: "Betrachte, meine Seel"
No. 19[II]	Aria: "Ach, windet euch nicht so, geplagte Seelen"
No. 20	Aria: "Erwäge, wie sein blutgefärbter Rücken"
No. 21a	Evangelista: "Und die Kriegsknechte flochten eine Krone"
No. 21b	Chorus: "Sei gegrüßet, lieber Jüdenkönig"
No. 21c	Evangelista: "Und gaben ihm Backenstreiche"
No. 21d	Chorus: "Kreuzige, kreuzige"
No. 25a	Evangelista: "Allda kreuzigten sie ihn"
No. 25b	Chorus: "Schreibe nicht: der Jüden König"
No. 25c	Evangelista: "Pilatus antwortet"
No. 33	Evangelista: "Und siehe da, der Vorhang im Tempel zerriß"
No. 34	Recitativo: "Mein Herz, indem die ganze Welt"
No. 35	Aria: "Zerfließe, mein Herze"

and in the discussion that follows, I refer to them as i 361 and i 363, respectively.[3] The two inserts contain the treble obbligatos to No. 19, the arioso "Betrachte, meine Seel," and No. 20, the aria "Erwäge, wie sein blutgefärbter Rücken," as well as portions of the following Gospel scene, No. 21. Watermarks and other evidence indicate that they come from the third performance of the St. John Passion, which Yoshitake Kobayashi has assigned to the year 1732.[4] Before considering them any further, however, we must fill in some background.

---

[3] On the pagination, see Mendel, p. 28. My nomenclature for the inserts differs from that used by Mendel (see especially p. 100), for reasons that I hope will become clear in the further course of discussion; see also n. 6, below.

[4] See Mendel, pp. 42 (but with reference to pp. 25 and 48) and 89–100, and Kobayashi, p. 20. Although I shall adhere to Kobayashi's dating—which rests chiefly on a detail in the development of Bach's script—throughout this article, I find it harder than he to exclude the possibility of a performance in 1730, given both the slender body of relevant autograph documents and the lack of a clear indication that the St. Luke Passion copied in score by Bach and Carl Philipp Emanuel Bach actually saw use that year; on this last point, cf. Andreas Glöckner, "Neuerkenntnisse zu Johann Sebastian Bachs Aufführungskalender zwischen 1729 und 1735," *Bach-Jahrbuch* 67 (1981): 48.

I

The performing materials for Bach's Leipzig sacred works typically included two copies each of Violin I and Violin II, a principal copy and a duplicate drawn directly from it.[5] By all indications, Bach had this complement at the first performance of the Passion, in 1724; but only the duplicate parts—which bear the labels B 5 and B 8, respectively, in Mendel's critical report—still exist. Indeed, all but a handful of the parts from the first performance appear to have vanished by the time Bach gave the Passion a second time only a year later; for he now had an almost complete new set prepared, including parts for the two violins—B 6 and B 9 in Mendel's labeling. In both the performance of 1725 and that of 1732, these new parts appear to have served as the principal ones while B 5 and B 8 retained their secondary position, as shown in Table 2.[6]

---

[5] See, among other sources, Alfred Dürr, *Zur Chronologie der Leipziger Vokalwerke Johann Sebastian Bachs*, 2nd ed., Musikwissenschaftliche Arbeiten, 26 (Kassel: Bärenreiter, 1976), p. 9, or the handy overview of the original parts to Bach's vocal works in Laurence Dreyfus, *Bach's Continuo Group: Players and Practices in his Vocal Works*, Studies in the History of Music, 3 (Cambridge, MA: Harvard University Press, 1987), pp. 183–207.

[6] The reasons for this assessment will, I hope, become self-evident in the further course of this study; see especially Tables 5 and 7. In Table 2 and elsewhere, I label the respective copies of each violin "a" and "b." This runs the risk of a certain confusion, as the Bach-Gesellschaft edition used similar labels to distinguish the different violin parts—referring, however, to their chronological position rather than their function within the string section (cf. Mendel, p. 27). As it happened, the Bach-Gesellschaft reversed the relative chronology of the parts from 1724 and 1725 (cf. Mendel, pp. 67–68), with the result that its "a" and "b," while chronologically inaccurate, do in fact coincide in function with ours. But as we shall see, the Bach-Gesellschaft's Violino I^c— Mendel's B 7—does not. Mendel's nomenclature, as distinct from his systematic labeling, adopts a strictly chronological stance, relating the parts to each of his four versions of the Passion: hence Violino I^1 means the surviving Violin I part of 1724 (B 5), Violino II^{II} the second-violin part copied in 1725 (B 9), and so forth. But Mendel's nomenclature says nothing about function. In fact, keeping function separate from chronology proves wise, as we shall see that the violin parts and their various components did not inevitably retain the same function from one performance to another.

Table 2

Distribution of violin parts in BWV 245, 1724–1732

	1724	1725/1732
Violin Ia	lost	B 6
Violin Ib	B 5	B 5
Violin IIa	lost	B 9
Violin IIb	B 8	B 8

Thanks to the loss not only of so many parts but of the composing score as well, we cannot reconstruct the earliest history of Nos. 19 and 20 in every detail. It seems clear, though, that Bach originally had the treble parts played by two viole d'amore. The surviving score heads No. 19 with the inscription "Viole d'Amour e Lieuto accomp:," No. 20 with the words "Aria 2 Viol. d'Amour Alt:" [sic]; the duplicate first-violin part, B 5, marks the omission of No. 20 with the rubric "Aria Viola d'Amore tacet."[7] B 8, the duplicate second-violin part, also proves informative. While it predictably omits No. 20, it includes the lower obbligato line of No. 19—erroneously, without doubt, and crossed out, most likely at once.[8] The mistake suggests that Bach had placed the obbligatos in the principal violin parts, the upper one in Violin I, the lower in Violin II; this in turn would mean that he had the viole d'amore played by the two section leaders of the violins. Table 3 summarizes the situation.

---

[7]For the headings, see Mendel, pp. 17 and 96–97; Nos. 19 and 20 belong to the later, non-autograph portion of the score. The continuo part B 21 refers to No. 20 with the marking "Aria Viola da Gamba tacet." Unlike Mendel (p. 97), I do not take this necessarily to mean that Bach had the continuo line played by a viola da gamba; very likely the instrumental indication represents a slip of the pen for "Viola d'Amore."

[8]See Mendel, pp. 92–93.

Table 3

Distribution of violin parts in Nos. 19/20, 1724

Violin Ia	lost	[Viola d'amore 1]
Violin Ib	B 5	tacet
Violin IIa	lost	[Viola d'amore 2]
Violin IIb	B 8	~~19~~/(20)

( ) = tacet marking

In 1725, Bach dropped Nos. 19 and 20 in favor of a substitute aria, No. 19[II]; as originally copied, therefore, B 6 and B 9 contain neither movement. The decision to reinstate Nos. 19 and 20 in 1732 thus obliged Bach to write out the obbligatos afresh and insert them in the violinists' parts—hence the creation of i 361 and i 363.[9] As we see from Plates 1 and 2, the new inserts no longer call for viole d'amore but instead simply mark the arioso "con Surdino."[10] In preparing the inserts, Bach evidently decided to modify the scoring of two further numbers as well: the Gospel chorus No. 21b, "Sei gegrüßet, lieber Jüdenkönig," and its restatement, "Schreibe nicht: der Jüden König," No. 25b. In 1724 and 1725, Violins I and II had doubled the soprano and alto, respectively. Now, it appears, Bach decided to have at least some of the violins double the two woodwind obbligato lines. Hence the inserts for Nos. 19 and 20 go on to include the wind lines of No. 21b. At the same time, B 9, which originally contained the alto line, received an autograph cover-sheet—pp. 365–66, or i 365—which doubled the soprano of No. 21b. For No. 25b, Bach proceeded in much the same fashion: he wrote the upper wind line on pp. 377–78—I shall call it i 377—and the soprano line on pp. 379–80, or i 379. An insert containing the second wind line does not survive, but Mendel demonstrates that it did once exist.[11]

---

[9]Indeed, Bach had to create similar inserts for virtually all the voices and instruments involved in the two movements: tenor, bass, organ, and, with one exception (B 21), continuo as well; for details, see Mendel, pp. 89–91.

[10]Bach appears to have handled the replacement of viola d'amore with violin similarly in adopting the Advent cantata *Schwingt freudig euch empor*, BWV 36, from the secular cantata of the same name, BWV 36c. In the autograph score of the earlier work—the parts do not survive—Bach assigns the aria "Auch mit gedämpften, schwachen Stimmen" to viola d'amore; in the sacred version, the autograph prescribes "Violino Solo col Sordino." The marking "col Sordino," however, represents a subsequent addition and does not appear in the part; cf. *NBA*, 1/1, *Kritischer Bericht*, p. 48.

[11]See below, p. 318.

Plate 1. Insert (i 361) containing upper obbligato part of Nos. 19/20 and portions of No. 21 (Staatsbibliothek zu Berlin—Preußischer Kulturbesitz, Mus. ms. Bach St 111, pp. 361–62)

Plate 1 (*continued*)

Violins in Bach's St. John Passion 315

Plate 2. Insert (i 363) containing lower obbligato part of Nos. 19/20 and portions of No. 21 (Staatsbibliothek zu Berlin—Preußischer Kulturbesitz, Mus. ms. Bach St 111, pp. 363–64)

Plate 2 (*continued*)

At this point, we at last approach the central question of this study. The Berlin library preserves i 361, the first-violin insert for Nos. 19–21b, as part of B 6. Since, as we have seen, B 6 served as the lead violin part both in 1725 and in 1732, this assignment would seem logical and beyond dispute. But the position of i 363, the second violin insert for Nos. 19–21b, has proved less obvious. When Mendel first examined the materials, the library had placed i 363 in B 9, the principal second-violin part. This would also seem logical. As Mendel noted, however, B 9 does not include a cue sign or any other indication connecting it to i 363, even though the insert has a quite prominent cue sign at its start.[12] Mendel concluded instead that the insert, like its companion i 361, belonged in B 6: both inserts, he wrote, have cue signs linking them to the part.[13] Table 4 shows Nos. 19–21b as Mendel imagined them.[14]

Table 4

Mendel's distribution of violin parts in Nos. 19–21b, 1732

		Nos. 19–20	No. 21b
Violin Ia	B 6	V obl 1 = i 361	WW 1 = i 361
		V obl 2 = i 363	WW 2 = i 363
Violin Ib	B 5	tacet	Soprano
Violin IIa	B 9	tacet	Soprano = i 365
Violin IIb	B 8	tacet	Alto

V obl = Violin obbligato
WW = Woodwind (Flute & Oboe)

Mendel's assignment of i 363 to B 6—or, to get at the nub of the issue, his idea that Bach intended both i 361 and i 363 to go into B 6—has its problems. Let us start with perhaps the least compelling of the arguments against it. Mendel imagined two violinists reading together from B 6 but playing Nos. 19–21b from individual inserts. This seems rather cumbersome, especially when we think that Bach could easily have notated the two obbligato parts on a single insert in score fashion, much as modern orchestral parts do. Bach clearly understood this notational practice, as we

---

[12]Mendel, p. 90.

[13]See Mendel, pp. 42 and 90.

[14]See Mendel, p. 100.

learn from the bassoon part to the *Missa* of 1733: when the music reaches the "Quoniam," which requires two bassoons, he shifts to a two-stave layout with the lines labeled "Bassono 1(mo)" and "Bassono 2(do)," respectively, and signals the change with the notice "Quoniam, seq(ui)t(u)r à 2 Bassoni."[15] It does not make much sense to think that something of this kind would not have occurred to him a year or so earlier.

A second problem arises when we consider the two inserts in their larger context. As we have already observed, Bach prepared other violin inserts for the performance of 1732 as well. We have referred to one set, those for No. 25b, in passing, and must now do so in more detail. The two surviving inserts, the cover-sheets i 377 and i 379, contain the music to the first wind line and the soprano line, respectively; i 377 fits straightforwardly in B 6, i 379 in B 9.[16] As for the missing insert with the second wind line, Mendel both demonstrates its existence and shows where it belonged through the presence in B 5 of stitching holes that match none of the existing cover-sheets.[17] The distribution of music for No. 25b in the violin parts would thus have looked like what we see in Table 5.

Table 5

Distribution of violin parts in No. 25b, 1732

Violin Ia	B 6	WW 1 = i 377
Violin Ib	B 5	WW 2 = lost cover-sheet
Violin IIa	B 9	Soprano = i 379
Violin IIb	B 8	Alto

WW = Woodwind (Flute & Oboe)

A further pair of inserts from 1732 evidently contained a sinfonia that took the place of Nos. 33–35. Although the movement no longer exists, we can infer its character from the remark "Sinfonia tacet" in several voice parts. But actual cues to the music—clearly to inserts—appear only in four

---

[15]Readers can easily consult the facsimile of the Dresden parts: *Johann Sebastian Bach: Missa h-Moll BWV 232¹. Faksimile nach dem Originalstimmensatz der Sächsischen Landesbibliothek Dresden*, ed. Hans-Joachim Schulze (Neuhausen–Stuttgart: Hänssler, 1983).

[16]Cf. Mendel, pp. 99–100.

[17]Mendel, pp. 99–100.

places: in two of the continuo parts and in the two first violins, B 6 and B 5.[18] With both this sinfonia and No. 25b, in other words, Bach placed an insert in each copy of Violin I, rather than bunching two inserts together in B 6. Hence the solution for i 363 proposed by Mendel conflicts with Bach's practice elsewhere in the same set of parts.

Yet another inconsistency lies within the two problematic inserts themselves. While both, as Mendel observed, have cues relating to B 6, a glance at Plates 1 and 2 will show that these cues provide their players with contradictory information. Insert i 361 shifts back to the main part directly after No. 21b; i 363, on the other hand, includes rests for the twelve and a half bars of recitative, No. 21c, that follow the chorus. A look at the relevant portion of B 6, reproduced in Plate 3, shows a predictably confused situation: while a player reading from i 363 would have had little trouble finding his way back to the "NB" on the ninth staff of the main part, anyone playing from i 361 would have had a harder time, having to pick out both a "bombsight" cue and the rests for No. 21c under a thick swatch of crossing out.[19] According to Mendel, this represents "just one of the numerous similar oversights that have crept into the parts."[20] But while the parts doubtless contain their share of misleading information, we might hesitate to accept such an anomaly unless we absolutely have to. Most of the errors in the parts, moreover, appear to stem from Bach's copyists, not the composer himself. In this instance, especially if we consider the length and complexity of the piece, we would at the very least have to accuse him of bad planning.

A final set of difficulties emerges with the last performance of the Passion, which Kobayashi has pinpointed to 1749.[21] Here, we may first turn our attention to a small detail in B 5. In 1732, according to Mendel, this part doubled the soprano of No. 21b, just as it had done in the performances of 1724 and 1725.[22] Yet in 1749, Bach had B 5 fitted with an cover-sheet—pp. 507–508, or i 507—containing the very line it had supposedly played on every previous occasion.[23] As we can see from Plate 4, moreover, the part itself shows the chorus crossed out to the point of illegibility. In the scenario proposed by Mendel, neither the deletion nor the reinstatement of the chorus makes any sense; Mendel's ascription of both to a flurry of indecision just before the performance of 1749 betrays evident discomfort.[24]

---

[18]See Mendel, pp. 101–11, especially the table on p. 105.

[19]Cf. Mendel, pp. 90–91.

[20]Mendel, p. 91; see also p. 90, n. 38.

[21]See Kobayashi, p. 63.

[22]See above, p. 317, and Table 4.

[23]See particularly Mendel, pp. 32 and 100.

[24]Mendel, p. 100.

Plate 3. Violin I (B 6), fol. 3ᵛ (Staatsbibliothek zu Berlin—Preußischer Kulturbesitz, Mus. ms. Bach St 111, p. 146)

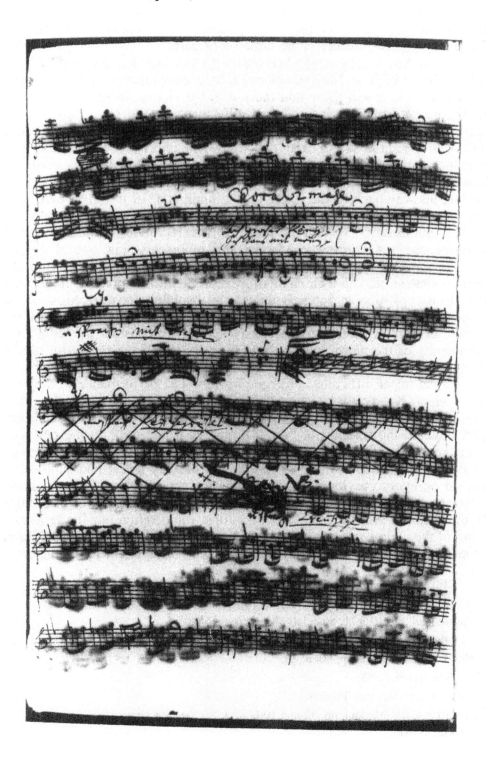

Plate 4. Violin I doublet (B 5), fol. 5, with cover-sheet (p. 507) removed (Staatsbibliothek zu Berlin—Preußischer Kulturbesitz, Mus. ms. Bach St 111, p. 9)

In 1749, Bach also had a third copy of Violin I prepared.[25] This copy—B 7 in Mendel's numbering—includes Nos. 19–21 as they read in B 6 with i 361 in place: it contains, in other words, the upper obbligato line for Nos. 19 and 20, and the upper woodwind line of No. 21b.[26] The reinforcement of the wind obbligato in No. 21b seems unproblematic enough. Not so, however, the doubling of the obbligato in Nos. 19–20. Bach surely meant both lines of both numbers for solo performance—a view held by Mendel as well, who labels them "solo," in editorial italics, in his score and writes in his critical report that they "were probably always performed solo."[27] So the presence of Nos. 19–20 in B 7 seems, at the very least, an oddity; indeed, Mendel regards it simply as an error.[28] By this point, however, we may well wonder how many errors, inconsistencies, and improbabilities Mendel's hypothesis can reasonably sustain, and whether we should not look for an alternative explanation. Such an explanation, I shall now try to show, lies readily to hand. It begins where we just left off: with B 7.

II

Bach clearly intended B 7 not to replace, but to supplement the other first-violin parts; for at the same time he had it prepared, he also made revisions to B 6 and B 5 that prominently concerned their inserts—a matter to which we shall return before long. We can readily see, moreover, that he intended B 7 to serve as the principal part, supplanting B 6 in that role. In addition to Nos. 19–20, B 7 also contains an insert with a muted doubling of the flute line in No. 35, the aria "Zerfließe, mein Herze."[29] None of the other violin parts contains this aria, and as Mendel recognizes, Bach surely meant only one violinist to double the flute.[30] In the performance of 1749, therefore, the violin parts—five in all—would presumably have served in

---

[25] See the description in Mendel, p. 49. Bach also had a new viola part copied (Mendel, p. 50), and, according to Hans-Joachim Schulze, "J. S. Bachs Johannes-Passion: Die Spätfassung von 1749," in *Johann Sebastian Bach, Johannes-Passion, BWV 245: Vorträge des Meisterkurses 1986 und der Sommerakademie J. S. Bach 1990*, Schriftenreihe der Internationalen Bachakademie Stuttgart, 5 (Kassel: Bärenreiter, 1993), p. 124, one for Violin II as well. But no such part survives, and I see less reason than Schulze to take its existence for granted; at the very least, it could scarcely have occupied the same position among the second-violin parts that B 7 does among the firsts (see n. 31, below). The question does not, in any event, materially affect the present inquiry.

[26] Cf. Mendel, pp. 49, 97, 100, 221, and 224; on p. 97, Mendel appears to overlook the presence of No. 19 in the part. The scribe of B 7 seems in fact to have copied Nos. 19–21 directly from i 361; see Mendel, pp. 137–38.

[27] Mendel, p. 97.

[28] See Mendel, p. 97.

[29] See Mendel, p. 49.

[30] See Mendel, p. 111.

the distribution shown in Table 6. With this established, at least provisionally, we can sort out what actually happened with our two inserts.

Table 6

Distribution of violin parts in BWV 245, 1749

Violin Ia	B 7
Violin Ib	B 6
Violin Ic	B 5
Violin IIa	B 9
Violin IIb	B 8

Let us return to 1732, when the distribution of the violin parts looked as it does in Table 2; let us also imagine a disposition of the two first-violin inserts i 361 and i 363 corresponding to what we saw with No. 25b and the lost sinfonia. If we add to this the position of i 365 in No. 21b, then the analogy with the parallel movement No. 25b becomes complete, as readers can see by comparing Table 7 with Table 5.

Table 7

Proposed distribution of violin parts in Nos. 19–21b, 1732

		Nos. 19–20	No. 21b
Violin Ia	B 6	V obl 1 = i 361	WW 1 = i 361
Violin Ib	B 5	V obl 2 = i 363	WW 2 = i 363
Violin IIa	B 9	tacet	Soprano = i 365
Violin IIb	B 8	tacet	Alto

V obl = Violin obbligato
WW = Woodwind (Flute & Oboe)

We shall test this proposition momentarily. First, though, let us consider a second question: what would have happened to this arrangement in 1749? With five violin parts in all, it seems simplest to imagine that Bach simply moved everything "up a notch": if, as we have already seen, B 7 included the first obbligato line of Nos. 19–20, then the second line could well have migrated from B 5 to B 6. In No. 21b, B 7 and B 6 would have continued as in the preceding movements, while B 5 would have reverted to its original function of doubling the soprano. Table 8 shows the presumed result.[31] If we compare this situation with that of 1732, we must imagine Bach to have taken the following measures: shifting i 363 from B 5 to B 6; setting i 361 aside; and modifying B 5 both to show the tacet markings for Nos. 19–20 and to reinstate the soprano line in No. 21b.

Table 8

Proposed distribution of violin parts in Nos. 19–21b, 1749

		Nos. 19–20	No. 21b
Violin Ia	B 7	V obl 1	WW 1
Violin Ib	B 6	V obl 2	WW 2
Violin Ic	B 5	tacet	Soprano
Violin IIa	B 9	tacet	Soprano
Violin IIb	B 8	tacet	Alto

V obl = Violin obbligato
WW = Woodwind (Flute & Oboe)

At this point, we should turn back to the sources to see whether they bear out these suppositions. Let us start with B 5. A look at Plate 4 shows several layers of correction that we must disentangle. We may begin with those in the third system.[32] The crossed-out material here originally read "Arioso tacet" and "Aria Viola d'Amore tacet," referring to Nos. 19 and 20, respectively. The deletion—or at least a first phase of it—occurred in 1725, when Bach replaced these two movements with No. 19[II]. He thus crossed out "Arioso tacet" and the words "Viola d'Amore tacet" but inserted an additional "tacet" indication beneath the "Aria" that remained, as schematically represented in Table 9. Mendel suggests further that the

---

[31]If the additional second-violin part hypothesized by Schulze (see n. 25, above) actually existed, it would presumably have corresponded in content to B 8 and occupied a position we may call Violin IIc; cf. also Table 10, below.
[32]For all of the following, cf. Mendel, pp. 92–93.

Table 9

Tacet markings for Nos. 19–20 in B 5

(a) before revision:

Arioso tacet ‖ Aria Viola d'Amore tacet ‖

(b) after revision:

~~Arioso tacet~~ ‖ Aria ~~Vi~~‖~~ola d'Amore tacet~~ ‖

tacet ‖

---

space at the right-hand end of the preceding system, immediately following No. 18, may have contained a notice such as "Sequitur Aria," which Bach subsequently erased.[33] On the basis of photographs, at least, I do not see this, although I do plainly see an erasure at the start of the space in question. But to my eyes, this erasure cancels a "bombsight" cue-sign—precisely the mark we would expect to find if Bach fitted an insert to this part at some point in its history. We find a corresponding cue for re-entry, in the form of an X, right at the start of No. 21d, the chorus "Kreuzige, kreuzige." If, as I suggest, Bach fitted i 363 to this part in 1732, we should naturally expect to find both cue-signs in the insert as well. In fact we do: the "bombsight," drawn with a firm hand, nestles within a shakier bracket-like sign at the head of the page, while at the end of the insert, we can readily discern the "X" in what now looks like a "NB."[34] Thus far, at least, our proposed solution to the problem seems to hold up.

It now becomes easy to see what happened to B 5 in 1749. Since, as we have proposed, Bach removed i 363 from this part, he wiped out the "bombsight" cue and inserted instead the words "Arioso et Aria tacent" in his stiff late script. This now left him with the problem of 21b, which—as we can now recognize—he had crossed out in 1732. He solved it, of

---

[33]Mendel, p. 92.

[34]On the bracket and the "NB," see below, p. 326.

course, by having i 507 written and sewn over the part, producing a result approximately like what we see in Plate 5.[35]

The same process that we have traced here occurred with B 6 as well, with the principal difference that the part went through one less stage—dating as it does from 1725, it did not originally contain Nos. 19–20 or references to them. In 1732, therefore, Bach had only to cross out the tacet marking for No. 19^{II} and insert a cue sign directing the player to i 361. He marked this insertion with a double-pronged bracket such as we still see on the insert itself, and marked the return with the "bombsight" still visible at the transition from No. 21b to 21c. Significantly, i 361—in contrast to i 363—underwent no further modification, which confirms our assumption that Bach did not use it in 1749.

In 1749, Bach only had to make two minor changes to B 6—both easily visible in Plate 3—for the part to accomodate i 363. At the cue for Nos. 19 and 20 in the sixth staff, he inserted a "bombsight" into the original bracket—at the same time, obviously, as he added the shakily drawn bracket in the insert. Since i 363 returned to the main part at a different juncture from its predecessor, he crossed out the original cue sign and the twelve bars rest for No. 21b, and instead added an "NB" at the start of No. 21c—making a corresponding change in i 363 to convert its "X" into an "NB."[36]

We can thus represent the entire progress of Nos. 19–21b between 1732 and 1749 as in Table 10. This solution resolves all the various problems with Mendel's and, for that matter, offers a tighter interpretation of

Table 10

Distribution of violin parts and inserts in Nos. 19–21b/c, 1732–49

	1732	1749
Violin Ia	B 6 + i 361	B 7
Violin Ib	B 5 + i 363	B 6 + i 363
Violin Ic	—	B 5 + i 507
Violin IIa	B 9 + i 365	B 9 + i 365
Violin IIb	B 8	B 8

---

[35] See Mendel, p. 32. The library has attached i 507 to B 5 in a way that makes it impossible to fit the insert over the part exactly as Bach placed it; the reader must imagine the cover sheet a stave higher than it appears in Plate 5.

[36] Just why Bach did this remains unclear; an "X" would have served just as well.

Violins in Bach's St. John Passion 327

Plate 5. Violin I doublet (B 5), fol. 5, with cover-sheet in place (Staatsbibliothek zu Berlin—Preußischer Kulturbesitz, Mus. ms. Bach St 111, p. 9 + p. 507)

the strictly visual evidence as well. Admittedly, one small inconsistency remains. Given the parallels between Nos. 21b and 25b, we might expect Bach in 1749 to have altered the distribution of inserts and doublings for the second chorus in precisely the same fashion as he did with the first. In fact, he treated this movement somewhat differently. B 7, rather than doubling the upper woodwind line, contains the lower one; B 6, meanwhile, retains the upper line; and B 5 does not revert to the soprano line but receives a new insert—pp. 513–14, or i 513—containing yet another copy of the lower wind obbligato. Table 11 shows the result.

Table 11

Distribution of violin parts in No. 25b, 1749

Violin Ia	B 7	WW 2
Violin Ib	B 6	WW 1 = i 377
Violin Ic	B 5	WW 2 = i 513
Violin IIa	B 9	Soprano = i 379
Violin IIb	B 8	Alto

WW = Woodwind (Flute & Oboe)

On closer inspection, however, this strangely imbalanced disposition proves a degree less chaotic than it initially seems. The presence of the second wind line in B 7 in fact makes sense. In contrast to the insert that contained Nos. 19–21, Bach had attached i 377 to B 6 with sewing thread. He could thus less easily remove it from the part—and in fact had no compelling reason to do so: by having the lower wind line copied into B 7, he still achieved the desired doubling, even if he had the two violin parts switched. This does leave a problem with B 5. Clearly, if Bach meant this part to double the wind line, he could simply have left the insert of 1732 in place—assuming it still existed.[37] Perhaps, then, Bach really intended i 513 to contain the soprano line, but his son Johann Christoph Friedrich, who copied the insert, got his signals crossed. In any event, the error surely did not have grave consequences. More important, it cannot really affect the interpretation of No. 21b: the fate of No. 25b in 1749 remains as anomalous under Mendel's hypothesis as under ours.

---

[37]This would seem likely given the stemmatic relationship for No. 25b between B 7 and i 513; cf. Mendel, p. 144.

III

It may seem that we have gone to a lot of effort to clarify a modest philological detail. But this detail turns out to have consequences of more than philological importance. Mendel's interpretation of the inserts i 361 and i 363 presupposes that the violinists in the St. John Passion played two from a part, just as their successors in modern symphony orchestras do. To many, this would appear self-evident: tradition has long inclined us to regard the St. John Passion, like all of Bach's concerted vocal works, as "orchestral" music. Even the critical reports of the *Neue Bach-Ausgabe* commonly refer to violins in terms of "desks."[38] Yet proof of this arrangement remains curiously hard to come by.[39] The Sanctus BWV 238 has a treble obbligato labeled "Violini Unisoni" in both the score and the parts; but since the parts include two copies of the line, the rubric does not necessarily say anything about the number of performers reading from each copy.[40] None of Bach's violin parts contains divided writing; and while the

---

[38] See, for instance, Mendel, pp. 99–100.

[39] This does not mean that we have no evidence whatever for the practice of sharing violin parts in Bach's time. A passage in a letter of Johann Gottfried Walther brought to my attention by Hans-Joachim Schulze certainly appears to describe just such a situation; see *Johann Gottfried Walther: Briefe*, ed. Klaus Beckmann and Hans-Joachim Schulze (Leipzig: Deutscher Verlag für Musik, 1987), p. 72, and, for a translation, Joshua Rifkin, "Bach's Chorus: Some Red Herrings," *Journal of Musicological Research* 14 (1995): 225. Records detailing the numbers of players, parts, and even music stands at Roman oratorio performances in the early eighteenth century leave no doubt that at least some of the violinists must have read from the same music; see Ursula Kirkendale, *Antonio Caldara: Sein Leben und seine venezianisch-römischen Oratorien*, Wiener musikwissenschaftliche Beiträge, 6 (Graz: Hermann Böhlaus Nachfolger, 1966), pp. 360–61, and idem, "The Ruspoli Documents on Handel," *Journal of the American Musicological Society* 20 (1967): 234, 237–38, 256–57, and 262. But none of this proves either the universal adoption of the practice to the exclusion of all others or, more particularly, that Bach followed it in his own performances.

[40] Cf. *NBA*, 2/2, *Kritischer Bericht*, pp. 184 and 188–90. Bach typically used the words "violini unisoni" to indicate that first and second violins play the same music; in the Sanctus, where the unison covers an entire piece rather than one of several movements, it would have made no sense to assign different labels to parts of identical content. The scribe of the duplicate obbligato part nevertheless headed it "Violino" rather than "Violini Unisoni"; this created some potential for confusion, as the set contains an additional violin part, labeled "Violino 2.do," that exercises no independent function but simply doubles the alto voice. Bach thus changed the title of the second obbligato part to match that of the principal copy, simultaneously clarifying the identity of the two parts and differentiating them from the "Violino 2.do" The terminological pitfalls inherent in the Sanctus also affect a set of parts written by Johann Ludwig Dietel for the Neue Kirche in Leipzig: here the first copy of the obbligato line has the heading "Violin. I.^{mo}," while both the second copy and the part doubling the alto carry the label "Violino II.^{do}"; cf. *NBA*, 2/2, *Kritischer Bericht*, pp. 191–92, and, for the scribe and on the provenance of the parts, Glöckner, "Neuerkenntnisse," pp. 57–60, 65, and 75. I wish to thank Michael Marissen for valuable discussion of this problem.

word "solo," found often over obbligato numbers, doubtless implies an absence of other players, this does not inevitably mean another player reading from the same music—both "solo" and "tutti" appear with some frequency in parts explicitly meant for a single performer.[41] Hence Mendel, if correct about the placement of our two inserts, would have provided the first real evidence I know for the proposition that Bach's violinist shared their parts.[42] With the inserts assigned to separate locations, the situation changes.

---

[41] The double concerto BWV 1043 offers a particularly instructive example; as Christoph Wolff observes in his Introduction to the facsimile edition (New York: C. F. Peters, 1990), markings of "solo" and "tutti" in the two *concertino* parts provide "cues for the performers to play either with the ripieno or against it without necessitating additional dynamic differentiation." The opening movements of two cantatas, *Ich glaube, lieber Herr, hilf meinem Unglauben*, BWV 109, and *Ihr Menschen, rühmet Gottes Liebe*, BWV 167, do show "solo" and "tutti" used in a way that could well suggest an alternation between one player and more than one player. In both instances, however, the markings appear in the duplicate part as well as the first copy (for BWV 167, where only the duplicate survives, cf. *NBA*, 1/29, *Kritischer Bericht*, pp. 10–11 and 18–19); in principle at least, they could have served as guides for two separate players—one reading from the first exemplar and, like the soloists in the double concerto, playing everything, regardless of its marking, the other reading from the second exemplar and pausing at the word "solo." Cf., on this last point, the observations in Joshua Rifkin, "'...wobey aber die Singstimmen hinlänglich besetzt seyn müssen...' – Zum Credo der h-Moll-Messe in der Aufführung Carl Philipp Emanuel Bachs," *Basler Jahrbuch für historische Musikpraxis* 9 (1985): 162, n. 18, and idem, "The Bach Compendium," *Early Music* 17 (1989): 83.

[42] I should perhaps amend this to read, "shared parts with one another in the performance of concerted music." Violins and oboes conceivably read from the same music in the three wedding chorales BWV 250–52—the autograph parts include two labeled "Violino è Hautbois 1" and "Violino è Hautbois 2. d'Amour," respectively (cf. *NBA*, 3/2.1, *Kritischer Bericht*, pp. 15–16). Yet the implications of this rather unusual example would seem anything but clear. The dual nomenclature does not itself ensure that players shared these materials: virtually all of Vivaldi's instrumental publications include two copies of a continuo partbook labeled "Organo e Violoncello," one of which clearly served for the stringed instrument, the other for the keyboard; see the descriptions in Peter Ryom, *Répertoire des œuvres d'Antonio Vivaldi: Les Compositions instrumentales* (Copenhagen: Engstrøm & Sødring, 1986), pp. 9–11, 20–34, and, for a particularly illuminating case, 380. Although the parts for BWV 250–52 survive only in single copies, we cannot rule out the possibility—familiar from so many of Bach's vocal works—that duplicates for the treble parts and the continuo vanished with the original score (cf. Dürr, as in n. 5, above); and this, in turn, opens the way to the possibility that violinists and oboists played from separate music after all. Of course, these simple chorales lie at some distance from more elaborate pieces like cantatas or Passions, which makes it risky to assume that patterns of transmission governing the latter repertory must also apply here; cf. Joshua Rifkin, "More (and Less) on Bach's Orchestra," *Performance Practice Review* 4 (1991): 8. But by precisely the same token, we might think twice about drawing analogies in the other direction as well and concluding that anything strings and winds might have done in the wedding chorales sets a precedent for what violinists did in concerted works. A forthcoming article by Michael Marissen, "Performance Practice Issues that Affect Meaning in Selected Bach Instrumental Works," in *Perspectives on Bach Performance*, ed. Robin Stowell (Cambridge University Press), offers valuable insights into this and related problems.

Strictly speaking, we might just as well imagine one violinist reading from each part—as violinists still do in chamber music. As it happens, the St. John Passion offers some provocative insights in precisely this regard.

Let us first consider the distribution of the inserts. As Mendel, an experienced orchestral practitioner, recognized, the arrangement that he proposed for i 361 and i 363 made good sense in at least one respect: entrusting the obbligatos of Nos. 19–20 to "the two violin soloists of the first desk" meant placing them in the hands of "surely the best players."[43] The pattern exemplified by Bach's treatment of the viole d'amore in 1724 also seems logical, as it assigns the two obbligato lines to the respective section leaders.[44] But unless Bach had a very different notion of violinistic ranking from ours, the procedure that we have seen him adopt throughout the St. John Passion proves hard to fathom—if two violinists read from each part. With one player to a part, however, it becomes eminently comprehensible.[45]

We get a similar message when we examine the parts and inserts themselves. Let us start with B 7. As we have seen, Bach intended this to serve as the lead part in the performance of 1749. As we have also seen, it contains three numbers all but certainly meant for solo performance: Nos. 19, 20, and 35. Yet at no place does B 7 show the word "solo" or any comparable term, nor does the marking "tutti" ever appear. No. 19 and No. 35 do call for muted playing—in the latter instance, in Bach's own hand.[46] But we have no reason to think that violinists would automatically have read his "col sourdino" to imply "solo" as well.[47]

The two autograph inserts for Nos. 19–20 present exactly the same picture. Once again, Bach took the trouble to specify mutes at the start of No. 19 but did not write "solo" or anything similar. Hence for all the pains he

---

[43]Mendel, p. 90.

[44]Obviously, this point would hold whether one or more than one player read from each part. Splitting the obbligato lines between sections seems the most frequent means of distributing such duos in Bach's violin parts; we find it documented in the performing materials to the cantatas BWV 17 and 51, as well as in Part IV of the Christmas Oratorio. The arias with two violins in the cantatas BWV 52, 72, and 125 do not really enter into consideration here, as each line of the duo appears in both copies of the part.

[45]Bach appears to have divided the lines of obbligato duos in the same fashion on at least two other occasions. In the cantata *Am Abend aber desselbigen Sabbaths*, BWV 42, the two obbligato violin parts of the aria "Jesus ist ein Schild der seinen" appear in Violin Ia and Ib, respectively. In *Wohl dem, der sich auf seinen Gott*, BWV 139, the aria "Gott ist mein Freund" calls for two concerted violins, although only the first of them survives; see William H. Scheide, "The 'Concertato' Violin in BWV 139," in *Bach-Studien 5: Eine Sammlung von Aufsätzen*, ed. Rudolf Eller and Hans-Joachim Schulze (Leipzig: Breitkopf & Härtel, 1975), pp. 123–37. As we still have the principal copy of Violin II, the missing obbligato must have appeared in the second exemplar of Violin I, which no longer exists.

[46]Mendel, p. 49.

[47]Bach used muted violins on more than one occasion where the parts call for the entire section, as in the "Domine Deus" of the B-minor Mass or the aria "Sanfte soll mein Todeskummer" in the Easter Oratorio; see also the following note.

clearly took over these inserts—as anyone can see from their full and careful articulation—he neglected to provide information that we might think all but essential if his players had used his violin parts in orchestral fashion.

In other words, the notational procedures in the violin parts of the St. John Passion make little sense in the context of an "orchestral" string practice but appear well suited to another mode of performance. Obviously, we cannot say that this "proves" anything. Nor can we pretend that reading the parts as if used by one player each will rid them of every inconsistency or insufficiency. To take just one example: Bach's evident pains to specify the addition of mutes did not extend to specifying their removal—we find "senza sordino" neither after No. 20 in any of the parts nor after No. 35 in B 7. Still, we may well suspect that the failure to remove a mute will have a less substantial impact on a performance than confusion over how many violinists should play a given line at a given moment; and in any event, as I have already stressed, the undeniable existence of anomalies in Bach's performing materials should not really encourage us to favor interpretations that have the effect of increasing, rather than diminishing, their number.[48]

Seen in this light, the violin parts to the St. John Passion send a clear and simple message. In this piece at least, the cautious scholar and performer would do better to imagine Bach's violinists reading one to a part rather than sharing their music. Whether, and to what extent, this conclusion holds elsewhere in Bach will obviously require further investigation—investigation, we may hope, that shows the epistemological scrupulousness and freedom from preconception that Mendel himself so vigorously urged upon us, and that Paul Brainard has so gracefully exemplified.[49]

---

[48]Conceivably, convention would have dictated the removal of mutes in most circumstances. If we count "Betrachte, mein Seel" and "Erwäge" as an integral pair, only a single Bach movement that calls for muted playing does not lead either to a number marked *tacet* or to a final chorale; significantly, the exception—the "Domine Deus" of the B-minor Mass—leads to the sole piece known to me that Bach actually marked "senza sordino." Those who might wish to argue, however, that a similar convention could have governed shifts between solo and tutti playing, especially in the St. John Passion, must reckon with the fact that the parts contain no indications of this kind to begin with.

[49]For some preliminary findings, see my notes to the Bach Ensemble's recordings of the Mass in B minor (Nonesuch D–79036) and cantatas BWV 140 and 51 (L'Oiseau-Lyre 417 616–1OH), as well as the example from BWV 59 communicated by Matthias Wendt, "Solo – Obligato – Concertato. Fakten zur Terminologie der konzertierenden Instrumentalpartien bei Johann Sebastian Bach," in *Beiträge zur Geschichte des Konzerts. Festschrift Siegfried Kross zum 60. Geburtstag*, ed. Reinmar Emans and Matthias Wendt (Bonn: Gudrun Schröder, 1990), p. 57.

French Opera in Transition: *Silvie* (1765) by Trial and Berton

Lois Rosow

The period that separated the Querelle des Bouffons (1752–54) from Gluck's arrival in France (1773) was a time of uncertain direction for the Académie royale de musique, more familiarly known as the Paris Opéra. Rameau composed few new works, yet no composer of similar stature appeared to replace him. At the fair theaters and Comédie-Italienne, a new genre of *opéra-comique* flourished, but it was not adopted by the Opéra. Since new librettos were scarce, Dauvergne and others experimented with the Italianate practice of making fresh settings of old librettos, but few such pieces succeeded at the box office.[1] Indeed, few new pieces of any kind were written for the Opéra; the institution filled its calendar mainly with revivals of old works by Rameau and others. Editors even breathed new life into some of Lully's *tragédies en musique* by reworking them to fit contemporary taste, and these productions did well financially. Still, an increasingly large part of the Opéra's schedule had to be filled by so-called "fragments"—independent *actes de ballet* and individual acts from *opéra-ballets* grouped together to make an evening's entertainment. Not even Philidor's *tragédie-lyrique Ernelinde* (1767) established a new direction for French serious opera, despite its innovations. In the end, it was Gluck who brought renewed vigor to the Paris Opéra by converting it "from a museum into a place of musical novelty and dramatic vitality."[2]

---

[1] Pierre J. B. Nougaret, *De l'art du théâtre en général* (Paris: Cailleau, 1769), 1:178, 2:237–44, attributed the scaraity of good poets willing to write librettos for the Opéra in part to the Académie's insistence on copyright: while the composer had the right to have his score engraved, the librettist was forced to relinquish his text to the Académie; the librettist thus profited from the performances but not the printing of his piece. Nougaret urged that the Italian practice of resetting good librettos from the past be fully embraced (as it indeed would be during the 1770s and '80s).

[2] Quotation from Julian Rushton, *Classical Music: A Concise History from Gluck to Beethoven* (London: Thames and Hudson, 1986), p. 62; see also pp. 52–53. Regarding repertory, see Théodore de Lajarte, *Bibliothèque musicale du théâtre de l'Opéra: catalogue historique, chronologique, anecdotique* (Paris: Librairie des bibliophiles, 1878), vol. 1, passim. A more complete overview of repertory, performance schedules, and box

Nevertheless, it would be a mistake to view the Opéra as moribund in those years. The institution's conservatism and curatorial function reflected an important side of public taste.[3] In addition, within an essentially conservative aesthetic framework, modifications of stylistic detail were welcome; they were regarded not as desperate attempts to save a dying art form but as creative innovations. Finally, the Opéra did respond to the general changes affecting musical style in the mid-eighteenth century. This study aims to illustrate the atmosphere at the Paris Opéra in the mid-1760s by concentrating on a single successful, historically important new opera: the *pastorale-héroïque Silvie* by Jean-Claude Trial and Pierre-Montan Berton.

Trial (1732–71), who began his career in the provinces, had gone to Paris originally for the purpose of meeting Rameau; the date of the trip is unknown. Although his intention had been to return to Montpellier, he remained in Paris instead, accepting the position of *premier violon* (in effect, leader of the orchestra) of the Opéra-Comique around 1759. Shortly thereafter, the prince de Conti, a former courtier who was now in disgrace and unwelcome at the royal court, undertook to make his home a principal center of Parisian music-making. He hired Trial as second violinist around 1761 and soon thereafter promoted him to the position of composer and music director. Under Trial's direction, an excellent ensemble of singers and instrumentalists (including, incidentally, the Silesian composer Johann Schobert as harpsichordist) entertained the most important members of high society.[4] As for Berton (1727–80), he was a former opera singer who

---

office receipts is available in the manuscript "Journal de l'Opéra," Paris, Bibliothèque de l'Opéra [hereafter F-Po], Usuels 201; vol. 5 covers 1751–70. Regarding *Ernelinde*, which avoids supernatural elements and contains Italianate arias and recitative, see facs. ed. with intro. by Julian Rushton, French Opera in the Seventeenth and Eighteenth Centuries, 16 (Stuyvesant, NY: Pendragon Press, 1994) and Daniel Heartz, "Diderot et le Théâtre lyrique: 'le nouveu stile' proposé par *Le Neveu de Rameau*," *Revue de Musicologie* 64 (1978): 245–51.

[3]See William Weber, "Lully and the Rise of Musical Classics in the Eighteenth Century," in *Jean-Baptiste Lully: Actes du Colloque / Kongressbericht: Saint-Germain-en-Laye—Heidelberg 1987*, ed. Herbert Schneider and Jérôme de La Gorce (Laaber: Laaber Verlag, 1990), pp. 581–90.

[4]On Trial's biography, "Eloge de Monsieur Trial," *Les Spectacles de Paris* 21 (1772): 17–23; Jean-Benjamin de Laborde, *Essai sur la musique ancienne et moderne* (Paris: E. Onfroy, 1780), 3:486–87. (I established Trial's dates of service in the Opéra-Comique according to repertory he is known to have directed there.) On Conti's salon (and a well-known painting of the child Mozart performing there), G. Capon and R. Yve-Plessis, *Vie privée du prince de Conty: Louis-François de Bourbon (1717–1776)* (Paris: J. Schemit, 1907), pp. 111–36; Barbara Russano Hanning, "The Iconography of a Salon

had left a conducting position in Bordeaux in 1753, planning merely to spend some time with his family in Paris but in fact staying there permanently; in 1758, he competed for and won the post of *batteur de mesure* (orchestra conductor) at the Paris Opéra. By 1759, he had begun to display his considerable talent for sensitively reworking old operas, and this activity joined the duties he already performed as conductor of the orchestra. In 1763, his title was changed from *batteur de mesure* to *maître de musique*, and his formerly modest salary increased dramatically.[5] It was at this stage of their careers, in 1765, that Trial and Berton completed *Silvie*, their first collaborative project.

The libretto for *Silvie*, by Pierre Laujon, antedates the première of Trial's and Berton's opera by some sixteen years. Laujon wrote it in 1749 for the composer Pierre de Lagarde, with whom he had recently collaborated on *Aeglé*, another *pastorale-héroïque*. Both *Silvie* and *Aeglé* were written for the Théâtre des Petits Appartements (or Petits Cabinets) at Versailles, the celebrated amateur opera company run by Louis XV's talented mistress, the marquise de Pompadour. Despite its temporary stage and modest performing forces, this theater was a major center of French operatic activity during its four years of existence; even one of Rameau's operas, *Les Surprises de l'Amour*, had its première there.[6] *Silvie* was performed twice at Versailles during the winter of 1749, with Madame de Pompadour in the title role, and in 1751 *Aeglé* and *Silvie* were among a small number of works from the Versailles repertory that were selected for production at the Paris Opéra itself. In the case of *Silvie*, however, no such production ever took place. Many years later Laujon explained that this situation had been caused by his collaborator, Lagarde, who not only held a conducting

---

Concert: A Reappraisal," in *French Musical Thought: 1600–1800*, ed. Georgia Cowart (Ann Arbor: UMI Research Press, 1989), pp. 129–48.

[5] Laborde, 3:387–90; "Eloge de Berton," *Les Spectacles de Paris* 30 (1781): 18–20; "Notice de la vie et des ouvrages de M. Berton...," *Le Nécrologe des hommes célebres de France*, vol. 17 (Paris: Moreau, 1782), pp. 43–56. Berton's starting salary of 1000 *livres* was raised to 1200 in 1760, then to 1500 in 1763, at which time he was also assigned a *gratification annuelle* of 300 *livres* (Paris, Archives nationales, AJ^{13}15, dossiers 2–3).

[6] Adolphe Jullien, *Histoire du théâtre de Madame de Pompadour dit Théâtre des Petits Cabinets* (Paris: J. Baur, 1874). For an excellent discussion of the scenic capabilities of the theater, which included some stage machinery, see Antonia Banducci, "Staging a *Tragédie lyrique*: A 1748 Promptbook of Campra's *Tancrède*," *Early Music* 21 (1993): 180–90.

position with the Opéra orchestra but, in addition, had recently been named *maître des enfants* of France:

> The tasks connected with these two positions were so numerous that Lagarde could hardly manage them. Also, when *Aeglé* was given, in order better to ensure its success, he borrowed the most outstanding choruses and portions of *divertissements* from our latest works. He left them impoverished, and when it became a question of presenting them, it was impossible for him to get away from his two jobs for a single instant... Always waiting hopefully for a few favorable moments, I used my spare time to repair the gaps that my musician had left in our works, especially those in *Silvie*; to reinforce those roles that Madame de Pompadour had wanted me to weaken so that hers would seem more brilliant; and, finally, to give that work all the pomp that it could hold—pomp that was not possible at the Théâtre des Petits Cabinets, that could only take place in the theater at Fontainebleau, and still more easily in the one in Paris. It was only after at least three years of patience—or, more accurately, of impatience— on my part that Lagarde, embarassed and sorry not to be able to cut short the delay, begged me to entrust my opera *Silvie* to Trial and Berton, who began to work on it then but took a long time to finish it...[7]

Laujon (who was twenty-two years old when Lagarde's *Silvie* was produced and eighty-four when he published his reminiscences) implied that he gave Trial and Berton the revised libretto around 1755; Lagarde's retire-

---

[7]"Les occupations attachées à ces deux places étaient si multipliées, que Lagarde avait peine à y suffire. Aussi quand on donna son acte d'*Aeglé*, pour mieux en assurer le succès, il emprunta, tant en choeurs qu'en divertissemens, ce qu'il avait de plus saillant dans nos ouvrages derniers: il les avait donc tellement appauvris, que lorsqu'il fut question de les donner, il lui était impossible de dérober un seul instant à ses deux places ...Leurré toujours dans l'attente de quelques momens favorables, j'employais mes instans à réparer les brèches que mon musicien avait faites à nos ouvrages, surtout à celui de *Silvie*; à renforcer les rôles que madame de Pompadour avait voulu que j'enervasse pour donner au sien plus d'éclat; à ménager enfin à cet ouvrage toute la pompe dont il était susceptible; pompe à laquelle ne pouvait se prêter le dernier théâtre des petits Cabinets, et qui ne pouvait avoir lieu que sur le théâtre de Fontainebleau, et plus facilement encore sur celui de Paris: ce ne fut guères qu'après trois ans au moins de patience, ou, pour mieux dire, d'impatience, de ma part, que Lagarde, confus lui-même, et désolé de ne pouvoir l'abréger, me pria de confier mon opéra de *Silvie* à Trial et Berton, qui s'en occupèrent alors et furent long-temps à le finir..." Pierre Laujon, *Oeuvres choisis* (Paris: Patris et Cie, 1811), 1:175–76. All translations in this article are my own. Extant sources at F-Po for Lagarde's *Silvie* and *Aeglé* contain no evidence of the cannibalization that Laujon described.

ment in 1756 from his post at the Opéra[8] seems to support this early date. On the other hand, there is no clear evidence of Trial's presence in Paris before approximately 1759. At all events, no matter when they began collaborating on *Silvie,* it is understandable that these two successful, busy musicians had no time to complete the job quickly.

Eventually they finished the project, Trial as principal composer of the Prologue and first two acts, and Berton as principal composer of Act 3.[9] On November 17, 1765, the work had its première at the royal court at Fontainebleau. About a year later, on November 18, 1766, *Silvie* began a highly successful run at the Paris Opéra, comprising twenty-four performances in the first two months, another eight later that winter, and a dozen more in the spring (during which it was reported that "the crowd does nothing but grow at each performance"). In April, Trial, who held a royal *privilège* to print his own compositions, had the score published. After a ten-month hiatus, *Silvie* closed the season (three performances in March 1768) and opened the next one (on April 12); though records for that season are incomplete, the piece is known to have been on the boards in April and November 1768.[10] It was early in the initial Paris run that Berton and Trial were chosen by the *bureau de la ville* to replace François Francoeur and François Rebel as co-directors of the Opéra, a position they assumed jointly in April 1767. While it is tempting to attribute the choice to

---

[8]Paris, Archives nationales, AJ[13]21, dossier 6.

[9]Laborde, 3:487; Louis-François Beffara, "Dictionnaire de l'Académie royale de musique," F-Po, Rés. 602 (MS, 1783–84), s.v. "Silvie," n. pag.

[10]Performance dates in "Journal de l'Opéra" (cited in n. 2), and Beffara. (As late as 1781, excerpts from *Silvie* still appeared in programs of "fragments.") Assertions of *Silvie*'s public and financial success in Beffara; *Le Mercure de France*, December 1766, p. 184; January 1767, p. 136; March 1767, p. 166; April 1768, part 2, p. 195; *Lavantcoureur*, December 8, 1766, p. 781; May 25, 1767, p. 331 (including the remark quoted above: "l'affluence n'a fait qu'augmenter à chaque représentation"); April 25, 1768, p. 265. Announcement of engraved score, *Silvie, opéra en trois actes...* (Paris: La Chevardière, n.d.), in *Le Mercure de France*, April 1767, pp. 146–47 and *Lavantcoureur*, May 11, 1767, p. 293; facsimiles in this article are from F-Po, A.212. Regarding the score's complicated publication history, see my introduction to facs. ed., French Opera in the Seventeenth and Eighteenth Centuries, 60 (Stuyvesant, NY: Pendragon Press), in preparation. Other important sources for the music are autograph fragments, Paris, Bibliothèque nationale, Cons. MS 1595, and the set of parts for the Paris production, F-Po, Mat.18.[73.

the success of *Silvie,* it had more to do with pressure placed on the *bureau* by Trial's patron, the prince de Conti.[11]

* * *

Silvie is a *pastorale-héroïque*. Plots in this genre typically revolve around a love triangle in which the principal lovers are a deity and a pastoral human. Unlike the *tragédie-lyrique,* the *pastorale-héroïque* rarely includes heroic (i.e., high-born) human characters; instead, the term "héroïque" usually refers only to the gods of Olympus and the minor deities of Arcadia—all of whom can be found in the *tragédie-lyrique* as well, of course. The "heroic" population of *Silvie,* for instance, consists of nymphs, fauns, dryads, naiads, Graces, "laughter and games" (*les Ris et les Jeux*), and several major gods; the only humans present are hunters and shepherds. The genre thus permits all of the *galanterie* of the mid-eighteenth-century *tragédie-lyrique* but requires none of its political implications or lofty attitudes; in this way, the mid-century *pastorale-héroïque* easily avoided those long, pompous speeches that Rococo sensibilities found so tiresome—"our eternal recitative," in the words of one critic.[12]

It is thus not surprising that this genre, invented in the seventeenth century, enjoyed a period of particular popularity—demonstrated by revivals as much as by new compositions—from the late 1740s to the early 1770s. By this time the more general term *ballet-héroïque,* which had originally indicated only a special type of *opéra-ballet,* had broadened in meaning to include the *pastorale-héroïque*.[13] *Silvie* is called a *pastorale-héroïque* in the libretto of 1749, merely an "opéra" in the libretto of 1765, and a *ballet-héroïque* in the libretto of 1766.

The plot of *Silvie,* based loosely on the pastoral play *Aminta* (1573) by Torquato Tasso, concerns Silvie and Amintas—she, a nymph of Diana, pledged to chastity, and he, a hunter who loves her but pretends to offer only friendship in order not to frighten her. After the goddess Diane (Diana)

---

[11] See Louis Petit de Bachaumont, *Mémoires secrets* (London: J. Adamsohn, 1777), 2:133–43.

[12] Nicolas Bricaire de la Dixmerie, *Lettres sur l'état présent de nos spectacles...* (Amsterdam and Paris: Duchesne, 1765), p. 55: "notre éternel récitatif."

[13] Paul-Marie Masson, "Le ballet héroïque," *Revue musicale* 9 (1928): 132–54. Regarding some related issues of genre definition, see my review of the facs. ed. of Destouches's *Issé,* in *Journal of the American Musicological Society* 40 (1987): 552–54. (I erroneously omitted a word on p. 552: *Acis* and *Issé* were not the first *pastorales-héroïques* but the first *important* ones.)

rescues Silvie from the faun Hilas, who has attempted to abduct her, Amintas challenges Hilas and kills him. L'Amour (Cupid), in disguise as a hunter, visits Silvie and lies to her about the outcome of the fight. Imagining that Amintas has died for love of her leads Silvie to discover her own love for him. Amintas arrives just in time to prevent her suicide. Mutual declarations of love are answered by thunder and an earthquake—but just as Diane's vengeance seems at hand, L'Amour descends from the heavens to announce that he has triumphed over her. The Temple of Diana is magically transformed into the Temple of Love.

The libretto contains all the conventional elements that Opéra audiences had come to expect. The sentiments are tender and precious; Amintas, for instance, assures Silvie that if he were in love with her, he would find it "charming" to "vanquish" his desires, for he would much rather "lose all my pleasures than pay for them with your tears" (Act 1, Scene 2: see Plate 2 below). Dramatic turning points are frequent, and they sometimes involve the abrupt juxtaposition of charming, pleasant scenes with horrific ones. Humans and minor deities are mere pawns in a power struggle between gods, and the capabilities of the gods provide the excuse for descents, transformations, and other supernatural spectacle. For instance, Diane arranges for Hilas's vehicle of abduction—a chariot drawn by tigers—to be enveloped in a cloud of mist and then swallowed by the earth. (In reworking the Versailles libretto for the theaters equipped with more elaborate machinery, Laujon greatly enlarged the roles of L'Amour and Diane. These were undoubtedly the soprano parts that he had kept weak to appease the jealous Madame de Pompadour.) Finally, poetic structures are traditional: Act 1 opens with a monologue in ternary form for the troubled Amintas, a conventional gesture that can be traced back to Lully;[14] the dialogues permit a flexible mixture of recitative, little airs, and brief ensembles of traditional types; there are ample opportunities for choral singing; and each of the three acts contains an elaborate ballet *divertissement*.

Laujon made plenty of provision for the visual splendor that so delighted Opéra audiences, and it is clear from contemporaneous reviews that the Paris production took advantage of these opportunities. For instance, the scenery for the Prologue, designed (presumably for the Fontainebleau production) by the King's painter François Boucher, made "the spectator believe himself to be in Vulcan's den"; to complete the illusion, the Opéra's director of machinery invented a sort of liquid fire for the forge.[15] Highest

---

[14]The 1749 version had opened with a monologue in ternary form for Silvie.
[15]*Lavantcoureur*, December 8, 1766, p. 781 ("Le Spectateur croit être dans l'antre de Vulcain"); *Le Mercure de France*, December 1766, pp. 179–80.

praise was reserved for the Temple of Love that replaced the Temple of Diana at the end of the opera—a design that was, on the one hand, original and, on the other, indicative of eighteenth-century scenographers' longstanding fascination with architectural illusion:

> This last piece of scenery, composed by Monsieur Boquet, Painter and Designer of the Académie, is entirely new for the theater, not only in its material but in its composition, in that the entire front area of the stage represents a rotunda formed by lapis columns and topped by an entablature, an attic, and a ceiling. The normal shape of the theater is changed, and the natural design of the building is entirely lost from view. People particularly admire—in fact, they cannot overpraise—the beauty of the ceiling, which shows some of the gods of Olympus, of the earth, and of the water. The design, the composition of the groups, the strength, beauty, and harmony of the colors, all make it one of the most beautiful pieces in this genre, one which would enrich a real palace of the greatest beauty.[16]

Despite Laujon's adherence to poetic tradition in *Silvie*, as an old man he remembered the Paris production as a moment of personal rebellion against some established conventions of visual presentation:

> It was an unusual time because of changes that I brought to that theater. I insisted on—I will say moreover that I secured right from the beginning—the suppression of the *masks* (granted to me as early as the trip from Fontainebleau) and the introduction of essential costumes for *all characters*, making no exception for *the dancers and chorus*. Before this time the chorus arrived on stage in an orderly *march*. The men on one side and the women on the other passed each other as they arrived and then re-entered the wings; then, in order of seniority they came on stage once again, this time to place themselves in line on each side, singing, the men with their arms crossed and the women holding fans, which meant that

---

[16]"Cette dernière décoration, de la composition de M. [Louis-René] BOQUET Peintre & Dessinateur de l'Académie, est entièrement neuve pour le théâtre, non-seulement par la matière, mais par sa composition; en ce que toute la scène antérieure représente une rotonde formée par des colonnes de lapis, surmontées de l'entablement, d'un attique & d'un plafond. La forme ordinaire du théâtre se trouve changée & le plan naturel du local entièrement perdu de vue. On admire particulièrement, & l'on ne peut en effet trop admirer la beauté du plafond, qui représente une partie des Dieux de l'olympe, de la terre & des eaux. Le dessein, la composition des grouppes, la force, la beauté & l'harmonie de la couleur peuvent le faire regarder comme un des plus beaux morceaux en ce genre, & qui enrichiroit le plus beau palais d'une construction réelle." *Le Mercure de France*, December 1766, pp. 183–84.

they could make not a single gesture. To bring them to do those things that the stage required, to get all of them to take part in the action, was a most challenging goal, but I succeeded. The chorus members, who until then had been automatons, no longer thought of themselves as anything but actors; the dancers gave to their different situations the expression that masks had not permitted them to show; and the effect was so immediate that a *pas de deux*, danced by Mademoiselle Allard and Monsieur Dauberval, was engraved, showing the impression that they made.[17]

Laujon's memories notwithstanding, he was not the first to put the formerly stationary Opéra chorus into action. The librettist Louis de Cahusac claimed to have introduced choral action in Rameau's operas starting in 1747;[18] furthermore, when Lully's *Armide* was revived in 1761, the periodicals *Lavantcoureur* and *Le Mercure de France* both described the way the chorus participated in "the action of the moment..., making a tableau in accord with the actors, especially in the chorus of the first act, 'Poursuivons jusqu'au trépas.'"[19] In that piece, "a fast, tightly woven, and precise song is accompanied by tumultuous actions on the part of all the members

---

[17]"L'époque en est assez singulière par les changemens que j'amenai sur ce théâtre; j'exigeai, je dirai plus, j'obtins d'abord, la suppression des *masques*, (ce qui m'avait été accordé dès le voyage de Fontainebleau), l'introduction des costumes nécessaires à *tous les personnages*, sans excepter *la danse et les choeurs*. Antérieurement à cette époque, les choeurs arrivaient sur la scène en *marche* réglée; les hommes d'un côté, les femmes de l'autre, se croisaient en arrivant, descendaient ainsi, en longeant les coulisses, et par ordre d'ancienneté, venaient repasser devant le théâtre, pour se mettre en file de chaque côté, chantant, les hommes les bras croisés, et les femmes un éventail à la main; tous enfin ne se permettant aucun geste. Les amener à faire ceux qu'exigeait la scène, obtenir d'eux tous, de prendre part à l'action, fut l'objet le plus difficile, mais j'en vins à bout. Les choeurs, qui n'avaient été jusque-là que des automates, ne se regardaient plus que comme des acteurs; les danseurs donnèrent à leurs situations différentes, l'expression que les masques ne leur permettaient pas d'indiquer; et l'effet en fut si prompt, qu'un pas de deux, dansé par mademoiselle Allard et Dauberval, d'après l'impression qu'ils firent, fut gravé." Laujon, *Oeuvres choisis*, 1:176–77.

[18]See Paul-Marie Masson, *L'Opera de Rameau* (Paris: Henri Laurens, 1930; repr. New York: Da Capo, 1972), p. 294. More evidence of mid-eighteenth-century choral action is found in Banducci and in Mary Cyr, "The Dramatic Role of the Chorus in French Opera: Evidence for the Use of Gesture, 1670–1770," in *Opera and the Enlightenment*, ed. Thomas Bauman and Marita P. McClymonds (Cambridge: Cambridge University Press), in press.

[19]"...l'action du moment...& faire tableau par leur accord avec les acteurs, sur-tout dans le choeur du premier acte, *Poursuivons jusqu'au trépas*, &c." *Lavantcoureur*, November 9, 1761, p. 713. The anonymous reviewer thought this was the first time such choral action had ever occurred at the Opéra.

of the chorus, who make one feel the ardor and zeal with which they share the fury of the main characters. Nothing is better imagined, nothing more striking, and nothing makes a greater impression on the public."[20] In contrast, some five years later the same two publications said not a word about choral action in the production of *Silvie*,[21] perhaps because none occurred or none seemed interesting, but perhaps because it was no longer such a novelty. In short, Laujon's memories can be neither confirmed nor denied: there might have been choral action in *Silvie* at his insistence, and he might well have found it difficult to make the singers engage in behavior that was not yet routine, and to which they were little accustomed.[22]

On the other hand, the librettist's claim regarding the dancers' traditional masks, which had covered most of the face, enjoys some external support: Louis Joseph Francoeur, who was a violinist and assistant conductor in the Opéra orchestra in 1766, later wrote, "It was in the opera *Silvie*...that one saw for the first time in this theater a dancer without a mask. Starting at that time, the solo dancers gave them up little by little, followed by the figurants."[23] The press, oddly enough, said nothing about

---

[20]"Un chant vif, serré & précis est accompagné d'actions tumultueuses par tous les Acteurs du Choeur, qui font sentir avec quelle ardeur & quel zèle ils partagent la fureur des principaux Personnages. Rien de mieux imaginé, rien de plus frappant & qui fasse plus d'impression sur le Public..." *Le Mercure de France*, December 1761, pp. 171–72. This reviewer indicates that the technique had been tried before, though without much success.

[21]One sentence in *Lavantcoureur*, December 8, 1766, p. 781, is partially ambiguous: "The musical form [*coupe*] and tempo [*mouvement*] of the chorus of Cyclops are in perfect agreement with the meaning of the words and the action that accompanies them." ("La coupe & le mouvement du choeur des Cyclopes sont parfaitement d'accord avec le sens des paroles & l'action qui les accompagne.") The end of the sentence might refer to choral action but is just as likely to refer to action by dancers; choral pieces in French opera had traditionally been danced.

[22]In an article published in the *Encyclopédie* in 1765, Grimm ridiculed the Opéra chorus for its normal manner of singing, "without action, arms crossed." However, in view of the complex history of the *Encyclopédie*—including a suspension of publication from 1757 to 1765—it is impossible to know when Grimm actually wrote the article. Friedrich Melchior, Baron von Grimm, "Du poème lyrique" (taken from *Encyclopédie raisonné des sciences, des arts et des métiers*, vol. 12), *Correspondance littéraire, philosophique et critique par Grimm, Diderot...*, ed. M. Tourneux, vol. 16 (Paris: Garnier frères, 1882), p. 392. See John Lough, *The Encyclopédie* (London: Longman, 1971), pp. 17–30 and idem, *Essays on the Encyclopédie of Diderot and d'Alembert* (London and New York: Oxford University Press, 1968), pp. 1–9.

[23]"Ce fut dans L'Opera de *Silvie*... qu'on vit pour la premiere fois sur ce théâtre un danseur sans avoir un Masque. Depuis cette Epoque peu à peu Les Danseurs seul [sic] Les quitterent et de suite tous Les figurants." Louis-Joseph Francoeur, "Essai historique sur l'etablissement de l'Opéra en France...." (autograph MS, ca. 1801), F-Po Rés. 591, p. 20.

the suppression of masks in *Silvie*—it must surely have been a startling development—but the reviews of the Paris production did comment favorably on several passages of pantomime in the *divertissements*, including the one in Act 2 to which Laujon would later allude:

> Monsieur Dauberval and Mademoiselle Allard execute, with such perfection, a *pas de deux*, representing the tender eagerness of a hunter for a nymph who is troubled by the attraction that leads her astray—resisting that attraction, fleeing him who is its object, resisting him with great firmness, and finishing in the end by [both] giving in to each other. This interesting dance is presented with such command and by two such superior individuals that it is perpetually applauded....[24]

Even Baron von Grimm, who generally had no sympathy for traditional French opera and dismissed *Silvie* in a few insulting words, wrote complimentary remarks about this particular pantomime *pas de deux*: "That nymph and that shepherd [sic] are two charming and first-rate performers at the Opéra. The hope of seeing them dance allows one to endure up to two scenes of the bellowed psalmody that is called singing in this theater."[25]

Although pantomime ballet had been part of occasional group actions in Lully's operatic *divertissements*, and had been further developed by Cahusac in his librettos for Rameau, it was Noverre in 1760 who made pantomime the centerpiece of a thoroughgoing and ultimately influential plan to reform ballet: he wanted the portrayal of unfolding events and relationships to replace static symmetry, dramatic truth to take precedence over traditional displays of virtuosity, and costumes to become less physically constraining and more natural looking.[26] Thus it is appropriate that Noverre

---

[24]"M. DAUBERVAL et Mlle ALLARD exécutent, avec tant de perfection, un pas de deux, figurant le tendre empressement d'un chasseur pour une nymphe affligée du penchant qui l'entraîne, résistant à ce penchant, fuyant celui qui en est l'objet, lui résistant avec la plus sévère fermeté, & finissant enfin par céder à l'un & à l'autre. Ce pas intéressant est rendu avec tant de conduite & par deux Sujets si supérieurs, qu'il est perpétuellement applaudi..." *Le Mercure de France*, December 1766, p. 182.

[25]"...Cette nymphe et ce berger [sic] sont deux sujets charmants et de la première force du théâtre de l'Opéra. L'espérance de les voir danser fait supporter jusqu'à deux scènes de psalmodie braillée, qu'on appelle chant à ce théâtre." Grimm, *Correspondance littéraire*, 7:458. For other brief remarks on *Silvie*, see 6:397 and 7:200.

[26]Jean-Georges Noverre, *Lettres sur la danse, et sur les ballets* (Stuttgart and Lyons: Delaroche, 1760). See Masson, *L'Opéra de Rameau*, pp. 368–82. It is ironic that Baroque dance—understood in its heyday as the expression of the passions through gesture—had come to seem too abstract.

himself, in 1807, finally placed *Silvie*'s special *pas de deux* in historical perspective:

> Dauberval, my student, a man of excellent taste, declared himself the zealous apostle of my theories, and was in no way a martyr because of it. For the opera *Silvie*, he composed a *pas de deux* filled with action and interest; this isolated excerpt offered the image of a "dialogued" scene, dictated by passion and expressed by all the sentiments that love can inspire. This *pas de deux*, embellished by the talents of the dancer Mademoiselle Allard..., obtained a justly merited success. It was thus Dauberval who first had the courage to battle against received opinion, to vanquish old prejudices, to triumph over the old prescriptions for opera, to break out of the masks, to adopt a more realistic costume, and to present himself in a manner true to nature.[27]

It is ironic that such a famous dance cannot be located with certainty in the score: none of the published remarks includes anything at all about its music. The Act 2 *divertissement* (Act 2, Scene 5) can be divided into three sections: a victory celebration for the nymphs and hunters, who have vanquished the fauns; a celebration by naiads and dryads, who had hidden in fear during the fighting; and, finally, gentle wooing by the hunters and resistance by the nymphs. This last section includes a chorus (presumably danced by the troupe), followed by two dances that bring the *divertissement* to a close: a traditional musette over a drone bass, in duple meter "sans lenteur" ("not slowly"); and an "air gai" (i.e., a dance piece at a "gay" tempo) in gigue rhythm. They are identical in form: rounded binary, followed by a contrasting eight-bar period in minor, and by a return to major for the final eight-bar period. In all likelihood, the famous *pas de deux* was danced to the gentle pastoral musette.

---

[27]"*Dauberval*, mon élève, homme rempli de goût, se declara l'apôtre zèle de ma doctrine et n'en fut point le martyr; il composa pour l'opéra de *Sylvie* un pas de *deux* plein d'action et d'intérêt; ce morceau isolé offrit l'image d'une scene dialoguée, dictée par la passion, et exprimée par tous les sentimens que l'amour peut inspirer. Ce pas de deux embelli par les talens de mademoiselle *Alard* [sic]...obtint le succès le plus justement mérité. Ce fut donc Dauberval qui le premier eut le courage de lutter contre l'opinion reçue; de vaincre les anciens préjugés, de triompher des vielles rubriques de l'opéra, de briser les masques, d'adopter un costume plus vrai, et de se montrer avec les traits intéressans de la nature." J.-G. Noverre, *Lettres sur les arts imitateurs en général, et sur la danse en particulier* (Paris: L. Collin, 1807), 1:146–47.

The engraving mentioned by Laujon, based on a watercolor by Carmontelle, shows a moment when the nymph recoils from the hunter.[28] The hunter's feathered headdress, elaborate animal-skin drapery, and stylized pose do not suggest realism and naturalism by twentieth-century standards. On the other hand, Dauberval wears ordinary pants—knee breeches—rather than the traditional short hoop skirt of the mid-eighteenth-century male dancer. In any case, it was surely the choreography rather than the costumes that gave this episode its powerful effect, especially on audiences who saw dancers' facial expressions for the first time at the Opéra.

* * *

In view of the traditional nature of the libretto, it is not surprising that most of the musical structures in *Silvie* are traditional as well. The simple recitative (see Plate 1) is little different in general structure from that of Lully (though of course there are differences in personal style); this example even includes archaic cadential bass line doubling (see "il seroit le vengeur," mm. 9–10). Only the use of the Italianate time signature $\frac{2}{4}$ gives away the late date of this recitative.[29] The recitative is broken up by little airs in miniature forms (Plate 2), whose largely syllabic text-setting, occasional brief word-painting melismas (not shown in this passage), ornamental melodic surface, and obbligato instrumental parts reflect French operatic practices of the preceding half-century. Instrumental passages reflect longstanding traditions as well; for instance, the "bruit de tonnerre" ("noise of thunder") in Act 3,

---

[28] A reproduction of the engraving accompanies Ingrid Brainard's article in this volume, p. 53. Color reproductions are available for two watercolor versions, both attributed to Carmontelle (though since one is a mirror image of the other, it seems likely that one was based on the engraving): François Lesure, *L'Opéra classique français* (Geneva: Minkoff, 1972), pl. 86 (original in Collection André Meyer); and Marian Hannah Winter, *The Pre-Romantic Ballet* (London: Pitman, 1974), pl. 2 (original in the Boston Museum of Fine Arts). Louis Carrogis, known as Carmontelle, was an author and prolific artist whose paintings often show the importance of music to French high society of his time.

[29] As is always the case in this sort of recitative, bar-line placement is related to verse structure. Trial appears to use ¢ in recitative as a quadruple rather than a duple meter. In this example, he apparently juxtaposes duple and quadruple at a slow tempo in the first system (2 and C, the beat of one roughly equal to the beat of the other), then juxtaposes them again at a slightly faster tempo in the third system ($\frac{2}{4}$ and ¢); a strict proportion between the two tempos is probably not involved. On this topic in general, see Lois Rosow, "The Metrical Notation of Lully's Recitative," in *Jean-Baptiste Lully: Actes du colloque / Kongressbericht: Saint-Germain-en-Laye—Heidelberg 1987*, ed. Herbert Schneider and Jérôme de La Gorce (Laaber: Laaber-Verlag, 1990), pp. 405–22.

painted by string tremolos and runs as well as sudden dynamic shifts, represents a *topos* that originated with the tempest in Marais's *Alcyone* of 1706. As for the *divertissements*, they contain traditional dance types, such as gavottes, rigaudons, and passepieds;[30] an old-fashioned *choeur en rondeau* (Act 2); and two large-scale *ariettes* whose conventional topics (the triumph of love and the singing of birds, Prologue and Act 2 respectively) allow lengthy melismas on conventional words. (See Plate 3: "ramages" means "warbling.") In short, nearly every page of the score makes clear the tenacity of *Silvie*'s venerable heritage.

In general, Trial and Berton chose a more colorful palette of expressive devices than Lagarde had used in 1749. Plate 4 shows an accompanied recitative from the Prologue, in which the god Vulcan describes his activities to Diana before declaring himself powerless to obey her request that he not make new arrows for Cupid. Trial had apparently used Lagarde's more subdued setting (Ex. 1) as a starting point; the similar vocal incipits and key plans are surely not coincidental.[31] At the beginning of Trial's version, the vocal line steadily climbs to the word "Guerre" ("war")—a more compelling reading of the initial decasyllable than Lagarde's—and that word is further emphasized by a military fanfare including double reeds and horns.[32] Soft strings then introduce a secondary dominant as the text focuses on Vulcan's gloomy den. A weak cadence at "Dieux" ushers in a brief thunderstorm: the word "foudre" ("thunderbolt") is painted by an ornate melisma and stormy string figuration. After an elaborate extended cadence, Cupid, the child from Cythera, is mentioned; here the texture is abruptly simplified, and modulation begins anew. There was nothing innovative about these dramatic gestures. Trial simply followed a traditional formula—but one that was traditional precisely because audiences had long found it effective.

---

[30]Within a month of the première, the lengthy chaconne at the end of the opera had been replaced in performances by the celebrated chaconne that Berton had written for the 1762 revival of *Iphigénie en Tauride* by Campra and Desmarets. (*Lavantcoureur*, December 15, 1766, p. 798.) The engraved score of *Silvie* does not reflect this revision, but the parts used by the members of the orchestra (F-Po, Mat.18.[73]) do.

[31]Such passages are exceptional. The Trial and Berton version of *Silvie* does not in general seem dependent on Lagarde's—not a surprising observation in view of the substantial changes Laujon had made throughout the libretto.

[32]As in many other published scores from this period, instrumentation is indicated by shorthand. "Haub" here indicates oboes and bassoons. The ensuing change of dynamic level, coupled with a change of figuration, indicates a return to strings alone.

Example 1. Lagarde's setting of accompanied recitative in Prologue, Scene 2 (transcribed from F-Po, MS 𝄞1176, pp. 28–29)

On the other hand, not all elements of the music in this opera are old-fashioned. In *Silvie,* the most up-to-date musical language—that is, the early classical style—coexists comfortably with conventional formal structures and expressive devices inherited from the past. In its initial review of the Paris production, the *Mercure* included the remark that the music of *Silvie* was composed "in the modern style."[33] It is interesting that the *Mercure* thought this worthy of mention; after all, even though the new style had come to France relatively late in comparison with other countries,[34] it was well established in French concert and operatic music by 1766. Surely the remark in the *Mercure* is a commentary on the total repertory of this particular institution: not only did audiences hear relatively little brand-new music at the Opéra in those days, but the newly composed dance pieces with which Rebel and Francoeur had "modernized" Lully's operas manifested an old-fashioned, essentially Baroque style.[35] It is noteworthy in this context that cosmopolitan (i.e., Italian) notation—exemplified here by such words as "Andante," "rinforzando," and "crescendo" (see Plates 5 and 6) and by the use of treble rather than French violin clef—did not become normal and expected in sources prepared for the Paris Opéra until Berton's influence increased in the mid-1760s.[36] The engraved score of *Silvie* uses both the French *d* (*doux*) and the Italian *p* to indicate a soft dynamic level, apparently interchangeably.

"The modern style" is indeed evident throughout the score. Plate 5 shows the first section of a dance piece in binary form; "modern" features include the scoring (about which further comment will appear below), the homophonic texture with slow harmonic rhythm and harmonization of the melody in parallel thirds, the internal division of the phrase into paired

---

[33]"Dans le goût moderne." *Le Mercure de France,* December 1766, p. 176.

[34]The early classical style took hold in the 1750s, with Antoine Dauvergne's opera *Les troqueurs* (1753), written in direct response to the Querelle des Bouffons; Johann Stamitz's visit to Paris (1754–55); and François-Joseph Gossec's first symphony (1756).

[35]Lois Rosow, "How Eighteenth-Century Parisians Heard Lully's Operas: The Case of *Armide*'s Fourth Act," in *Jean-Baptiste Lully and the Music of the French Baroque: Essays in Honor of James R. Anthony,* ed. John Hajdu Heyer (Cambridge and New York: Cambridge University Press, 1989), pp. 228–32.

[36]Obervation based on study of datable parts in F-Po, Matériel. While Francoeur added old-fashioned pieces to Lully's *Armide* in 1761 (see Rosow, "How Eighteenth-Century Parisians Heard Lully's Operas"), Berton added thoroughly modern ones to that same opera in 1766; see Lois Rosow, "From Destouches to Berton: Editorial Responsibility at the Paris Opéra," *Journal of the American Musicological Society* 40 (1987): 303–304.

symmetrical units, the appoggiatura figures, the augmented sixth of the closing half-cadence, and the repetitive extension of that closing cadence.

A very different side of modernity is illustrated by Plate 6, the beginning of the massive introduction to Act 2. Here the troupe of nymphs scurries down the crags in fright, pursued by the troupe of fauns; the brief C-major horn call (third system) indicates that the hunters are not far behind.[37] The action is painted by busy textures, dramatic dynamic changes and harmonic gestures, sudden shifts of tempo and meter, and rapid movement through different key areas. Near the end of the first system, the root C of a dominant chord in F minor is displaced in both directions by B♭ and D♭, against a sustained E♮ in the treble. Both the placement in the bass of what would have been the seventh of the dominant chord and the irregular voice-leading of the resolution in the next measure indicate that the phrase has not ended; the dominant is reiterated at the beginning of the second system, and a sweeping chromatic scale rushes upward to a firm resolution in root position.[38] After a brief tonic pedal (enlivened by the diminished seventh chord) and a sudden shift of key and meter for the hunting horn call, the piece appears to return to F minor by way of the same C–B♭–A♭ bass motion heard earlier—compare the end of the first system with the beginning of the fourth system—but this time the expected resolution of the E♮ is replaced by a surprising chromatic move to an A♭ triad. The ensuing oblique augmented sixth progression (including interplay between A♭ in the bass and A♮ in the bassoon) points out the key of C, but resolution is again thwarted by a chromatic surprise. The piece continues in this vein, but with still other textural, metrical, and harmonic surprises, for an additional forty-one measures.

The new style, of course, involved new ways of using the orchestra. In his combined roles of composer, arranger, and conductor, Berton was particularly sensitive to these developments, and he evidently took advantage of his new position as co-director of the Académie to do something in response to them. In May 1767, *Lavantcoureur* published a brief commentary

---

[37]Context enhances the dramatic effect. Act 1 ends with an ominously threatening chorus of fauns. During the brief entr'acte—a lively *chasse* in F major—stage machinery would have changed the scenery instantaneously to the spectacular crags and distant waterfall of Act 2. Finally, the entr'acte is interrupted in mid-phrase by the passage shown in Plate 6.

[38]This device—a weak cadence followed by a dramatic sweep to a firm cadence—foreshadows similar gestures by Beethoven (e.g., the piano sonata, Op. 2, No. 1, first movement, mm. 33–41).

on the ongoing production of *Silvie*. A discussion of changes that had been introduced since the November première included the following:

> We have also noticed the increase that has been made in the number of musicians, both in the chorus and in the orchestra. The effect is most perceptible. This is an increase in expense that proves the zeal of the new directors of the Opéra.... The increase in the orchestra consists of fifteen musicians in different instrumental categories, and all well chosen. Included among them is the celebrated Monsieur Rodolphe, who draws such lovely and varied sounds from the hunting horn. The orchestra is now turned as in Italy; that is, half of the musicians are face-to-face with the other half, and all present their profiles to the public instead of turning their backs to the audience as before. This arrangement is more favorable than the old one, both for its visual appearance and for the effect of the instruments, two considerations that must not be neglected in an entertainment like the opera.[39]

Prior to this time, the conductor had stood at the edge of the stage, just beneath it, and faced the singers; the members of the orchestra, in order to watch the conductor, did indeed sit with their backs to the audience.[40] The new seating plan does not, however, appear to conform to Italian practice as the commentary states.[41] As for the increased size of the orchestra, documents survive that permit comparison of the Opéra orchestra in March

---

[39] "On s'est aussi très-bien apperçu de l'augmentation qui a été faite dans le nombre des Musiciens tant des Choeurs que de l'Orchestre. L'effet en est des plus sensibles. C'est un accroissement de dépense qui prouve le zèle des nouveaux Directeurs de l'Opéra.... L'augmentation de l'Orchestre est de quinze Musiciens dans différens genres, & tous bien choisis. On compte parmi eux le célèbre M. Rodolphe, qui tire du Cor-de-Chasse des sons si agréables & si variés. L'Orchestre est actuellement tourné comme en Italie; c'est-à dire, qu'une moitié des Musiciens regarde l'autre en face, & que tous présentent le côté au Public, au lieu de lui tourner le dos comme auparavant. Cette position est plus favorable que l'ancienne, & pour le coup d'oeil, & pour l'effet des Instrumens: deux motifs qui ne sont point à négliger dans un spectacle tel que l'Opéra." *Lavantcoureur*, May 25, 1767, pp. 331–32.

[40] This arrangement is clearly visible in a drawing showing the production of Rameau's *La princesse de Navarre* at the royal court at Versailles in 1745; presumably the orchestral seating plan at Versailles reflected the one in Paris. The same old-fashioned arrangement appears in a diagram of the Versailles opera orchestra in 1773. Lesure, *L'Opéra classique français*, pls. 5 and 9.

[41] See Neal Zaslaw, *Mozart's Symphonies: Context, Performance Practice, Reception* (Oxford: Oxford University Press, 1989), pls. 7, 8, 15 and idem, "Toward the Revival of the Classical Orchestra," *Proceedings of the Royal Musical Association* 103 (1976–77): 160–63.

Table 1.

Membership of the Paris Opéra Orchestra[42]

1766–67	1769
5 *hautbois et flûtes*	6 *hautbois et flûtes*
—	2 *clarinettes*
(*musette*: see *parties* below)	1 *musette*
5 *bassons*	6 *bassons*
1 *trompette*	2 *trompettes*
(*cor-de-chasse*: see *parties* below)	4 *cors-de-chasse*
(*timballe*: see *dessus de violon* below)	1 *timballe*
—	1 *tambourin*
16 *dessus de violon*, 1 doubling on *timballe*	24 *violons*; 4 *violons surnuméraires*
6 *parties* (i.e., violas), 1 doubling on *musette* and 2 doubling on *cor-de-chasse*	4 *altos* (violas)
8 *basses du grand choeur* (cellos)	12 *violoncelles*
4 *basses du petit choeur* (3 continuo cellos and 1 *contrebasse*)	4 *contrebasses*
1 *clavecin*	2 *clavecinistes*

1767—just before Berton and Trial assumed the directorship—with that established by royal decree in June 1769 (see Table 1). (It should be kept in mind that these lists enumerate people, not instruments; thus, for instance, there were two salaried harpsichordists in 1769, but there was never more than one harpsichord in the orchestra.) The orchestra not only grew enormously and came to include instruments that had been played only by supernumeraries before, but the balance of strings to woodwinds shifted

---

[42]"Reglement pour servir au paîment des appointements et gratiffications annuelles...du 1er avril 1766 au d^{er} mars 1767," F-Po, Archives; "Suivant les Lettres Patentes du Roi, en faveur de l'Académie royale de musique...juin 1769..." Paris, Archives nationales, O^{1}623, no. 1.

dramatically in favor of strings. Berton thus eliminated the last vestige of Lully's orchestra. The increased importance of the French horn—an instrument that Rameau had cultivated and that had become an indispensable element of the classical orchestra—is obvious as well.

Around the time of his death, Berton was best remembered for two of his activities at the Opéra: the skill with which he had modernized works by earlier masters, and the transformation of the Opéra orchestra into one of the best in Europe.[43] It is clear from the information presented here that a reorganization of the orchestra began at almost the moment he and Trial took over the direction of the institution, and that it continued at a brisk pace. *Silvie*, though it makes no use of clarinet or trumpet, obviously profited from this development and perhaps even served as a laboratory for it.

Not surprisingly, *Silvie*'s orchestration reflects the trends in French concert and operatic music of the 1750s and '60s.[44] The double reeds sometimes perform their old-fashioned role of reinforcing the strings on treble and bass lines (and traditional florid flute parts decorate many lightly scored passages); on the other hand, *divisi* oboes often form a textural group with *divisi* horns, providing sustained harmonic support rather than melody, and *divisi* bassoons often play in the tenor range, also helping to fill out the harmony. The full tuttis frequently include six or seven voices. As for the strings, old-fashioned *divisi* writing for violas occurs occasionally—a vestige of much earlier French practice, in which there had been three viola parts—but Berton and Trial preferred the modern string scoring shown in Plate 5.

One of the most modern aspects of *Silvie*'s scoring, a high degree of textural flexibility, is evident even where orchestration is light and includes traditional doublings. In Plate 7, a duet for first violins (doubled by oboes) and violas is succeeded by a trio for two violin parts and violas, then by a duet for violins in unison and cellos with violas at the octave, and finally by

---

[43] Laborde, 3:389; Beffara, "Dictionnaire," s.v. "Berton," cahier 8, f. 23^v.

[44] Regarding the development of Rameau's orchestration in his later operas, see Graham Sadler, "Rameau and the Orchestra," *Proceedings of the Royal Musical Association* 108 (1981–82): 47–68. Sadler points out that orchestration was often silently modernized by the editors of the *Oeuvres complètes* of Rameau (Paris, 1895–1924); for instance, the classical-style sustained winds shown in the early operas are spurious. On this subject, see also Graham Sadler, "Vincent d'Indy and the Rameau *Oeuvres complètes*: A Case of Forgery?" *Early Music* 21 (1993): 415–21. Regarding organization and membership in the Opéra orchestra from 1704 to 1764, see Jérôme de La Gorce, "L'orchestre de l'Opéra et son évolution de Campra à Rameau," *Revue de musicologie* 76 (1990): 23–43.

a trio for violins in unison, violas, and cellos—all in the space of a four-measure phrase. Opéra audiences were long accustomed to hearing the simple alternation of contrasting instrumental textures and timbres; they were much less accustomed to subtle textural shifts of this sort.[45] Textural flexibility is used on a grander scale in such pieces as the chorus of fauns at the end of Act 1, praised by the reviewers for its effective music; there a kaleidoscope of shifting textures—including idiomatic string figuration—is presented by an ensemble made up of three-part male chorus (*hautes-contre*, tenors, basses), four-part strings, and brilliant *divisi* piccolos ("petites flûtes").

* * *

In October 1765, *Silvie*'s première at Fontainebleau was reported in the press. After summarizing the plot and naming the performers, *Lavantcoureur* continued as follows:

> As we have seen, this opera has as much stage machinery and pomp as the subject can hold. Its style is very lyrical and offers much to the musicians [i.e., to the composers]; both have in fact turned it to the best account. This opera is in an almost new style, and might give rise to very favorable innovations in our musical theater.[46]

Unfortunately, no clarification is offered for the enigmatic final sentence. The libretto for *Silvie* is manifestly not in "un genre presque neuf." Still, it did give rise to one true innovation—the appearance of dancers without masks—and to considerable ingenuity in scenery, machinery, and choreography. As for the music, the classical style was indeed "almost new" to France in 1765, and the composers used it effectively. The principal innovation it inspired, an expansion and reorganization of the orchestra, would surely have happened in any case when control of the Académie's budget passed from Rebel and Francoeur to Berton and Trial; still, the fact that the new directors themselves had composed an opera that was then on the boards probably led it to happen especially quickly.

---

[45]Compare with Rameau's "counterpoint of timbres" (Masson's term); see Sadler, "Rameau and the Orchestra," pp. 65–68.

[46]"Il y a, comme on le voit, dans cet Opéra autant de machines & d'appareil que le sujet en pouvoit comporter. Le style en est très lyrique, & fournit beaucoup aux Musiciens. L'un & l'autre en ont effectivement tiré le plus grand parti. Cet Opéra est dans un genre presque neuf, & peut occasionner sur notre scène lyrique des innovations très-avantageuses." *Lavantcoureur*, October 28, 1765, p. 679.

Yet perhaps the most important message of *Silvie*'s success has less to do with innovation than tradition. There was apparently still a strong market in Paris for good new operas that adhered to the old-fashioned conventions of genre. By injecting the right degree of modernity and innovation into an otherwise conservative piece, and by handling both traditional conventions and new devices skillfully, Laujon, Trial, and Berton wrote an opera that inspired artistic creativity in those involved in its production and, moreover, drew a large and enthusiastic audience; *Silvie* held its own in the face of competition from the *opéra-comique*. On the other hand, new works capable of such success were in very short supply at the Paris Opéra in the 1760s. While contemporaneous writings make clear that *opéra-comique* was perceived to be popular and traditional opera unpopular,[47] the crisis for the Opéra probably had less to do with a fickle audience than with the scarcity of good composers and poets willing to provide new pieces for an institution thought to be in decline. Presumably the same public that appreciated *Silvie* would have flocked to the Opéra routinely to hear new works, had such works been available in larger numbers.

---

[47]For instance, Bricaire de la Dixmerie, *Lettres* (cited in n. 12), pp. 67–69 and Nougaret, *De l'art du théâtre en général* (cited in n. 1), passim, especially 2:243–44. Bricaire's essay includes an extended prescription for saving traditional opera by retaining some features (e.g., choruses) while avoiding others (e.g., lengthy recitatives); *Silvie* is entirely compatible with his recommendations. Nougaret's prescriptions include reusing old librettos and creating a "spectacle lyrique complet" by placing *opéra-comique* and "grand-Opéra" in the same theater.

French Opera in Transition 355

Plates

Plate 1. Simple recitative (headed "Un chasseur aux Faunes enchaînés") in Act 2, Scene 5; engraved score published by La Chevardière in 1767 (F-Po, A.212, p. 190)

Plate 2. Air in Act 1, Scene 2 (F-Po, A.212, p. 86)

French Opera in Transition 357

Plate 3. Excerpt from *ariette* in Act 2, Scene 5 (F-Po, A.212, p. 199)

Plate 4. Accompanied recitative in Prologue, Scene 3 (F-Po, A.212, pp. 59–60): "I arm Bellone and the god of war; it is in this gloomy den that I prepare thunder for the king of the gods, with which he knows how to terrify the world."

French Opera in Transition 359

Plate 4 (*continued*)

Plate 5. Excerpt from dance in Act 2, Scene 5 (F-Po, A.212, pp. 205–206)

French Opera in Transition   361

Plate 6. Beginning of introduction to Act 2, Scene 1 (F-Po, A.212, pp. 140–41)

Plate 6 (*continued*)

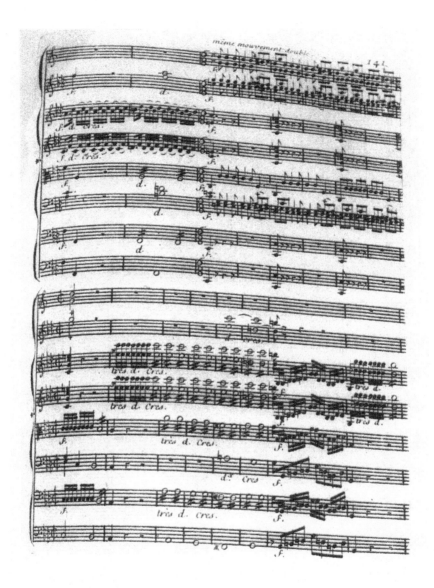

Plate 7. Beginning of dance in Prologue, Scene 2 (F-Po, A.212, p. 54)

Kindling the Compositional Fire: Haydn's Keyboard *Phantasiren*[*]

Hollace A. Schafer

A portrait of Joseph Haydn by Ludwig Guttenbrunn[1] shows the composer deep in thought, working at the keyboard (Plate 1). His eyes are focused in the distance, a quill poised for writing in his right hand, his left hand resting on the keyboard. Before him on the music stand is an open manuscript ruled with staves and containing some musical notation. On the instrument rests an ink well atop additional manuscript paper. The pose is by no means common in the contemporary portraits of the composer.[2] In his surviving letters and personal papers, Haydn never mentions using the keyboard to create his musical works. Haydn's pose in the portrait could of course be an iconic representation, meant to inform the viewer of the subject's profession, and not to portray a scene from Haydn's life. However, abundant contemporary evidence of Haydn's composing at the keyboard comes from his biographers, Georg August Griesinger and Albert Christoph Dies.[3]

---

[*] An earlier version of this paper was read in Spring, 1990, at "Haydn's Piano Sonatas: A Conference and Festival of Recitals," at Smith College. I would like to thank Dr. Merle C. Krueger of the Ãenter for Language Studies at Brown University for his advice in translating the German texts. My interest in Haydn sketches owes much to a seminar at Brandeis University with Paul Brainard, to whom I am grateful.

[1] The version of the portrait reproduced here is in the Haydn-Museum in Eisenstadt, Austria; a more finished version belongs to Mrs. Eva Alberman, London,.

[2] See reproductions of the authenticated representations of Haydn in László Somfai, *Joseph Haydn: Élete Képekben és Dokumentumokban* [Joseph Haydn: His Life in Pictures and Documents] (Budapest: Zenemukiadó, 1977), pp. 213–17.

[3] Georg August Griesinger, *Biographische Notizen über Joseph Haydn* (Leipzig: Breitkopf & Härtel, 1810); Albert Christoph Dies, *Biographische Nachrichten von Joseph Haydn* (Vienna: Camesinaische Buchhandlung, 1810; repr., ed. Horst Seeger, Berlin: Henschelverlag, 1959). All page numbers for Dies's biography refer to the reprint.

Griesinger observed Haydn with papers and music on his keyboard instrument, just as portrayed by Guttenbrunn:

> Haydn set great store by order and regularity in everything he did and in everything that surrounded him. His rooms were always neat and clean, every implement stood in its place, and not even on the fortepiano did the papers and music lie mixed up together. ("Haydn hielt in allem, was er that und was ihn umgab, viel auf Ordnung und Regelmäßigkeit. Seine Zimmer waren immer reinlich und sauber, jedes Geräthe stand an seiner Stelle, und sogar auf dem Fortepiano lagen die Papiere und Noten nicht verworren unter einander" [Griesinger, p. 109].)

366 Hollace A. Schafer

Plate 1. Portrait of Franz Joseph Haydn by Ludwig Guttenbrunn, Haydn-Museum, Eisenstadt

In this paper, I shall investigate Haydn's use of the keyboard while composing, basing the study on the biographers' accounts of the composer's own words, as well as on the biographers' observations of the composer. Published in the year following Haydn's death in 1809, these descriptions remain fresh, exciting, and vivid, bringing the viewpoint of eyewitnesses to our understanding of Haydn and his compositional techniques.

As the agent of Breitkopf & Härtel in Vienna, Griesinger visited Haydn often during the last ten years of the composer's life. In addition to his business relationship, he made copious notes for a biography of the composer, a biography in which he wrote:

> ...I regarded it as my duty frequently to insert Haydn's own words just the way I wrote them down on returning home from [visiting] him.[4]

Dies, who was a landscape painter, began visiting Haydn in 1805 for the purpose of writing the composer's biography. In addition to noting the events of Haydn's life, Dies included information about Haydn's current health. Like Griesinger, Dies quoted conversations with the composer.

However, as Gotwals notes,[5] Griesinger and Dies have important limitations as witnesses. They apparently did not take notes during their visits, but waited until afterward to record what had happened. Thus we do not know how accurately they recalled the events and conversations. It seems that the composer never edited their work; indeed, when Dies asked Haydn to review his notes for accuracy, the composer responded by suggesting that Dies check his notes with Griesinger's.[6] This he did. Dies and Griesinger had the means, motive, and opportunity to exchange stories and borrow from one another. So, even if they did visit Haydn independently, they cannot be regarded as independent witnesses. In a great many of the stories can be found echoes of the other's words. Nevertheless, the verisimilitude of their anecdotes is supported by other independent documents.

An additional limitation to their testimony is that both biographers concentrated more on the man, his career, and his social milieu, than on a description of his creative activities.[7] This focus is understandable (if also frustrating): Griesinger began his visits just prior to Haydn's retirement; Dies's visits began well into that retirement. However, enough can be glimpsed to gain a sense of Haydn's creative methods, especially since we

---

[4]"...ich hielt es für Pflicht, öfters Haydns eigene Worte, so wie ich sie nach der Rückkehr von ihm zu Hause niederschrieb, einzuschalten" (Griesinger, p. 6).

[5]Vernon Gotwals, "The Earliest Biographies of Haydn," *Musical Quarterly* 45 (1959): 439–59.

[6]Dies, pp. 109–10.

[7]In his forward (p. 13), Dies confesses that he will speak little about Haydn as composer: "I have allowed myself to say little about his musical genius. To properly judge this, to follow it in flight, to accompany it everywhere—this would demand knowledge that might often surpass my powers." ("Über sein musikalisches G e n i e habe ich mir wenig zu sagen erlaubt. Dieses richtig zu beurteilen, ihm im Fluge zu folgen, es überall zu begleiten: dazu werden Kenntnisse erfordert, die oft meine Kräfte übersteigen dürften.")

can corroborate the descriptions by comparing them to the surviving compositional documents.

* * *

Griesinger states categorically: "Haydn always devised [dichtete] his works at the keyboard." The verb Griesinger uses, *dichten*, resists translation. The word frequently used for "crafting" poetry, *dichten*'s musical applications are not very clear, so many questions remain. In what manner did Haydn use the keyboard? When did he use it: from the time he started work to the time he finished preparing a score, or just for specific parts of that compositional continuum? What was the end result of his keyboard work? None of this is revealed by Griesinger's provocative sentence, nor by its context in the full paragraph, which reads:

> Haydn always devised his works at the keyboard. "I sat down, began to improvise depending on whether my mood was sad or happy, serious or playful. When I got hold of an idea, my entire effort went toward carrying it out and sustaining it according to the rules of art. That is how I sought to help myself, and that is what so many of our young composers lack; they string one bit next to another, they break off when they have scarcely begun: but nothing stays in the heart after you have listened to it."[8]

This paragraph will serve as a point of departure. By explicating it one sentence at a time, referring to supporting descriptions elsewhere in the biographies by both Griesinger and Dies, and by observing the composer's procedures in his autograph manuscripts, I hope to demonstrate the nature of Haydn's work at the keyboard.

"Haydn always devised his works at the keyboard."

Griesinger's first sentence indicates that Haydn did not limit himself to working at the keyboard only while devising keyboard pieces. The sentence implies that he worked this way in all genres of composition.

---

[8]"Haydn dichtete seine Werke immer vor dem Klavier. 'Ich setzte mich hin, fing an zu phantasiren, je nachdem mein Gemüth traurig oder fröhlich, ernst oder tändelnd gestimmt war. Hatte ich eine Idee erhascht, so ging mein ganzes Bestreben dahin, sie den Regeln der Kunst gemäß auszuführen und zu soutreniren. So suchte ich mir zu helfen, und das ist es, was so vielen unserer neuen Komponisten fehlt; sie reihen ein Stückchen an das andere, sie brechen ab, wenn sie kaum angefangen haben: aber es bleibt auch nichts im Herzen sitzen, wenn man es angehört hat'" (Griesinger, p. 114).

"I sat down, began to improvise [phantasiren] depending on whether my mood was sad or happy, serious or playful."

Griesinger's second sentence names the composer's work at the keyboard; he calls it *Phantasiren*, roughly translated as "improvise." Apparently, it was with *Phantasiren* at the keyboard that Haydn began his creative work. Dies corroborates this, using the same word, and tells us the usual time of day for Haydn's *Phantasiren*:

> At eight o'clock, Haydn had breakfast. Then he sat down at the keyboard and improvised until he found ideas serving his purpose, which he immediately put on paper. That is how the first sketches for his compositions came into being.[9]

Phantasiren is mentioned in anecdotes concerning Haydn at widely varying stages of his career. Griesinger relates an amusing story from about forty years previously of Haydn using the keyboard at the beginning of his compositional process. The circumstances make it exceptional, but nevertheless the outline is familiar:

> Around 1770, Haydn had fallen into a high fever, and the doctor had strictly forbidden him to occupy himself with music during his gradual recovery. Shortly afterwards, Haydn's wife went to church, having first impressed upon the maid to see that her master should not go to the keyboard. Haydn, in his bed, pretended that he had heard nothing of this order, and scarcely had his wife left when he sent the maid out of the house on an errand. Then he quickly leapt over to his keyboard; with the first chord, the idea for an entire sonata stood before his soul, and the first part was completed while his wife was at church. When he heard her come back, he quickly threw himself back into bed where he composed the rest of the sonata—Haydn could no longer identify it for me precisely except that it had five sharps.[10]

---

[9]"Um acht Uhr nahm Haydn sein Frühmahl. Gleich nachher setzte er sich an das Klavier und phantasierte so lange, bis er zu seiner Absicht dienende Gedanken fand, die er sogleich zu Papier brachte. So entstanden die ersten Skizzen von seinen Kompositionen" (Dies, pp. 209–10).

[10]"Um das Jahr 1770 war Haydn in ein hitziges Fieber verfallen, und der Arzt hatte ihm während seiner allmäligen Genesung aufs strengste verboten, sich mit Musik zu beschäftigen. Bald darauf ging Haydns Gattin in die Kirche, nachdem sie vorher der Magd ernstlich eingeschärft hatte, ihren Herrn zu bewachen, daß er nicht ans Klavier komme. Haydn that in seinem Bette, als ob er nichts von diesem Befehle gehört hätte, und kaum war seine Gattin fort, als er die Magd mit einem Auftrage aus dem Hause schickte. Nun schwang er sich eilends an sein Klavier; mit dem ersten Griffe stand die Idee einer

Whether Haydn always began composing with *Phantasiren* is impossible to say, but these accounts imply that such activity was customary.[11] The following story strengthens this impression. Here Dies reports on Haydn's morning work at the keyboard:

> Haydn was at that time in Vienna where he spent his study hours each morning behind closed doors. The servant meanwhile guarded the antechamber, tiptoeing over to all who came, indicating by gestures that no noise should be made, and then saying very softly: "Sh! Sh! the master is studying."
>
> Three strangers who wanted to make Haydn's acquaintance were received in this manner by the servant and had to consent to wait until the end of the study period. Indeed they made many protestations and opined that surely an occasional exception to the rule could be made. But the servant could not be persuaded, [he] placed his ear against the closed door several times with a meaningful air, and put off the strangers from one quarter hour to the next. Finally he said with a sort of certainty: "It will surely be soon; the master is already working in the rough." The servant had commented that Haydn at the conclusion of his improvisations liked to hurry to get to the bass and end there.[12]

---

ganzen Sonate vor seiner Seele, und der erste Theil wurde beendigt, während seine Frau in der Kirche war. Als er sie zurückkommen hörte, warf er sich geschwind wieder ins Bett, und hier komponirte er den Rest der Sonate, die mir Haydn nicht mehr genauer zu bezeichnen wußte, als daß sie fünf-Kreutze habe" (Griesinger, pp. 27–28). The piece in question could be the lost sonata Hoboken XVI:2c.

[11]No anecdote describes Haydn returning to the keyboard once he had finished with *Phantasiren*.

[12]"Haydn war eben in Wien, wo er wie gewöhnlich an jedem Morgen bei verschlossener Tür seine Studierstunden hielt. Der Bediente hütete indessen das Vorzimmer, ging jedem Kommenden auf den Zehen entgegen, bedeutete durch Gebärden, daß man keinen Lärm machen möchte, und sagte dann ganz leise: 'St! St! der Herr studieret.'

Drei Fremde, die Haydns Bekanntschaft zu machen wünschten, wurden von dem Bedienten auf obige Art empfangen und mußten sich gefallenlassen, das Ende der Studierstunden abzuwarten. Sie machten zwar mehrere Vorstellungen und meinten, es könne doch zuweilen eine Ausnahme in der Regel gemacht werden. Aber der Bediente ließ sich nicht überreden, legte mehrmals mit bedeutender Miene das Ohr an die verschlossene Türe und vertröstete die Fremden von einer Viertelstunde zu der andern. Endlich sagte er mit einer Art von Gewißheit: 'Es wird bald gar sein; der Herr arbeitet schon im Groben.' Der Bediente hatte die Bemerkung gemacht, daß Haydn am Schlusse seiner Phantasien gerne dem Basse zueilte und darin endigte" (Dies, p. 68).

Griesinger tells the same story, which helps to clarify what the servant meant by "working in the rough":

> [Haydn] once had an urgent composition to write, and thus ordered his servant to admit nobody. Shortly thereafter, as chance would have it, some strangers appeared; the servant informed them of his master's order, but they explained that they had travelled to Hungary expressly to meet Haydn, and that it would make them very sorry not to have attained their purpose. The servant bade them sit down in the antechamber, and stood listening at the door of the room where Haydn was improvising at the keyboard. When in the course of his ideas, [Haydn] began thundering loudly in the bass, the servant called out at once to the strangers: Now, you will be able to see my master soon "because he is already working in the rough."[13]

From these stories we learn also that the composer did this sort of work behind closed doors. Thus translating "phantasiren" as "improvise" may be slightly misleading if "improvise" is taken to mean "perform extemporaneously." Haydn explicitly avoided performance conditions during *Phantasiren*. I use "improvise" here only because the other logical choice, "fantasize," carries too many non-musical connotations.

Describing their visits to the retired composer in his twilight years, both biographers took for granted Haydn's practice of generating ideas at the keyboard. In sobering contrast to the previous story, Griesinger writes:

> In the summer of 1806 the little keyboard was also removed from Haydn's living room because the doctor forbade him all exertion, and wanted thus to remove every temptation from him. Haydn himself felt how necessary it was for the maintainance of his health to follow this advice, for when he sat down from time to time to improvise at his English fortepiano, dizziness overtook him after just a few minutes. "Never would I have believed," said Haydn on the third of September, 1807, "that anyone could deteriorate as much as I feel myself now doing. My memory is gone, I still occasionally have good ideas at the keyboard, but I could just cry because I am not even capable of repeating them and writing them down."[14]

---

[13] "[Haydn] hatte einst eine dringende Komposition zu verfertigen, und befahl daher seinem Bedienten, Niemanden vorzulassen; kurz darauf führte der Zufall einige Fremde herbey, der Bediente machte ihnen den Befehl seines Herrn kund, sie erklärten aber, daß sie, nur um Haydn kennen zu lernen, nach Ungarn gereist wären, und daß es ihnen sehr leid thun würde, diesen Zweck nicht erreicht zu haben. Der Bediente hieß sie im Vorzimmer niedersitzen, und stellte sich horchend an die Thüre des Zimmers, wo Haydn am Klavier phantasirte. Als er im Laufe seiner Ideen stark im Basse rauschte, rief der Bediente auf einmal den Fremden zu: nun werden Sie meinen Herrn bald sehen können, 'denn er arbeitet schon im Groben'" (Griesinger, pp. 26–27).

[14] "Im Sommer 1806 wurde auch das kleine Klavier aus Haydns Wohnzimmer entfernt, weil ihm der Arzt alle Anstrengung untersagte, und ihm jede Versuchung dazu beneh-

> *"When I got hold of an idea, my entire effort went toward carrying it out and sustaining it according to the rules of art."*

How would Haydn "carry out and sustain" an idea? What was the content of his *Phantasiren*? The story of Haydn's illness in 1770 addresses these questions, as does the anecdote concerning the visit of the strangers. When Haydn leapt to the keyboard in 1770, he found in the first chord an idea for the entire sonata. And Haydn's servant reported to the strangers that his master ended his work behind closed doors only after he was able to play a roughed out version of the piece. These are intriguing stories, but what was the actual substance of the music that Haydn played in *Phantasiren*? What was meant by "the idea for an entire sonata"? Does anything survive of Haydn's work behind closed doors?

When Dies wrote of Haydn's disciplined search for ideas in *Phantasiren*, he claimed that Haydn wrote his first sketches for a piece immediately following his work at the keyboard (see page 369, n. 10, above). Thus, if these first sketches could be identified, we could study the content of *Phantasiren*.

Many obstacles stand in the way of finding these sketches. The end product of *Phantasiren* involved committing ideas to paper, but as Haydn continued his written work, expanding and altering his original ideas, the page filled with additional sketches. Distinguishing the initial layer from the layers that were written later is usually possible, though only after lengthy deliberation about overlapping and replacement versions. Luckily a group of sketches in the Austrian National Library obviates these deliberations. These sketches, for the Finale of Symphony 99,[15] contain a readily perceptible first layer, distinguished by a unique shade of ink.[16]

---

men wollte. Haydn fühlte selbst, wie nötig es zur Erhaltung seiner Gesundheit sey, diesen Rath zu befolgen, denn wenn er sich von Zeit zu Zeit an sein englisches Fortepiano setzte, um zu phantasiren, so überfielen ihn Schwindel nach wenigen Minuten. 'Nie hätte ich geglaubt,' sagte er am 3ten Sept. 1807, 'daß ein Mensch so sehr zusammensinken könnte, als ich es jetzt an mir fühle; mein Gedächtniß ist dahin, ich habe an dem Klavier zuweilen noch gute Ideen, aber ich möchte weinen, daß ich nicht im Stande bin, sie nur zu wiederholen und aufzuschreiben'" (Griesinger, p. 87).

[15]Vienna, Österreichische Nationalbibliothek, Musiksammlung Cod. 16835, ff. 24ᵛ and 25.

[16]Leopold Nowak notes this unique ink color and considers it the earliest stage of writing as well: "Die Skizzen zum Finale der Es-dur Symphonie GA 99 von Joseph Haydn," *Haydn-Studien* 2 (1970): 137–67.

When beginning to write the Finale, Haydn entered three sketches on two facing pages (see Figure 1):

1. The first theme (f. 24^v, staves 1/2–3/4, beginning at the top left; see Ex. 1)

2. An outline for the harmonic progression of the second theme (f. 24^v, middle of staves 10/11)

3. A version of the second theme (f. 25, staves 1/2, beginning at the top left; see Ex. 2)—this original version of the second theme was subsequently changed almost beyond recognition.

Figure 1: Three early sketches for Symphony No. 99, 4th Movement

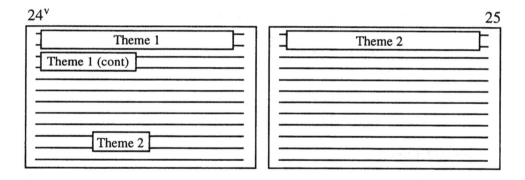

In other words, Haydn initially laid out his ideas for the main melodic, harmonic, and structural events of the first half of the movement. In between them, he left empty staves to accommodate the passages that would subsequently join one event to the next. This procedure was followed in most of Haydn's surviving sketches,[17] and is remarked on by Griesinger:

> Haydn always constructed his compositions as an entity; in each part, he completely laid out the plan for the principal voice, marking the prominent places with only a few notes or numbers; afterwards, he breathed spirit

---

[17]László Somfai noted this procedure first, in his article on the String Quartet, Op. 20, No. 3/3: "'Ich war nie ein Geschwindschreiber...' Joseph Haydns Skizzen zum langsamen Satz des Streichquartetts Hoboken III:33," in *Festskrift Jens Peter Larsen* (Copenhagen: Hansen, 1972).

and life into the dry skeleton with the accompaniment of counter melodies, and dexterous transitions."[18]

This sketch also allows the opportunity to investigate what Haydn meant by "carrying out and sustaining an idea." At first glance, the melodic and harmonic materials of the first theme and the earliest version of the second theme seem to have little in common. However, the similarities become apparent when we analyze the entries.

First Theme

The phrasing of the opening binary theme is illuminated in the sketch by the accompanimental motive—a scalar run in thirds that is three eighth notes in length (Ex. 1). This accompanimental motive appears four times—every four measures (mm. 1, 5, 9, 13)—until the texture is simplified and the motive is extended and displaced by an eighth rest (mm. 17–18). Two characteristics are noteworthy:

a. In the first half of the theme, the accompanimental motive descends.

b. In the second half (m. 9), the motive ascends, but when the tonic returns (m. 13), so does the original contour of the motive.

Second Theme

In the earliest version of the second theme (Ex. 2), Haydn again used the scalar motion harmonized in thirds:

a. When the first phrase moves away from its initial sonority (mm. 2–4), it descends with half notes in thirds (F–E♭–D), echoing the accompanimental motive from the opening of the movement.

---

[18]"Haydn verfertigte seine Kompositionen immer in Einem Guß; er legte bey jedem Theil den Plan zur Hauptstimme ganz an, indem er die hervorstechenden Stellen mit wenigen Noten oder Ziffern bezeichnete; nachher hauchte er dem trockenen Skelett durch Begleitung der Nebenstimmen und geschickte Uebergänge Geist und Leben ein" (Griesinger, p. 116).

Kindling the Compositional Fire 375

Example 1. Sketch for first theme, f. 24^v, staves 1/2–3/4

Example 2. Sketch for second theme, f. 25, staves 1/2: original layer

b. When the second phrase moves away from its initial sonority (mm. 9ff), it makes a decorated scalar ascent in thirds (F–G♭–A♭).[19] The contour inversion of these two phrases recalls Haydn's contour inversion of the accompanimental motive in the first and second parts of the opening theme.

There are other examples of Haydn creating such connections within this movement. In the original version of the first theme, the surprise G♭ (Ex. 1, m. 3), a passing chromaticism, reappears in the vii°7 chord that tonicizes the dominant (Ex. 3a), and prepares the cadence on V at the first double bar. In the original version of the second theme, the G♭ and its enharmonic equivalent, F♯, appear again, this time substantially prolonged. They accompany the openings of the two phrases (Ex. 2, mm. 3, 11; Exx. 3b, 3c), and each is a part of a tonicizing seventh chord. To use a mechanistic metaphor, the G♭/F♯ "triggers" tonicization in both themes.

Example 3. Uses of G♭ (F♯) in first-movement sketch

Haydn created another connection, using the repercussive eighth notes in the opening measure of the first theme (see Ex. 1). They are echoed in the last measure of the first half (m. 8), and metrically shifted in the measure leading to the return of the tonic in the second half (m. 12). In the original version of the second theme (Ex. 2), these eighth notes are extended and used in imitation in the first phrase, and gradually proliferate through the texture in the second phrase. Thus, in these sketches, we see Haydn using a limited set of ideas to help denote phrase structure, to strengthen the sense of temporal progression, and to establish connections between seemingly contrasting melodies—"carrying out and sustaining" his ideas.

Interestingly enough, most of these original connections were dropped in Haydn's subsequent work on the movement. Only the repeated notes in the second theme were preserved in the final version. Haydn characteristically

---

[19] The origin of the figure in mm. 10–13 as a scalar ascent without decoration can be seen in the preliminary harmonic outline for the second theme on staves 10/11 of folio 24ᵛ (see page 373 above). This sketch is discussed and transcribed in my Ph.D. dissertation, *"A wisely-ordered* Phantasie*": Joseph Haydn's Creative Process from the Sketches and Drafts for Instrumental Music* (Brandeis University, 1987), p. 127 and illustration IV.12.

made such changes, often revising dense, complicated, or ear-catching ideas in subsequent work. I have mainly discussed ideas that were eventually abandoned, but the ideas Haydn kept were expanded and transformed to construct the "counter melodies and dexterous transitions" of Griesinger's description. Apparently when "the idea for an entire sonata" stood before Haydn's soul, that idea was multifaceted and subject to change in treatment and emphasis. Griesinger's generalization might explain the composer's motives for such changes:

> [Haydn's] theoretical reasoning was of the simplest sort, that is: a piece of music should have a flowing melody, coherent ideas, no frilly ornamentation, nothing bombastic, no deafening accompaniment, and so forth.[20]

"[By carrying out and sustaining an idea] I sought to help myself, and that is what so many of our young composers lack; they string one bit next to another, they break off when they have scarcely begun; but nothing stays in the heart after you have listened to it."

By limiting himself to rather closely related ideas, Haydn avoided the results that he deplored in the work of younger composers. He was convinced that this manner of composition made a piece more effective. Yet his thoughts about winning the audience's favor were not coldly calculated; he attributed his good reception to the harnessing of his passionate impulses. Dies reports this conversation with Haydn:

> "Have you ever," I asked, "made a system or rules that you could count on helping you gain the approval of the audience?" Haydn made no response. I continued speaking: "You know," I said, "that our philosophers analyse everything and are not satisfied with 'it pleases' until they have found the reason why it pleases. Should they discover the reason, then they know the components of beauty and can set out rules that one must follow strictly if one hopes to produce anything that will please."
>
> Haydn answered: "In the fire of composition, I never thought about that; I wrote what seemed good and corrected it afterwards according to the laws of harmony. I used no other devices."[21]

---

[20]"Seine theoretischen Raisonnements waren höchst einfach; nämlich: ein Tonstück soll haben einen fließenden Gesang, zusammenhängende Ideen, keine Schnörkeleyen, nichts Ueberladenes, kein betäubendes Accompagnement u. dgl. m." (Griesinger, p. 113).

[21]"'Haben Sie,' fragte ich, 'sich je ein System oder Regeln gemacht, mit deren Hilfe Sie den Beifall des Publikums zu erzwingen wußten?' Haydn schwieg. Ich fuhr daher in

We have witnessed Haydn using the keyboard throughout his career to kindle his "fire of composition." The keyboard was the means of igniting his passions and ideas, the medium for translating his mood into music that would stir the emotions of his listeners, and stay in their hearts even after it was over.

Owing to his failing health, Haydn played the keyboard less and less in old age and no longer sought ideas at his keyboard. But the experience of the instrument throughout his creative life abided with him; its power waned but was too strong to disappear as long as the light of his imagination and intellect still burned. Haydn complained to Dies of music's restless drive, and of the reversal of his role from the pursuer to the pursued:

> "Usually musical ideas persecute me to martyrdom, I can't get rid of them, they stand before me like walls. If it's an allegro that persecutes me then my pulse beats harder and harder, I can't sleep. If it's an adagio then I notice that my pulse beats slowly. My *Phantasie* plays me as if I were a keyboard." Haydn smiled, suddenly blushed, and continued: "I am really just a living keyboard."[22] †

---

meiner Rede fort: 'Sie wissen,' sagte ich, 'daß unsere Philosophen alles zergliedern und mit dem "es gefällt" so lange nicht zufrieden sind, bis sie die Ursache gefunden, warum es gefällt. Haben Sie die Ursache entdeckt, so kennen Sie die Bestandteile des Schönen und können dasselbe unter Regeln bringen, die in dem Fall, wo einer die Absicht hat, etwas hervorzubringen, das gefallen soll, auf das strengste beobachtet werden müssen.'

Haydn antwortete: 'Daran habe ich im Feuer der Komposition nie gedacht; ich schrieb, was mich gut dünkte und berichtigte es nachher nach den Gesetzen der Harmonie. Andere Kunstgriffe habe ich nie gebraucht'" (Dies, p. 61).

[22] "'Gewöhnlich verfolgen mich musikalische Ideen bis zur Marter, ich kann sie nicht loswerden, sie stehen wie Mauern vor mir. Ist es ein Allegro, das mich verfolgt, dann schlägt mein Puls immer stärker, ich kann keinen Schlaf finden. Ist es ein Adagio, dann bemerke ich, daß der Puls langsam schlägt. Die Phantasie spielt mich, als wäre ich ein Klavier.' Haydn lächelte, das Blut färbte plötzlich sein Gesicht röter, und er sagte: 'Ich bin wirklich ein lebendiges Klavier'" (Dies, p. 111).

† Holly Schafer died on April 26, 1995 after a long illness. At her request, this essay was edited by Dennis Slavin and John Knowles, based on the paper she read in Spring, 1990. The sketches and compositions discussed above are treated in greater detail in Schafer, *"A wisely-ordered Phantasie."*

When Sources Seem to Fail: The Clarinet Parts in Mozart's K. 581 and K. 622

Joel Sheveloff

Present practitioners of musical scholarship have gained fresh respect for source evaluation as an art, a central technical skill in discriminating the useful from the peripheral. In the last forty years, a flood of sources, even many that had been previously pored over, have undergone reexamination, revaluation, recategorization, and have then yielded fresh, sometimes startling data. We have learned about the stages of a work's composition and performance, about its reception by audiences and critics, about its functions and reuses in late environs, about analysis then and now, and about innumerable ancillary details. Specific places in a work reveal themselves as problematical, often insoluble; sometimes we cannot divine the composer's ultimate intention, though we can now come closer to that ideal than ever before.

This work has hardly begun; so many lesser composers have been dealt with only superficially, so many documents remain to be sifted, so many icons to be identified—and the integration of phonograph or mechanically recorded music has barely passed its infancy. So much of the new scholarship has appeared that the "Early Music Movement" has not been able to catch up with it. An embarrassment of riches has overwhelmed those whom we expect to serve as intermediaries between the composer on the one hand, and the great audience on the other, an audience that only *thinks* it has heard this music. It must be interpreted and reworked, and tried again and again, until all the promise unearthed has reached as much of its potential audience as possible. This adventure, fairly well begun in the last score years, ought to be allowed to proceed naturally, warts and all, so far as reconstruction and enthusiasm allows. Recently, a group of backlashers has arisen, challenging even whether what these performers do can in any way be defined as reawakening past practices.[1] Happily, this criticism has not slowed

---

[1]The anti-performance-practice tide turned against performers through a large portion of the 1980s, reaching its plateau of intensity with the publication of a flood of combative articles collected in Nicholas Kenyon, ed., *Authenticity and Early Music: A Symposium*

down the number or extent of such performances nor dampened the players' dedication or spirit of adventure. Undoubtedly the present state of rendition leaves enormous room for improvement: that will come in time. The next edition will correct errors, and the next performance will reach back and capture the essence of the composer's milieu, and maybe even the core of his intentions. It can only happen if we don't lose faith in the process, from finding a source to testing it in public.

Obstacles sometimes surface that interfere with traditional source evaluation methods, making them inadequate to the tasks usually expected of them. We must develop new questions to pose before essaying new techniques: without a clear sense of purpose, we cannot fail to grope about helplessly, trying to gain information the sources cannot provide. What can we do when the only sources for music under scrutiny lack authentic provenance, or transmit a text known to distort *any* master composer's intentions? How can we satisfy our justifiable desire to find a true text when none of the paper before us can be trusted? What can we do when the music involved has long since been accepted as a masterpiece, even in its messy condition? How do we convince ourselves that something must be done, even if a scientifically controlled solution cannot be achieved? And how do we convince performers to go along with us?

Such a despicable situation prevails in the cases of Mozart's two masterworks featuring the virtuoso clarinet: the Quintet, K. 581, and the Concerto, K. 622. Credible though impeachable sources exist for the accompanying parts, but the clarinet solo music has disappeared, and the late-copied parts have long been known to have been grossly altered.[2] Generations of avid searchers have been unable to find Mozart's manuscripts. If his clarinetist Anton Stadler really bore the responsibility for their disappearance, as

---

(Oxford: Oxford University Press, 1988), particularly its finale: "The Pastness of the Present and the Presence of the Past," by Richard Taruskin, pp. 137–210. Taruskin followed this with several naked attacks in the Sunday Arts sections of *The New York Times* that shifted the focus from the scholarly milieu to the arena of public opinion. He argues that performance-practice reconstruction has hardened into a neo-classic, anti-expressive rendition that conveys the sensibilities of our time with greater accuracy than the music being created now. He errs on two grounds: that all performers of old music have forgotten the ideal after which they strive; and that contemporary composition fails to satisfy our need for a sound of our own time. The backlash he leads against authentic performance practice can hardly slow the impetus to an ever-improving sense of how the music sounded to the composer. This soufflé will continue to rise.

[2]The enormous bibliography on this subject has been best summarized, annotated, and reviewed by Colin Lawson, "The Basset Clarinet Revived," *Early Music* 15 (1987): 487–501, and thus need not be retailed here.

Constanze Mozart alleged,[3] then *He who reserved vengeance unto himself* has certainly exacted it, upon Stadler, Mozart, all subsequent clarinetists, and the rest of us. The "correct" texts of these works deserve to be sought after—but just how do we do it?

The divination process began back in 1948, when George Dazeley pointed us in the right direction, and also threw a Molotov Cocktail into the mess, for it turned out that the problems extended well beyond the text to the very nature of the solo instrument itself.[4] A fair amount has been accomplished since then, more on the organological than on the text-explicatory front. By 1780, the evolution of the clarinet had proceeded so rapidly that its compass and chromatic utility already exceeded that of the other members of the 18th-century woodwind family. Players of this instrument, originally oboists who doubled it as an added attraction, now felt able to concentrate on the newly accepted sonority. But by 1790, when K. 581 and 622 appeared, the normal clarinet could no longer meet the demands of Mozart's conception of a vehicle for concerted solo music, so Theodor Lotz (or Lodz, the orthography remains uncertain) built a special instrument, presumably at the instigation of Anton Stadler, Mozart's close friend and performer of the master's clarinet and basset-horn music. Lotz's machine extended the clarinet range in a fully chromatic manner, four semitones beyond the usual lowest E of the *chalumeau,* all the way to the C below middle C.[5] The utility of such an extension depended on the size of the instrument, of course. A soprano or alto clarinet gains very little in richness from such an extension, but an instrument pitched lower than Concert C would gain considerable sonic advantage over the intestined basset-horn in this lowest portion of its range. In the 18th century, tenor- and baritone-range clarinets appeared in

---

[3]Constanze's spite was conveyed into print first through her husband Georg Nikolaus Nissen and repeated by Otto Jahn, but has been called into question many times since, perhaps most thoughtfully by Martha Kingdon-Ward, "Mozart's Clarinetist," *Monthly Musical Record* 85 (1955): 10. The fact remains, however, that these are the only two Mozart works of the period in so sorry a source condition—perhaps Stadler might at least be regarded as involved with their loss, if not directly responsible for it.

[4]George Dazeley. "The Original Text of Mozart's Clarinet Concerto," *Music Review* 9 (1948): 166–72. Perhaps the principles enunciated there may in themselves be insufficient for a thorough reworking, but most of the examples he intuits stand up remarkably well indeed.

[5]Lawson, "The Basset Clarinet Revived," seems to me far too cautious in granting the clarinetist and composer the existence of the full chromatic extension by the time of the composition of K. 581, rejecting even the most logical explanation of his own Example 3, p. 491, on the basis of organological evidence far more tenuous than the very nature of this passage, an unequivocal musical construct.

far more keys than now, with that in A being the most likely candidate for this extension.[6]

Reconstructed editions, live renditions, and phonograph productions (and a plethora of all these exist), demonstrate how far this process of divination has progressed. I find the results unsatisfactory in several respects, mostly due to the great number of unknowns in the surviving equation. The music, even distorted as much as the present sources do, has long been known and loved; the musical public has grown so used to it that demonstrating the superiority of any reconstruction demands far more than a convincing instrument and a Mozart-worthy text. The former has almost been attained, though players need to master its idiosyncrasies beyond the levels thus far displayed. The level of deduction thus far applied to the text seems to have been almost entirely restricted to circumstantial evidence, building the sort of case frighteningly similar to the kind reached by the legendary Inspector Lestrade.

Though we know the instrument existed, and possess evidence of other music written for it, both by Mozart and by other composers, no exemplar comes down to us, nor any particulars about the specific mechanisms that enabled it to press the clarinet's range so far below the natural limit we still believe in and employ.[7] All recent attempts to build a similar device have been largely based on the sort of keywork improvement that arose in the 19th and 20th centuries.[8] Even the name we have given this thing seems suspect. As part of the most seminal article about the problem and its solution, Jíri Kratochvil offered the appellation of "basset clarinet" to his vehicle for this *Klangideal*.[9] The persistence of this awkward name has caused confusion and dismay in the clarinet world, for non-clarinetists

---

[6]Francis Geoffrey Rendall, *The Clarinet: Some Notes upon Its History and Construction*, 3rd rev. ed., ed. F. Bate (London: E. Benn, 1971), covered well the known information up to 1970. Since then, as one tiny piece after another has been added to the picture, a lively discussion in the periodical literature has been engaged in by Nicholas Shackleton, John Newhill, Gary Karp, Albert R. Rice, David Charlton, and Colin Lawson.

[7]Lawson, "The Basset Clarinet Revived," pp. 488–89, reveals this very clearly and cogently, though the practical consequences of this problem seem even more crystalline in Colin Lawson, "Alan Hacker's Recording of K. 581, Amon Ra S A R 17 [review]," *Early Music* 14 (1986): 309–10.

[8]The most unashamed "makeshift" in clarinet building and adapting is described and illustrated by its perpetrator, Alan Hacker, in "Mozart and the Basset Clarinet," *Musical Times* 110 (1969): 359–62.

[9]Jíri Kratochvil, "Betrachtungen über die Urfassung des Konzerts für Klarinette und des Quintetts für Klarinette und Streiche," in *Internationale Konferenz über das Leben und Werk W. A. Mozarts: Bericht (Prag 27—31 Mai, 1956)* (Prag: Czechoslovakischer Komponisten, 1958), pp. 263–64.

consistently confound this instrument with the basset-horn (yet another member of the clarinet family, and not a horn, any more than the *Cor anglais*), and because *bassetto* arose as the sort of pejorative term that contradicts the most manifest virtues of this ideal clarinet. This locution has always explicitly meant "disappointingly weak just at the very place at which one might have expected, or at least hoped for, great strength," as in *voce bassetto*, a bass voice with a puny lowest tessitura, or *violone bassetto*, a name for the diminutive string bass with its clear but relatively unresonant sonority.[10] The linguistic origin of *corno di bassetto* has not been established beyond doubt, but I venture to concur with those who claim that it might refer to the generally thin and weak sound of its lowest tones, despite the makers' attempts to compensate for it by appending to its base a flamboyantly flaring metallic bell.[11] The extended straight tube clarinet built for Stadler, on the contrary, apparently maintained the warmth and power of the *chalumeau* register through its fully mechanized appendage. So the basset clarinet may be the very opposite of the basset-horn!

We know that Stadler began as an oboist, but gradually added to his accomplishments the basset-horn, and clarinets of several sizes and types. This extended clarinet seems to have occupied him from about 1788 to about 1794, after which, for some unknown reasons, he abandoned it. Allow me to hypothesize that neither Lotz nor Stadler had much reason to force the range all the way down to C. The cylindrical pipe's natural limit was G. Adding keywork to get down to F♯, F, and E presented great difficulties in manipulation for the little fingers of both hands as well as of breath control for the demands of the tone; any further lowering of the limit would not have seemed worth the trouble it would take, at least to builder and player. The one person who would find purpose and gain in attaining the lowest C, who would pester Lotz and Stadler for it, would be none other than Johann Chrysostom Wolfgang Theophilus Sigismund Mozart himself!

Several rationales support this theory, though none of them can be dignified by the term "evidence." The composer had met Stadler early in the 1780s, possibly late in 1781, and by 1786, had written a covey of pieces displaying various combinations of clarinets, basset-horns, bassoons, and

---

[10]Nicholas Shackleton, "Basset-horn," *New Grove Dictionary of Music and Musicians;* 6th ed., ed. S. J. Sadie (London: Macmillan, 1980), 2:260–61. Any *Dizionario de la lingua italiana* will confirm this assertion, some more unequivocally than others.

[11]A detailed supplement about experimental devices to mitigate anomalies on this instrument can be found in Albert R. Rice, "The Clarinette d'Amour and Basset Horn," *Galpin Society Journal* 38 (1989): 97–112.

vocal ensembles (especially trios).[12] He grew very close to Stadler, and became both professionally and financially interdependent with him in ways that exasperated Constanze, who never liked nor trusted Stadler, almost from the day they met. Wolfgang and Anton had plenty of opportunity to discuss the clarinet's suitability as a vehicle for concerted music as well as for other assorted solo functions. I theorize that Mozart would maintain that he required, nay, absolutely demanded, an instrument that could at least duplicate the advantages of the bassoon and horn, for which he produced so much concerted and chamber music. The prerequisites of this clarinet would focus upon its ability to serve both high-register-melodic and bass-ic functions:[13] its middle and high registers should be able to cut through any number of violins and violas, and soar above all but the heaviest orchestral tuttis, while its lowest register should be able to double or substitute for any bass line carried by cellos, basses, bassoons, or low horns. Almost everyone with enough background to read this paper can recall places in Mozart's bassoon concerto, or in any of his four horn concertos, or the horn quintet, where he suddenly shifts from high to low register or the reverse, thus changing the solo instrument's musical and textural role. The piano concertos also do this, of course, with their range being the very largest of all. Among solo instruments Mozart employed, only the flute and violin lacked the bass to fulfill this dual role, which may in part explain why the composer never used them after his earliest compositional years. But one can not, and should not push this last argument too far....

I further envision Mozart complaining that the low end of the clarinet came up far short of his minimal needs. The key of a given work need not matter, for the clarinet could be built in most any key to match; Mozart just wanted to write in the C major or C minor that fit the natural tube of the vehicle, and descend to its tonic C at its very bottom, the rich climactic bottom of the cylinder, the *chalumeau* register taken to its wondrous extreme, the *sub-chalumeau*. His first excursion into the realm of clarinet-featured music, the so-called "Kegelstatt" Trio, K. 498, for clarinet, viola, and piano, had to be set in E♭ major, though its clarinet's natural tube and key was pitched in B♭, precisely because the normal clarinet could not reach to the *sub-chalumeau*. A few eventful years later, when first K. 581 and then K. 622 saw the light of day, both ended up in A major for a clarinet also

---

[12]Save for some minor revision in K. numbers, the listing and categorization in Martha Kingdon-Ward, "Mozart and the Clarinet," *Music & Letters* 28 (1947): 151–53, has remained sound and useful.

[13]It seems startling how effectively Mozart exploited this dichotomy even as early as the Bassoon Concerto, K. 191, though models for this in other composers' treatment of the bassoon are all but impossible to find.

pitched in A, precisely because this extended clarinet could fulfill what I claim to be Mozart's dream, to sweep magnificently down to its lowest C, a pitch corresponding to the A on the lowest space of the bass staff. Mozart has been reported to call this monstrous prodigy amongst cylindrical single-reed pipes, his "bass clarinet", because it penetrated so far into the bass register, but we cannot call it that for obvious reasons. I propose, therefore, that it would be most appropriate to name this very special achievement the "Mozart clarinet," after the person who may very well have inspired or commissioned it, and who undoubtedly composed the very best music for it.

Dazeley first noted that many passages in the traditionally transmitted clarinet parts of both works under review here amounted to "makeshifts," to conform to the reduced range of the ordinary clarinet,[14] in much the same way that the alternate violin part that often substitutes for the clarinet in the Kegelstatt Trio, from Mozart's time to ours, had to be adjusted every time the clarinet part descended below the violin's lowest G. So far as I can tell, almost all the work of recent scholars attempting to reconstruct the lost original text has consisted of the direct application of Dazeley's first principle. In fact, most editorial changes offered in print up to now simply follow the very ones intuited by Dazeley himself.

But what of places in which the part has been altered wholesale, and thus no clear evidence of makeshift remained? What about places in which the original so intricately interwove through the registers that extensive recomposition had to be undertaken by the nameless reviser, to avoid hopelessly awkward passages? What about places in which the ensemble role of the clarinet part took precedence over its soloistic functions? Whatever one may say about this nameless person (or persons) who altered the original Mozart-clarinet parts back into ordinary clarinet parts, he did not lack musicianship, resourcefulness, nor quite a bit of common sense. Several of the makeshifts already uncovered and accepted now by consensus show him employing considerable skill in the handling of the material entrusted to his judgment. Doesn't it seem reasonable that he would sometimes have succeeded so thoroughly, so completely, in making his changes, that many of them might defy all but the most creative, liberal, unstinting, and indefatigable efforts at reconstruction? I am absolutely certain of this—my respect for the skill of the reviser has grown apace through the many years I have studied this situation and lived with the distorted source. I thus maintain that we must reach far beyond simple makeshifts to complete any really artistic reconstruction, in order to disinter Mozart's most interesting gambits.

---

[14]Dazeley, p. 167.

At the same time, we must be careful not to allow our imaginations so much free play that we risk the perpetration of a radical travesty of the magical musical language of Mozart.

Treading this thin line between creative divination and uncontrolled fantasy is a dangerous enterprise; I or anyone walking it should admit this to be the case, rather than advertising his or her reconstruction as a labor of pure scholarship unencumbered by personal ideas or judgment. The results must be allowed to justify themselves. Contrast this ideal with the publication of K. 622 in the *Neue Ausgabe sämtlicher Werke* (the *NMA*) of Mozart edited by Franz Giegling, who speaks very confidently and firmly about his changes in his introduction and critical notes, and who saw fit to print this concerto twice in full score, first in his reconstruction of the lost solo part, and then in the "traditional" version; the gorgeously executed tangibility of this volume gives the reader or performer the impression that each reading exists independently, that both partake of the same degree of reality.[15] This false impression should be condemned as wasteful as well as misleading. The orchestral parts, identical, need only have been printed once. Giegling should have done so, then juxtaposing the two readings of the solo part on adjoining staves, so the performer, conductor, scholar, or other user could instantly see how, and perhaps why, Giegling chose his reconstructed readings. At times (even to Giegling), more than one way of solving a particular passage might suggest itself; he should have then placed alternate solutions in a footnote, thus allowing the user to feel free to select the solution that most appealed to him. In an unusual musical situation like this one, the role of an editor like Giegling should never have been to provide the one true, finished, polished reconstruction, but to print the starting point for a process of rediscovery that might continue with later editors and clarinetists, perhaps indefinitely.

Recently, a player of replicas of 18th-century clarinets looked at my latest reading of the Quintet, K. 581, and asserted that some of my solutions would have been unplayable on all the instruments he knew and played. I replied that the Mozart clarinet of Lotz and Stadler may have possessed abilities far, far beyond those of any other instrument; he refused to believe that the technology of the time could have allowed anyone to build so efficient and noble an instrumentality. When I showed him the obbligato Mozart-clarinet part to the aria "Parto, parto, ma tu ben mio," from the opera seria *La clemenza di Tito,* he admitted that several places in this undoubtedly

---

[15]Franz Giegling, ed., *Klarinettenkonzert KV 622, Wolfgang Amadeus Mozart: Neue Ausgabe sämtlicher Werke* (*Neue Mozart Ausgabe;* hereafter *NMA*), Serie 5, Werkgruppe 14, Band 4 (Kassel: Bärenreiter, 1977).

authentic Mozart score challenged the instruments and players of the era almost as much as my text did. If I had shown him the texts of the Mozart-clarinet concertos by Süssmayr and Cimarosa, not then available to me, his wonderment would have known no bounds. This point needs to be driven home most forcefully, because the Mozart clarinet, however it actually did work, seems to have been as startling a rethinking of the clarinet of its time as the Boehm-system instruments of the 1840s would come to be.

The place in my text that my interlocutor most distrusted appears in the Quintet, K. 581, mvt. 1, m. 36, where I take the traditional text (Ex. 1a) and lower it, in its entirety, two octaves (Ex. 1b). The resultant figuration's first six notes, all below the clarinet's low G, would require heroic effort from both pinkies of the Mozart clarinetist to negotiate, for, whatever mechanical attributes the Mozart clarinet did have, these did not include the Boehm system's redundancies, which allow the player several choices for negotiating a passage between left and right little fingers. My critic claimed that, whichever pinky mechanisms the extended clarinet had, they could not have allowed just a workable combination of left and right hands to execute all six notes in Example 1b. He agreed that mm. 37–38's simple repetition of mm. 35–36 violates his sense of dramatic fitness as it does mine, so he suggested that the passage be lowered only one octave. If the original had been just one octave below its notated version, I reminded him, the nameless reviser would have had no need to alter it, for it would have been playable on the regular clarinet. The long-held C in m. 36, moreover, if notated one octave below the present, would impede the first violin's *Hauptstimme* at that point, being in the same register. We must believe that the first six notes of the passage in my realization could be executed with alternate hands for each note, even if we cannot verify it; with the two Ds two notes apart and the two Es four notes apart, this remains a possibility.

Example 1. K. 581, 1st movement, mm. 35–36

a. Traditional version

b. Original version, reconstruction

Previous editors' reconstructions have been based almost entirely upon factors derived from the solo clarinet part alone. A factor largely ignored has been the balance between the solo and accompanying parts, and all the stylistic conditions arising therefrom. Redesigning the clarinet part without regard for the whole of the musical fabric must be regarded as a recipe for failure. The clarinet part remains just one part: of all composers, Mozart would have been most sensitive to every aspect of its interaction with the others—and some of the solutions offered up as musically satisfying out of context can be easily shown to be the reverse in connection with the other parts.

Perhaps the clearest example of such a misguided solution occurs not far from the preceding example, in the Quintet's mvt. I, m. 41 (see the context in Ex. 2a, which shows the solo part in its traditional realization). The solo clarinet melody has just reached its climactic C in alt in m. 38, then prolongs it with looping half-scales in m. 39, after which it sweeps through descending scales in m. 40 from the C in alt to middle C, where it again sustains itself an eighth. At this point, the usually-transmitted notation shows the line suddenly changing direction to go back up to treble C where the clause concludes. This abrupt change of direction drew suspicion from those seeking out places to restore from the "ravages" of the nameless reviser, as a sure sign that the line had originally been meant to continue down into the *sub-chalumeau*. Of course, I cannot but accept this judgment; the change of direction violates the most fundamental Mozartian principles of wind writing. The solution chosen by every editor who has "restored" the text in this place, on the other hand, violates the most basic concepts of voice-leading, and conduct of a cadence, and, while looking straightforward enough, must be rejected; its text appears as Example 2b.[16]

Let me explain: within this movement's sonata-allegro form, this passage serves the exposition as the close of its transition, just before the onset of the second-theme group in m. 42, with the first violin then taking up the melody. In this eventful exposition, Mozart modulates from the tonic A major to the dominant in m. 42, using as pivotal vehicle the dominant of the dominant, reached as early as m. 35. Just after this point, the clarinet reaches the climactic C in alt (concert A) while the V of V alternates with a semi-chromatic upper-neighbor chord. So, this clarinet's written C, brought into

---

[16]Dazeley, p. 171, does not offer the actual realization of his suggested emendation, but merely indicates the measure in which it ought to occur. Gerhard Croll & Kurt Birsak, "Anton Stadlers 'Bassetklarinettte' und des 'Stadler-Quintett' K. 581: Versuch einer Anwendung," *Österreichisches Musikzeitschrift* 24 (1969): 7, clearly spell out the reverse all the way to the lowest C in their Example 1.

When Sources Seem to Fail   389

Example 2. K. 581, 1st movement

a. mm. 38–44: traditional version

b. m. 41: original version, incorrect reconstruction

c. m. 41: original version, possible reconstructions

sharp relief through a prolongation that lasts all these measures and through all these shifts of register, must be understood as the seventh of the V of V built on the root B; in all its earlier appearances in the upper three octaves, this seventh behaves properly and with musical tact—but when the note sounds forth at the close of its great descent, on the third quarter of m. 41, it becomes the worst possible bass tone for a chord about to resolve to one in root position in m. 42. At this very moment, the violoncello leaps up an octave, from bass B to middle B, leaving the clarinet alone to serve as the true bass, and if that bass actually sounds concert A, a major ninth below the cello, we are faced with the anomaly of a local dominant seventh in third inversion resolving to a tonic in root position at the most important cadence in the entire exposition! Such a progression violates every practice of Mozart, Haydn, and Beethoven. So, while I accept the notion that the scale must descend in this measure, I submit that it must finish on the written *sub-chalumeau* tone D (concert B), the root tone of the V^7.

Listen to any concert or recording thus far made of K. 581 on what is advertised as the "basset clarinet," and you will hear a soloist playing this incorrect solution with great gusto.[17] With some of these clarinetists, one wonders whether they take the trouble to listen to the remainder of the ensemble; with others, one gets the idea that they believe their special tone color so ostentatiously contrasts with those of the accompanying instruments that the rules of voice leading need not apply to them. Perhaps I overstate this case, but continued listening to such performances, live and recorded, tends to engender an incommensurate level of anger. How can good musicians commit so grievous an error, I wonder?

That the clarinet, alone of all orchestral instruments, overblows at the twelfth rather than the octave on the overtone series, seems to inspire the sort of chauvinism about its interaction resulting in situations like that just cited. Again and again, the judgment of clarinetists has to be questioned. I know still another "basset clarinetist" who has played in the opera orchestra in a performance of *La clemenza di Tito,* and who, in the aforementioned aria "Parto, parto," adds *sub-chalumeau* Cs where Mozart does not call for them. A notable example occurs in mm. 18–19, where an unwinding line in the treble falls all at once to middle C (concert B♭). When my acquaintance substituted his lowest C at this point, the conductor could not help but notice it, but after a brief discussion, assented, admitting the amended note to be more exciting than the one written. *Tito* comes undistorted from Mozart's pen; if he had wanted the lowest C at this point, he would surely have written it. A cursory examination of the place reveals, moreover,

---

[17]It has been recorded this way by Kurt Birsak (Claves D 8007, 1980); Antony Pay (Philips 9500772, 1981); Eric Hoeprich (Philips 420242, 1983); Alan Hacker (Amon Ra S A R 17, 1984); Lawrence McDonald (Smithsonian N 031, 1986); Colin Lawson (Nimbus 35228-2, 1987); and W. Pencz (Saphir INT 830868, [after 1981]). There have probably been others as well that I have missed, and I am sure the process is ongoing.

that this decision once more places the seventh of a dominant seventh in the bass, where only a root ought to be. While this root does sound in the cellos and basses, their eighth note tends to get overpowered by the clarinet's quarter. Only a truly solid musical rationale can justify redaction, and any editor or performer who violates this aesthetic law does so at the peril of himself, his performance, and the respect in which the laity hold us.

To return to this awkward place in K. 581: one problem remains—since written C had been the emphasized tone in all the upper octaves, a shift from it to the lowest written D must be engineered to make the alighting convincing. To accomplish this, one may choose to break the flow of sixteenth notes at some point, or to insert a chromatic or repeated note into the scale, in a manner illustrated in five ways in Example 2c. In my edition of the Quintet, I would offer the first reading, with its special braking action derived from the extra pause on the G in the middle of the scale as my principal text, but add the others in a footnote, for only my taste and my sense that the simplest, most elegant solution usually works best leads me to prefer the first reading. In a case like this, every clarinetist should be free to choose the realization, among those ending on D, that most appeals to his taste. Nor would I take it amiss if he devised another solution that landed on D: who knows? his guess may be more convincing than mine—it may even be correct! This type of situation recurs throughout K. 581 and K. 622, and again and again, a mere glance at the harmony, the spacing, or the disposition of the other parts will reveal not only whether a change in the traditional text is warranted, but how to make it work out best.

My constant chiding of performers who get carried away by their enthusiasm for the *sub-chalumeau* and go too far in making emendations makes me fair game for my critics, who have already accused me of the same, and of others who will surely join the chorus once they see my edition. One example already attacked occurs very early in K. 581; the first movement of the Quintet opens with a lyrical gambit strikingly reminiscent of the first line of *The Sidewalks of New York,* entrusted to the strings in some unusual spacings, after which the solo clarinet appends a kind of *jubilus;* the return of the string melody exhibits an intensification of inner-voice tension and melodic variation leading to a second, similar clarinet outburst. Though these two subdivisions, respectively occupying mm. 1–8 and 9–16, both cadence on the tonic, they sound like an antecedent and consequent, because the clarinet figure's tail arrives at tonic somewhat awkwardly the first time, but much more smoothly the second. The second outburst, being much higher than the first, seems to reach a climax on its highest tone, one that brings the whole sixteen-measure complex to a proper balance. So far so good.

Example 3. K. 581, 4th movement., mm. 15–17: original version, reconstruction

I propose to drastically alter the effect, and yet enhance it as only Mozart, in my opinion, could have calculated it. As Example 3 clearly reveals, my reconstruction takes the entirety of the clarinet part from m. 15 to the downbeat of m. 17 and lowers it an octave. Why do I lower the second clarinet passage and not the first, or both of them? To lower the first one, it would have to be largely rewritten, while the second requires not a single adjustment. When the second gets lowered, do we not lose the aforementioned climax? Absolutely true—but a new sort of climax reveals itself at the very end of the passage, as well as at its very outset, when the low Cs, notes never before heard on a clarinet, sound forth in all their glory. Objectors will immediately point out that this lowering forces the last four sixteenths of the clarinet line down beneath the root of the chord, bass E, performed here by the viola. I must accept the point. While I take this kind of objection most seriously, I ask you to remember that the string parts may have been altered as well, for their provenance has not been established beyond doubt. It seems singularly strange that, after the string texts of mm. 3–7 have undergone significant alteration in every measure of the parallel phrase, mm. 11–15—the texts of mm. 8 and 16 would be identical. This does not work when the traditional text is set against it: the balance of second-violin double-stop and viola bass seems strained against the traditional "high" clarinet part. If, as a minimal change, we add the resting cello in m. 16, doubling the root E at the lower octave, either for the whole measure, or at least the final quarter-note value of it, the result would more than adequately undergird the Mozart clarinet's first plummet to its base; the cello had already stated this profundo E in m. 14, rather than the bass E in the parallel place in m. 6. This cello part might also serve as proleptic of the cadential statement in mm. 18–19: having these two same passing 16ths at the close of m. 16 would work as well with the clarinet descent as it does with the subsequent violin duet. The Mozart clarinet reveals its new powers for the very first time in mm. 15–17, and the two violins seem to react to it in startled, frenzied amazement. With this one small alteration in the cello part, it can serve as foundation to both clarinet event and violin reaction with that Mozartian sort of perfection that we have come to take for granted.

The central point I have taken particular pains to hammer home here remains the motivation for every alteration: each one must arise from the inner workings of the music itself rather from the new possibilities, the very nature of the Mozart clarinet. With his customary command over even this newest, most experimental mechanism, Mozart would have employed its special powers in almost every place in which he could make it musically appropriate; the motivic chains, the flow of musical prosody, the balance of the ensemble, and the rich unfolding of the formal designs of every movement of K. 581 and K. 622 must be the decisive considerations in any recasting of the traditional musical fabric.

To continue this disquisition in this same vein, however, citing a flood of further examples, would be to give way to the temptation of turning this paper into a histrionic, perhaps even a hysterical *kritische Bericht* of my upcoming edition. For one who has spent so long agonizing over every potential and actual rethinking of the text, such shameless advertising would be an easy way out. The reader has the right to demand a level of argumentation beyond anecdotal and circumstantial evidence. He needs to know what principles, based upon what observations of Mozart's style, serve as foundation for this reconstruction. I offer seven of them, each accompanied by a few words or an example.

1) On the Mozart clarinet, *clarino* material links itself to melody instruments while *chalumeau* material tends to interact with the accompanying bass.

Though demonstrated over and over again in the bassoon and horn concertos, this element is the one that Giegling neglects most in his score of K. 622. Exceptions to this principle do occur in the most subtle places, in the thinnest textures, and in passages set at soft, especially very soft dynamic levels. Since clarinets of whatever size, shape, or compass excel at just these nuances, quite a few of these exceptions may be noted. At key moments in the form, this principle nevertheless stands out as a beacon for the would-be resuscitator, which accounts for this principle's pride of place in my listing.

Giegling violates this principle in his version of the Concerto, K. 622, several times, notably in the coda of the first movement, (mm. 337–40). I give the traditional text for this place in Example 4a; the way the clarinet solo part starts downward only to change direction in the middle and press upward to the high E betrays the presence of the reviser's hand, and Giegling correctly sets out to neutralize the effect. His solution appears as Example 4b; he lowers the first eight 16ths an octave, keeping the remainder of the phrase as it stands. In so doing, he locks the clarinet line in a collision course with all the high strings, as it proceeds to a very brief climax on E in alt, followed by a particularly unsatisfactory rest. But all of this carping about small points pales beside his failure to note that the first note of each clarinet arpeggio thrust, from the second half of m. 337 through all of m. 338 duplicates the notes of the descending line in the cellos and string basses. My solution, Example 4c, leaves the first eight 16ths alone, proceeds downward with the bass line in the strings, leaving the next eight 16ths alone as well, and then drops the next eight 16ths *one* octave to keep the pattern in line with the bass, and the final 16ths two octaves down to complete the pattern. This clears the clarinet out of the way of the ascending strings, and sets up a link to the final cadential pattern, a link that, in my opinion, connects far more compellingly than the high E and rest of the traditional text that sounded much like a syntactical hiccough. The climactic C in m. 339, prolonged by its lower neighbors, leads to the conclusion with far greater grace than had the E.

Example 4. K. 622, 1st movement, mm. 337–38

a. Traditional version

b. Original version, reconstruction (*NMA*, Giegling)

c. Original version, reconstruction (Sheveloff)

2) Avoid literal repetition of a melodic idea in the same register.

This prescription may seem baseless to most observers of Mozart's style, since examples of such repetitions abound, particularly in vocal music, but in several instrumental genres as well. The notable exception, relevant to these pieces, is the concerto, especially those for bassoon and horn. In an environment where the featured instrument's large compass and different registral characters serve as essential elements in the form-building process, simple repetition at the same pitch level seems to be a negation of its principal method of locomotion. Only the piano possesses a greater total range than the Mozart clarinet, and the startling color contrasts between the clarinet's registers have no counterpart on the keyboard. In the Concerto, the traditional text shows repetition many, many times (the preponderance of the examples happen in the first movement), so I found myself making changes based upon this second principle more often than upon any other. It happens often in the Quintet as well, as Examples 1a and 1b demonstrate. In the Concerto, these changes often force me to take some part of the text down two octaves, a rare expedient in the Quintet.

3) The clarinet's integration into dialogues and imitative passages ought to be as literal as possible.

Dialogues between the clarinet and other instruments in the ensemble, most often the first violin(s), occur every so often (mostly in the two slow movements). In some places where the clarinet appears to accept the idea from the accompaniment in an incomplete or altered manner, I have altered it to match, citing the usual range rationale. Delaying the clarinet's entrance by a sixteenth-rest in m. 63 of the first movement of K. 581 may not be a range matter, but sometimes the reviser seems to want to bring the solo part into higher relief than the overall musical texture and imitative situation warrant.

4) Rules of spacing, voice-leading, and harmonic doubling apply to the solo clarinet on an equal footing with all the other instruments.

This matter has already been discussed. Rarely does this seem the first principle for a change, but its application often cements a choice made along other lines. One need only review the examples cited thus far to observe that this principle has played some role in each and every one of them.

> 5) **Registral change can enhance a motivic or a structural point in the form; analyze with care, to see just how you can best make the change of register work to highlight the music's drama.**

This formulation has been especially useful as a counterweight against overindulgence in alteration, rather than as a cause for change. If making a change would have caused far too much attention to be drawn to a location within the form that could not stand it, having its outline before me helped me to realize this. At the same time, this has been the vaguest of all these ideas, for a higher degree of uncertainty exists on matters of priority in structural weight and center of musical gravity than on any other parameter in this list.

> 6) **Beware of unusual metric units, such as triplets, suddenly intruding in a movement in which they played no previous role.**

Early and middle Mozart often employs such triplets, especially at cadential passages, just before concluding with a big trill. Like the literally repeated phrase, this element has seemed to me to gradually fade out of Mozart's style, though it still has uses in some late works. In the Quintet's first movement, for example, no triplets appear until m. 122 (Example 5a). The makeshift at movement's end makes it clear that the composer (or the nameless reviser) used the triplets to avoid an excursion all the way up to altissimo G (as in Example 5b). This would not have worked anyway, as the main notes of the melody being recapitulated here must remain in the treble octave. Mozart could have avoided the makeshift while keeping the melody in line by employing the notes in Example 5c, notes well within the compass of the normal clarinet. But this solution keeps the triplets that offend against the momentum of the movement. Only the reading in Example 5d satisfies every requirement, and it contains one *sub-chalumeau* tone, so the nameless reviser could not allow it to stand as it was. One might object that the difference between Examples 5a and 5b is far too great for the latter to be a proper solution to the former, but the logic of this paragraph's argument demonstrates that workable solutions can end up being very, very different from the traditional text, once these principles exert their logic. The change looks more radical than it sounds, and it helps signal a point in the recapitulation in which the first theme must take a fresh turn, both tonally and materially. Once one gets used to the way this example sounds, one discovers that it aids the melody in projecting its full

When Sources Seem to Fail 397

form, heard for the first time since the very outset of the Quintet. It is exactly the sort of change represented by Example 5, in which several logical steps must be taken before a truly workable text can be achieved, that Giegling and other previous redactors never even approach. Over fifty examples within K. 581 and K. 622 illustrate this process. The most dramatic changes in the first movement of the Concerto all seem to arise in this way.

Example 5. K. 581, 1st movement, mm. 122–23

a. Traditional version

b. Possible original version

c. Possible original version

d. Original version, reconstruction

7) All previous principles apply to potential changes in the clarinet's highest notes as well as its lowest ones.

Anton Stadler played second clarinet in orchestras because of his great expertise in producing great beauty of sound in the *chalumeau,* while his brother Johann Nepomuk Franz Stadler specialized in the high registers and thus played first clarinet. This does not mean that Anton could not play in the highest registers, or that, in a concerted context, would not wish to show off the highest portion of his compass. Even the basic clarinet cylinders of the 18th century could theoretically reach all the way up to C in altissimo, and we possess a wonderful example of a scale running all the way from the Mozart clarinet's very lowest C to this highest possible C, in a concerto by Mozart's disciple Süssmayr.[18]

I have long believed, as no other writer before me has ever suggested, that the nameless reviser also smoothed out and eliminated some very high places as well as the already demonstrated large number of low ones, perhaps to make K. 581 and K. 622 negotiable by the average clarinetist. Notes above C in alt seem especially rare throughout these two masterworks. While notes in the highest octave require extraordinary lip pressure in order to gain control, players of the highest caliber, players like the Stadler brothers, would doubtless possess the requisite skill. One must be sure, in writing for the highest octave, however, to avoid notes of any real length—from two usual beats onwards, for then the sound of the note tends to get out of the player's control, to grow harsh, or flat, or squeaky, or even give out altogether. I have thus contrived, in all the places where I add something in the highest register, to make all these notes short; still, I fully expect every new reading involving the highest register (see three such examples chosen at random as Exx. 6, 7, and 8) to be among the most controversial in my version of these pieces.

Example 6. K. 581, 1st movement, mm. 190–93: original version, reconstruction

Example 7. K. 622, 1st movement, mm. 198–200: original version, reconstruction

---

[18]The text of this scale traversing the entirety of the Mozart clarinet's compass can be seen in partial facsimile at the top of p. 360 in Hacker.

Example 8. K. 622, 1st movement, mm. 303–07: original version, reconstruction

My version of K. 622 differs from Giegling's in about 150 particulars, some of them extensive. Ernst Fritz Schmid's treatment of K. 581, in one of the earliest-appearing volumes of the *NMA*,[19] employs only the traditional text. Even after one includes his rather reluctant gestures towards reconstruction, mentioned only in his Einleitung,[20] I make some eighty or so further emendations. Any Mozart clarinetist performing my texts would be called upon to reach down into the *sub-chalumeau* register about four times as often as in the presently available publications. And he would find himself ascending to new heights in about thirty places not now so disposed. Of these changes, the musical logic brought to bear to undergird them seems at least compelling, and sometimes convincing, even to me, about three-quarters of the time. My arguments sound strained, at least somewhat, in another fifth of the changes. Each one must stand on its own, and may be rejected or accepted or altered by a Mozart clarinetist as he desires. My full-score edition will place the traditional text and my reconstruction on adjacent staves, so this player's choice will always be easily available and convenient. As for the other 5% of the places in these two scores, I will admit them to be quite troublesome, and ask for help in finding more satisfactory ways out! I do so now, and will retain this policy in the future—any editor of a work in this source condition cannot help but retain his full degree of humility in the face of the enormity of the problem, or go mad!

The most maddening passage, and one that I have never dealt with satisfactorily, after attempting more than a dozen realizations, consists of the entirety of the first variation of the Theme-and-Variations that make up the Quintet's fourth movement. Nothing seems to work out—the existent clarinet line appears far more awkward and angular than anything else in these two works, but every emendation that I can devise sounds about equally

---

[19]Ernst Fritz Schmid, ed., *Quintett KV 581, NMA,* Serie 8, Werkgruppe 19, Abteilung 2. (Kassel: Bärenreiter, 1958). K. 581 occupies pp. 15–38.

[20]Schmid, *Quintett KV 581,* pp. vii–xiii, especially pp. viii–ix.

unconvincing, though in an entirely different way (one version appears as Ex. 9). That the opening gesture of this variation cyclically recalls the opening gesture of the *Trio II* of the preceding *Menuetto,* does not seem to help in any way. My by now overtaxed musical intuition tells me that the nameless reviser has been extraordinarily busy here, altering this variation so much, and in so many ways, that I cannot penetrate all his twists and turns. I feel sure that the solution stares out at me from this flawed text, but my inability to find it in thirty years, half my lifetime, has caused me enormous discomfort. Some other musician will see it straight-away, and I will kick myself for not having the musicianship he possesses. God teaches us humility in many ways.

Example 9. K. 581, 4th movement, variation 1, mm. 17–32: reconstruction

Opportunities for the kind of musical detection that can only be accomplished by deduction come along so rarely that one finds oneself constantly reviewing the ethics and morals of the project. I sometimes compare this task to Robert Levin's several "completions" of unfinished Mozart works; I have never been satisfied with a single one of Levin's recompositions—so why should a musically sensitive person be tolerant of mine? At least K. 581 and K. 622 stand as completed compositions, to which recasting had been applied some time in the first decade of the 19th century, by a person or persons who will almost certainly never be identified. Levin's subjects, to the contrary, seem to have been dropped by Mozart himself for what the great composer must have seen as good and sufficient reason; at any rate,

Levin found a piece abandoned at so early a stage that to finish it required considerable fresh composition, so much that the term "completion" seems a less pertinent appellation than "fantasy." When, on the other hand, I print the nameless reviser's text next to my own, the reader possesses a constant control.

A project such as this can maintain a semblance of ethical control, so long as its author focuses upon his love for Mozart's vision, so long as he can sustain that minimal belief in his own musical intuition in dealing with music where his chances of being incorrect remain uncomfortably high, and so long as he accepts the ultimate limitation—that the glory of the task grows out of the seeking rather than the finding. "The answers may make us wise, but the questions make us human."[21] We must derive every morsel we can from the sources, no matter how corrupt they may be, and when the sources seem to fail, we must fall back on logic, on secondary methods of investigation, and finally, upon our own musicianship. After a lifetime spent in developing this supposed virtue, it ought to be useful for something!

The ideas for and impetus towards this project began in a Classic Era Seminar conducted by Paul Brainard some three decades ago. This little paper must thus be regarded as a progress report by the slowest, most painstaking and deliberate student in that group. All future publication and recording and live performance of the results of this work I hereby dedicate to the person whose leadership and example made it all possible; whatever good may come of it derives from his steady hand and kindly heart.

---

[21]This line is spoken by the psychiatrist in Alan Jay Lerner's Broadway musical *On a Clear Day, You Can See Forever,* just before the title song appears as finale.

From Madrigal to Toccata: Frescobaldi and the *Seconda Prattica*

Alexander Silbiger

The assertion that Frescobaldi's keyboard toccatas can be fully comprehended only within the framework of the *seconda prattica* will at first appear paradoxical. The fundamental tenet of this practice is that the words shall rule the music—"l'oratione sia padrone del armonia e non serva"[1]—and an instrumental genre would seem to hold little promise for realizing that aesthetic. However, attempts to understand the toccatas as realizations of an autonomous instrumental form governed by abstract musical principles have been problematic at best. In this respect Frescobaldi's toccatas differ from the toccatas of Froberger and of later composers, which generally exhibit an orderly succession of clearly differentiated free and contrapuntal segments. Frescobaldi's own works in other genres also usually possess common formal principles; for example, his canzonas are structurally defined by the regular alternation of imitative sections in contrasting meters, and are musically unified by thematically related subjects.

Even Willi Apel, who brought to his comprehensive study of early keyboard music a firm conviction that each genre is defined by demonstrable principles of musical organization and cohesion, appears to have been perplexed by Frescobaldi's toccatas. He hears in some passages only "a splintering into small fragments, which seem to follow no other law than that of momentary inspiration," and "a plethora of nervous formulae, which change from moment to moment."[2] Should we then cease our search for organizing principles, and regard these pieces merely as written-down, spontaneous improvisations? Apel clearly did not think so. In spite of his failure to detect such principles in Frescobaldi's toccatas, his faith was unshaken that "as is to be expected from a great master, [Frescobaldi] possesses not only the talent to invent the most diverse figures but also the insight and the faculty to join them into an organic, meaningful whole."[3]

---

[1] Claudio Monterverdi, *Scherzi musicali* (Venice, 1607), "Dichiaratione della lettera...," facs. in Monteverdi, *Tutte le opere*, vol. 10 (Asolo, 1929), p. 69.

[2] Willi Apel, *The History of Keyboard Music to 1700*, trans. and rev. Hans Tischler (Bloomington: Indiana University Press, 1972), p. 457.

[3] Apel, p. 457.

Besides, that a composition might be a written-down improvisation has little bearing on the presence of organizing principles. These can operate regardless of whether the piece has been worked out on paper or was composed "in real time" at the keyboard. Unquestionably, Frescobaldi's toccatas with their constant motivic whirl owe much to an improvising tradition, but this is also true of many works in genres in which the structural procedures are easy to define, such as the romanesca and passacaglia variations, and the plain-chant versets. In fact, one scholar, Murray Bradshaw, has proposed that early toccatas are constructed according to a technique somewhat similar to that of variation and cantus firmus settings; he believes them to be settings of hidden (that is, not explicitly stated) cantus firmi corresponding to psalm-tone formulas. Although that model works for some of the brief 16th-century intonations, it breaks down when applied to the toccatas of Frescobaldi and others.[4]

Another key to the workings of these toccatas has been sought in the models of rhetoric.[5] In recent years, there has been much interest in the role rhetoric theory may have played in Renaissance and Baroque compositional practices, and analogies to rhetorical concepts have been detected in a broad range of repertories, from early sixteenth-century quasi-improvisational lute ricercars to large eighteenth-century constructions like Bach's *Musical Offering*.[6] Rhetoric provides oratorical analogues both for the formal arrangement of component parts and for the expressive figures, but I am not sure how the mere identification of the parts and figures of Frescobaldi's toccatas with these analogues will clarify the special nature of those pieces, that is, yield insight into what distinguishes them from his other works and from

---

[4] See Alexander Silbiger, *Italian Manuscript Sources of Seventeenth-Century Keyboard Music* (Ann Arbor: UMI Research Press, 1980), pp. 191 (n. 1), 192 (n. 4). Others who have questioned Bradshaw's theory include Frits Noske, *Sweelinck* (Oxford: Oxford University Press, 1988), p. 103 (with reference to Sweelinck's toccatas); Paul Anthony Luke Boncella, *The Classical Venetian Organ Toccata (1591–1604): An Ecclesiastical Genre Shaped By Printing Technologies and Editorial Policies* (Ph.D. dissertation, Rutgers, The State University of New Jersey, 1991), pp. 8–15 (with reference to the Venetian toccatas); and Vincent Joseph Panetta, *Hans Leo Hassler and the Keyboard Toccata: Antecedents, Sources, Style* (Ph.D. dissertation, Harvard University, 1991), pp. 29–32 (also with reference to the Venetian repertory).

[5] See for example, Emilia Fadini, "The Rhetorical Aspect of Frescobaldi's Musical Language," *Frescobaldi Studies*, ed. Alexander Silbiger (Durham: Duke University Press, 1987), pp. 284–97.

[6] Warren Kirkendale, "Ciceronians versus Aristotelians on the Ricercar as Exordium from Bembo to Bach," *Journal of the American Musicological Society* 32 (1979): 1–44; Ursula Kirkendale, "The Source for Bach's *Musical Offering*: The *Institutio oratoria* of Quintilian," *Journal of the American Musicological Society* 33 (1980): 88–141.

other kinds of music. The idea that rhetorical analogues played an active role in the compositional process, not just in theoretical speculation after the fact, remains a fascinating one, but I will not pursue it here, the more so since I do not know of any writer of the time who specifically related rhetoric to the toccata genre. Instead I will turn to another, admittedly related theory for which I believe Frescobaldi did leave us some concrete support: the application of the *seconda prattica* aesthetic to instrumental music.

Today the *seconda prattica* usually is associated with those aspects of 17th-century composition that proved most significant from our own historical vantage point: the new concerted style and monody, freer dissonance treatment and heightened chromaticism, and the replacement of modal polyphony by chordal harmony. It is clear though from Monteverdi's defense of the practice that these phenomena, when recognized at all, were regarded at most as symptomatic consequences of the basic premise that distinguished the second from the first practice: that demands of the text have priority over purely musical considerations, meaning, over the principles derived from codified music theory. Monteverdi takes pains to show that he is not necessarily defending new against old music, and that the *seconda prattica* was practiced by a long line of distinguished predecessors, among them Rore, Wert, Marenzio, Luzzaschi, and Gesualdo.[7] Evidently, Monteverdi saw the embodiment of the second practice as much in the polyphonic madrigals by these composers as in the new monodies; in fact, we do not know whether Monteverdi had written any monodies when he published the historic *Lettera* in his fifth book of madrigals (1605).

In view of the governing role assigned to the text, was there a place within the *seconda prattica* for instrumental music? This question never seems to have been addressed in the theoretical literature of the time. The leading practitioners like Monteverdi, perhaps as a result of their pursuit of this new aesthetic, showed little interest in instrumental genres *per se*, and confined their purely instrumental writing to functional movements within larger vocal compositions, such as introductory sinfonias and toccatas, ritornellos, and dance numbers. The belief in the preeminence of the text, and hence of vocal music, continued to pervade the Italian musical scene during the later seventeenth century, and even affected Northern composers like Heinrich Schütz. Of course, instrumental composition did not disappear; works in the traditional genres of the *prima prattica* such as ricercars and liturgical organ versets, as well as other traditional types like dances and canzonas, continued to be written in large numbers, but these showed few traces of the new style.

---

[7]Monteverdi, *Scherzi musicali*, p. 70.

There was however one instrumental genre that, at least indirectly, had a connection with a literary text: the intabulation. It is my thesis that techniques developed with the embellished intabulations of madrigals and subsequently introduced into another tradition, that of the improvisational, preluding toccata, showed the way to the creation of an authentic instrumental genre within the aesthetic of the *seconda prattica*.[8]

* * * * *

Frescobaldi's intabulation of Arcadelt's *Ancidetemi pur* appears in his *Secondo libro di toccate* (Rome, 1627), and is his only known contribution to the genre;[9] its placement within the volume is of special interest.[10] His first book of *Toccate* (Rome, 1615–16) had opened with twelve toccatas, a traditional number probably derived from the earlier practice of providing a set of toccatas in all the church modes. The second book contains, however, only eleven toccatas, the position of the twelfth being taken by the intabulation. This suggests that Frescobaldi intended his "Ancidete mi pur d'Archadelt" to form the crowning end-piece for the magnificent series of toccatas of the *Secondo libro*.[11]

The connection between toccatas and the art of embellishment was well recognized at the time. Diruta, in his *Transilvano* of 1593, had written "the toccatas are all divisions" ("le Toccate sono tutte Diminutioni") and in its *Seconda parte* of 1609 mentioned Merulo's toccatas among the inspiring models for the "fine art of intabulating with divisions" ("bell'arte d'intavolature diminuito").[12] Furthermore, a connection between the toccata and the madrigal, albeit only with regard to performance, was made by Frescobaldi himself in the prefatory notes to the first book of *Toccate*, in which he stated

---

[8]A similar process may well tie the madrigal *passaggi* for strings and winds to the creation of the instrumental sonata, but that topic will not be pursued here.

[9]Modern edition in Girolamo Frescobaldi, *Opere complete 3: Il secondo libro di toccate*, ed. Etienne Darbellay, Monumenti musicali italiani, 5 (Milan: Suvini Zerboni, 1979), pp. 49–54.

[10]In the following, I shall understand by "intabulation" an embellished intabulation (*intavolatura diminuito* or *passaggiato*) rather than a simple scoring of a polyphonic work on two staves for keyboard use.

[11]The position of *Ancidetemi* and the relationship between toccatas and madrigal intabulations were briefly discussed in my *Italian Manuscript Sources*, pp. 31–32, but not the connection with the *seconda prattica*; another aspect of the relationship is treated in my article "Is the Italian Keyboard 'Intavolatura' a Tablature?," *Recercar* 3 (1991): 81–101.

[12]Girolamo Diruta, *Il Transilvano* (Venice: Giacomo Vincenti, 1593), p. 36, and *Seconda parte del Transilvano* (Venice, 1609), Libro primo, p. 10.

that his toccatas "must not be subject to a rigid beat, but performed, as is the custom with modern madrigals, now languidly, now fast, now as if they were suspended in the air—all according to the 'affetti' or sense of the words."[13] Frescobaldi was of course intimately familiar with the modern madrigal tradition; he had been trained by one of its foremost practitioners, Luzzasco Luzzaschi—the only teacher he ever acknowledged—and his first publication was a book of madrigals for five voices.[14] But how do the *affetti* in a toccata relate to the words set in a madrigal?

I propose that we look for answers in the aforementioned example of the ancient intabulation practice that for some curious reason Frescobaldi decided to append to the modernist essays of his 1627 collection. Since the turn of the century, the only other madrigal intabulations published for keyboard had come from Naples: two other settings of *Ancidetemi,* by Ascanio Mayone (1603) and by Giovanni Maria Trabaci (actually for harp, 1615), with a third setting by Gregorio Strozzi appearing not until 1687, and two intabulations of Domenico Ferrabosco's *Io mi son giovinetta,* by Trabaci (1603) and by Mayone (with segments by Giovanni Domenico Montella and Scipione Stella, 1609).[15] Some connection between the Neapolitan tradition of "Ancidetemi" keyboard settings and Frescobaldi's contribution to the genre seems more than likely, although his version differs in at least one significant respect.[16] The Neapolitans follow the time-honored procedure, described in some detail by Diruta, of applying diminutions to each of the voices of the polyphonic model. Although their elaborations are much more fanciful than Diruta's stereotypical formulas—indeed, some ornaments are quite bizarre—the integrity of each voice is never lost, even when several voices are decorated simultaneously.

Frescobaldi's ornaments are not nearly as extravagant, but to trace the individual voices through his setting proves impossible, even if one allows for octave transfers. Neither the bass line nor the harmonic progressions are consistently preserved in his version; the only element of the original madrigal framework never distorted is the metric structure (with the exception of the penultimate chord, which is stretched to three times its original

---

[13]"che non dee questo modo di sonare stare soggetto à battuta, come ueggiamo usarsi ne i Madrigali moderni, i quali quantunq[ue] difficili si agevolano per mezzo della battuta portandola hor languida, hor veloce, è sostenendola etiandio in aria, secondo i loro affetti, ò senso delle parole," *Toccata e partite d'intavolatura di cimbalo (*Rome, 1615–16), as quoted in Frederick Hammond, *Girolamo Frescobaldi; a Guide to Research* (New York: Garland Publishing, 1988), p. 188.

[14]Girolamo Frescobaldi, *Il primo libro de madrigali* (Antwerp: Phalèse, 1608).

[15]Ascanio Mayone, *Primo libro di diversi capricci* (Naples: Vitale, 1603) and *Secondo libro di diversi capricci* (Naples: Gargano, 1609); Giovanni Maria Trabaci, *Ricercate* (Naples: Vitale 1603) and *Il secondo libro de ricercate* (Naples: Carlino, 1615); Gregorio Strozzi, *Capricci* (Naples: Novello de Bonis, 1687).

[16]See also Examples 4 and 5, and the accompanying discussion below (p. 411).

length).[17] Frescobaldi's intabulation is essentially a free interpretation of the madrigal, and, as I hope to show, an interpretation not only of its notes but also of its words.

* * * * *

The model for Frescobaldi's intabulation is a four-part madrigal from Arcadelt's celebrated *Primo libro di madrigali*.[18] This collection, although first published around 1540, continued to be much admired in Frescobaldi's time. Some fifteen editions were still issued during the first half of the seventeenth century, including one prepared by no other than Monteverdi and published in Rome in 1627, the year of the *Secondo libro di toccate*.[19] Conceivably that edition served as Frescobaldi's source;[20] in any case, it would have provided him with the untransposed version in D rather than the transposed version in G used by Trabaci and Mayone.[21]

The text is a typical example of the sixteenth-century literary madrigal genre:

> Ancidetemi pur, grievi martiri,
>   ch'el viver mi sia noia,
>   che'l morir mi sia gioia;
> ma lassat' ir gli estremi miei sospiri
>   a trovar quella ch'è cagion ch'io muoia,
> e dir a l'empia fera,
>   ch'onor non gli'è, che per amar l'io pera.

> Kill me then, heavy torments,
>   since living brings me pain,
>   and dying will bring me joy;
> but let my last sighs go,
>   to find her, who is the reason I die,
> and tell the heartless creature,
>   that it brings her no honor, that for loving her I perish.

(author unknown)

---

[17]In Gregorio Strozzi's very late setting (see note 15), chords are prolonged at several points.

[18]Modern edition in Jacobus Arcadelt, *Collected Works, vol. 2: Madrigali, Libro Primo*, ed. Albert Seay, Corpus mensurabilis musicae, 31 (n. p.: American Institute of Musicology, 1970), pp. 9–11

[19]For a list of editions, see Arcadelt, *Madrigali*, xvii.

[20]In addition to the coincidences of time and place, the following year Monteverdi's publisher Paolo Masotti brought out an edition of Frescobaldi's ensemble canzonas.

[21]Strozzi in 1687 also used thè original version in D and thought this worth noting in his title: "Ancidetemi dell' Arcadelt, diminuto nel suo proprio tono."

Generally a madrigal consists of an extended declamatory sentence, divided into a number of verses of either seven or eleven syllables. However, there is no fixed form, that is, no set convention about either the number and order of the lines or the rhyme scheme.[22] The unique form resulting from the irregular alternation of long and short lines and the continuity of thought due to the lack of distinct stanzas are very much part of the essence of madrigal poetry, and usually are reflected in the corresponding musical settings.

The madrigal poets did not search for originality in their choice of subject matter; like most madrigals, *Ancidetemi* presents the lament of a forsaken lover. Instead, the poet displayed his skill by the inventiveness of his conceits. Similarly, the *seconda prattica* composers were concerned not so much with an interpretation of the overall sense of the poem as with a translation into musical terms of the individual words—the "imitazione delle parole." Monteverdi parodies this practice in a letter to Alessandro Striggio (1627), where he writes regarding the role of Licoris in his opera *La finta pazza Licori*, "imitation is based on the single word rather than the sense of the phrase. When, therefore, war is mentioned, it will be necessary to imitate war, when peace [is mentioned], peace, when death, death, and so on," and he goes on to prescribe that when these transformations happen in a very short space of time, so must their imitation.[23] Hence, to the composer, the attractiveness of the madrigal poems lay in the opportunities these afforded for the musical rendition not only of their extravagant images, but also of their startling juxtapositions (as "living is pain, but dying is joy").

When Monteverdi named his predecessors of the *seconda prattica*, he began his list with Rore and did not include Arcadelt. Despite the importance he must have attached to the earlier composer's work—witness his subsequent edition of the *Primo libro di madrigali*—he evidently considered Rore to be the first composer to transgress musical norms in order to respond more effectively to the text. Indeed, Arcadelt is quite restrained in this madrigal and does not exploit words such as "ancidete" ("kill"), "morir"

---

[22]"Non hanno alcuna legge o nel numero de' versi, o nella maniera del rimargli" according to Pietro Bembo, as quoted in Don Harran, "Verse Types in the Early Madrigal," *Journal of the American Musicological Society* 22 (1969): 36, n. 33. This applies only to the sixteenth-century madrigal proper, not to many song texts that were loosely referred to as madrigals.

[23]I am quoting here from the translation given by Gary Tomlinson in his article "Madrigal, Monody, Monteverdi's 'Via Naturale alla immitazione,'" *Journal of the American Musicological Society*, 34 (1981): 101–102. Tomlinson evidently believed this expressed Monteverdi's philosophy of text setting at the time; a rather different interpretation was offered by Lorenzo Bianconi, who took Monteverdi's point to be that Licoris is mad, and that therefore the music should express the incoherence of his thinking—see his *Music in the Seventeenth Century*, trans. David Bryant (Cambridge: Cambridge University Press, 1987), p. 40.

("dying"), "sospiri" ("sigh"), or "pera" ("perish") in the manner of later madrigalists.

Arcadelt's setting is like a dramatic reading of the poem (Ex. 1). Each line is given a distinct musical sentence, usually terminating in some sort of cadence. As with a recitation, some lines connect smoothly to their successors, while between others there is distinct pause. Nevertheless, the succession of musical phrases—paralleling the poetic lines—is always clear.

Much of the time the voices declaim their syllables together, in a manner bordering on choral recitation. Here and there the voices become more independent and a bit of imitation is introduced, but at no point does this independence interfere with the intelligibility of the text. Because of the sobriety of the musical setting, much of the impact of the madrigal depends on the emotional effect of the text itself and on how it is sung and declaimed.

If Arcadelt's setting is played on a harpsichord, all those elements are missing: there is no text, and instead of the variety of attacks provided by the consonants and the expressive colorings of the voices, one only hears the more or less unalterable pluck of the harpsichord. Clearly, to communicate the "affetti" the intabulator must resort to other means. How this can be achieved is what I believe Frescobaldi illustrates with his intabulation, as will be shown by the following comparisons of selected excerpts of his version with the corresponding passages of the original madrigal.

The startling opening exclamation, "Ancidetemi pur" ("Kill me then!") is rendered by Arcadelt by a succession of root position chords (Ex. 2b). His setting is effective when declaimed vocally, but has little impact if played as it stands on a harpsichord. In contrast, Frescobaldi's version produces in the listener a shock and horror similar to that evoked by these words (Ex. 2a). Upon the opening incomplete A-major chord the alto intrudes with an F-natural, producing an unsettling augmented sonority (which, like most dissonances, will have an even more biting effect in a mean-tone temperament). This F continues to oscillate with its resolution on E, intensifying the effect through reiteration—a highly affective use of a typical rhetorical device. After the third iteration it "overshoots" its goal and comes momentarily to rest on another dissonance, D, pulling along the tenor to an equally dissonant B. By the third beat the voices finally settle on the A-major chord, but no sooner is this consonant sonority achieved, than, like the thrust of a dagger, a high voice enters and aims for yet another dissonance (G). Other entries follow—successively lower thrusts of the dagger—with the second voice entering on B at a diminished fifth with the highest voice. Gradually the tension subsides, and the voices come to rest on an incomplete C-major chord.

An opening exclamation like "Ancidetemi pur," which at once arouses the interest of the listener, is a common device for beginning a madrigal poem. Frescobaldi often achieves a similar effect at the beginning of his toccatas by purely musical means. While earlier composers usually commence their toccatas with a series of smooth consonant chords, Frescobaldi often throws the listener off balance by the introduction of unexpected dissonances or harmonies, marked by asterisks in Example 3. Thus, he transgresses convention to serve an imaginary text and produce the desired effect upon the listener, as decreed by the *seconda prattica.*

In the madrigal, the next phrase identifies the parties to whom the suicidal plea is addressed: the "grievi martiri," ("heavy torments"). Again, Arcadelt's setting is relatively sober, involving only a few orthodox suspensions (Ex. 4b), but not so Frescobaldi's treatment. The tormentors enter like an angry mob in a dense chorus of stretto imitation (Ex. 4a); there are altogether nine entries!

This passage is rather similar to an imitative point in the cooperative Neapolitan intabulation of *Io mi son giovinetta*—too much so to be mere coincidence—but there is a notable difference in the way both points relate to their unembellished models.[24] Montella, responsible for this segment, merely decorates the imitation in his model with neighbor and passing notes (Ex. 5), but even though imitation is also present in Frescobaldi's model,[25] it is not related to the point developed in his intabulation. The latter is superimposed on the madrigal framework, and might be called "ornamental imitation" as opposed to the "structural imitation" of the original. Today we tend not to think of imitation as an ornament, but *fuga* was in fact an often cited rhetorical figure.

The imitation found in Frescobaldi's toccatas is frequently of this ornamental type, and differs in this respect from the imitation in his canzonas or from the imitative sections in the toccatas of other composers, notably those by Froberger. Characteristically, in such imitative passages in Frescobaldi's toccatas the underlying polyphonic lines are not imitative, and the voices in such ornamental imitation usually do not enter in an orderly exposition at the interval of a fourth, fifth or octave, but may commence on any scale degree.

A second, even more extended point of imitation, not present in the model and clearly text related, appears in mm. 37–47 on the line "ma lassat'ir gli estremi miei sospiri" ("but let my last sighs go") (Ex. 6a). The motive begins on a", the highest pitch used in this piece, and gradually works its way down to low F, near the bottom of the range—perhaps a pun on "estremi" ("last," but also "extreme"). This passage, with its systematic development of imitation, does begin to resemble a segment from a canzona, although even here the voices do not enter at the customary intervals (the

---

[24] A modern edition of both the intabulation and the model can be found in Ascanio Mayone, *Diversi capricci per sonare, Libro II*, ed. Christopher Stembridge (Padua: Zanibon, 1984), pp. 40–47.

[25] It is most evident between alto and bass, but the three descending scale steps also appear twice in the soprano, and in contrary motion in the tenor.

entries of the repeated eighth-note subjects begin on a', c", e', g', d', and again on c' and e').

Sometimes one encounters the reverse procedure, that is, a point of imitation presented in the model is obscured in the intabulation. An example can be seen in mm. 47–59, on the words "a trovar quella" ("to search for her..."), in which a little "sigh" motive goes searching across the keyboard (Ex. 7a). An imitative point on *re, mi, fa, sol, mi, fa, mi, re* is heard in the parallel passage of the madrigal (alto, bass, soprano, then again bass, soprano) (Ex. 7b). In the intabulation, at first the alto and bass are given nearly identical figurations, resulting in a close canon, which breaks down, however, when the soprano enters (m. 50); from there on the model's imitative structure is no longer discernible. Note the quick imitations passing through the voices in mm. 52–54, in m. 55, and again in mm. 57–58, none relating to the much slower imitation that continues to move through the madrigal.

In Example 8, a dramatic shift of affect midway through a text phrase is reflected in the keyboard figuration. On the word "viver" ("living") one hears a playful figure, set against a relatively consonant texture, but on the word "noia" ("pain") the lines jump down to a succession of diminished sonorities—a clear example of an imitation of the individual words rather than of the meaning of the entire phrase. A similar shift can be found in mm. 63–70 (Ex. 9): the bright, diatonic C-major texture of "onor" ("honor") becomes more pressing with "amar" ("loving"), giving way to chromaticism and crushing dissonances on "pera" ("perish").

A final, particularly striking example of the "imitazione delle parole" is provided by Frescobaldi's settings of lines 3 and 5 of the poem. Although these two lines end, respectively, on the words "gioia" ("joy") and "muoia" ("die"), they are concluded by Arcadelt in identical fashion (Exx. 10b and 11b). Frescobaldi, on the other hand expresses the contrasting affects evoked by these two words; at the end of the setting of "gioia," the soprano suddenly moves up an octave before resolving the suspended d', while in the setting of "muoia" the bass descends abruptly to a low E (Exx. 10a and 11a).

Analogous musical features can be found in Frescobaldi's toccatas, and, as is the case with the poems and the vocal settings, each toccata has a unique and unpredictable form. I do not mean to suggest that the toccatas are hidden madrigals—that if one peels away the ornamentation one is left with the structural framework of a polyphonic madrigal. Such a procedure would not even work with Frescobaldi's intabulation of *Ancidetemi pur*. As was noted earlier, Frescobaldi, unlike many of his predecessors, frequently disregards the actual voicing of the original in his setting, and it would have been virtually impossible to reconstruct the madrigal if it were not known from other sources. Rather, Frescobaldi's toccatas resemble madrigals in their succession of phrases of irregular length and unpredictable, often startling content. The overall continuity is not a musical one, but that of an impassioned speech, designed to carry us to the extremes of emotion.

* * * * *

Postscript (1993)

I first presented this paper in 1981 at a meeting of the Midwest Chapter of the American Musicological Society in Chicago, and then, in a slightly revised version, at the Frescobaldi Symposium of the 1983 Boston Early Music Festival. My presentation included live musical illustrations, and at the time I was unsure how a printed version of the paper, lacking the support of those illustrations, would fare. In the intervening years the paper has circulated informally among a few colleagues and students, and their responses led me to think that a wider distribution was called for.[26] I welcome the opportunity to include it among these essays honoring my dissertation godfather, Paul Brainard; I hope that he too will find it of some interest.

Astonishing as it may seem, there probably has been more research on Frescobaldi during the past decade than during the preceding three-and-a-half centuries. At the time I wrote my paper, few scholars other than Willi Apel had published any serious work on the toccatas, but in the intervening years quite a few studies on them have appeared in print, including two monographs specifically dedicated to these works.[27] It might be worthwhile to touch upon some of the more significant efforts to penetrate their mysteries, with specific reference to the preceding paper.

Despite Willi Apel's failure, scholars have not given up the hope of discovering how Frescobaldi joined his "most diverse figures" into "an organic, meaningful whole." Their search is directed, on the one hand, toward establishing motivic and other musical connections between different sections of a toccata, and, on the other, toward uncovering a characteristic structural plan that underlies these works. Most impressive among these attempts is one by Anthony Newcomb, in which he proposes a scheme based on a standard succession of five cadentially articulated sections, differentiated

---

[26] I specifically would like to thank Claudio Annibaldi for his encouragement and his suggestions.

[27] The monographs are: Loris Azzaroni, *Ai confini della modalità: le toccate per cembalo e organo di Girolamo Frescobaldi* (Bologna: Editore CLUEB, 1986) and Heribert Klein, *Die Toccaten Girolamo Frescobaldis* (Mainz: Schott, 1989); see also the reviews by Frederick Hammond in *Music & Letters* 68 (1987): 367–69 and *Notes* 48 (1991): 479–80.

mostly by figurational and rhythmic texture.[28] He illustrates this scheme with a discussion of *Toccata nona* of the first book, showing how control of motivic development, phrase structure, harmonic prolongation, and cadential preparation work together to provide a compelling unity.[29]

Newcomb's analysis appears to be context-free; that is, he approaches the toccata as a pure musical text divorced from its original seventeenth-century context. However, in any seemingly context-free analysis, a context is usually substituted from the analyst's own experiences—in this case the context of the later eighteenth- and nineteenth-century standard repertory with its clear, harmonically defined structures and associated motivic relationships (and, furthermore, of a late twentieth-century analytical understanding of that repertory). Unfortunately, Newcomb's toccata scheme will not work like a sonata or rondo form, because early seventeenth-century music is not strongly organized by key areas and modulatory progressions. Without the support of a tonal procedure, his differentiating traits for the sections are too weak and too subjective to provide a clear formal paradigm for the toccata; he makes his scheme even more elusive by allowing repeats or skips of characteristic section types, as well as loops, that is, interruptions followed by varied retakes from earlier points in the sequence. Nevertheless, his analysis contributes perceptive and useful descriptions of the types of events encountered in the toccatas.

With regard to motivic interconnections, however, Newcomb has stacked the deck by his choice of *Toccata nona*, since within Frescobaldi's toccata practice this work is far from the norm.[30] While in other toccatas one does come across motivic or other, more subtle cross-references between remote sections (e.g., the minor-third/major-third juxtapositions in *Toccata undecima* of the first book), the surprise is how much Frescobaldi avoids them, particularly the more obvious kinds of allusions.[31] In this respect his toccatas

---

[28] Anthony Newcomb, "Guardare e ascoltare le toccate," in *Girolamo Frescobaldi nel IV centenario della nascita*, ed. Sergio Durante and Dinko Fabris (Florence: Olschki, 1986), pp. 281–300.

[29] In a single reference to Frescobaldi's intabulation, Newcomb comments that, reflecting the even pace of its model, it lacks the wide variety in speed of harmonic change encountered in the toccatas (p. 88). Although it is true that the fast-moving root progressions found especially in some toccatas of the second book are absent in the intabulation, its figurations often create the effect of chord changes during the sustained harmonies of the madrigal.

[30] Newcomb recognizes this, stating that it shows a particularly highly developed form of motivic interconnection.

[31] Much effort to establish motivic connections, both within individual toccatas and with other music, especially plainchant melodies, is shown in Klein, *Toccaten Girolamo Frescobaldis*. For the most part Klein's treatment of the toccata falls in the context-free category; he attempts to circumvent the "toccata problem" by classifying Frescobaldi's

differ not only from those of Froberger, but also from Frescobaldi's own works in other genres like the canzonas and capriccios. To my mind it suggests that he tried to avoid imposing a strong musical organization, since he was striving for a poetical organization instead.

In a companion article, a wide-ranging study that pulls together the many stylistic strands leading to Frescobaldi's toccatas, Newcomb makes an analogy between the "standard sections" of his scheme and the parts of speech as defined in rhetoric theory.[32] Other authors continue to look toward rhetoric in the hope of finding a model more in accordance with the seventeenth-century mind-set. An excellent critique of these attempts has been provided by Luigi Fernando Tagliavini, along with a survey of insights to be gained and pitfalls to be avoided.[33] Tagliavini remarks, however, that more profound analogies than between music and rhetoric can be found between music and poetics,[34] and he is one of several recent writers who relate Frescobaldi's toccatas and their *affetti* to the modern madrigals.[35] In this context, he refers to the Arcadelt intabulation and its position at the end of the toccatas in the *Libro secondo*; it is evident that his understanding of the toccatas is close to the one proposed in the present paper.

Connections between the toccata and the period's vocal art are also explored by Francesco Tasini, with ample reference to contemporary writings.[36] However, while Tagliavini and Tasini provide a rich contemporary context, they offer few specific connections between that context and the actual texts of the toccatas. I continue to believe that in his "Ancidetemi passaggiata" Frescobaldi has presented us with a kind of Rosetta stone for making those connections, that is, for showing through the art of the embellished madrigal intabulation how the art of the toccata relates to the arts of oratory and poetry.

---

toccatas into a series of distinct types, thus in a sense anihilating the genre, but his classification criteria are rather shaky.

[32]Newcomb, "Frescobaldi's Toccatas and their Stylistic Ancestry," *Proceedings of the Royal Musical Association* 3 (1984–85): 28–44.

[33]Luigi Fernando Tagliavini, "Varia frescobaldiana," *L'Organo* 21 (1983; publ. 1987): 83–128; see specifically pp. 90–117.

[34]"Ma più profonde ancora sono le analogie tra arte musicale e arte poetica," Tagliavini, p. 88.

[35]See also Klein, *Toccaten Girolamo Frescobaldis,* p. 27. Klein cites as evidence for an affinity between the toccata and madrigal, an observation attributed to W. Richard Shindle that the beginning of Giovanni de Macque's *Toccata a modo di trombette* is identical to that composer's madrigal *Io piango, o Filli.* However, Klein appears to have misinterpreted Shindle's remark, which merely noted similarity in the handling of chromaticism (letter of July 25, 1992 from Dr. Shindle).

[36]Francesco Tasini, "'Vocalità' strumentale della toccata frescobaldiana: un linguaggio tradito," *Musica/Realtà* 4 (1983): 143–62; see especially pp. 153–54.

416 Alexander Silbiger

Musical Examples

Example 1. Arcadelt, *Ancidetemi pur*

From Madrigal to Toccata 417

Example 1 (*continued*)

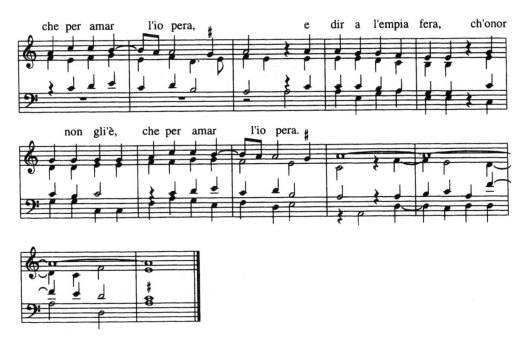

Example 2. Frescobaldi/Arcadelt, *Ancidetemi,* mm. 1–4

Example 3. Frescobaldi, *Secondo libro de toccate*: Openings of Toccatas III, IV, V, X, and XI

Example 4. Frescobaldi/Arcadelt, *Ancidetemi*, mm. 4–10

Example 5. Montella/Ferrabosco, *Io mi son giovinetta,* mm. 4–6

422 Alexander Silbiger

Example 6. Frescobaldi/Arcadelt, *Ancidetemi,* mm. 37–47

From Madrigal to Toccata 423

Example 6 (*continued*)

424 Alexander Silbiger

Example 7. Frescobaldi/Arcadelt, *Ancidetemi,* mm. 47–59

From Madrigal to Toccata 425

Example 7 (*continued*)

Example 8. Frescobaldi/Arcadelt, *Ancidetemi*, mm. 1–4

From Madrigal to Toccata 427

Example 9. Frescobaldi/Arcadelt, *Ancidetemi*, mm. 63–70

Example 10. Frescobaldi/Arcadelt, *Ancidetemi,* mm. 34–36

Example 11. Frescobaldi/Arcadelt, *Ancidetemi,* mm. 57–59

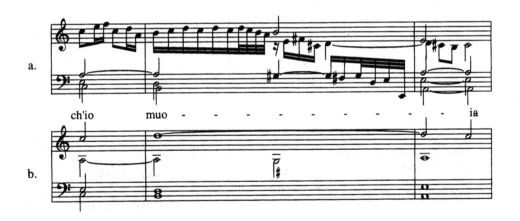

Beethoven and Shakespeare

Caldwell Titcomb

The yoking of the names of Beethoven and Shakespeare is far from novel. Indeed the composer himself was aware of such pairings, and copied one example into the so-called *Tagebuch*, a combination of diary and commonplace book he kept from 1812 to 1818. In 1816, Beethoven wrote down in French a quotation, hitherto unidentified: "Unfortunately, mediocre talents are condemned to imitate the faults of the great masters without appreciating their virtues—whence the harm that Michelangelo does to painting, Shakespeare to dramatic art, and nowadays Beethoven to music."[1]

Already in 1810, E. T. A. Hoffmann had made the comparison in his pioneering review-essay of the Fifth Symphony (the first of five such articles on Beethoven):

> Just as the aesthetic surveyors have often complained of a complete lack of true unity and inner coherence in Shakespeare, while only those of deeper vision have witnessed the springing forth of a beautiful tree, buds and leaves, blossoms and fruits, from a germinal seed—so too will only a very deep penetration into the inner structure of Beethoven's music reveal the great extent of the master's self-possession.[2]

A reviewer who signed himself "K. B." [Karl Bernard] said of Beethoven in 1814: "Perhaps the originality of his most accomplished works is to be compared only with the originality of Shakespeare's." The next year, Amadeus Wendt wrote a lengthy article on Beethoven, in which he spoke of calling the composer "the musical Shakespeare" and iterated the comparison later. In 1816, Friedrich Mosengeil referred to Beethoven as "the

---

[1] An annotated translation of the whole *Tagebuch* is contained in Maynard Solomon, *Beethoven Essays* (Cambridge: Harvard University Press, 1988), pp. 233–95. The French text is printed in George Marek, *Beethoven* (New York: Crowell, 1969), p. 426, and, with a facsimile of the earliest surviving manuscript copy, in Maynard Solomon, *Beethovens Tagebuch*, ed. Sieghard Brandenburg (Bonn: Beethoven-Haus, 1990), pp. 84–85.

[2] Translation by F. John Adams Jr. in Elliot Forbes's edition of the symphony (New York: W. W. Norton, 1971), p. 153; a different translation is in Oliver Strunk, *Source Readings in Music History* (New York: W. W. Norton, 1950), p. 778. The German is reprinted in Stefan Kunze, ed., *Ludwig van Beethoven: Die Werke im Spiegel seiner Zeit* (Laaber: Laaber-Verlag, 1987), p. 102.

Shakespeare of the musical world." And, looking back shortly after Beethoven's death, Gottfried Wilhelm Fink in 1828 stated: "We might thus compare him not with Byron, but preferably with Shakespeare and with our Goethe."[3]

Wearing his critic's hat, Schumann, appraising a batch of new symphonies in 1839, opened by saying: "When the German speaks of symphonies, he is speaking of Beethoven." And after references to Italy, France, and England, he tops off by saying that the German "even dares to put him on a par with Shakespeare." About the same time, Wolfgang Griepenkerl published a novel entitled *Das Musikfest oder die Beethovener*. At one point there is talk of some scenes in *King Lear*, whereupon the character Adalbert exclaims, "Beethoven is Shakespeare's brother!" And in 1854, the British critic Henry Chorley looked back on hearing Beethoven's symphonies played in Leipzig during 1839, and called them "works of the Shakespeare of Music."[4]

Three of the titans of 19th-century composition chimed in. Berlioz, speaking of revelations at the outset of his career in 1828, wrote in his memoirs: "Directly, at another point on the horizon, I saw Beethoven's giant form looming. The shock I received from it was almost comparable to what Shakespeare has given me. Beethoven opened up to me a new world of music, as the poet had unveiled a new universe of poetry." Then, late in life (1864), he dined with his son Louis and the musician Stephen Heller: "Towards evening, while strolling along the bank of the Seine, we talked of Shakespeare and Beethoven, and we arrived, I recall, at a state of extreme exaltation."[5]

Similarly, Wagner in his autobiography reported being overwhelmed by Beethoven at the age of 15:

> There arose in me an image of the sublimest unearthly originality, with which absolutely nothing could compare. This image fused in me with that

---

[3]German texts in Kunze, pp. 601, 177–78, 312, 616.

[4]Robert Schumann, *Gesammelte Schriften über Musik und Musiker* (Leipzig: Georg Wigand, 1854), 3:133; W. R. Griepenkerl, *Das Musikfest oder die Beethovener*, enlarged ed. (Braunschweig: Eduard Leibrock, 1841), pp. 80–81 [1st ed. 1838]; Henry F. Chorley, *Modern German Music*, 2 vols. (London: Smith, Elder & Co., 1854; repr. New York: Da Capo, 1973), 2:32.

[5]Hector Berlioz, *Mémoires* (Paris: Calmann-Lévy, 1870), 1:110, 2:393. The best English edition is that of David Cairns (New York: Knopf, 1969; rev. New York: W. W. Norton, 1975).

of Shakespeare: in ecstatic dreams I met both, saw and spoke to them; on waking up I was bathed in tears.[6]

In honor of the composer's centennial in 1870, Wagner wrote a long essay, "Beethoven," in the middle of which he refers to Shakespeare more than a dozen times, as here: "Thus Shakespeare remained wholly incomparable until German genius brought forth in Beethoven a being analogically explicable only in comparison with him."[7] In the same year Cosima Wagner records in her diary that the mention of a line from *Hamlet* "brings [Wagner] to a comparison between Shakespeare and Beethoven; as in Shakespeare the characters, so in Beethoven the melodies—unmistakable, incomparable, an entire, inexplicable world." In 1872, she says, he exclaimed: "Oh, to meet someone like Beethoven! That was the dream of my early youth; not being able to do it, no longer seeing such men as Shakespeare and Beethoven about, has made me melancholy throughout my life." And, towards the end of his life, he once more talked of Beethoven: "If only one had known, had seen a being like that!...I have seen both him and Shakespeare in my dreams—towards me always gently consoling."[8]

Brahms, speaking in a letter of owning the works of Beethoven and Shakespeare, said; "For this pair no youth should have to wait long; but, once he owns them, he need not run rapidly after any others. In these two he has the whole world."[9] And Brahms's close friend Joseph Joachim, violinist and composer, wrote in a letter: "Beethoven...more than any other has a deep understanding of the human soul. He is the Shakespeare of music."[10]

Such comparisons were by no means restricted to musicians. Delacroix, in a journal entry, recorded that a painting student visited his studio and their talk turned to Beethoven: "We compared him to Shakespeare." Victor Hugo's 1864 volume *William Shakespeare*, which roams far beyond its title, contains a book on "Geniuses." He states there: "Music is the Verb of Germany....Germany's greatest poets are her musicians, of which wonderful family Beethoven is the head." He proceeds to name what he considers the supreme figure in each of a series of cultures, and ends with "Shakespeare, the great Englishman; Beethoven, the great German." And T. S. Eliot, in his 1930 essay "Poetry and Propaganda," states that "the

---

[6]Richard Wagner, *Mein Leben*, 2 vols. (Munich: F. Bruckmann, 1911), 1:41.

[7]Richard Wagner, *Gesammelte Schriften und Dichtungen*, 2nd ed., 10 vols. (Leipzig: E. W. Frietzsch, 1887–88), 9:106–107.

[8]Geoffrey Skelton, trans., *Cosima Wagner's Diaries,* 2 vols. (New York/London: Harcourt Brace, 1978), 1:250 [31 July 1870], 527 [23 Aug. 1872]; 2:614 [4 Feb. 1881].

[9]Quoted in Robert Haven Schauffler, *The Unknown Brahms* (New York: Crown, 1933), p. 216.

[10]Nora Bickley, trans., *Letters from and to Joseph Joachim* (New York: Macmillan, 1914; repr. New York: Vienna House, 1972), p. 19 [7 Apr. 1853].

philosophy of Shakespeare is quite a different thing from that of Dante; it really has more in common with, let us say, the philosophy of Beethoven."[11]

But enough of these prefatory comparisons. Let us proceed to ask exactly how familiar Beethoven was with Shakespeare and what impact the British playwright had on him.

As is well known, Beethoven's formal education was skimpy, probably covering no more than the years from six to eleven. He never managed to master spelling or elementary arithmetic.[12] But he did develop considerable intellectual curiosity, and in the course of time acquired some French along with a little Latin, Italian and English.[13] The greatest early stimulus came from his association with the von Breuning family, whom he met when he was 14 or 15. The widow Hélène became a second mother to Beethoven, and it was in her family and circle of friends that he was introduced to the world of books—classics, poetry, modern literature.[14]

During Beethoven's youth, the Bonn theater was only intermittently active. There were a few performances of Shakespeare. Frida Knight tells us: "As a 12-year-old boy at the court of Bonn he must have seen Shakespeare performed: *Lear, Falstaff* [based on *Merry Wives of Windsor*], *Richard III* were played there in the year 1783 alone."[15] There is, however, no evidence for his attendance; the "must have seen" could just as well read "likely did not see."

It is more probable that Beethoven first came into contact with Shakespeare at second hand, through musical adaptations. He could have seen Georg Benda's 1776 opera *Romeo und Julie* (libretto by Friedrich Gotter), the first of a long series of musical versions of the play, which was staged in Bonn on 8 May 1782. We are on firmer ground, however, when we recall that the Elector established a National Theater with an emphasis on opera, opening in January of 1789. Beethoven played the keyboard at rehearsals

---

[11]Eugène Delacroix, *Journal*, 3 vols. (Paris: E. Plon, 1893–95), 1:274 [27 Feb. 1847]; Victor Hugo, *William Shakespeare*, trans. A. Baillot (Boston: Dana Estes, 1892?), pp. 74–75 [Part I, Book 2, Chap. 4]; Morton Zabel, ed., *Literary Opinion in America*, 3rd ed., 2 vols. (Gloucester, Mass.: Peter Smith, 1968), 1:105 [the Eliot essay reprinted here originally appeared in *The Bookman* 70 (Feb. 1930): 595–602].

[12]Elliot Forbes, ed., *Thayer's Life of Beethoven*, rev. ed. [hereafter Th-F] (Princeton: Princeton University Press, 1970), pp. 58–59; Marek, pp. 41–42.

[13]One extensive account is J. G. Prod'homme's "Beethoven's Intellectual Education," *Musical Quarterly* 13 (1927): 169–82.

[14]Th-F, pp. 108–109; Marek, pp. 65–67.

[15]Frida Knight, "Britain in Beethoven's Mind," *Bericht über den Internationalen Beethoven-Kongress 1977*), ed. Harry Goldschmidt, Karl-Heinz Köhler, and Konrad Niemann (Leipzig: VEB Deutscher Verlag, 1978), p. 285.

and the viola in performances. We know that Beethoven was in the orchestra when the Benda opera was performed in the spring of 1789 and again during the following season. And he would have participated in Captain Ferdinand d'Antoine's (now lost) two-act Singspiel *Ende gut, Alles gut*, based on Shakespeare's *All's Well That Ends Well*, which had its premiere on 9 May 1792.[16] In November of that year, Beethoven left Bonn forever and took up residence in Vienna.

It was during his decades in Vienna that Beethoven truly came to value Shakespeare. A number of people who knew him bore witness. For instance, the French diplomat Baron de Trémont reported visiting the composer in 1809: "We would talk philosophy, religion, politics, and especially of Shakespeare, his idol." The Baron postulated some reasons that led Beethoven "to make a study of the Greek and Latin authors and, enthusiastically, of Shakespeare."[17] Recounting an 1825 visit to Beethoven, Sarah Burney Paine stated that "his admiration for Shakespeare is indeed very great."[18] And the composer's factotum Anton Schindler included in the 1840 edition of his biography (but deleted from the 1860 edition) his assertion that "Shakespeare and no other was his *poète de prédilection*," and that he knew Shakespeare "as thoroughly as he did his own scores."[19]

Beethoven's knowledge of the dramatist came above all from reading him in translation.[20] The story of German Shakespeare translations, in the wake of the first attempt, Caspar von Borck's version of *Julius Caesar* in 1741, is rather complex.[21] For Beethovenian purposes, the translations listed in Table 1 will suffice.

---

[16]Th-F, pp. 31, 97–98; Marek, pp. 60–61.

[17]Oscar G. Sonneck, ed., *Beethoven: Impressions by His Contemporaries* (New York: G. Schirmer, 1926; repr. New York: Dover, 1967), p. 72.

[18]Donald MacArdle, "Shakespeare and Beethoven," *Musical Times* 105 (Apr. 1964): 260.

[19]Anton Schindler, *Biographie von Ludwig van Beethoven* (Münster: Aschendorff, 1840), p. 261.

[20]For an overview of his general reading, see the Prod'homme article already cited, and Archibald M. Henderson, "Beethoven as a Reading Man," *Monthly Musical Record* 58 (1 Dec. 1928): 355–56, essentially reprinted as "Beethoven as a Reader," *Musical Opinion* 79 (Apr. 1956): 407.

[21]A particularly useful survey is Gisbert Freiherr Vincke, "Zur Geschichte der deutschen Shakespeare-Übersetzungen," *Shakespeare Jahrbuch* 16 (1881): 254–73. See also F. W. Meisnest, "Wieland's Translation of Shakespeare," *Modern Language Review* 9/1 (Jan. 1914): 12–40; George Leuca, "Wieland and the Introduction of Shakespeare into Germany," *German Quarterly* 28/4 (Nov. 1955): 247–54; John A. McCarthy, *Christoph Martin Wieland* (Boston: Twayne, 1979), pp. 39–41; Marion Candler Lazenby, *The Influence of Wieland and Eschenburg on Schlegel's Shakespeare Translation* (Baltimore: Johns Hopkins University, 1942); Henry Lüdeke, "Ludwig Tieck's erste

In a letter of 1809 to his Leipzig publisher, Beethoven asks to be told what the cost would be for "the complete works of Wieland in a small format—If I decide to buy them, I would rather purchase them in Leipzig, for all the editions here are garbled and expensive."[22] Of course, Wieland was a noted poet and novelist as well as a translator of Shakespeare.

The next spring, in a letter to Therese Malfatti, with whom Beethoven was then infatuated and who was staying at the family estate in Mödling a few miles south of Vienna, he asked: "Have you read Goethe's *Wilhelm Meister* and Shakespeare in Schlegel's translation? One has so much leisure in the country. Perhaps you would like me to send you these works."[23] Clearly the composer owned or had access to the Schlegel edition (Table 1, No. 4), whose final volume appeared that year. This gives the lie to the notoriously unreliable Schindler's assertion that Beethoven "refused to have anything to do with Schlegel's translation of the great Briton: he pronounced it stiff, forced, and at times too far from the original, which he could deduce only by comparing it with Eschenburg's version."[24] In 1816, Fanny Giannatasio recorded in her diary that Beethoven came to spend the evening with her family and brought his Shakespeare along with him.[25]

We find further information in several of the 137 Conversation Books that survive from Beethoven's last decade; through these it was possible to carry on a dialogue with the increasingly deaf composer. In June of 1824, Beethoven's young nephew Karl wrote that a bookseller was advertising a subscription for a new Shakespeare translation—that by Meyer (Table 1, No. 7). Beethoven had clearly seen the same notice, for he scribbled down: "and pure English with German annotations"—a reference to the same publisher's companion edition providing the Bard's original text along with

---

Shakespeare-Übersetzung," *Shakespeare Jahrbuch* 57 (1921): 54–64; Alois Brandl, "Ludwig Fulda, Paul Heyse und Adolf Wilbrandt über die Schlegel-Tiecksche Shakespeare-Übersetzung," *Shakespeare Jahrbuch* 37 (1901): xxxvii–lv; J. G. Robertson, "Shakespeare on the Continent," *Cambridge History of English Literature* 5 (1910): 322, 327–34, 337–40; Lawrence M. Price, *English Literature in Germany* (Berkeley: University of California Press, 1953), pp. 234–39, 270–81; Roy Pascal, *Shakespeare in Germany 1740–1815* (Cambridge: Cambridge University Press, 1937), pp. 191–99 (chronological table).

[22]Emily Anderson, ed., *The Letters of Beethoven,* 3 vols. (New York: St. Martin's Press, 1961), 1:243 (Letter No. 226, 19 Sept. 1809).

[23]Anderson, 1:273 (Letter No. 258, May 1810).

[24]Anton Schindler, *Beethoven as I Knew Him,* ed. Donald MacArdle & trans. Constance Jolly [hereafter Schindler/MacArdle] (New York: W.W. Norton, 1972), pp. 378, 393.

[25]A. W. Thayer, *Ludwig van Beethovens Leben,* ed. Hermann Dieters & Hugo Riemann (Leipzig: Breitkopf & Härtel, 1907), 4:528 (23 Mar. 1816) [Anhang II].

Table 1

German translations of Shakespeare

1. Christoph Wieland, 8 vols. (Zürich: Orell, Gessner & Co., 1762–66).

    Twenty-two plays, all in prose except *Midsummer Night's Dream*; many omissions, with summaries substituted.

2. Johann Eschenburg, 13 vols. (Zürich: Orell, Gessner, Füesslin & Co., 1775–77 & 1782).

    Incorporated Wieland, filling gaps and adding 15 plays (plus 6 spurious ones); all in prose except *Richard III*.

3. Gabriel Eckert, ed., 22 vols. (Strassburg & Mannheim: Franz Levrault, 1778–79 & 1783).

    Pirated version of Eschenburg, with corrections.

4. August Wilhelm Schlegel, 9 vols. (Berlin: G. Reimer, 1797–1801 & 1810).

    Seventeen plays in blank verse.

5. A. W. Schlegel & Ludwig Tieck, 9 parts (Berlin: G. Reimer, 1825–33).

    Ludwig oversaw the project, but the actual translations added to Schlegel's 17 were 6 by his daughter Dorothea Tieck and 12 by her husband Wolf von Baudissin.

6. The Voss family, 9 vols. (Leipzig: F. A. Brockhaus [1–3] and Stuttgart: J. B. Metzler [4–9], 1818–29).

    Verse translations by Johann Heinrich Voss (13 plays), and his sons Heinrich (14 plays) and Abraham (9 plays).

7. Joseph Meyer [and others], 52 booklets (Gotha: Hennings, 1824–33).

    Cheap pocket edition; free adaptations of the entire canon plus the spurious plays.

a German critique and notes for each play by Meyer.[26] The next month Beethoven jotted down this entry: "& Shakespeare / remit money" (*KH* 6:308), so it would appear that he had decided to subscribe to the edition. Or at least *some* edition, since Karl in late June of 1825 wrote down the amount paid for Shakespeare, the amount due later, and the overall total. (*KH* 7:306) In the meantime (December, 1824), Karl had informed his uncle that there was an advertisement for a mammoth edition of classic foreign drama, which proclaimed Shakespeare "the greatest of the poets"— the publication incorporating Meyer's versions of the Bard along with works of Corneille, Calderon, etc. (*KH* 7:36, 354)

In June of 1823, the 16-year-old lad told Beethoven that, on his nameday, he had to recite in English the "To be or not to be" soliloquy from *Hamlet*. (*KH* 3:336) At the end of August he asked his uncle, "Are you of the opinion that Shakespeare was a greater genius than Schiller?" Beethoven obviously gave his vote to the Briton, for Karl replied, "That's what people generally say. But I prefer Schiller." (*KH* 4:47)

The youth was not the only person to talk with Beethoven about Shakespeare. The composer's friend Franz Oliva referred to the playwright's *King John* in December of 1819; and the next month Oliva gave Beethoven the traditional explanation that Shakespeare wrote *The Merry Wives of Windsor* because Queen Elizabeth wanted to see *Henry IV*'s Falstaff in love. (*KH* 1:111, 228, 443, 471) Beethoven's intimate friend Karl Holz commented in August of 1825 that "Shakespeare is the eternal paragon," and asserted the next April: "I think that Beethoven is as little likely to be surpassed as Raphael or Shakespeare." (*KH* 8:35; 9:172) And in one of the last recorded chats, a few days before Beethoven's death in March 1827, Schindler talked with the composer about Aristotle's theory of tragedy and how Euripides fell short. As to any pitfall, Schindler commented, "Shakespeare has at all times avoided this."[27]

On 5 November 1827, an auction was held to dispose of Beethoven's estate. The inventory listed "Shakespeare's Plays," without specifying the edition.[28] Prior to this, however, Schindler had taken some books from Beethoven's personal library for his own purposes. About a dozen of these

---

[26]Karl-Heinz Köhler, Grita Herre, and Dagmar Beck, eds., *Ludwig van Beethovens Konversationshefte* [hereafter *KH*], 10 vols. so far (Leipzig: VEB Deutscher Verlag, 1968–93), 6:261, 418.

[27]Martin Hurlimann, ed., *Beethoven: Briefe und Gespräche* (Zürich: Atlantis, 1944), pp. 215–16. See also Marek, p. 626. (The definitive *KH* edition has, at this writing, reached only to early December of 1826.)

[28]Albert Leitzmann, *Ludwig van Beethoven*, 2nd ed. (Leipzig: Insel-Verlag, 1921), 2:383.

have survived to the present and are now in the German State Library in Berlin. One of the books is an 1825 reprint of Schlegel's translation of Shakespeare's *The Tempest*. Also included are two double volumes (3/4 and 9/10) of the pirated Eschenburg translation (No. 3 in my list).[29]

What is most noteworthy about the Eschenburg volumes, which contain eight plays, is that six of the dramas show heavy use by Beethoven through such things as dog-ears, underlinings, question marks and exclamation points. Credit belongs to one of Beethoven's early biographers, Ludwig Nohl, for gathering and first publishing in a small book the passages—from Homer, Shakespeare, Goethe and others—marked by Beethoven himself, with occasional notations by Nohl as to their probable significance.[30] Nohl numbered the Shakespearean passages from 1 to 31, a total passed on by subsequent scholars. But a check against the English originals shows that the proper total is 37, distributed as follows:

Othello	10
Romeo and Juliet	3
Much Ado About Nothing	1
All's Well That Ends Well	2
The Merchant of Venice	19
The Winter's Tale	2

The excerpts range from half a line to 20 lines.[31] In *Othello*, Beethoven marked Brabantio's line (1.3.191) "I had rather to adopt a child than get

---

[29]The whole list of these books is in Leitzmann, 2:380; also in Eveline Bartlitz, *Die Beethoven-Sammlung in der Musikabteilung der Deutschen Staatsbibliothek: Verzeichnis* (Berlin: Deutsche Staatsbibliothek, 1970), pp. 207–18. See also Paul Nettl, *Beethoven Encyclopedia* (New York: Philosophical Library, 1956), pp. 185–87 (entry: "Reading").

[30]Ludwig Nohl, ed., *Beethovens Brevier* (Leipzig: E. J. Günther, 1870).

[31]I use the text and act/scene/line numbering of *The Riverside Shakespeare*, ed. G. Blakemore Evans (Boston: Houghton Mifflin, 1974), which Marvin Spevack adopted as the basis for his *Harvard Concordance to Shakespeare* (Cambridge: Harvard University Press, 1973). Here are the passages marked by Beethoven. *Othello*: 1.2.19–20; 1.3.106, 113–14, 191, 204–207, 218–19, 224–25; 2.1.187–89; 4.3.104–105; 5.2.7. *Romeo*: 2.2.68; 2.5.4–6; 2.6.9–15. *Much Ado*: 1.3.5–7. *All's Well*: 1.1.39–45, 65–66. *Merchant*: 1.1.74–75, 114–18; 1.2.8–9, 18–19; 1.3.179; 2.3.18–19; 2.6.36–39; 2.9.41–49; 3.2.131–38; 3.3.18–23; 4.1.68, 115–16, 130–32, 163–64, 184–87, 267–71; 5.1.69–88, 90–91, 107–108. *Winter's Tale*: 1.2.92–94; 3.2.54–57.

[i.e. beget] it" with "???!" Nohl and Marek (who reprints some of the marked passages) are surely correct in associating this with the composer's stormy custody battle over his nephew Karl.[32] Half of the excerpts come from *The Merchant of Venice*. It is easy to understand why Beethoven might repeatedly turn to a play in which society bands together against the solitary Shylock. One thinks of a sentiment such as Beethoven expressed in his "Heiligenstadt Testament" of 1802: "I must live almost alone like one who has been banished, I can mix with society only as much as true necessity demands."[33] The composer marked the merchant Antonio's statement, "The weakest kind of fruit / drops earliest to the ground" (4.1.115–16)—of which Marek rightly says that "the need for being strong" was one of Beethoven's "dominant beliefs." Beethoven's *Tagebuch* entry "Endurance. Resignation. Resignation." is only one of many echoes.[34] The longest passage marked (Nohl, 12–13) is Lorenzo's arietta about "the sweet power of music" (5.1.69–88)—an excerpt that ought to appeal to any musician. There can be no doubt how Beethoven responded to his nephew's question in an 1823 Conversation Book: "How do you like *The Merchant of Venice*?" (*KH* 3:322)

His acquaintance with Shakespeare led Beethoven to some of his little jests. In April of 1820, he had occasion to write to Carlo Boldrini, a partner in the Artaria publishing firm, who, like Shakespeare's "fat knight," was extremely corpulent. Beethoven's handwritten address said: "To Sir John Falstaff / deliver to H. Artaria / and Company." The letter's salutation is: "Most Excellent Falstaff!" And towards the end, the composer says: "All good wishes, Sir Falstaff, do not be too dissolute." The next autumn, another letter to the firm bears the salutation: "Highly born Herren Artaria, Falstaff & Kompagnie."[35]

A close member of Beethoven's circle was the violinist Ignaz Schuppanzigh, who played much of the composer's music and admired him enormously. Like Boldrini, Schuppanzigh was excessively fat. In a letter to another intimate, Ferdinand Ries, Beethoven said that the violinist "might be grateful to me if my insults were to make him slimmer." When in 1823 Schuppanzigh returned to Vienna from several years in Russia, Beethoven welcomed him back by sending him a five-voice canon (WoO 184), whose

---

[32] Nohl, p. 3; Marek, p. 182.

[33] Th-F, p. 304.

[34] Marek, p. 182; Solomon, *Beethoven Essays*, p. 272. For some highly speculative interpretations of Beethoven's markings, see Luigi Magnani, "Beethoven as a Reader of Shakespeare," *English Miscellany* 24 (Rome, 1973–74): 331–46.

[35] Anderson, 2:888 (Letter No. 1017, 8 Apr. 1820), 904 (Letter No. 1036, 26 Oct. 1820).

entire text was: "Falstafferel, let us see you." The composer addressed it thus: "To the Highly Born / Mr. von Schuppanzig / sprung / from the old English / noble family / of Milord Fallstaf. / See Schakespeare's biography / of Mylord Fallstaf."[36]

In February of 1825, Beethoven sent the violinist a letter that concluded: "I shall let you know as soon as that machine of mine is ready enabling you to be lifted up quite comfortably to me on the fourth floor"—an apparent reference to the query Falstaff put to Prince Hal in *1 Henry IV:* "Have you any levers to lift me up again, being down?"[37] Sir George Smart recorded in his diary that he had attended a dinner party in Vienna on 11 September 1825, with Schuppanzigh at the head of the table. Smart reported that "Beethoven calls Schuppanzigh Sir John Falstaff, not a bad name considering the figure of this excellent violin player."[38]

Beethoven had not always spoken laudatorily or jocularly of Schuppanzigh. In an 1801 letter to his friend Karl Amenda, Beethoven called Schuppanzigh and cellist Nikolaus Zmeskall "miserable egoists," adding that "I regard [them] merely as instruments on which to play when I feel inclined....I value them merely for what they do for me." Here he seemed to be thinking of Hamlet's musically punning speech ending, "Call me what instrument you will, though you fret me, yet you cannot play upon me."[39]

Beethoven took another nickname from Shakespeare. In the summer of 1825, he met little Gerhard von Breuning, then 12 years of age, to whom he took a great fancy. Unlike most adults, the boy enjoyed free rein of the composer's lodgings, and during Beethoven's last months gladly ran all sorts of errands around town. Because of the lad's "lightness of foot" and his service as a "tireless messenger," Beethoven called him Ariel in honor of the sprite who served Prospero in *The Tempest.*[40]

The Vienna in which Beethoven lived from 1792 until his death was theatrically the most active city in the German-speaking world. It was able to support a half dozen important theaters: the court theater in the Hofburg

---

[36]Anderson, 1:111 (Letter No. 92, 14 July 1804); 3:1027–28 (Letter No. 1168, 26 Apr. 1823). The misspellings are Beethoven's. For the German text of the Schuppanzigh inscription, see Georg Kinsky, *Das Werk Beethovens* (Munich/Duisburg: G. Henle, 1955), p. 687.

[37]Anderson, 3:1177 (Letter No. 1350, Feb. 1825); *1 Henry IV*: 2.2.34–35.

[38]H. Bertram Cox & C. L. E. Cox, eds., *Leaves From the Journals of Sir George Smart* (London: Longmans, Green, 1907; repr. New York: Da Capo, 1971), p. 114. For a lithograph and caricature of Schuppanzigh, see H. C. Robbins Landon, ed., *Beethoven: A Documentary Study* (New York: Macmillan, 1970), p. 117.

[39]Anderson, 1:64 (Letter No. 53, 1 July 1801); *Hamlet*: 3.2.364–72.

[40]Th-F, p. 968; Marek, p. 600.

(opened 1700; renovated 1748; established by Emperor Josef II in 1776 as the National Theater, known as the Burgtheater; site of the premieres of Beethoven's *Prometheus* ballet and *Egmont* music; demolished 1888); the Kärntnerthor Theater (1709; enlarged after a fire, 1763; site of Ninth Symphony and *Missa Solemnis* premieres; operated until 1869); the Leopoldstadt Theater (1781; headed for a decade by the playwright Karl Friedrich Hensler, a friend of Beethoven's; demolished 1847); the Freihaus Theater auf der Wieden, known as the Wiedner Theater (1787; site of Mozart's *Magic Flute* premiere during reign of impresario Emanuel Schikaneder, who headed the theater from 1789 until its closing in 1801); the Josefstadt Theater (1788; frequently rebuilt and enlarged, notably in 1822, for which occasion Beethoven wrote *The Consecration of the House* Overture; still in use); and the Theater-an-der-Wien (1801; built by Schikaneder with *Magic Flute* profits; site of numerous Beethoven premieres; still in use).[41]

Beethoven maintained a lively interest in theatrical activities. Indeed, for much of the period 1803–1808 he enjoyed free lodging in the Theater-an-der-Wien itself,[42] and could not possibly have remained unaffected by its offerings. It is not certain how long he continued to attend plays, owing to his hearing difficulties. But in a letter of 1812, he wrote of seeing Zacharias Werner's romantic tragedy *Wanda*.[43] And as late as 1818, he wrote to the head of the Burgtheater, Josef Schreyvogel, returning some unused tickets and asking for new ones: "If hitherto I have not frequented the theater as often as formerly, my poor health is chiefly the reason. But now I am feeling better and shall be able to take more interest in the theater."[44] Yet this was the time he began to resort to Conversation Books.

The Conversation Books are nonetheless peppered with references to actors, actresses, playwrights, and managers—some of whom Beethoven knew personally. For instance, there was Friedrich Baumann, especially admired for his comic roles, who acted in the Leopoldstadt Theater, the Kärntnerthor Theater, and the Burgtheater from 1781 to 1822. Beethoven sent him a letter in 1807, which carried the salutation "Friend, great phi-

---

[41]See Marvin Carlson, *The German Stage in the Nineteenth Century* (Metuchen, N. J.: Scarecrow Press, 1972), pp. 52–53; Andrea Seebohm, ed., *The Vienna Opera* (New York: Rizzoli, 1987), pp. 9–30; Kurt Honolka, *Papageno: Emanuel Schikaneder*, trans. Jane Mary Wilde, (Portland, Ore.: Amadeus Press, 1990), pp. 73–76, 187–88. For views of the interiors, see Robbins Landon, pp. 123 (Burgtheater), 234 (Theater-an-der-Wien), 343 (Josefstadt Theater), and Robert Winter & Bruce Carr, eds., *Beethoven, Performers, and Critics* (Detroit: Wayne State University Press, 1980), p. 85 (Kärntnerthor Theater).
[42]Th-F, p. 1109.
[43]Anderson, 1:369 (Letter No. 367, Mar. or Apr. 1812).
[44]Anderson, 2:774 (Letter No. 908, 24 Nov. 1818).

losopher and comedian!!!" And in 1813, Beethoven reported getting oral advice from Baumann on what prices to charge for his impending concerts.[45]

Shakespeare in Vienna began in 1771–73, when five plays were mounted, most famously the premiere of Franz von Heufeld's "happy ending" version of *Hamlet* with Josef Lange in the title role (16 Jan. 1773). A still brighter period came in 1780–1785, when Friedrich Ludwig Schröder, the foremost German actor of his time (some would say of *all* time), was guest artist at the Burgtheater. Under his auspices ten Shakespeare plays took the stage there.[46]

But during Beethoven's early Vienna years, Shakespeare turned up only sporadically. The composer might have seen *Die Quälgeister*, an adaptation of *Much Ado About Nothing*, in 1793; *King Lear*, with the visiting star Ferdinand Iffland, in 1801; and *Merry Wives of Windsor* in 1806. The aforementioned Josef Lange had the title role in an important production of Schiller's *Macbeth* adaptation in 1808, followed by his Othello in 1810, just prior to his retirement, with Nikolaus Heurteur taking on this part in the 1814 revival. Schikaneder, who had himself acted Hamlet, Macbeth, Iago, and Richard III in 1777 as a young man in Nuremberg, mounted a *Hamlet* in 1802 on the stage of his new Theater-an-der-Wien, which would later house productions of *Henry IV* (1807), *King Lear* (1808), and *Julius Caesar* (1810, with incidental music by Beethoven's friend Ignaz Seyfried, conductor of the *Fidelio* premiere).[47]

The high point came during the reign of Josef Schreyvogel, who ran the Burgtheater from 1814 to 1832. Not only did he insist on fielding an ensemble of absolutely sterling players, but he also brought an unusually serious attitude to the presentation of Shakespeare—and this in the face of strictures by the Viennese censors. He mounted brand new and reasonably faithful productions of eight works by Shakespeare: *Romeo and Juliet* (1816), *King Lear* (1822), *Othello* (1823), *Hamlet* (1825), and, after Beethoven's death, *The Merchant of Venice* (1827), *All's Well That Ends*

---

[45]Anderson, 1:178 (Letter No. 155, Oct. 1807), 431 (Letter No. 443, Dec. 1813).

[46]Eduard Wlassack, *Chronik des k.k. Hof-Burgtheaters* (Vienna: L. Rosner, 1876), pp. 53–59; Hans Knudsen, *Deutsch Theater-Geschichte*, 2nd ed. (Stuttgart: Kröner, 1970), pp. 205–209; Simon Williams, *Shakespeare on the German Stage* (Cambridge: Cambridge University Press, 1990), 1:108–11.

[47]Wlassack, pp. 77, 119; Williams, p. 111; Honolka, pp. 40–41, 206; Knudsen, pp. 247–51. See also Monty Jacobs, ed., *Deutsche Schauspielkunst: Zeugnisse zur Buhnengeschichte klassischer Rollen* (Leipzig: Insel-Verlag, 1913), an anthology of critiques (pp. 255–481 devoted entirely to Shakespeare).

Well (1828), and *1 Henry IV* and *2 Henry IV* (both in 1828). In 1821, he also revived the Schiller *Macbeth*.[48]

The *Lear* was the crown jewel of the series. Schreyvogel retained about 2800 lines of Shakespeare's approximately 3300—a far more nearly complete text than most productions of the time. Above all, the title role was in the hands of Heinrich Anschütz, whom Schreyvogel recruited from Breslau in 1820, and who was a mainstay of the Burgtheater until 1864. Beethoven's nephew attended a later performance in 1824, and had a lengthy talk about it with the composer, since (as we shall see later) Beethoven knew Anschütz well. In the Conversation Book young Karl wrote: "This is as is well known his most splendid role." Indeed it was, for no 19th-century German performance elicited more commentary. Anschütz went on playing it for decades, and it was even hailed as possibly the greatest performance in the German language on any stage. Karl reported that Goneril, Lear's eldest daughter, was played by Sophie Schröder, who was the foremost tragedian of her time (and whose name crops up several times in the Conversation Books). The part of the Fool "was masterfully taken by [Ludwig] Costenoble. He played the whole role with an overlay of bitterness." Imported from Hamburg in 1818, Costenoble was famous for his comic and character parts; he had played Cornwall in the *Lear* premiere, and would portray Shylock in *The Merchant of Venice*, with Anschütz as Antonio. Josef Koberwein, who acted at the Burgtheater from 1796 to 1847 and had played Kent at the premiere, this time "had the role of one of the sons-in-law. He seems to be better equipped for drawing-room comedy." The translation, Karl said, was by Johann Heinrich Voss (No. 6 in my list above), which gave the whole play a different flavor "if one compares it with the Eschenburg or Schröder version." This is the Friedrich Schröder I cited before. In a chat the previous year, Beethoven himself had written down details of an advertisement he had read for the 1821 acting manual by Antoine-François Riccoboni and the selfsame Schröder.[49]

---

[48]Rudolf Fischer, "Shakespeare und das Burgtheater: Eine Repertoirestudie," *Shakespeare Jahrbuch* 37 (1901): 136–37, 158–59; Eugen Kilian, "Schreyvogels Shakespeare-Bearbeitungen," *Shakespeare Jahrbuch* 39 (1903): 87–120, 41 (1905): 135–62, 43 (1907): 53–97 [these detailed discussions curiously overlook *All's Well*]; Alexander von Weilen, "Shakespeare und das Burgtheater," *Shakespeare Jahrbuch* 50 (1914): 60–65; Robert Proelss, *Kurzgefasste Geschichte der Deutschen Schauspielkunst* (Leipzig: F. A. Berger, 1900), pp. 347–52; Knudsen, pp. 251–54; Carlson, pp. 59–63; Williams, 1:111–19; Wlassack, pp. 138–75. On censorship, see Knudsen, pp. 254–58, Williams, 1:112–14, and *KH* 2:143 and 3:21. For a collection of contemporary appraisals, see Richard Smekal, ed., *Das Alte Burgtheater (1776–1888)*, 2 vols. (Vienna: Anton Schroll, 1916), 1:59–105.

[49]*KH* 7:37, 355–56; 4:54, 340; Carlson, pp. 60–62; Williams, 1:115–19; Wlassack, pp. 162, 173.

In addition to what Beethoven knew of Shakespeare through reading and productions in Vienna, he also had access to a number of operatic works based on the Bard's plays. In March of 1794, the Wiedner Theater opened a production of Georg Benda's *Romeo und Julie*, the same piece Beethoven had played during his Bonn days. In April the same theater mounted *Die bezähmten Widerbellerin*, a Singspiel to a libretto by Johann Friedrich Schink based on *The Taming of the Shrew*; the composer's name is today unknown. In April of 1797, Nicola Zingarelli's three-act *Giulietta e Romeo* (libretto by Giuseppe Foppa), the first Italian opera on the subject, opened at the Kärntnerthor Theater and had numerous performances over the next few years. In November of 1798, the Leopoldstadt Theater put on Wenzel Müller's heroic comic opera *Der Sturm*, based on *The Tempest*, with a libretto by Karl Friedrich Hensel, whom Beethoven would come to know well. Antonio Salieri's *Falstaff, ossia Le tre burle*, a two-act comic opera with a C. P. Defranceschi libretto adapted from *The Merry Wives of Windsor*, had its world premiere at the Kärntnerthor Theater on 3 January 1799, and proved to be an enormous success. Beethoven had to have heard it, since he used its duet "La stessa, la stessissima" as the theme for a set of ten piano variations in B♭ (WoO 73) that were already in print by the beginning of March. Shakespeare's Falstaff was also the subject of the Singspiel *Ritter Hans von Dampf*, which opened at the Leopoldstadt Theater in November of 1800; the librettist is unknown, and all we know of the composer is that his last name was Hofmann. And *The Tempest* was the source of Franz Volkert's Singspiel *Der Schiffbruch* (libretto by Karl Hampel), which had its premiere at the Leopoldstadt Theater on 12 May 1815.[50]

We are led to wonder whether Shakespeare was an admitted source for any of Beethoven's music—as he would soon be for some nine works by Berlioz. Mindful of the fact that, in Beethoven's only completed opera, the heroine (Leonore) seeks her husband (Florestan) by disguising herself as a young man named Fidelio, Donald MacArdle stated that it was more than "merely a coincidence" that, in Shakespeare's *Cymbeline*, the heroine (Imogen) had sought her husband (Posthumus) by presenting herself on three occasions in male attire as a person going by the name of "Fidele, sir." MacArdle was right. But there was an intermediate step: Beethoven and his librettist Joseph Sonnleithner were adapting Jean Nicolas Bouilly's French libretto *Léonore, ou l'amour conjugal* (which had been set to music

---

[50]Anton Bauer, *Opern und Operetten in Wien* (Graz/Köln: Hermann Böhlaus, 1955), Nos. 531, 3598, 3628, 3762, 4092 (the Salieri opera was overlooked here); Th-F, pp. 215, 218.

by Pierre Gaveaux in 1798), in which the title character passed herself off as Fidélio.[51]

Donald Francis Tovey opens his commentary on Beethoven's Op. 62 with these words:

> It does not greatly matter that the *Coriolanus* for which this overture was written is not Shakespeare's nor a translation or adaptation of Shakespeare's, but an independent German play, by Collin.

Tovey proceeds to say, however, that Wagner, in his analysis of the piece, "did well to ignore everything but Shakespeare and Beethoven." In fact, Wagner discussed the overture twice (in 1852 and 1870), and assumed that Beethoven was dealing with one particular scene (5.3)—that between Coriolanus, his mother, and his wife in the enemy camp before the gates of Rome. Thayer said that "the admirable adaptation of the overture to the play is duly appreciated by those only who have read Collin's almost forgotten work." Willy Hess has recently explained in some detail why "Beethoven's composition is intrinsically difficult to bring into a relation to Shakespeare's work."[52]

The same German playwright, Heinrich Joseph von Collin, did become involved with Beethoven on a real Shakespearean project—an opera based on *Macbeth*. Joseph Röckel, who had sung the role of Florestan in the 1806 version of *Fidelio,* much later wrote a letter in which he stated that Beethoven "could scarcely wait for his friend Collin to make an opera book for him of Shakespeare's 'Macbeth.' At Beethoven's request, I read the first act and found that it followed the great original closely." The Beethoven scholar Gustav Nottebohm was the first to publish two musical

---

[51]MacArdle, "Shakespeare and Beethoven," p. 260; *Cymbeline*: 3.6.60; 4.2.379; 5.5.118. On Bouilly's work, see Adolf Sandberger, *Ausgewählte Aufsätze zur Musikgeschichte* (Munich: Drei Masken Verlag, 1924), 2:141–53, and Willy Hess, *Das Fidelio-Buch* (Winterthur: Amadeus Verlag, 1986), pp. 37–54. The complete Bouilly libretto is reprinted as an appendix in both Sandberger (pp. 283–324) and Hess (pp. 327–63). For an extended comparison of Shakespeare's play and Beethoven's opera, see Johanna Rudolph, "*Cymbeline* und *Fidelio*: Ein Beitrag zur Wechselbeziehung der Künste," *Shakespeare Jahrbuch* 108 (Weimar, 1972): 64–80. The Bouilly work, translated into Italian, provided the libretti for two other operas written at the same time Beethoven was working on *Fidelio*: Ferdinando Paër's *Leonora ossia L'Amor conjugale* (Dresden, 1804; Vienna public premiere 8 Feb. 1809, attended by Beethoven), and Simon Mayr's *L'Amor conjugale* (Padua, 1805).

[52]Donald Francis Tovey, *Essays in Musical Analysis* (London: Oxford University Press, 1937), 4:43; Wagner, *Gesammelte Schriften* 5:173; 9:107; Th-F, p. 417; Willy Hess, *Beethoven-Studien* (Bonn: Beethovenhaus, 1972), pp. 115–17.

sketches for the opera, from 1808, with some commentary. The first, labeled "Macbeth" by the composer, was a passage in $\frac{6}{8}$ meter in the key of D minor; the second, right beneath, wound up a little later as the opening theme of the D-minor Largo in the Piano Trio, Op. 70, No. 1. In another sketchbook Beethoven wrote in an upper margin, "*Macbeth* Overture leads directly into the Chorus of Witches." Nottebohm printed the opening of Collin's rhymed, incantatory chorus:

> The wild storms rage,
> First on high;
> Now here below
> In the motley
> Bustle on earth!
> Never quiet!
> Huhuhuhu!
> Round about,
> Round and round!
> Lightning flashes, thunder cracks;
> The jaws of hell open wide!

Collin published the entire first act in 1809; but he laid his libretto aside in the middle of the second act, according to his brother, "because it threatened to become too gloomy." At any rate, the playwright died in 1811, putting an end to the effort.[53]

But Beethoven did not forget the possibility, as we learn from the memoirs of the actor Heinrich Anschütz, whom we have already met. The Burgtheater star wrote of first running into the composer in the summer of 1822 and gradually becoming friendly with him:

> One day I accompanied him for a distance. We spoke about art, music, and finally about Lear and Macbeth. How casually I dropped the remark that I had often busied myself with the notion whether he should not treat *Macbeth* musically as a counterpart to the *Egmont* music! The thought seemed to electrify him. He stopped as though nailed to the spot, looked at

---

[53]Th-F, p. 441; Gustav Nottebohm, *Zweite Beethoveniana* (Leipzig: C. F. Peters, 1887; repr. New York: Johnson Reprint Corp., 1970), pp. 225–27. The leaf of musical sketches (page 133 of the Landsberg 10 sketchbook) is reproduced in facsimile in Paul Bekker, *Beethoven* (Berlin/Leipzig: Schuster & Loeffler, 1911), p. 65 of the supplementary plates. Concerning the composer's verbal reminder (folio 9ᵛ of the Petter Sketchbook), see Hans Schmidt, "Die Beethovenhandschriften des Beethovenhaus in Bonn," *Beethoven-Jahrbuch*, Jg. 1969/70 (Bonn: Beethovenhaus, 1971), pp. 286–87 (item No. 639). And see Douglas Johnson, ed., *The Beethoven Sketchbooks: History, Reconstruction, Inventory* (Berkeley: University of California Press, 1985), pp. 171, 213–15.

me with a penetrating, almost demoniacal gaze and shot right back: "I have already occupied myself with that very thing. The witches, the murder scene, the spectral banquet, the cauldron apparitions, the sleepwalking scene, Macbeth's fatal frenzy!" It was fascinating in the highest degree to follow his grimaces and gestures, in which lightning-swift ideas raced by. In a few minutes his genius had worked through the entire tragedy. At the next question I put to him, he turned and with a hasty greeting ran off. Unfortunately action did not follow his stormy excitement. When I alluded to the topic sometime later, I found him out of humor and kept quiet.... What *Macbeth* might have been with the support of his music!

But Beethoven did not drop the idea. In fact, from then on, the composer solicited a libretto on a host of subjects from the eminent poet Franz Grillparzer, whom Beethoven had known from at least as early as 1805. Among the many opera subjects considered were at least two Shakespeare plays, for in early 1823 Count Moritz Lichnowsky wrote in a Conversation Book, "I shall definitely get together with Grillparzer concerning *Macbeth* or *Romeo and Juliet*." But Beethoven's pen never produced a second opera. Anschütz, Grillparzer, and Beethoven would come together one final time: at Beethoven's obsequies on 29 March 1827, it was Anschütz who delivered the funeral oration written by Grillparzer. And the first of two memorial services would take place on 3 April, the day that Anschütz debuted in the title role of *The Merchant of Venice*, that play so dear to Beethoven's heart.[54]

Writing in the *Allgemeine musikalischer Zeitung* (which over the years published an enormous amount of commentary on Beethoven's music), the critic "K. B.," whom I cited at the outset, in 1813 devoted substantial space to a plea that Beethoven deal with the Bard:

> Would that the greatest musical romantic, L. v. Beethoven, would enrich us with a musical Shakespeare Gallery!...With what gigantic power, for example in a *Macbeth* overture, would Beethoven let us look down into the depths of the realm of darkness! How he would, in a composition on *Romeo and Juliet*, raise to a heavenly crest the fusion of love and pain, death and transfiguration! Or in *The Tempest* how he could transport us to a fairyland full of lovely melodies, strange, airy sounds, and fantastic illusions! But enough suggestions! What we would be entitled to wait for from the

---

[54]Friedrich Kerst, ed., *Die Erinnerungen an Beethoven*, 2 vols. (Stuttgart: Julius Hoffmann, 1913), 2:38–39; *KH* 3:79 [late Feb. 1823]; Th-F, pp. 1052–60; Wlassack, p. 173. On Beethoven's abortive operas, see Winton Dean, "Beethoven and Opera," in *The Beethoven Companion*, ed. Denis Arnold & Nigel Fortune (London: Faber & Faber, 1973), especially pp. 381–86.

master genius in this sphere he has shown through his *Coriolan* overture and above all through his *Egmont* music—a work wherein the artist appears in full greatness and grandeur.[55]

When we look at the music that Beethoven actually did leave us, extramusical influences are particularly risky to posit in the purely instrumental pieces. Yet people who knew the composer—such as Schindler, Ferdinand Ries, Carl Czerny, and Charles Neate—maintained that Beethoven in writing music usually had in mind a "poetic idea," "a particular object," or "a picture from his reading or imagination." Especially enlightened discussions of the matter have recently issued from the pen of Frank E. Kirby, in dealing with the "Pastoral" Symphony; and from that of Barry Cooper, who cautions us against accepting pure speculation, uncorroborated hearsay evidence, and the idea that Beethoven's music closely parallels his life.[56]

The most notoriously incautious and presumptuous interpreter of all time was the musicologist Arnold Schering, who, in two fat tomes in the 1930s, claimed to have incontrovertibly uncovered the literary works that Beethoven consciously portrayed in more than three dozen instrumental pieces. In the later volume he conveniently tabulated the sources, of which fourteen were plays of Shakespeare (see Table 2).[57]

In Schering's view, the slow introduction of Op. 74 is Romeo yearningly waiting in front of Juliet's window (2.2), the *Allegro agitato* in the finale of Op. 95 is the scene of Desdemona's murder by Othello (5.2), the *Cavatina* of Op. 130 is Puck's nocturnal conjuring near the end (5.1.371*ff.*), and so forth.[58]

---

[55]Reprinted in Kunze, p. 623.

[56]Schindler/MacArdle, pp. 400–408; Th-F, pp. 436, 620; Frank E. Kirby, "Beethoven's Pastoral Symphony as a *Sinfonia caracteristica*," in *The Creative World of Beethoven*, ed. Paul Henry Lang (New York: W. W. Norton, 1971), pp. 103–21; Barry Cooper, *Beethoven and the Creative Process* (Oxford: Clarendon Press, 1990), pp. 42–58. In *Refractions of the Pastoral Myth: Shakespeare and Beethoven* (Ph.D. dissertation, University of Texas at Austin, 1975), Nancy Ann Cluck argued a relationship between the playwright's *As You Like It* and the composer's "Pastoral Symphony," and between *The Tempest* and the Ninth Symphony (see *Dissertation Abstracts International* 36/5, 2789-A).

[57]Arnold Schering, *Beethoven in neuer Deutung* (Leipzig: C. F. Kahnt, 1934); idem, *Beethoven und die Dichtung* (Berlin: Junker & Dünnhaupt, 1936; repr. Hildesheim: Georg Olms, 1973) [table, pp. 560–61].

[58]Schering, *Beethoven und die Dichtung*, pp. 295, 50, 351.

Table 2

Schering's literary "sources" for Beethoven's music

Opus	Work	Shakespeare Source
Op. 27, No. 1	Piano Sonata, E♭ Major	*The Merchant of Venice*
Op. 27, No. 2	Piano Sonata, C♯ Minor	*King Lear*
Op. 28	Piano Sonata, D Major	*The Winter's Tale*
Op. 31, No. 1	Piano Sonata, G Major	*The Taming of the Shrew*
Op. 31, No. 2	Piano Sonata, D Minor	*The Tempest*
Op. 31, No. 3	Piano Sonata, E♭ Major	*As You Like It*
Op. 54	Piano Sonata, F Major	*Much Ado About Nothing*
Op. 57	Piano Sonata, F Minor	*Macbeth*
Op. 74	String Quartet, E♭ Major	*Romeo and Juliet*
Op. 95	String Quartet, F Minor	*Othello*
Op. 111	Piano Sonata, C Minor	*Henry VIII*
Op. 127	String Quartet, E♭ Major	*The Merry Wives of Windsor*
Op. 130	String Quartet, B♭ Major	*A Midsummer Night's Dream*
Op. 131	String Quartet, C♯ Minor	*Hamlet*

It did not take long for Schering to become the butt of uninhibited condemnation. The first book, for instance, elicited an essay, "Lurid Light on Beethoven," from Eric Blom, who hurled at Schering such words as "wrongheaded," "dangerous," "insidious," and "arbitrary," and concluded that the claims "rest on the flimsiest foundations." In a lengthy discussion of the second volume, Alfred Einstein said that "absurdities may be found by the dozen," and asserted: "This book stands in the same relation to true musical research as modern astrology stands to physical astronomy, and I do not think that the printed conclusions of astrological endeavours are reviewed in astronomical journals."[59]

Two oft-cited Shakespearean associations warrant repetition here. The first involves the D-minor Adagio of the early F-major string quartet (published as Op. 18, No. 1). Beethoven played the movement for his friend Karl Amenda and then asked what thought had been awakened by it. "It pictured for me the parting of two lovers," said Amenda. Beethoven remarked, "Good! I thought of the scene in the burial vault in *Romeo and Juliet*." Beethoven presented Amenda (who was a violinist) with a copy of the quartet parts, inscribed on 25 June 1799. Two years later, at the end of a long letter to Amenda, the composer wrote: "Be sure not to hand on to anybody your quartet, in which I have made some drastic alterations. For only now have I learnt how to write quartets."[60]

The invocation of Romeo and Juliet here cannot readily be dismissed, for Beethoven himself made five jottings in his sketches for the Adagio: "et après cela le majeur" ("and after that the major [mode]"), "il prend le tombeau" ("he approaches the tomb"), "dése[s]poir" ("despair"), "il se tue" ("he kills himself"), "les derniers soupirs" ("the last gasps").[61]

The most convincing and detailed case for the validity of this association came in an illustrated lecture given by Owen Jander in 1988. He rightly stated that the whole piece has "a narrative quality," and believed the early version to be "more theatrical" (ten fortissimi, for instance, as compared with only one in the 1801 revision). He said that the proportions of the sonata-form piece followed the play, and assigned the movement's sections to specific lines in the text (5.3.85–170) and to the French jottings. (Incidentally, he suggested that Beethoven might have used French as a result of having studied the French opera *Roméo et Juliette* by Daniel Steibelt (libretto by J. A. P. de Ségur), of which a full score had been published in 1793.) Jander included some of his argument in a feature for *The New York Times* a year later:

> The parallels are clear: exposition, Romeo contemplates the form of his "dead" bride, Juliet [5.3.85–112]; development, in his despair Romeo poisons himself and expires [5.3.112–120]; recapitulation, Juliet revives, and

---

[59]Eric Blom, *Beethoven's Pianoforte Sonatas Discussed* (London: J.M. Dent, 1938; repr. New York: Da Capo, 1968), pp. 155–59 (Interlude VII); Alfred Einstein, review in *Music and Letters* 18/2 (April 1937): 206–11.

[60]Th-F, pp. 261–62; Anderson, 1:65 (Letter No. 53, 1 July 1801) and 3:1412 (inscription). The early and revised versions of the quartet may be found in the new collected *Beethovens Werke*, part 6, vol. 3, ed. Paul Mies (Munich/Duisburg: G. Henle, 1962); for the slow movement, see pp. 8–13, 133–38.

[61]Beethoven: *Ein Skizzenbuch zu Streichquartetten aus Op. 18*, facsimile and transcription by Wilhelm Virneisel, 2 vols. (Bonn: Beethovenhaus, 1972–74), folios 8 and 9. See also Nottebohm, p. 485.

discovers the lifeless body of Romeo [5.3.148–167]; coda, in her anguish Juliet grabs Romeo's dagger and stabs herself [5.3.169–170]. It fits.

Lamenting the lugubrious tempos of recorded performances, Jander added: "Here is a situation in which an awareness of Beethoven's poetic inspiration will urge performers to respect his metronome marking, leading to a more dramatic and wonderful musical experience."[62]

The second instance arose from an anecdote reported by Schindler:

> One day when I was telling the master of the great impression that Carl Czerny's playing of the D-minor and F-minor sonatas opp. 31 [no. 2] and 57 had made upon the audience, and he was in a cheerful mood, I asked him to give me the key to these sonatas. He replied, "Just read Shakespeare's *Tempest*." It is, therefore, to be found in that play.

Many hold that the composer was merely indulging, to use Robert Haven Schauffler's words, in "a harmless mystification intended to seal the mouth of a bore." It seems hard to accept that two such different pieces could both have sprung from the same source. But plenty of people have taken the matter seriously and latched onto one piece or the other. The D-minor work has indeed acquired the nickname of the "Tempest Sonata." Even Tovey, in his technical bar-to-bar analysis of this piece, did not discount a modicum of "illumination" in yoking the music and the play, "though the two works have not a single course of events on any parallel lines and though each contains much that would be violently out of place in the other. But there is a mood that is common to both." And he added that "it will do you no harm to think of Miranda at bars 31–38 of the slow movement." In a lecture some years later, however, Tovey commented:

> The advice [to Schindler] was perhaps not one of Beethoven's practical jokes: though I myself find both *The Tempest* and the D-minor Sonata very much clearer when I do not compare them.[63]

---

[62]Owen Jander, "The Crypt Scene in *Romeo and Juliet*: Inspiration for the Slow Movement of Beethoven's String Quartet Op. 18, No. 1," New England chapter meeting of the American Musicological Society, Wellesley College, 24 Sept. 1988; idem, "Putting the Program Back in Program Music," *The New York Times*, 3 Sept. 1989, sect. II, pp. 17 and 27. (For a companion study, see Jander's "Beethoven's 'Orpheus in Hades': The *Andante con moto* of the Fourth Piano Concerto," *Nineteenth-Century Music* 8/3 (Spring, 1985): 195–212.)

[63]Schindler/MacArdle, p. 406; Robert Haven Schauffler, *Beethoven: The Man Who Freed Music* (Garden City: Doubleday, 1933), p. 107; Donald Francis Tovey, *A Companion to Beethoven's Pianoforte Sonatas* (London: Royal Schools of Music, 1931), p. 121; idem, "Absolute Music," in *A Musician Talks*, 2 vols. (London: Oxford University Press, 1941), 2:71. For a further discussion, see Theodore Albrecht, "Beethoven and Shake-

Schauffler opted for Op. 57, saying that "the first movement of the '*Appassionata*' might well characterize a benignant amateur sorcerer like Prospero," and adducing two specific passages (1.2.25–32, 451–53). The theme-and-variations movement, he said, "might well have been inspired by" lines of Caliban (3.2.135–40) or Prospero (4.1.148–58). Marion Scott pushed the pairing to an extreme: the *Tempest* reference "may even be taken as a faint shadow of evidence for the first subject of the *Appassionata* having been deliberately adapted from the tune *On the Banks of Allan Water*." British folksongs were well known in Vienna, she said, and "there is reason to believe [Beethoven] knew the tune" and "linked it with Shakespeare in his mind because it too was British." The piece was indeed a favorite in the 19th century; but, unluckily for her, it was not an old folksong. With a new text by Matthew "Monk" Lewis and music by Charles Edward Horn, it made its debut in the opera *Rich and Poor* in 1812, some seven years *after* the *Appassionata*.[64]

Schering, having propounded *The Tempest* as the source of the D-minor sonata, settled on *Macbeth* as the basis of Op. 57. In "Beethoven, Shakespeare, and the *Appassionata*," a stimulating and insightful paper delivered in 1988, Thomas Sipe provided a serious discussion of Schering's view of the sonata, and compared it with the Shakespearean correlations made by Griepenkerl (in the musical novel I mentioned at the outset) and Tovey (in his posthumously published book on Beethoven). Sipe summarized the underpinning that Schering took from Schopenhauer by way of Wagner, and proceeded to characterize Schering's view as one in which Beethoven produced "a musical realization of Shakespeare's dramatic program" with melody as "the principal means by which music expressed psychological significance." Accordingly, each section of Op. 57, Sipe stated, "corresponds to a line, phrase, or mood" from the play. In the first movement, the opening F-minor theme is Macbeth, the rhythmically related A♭ theme is Lady Macbeth, and the four-note motive (bar 10 and later) is Banquo's ghost.

For Griepenkerl, this movement "evoked such a picture as could remind one of the [mock-trial] scene in *King Lear* [3.6.20–85]." Tovey, in

---

speare's *Tempest*: New Light on an Old Allusion," *Beethoven Forum 1* (Lincoln, Neb.: University of Nebraska Press, 1992): 81–92.

[64]Schauffler, *Beethoven*, pp. 154–55; Marion M. Scott, *Beethoven*, rev. Jack Westrup (London: J.M. Dent, 1974), pp. 142–43; Louis F. Peck, *A Life of Matthew G. Lewis* (Cambridge Mass.: Harvard University Press, 1961), p. 136. The curious can find the Lewis/Horn piece in John L. Hatton, ed., *The Songs of England* (London: Boosey & Co., 1873), pp. 78–80, and Helen Kendrick Johnson, ed., *Our Familiar Songs* (New York: Henry Holt, 1881), pp. 300–303.

discussing the left hand's ascent through two octaves in the development (bars 109–23), thought of the same play:

> His rising bass is the *hysterica passio* to which Lear, already dreading the approach of madness, cries "Down!" [2.4.56–58] Its climax is inarticulate. Melody disappears and harmony becomes ambiguous [bars 124–31].

Sipe clearly distinguished what he called "Griepenkerl's metaphorical mode, Schering's psychological mode, and Tovey's structural mode of interpretation."[65]

There is of course an enormous difference between claiming that a piece of music is a conscious depiction of Shakespeare and saying that it "could remind one of" such and such a play. Griepenkerl and Tovey were doing the latter—merely trying, through an analogy with literature, to put into words the effect of certain sounds on one listener. Examples of this practice are endless. So we find Wagner saying, in a conversation with his wife about Beethoven's Ninth Symphony: "When the theme in fifths recurs in the middle of the first movement, it always strikes me as a sort of Macbethian witches' cauldron in which disasters are being brewed—it does literally seethe." And in our time Wilfred Mellers has repeatedly linked the two men, such as here:

> The supreme greatness of Beethoven's work is attributable precisely to this risky equilibrium between the sublime and the ridiculous, the tragic and the bizarre....Again the only [?!] valid comparison is with Shakespeare's *King Lear*, whose tragedy encompasses, along with pity and terror, pathos that is near to bathos ("Thou'lt come no more, / Never, never, never, never, never. / Pray you, undo this button" [5.3.308–10], and savage farce (Gloucester's self-precipitation off the non-existent cliff [4.6.1–80]).[66]

Space precludes further instances, which could by themselves fill a book.

The last subject I want to touch on involves a comparison between the later creative efforts of Shakespeare and Beethoven. Nearly a century ago, John S. Shedlock, editor of the *Monthly Musical Record*, published in his magazine a short article assigning to the two men "three periods...of Imita-

---

[65] I am most grateful to Thomas Sipe for providing me with a copy of his 26-page paper, presented at the Annual Meeting of the American Musicological Society, Baltimore, 1988. And see Griepenkerl, p. 80; Donald Francis Tovey, *Beethoven* (London: Oxford University Press, 1945), p. 44.

[66] Skelton/Cosima Wagner, 1:450 (17 Jan. 1872); Wilfred Mellers, *Beethoven and the Voice of God* (New York: Oxford University Press, 1983), p. 365 (see also pp. 275–76, 315, 366, 417).

tion, Self-Reliance, and Aspiration." I suppose one could argue a similar tripartite division for the output of most creative artists, though in some cases, such as Stravinsky and Picasso, three periods will not suffice. The three-period division for Beethoven was already widely established by the middle of the 19th century, and has remained the prevailing view, although in our own time proposals have been made for four, five, or even eight periods.[67]

For Shakespeare the question has been complicated by the special difficulties in determining the proper chronology, ever since the first important study by Edmond Malone in 1778. Edward Dowden, in his classic and oft-reissued 1875 survey (*Shakspere: A Critical Study of His Mind and Art*), reprinted the 1874 table of Frederick Furnivall, which assigned four periods to the dramatist—a division widely adopted to the present. In the decades since Sir Edmund Chambers's detailed study in 1930, there has been pretty general agreement about the dates, most demurrers relating only to the earliest plays.[68]

I have for some decades been struck by the uncanny parallelism between Shakespeare's final efforts and the string quartets that concluded Beethoven's career[69]—beyond the fact that both groups were exceedingly slow

---

[67] John S. Shedlock, "Shakspere and Beethoven," *Monthly Musical Record* 29, No. 339 (1 Mar. 1899): 49–51. The most convenient summary for Beethoven is Maynard Solomon, "The Creative Periods of Beethoven," in *Beethoven Essays*, pp. 116–25, 323–26.

[68] Edward Dowden, *Shakspere: A Critical Study of His Mind and Art* (London: H. S. King, 1875; it reached a 13th edition in 1906); Edmund Chambers, *William Shakespeare: A Study of Facts and Problems,* 2 vols. (Oxford: Clarendon Press, 1930), 1:243–74. Other important contributors to the dating discussion include George Chalmers (1799), Nathan Drake (1817), Georg Gervinus (1850), Nikolaus Delius (1852), Wilhelm König (1875), Frederick Fleay (1876), Henry Paine Stokes (1878), Gregor Sarrazin (1894, 1896), Hermann Conrad (1909), Eilert Ekwall (1911), James McManaway (1950), and Peter Alexander (1964).

[69] The best book on the string quartets is Joseph Kerman, *The Beethoven Quartets* (New York: W. W. Norton, 1979). There is still value in Joseph de Marliave, *Beethoven's Quartets*, trans. Hilda Andrews (London: Oxford University Press, 1928; repr. New York: Dover, 1961). Other particularly useful studies are Ivan Mahaim, *Beethoven: Naissance et Renaissance des Derniers Quatuors,* 2 vols. (Paris: Desclée De Brouwer, 1964); Philip Radcliffe, *Beethoven's String Quartets* (New York: E. P. Dutton, 1965); and Basil Lam, *Beethoven String Quartets,* 2 vols. (London: British Broadcasting Corporation, 1975). The most detailed treatment of dating will be found in Douglas Johnson, passim. Overviews of late-quartet chronology, which is not reflected in the published opus numbers, can be found in Kinsky, pp. 753–54; Mahaim, 1:23–35; Kerman, pp. 224–25; Maynard Solomon, *Beethoven* (New York: Schirmer, 1977), p. 317.

to win widespread admiration. This can best be indicated by the following chart (Table 3):

Table 3

A comparison of the last works of Shakespeare and Beethoven

Shakespeare		Beethoven		
Coriolanus	1607–08	Op. 127	May 1824–Feb. 1825	4 mvts.
Pericles	1608–09	Op. 132	Feb. 1825–Aug. 1825	5 mvts.
Cymbeline	1609–10	Op. 130	Aug. 1825–Dec. 1825	6 mvts.
Winter's Tale	1610–11	Op. 133	Sep. 1825–Dec. 1825	
Tempest	1611	Op. 131	Dec. 1825–July 1826	7 mvts.
Henry VIII	1612–13	Op. 135	Aug. 1826–Oct. 1826	4 mvts.
Two Noble Kinsmen [part only]	1613	Op. 130: Finale II	Oct. 1826–Nov. 1826	1 mvt.

Shakespeare, in *Coriolanus*, for the last time penned a tragedy. He then proceeded to write a series of four plays that virtually all commentators, in one way or another, describe as the most unified group of works in the entire canon. They are all tragicomedies—that is, they begin as serious dramas but veer in the middle away from the tragic genre and move to a happy ending. Ever since the aforementioned book by Dowden, these plays have most commonly been known as "romances."[70]

---

[70]The most insightful books on the romances are E[ustace] M. W. Tillyard, *Shakespeare's Last Plays* (London: Chatto & Windus, 1954); Derek Traversi, *Shakespeare: The Last Phase* (New York: Harcourt, Brace & Co., 1955); Frank Kermode, *Shakespeare and the*

What makes these four plays related? Consider their plot skeletons:

Pericles. Prince Pericles, on one of many voyages, loses his wife Thaisa in childbirth. She is buried at sea, washed ashore, and restored to life. Their infant daughter Marina is left in foster care at a remote location, and raised to womanhood, when she is courted by governor Lysimachus. Marina is providentially brought to Pericles to cheer him up; they realize they are father and daughter, and are persuaded to journey to a distant temple, where they find Thaisa alive. There is a joyous family reunion, with Marina betrothed to Lysimachus.

Cymbeline. King Cymbeline unjustly banishes a lord, who takes the king's two infant sons with him to a remote location and raises them to manhood as his own offspring. The king's daughter Imogen (or more accurately Innogen, it now seems certain[71]), against her father's wishes, marries Posthumus, who is banished. She escapes from imprisonment, and (in male disguise) providentially takes up with the two brothers. When she mistakenly swallows a trance-inducing drug, she is left for dead by the men but revives after they have left for battle. They and a disguised Posthumus fight for the king with valor. Imogen/Innogen is brought in, and her true identity revealed. There is a joyous family reunion of father and sons, sister and brothers, wife and husband.

Final Plays (London: Longmans, Green, 1963); G[eorge] Wilson Knight, *The Crown of Life* (New York: Barnes & Noble, 1966); Joan Hartwig, *Shakespeare's Tragicomic Vision* (Baton Rouge: Louisiana State University Press, 1972); Howard Felperin, *Shakespearean Romance* (Princeton: Princeton University Press, 1972); Douglas L. Peterson, *Time, Tide and Tempest: A Study of Shakespeare's Romances* (San Marino: Huntington Library, 1973); Frances A. Yates, *Shakespeare's Last Plays: A New Approach* (London: Routledge & Kegan Paul, 1975); Barbara A. Mowat, *The Dramaturgy of Shakespeare's Romances* (Athens: University of Georgia Press, 1976); John Dean, *Restless Wanderers: Shakespeare and the Pattern of Romance* (Salzburg: Universität Salzburg, Institut für Anglistik und Amerikanistik, 1979); Robert M. Adams, *Shakespeare: The Four Romances* (New York: W.W. Norton, 1989); Maurice Hunt, *Shakespeare's Romance of the Word* (Lewisburg, Penn.: Bucknell University Press, 1990); Roger Warren, *Staging Shakespeare's Late Plays* (Oxford: Clarendon Press, 1990); H[arald] W. Fawkner, *Shakespeare's Miracle Plays* (Rutherford, N.J.: Fairleigh Dickinson University Press, 1992); Marco Mincoff, *Things Supernatural and Causeless: Shakespearean Romance* (Newark, Del.: University of Delaware Press, 1992); and Maurice Hunt, *Shakespeare's Labored Art: Stir, Work, and the Late Plays* (New York: Peter Lang, 1995). See also Philip Edwards, "Shakespeare's Romances: 1900–1957," *Shakespeare Survey 11* (1958): 1–18, and F. David Hoeniger, "Shakespeare's Romances Since 1958: A Retrospect," *Shakespeare Survey 29* (1976): 1–10.

[71] See, for instance, Warren, pp. xi–xii. Furthermore, the Innogen spelling was adopted for the complete works edited by Stanley Wells and Gary Taylor (Oxford: Clarendon Press, 1986); and see their *William Shakespeare: A Textual Companion* (Oxford: Clarendon Press, 1987), p. 604.

The Winter's Tale. King Leontes unjustly accuses his pregnant wife Hermione of adultery with his longtime friend King Polixenes, who flees. The imprisoned queen gives birth to a daughter, whom Leontes orders taken to a remote location and left to die. When news is brought of the death of his young son and then that of Hermione, he is persuaded of his errors. The daughter, Perdita, is found by a shepherd and raised as his own offspring to womanhood, when she is courted by Polixenes's son, Florizel, against his father's wishes. All wind up at Leontes's court, and true identities are revealed. When a statue of Hermione is exhibited, it turns out to be the living queen, who has been living in seclusion all these years. There is a joyous reunion of the two families, with three pairs of spouses.

The Tempest. Antonio, with King Alonso's help, usurps the dukedom of his brother Prospero, whom he sets adrift to drown. Prospero, with his little daughter Miranda, is washed ashore a remote enchanted island, where they are the only human beings. Years later a shipwreck brings the villains and their retinue to the island, Alonso thinking his gallant son Ferdinand drowned. Ferdinand comes across Miranda and they fall in love. After several plots are foiled, all persons wind up in the same spot, Prospero forgives the traitors, and there is a joyous reunion of the two households, with Miranda betrothed to Ferdinand.

These plays ring different changes on one theme: error causes a rupture in the bonds of royal friendship and blood; the resulting estrangement leads through a parade of ordeals to eventual remorse, forgiveness, and harmonious reconciliation. In each the restoration is effected to a great extent by a virtuous daughter, assisted by a supernatural power. They all exhibit an enormous temporal and geographical reach, and all contain theophanies (Diana in *Pericles*; Jupiter in *Cymbeline*; the oracle of Apollo in *The Winter's Tale*; Juno, Ceres, and Iris in *The Tempest*).

In addition, as hybrids they incorporate fairytale, myth, dream, tales-within-tales, epic of quest and return (the ancient Greek *nóstos*), episodic adventure, grotesquerie, storms, and marvels. They also contain an unusual abundance of music and masque.[72]

Beethoven, returning to the string quartet after a hiatus of more than a dozen years, eased himself back into the medium by writing Op. 127 in traditional Classical-period format, corresponding to the playwright's classical tragedy. So the composer gave us an independent work in the standard four movements: a sonata-form first movement, slow theme-and-variations, scherzo, and folklike sonata-form finale. (I am not denying the work's stylistic advance over his earlier quartets.)

Then the picture changes drastically. Beethoven goes on to write what Joseph Kerman calls his "two most radical and extreme compositions" and

---

[72]See especially Dean, pp. 3–4, 89–115, 211–14; also Traversi, pp. 2, 43–44, 106–107, 206; Yates, pp. 12–13; Adams, pp. 4–8, 14–16.

what Maynard Solomon terms "three experimental works (Opuses 132, 130, 131) which create a variety of new formal structures."[73] From four movements, Beethoven expands the format to five, then six, then seven. In Op. 131, which begins in unorthodox fashion with a slow fugue, we get no sonata-form design until the seventh movement. Op. 130 originally ended with a fugue-to-end-all-fugues. This piece grew to such mammoth, multipartite proportions (taking more than a quarter hour in performance) that Beethoven decided to substitute a new finale and issue the fugue as a separate work (the *Grosse Fuge*, Op. 133).

More than a century ago, Nottebohm demonstrated that the four opus numbers were rattling around in Beethoven's mind at the same time, and that the sketches for these works were all mixed up. Moreover, he discovered that the fourth of the six movements in Op. 130, the *Alla danza tedesca*, now in G major, was at first to be in the quartet's main key of B♭ major, and still earlier had been planned in A major as the fourth of the five movements in Op. 132. Still more important, he pointed out evidence of thematic interrelation between Op. 132 and 133.[74]

Nottebohm's research led Bekker to consider Opp. 132, 130 and 131 as a sort of triptych separating Opp. 127 and 135.[75] Many have followed Bekker's lead, though I prefer, with the Grosse Fuge now detached, to look at Opp. 130–33 as a tetralogy. As to the thematic connections, consider some of the things that happen to the first two ideas in Op. 132 (Ex. 1).

Although Kerman admits that "thematic parallels among the quartets are quite unmistakable," he considers it "dangerously mistaken" to view these works as "a specially unified group"—an idea that for him has an "*echt* Wagnerian flavor." He even makes a case for pairing Op. 127 and Op. 132 instead. He doth protest too much, methinks. His error lies in asserting that Bekker & Co. believe that Opp. 130–33 "are to be experienced on some level as a continuity." The works can be a tetralogy without somehow anticipating Wagner's *Ring* cycle. And one can agree with Kerman that "we should be attending to each separate work of art in its own private intensity." But this should not prevent us from appreciating that Beethoven created individual works that were at the same time related treatments of similar material—just as Shakespeare's four romances deal with the same theme without constituting four installments of one continuous story. Nevertheless, Basil Lam goes so far as to state, "There is no evidence of any kind to

---

[73]Kerman, p. 267; Solomon, *Beethoven*, p. 321.
[74]Nottebohm, pp. 1–13. For four scholars' guesses why Beethoven transplanted the dance movement from one quartet to another, see Sieghard Brandenburg, "The Autograph of Beethoven's String Quartet in A Minor, Opus 132," in *The String Quartets of Haydn, Mozart, and Beethoven: Studies of the Autograph Manuscripts* (Cambridge: Harvard University Department of Music, 1980), p. 301.
[75]Bekker, pp. 422–23.

Example 1. Thematic connections in Beethoven Opp. 132, 130, 133, and 131

Op. 132/1, mm. 1–4

Op 132/1, mm. 13–16

Op. 132/2, mm. 1–8

Op. 130/1, mm. 1–4

Op. 130/1, mm. 55–57

Op. 130/5, mm. 1–3

Beethoven and Shakespeare 459

Example 1 (*continued*)

Op. 133/1, mm. 4–10 (Fugue theme)

Op. 131/1, mm. 1–4 (Fugue Theme)

Op. 131/4, mm. 107–109

Op. 131/7, mm. 2–3

Op. 131/7, mm. 21–25

Op. 131/7, mm. 169–71

suggest that these three quartets were considered by Beethoven to be connected or related"—which is pure nonsense. Kerman and Philip Radcliffe are both right, however, to caution against Deryck Cooke's attempt to prove, through forced and strained motivic resemblances, that *all* the late quartets make up a "self-contained unity." Cooke skates perilously close to the absurdities promulgated by Rudolph Réti (in *The Thematic Process in Music*, notably), by which virtually anything can be derived from anything else. But if much of Cooke's supposed evidence is not audible, I would maintain that the kinds of relatedness I showed in Example 1 are such as, to use the comment attributed to Brahms on another Beethovenian occasion, "any ass can see."[76]

After writing the four romances, Shakespeare in *Henry VIII* reverted to British history—a genre that he had used nine times in the first half of his career. In like fashion, Beethoven produced, in the F-major Op. 135 quartet, a compact work of four-movement 18th-century design: a sonata-form first movement and finale enclosing a scherzo and slow theme-and-variations. The piece employs fresh thematic material throughout. Lam describes it as "music less exploratory than recreative." Kerman rightly speaks of its "successful evocation of the style of Haydn and Mozart," and its "self-conscious classicism," while Radcliffe also points to "a decidedly Haydnesque feeling."[77] Finally, Shakespeare concluded his writing career by penning part of a larger work, *The Two Noble Kinsmen* (the rest of it was by John Fletcher); and Beethoven, having cut loose the *Grosse Fuge*, also wound up by writing part of a larger work—namely, a new finale for Op. 130.

There is of course no question of influence here. It just strikes me as one of the most extraordinary coincidences in cultural history that the careers of the foremost western writer and the foremost western composer should finish in the same way. It seems as though Providence wanted to underscore the validity of Griepenkerl's mot that Beethoven is indeed Shakespeare's brother.

---

[76]Kerman, pp. 225–28; Lam, 2:21; Radcliffe, pp. 109–10, 175–78; Deryck Cooke, "The Unity of Beethoven's Late Quartets," in *Vindications* (Cambridge: Cambridge University Press, 1982), pp. 143–70 [originally published in *The Music Review* 24, No. 1 (Feb. 1963): 30–49]; Rudolph Réti, *The Thematic Process in Music* (New York: Macmillan, 1951). For the oft-cited Brahms quip, see for instance Schauffler, *Unknown Brahms*, p. 423; Florence May, *The Life of Johannes Brahms* (London: E. Arnold, 1905), 2:150–52; Jeffrey Pulver, *Johannes Brahms* (New York: Harper & Bros., 1926), p. 221; Richard Specht, *Johannes Brahms* (Hellerau: Avalun-Verlag, 1928), p. 299; Hans A. Neunzig, *Brahms* (Vienna: Amalthea-Verlag, 1976), p. 78; Ivor Keys, *Johannes Brahms* (Portland, Ore.: Amadeus Press, 1989), p. 168; Malcolm MacDonald, *Brahms* (New York: Schirmer Books, 1990), p. 384.

[77]Lam, 2:66; Kerman, p. 354; Radcliffe, p. 166.

Tenors Lost and Found: The Reconstruction of Motets in Two Medieval Chansonniers*

Mary E. Wolinski

The chansonniers of the Bibliothèque Nationale, f. fr. 844 and 12615, known as *R* and *N*, respectively,[1] preserve one of the major collections of French motets for two voices.[2] Dating from the late thirteenth or early fourteenth century,[3] these manuscripts are also important sources of the monophonic chanson and are among the few anthologies of thirteenth-century music that preserve both chansons and motets side by side. Other collections include the chansonnier Paris, Bibliothèque Nationale, f. fr. 845 with its monophonic *motets entés*;[4] the chansonnier *V*;[5] the manuscript *Ha*, which preserves the chansons and polyphony of Adam de la Halle;[6] and

---

*An earlier version of this article was read at the Annual Meeting of the American Musicological Society, Vancouver, 1985. My thanks to Professor Paul Brainard for sharing with me his inventories of the Parisian chant manuscripts cited in this article.

[1] Also known as the Manuscrit du Roi and the Manuscrit de Noailles. For a complete facsimile of *R* with commentary, see Jean Beck and Louise Beck, *Le Manuscrit du Roi: Fonds français n° 844 de la Bibliothèque Nationale: Reproduction phototypique publié avec une introduction*, 2 vols. (Philadelphia: University of Pennsylvania Press, 1938; repr. New York: Broude Brothers, 1970). A list of manuscript sigla is provided at the end of this article.

[2] The other collections are the fascicles of two-voice French motets in W_2, ff. 216–53ᵛ and *Mo*, ff. 231–69ᵛ, and the fragments *MüA*, which contain two-voice French and Latin motets mixed together. See the catalogue descriptions in Friedrich Ludwig, *Repertorium organorum recentioris et motetorum vetustissimi stili*, 2 vols. in 3 (New York: Institute of Mediaeval Music and Hildesheim: Georg Olms, 1964–78), 1/1:206–22, 279–85; 1/2:355–64, 760–72.

[3] For a discussion of dating, see Mark Everist, *Polyphonic Music in Thirteenth-Century France: Aspects of Sources and Distribution* (New York: Garland Publishing, 1989), pp. 175–87.

[4] The *motet enté*, literally "grafted motet," begins and ends with lines of verse that together form a coherent couplet. See Ludwig, *Repertorium*, 1/1:306–307.

[5] Ludwig, *Repertorium*, 1/2:569–90.

[6] For recent bibliography on Adam's works, see Deborah Hubbard Nelson and Hendrik van der Werf, *The Lyrics and Melodies of Adam de la Halle* (New York, London:

Gautier de Coinci's *Les Miracles de Nostre-Dame,* which is a lengthy narrative poem with musical interpolations of polyphony, chant, and chansons.[7]

The chansonniers *N* and *R* preserve an exceptionally large number of polyphonic motets, totaling ninety-eight upper voices in *N,* the larger of the two collections. Only the major motet sources *F, Mo, W$_2$, Cl,* and *Ba* exceed this number. Yet, at the same time, the tenor voices of the motets of *N* and *R* are mostly faulty. Their rhythmic patterns have been altered to such an extent that the tenors no longer fit with the upper voices. One tenor may have been substituted for another in a different rhythmic pattern or mode, or the pattern of ligatures and strokes in a tenor may not have been copied exactly. While in a monophonic chant the number of notes joined in a ligature is only a matter of graphic convention, in the tenor of a polyphonic motet the number of notes in a ligature indicates the relative durations of the notes, and the strokes represent rests. Scribes knowledgeable in rhythmic notation copied these ligatures and rests in accordance with precise rules. The failure to preserve the tenor notation exactly makes it difficult or impossible to read the rhythm.

The tenor errors in *N* and *R* have led scholars to the conclusion that their scribes had little or no competence in mensural polyphony, a view with which I agree. Nevertheless, the tenor errors have never been studied closely. In this article, I shall show that not all the tenors were copied mindlessly. Some of them were carefully borrowed or pieced together from others. I shall also discuss the reasons for these borrowings, which lie not only in the polyphonic incompetence of the scribes, but in the centonate practices of the chansonnier tradition.

Borrowed Tenors. Scribes or editors created some of the tenors by borrowing them from other tenors in the same collection. Table 1 lists the motets in question with the sources of their tenors.[8] The tenors of *N* 13

Garland Publishing, 1985) and Sylvia Huot, "Transformations of Lyric Voice in the Songs, Motets, and Plays of Adam de la Halle," *Romanic Review* 78 (1987): 148–64.

[7] See V. Frederic Koenig, *Les Miracles de Nostre Dame par Gautier de Coinci,* 4 vols. (Geneva: Librairie Droz, 1955–70); Jacques Chailley, *Les Chansons à la Vierge de Gautier de Coinci (1177[78]–1236)* (Paris: Heugel, 1959); and Ludwig's *Repertorium,* 1/2:594–602.

[8] For a catalogue of the motets, see Ludwig, *Repertorium,* 1/1:285–305. In referring to all motets, I adopt Ludwig's numbering of *N,* since *N* contains all motets discussed here and because the numbering conveys a sense of the motets' order within the collection. Note that Ludwig numbers each of the upper voices, but not the tenor. Thus, a two-voice

Table 1

Reconstructed tenors and their sources in manuscripts *N* and *R*

Motets with Borrowed Tenors	Sources of Tenor
No. 13, *Bone amour sans trecherie / Flos* (*R* lacks motet)	No. 10, *Puuis ke belle dame m'aime / Flos filius eius;* No. 11, *Dame tous jors m'avés pramise joie / Flos filius;* No. 12, *Molt m'abellist l'amourous pensament / Flos filius*
No. 14, *Novellement m'a sospris / Et [super]*, second tenor statement borrowed (*R* lacks motet)	No. 14, first tenor statement
No. 23, *Chascuns dist ke je foloi / In seculum* (*R* lacks motet)	No. 22, *Ma loiautés m'a nuisi / Seculum;* No. 20, *Ma loiaus pensee / In seculum;* and No. 19, *Je quidai mes maus celer / In seculum*
No. 30, *Main s'est levee Aelis / [Et tenuerunt]* (*R* lacks tenor)	Source common with No. 31, *Quant voi la flour en l'arbroie / [Et tenuerunt]*
Nos. 40–41, *De la vile issoit pensant / A la vile une vieille a / Manere*	No. 3, *D'amor trop lontaigne / Manere*
No. 84, *Quant se siet belle Ysabeaus / Propter veritatem* (*R* lacks motet)	Possibly No. 69, *A vous pens, belle douce ami / Propter veritatem,* or a lost model
No. 86, *D'amors sont en grant [esmai] / Et super* (*R* lacks motet)	No. 14, *Novellement m'a sospris / Et [super]*
Possibly No. 89, *C'est la jus en la roi pree / Pro patribus* (*R* lacks motet)	Possibly No. 62, *Je n'amerai autrui ke vous / Pro patribus*

---

motet receives a single number (*N* 13); a three-voice motet has two numbers (*N* 40–41). For a complete list of concordances, see Hendrik van der Werf, *Integrated Directory of Organa, Clausulae and Motets of the Thirteenth Century* (Rochester, N.Y.: By the author, 1989). For an edition of *N* and *R*'s motets, see Hans Tischler, *The Earliest Motets (to circa 1270): A Complete Comparative Edition*, 3 vols. (New Haven: Yale University Press, 1982).

and 23 are remarkable for being constructed of preexistent tenor sections strung together like pearls on a string. The situation with *N* 13, *Bone amour sans trecherie* is illustrated in Example 1. The correct version of the

Example 1. Versions of the tenor *Flos filius eius*:
  (a) No. 13, *Bone amour sans trecherie*, W_2, f. 251
  (b) No. 13, *Bone amour sans trecherie*, *N*, f. 181^v
  (c) No. 10, *Puuis ke belle dame* and No. 11, *Dame tous jors m'avés*, *N*, ff. 180^v–181
  (d) No. 12, *Molt m'abellist*, *N*, f. 181

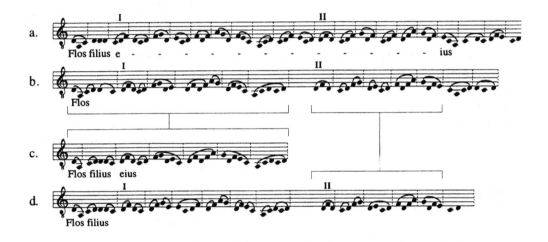

tenor *Flos filius eius*, based on the manuscript W_2, appears in Example 1a.[9] Example 1b gives *N*'s very different reading. *N* 13 differs from W_2 not only in the placement of rests and notation of ligatures, but also in the omission of the tag F–E–C–D at the end of each statement of the chant melisma, labeled I and II in the example. The sources of *N* 13's version are *N* 10, 11, and 12 of the same collection. The tenors of *N* 10 and 11, which are identical, provided statement I of *N* 13 (cf. Exx. 1b and c), while *N* 12 furnished statement II (cf. Exx. 1b and d). Although there are some minor differences

---

[9] W_2's notation is not explicit enough for us to know whether it is in first or second mode. For a facsimile, see Luther A. Dittmer, *Facsimile Reproduction of the Manuscript Wolfenbüttel 1099 (1206)*, Publications of Mediaeval Musical Manuscripts. No. 2 (Brooklyn: Institute of Mediaeval Music, 1960). Hans Tischler (*The Earliest Motets*, 2:1148–50) transcribes it in second mode. I have transcribed the tenors using unmeasured noteheads with slurs representing the original ligatures and strokes representing rests.

between *N* 13 and *N* 10, 11, and 12,[10] I believe that their resemblances are too strong to be coincidental.

Another centonate type of tenor occurs in *N* 23, *Chascuns dist ke je foloi*. In this case the first statement of *In seculum* was pieced together from three different sources. Example 2a shows the correct version as

Example 2. Versions of the tenor *In seculum*:
  (a) Statement I of No. 23, *Chascun dist que je foloie*, W_2, f. 211; *Cl*, f. 384^v
  (b) Complete tenor of No. 23, *Chascun dist que je foloie*, *N*, f. 183^v
  (c) Complete tenor of No. 22, *Ma loiauté m'a nuisi*, *N*, f. 183^v
  (d) Statement I of No. 20, *Ma loiaus pensee*, *N*, f. 183

preserved in manuscripts W_2 and *Cl*.[11] Example 2b illustrates how *N* 23 consists of the first four phrases of the correct version, followed by nine

---

[10] Statement I of *N* 13 is missing some notes and differs slightly from *N* 10 and 12 in the placement of rests and ligatures. The ending of statement II of *N* 13 differs from that of *N* 12, and, indeed, from that of any other *Flos filius* tenor in the collection.

[11] The motet is edited in Tischler, *The Earliest Motets*, 2:987–90 and in Gordon A. Anderson, *Motets of the Manuscript La Clayette*, Corpus Mensurabilis Musicae, 68 (American Institute of Musicology, 1975), p. 49. For facsimiles of *Cl*, see Luther A. Dittmer, *Paris 13521 and 11411. Facsimile, Introduction, Index and Transcriptions from the Manuscripts Paris, Bibl. Nat. nouv. acq. fr. 13521 (La Clayette) and lat. 11411*, Publications of Mediaeval Musical Manuscripts, 4 (Brooklyn: Institute of Mediaeval Music, 1959); and Friedrich Gennrich, *Ein altfranzösischer Motettenkodex. Faksimile-Ausgabe der Hs. La Clayette, Paris, Bibl. Nat. nouv. acq. fr. 13521*, Summa Musicae Medii Aevi, Bd. 6 (Darmstadt: By the author, 1958).

phrases of *N* 22 and the last two phrases of *N* 20 (or possibly *N* 19, which ends in a similar way).

Further cases of tenor borrowing include the following. The tenor of *N* 30, *Main s'est levee Aelis,* was copied from the tenor of *N* 31. In the double motet Nos. 40–41, *De la vile issoit pensant / A la vile une vieille a,* the tenor *Manere* of *N* and *R* uses the tenor of motet No. 3 instead of following the version of manuscripts W_2, *StV, Mo,* and *Fauv*.[12] The tenor *Et super* of *N* 86, *D'amors sont en grant esmai,* resembles and may have been copied from the first statement of the tenor of *N* 14. In addition, *N* 14, *Novellement m'a sospris novelle amours,* borrows from its own first tenor statement in order to complete the second statement.

The sources of two other tenors in *N* are somewhat more difficult to trace. The tenor *Propter veritatem* of *N* 69 may have supplied the first four phrases of the tenor of *N* 84, *Quant se siet belle Ysabeaus,* but I shall explain my doubts about this later in this article. In *N* 89, *C'est la jus en la roi pree,* the tenor *Pro patribus* does not exactly resemble any other tenor on this chant either. The tenor of *N* 89 (Ex. 3a) most resembles the tenor of *N* 62 (Ex. 3b), because both share the ascent to B in phrase 5 (as opposed to C in the tenor of *N* 4, Ex. 3c) and the repetition of G in phrase 7 (lacking in *N* 4 and 78, Exx. 3c and d, respectively).

The reconstruction of missing tenors. The reason that tenors were quoted or borrowed from other motets undoubtedly was to replace missing or incomplete tenors, which posed a major problem. *R* lacks seventeen, or forty percent, of the tenors needed to go with its forty-one preserved upper voices, and *N* is missing ten of the tenors needed to go with its ninety-eight upper parts. In eight cases the tenors of *N*[13] and in four cases the tenors of *R*[14] end well before the first statement of the melody is complete. In many

---

[12]There are many rhythmic discrepancies among the mensural sources. The motet is edited in Tischler, *The Earliest Motets,* 2:973–76. Facsimiles of *StV* and *Fauv* are, respectively, Ethel Thurston, *The Music in the St. Victor Manuscript Par. lat. 15139: Polyphony of the 13th Century* (Toronto: Pontifical Institute of Mediaeval Studies, 1959); and *Le Roman de Fauvel in the Edition of Mesire Chaillou de Pesstain: A Reproduction in Facsimile of the Complete Manuscript, Paris, Bibliothèque Nationale, Fonds Français 146,* Introduction by Edward H. Roesner, François Avril, and Nancy Freeman Regalado (New York: Broude Bros., 1990).

[13]Nos. 9, 31, 38, 51, 71, 79–80, 81, and 96.

[14]Nos. 44, 46, 58, and 71.

more instances—twenty-four cases in N^{15} and six cases in R^{16}—the second or third statements of the tenor melody are omitted or left incomplete.

Nevertheless, there are few tenors in N that cannot be completed, either by repeating the previous statement or by consulting other tenors in the

Example 3. Versions of the tenor *Pro patribus*:
(a) No. 89, *C'est la jus en la roi pree*, N, f. 195
(b) No. 62, *Je n'amerai autrui ke vous*, N, f. 191
(c) No. 4, *Trop longement m'a failli*, first statement, N, f. 179ᵛ
(d) No. 78, *L'autr'ier quant me chevaucoie*, first statement, N, f. 193

collection.[17] An interesting clue as to how some of these reconstructions were facilitated appears in the practice of clustering together certain motets on the same tenor chant, as illustrated in Table 2. The clusters consist of two motets on the chant *Balaam*, four motets on *Flos filius eius*, three motets

---

[15]Nos. 6, 10, 11, 15, 20, 21, 22, 23, 25, 27, 28, 29, 32, 33, 34, 47, 48, 56, 58, 59, 84, 85, 92, and 98. In No. 42, the first of three tenor statements is omitted.

[16]Nos. 5, 33, 34, 42, 48, and 56.

[17]The exceptions include the tenors lacking both text and music of Nos. 24, 61, 73, and 97. Also lacking models within the collection are the abbreviated and missing tenors on *Fiat* of Nos. 81 and 94, and the abbreviated tenors on *Tamquam*, No. 51, and *Hic factus est*, Nos. 79–80.

Table 2

Groups of consecutive motets having the same tenor chant in manuscripts *N* and *R*

	Upper Voices	Tenor	Source
Nos. 7–8	*Haré, haré, hïe / Balaan Goudalier ont bien*	*Balaam*	*N*
No. 9	*Li dous termines*	*Balaam*	*N, R*
No. 10	*Puuis ke belle dame*	*Flos filius eius*	*N, R* table of contents
No. 11	*Dame tous jors m'aves*	*Flos filius*	*N, R* table of contents
No. 12	*Molt m'abellist*	*Flos filius*	*N*
No. 13	*Bone amour sans trecherie*	*Flos*	*N*
No. 19	*Je quidai mes maus celer*	*In seculum*	*N*
No. 20	*Ma loiaus pensee*	*In seculum*	*N*
No. 21	*Ne m'en blasmes pas*	*Docebit*	*N*
No. 22	*Ma loiautes m'a nuisi*	*Seculum*	*N*
No. 23	*Chascuns dist ke je foloi*	*In seculum*	*N, R* table of contents
No. 30	*Main s'est levee Aelis*	*[Et tenuerunt]*	*N, R* lacks the tenor
No. 31	*Quant voi la flour*	*[Et tenuerunt]*	*N*
No. 32	*Hui matin a la jornee*	*Nostrum*	*N*
No. 33	*Au douç tans seri*	*Et tenuerunt*	*N, R*

on *In seculum* intersected by one on *Docebit,* and three motets on *Et tenuerunt* intersected by one on *Nostrum.* It is more than a coincidence that tenors on the same chant are grouped together. Since the rest of the motets in *N* and *R* are not ordered by tenor,[18] it seems unlikely that liturgical considerations played a part in their organization. Rather, the clusters resulted from an editor's gathering together the tenors in need of reconstruction with their potential models, as the following cases indicate.

The first tenor on *Balaam* of the double motet Nos. 7–8 in Table 2 appears in its complete form in *N.* The tenor of No. 9, *Li dous termines,* ends after the first nine phrases. It follows the same rhythmic pattern as the previous tenor, and easily could have been completed in performance by referring to the preceding tenor.[19] As far as the second cluster is concerned, we have already described in Example 1 how the two tenor statements of *N* 13 were pieced together from *N* 10 or 11 and from *N* 12. In the third cluster, the tenor of *N* 23 was constructed first from its own first four phrases, then the next nine phrases of *N* 22, and finally the ending of *N* 19 or 20, as illustrated in Example 2.

The question of how the tenor *Et tenuerunt* came to be matched with the motetus of *N* 30, *Main s'est levee Aelis,* in the fourth cluster is open to speculation and defies a certain answer. The proper tenor for this motet is *Ne,* according to the manuscript *MüA.*[20] Judging from its form and transmission, *Main s'est levee Aelis* was originally a chanson by Robert de

---

[18]There are, however, two clusters of motets based on genre: the rondeau motets Nos. 25–29, which do use different passages of the same chant, and the refrain motets Nos. 65–69.

[19]The manuscript *Mo* gives only the first fifteen phrases of this tenor, without indicating that phrases 1–10 must be repeated. It was uncharacteristic of *Mo*'s scribe not to have indicated the abbreviation. For an edition of the motet, see *The Montpellier Codex,* Parts 1–3, ed. Hans Tischler; Part 4, trans. Susan Stakel and Joel C. Relihan, Recent Researches in the Music of the Middle Ages & Early Renaissance, vols. 2–8 (Madison: A-R Editions, 1978–85), 3:29. For a facsimile, see Yvonne Rokseth, *Polyphonies du xiiie siècle; le manuscrit H 196 de la Faculté de Médecine de Montpellier,* 4 vols. (Paris: L'Oiseau-Lyre, 1935–39).

[20]For a transcription according to *MüA,* see Tischler, *The Earliest Motets,* 2:1386–88. For facsimiles of *MüA,* see Luther A. Dittmer, *A Central Source of Notre-Dame Polyphony: Facsimile, Reconstruction, Catalogue raisonné,* Publications of Mediaeval Musical Manuscripts, No. 3 (Brooklyn: Institute of Mediaeval Music, 1959); and Dittmer, "The Lost Fragments of a Notre Dame Manuscript in Johannes Wolf's Library," in *Aspects of Medieval and Renaissance Music: A Birthday Offering to Gustave Reese,* ed. Jan La Rue (rev. ed. New York: Pendragon Press, 1978), pp. 122–33.

Rains.[21] The tenor *Ne* preserved in the motet version of *MüA* suits the chanson-motetus well, but, except for its first seven or eight notes, it is quite different from the *Domine* tenors with which it is grouped in *MüA*. It appears that the tenor *Ne* was freely composed by a skillful polyphonic composer, who created, in effect, an accompaniment to the chanson. *N* 30's version of *Main s'est levee Aelis* lacks this tenor, and appears with a substitute tenor *Et tenuerunt,* which most resembles the tenor of *N* 31, *Quant voi la flour en l'arbroie.* Both tenors lack the text *Et tenuerunt* and both follow the same pattern of rests and ligatures. They differ in that *N* 30 is a fifth lower than *N* 31, and *N* 30 is complete, while *N* 31 is incomplete. In postulating that *N* 31 was the model for *N* 30, we would have to assume that (1) *N* 30 was transposed down a fifth from *N* 31 either during or after it was copied from *N* 31, and (2) *N* 31 was complete at the time it was used as the model for *N* 30. Therefore, sometime afterwards, *N* 31 was shortened and, as a result, a singer of the time would have had to rely on *N* 30 in order to complete *N* 31. Alternatively, *N* 30 may have used a different model altogether for its tenor.

In *N* 14, *Novellement m'a sospris novelle amours,* an editor completed the second statement of the tenor *Et super* by referring back to the first statement. For the sake of comparison, Example 4a illustrates a reliable version of the tenor as preserved in *Mo*'s musically identical motet, *Nonne san amour / Moine qui a cuer joli.* In *N*'s version (Ex. 4b), statement I is faithful to *Mo*'s reading, and statement II also begins correctly. But, after the first four phrases of statement II, at the point marked by the asterisk, *N*'s tenor reverts to the pattern of rests and ligatures of statement I. Thus, the editor reconstructed statement II by referring back to statement I.

We have seen how the tenors of Nos. 14, 23, 40–41 and 89 began correctly and subsequently strayed to passages quoted from elsewhere. I contend that those tenors had been incomplete, consisting only of the correct reading, and that they had been completed by copying other tenors on the same chant. However, in a reversal of this situation, the tenor *Propter veritatem* of *N* 84, *Quant se siet belle Ysabeaus,* begins with the first four phrases of the tenor of *N* 69 and ends with the correct version of the fifth phrase.[22] The combination of, first, the borrowed tenor and, then, part of

---

[21]See Hans Spanke, ed., *G. Raynauds Bibliographie des altfranzösischen Liedes* (Leiden: E. J. Brill, 1955; repr. 1980), p. 213, no. 1510; and Dittmer, *A Central Source of Notre-Dame Polyphony,* pp. 58–59.

[22]The correct version of *N* 84 is preserved among the *StV* clausulae. For an edition, see Tischler, *The Earliest Motets,* 2:1519.

Example 4. Versions of the tenor *Et super*:
  (a) *Nonne sans amour / Moine qui a cuer joli*, Mo, ff. 152ᵛ–153ᵛ
  (b) No. 14, *Novellement m'a sospris*, N, f. 181ᵛ. Dittographies in *N* are indicated by brackets.

the correct tenor, is difficult to explain. The very strangeness of the situation raises the possibility tht *N* 84 was modeled on a different tenor that is not in *N*'s collection.

The scribes' lack of competence in measured polyphony. In spite of the effort they made to fit together these combinations of quotations, it is clear that the editors did not understand mensural polyphony and that the scribes of *N* and *R*, who preserved this sorry state of affairs, were just as ignorant. There is strong evidence for this in the wide variety of problems found in most of the tenors in the collection.

The problems with the reconstructed tenors are numerous. In the correct version of the tenor *Flos filius eius* of *N* 13 (Ex. 1a), a constant first or second mode rhythm is maintained throughout. The first statement of the melisma on *eius,* beginning on D, falls on the second note of the third phrase. However, the second statement of the *eius* melisma begins on the first note of the phrase marked by Roman numeral II in Example 1a. By falling at a different point in the rhythmic pattern, the second statement behaves like a *color* that overlaps the *talea* in an isorhythmic motet. This subtlety is lost in *N* 13, whose two tenor statements are derived from *N* 10 or 11 and *N* 12. *N* 13's version is incompatible with its motetus not only because of the rhythm, but because it is missing the melodic tag F–E–C–D, which is required at the ends of both statements I and II.

A similar problem arises in the tenor *Et super* of *N* 14. In the correct version (Ex. 4a), there is a constant rhythm of first mode ternariae,[23] and statement II begins at a different point in the modal pattern than it did in statement I. In *N*'s version (Ex. 4b), however, after the first four phrases of statement II, at the asterisk the tenor reverts back to the pattern of rests and ligatures of statement I. Consequently an extra note, C, is added. In addition, there are two dittographies (repetitions, probably caused by eye-slip, which are enclosed in braces in Ex. 4b), which make the tenor even longer than it should be.

Other tenors encounter difficulties when they require two or more rhythmically different statements of the chant melisma and yet preserve only one. For example, in the tenor *In seculum* of *N* 85, *Trop m'a amours assailli*, the first statement consists of three-note phrases separated by rests, while the second statement should be phrased in groups of five notes, according to the versions in *Mo*, W_2 and *StV*.[24] Because *N* omits the second statement, its reading does not supply sufficient information to perform this motet in the manner indicated in the other polyphonic sources. Similar problems occur in *N* 23 (Ex. 2b) and *N* 84, in which not only is the first tenor statement incompatible with the motetus, but the second statement is also lacking.

In *N* 89, *C'est la jus en la roi pree,* the motetus follows a truncated rondeau form: aAabAB. The first four phrases of the tenor *Pro patribus* are to be repeated in the same form as the motetus, so that phrases 1 and 2 equal A and phrases 3 and 4 equal B, as Tischler has demonstrated.[25] The error occurs when the editor, ignoring the rondeau convention, continued with a garbled version of the *Pro patribus* chant at phrase 5 (see Ex. 3a).

The chant melisma *Et super* has a natural internal repetition of eighteen notes, which is maintained in the version of *N* 86, *D'amors sont en grant esmai* preserved in *Mo, StV* and W_2. However, *N*'s version deletes this necessary repetition with the result that *N*'s tenor is shorter than its motetus.

Finally, both tenors of *N* 30 and *N* 40–41 create too many dissonances with the upper voices. The tenor on *Manere* of *N* 40–41 is also notated a fifth too high and is rhythmically incorrect.

---

[23]Tischler, *The Earliest Motets,* 2:936–43.

[24]Tischler, *The Earliest Motets,* 2:1140–42.

[25]Tischler, *The Earliest Motets,* 2:1521–22. This synchronization of motetus and tenor is also followed in the five rondeau motets Nos. 25–29. For further discussion, see Mark Everist, "The Rondeau Motet: Paris and Artois in the Thirteenth Century," *Music & Letters* 69 (1988): 1–22.

In addition to the errors in the reconstructed tenors, problems abound in most of the other motets in *N* and *R*. The omission and abbreviation of numerous tenors has already been pointed out. Ligatures and rests frequently disagree with reliable mensural versions or standard modal patterns, a condition that is more the rule than the exception. There are also a number of transposed tenors. The tenor *In seculum* of *N* 22 is a fifth too high, as is the tenor *Manere* of Nos. 40–41 of *N* and *R*. However, in most cases incorrect pitch levels occur only in part of the tenor. The tenor *Amoris* of *N* 46 is a fifth too high from the third phrase to the end. In the tenor *Regnat* of No. 52, the last phrase is a second too high; in *Nobis* of No. 53, the last two phrases are a third too high; in *Et tenuerunt* of No. 55, the first phrase of the second statement is a fifth too low; in *Vitam* of No. 92, the fourth phrase is a third too high. The tenor *Regnat* of *N* 77 is a fifth too high when, suddenly, it jumps to the correct pitch notation for the last ten pitches. These transpositions seem to have resulted from reading from one clef and copying in another, or from eyeslip. *N* 58, however, is not so easily explained. The tenor *Perlustravit* is formed of passages variously transposed at levels a fourth, third, fifth and sixth higher than the correct version, so that no part of *N*'s tenor is written at the correct pitch. *R*'s version of the tenor is different: it begins at the correct pitch, but the last nine notes of its truncated version are a third too high.

In addition to these types of errors, there are numerous discrepancies in the melodies of the tenors. In several cases, *N* and *R* preserve versions of a chant melody that differ from those of the reliable polyphonic sources. For example, *N* and *R*'s version of the tenor *Hec dies* of No. 34, *Hui main au douç mois de mai*, conforms with the chant as preserved in Parisian missals[26] and an Arras gradual.[27] The mensural manuscripts *Mo*, W_2, and *F* follow the chant found in missals for use of the Augustinian abbey of Ste-Geneviève in Paris[28] and the Benedictine monastery of St-Vaast in Arras.[29] The tenors of *Mo*, W_2, and *F* do differ from each other, since W_2 does not have the phrase repetition present in *Mo* and *F*. However, the tenors of *Mo*, W_2, and *F* are still polyphonically compatible with the motetus, which demonstrates that the editors of these versions were competent to recompose tenors within a polyphonic structure. On the other hand, the truncated

---

[26]Paris, Bibliothèque Nationale, f. lat. 830, f. 132; lat. 1112, f. 105^v; lat. 9441, f. 91^v; lat. 15615, f. 147^v.

[27]Arras, Bibliothèque Municipale, MS 437, f. 48.

[28]Paris, Bibliothèque Ste-Geneviève, MS 1259, f. 105.

[29]Arras, Bibliothèque Municipale, MS 444, f. 130^v (Temporale).

and incompatible tenor of *N* and *R* betrays a lack of polyphonic control on the part of the editor.[30]

Attempts to preserve a chant melody at the expense of destroying polyphonic viability appear in two more motets of *N*. The last four phrases of the tenor *Justus* of *N* 16–18 as preserved in *Mo, Cl,* and *W*₂ are polyphonically suitable and mensurally correct, but at the same time they deviate substantially from the chant. *N* and *Her,* however, terminate their tenors just before this recomposed passage, in effect supressing a liturgically unsound reading. In addition, Klaus Hofmann has shown that the tenor *In seculum* of *N* 85 follows the chant ending G–G–F instead of the mensural version G–F.[31] On the other hand, the chant melody is highly distorted without being polyphonically viable in *N*'s readings of the rondeau motets Nos. 25 and 66, the refrain cento motet No. 91, the second tenor statement of No. 90, the double motet Nos. 82–83, and *R*'s version of the ending of motet No. 39.

The consequences of polyphonic incompetence. As a result of their lack of ability in rhythmic notation and polyphony, the scribes of *N* and *R* exerted no discernible control over the musical intelligibility of the motets they copied. There are no traces of any "house style" of mensural notation, no recurrent idiosyncracies that mark the work of the scribes or their ancestors.[32] As a consequence of the lack of scribal control, good and bad tenors were copied indiscriminately side by side.

One may well ask what purpose the reconstructed tenors served and how motets were performed in the chansonnier tradition. Using reliable concordances and, when these are lacking, a keen sense of the discant possibilities, Hans Tischler has been able to transcribe most of the motets in *N*

---

[30] The question of why these tenor variants occured in No. 34 is raised and left open to speculation in Gérard Le Vot, "La notation et l'oralité des musiques polyphoniques aux xiie et xiiie s.," *Cahiers de civilisation médiévale* 31 (1988): 142–47.

[31] *Untersuchungen zur Kompositionstechnik der Motette im 13. Jahrhundert durchgeführt an den Motetten mit dem Tenor "In Seculum,"* Tübinger Beiträge zur Musikwissenschaft, Band 2 (Neuhausen-Stuttgart: Hänssler, 1972), p. 49.

[32] For example, the motets of *W*₂ are notated in much the same way as in *N* and *R*: with mensurally undifferentiated notes in the upper voices and tenors that derive their durational values from the patterns of notes within ligatures. While *W*₂'s scribe doubtless knew the difference between first and second mode ligature patterns, he frequently alternated modal patterns midway in a tenor, as, for example, in the tenor *Letabitur* of *Ki leiaument sert s'amie,* f. 219^v. He also shares with *Mo* the habit of elongating penultimate noteheads to indicate they are longer in duration.

and *R* into polyphonically viable versions.[33] But his reconstructions are attempts to restore the ideal archetype, the source from which both the mensural manuscripts and chansonniers descended, and these ideal versions have corruptions and conflations of their own. Tischler's sturdy transcriptions do not, I think, represent the performing tradition of the chansonnier scribes. The lack of scribal control over the music makes it difficult to posit any single manner of performance that the chanson singers might have observed.

Richard Crocker has suggested that those who cultivated secular song viewed the motets as a new way of performing a familiar kind of song by means of tenor accompaniment.[34] Nevertheless, I find no indication that the chanson scribes of *N* and *R* knew how to perform the tenors with the upper parts, even in those motets that were copied correctly. Even motets in the simplest note-against-note texture, such as the rondeau motets, were copied poorly in the chansonniers.[35]

The common source. The motets of *N* and *R* descend from a common source,[36] which is indicated by the organization of motets and the trans-

---

[33] The exceptions are Nos. 3, 24, 54, 56, 60, 61, 73, 75, 76, and 97.

[34] "French Polyphony of the Thirteenth Century," in *The Early Middle Ages to 1300*, ed. Richard Crocker and David Hiley, vol. 2 of *New Oxford History of Music* (Oxford: Oxford University Press, 1990), p. 653.

[35] The rondeau motets *N* 25, 66, and 89 have substantial errors in the tenors.

[36] Hans Spanke ("Der Chansonnier du Roi," *Romanische Forschungen* 57 [1943]: 90) believed that *N* and *R* descended from a common exemplar. Hendrik van der Werf (*The Chansons of the Troubadours and Trouvères* [Utrecht: A. Oosthoek, 1972], pp. 31–32) has posited that their chansons were transmitted through a combination of oral tradition for melody and written tradition for text. A recent study of transmission in *N* (called *T* by chanson scholars) appears in J. H. Marshall, "The Transmission of the lyric *lais* in Old French *Chansonnier T*," in *The Editor and the Text: In Honour of Professor Anthony J. Holden*, ed. Philip E. Bennett and Graham A. Runnalls (Edinburgh: Edinburgh University Press, 1990), pp. 20–32. The principle by which *N* and *R*'s motets can be proven to derive from a common source is set forth in Paul Maas, *Textual Criticism*, trans. Barbara Flower (Oxford: Clarendon Press, 1958), pp. 4, 44. The limitations and value of applying the so-called Lachmannian principles of filiation are discussed in regard to chansonniers and early music in, respectively, István Frank, "The Art of Editing Lyric Texts," in *Medieval Manuscripts and Textual Criticism*, ed. Christopher Kleinhenz, North Carolina Studies in the Romance Languages and Literatures, Symposia No. 4 (Chapel Hill: University of North Carolina Department of Romance Languages, 1976), pp. 123–38; and Stanley Boorman, "Limitations and Extensions of Filiation Technique," in *Music in Medieval and Early Modern Europe: Patronage*,

mission of tenor errors. Both collections of motets are arranged in the same order, although *R*'s collection is only half the size of *N*'s. The gaps in *R* are randomly distributed, except towards the end where *R* stops at motet No. 72 and *N* continues on to No. 98. The identical organization of *N* and *R* sets them apart from other contemporary motet anthologies, such as *Mo* and W_2, which appear to have been copied from multiple exemplars and whose motets were reorganized along generic, alphabetical or liturgical lines.[37]

N and *R* also share errors that go back to the common exemplar. In five cases *N* and *R*'s tenors end prematurely at the same, or nearly the same, point, which testifies to the presence of these abbreviations in the common source.[38] Their tenors frequently share almost identically faulty ligatures and rests.[39] Another manuscript that may have descended from the same exemplar is *Her*, which shares some of *N*'s ligature discrepancies in three of its tenors.[40]

At the same time, *N* and *R*'s motet collections descended from the common source via two separate branches, because each manuscript has errors not found in the other. *N* could not have been copied from *R*, because *R*'s collection is smaller than *N*'s and has many errors not present in *N*, especially the omission of many of the tenors.[41] With only one excep-

---

Sources and Texts, ed. Iain Fenlon (Cambridge: Cambridge University Press, 1981), pp. 319–46.

[37] The state of the exemplars of *Mo* and W_2 is discussed in this author's *The Montpellier Codex: Its Compilation, Notation and Implications for the Chronology of the Thirteenth-Century Motet* (Ph.D. dissertation, Brandeis University, 1988), pp. 50–58. *Mo* is declared a "collection of collections" in James Heustis Cook, *Manuscript Transmission of Thirteenth-Century Motets*, 2 vols. in 3 (Ph.D. dissertation, University of Texas at Austin, 1978), 1:254.

[38] Motets Nos. 33, 34, 48, 56, and 71.

[39] Faulty ligatures and rests are almost identical in *N* and *R* in Nos. 40–41, 47, 51, 56, 57, 58, 70, and 71. Some of the same errors are shared in Nos. 5, 34, 35–36, and 39.

[40] Motets Nos. 1, 2, and 12. *Her* consists of only ten motets, eight of which it shares with *N* and two with *R*. It transmits some of the same errors as *N* and *R*, but its relationship to them is unclear due to its fragmentary nature, the scarcity of concordances, and the high degree of corruption in all the sources. The relationship of *Her* to *N* and *R* is discussed in E. F. Kossmann, "Ein Fragment einer neuen altfranzösischen Motetten-Handschrift," *Zeitschrift für Musikwissenschaft* 8 (1926): 193–95; and Friedrich Ludwig, "Versuch einer Übertragung der Motetten Herenthals Nr. 4 und 5," *Zeitschrift für Musikwissenschaft* 8 (1926): 196–200.

[41] *R*'s table of contents lists fifty of the ninety-eight motet upper voices of *N*. Of these, only forty-one motets are actually preserved in *R*.

tion,[42] all of the tenors missing in *R* are present in *N*. Therefore, these tenor omissions come from *R*'s branch and not the common source. *N* is also missing some tenors,[43] but since *R* preserves none of the motets to which *N*'s missing tenors belong, we cannot tell whether the tenors were lacking from the common source or from *N*'s branch of transmission. On the other hand, *R* was not copied from *N*, because *N* contains errors not found in *R*. For example, *R* preserves five of its tenors in more complete versions than does *N*.[44]

The reconstruction of tenors did not actually take place in *N* and *R*, but, rather, in their common ancestor, or perhaps the ancestors of their common ancestor. We know that the common source was defective polyphonically, because of the shared errors in *N* and *R*. The clustering of motets on the same chants also emanates from the common source, since vestiges of this clustering can be discerned in *R*, as well as *N*. It is also very likely that the tenor reconstruction was present in the common source, since *N* and *R* both preserve the borrowed tenor of Nos. 40–41. Unfortunately, all of the other reconstructed tenors are missing from *R*, which denies the opportunity for further substantiation.

The origin of the common source and its ancestors bears on the question of whether certain motets were written by Artesian composers. Mark Everist has argued that the rondeau motets Nos. 25–29, 66, 73, and 89 originated in Artois, based on their uniqueness to *N* and *R* and their relative simplicity.[45] Both *N* and *R* were copied by scribes speaking Picard dialects. *N* has been localized to Arras, or the county of Artois, based on the presence of poems that cite persons, places, and events connected with Arras and its environs.[46] However, even if the common source was also Artesian, this does not guarantee that the unique motets were written in Artois. In fact, it is highly unlikely that any motets originated with the common source, since it transmitted motets in such poor condition.

---

[42] The *Florebit* tenor of No. 43, which is missing in *R* and *N*.

[43] Nos. 24, 54, 60, 61, 73, 76, 94, 95, and 97.

[44] The tenors of motets Nos. 32, 37, 38, 47, and 51 are abbreviated and missing phrases in *N*. This disproves Gilbert Reaney's conjecture that the motets of *R* were copied from *N*; see his *Manuscripts of Polyphonic Music, 11th-Early 14th Century*, Répertoire international des sources musicales, B IV¹ (Munich-Duisberg: G. Henle, 1966), p. 374.

[45] "The Rondeau Motet," pp. 17, 21–22.

[46] For the localization of *N*, see Roger Berger, *Littérature et société arrageoises au xiiie siecle: Les chansons et dits artésiens* (Arras, 1981), pp. 17–24. In connection with *R*, see Jean Longnon, "Le Prince de Morée chansonnier," *Romania* 65 (1939): 97.

Determining the origin of the rondeau motets means determining the work of the author, as opposed to that of the scribe. Two methods can be employed. One is to establish whether or not there are dialectal traits in the rhyme and meter of the poems in question. These traits must be numerous and consistent, otherwise the results of such a study may be inconclusive.[47] It is beyond the scope of this article to attempt to analyze the language of the motet authors.

Another method of pinpointing origin is to analyze the "dialectal traits" of the chant melodies used in the tenors. This approach has been used in determining liturgical origin in studies by Husmann, Roesner, and Wright.[48] The results of my preliminary study were inconclusive. I consulted two Artesian sources: Arras, Bibliothèque Municipale, MSS 437 and 444. Both preserve chant for the Mass dating from the thirteenth century and both are described as issuing from the Benedictine abbey of St-Vaast in Arras.[49] There is no convincing pattern of agreement with Arras chant sources over Parisian sources, and it would appear that some agreements between tenors and Arrageois chants are only coincidental, or emanate from an unknown source that shared traits of Arras and Paris.

In motet No. 34, we have already noted that reliable mensural versions correspond with Arras 444, while *N* and *R* agree with Arras 437 (see page 473). In only two cases do motets Nos. 4 and 16–18 correspond better to Arras 444 than to Parisian chant books, and even these cases seem purely coincidental. In No. 4, *Trop longement m'a failli,* at phrase 5 the tenor *Pro patribus* rises to C, which agrees with Arras 444.[50] The

---

[47]See Alfred Foulet and Mary Blakely Speer, *On Editing Old French Texts* (Lawrence: The Regents Press of Kansas, 1979), p. 93.

[48]Heinrich Husmann, "The Enlargement of the *Magnus liber organi* and the Paris Churches St. Germain l'Auxerrois and Ste. Geneviève-du-Mont," *Journal of the American Musicological Society* 16 (1963): 176–203; idem, "The Origin and Destination of the *Magnus Liber Organi,*" *The Musical Quarterly* 59 (1963): 311–30; idem, "St. Germain and Notre-Dame," *Natalicia Musicologica Knud Jeppesen septuagenario,* ed. Bjørn Hjelmborg and Søren Sørensen (Copenhagen: Wilhelm Hansen, 1962), pp. 31–36; Edward H. Roesner, "The Origins of W_1," *Journal of the American Musicological Society* 29 (1976): 337–80; Craig Wright, *Music and Ceremony at Notre Dame of Paris 500–1550* (Cambridge: Cambridge University Press, 1989), pp. 243–58.

[49]In regard to Arras 437, see *Le graduel romain: II. Les sources* (Abbaye Saint-Pierre de Solesmes, 1957), p. 27. For Arras 444, see Victor Leroquais, *Les sacramentaires et les missels manuscrits des bibliothèques publiques de France,* 3 vols. and plates (Paris: n.p., 1924), 2:79–80.

[50]Folio 27 (Sanctorale).

Parisian sources reach only B at that point.[51] Nevertheless, there is little doubt that No. 4 is Parisian in origin, since it appears as a clausula in *F*. In motet Nos. 16–18, *Je ni puis / Par un matin / Le premier jour de mai,* the tenor *Justus germinabit* of the versions in *N, Mo,* and *Her* corresponds better to Arras 444[52] at a few points than to any Parisian chant.[53] Nevertheless, this motet is widely distributed,[54] which again suggests Parisian origin. Its tenor deviates quite a bit from any known chant and may have been deliberately changed, making its resemblance to Arras 444 also seem coincidental.

Sometimes it seems possible to penetrate the layers of corruption in the present sources to arrive at the original version of the author. One example suggests Artesian origin. No. 27 is a rondeau motet unique to *N*. In manuscript *N,* the tenor *Letabitur* begins on C, which is dissonant with the motetus, *J'ai mon cuer del tout abandouné,* which begins on D. The Parisian versions of the tenor chant[55] begin on A, which creates an acceptable fourth with the motetus on D. Tischler, in his edition, has corrected *N*'s tenor to conform to the Parisian chant.[56] However, the chant in Arrageois service books[57] is even better, because it begins on G, creating a more usual perfect fifth with the motetus. This, however, is the only case I could find in which an Arrageois, rather than a Parisian, chant seemed best suited for a motet. In addition, I could discern no consistent agreement of tenors as transmitted in *N* and *R* with Arrageois over Parisian chants.

The influence of the chanson tradition. The reason for the polyphonic ineptitude of *N* and *R* lies in the background of their scribes, who belonged to the chansonnier tradition. Both motet scribes had worked earlier on the chansons of their respective manuscripts. The single scribe who copied all

---

[51]Paris, Bibliothèque Nationale, f. lat. 830, f. 257; lat. 1112, f. 206^v; lat. 9441, f. 188^v; lat. 14452, f. 117^v; lat. 15615, f. 307^v; lat. 15616, f. 52 (Sanctorale); Bibliothèque de l'Arsenal, MS 197, f. 145; and Bibliothèque Sainte-Geneviève, MS 1259, f. 200^v.

[52]Folio 12 (Sanctorale).

[53]Paris, Bibliothèque Nationale, f. lat. 830, f. 269; lat. 861, f. 317; lat. 1112, f. 213^v; lat. 9441, f. 203^v; lat. 14452, f. 129; lat. 15615, f. 327; lat. 15616, f. 69 (Sanctorale); Bibliothèque de l'Arsenal, MS 110, f. 146; MS 135, f. 201; MS 197, f. 158^v; Bibliothèque Sainte-Geneviève, MS 1259, f. 244.

[54]It is present in *Mo, Cl, W$_2$,* and *MüB,* as well as *N* and *Her*.

[55]Paris, Bibliothèque Nationale, f. lat. 1112, f. 208 and Bibliothèque Sainte-Geneviève, MS 1259, f. 234.

[56]Tischler, *The Earliest Motets,* 2: 1465–66.

[57]Arras, MS 437, f. 67^v and MS 444, f. 71^v (Sanctorale).

of *R*'s motet collection (on ff. 205–10) also copied most of *R*'s chansons organized by trouvère attribution. Similarly, the sole scribe of *N*'s motets (on ff. 179–97) also copied the chansons on ff. 4ᵛ–20 and 59ᵛ–172ᵛ of *N*.[58] Thus, the scribes were very involved with the monophonic chanson repertory.

The scribes' ignorance of the conventions of rhythmic notation may reflect the general musical background of other musicians in their circle and within the tradition going back at least to their common source. Nor is the defective transmission of motets within the chansonnier tradition limited to *N* and *R*. In its motet section, the chansonnier *V* omits the notation and correct texts of all the tenors except one, and other motets were transformed into monophonic songs by stripping away their tenors and copying them into the chanson collections.[59] The *motets entés,* framed by verses at the beginning and the end to which the middle of the song is grafted, of the chansonnier Paris, Bibliothèque Nationale, f. fr. 845 are entirely monophonic. The motets added to the manuscript *ArsB,* which is devoted to Gautier de Coinci's *Les Miracles de Nostre-Dame* and other French devotional writings, are badly notated and occasionally lacking tenors.[60] The lack of consistent modal notation in the chansonniers' motets weakens Tischler's argument that measured rhythm was used in performing chansons as well as motets.[61]

The reconstructions of tenors in *N* and *R* were not of the philological sort, i.e., attempts to restore a lost archetype or to correct mistakes. The reason they were undertaken the way they were, by substituting or stringing together sections of other tenors, lies in the chanson tradition.

An important part of lyrical poetic technique was interpolating into one poem quotations from another. The monophonic *motet enté* of Paris, Bibliothèque Nationale, f. fr. 845, was framed by verses inserted or grafted onto the motet; the chanson with multiple refrains usually used a different quotation for each refrain; and the refrain cento, as it is termed by scholars, refers to a motet voice that consisted of a string of quotations placed end

---

[58] In regard to *N*, Berger (*Littérature et société,* 18) does not identify the motet scribe with any of the preceding chansons. My analysis also differs somewhat from that of Everist (*Polyphonic Music,* pp. 178–79).

[59] Ludwig, *Repertorium,* 1/2:569–90.

[60] Ludwig, *Repertorium,* 1/2:594–602; Chailley, *Les Chansons,* pp. 24–29.

[61] See Samuel N. Rosenberg and Hans Tischler, eds., *Chanter m'estuet: Songs of the Trouvères* (Bloomington: Indiana University Press, 1981), pp. xxi–xxii.

to end.[62] There is, in fact, a peculiar case of textual centonization in two tenors in *N*. The tenor of *N* 38 reads *Hec dies et florebit,* and *N* 88 *Adorabo flos filius eius.* Each tenor, in effect combines two different, unrelated texts in the manner of a refrain cento.[63]

For the scribes, copying was a linear process. In reconstructing tenors, the editors, too, were not recreating or restoring a harmonic edifice, but seem to have been interested only in melodic invention. The polyphonic implausibility of the solutions indicate that the polyphonic motet was not understood by the chansonnier compilers, but was preserved as a curiosity. The presence of motets in *N* and *R* perhaps reflects a retrospective attitude on the part of the compilers, who may not have understood or been interested in how motets were performed. It appears that they preserved the motets for their poetic and melodic charm, and because they made an impressive anthology that complemented the trouvère repertory.

---

[62]See Mark Everist, "The Refrain Cento: Myth or Motet?" *Journal of the Royal Musical Association* 114 (1989): 164–88; and Beverly J. Evans, "The Textual Function of the Refrain Cento in a Thirteenth-Century French Motet," *Music & Letters* 71 (1990): 187–97.

[63]*Hec dies* is appropriate for the tenor melody of No. 38, while *Et florebit* is properly the tenor text of motets Nos. 43 and 70. Only *Adorabo* suits the tenor chant of No. 88. *Flos filius eius* is the tenor of Nos. 10, 11, 12, 13, 35–36, and 93. Note that only the melody of the first chant text is used in the tenors of Nos. 38 and 88. There is no musical conflation of the two chants.

MANUSCRIPT SIGLA

ArsB Paris, Bibliothèque de l'Arsenal, 3517–3518
Cl Paris, Bibliothèque Nationale, nouv. acq. fr. 13521
F Florence, Biblioteca Laurenziana, Pluteus 29.I
Fauv Paris, Bibliothèque Nationale, f. fr. 146
Ha Paris, Bibliothèque Nationale, f. fr. 25566
Her Lost fragments, photographs of which are in Göttingen, Universitätsbibliothek, Ludwig Nachlass, portfolio IX, 14
Ma Madrid, Biblioteca Nacional, 20486
Mo Montpellier, Bibliothèque Interuniversitaire, Section Médecine, H 196
MüA Munich, Bayerische Staatsbibliothek, Mus. Ms. Nr. 4775 (olim gallo-roman 42) and lost fragments belonging to Johannes Wolf, photographs of which are in Paris, Bibliothèque Nationale, Département de Musique, Vma 1446
MüB Munich, Bayerische Staatsbibliothek, Cod. lat. 16444
N Paris, Bibliothèque Nationale, f. fr. 12615
R Paris, Bibliothèque Nationale, f. fr. 844
StV Paris, Bibliothèque Nationale, f. lat. 15139
V Rome, Biblioteca Apostolica Vaticana, Reg. lat 1490
W_2 Wolfenbüttel, Herzog August Bibliothek, Cod. Guelf. 1099 Helmst.

INDEX

Adam de la Halle 461
Aeschylus
   Prometheus Unbound 239
Agricola, Johann Friedrich 259
Allard, Marie 48, 341, 343, 344
allegory 226–27
Altnikol, Johann Christoph 270
Ambros, Wilhelm August 173
Amenda, Karl 439, 449
anabasis 72, 73
Andrieu, F. 282
Angiolini, Gaspero 15–47
   Don Juan 17–18, 24, 26–27, 29–32, 39, 43–45
   Semiramis 17–18, 27, 33–34, 43–46
Anne of Brittany 62
Anschütz, Heinrich 442, 445, 446
Arbeau, Thoinot 16, 25
Arcadelt, Jacques
   Ancidetemi pur 406–13
   "Ave Maria" 109
   Nous voyons que les hommes 109
Ariosto, Lodovico 145
Aristotle 234, 436
   Rhetoric 16
Artois 477
Attaingnant, Pierre 198
Aureli, Aurelio
   Ercole in Tebe 134
   Le fortune di Rodope e Damira 131
   Olimpia vendicata 126
autos sacramentales 2

Bach, Carl Philipp Emanuel 261, 309
Bach, Johann Christoph Friedrich 328
Bach, Johann Sebastian 279
   "Ächzen und erbärmlich Weinen" BWV 13/5 76–77
   Ascension Oratorio
      "Ach, bleibe doch, mein liebstes Leben," BWV 11/4 79–81
   Brandenburg Concerto No. 5 249, 256
   Concerto for Two Harpsichords 267
   "Dein Wetter zog sich auf von weiten," BWV 46/3 89–90
   "Der Priester und Levit," BWV 164/2 68–69
   "Die Armut, so Gott auf sich nimmt," BWV 91/5 69–70
   "Die schäumenden Wellen von Belials Bächen," BWV 81/3 73–74
   "Ich sehe schon im Geist," BWV 43/9 75
   "In Jesu Demut kann ich Trost," BWV 151/3 70–72
   "Italian" Concerto 266
   "Jesu, der aus großer Liebe," BWV 165/3 76
   Laß Fürstin, laß noch einen Strahl 275
   "Liebster Gott, erbarme dich," BWV 179/5 90–92
   Magnificat
      "Et misericordia" 73
   Mass in B Minor
      Agnus Dei 80
      Gloria 273
      Sanctus 274
   "Mein Erlöser und Erhalter," BWV 69a/5 90
   "Mein Gott, ich liebe dich von Herzen," BWV 77/3 79
   "Mein liebster Jesus ist verloren," BWV 154/1 78–79
   Musical Offering 404
   Organ Prelude and Fugue in G Major 267
   "Phoebus, deine Melodei," BWV 201/9 69
   St. John Passion
      "Mein teurer Heiland" 268
   St. Luke Passion 309
   St. Matthew Passion
      "Ach nun ist mein Jesus hin!" BWV 244/30 79
      "Aus Liebe will mein Heiland sterben," BWV 244/49 75
      "Ich will bei meinem Jesu wachen," BWV 244/20 74

Bach, Johann Sebastian (*cont*)
   "Stumme Seufzer, stille Klagen," BWV 199/2 73
   "Vergibt mir Jesus meine Sünden," BWV 48/6 92–94
   Well-Tempered Clavier 250, 270
   "Wie zweifelhaftig ist mein Hoffen" BWV 109/3 81–89
ballata 146–48, 150–54, 157, 164
ballet d'action 15, 36, 37, 40, 41
ballet de cour 37
Bardi, Giovanni de 234
barzelletta 147, 154–55, 157
Beauchamps, Pierre 21
Beethoven, Karl 434, 436, 438, 442
Beethoven, Ludwig van 103, 172, 173
   Consecration of the House, The 440
   conversation books 434, 436, 438, 440, 442, 446
   Coriolan 444, 447
   Egmont 440, 445, 447
   "Falstaff" canon 438
   Fidelio 441, 443, 444
   Heiligenstadt Testament 438
   late quartets 453–54, 456–60
   Macbeth opera 444–46
   Missa Solemnis 440
   Piano Sonata, Op. 31, No. 2 ("Tempest") 450
   Piano Sonata, Op. 57 ("Appassionata") 450, 451
   Piano Trio, Op. 70, No. 1 445
   Prometheus 440
   String Quartet, Op. 135 460
   String Quartet, Op. 18, No. 1 449–50
   style 181
   Symphony No. 5 97, 104, 429
   Symphony No. 6 ("Pastoral") 447
   Symphony No. 9 440, 447, 452
   Variations on "La stessa, la stessissima" 443
Belcari, Feo 145, 146, 150, 154, 164
Benda, Georg
   Romeo und Julie 432–33, 443

Berchem, Jachet 212
Berlin Philharmonic Orchestra 99
Berlioz, Hector 430, 443
   Harold in Italy 110
Bernard of Clairvaux 165
Berner, Felix 28
Bernhard, Christoph 227, 229, 242
Berton, Pierre-Montan 333–54
   Sylvie 48
Bianco da Siena 165
Boethius 234
Böhme, Jacob 234
Boldrini, Carlo 438
Boniventi, Giuseppe
   Almira 126
Boquet, Louis-René 340
Boretti, Giovanni Antonio
   Ercole in Tebe 134
   Marcello in Siracusa 131
Boucher, François 339
Bouilly, Jean Nicolas
   Léonore, ou l'amour conjugal 443
Brahms, Johannes 225, 431, 460
   Five Songs for Mixed Choir, Op. 104 186–91
   Four Serious Songs 180
   German Requiem 180
   Schenker on 178–91
   symphonies 181
Breitkopf & Härtel 367
Breuning, Gerhard von 439
Breuning, Hélène von 432
Bricaire de la Dixmerie, Nicolas 338, 354
Brossard, Sébastien 253
Buglhat, Johannes 211
Bulwer, John 35, 36
Burmeister, Joachim 245
Byron, George Gordon 430

Caccini, Giulio 234
Cahusac, Louis de 18, 25, 37, 46, 341, 343
Calderón de la Barca, Pedro 2
Camargo, Marie-Anne de Cupis 38

Cambio, Perissone 212
Camerata 234
Campra, André
   Iphigénie en Tauride 346
   Tancrède 335
cantus firmus 156
canzona 403
capitolo 145, 164
Cara, Marchetto 144, 155
Caravaggio, Michelangelo da 231, 234
Carmontelle, Louis Carrogis dit 48, 345
Carvalho, Léon 99
Casale Íonferrato 62
Castellani, C. 164
Castelli, Girolamo
   Almerico in Cipro 134
catabasis 72, 73
Cavalli, Francesco
   Artemisia 126, 129, 133
   Egisto 126
   Ormindo 128
   Scipione affricano 129
   Xerse 131
Cicero, Marcus Tullius
   De Oratore 16
Cicognini, Giacinto Andrea
   Orontea 129
Ciconia, Johannes 303
Cimarosa, Domenico 387
Collin, Heinrich Joseph von
   Coriolan 444
   Macbeth 444–46
Comes, Juan Batista 5
commedia dell'arte 29, 39–41, 126
Conti, prince de 334, 338
copyright 198–99
Cornazano, Antonio 22
Czerny, Carl 447, 450

d'Albizo, Francesco 167
d'Este, Isabella 155
d'Indy, Vincent 99, 352
Dante Alighieri 432
   Divine Comedy 145
Dauberval, Jean 48, 341, 343, 344, 345
Dauvergne, Antoine 333
   Les troqueurs 348

Davies, Sir John 25
de Hesse (Deshayes), Jean-Baptiste
   François 28
de Pure, Michel 18, 36
Delacroix, Eugène 431
Deschamps, Eustache 284
Destouches, André
   Issé 338
Dies, Albert Christoph 365, 367
Diruta, Girolamo 406, 407
Dolfin, Pietro
   Ermengarda 126, 131
Domenico da Piacenza 22
Dubos, Abbé Jean-Baptiste 18
Dukas, Paul 100
Dupré, Louis 21

Eliot, Thomas Stearns 431
Elizabeth I (England) 436
estribillo 2
Euripides 239, 436

Farrenc, Louise
   Piano Quintet No. 2 110
Faustini, Giovanni
   Ormindo 128
Favier, Jean 42
Ferrabosco, Domenico
   Io mi son giovinetta 407, 411
Festa, Costanzo
   Quis dabit oculis nostris 62, 63
   Super flumina Babylonis 62
Festa, Sebastiano 62
Feuillet, Raoul Auger 21, 23, 34, 42
Florence 148
Franck, Salomon 68
Francoeur, François 337, 348, 353
Francoeur, Louis Joseph 342
Freschi, Domenico
   L'incoronazione de Dario 138
   Olimpia vendicata 126
Froberger, Johann Jacob 403, 411
Froissart, Jean 284
frottola 143, 147, 156

Gabrieli, Giovanni 225
Gallini, Giovanni Andrea Battista 21

Gardano, Antonio 193–216
Gaudio, Antonio dal
    Almerico in Cipro 136
Gautier de Coinci
    Les Miracles de Nostre-Dame 462, 480
Gellandi, Claudius 61
Gero, Ihan 198, 212
Gesualdo, Carlo 405
Giannatasio, Fanny 434
Giustiniani, Leonardo 147, 148, 164
Gluck, Christoph Willibald 20, 44, 47, 333
    Don Juan 17–18, 24, 26–27, 29–32, 39, 43–45
    Semiramis 17–18, 27, 33–34, 43–46
Goethe, Johann Wolfgang von 172, 430, 437
    Wilhelm Meister 434
Gossec, François-Joseph 348
Griepenkerl, Wolfgang 430, 451–52, 460
Griesinger, August 365, 367
Grillparzer, Franz 446
Grimm, Friedrich Melchior, Baron von 342, 343
Guttenbrunn, Ludwig 365

Handel, George Frideric 100
    Messiah 254
Hanslick, Eduard 174, 177
Hassler, Hans Leo 404
Hasslinger, Joseph 28
Hausegger, Friedrich von 174, 175–76
Haydn, Franz Joseph 460
    Symphony No. 99 372–77
Hegel, Georg Wilhelm Friedrich 172
Hilverding, Franz 16, 38
Hoffmann, Ernst Theodor Amadeus 171, 429
Holz, Karl 436
Homer 437
Hugo, Victor 111, 431
hymn 155, 164

Incogniti 127

Jachet of Mantua 216
Jacopone da Todi 149, 165
Jeppesen, Knud 143
jeu-parti 292
Joachim, Joseph 431
Josquin Desprez 63
    Ave Maria gemma virginum 60
    Inviolata integra et casta es Maria 57–59, 60–61

Kircher, Athanasius 228, 235, 247
Kirnberger, Johann Philipp 262, 272
Kuhnau, Johann 229, 247

Lagarde, Pierre de 335–36, 346
    Aeglé 335, 336
Lambranzi, Gregorio 40, 48, 50, 52, 54, 56
Laujon, Pierre 335, 336, 339, 340, 343, 345, 354
Laval, Antoine Bandieri 38
leitmotives
    and Verdi 184
    in Schenker's thought 185–86
Lichnowsky, Moritz 446
ligatures 208–209
Liskin, Margaretha 28
Liszt, Franz 98
    Ce qu'on entend sur la montagne 97, 111
    Dante Symphony 108
    Die Hunnenschlacht 108
    Gran mass 108
    Legende von der Heiligen Elisabeth 108, 110
    Sonata in B-Minor 106
London Philharmonic Society 98
Lotz, Theodor 381, 383
Louis XII (France) 62
Lucian de Samosata
    De Saltatione 18
Lully, Jean-Baptiste 333, 339, 343, 345, 352
    Armide 341, 348
Lupus 212
Luther, Martin 67
Luzzaschi, Luzzasco 405, 407

Machaut, Guillaume de
    Dit dou Vergier 285
    Jugement du roy de Behaigne 293
    Le Livre du Voir-Dit 281, 283–86
    Remede de Fortune 283, 292
madrigal 409
Magri, Gennaro 23, 24, 29, 31, 32, 36, 40–42
Maistre Ihan 212
Malfatti, Therese 434
Manara, Francesco 211
Manchicourt, Pierre 212
Mantua 143, 155
Marais, Marin
    Alcyone 346
Marcello, Benedetto
    Teatro alla moda 141
Marenzio, Luca 405
Marx, Adolph Bernhard 170
masks 36–38
Matteo da Perugia 282, 303
Mattheson, Johann 26, 44–46, 229
Mayone, Ascanio 407, 408
Mayr, Simon
    L'Amor conjugale 444
Medici Codex 61, 62, 63
Medici, Lorenzo de' 167
Mendel, Arthur 249
Ménestrier, Claude François 18, 19, 20, 36
Merulo, Claudio 406
Michel, Pierre 23
Michelangelo Buonarotti 429
Minato, Nicolò
    Artemisia 126, 129, 133
    Orimonte 129
    Scipione affricano 129
    Seleuco 132
    Xerse 131
Moderne, Jacques 194, 211
Molière 17, 39
Montella, Giovanni Domenico 407, 411
Monteverdi, Claudio 403, 405, 409
    L'incoronazione di Poppea 126
    La finta pazza Licori 409
    Lettere amorose 128
Montpelier Codex 469, 476
Morales, Cristóbal de 205, 216

moresca 41
Morselli, Adriano
    L'incoronazione di Dario 138
motet 155, 280
Mouton, Jean 63
    Ave Maria gemma virginum 60
    Nesciens mater 60
    Quis dabit oculis nostris 62
Mozart, Constanze 380
Mozart, Wolfgang Amadeus 460
    Don Giovanni
        "Or sai che l'onore" 176
    La Clemenza di Tito
        "Parto, parto, ma tu ben mio" 386, 390
    Magic Flute 440
Müller, Wenzel
    Der Sturm 443

Noris, Matteo
    Diocletiano 131
    Marcello in Siracusa 131
    Numa Pompilio 137
Nougaret, Pierre J. B. 333, 354
Noverre, Jean-Georges 16, 17, 24, 27, 37, 38, 43, 44, 343, 344

oda 145, 164
Oliva, Franz 436
Opéra-Comique 99, 334
opéra-comique 333, 354
organicism 178–81
ottava rima 145

Paër, Ferdinando
    Leonora ossia L'Amor conjugale 444
Pagliardi, Giovanni Maria
    Numa Pompilio 137
Paien, Thomas 284
Pallaio, Simon 165
Pallavicino, Carlo
    Diocletiano 131
Panciri, Giulio
    Almira 126
partimen 292
pastorale-héroïque 338
Paul (Apostle) 239

Petrucci, Ottaviano 143, 148
Philidor, François-André
    Ernelinde 333, 334
Picardy third 74
Picasso, Pablo 453
Pilate, Pontius 239
Pindar 239
Plautus, Titus 126
Pompadour, Madame de 336, 339
prima prattica 405
prose 164

Quantz, Johann Joachim 251, 254
Querelle des Bouffons 333, 348
Quintilian
    Institutio Oratoria 16

Rameau, Jean-Philippe 333, 334, 341, 343, 352, 353
    La princesse de Navarre 350
    Les Surprises de l'Amour 335
Rameau, Pierre 21, 34, 35
Ramos de Pareia 251
Raphael Sanzio 436
Rebel, François 337, 348, 353
Rembrandt 234
Requeno, Abbate Vincenzo 36
rhetorical figures 227
Ries, Ferdinand 438, 447
Robert de Rains 469
Roman de la Rose 279, 285
Rore, Cipriano de 211, 212, 216, 405, 409

Sachs, Curt 254
Saint-Saëns, Camille
    Carnaval des animaux 98
    Danse Macabre 124
    Henri VIII 99
    La jeunesse d'Hercule 98
    Le rouet d'Omphale 98, 124
    Phaeton 98
    Piano Concerto No. 4 98, 103, 104, 107
    Violin Sonata No. 1 103, 104
Salazar y Torres, Agustin 7
Salieri, Antonio
    Falstaff, ossia Le tre burle 443

Sallé, Marie 38
Santlow, Hester 28
Sartorio, Antonio
    Ermengarda 126, 131
    Seleuco 132
Schelling, Friedrich Wilhelm 172
Schikaneder, Emanuel 440, 441
Schiller, Friedrich 436
    Macbeth adaptation 441, 442
Schindler, Anton 433, 434, 436, 447, 450
Schlegel, August Wilhelm 434, 435, 437
Schobert, Johann 334
Schoenberg, Arnold 103
Schuller, Johann Georg 28
Schumann, Clara 225
Schumann, Robert 430
Schuppanzigh, Ignaz 438–39
Schütz, Heinrich 405
Scotto, Girolamo 193–216
Sermisy, Claudin de 212
Seyfried, Ignaz 441
Shakespeare, William 173
    All's Well That Ends Well 433, 437, 441
    As You Like It 447, 448
    Coriolanus 454
    Cymbeline 443, 454–56
    Hamlet 431, 436, 439, 441, 448
    Henry IV 436, 439, 441, 442
    Henry VIII 448, 454, 460
    Julius Caesar 433, 441
    King John 436
    King Lear 430, 432, 441, 442, 445, 448, 451, 452
    Macbeth 441, 442, 444–46, 448, 451, 452
    Merchant of Venice, The 437, 438, 441, 442, 446, 448
    Merry Wives of Windsor, The 432, 436, 441, 443, 448
    Midsummer Night's Dream, A 435, 447, 448
    Much Ado About Nothing 437, 441, 448
    Othello 437, 441, 447, 448
    Pericles 454, 455, 456

Shakespeare, William (*cont*)
   Richard III 432, 435, 441
   Romeo and Juliet 432, 437, 441, 443, 446–50
   Taming of the Shrew, The 443, 448
   Tempest, The 437, 439, 443, 446, 447, 448, 450, 451, 454, 456
   Two Noble Kinsmen, The 454, 460
   Winter's Tale, The 437, 448, 454–56
Silva, Andreas de 212
Sleep scene 125
Société des Concerts du Conservatoire 100
Société Nationale de Musique 98
sonate cyclique 103
sonnet 144, 156, 164
Sonnleithner, Joseph 443
Sophocles 173
Spitta, Philipp 94, 228
Stadler, Anton 380, 381, 383, 397
Stamitz, Johann 348
Steibelt, Daniel
   Roméo et Juliette 449
Stella, Scipione 407
stile rappresentativo 226, 235
strambotto 145, 150
Stravinsky, Igor 453
Striggio, Alessandro 409
Strozzi, Gregorio 407, 408
Süssmayr, Franz Xaver 387, 398
Sweelinck, Jan Pieterszoon 404

Tasso, Torquato 145
   Aminta 338
Taubert, Gottfried 21
tenso 285
text underlay 206–208
Thuringus, Joachim 245
Tieck, Ludwig 435
Tomlinson, Kellom 21, 34, 35
Tornabuoni, Lorenzo 167
Trabaci, Giovanni Maria 407, 408
tragédie-ballet 20
tragédie-lyrique 338
Trial, Jean-Claude 333–54
   Sylvie 48
Tromboncino, Bartolomeo 155

Vaillant, Johannes 282, 295
Venice 148, 404
Verdelot, Philippe 203, 212
   Hesterna die dominus 213
Verdi, Giuseppe
   Aïda 183
   Don Carlos 132, 182, 183
   Falstaff 182, 183–84
   La Traviata 183
   Otello 175, 182–83
Vergelli, Paulo 212
Vestris, Gaetano 21
villancico 3
Viola, Francesco 211
Voltaire 17

Wagner, Cosima 431
Wagner, Richard 169, 172, 173, 430, 431, 444, 452
   Die Meistersinger von Nürnberg 184
   influence on Schenker 182–86
   Lohengrin 99
   Ring des Nibelungen 106, 457
   Siegfried 183
   Tannhäuser 109, 183
   Tristan und Isolde 183
Walther, Johann Gottfried 329
Weaver, John 19, 20, 30–31, 33–36, 38, 40, 42, 46–47
   The Loves of Mars and Venus 29
   The Tavern Bilkers 28–29
Werckmeister, Andreas 230
Werner, Zacharias
   Wanda 440
Wert, Giaches de 405
Wieland, Christoph 434, 435
Willaert, Adrian 212
   Canzone villanesche 202, 209, 216

Zarlino, Gioseffo 241
Zingarelli, Nicola
   Giulietta e Romeo 443
Zmeskall, Nikolaus 439